Health Policy
and
Nursing

Health Policy and Nursing

Crisis and Reform in the U.S. Health Care Delivery System

Edited by

Charlene Harrington

Carroll L. Estes

Institute for Health & Aging
Department of Social and Behavioral Sciences
School of Nursing
University of California, San Francisco

Ida VSW Red, Coordinating Editor

Jones and Bartlett Publishers
Boston   London

Editorial, Sales, and Customer Service Offices

Jones and Bartlett Publishers
One Exeter Plaza
Boston, MA 02116
1-800-832-0034
617-859-3900

Jones and Bartlett Publishers International
P.O. Box 1498
London W6 7RS
England

Library of Congress Cataloging-in-Publication Data

Health policy and nursing : crisis and reform in the U.S. health care
    delivery system / edited by Charlene Harrington and Carroll L. Estes;
    Tom Ferentz, photographer.
        p.   cm.
    Includes index.
    ISBN 0-86720-813-9
    1. Medical policy—United States.   2. Nursing—United States.
    3. Medical care—United States.   4. Medical care—United States—
    Finance.   I. Harrington, Charlene.   II. Estes, Carroll L.
    [DNLM: 1. Health Policy—United States.   2. Delivery of Health
    Care—United States.   3. Nursing Care.   WY 100H4338 1994]
RA395.A3H42554   1994
362.1'0973--dc20
DNLM/DLC
for Library of Congress   93-14285
                                                                      CIP

Photography by Tom Ferentz; photos on pages 53 and 267 courtesy of Children's Hospital, Boston; photo on page 91 courtesy of David U. Himmelstein; photo on page 463 courtesy of the American Nurses' Association.

Printed in the United States of America
98 97 96 95 94   10 9 8 7 6 5 4 3 2 1

Contents

Foreword

Health Policy and Nursing: Crisis and Reform in the U.S. Health Care Delivery System provides a broad spectrum of information about the vital issues affecting U.S. health care policy. The volume treats the problems and alternatives facing the health care system in sufficient depth to be of great value to all health professionals. The article authors, experts in their fields, present analyses of current problems and issues as well as forecast national programs and policies. The contents are rich in detail and cover the critical concerns of our country. Ranging from the financing and structure of our health care system to insurance mechanisms and managed care; to offering information on trends in the various modalities of care, such as hospitals, homes, nursing homes, and communities; to exploring health personnel issues; to examining outcomes of the health care system; and finally, to highlighting proposals and prospects for health care reform—this book is an invaluable compendium of what every educated health professional needs to know to function intelligently in today's health care world.

As this volume is published, the nation is still grappling with the shape and specific content of health reform. Part IV deals specifically with this topic, and the facts and interpretations presented will inform readers and help them reach their own conclusions. Struggles between and among groups have impeded reform in the past and will continue to do so. Political moves to win over one or another of these groups have an impact on the logic and effectiveness of proposed policies. Despite controversy, tough decisions are being made. The extent to which there is "give" as well as "take" on the part of health professionals will affect the degree of their genuine participation in these decisions.

The editors hope that *Health Policy and Nursing,* through its cogent and thorough interpretations of the major areas of daily concern to policymakers, will affect readers' participation in decision making. Nurses and other health care professionals cannot legitimately engage in the policy world without a broad understanding of the stakes, the stakeholders, the possible compromises, and the practicality of proposed solutions in the complex national scenario of health reform.

Claire Fagin, Ph.D., R.N., F.A.A.N.

Introduction

This edited volume grew out of our experience teaching health care policy and financing for the past decade to graduate students in nursing and sociology. Each year we selected our favorite articles for the reading list and developed an original syllabus because we could not find a book that encompassed all the key readings for the course. This book is designed to solve the need for a basic text and to complement *The Nation's Health,* which is also a valuable policy anthology. *Health Policy and Nursing,* designed especially for nurses and other health professionals, includes articles on nursing, women's health, and policy from a nursing perspective.

To introduce students and professionals to the current debates about health policy and health care organization, chapters treat the vital issues of cost, access, quality, health status, and system reform. Health policy, by necessity, must give attention to health financing, though not to the exclusion of other policy concerns. The rapid and relentless growth in health care costs since the 1980s, in spite of a number of important cost-cutting policy initiatives, remains crucial to the health policy debate. Health costs were a major topic of the 1992 general presidential election and are the driving force behind a large number of congressional and presidential legislative efforts. President Clinton correctly states that economic recovery and deficit reduction both require the control of health care costs. Even if health costs were not out of control, there would still be major problems with the U.S. health care delivery system. However, economics is the most powerful motivating force for change.

Because financing and economics dominate the current health policy agenda, nurses, physicians, and other health professionals have been relegated to a back seat behind economists and health service researchers. Full participation in the national debate requires an understanding of economic and research perspectives. This book includes articles by economists, sociologists, and a variety of health service researchers. Because much of the current policy debate hinges on complex arguments, the articles reprinted in this volume were selected to familiarize the reader with the central elements of key policy issues and the concepts that underlie policy-making debates.

The chapters in this book focus on many of the difficult problems of the U.S. health care system. Nurses and providers of health care are aware of the strengths of health care as promoted by marketing services and community relations experts and as provided in exemplary public services. Many health professionals, convinced that this country has the greatest health care system in the world, often overlook major problems that require solutions. Fortunately, the problems of the system are amenable to change and reform, but not without an understanding of their major dimensions and alternative solutions.

Problems in health care cost and the organization of the health industry are enormous and difficult to comprehend. The growth of the medical-industrial complex, which includes the nation's vast proprietary groups of providers and services, is driven by economic conditions and profit motives as well as a political climate that promotes competition. Profits in health care, which have become accepted practice in the United States, undeniably distort the service system in terms of quality, access, and cost of care. In their efforts to obtain health services, consumers become lost in a maze of providers. More important, consumer needs are overwhelmed by the economic considerations that drive the decision-making process about what care to provide or to withhold.

Improving access to needed and appropriate health care services is one approach to improving health status. Reducing unnecessary hospitalizations and inappropriate medical services can, in turn, ensure full access to primary care services. No health financing strategy or reform will overcome the delivery system problems. Every community needs a comprehensive system of services that includes a full range of primary care, prevention, long-term care, and related health and social services in addition to hospital services. Income, housing, education, the environment, child care, eldercare, and other social concerns outside the health system also need to be dealt with to improve the overall health status of the population; however, a detailed discussion of these vital issues is beyond the scope of this book.

Poor health status and limited access to services, particularly for people with low incomes and the 37 million uninsured, are the greatest health problems in the United States. High infant mortality, low immunization, and high maternal mortality rates, along with a lower-than-average life span for millions of disadvantaged people are unacceptable for one of the richest and most industrialized countries in the world. These trends are even less acceptable in light of the nation's large direct health expenditure per capita and the growing percentage of the gross national product spent on health care.

Developing a national health plan for the population ranks as one of the nation's top priorities along with strengthening the economy. Any such plan should address the problems of the uninsured, the under-insured, and the uninsurable. The 37 million uninsured residents, many of whom work for organizations that do not provide health insurance, urgently need access to health care services. Many people who would like to buy private insurance are not able to because of high premium rates and exclusionary provisions for applicants with medical problems. Small businesses cannot afford the premiums for their employees, and almost everyone is underinsured for long-term care and preventive services. Individuals with the greatest need for health care are often the least able to pay for insurance or obtain services. Medicaid often fails to cover the poor people it was designed to provide for because of the severe underfunding of the program. Medicare is limited by eligibility regulations and in the services it provides. Nothing short of major reform is needed to address these problems, which threaten the social and financial well-being of individuals, the business community, and the overall economy. Numerous studies have documented the negative effect that lack of access to health care may have on health status and service utilization. At particular risk are vulnerable population groups such as elders, people with disabilities, infants, children, adolescents, women, rural residents, people in poverty, and people of color. Health care services are rationed for all who cannot afford to purchase them privately.

Concerns about health care quality are increasing, particularly in relation to long-term care in nursing homes and home care settings. Unnecessary surgeries, overmedication, and overuse of expensive technologies and procedures plague health consumers. Reforms in reimbursement of hospitals have resulted in earlier hospital discharge and a shift from formal to informal care services. The lack of consumer information, the poor training and low wages of many health care workers, and the ineffective oversight of physician practices all contribute to problems in quality of care. Also, many service problems exist because of a lack of access to appropriate health personnel. The oversupply of physicians, particularly in specialties, and the undersupply and poor distribution of primary care providers are central problems.

Physicians are receiving increased criticism for their high incomes, conflict of interest, and ability to raise the demand for and volume of health care services provided. Physicians are increasingly monitored by insurance companies and by the hospitals and managed care systems in which they work. Malpractice claims and administrative costs are substantial. Controlling physician fees is just a beginning in greater regulation of physician expenditures and practices.

Nurses, who make up the largest component of the health care delivery work force, frequently are invisible, overlooked, and unappreciated. Nevertheless, they play a critical role in expanding access to services. Nurses in advanced practice, including clinical specialists and nurse practitioners, provide primary care and highly specialized technological care. Although nurses have critical skills and a strong commitment to service, they face many barriers to providing services—restrictive state practice laws; restrictive Medicaid, Medicare, and private insurer reimbursement rules; and discrimination from institutional and ambulatory care providers.

The U.S. health care financing and delivery system requires major restructuring. Changes in the political winds of the 1990s are likely to represent a window of opportunity not seen since the early 1960s. This book describes several of the many proposals made for reform. Through political mobilization, nurses can have an impact on changes in the health care delivery system and improvement in access to and quality of care.

Part I

Economics of the U.S. Health Care Delivery System

Health care economics is a subject that has the potential to induce sleep in any health care professional, yet it is the underpinning of the existing U.S. health care system. The combination of private and public financing for health services without a national plan has left millions of people without health care and created a system unique in the industrialized world. Providers usually are private but receive funds from third-party payers for health care. The cost of this relatively unregulated system, with 1,500 private and several governmental payers, is out of control. Medical care expenditures have created a crisis of unprecedented proportion for government agencies and corporations that provide health insurance. Methods to control costs have risen to the top of the domestic policy agenda and are the focus of numerous legislative proposals.

The trends presented in this part are the most accurate estimates available from the Health Care Financing Administration. The magnitude of the expenditures is almost impossible to grasp, but it is clear that many people are unable to pay for the average $2,500 annual cost per person. These trends are unacceptable even under the most conservative scenarios. The cost of Medicaid and Medicare is of grave concern to policymakers and threatens to bankrupt both state and federal government agencies.

1

The *total cost* also is problematic, as the need for a national health care system grows and the U.S. government struggles to develop a plan to insure the entire population.

Critics charge that the medical-industrial complex, with its emphasis on profit and growth, contributes to poor quality of care and inappropriate and expensive services. The emphasis on health as a business commodity rather than a vital public service diverts medical practice patterns away from preventive, primary, and chronic care and raises many ethical questions. Even more serious is the deteriorating administrative efficiency of the system, which now absorbs as much as one-fourth of all U.S. health expenditures.

When compared to the single public (government) payer system of health care in Canada, the high cost of health care in this country can be traced directly to the fee-for-service billing systems of the many private and public insurers in the U.S. multipayer system. Unnecessary layers of billing and accounting procedures are built in for providers and insurers in addition to the costs for marketing, computer systems, utilization control, and oversight costs—all part of the administrative overhead. Although there is some dispute regarding estimates of administrative costs and potential savings if they could be reduced, there is no disagreement that administrative costs are currently a major factor contributing to the current inefficiency of the system.

The competitive approaches to health care in the 1980s have not reduced the cost as many private-sector proponents predicted. In fact, the cost has continued to skyrocket under market competition models. Moreover, policymakers have been unwilling to regulate private health care prices, and an ineffective regulatory system for prices paid by government agencies remains intact.

The practice and ethics of the health insurance industry are receiving increased criticism. Private companies may select the healthiest clients and exclude applicants with serious health problems, which leaves these patients without any care at all or forces them to rely on public insurance systems and public providers. Health maintenance organizations (HMOs) are viewed by many as the way to develop effective delivery of care under capitated financing systems. HMO models are highly successful in attracting new enrollees because of competitive prices and comprehensive care delivery systems. Some such organizations, however, have limited access, lack continuity of care by providers, and display other serious delivery system problems. The barriers to use of HMOs are greatest for poor, frail, disabled, and elderly clients. Nevertheless, the HMO concept is growing in popularity with both consumers and public policymakers because of the cost advantage.

Part I addresses the critical economic issues that shape the U.S. health care system. Chapter 1 discusses the necessity of understanding health economics and presents basic economic tools and principles. Trends in U.S. private and public health care expenditures are presented to provide basic reference and background information on health costs and programs and to compare the U.S. health system with programs in other countries. Chapter 2 describes the enormous medical-industrial complex of private health care organizations and analyzes the effect of market values and high administrative costs on medicine and health care in the United States. Chapter 3 outlines trends and developments in private health insurance and managed care and illustrates how private insurance organizations form the basic structure of the U.S. health care financing system and, therefore, are principal targets in health reform efforts.

1

Financing Health Care

*Ph.D. nurses
conducting high-tech
research in a
university lab*

Lanis L. Hicks / Keith E. Boles

Why Health Economics?

The role of economics in health care has never been fully defined or totally accepted. In the past, structural characteristics of the system made the resources available to the health care industry virtually unlimited, thereby minimizing the need to economize the decision-making process. As long as resources were readily available and decisionmakers did not have to make hard choices among alternatives, it was not necessary for them to understand consumer behavior, producer behavior, or even industry performance. Consequently, economics, which deals with the efficient allocation of scarce resources, was generally viewed as superfluous or even irrelevant.

As pressures mount to contain rising health care costs and resources available to the health care industry become increasingly limited, decisionmakers are looking for ways to improve their allocation of those limited resources. As a result, economics is playing an ever-expanding role in health care. . . .

RELEVANCE OF ECONOMIC THEORY

As expenditures for health care services rose at an alarming rate and policymakers developed cost-containment strategies, more economists became involved (Feldstein, 1983; Fuchs, 1974; Ward, 1975). This involvement has not been without controversy, and much has been written about the pros and cons of economics and economists in the determination of health care policy. Debates are still being fought vigorously around the question "Should economic factors be given consideration in reaching a decision in health care?" (Fuchs, 1966) . . .

DEFINING THE SUBJECT

Economics is the study of the efficient allocation of scarce resources among competing uses. Basically, it addresses four aspects of any economic sys-

Lanis L. Hicks, Ph.D., and Keith E. Boles, Ph.D., are Associate Professors of Health Services Management at the University of Missouri—Columbia.

Abridged from Hicks, L.L., and Boles, K.E. (1984). Why health economics? *Nursing Economic$* 2(3):175—180. Used with permission.

tem: (a) What will be produced? (b) How will the output be produced? (c) How much will be produced? and (d) Who will get the output that is produced? A fifth aspect also can be included: (e) Who will produce the output? Microeconomics, the area of primary concern here, purports to explain and predict in a nonjudgmental fashion the behavior of the individual consumer, investor, worker, firm, or industry under various circumstances. Economic theories can be interpreted as describing how, under proper conditions (for example, conditions of economic rationality, competition, and laissez-faire), an unregulated market economy will produce optimum results. It is a positive, nonjudgmental approach that permits the analysis of what will happen under a given set of incentives.

An *economist* is an individual who applies the theories of economics to a specific situation or environmental condition. The elaboration of theoretical models of a market or price system serves a dual function: to describe and explain scientifically and to justify and advocate. A description or explanation of a result is relatively meaningless unless it is stated in terms of specified ethical or political criteria or definitions of what constitutes "good" or "bad" results. Economists are no more qualified to make the judgmental choice of relevant criteria for determining "good" or "bad" results than other individuals. The use of economic theories can, however, make explicit the implications of alternative public policies being considered. Under a normative approach the economist attempts to place a value judgment on what the results should be and, therefore, attempts to establish the incentive structure that will achieve the desired results in the most efficient manner.

ROLE OF ECONOMICS AND ECONOMISTS

Part of the controversy surrounding application of economics to the health care industry stems from a reluctance to separate economics from the economist. Such a separation is necessary if the full contributions of economics to the decision-making process are to be realized.

According to Fuchs (1974), the economic point of view deals with three fundamental observations about the world: (a) resources are scarce relative to wants; (b) these limited resources have alternative uses; and (c) people have different wants and place different values on these wants. As a result, choices about which wants to satisfy must be made and rationing must occur. The role of economics is to systematically provide information about the consequences of the available alternatives. It provides a mechanism for determining total costs and benefits as well as the marginal costs and benefits of specific decisions. Through the use of marginal (incremental) analysis, economics can assist in effectively allocating resources among alternatives.

While the results of an economic analysis provide valuable information about the most efficient way of achieving an objective, economics
cannot determine which alternative should be undertaken, which goal
should be pursued, or the amount of resources that should be allocated to
each alternative. Economic analysis provides information about the relative costs and benefits of the alternatives being considered, but other
factors—social, political, moral, ethical, and personal preferences—must
also enter into the decision-making process. . . .

RATIONING HEALTH CARE

The application of economic theories and models to the health care system
is becoming increasingly important (Salkever & Sorkin, 1983). No society,
no matter how affluent, can provide all of its citizens with all of the health
care and technology that they might wish to consume. Since resources
available to the health care system are limited, decisions must be made
about who gets how many of these scarce resources. Consequently, a system must be developed for rationing available resources. Rationing is
simply the distribution of scarce items by a system that "limits the quantity of product which can be purchased" (Nemmers, 1970, p. 349). Since
scarcity is a fact of life, a mechanism for distributing the limited resources
must be developed.

A variety of methods have been developed for allocating scarce resources. In a private, nongovernmental system, price and ability to pay are
the usual mechanisms for rationing. If an individual has sufficient resources, then health care services will be provided; if an individual does
not possess sufficient resources, those services will be denied. Such a
price-oriented, market system ignores the relative needs of the population
for health care and places full responsibility for obtaining necessary services on the individual. This type of market results in a multi-tiered system relative to ability to pay. It has generally been viewed as an inadequate system for health care because of social considerations (Rorem,
1982).

In most industrialized countries, health care is viewed as extremely
important to the general welfare of society. Given its importance, outside
intervention is necessary to ensure that individuals unable to afford at
least basic care are not denied access to the system. However, the approaches taken by various political systems to achieve this access differ
significantly.

To ensure access, many European countries have socialized their systems and made a central government agency responsible for delivering
necessary services. This approach assumes that either an individual or a
group of individuals can determine the appropriate allocation of scarce

resources in a more efficient manner than a price-driven delivery system. The types of services produced, how they are produced, the amount of services produced, and who receives the services all are determined by a central authority.

In the United States, a rationing method allows the private delivery system to continue to operate, but subsidizes the purchases of certain subsets of the population and regulates other aspects of the private system. In this quasi-private market or price system approach, it is assumed that the types and amounts of services being produced are what consumers want and are willing to pay for. Through subsidization, low-income individuals are able to compete economically for the purchase of available services and to obtain necessary services. This type of system assumes that consumer buying is an accurate reflection of consumer desires and that consumers possess sufficient information to make rational choices in the market. To ensure that decisions reached by consumers correspond to values established by society, certain regulatory measures have been introduced. These regulations are designed to protect the consumer from incompetent providers and to place restrictions on the production activities of producers. Within these restrictions, however, the market is allowed to ration available resources.

Under the European method the government explicitly rations health care, while under the U.S. method health care is more implicitly rationed. In either system, rationing is necessary.

TOOLS OF ECONOMICS

The primary tool used in developing a framework for comparative analysis is benefit-cost analysis (also called cost-benefit analysis). Benefit-cost analysis is a logical process of identifying the benefits and costs associated with alternative solutions and then attempting to quantify them. The basic premise of economic efficiency is that resources should be allocated to those projects or activities for which the benefits are greater than the costs, and that those projects with the largest benefit-cost ratio should be undertaken first. The necessary assumption for this premise is that society is rational and that decisions are made in a rational fashion (Salkever & Sorkin, 1983). In this case any actions that have greater costs than benefits (that is, a benefit/cost ratio less than 1) should never be undertaken.

There are essentially two categories of decisions represented by economics, although the dividing line between them is somewhat gray. The first category is called *positive economics* and determines what the outcome will be under a specific decision. There are no value judgments placed on the decision or the outcome. The second category is represented by what is called *normative economics*. Normative economics makes a value judgment, based on the premise of economic efficiency, that a specific decision should be made. By analyzing the distinction between normative and positive economics, the role and relevance of economics can be more accurately defined. . . .

Society, in effect, determines the extent to which resources are allocated to the provision of health services. When policymakers perceive (from a normative standpoint) that the industry is not functioning effectively in the provision of services, they make decisions that will have an impact on the industry and on the extent of resources going to the industry. A policy is made because the perceived benefits outweigh the perceived costs, at least to the individuals or entities involved in decision making.

For example, the decision at the society level may be that everyone has a right to at least a minimal amount of health services, regardless of ability to pay. Without defining minimal, the next step in the process is to establish an administrative structure to achieve the desired results. There will be alternative methods developed that may be expected to achieve the same results. A positive economic approach would then be used to evaluate and compare the relative benefits and costs associated with each alternative.

The administrative structure . . . defines the constraints to be placed on the delivery of health services. The benefits and costs are defined and constrained by the existence of the incentives previously established. This will determine the types of institutions and individuals involved in the delivery of health services. For instance, the administrative structure (representing the policy decisions) may discourage the existence of investor-owned providers of health services, may discourage the existence of hospitals over the size of 250 beds, or may prohibit any corporation from owning more than one facility. Within facilities, constraints are placed on the flexibility to act from a normative standpoint, and inputs for decision making have more positive and quantifiable aspects. . . .

PROVISION OF HEALTH SERVICES

Returning to the questions that economics addresses, it is easy to see that all decisions are based on economic rationality, at least implicitly. Explicit recognition of economic rationality in establishing an evaluative framework, however, results in a more complete attempt at considering all relevant aspects of any decision.

1. *What will be produced?* Society demands that health services be provided and that interventions occur to interrupt the course of disease and injury.

2. *How will the output be produced?* Providers of health services will rationally react to the incentives created by society to produce the services, weighing the relative benefits and costs of providing services in alternative ways.
3. *How much will be produced?* Once again, the providers, reacting to the incentives established by society, will deliver services as long as the perceived benefits are greater than the perceived costs.
4. *Who will get the output?* The answer to this is primarily normative, from a societal standpoint, and determined by social policy. The administrative structure establishes the boundaries for the application of benefit-cost analysis at the lower levels of the inverted pyramid. . . .

Once the amount of resources allocated to health care has been decided, the next level of decision involves determining which sectors of the health care system get what amounts. Again, it must be recognized that resources are limited and the more spent on sophisticated, acute care services, the less available to spend on prevention and chronic care. Hard choices must be made among the various services, and rationing occurs. The other aspect of this allocation process is deciding who will receive the services available. If it is decided that anyone gaining access to the system is entitled to all services that might be even marginally beneficial, then access to even minimal services will have to be denied to others (Schwartz & Aaron, 1984).

NURSING, NURSES, AND ECONOMICS

While a discussion of the role of nursing and nurses in the health services management environment is beyond the scope of this article, the role and relevance of economics to nursing and nurses can be addressed. . . . Nursing and nurses must become involved at all levels of decision making. As nurses are involved at all levels in the provision of health care, they also must become involved in answering the five economic questions previously mentioned.

. . . At the society level, nurses are concerned with the availability of health services to all individuals, regardless of ability to pay. This statement is a normative one that is adhered to in varying degrees by different professionals. To the extent that individuals in nursing have feelings about access to health services, they will be concerned with public policy proposals presented before national, state, and local governments.

The public policy decisions . . . determine the structure of the health services delivery system. . . . For example, if legislation is passed stating that nursing services will be paid for by Medicare or Medicaid only when they are provided in a duly licensed health services institution, the use of home health nursing services by these beneficiaries will diminish.

The health services delivery structure, which is determined by public policy decisions, may result in multi-institutional providers. At this level, . . . a vice-president of nursing services may be responsible for establishing appropriate staffing levels or standards, determining a provider for nursing supplies to guarantee consistency and quality at an efficient price across all institutions, reconciling and justifying budgets and expense reports submitted by member institutions, and establishing a procedures manual delineating responsibilities associated with the nursing staff's organizational structure.

. . . The director of nursing services is responsible for recruiting nursing staff or dealing with a strike situation. Questions . . . may include: "Under current budget constraints, nursing wages can only be raised by leaving vacant positions unfilled. How would this affect employee morale?"

At the departmental level, decisions are more centered on direct provision of nursing services. Determination of activities performed by nurses' aides as opposed to LPNs, who gives baths, who works what shift, how to best provide adequate services when there are staff shortages, or how to resolve conflicts are examples of decisions that need to be evaluated on a benefit-cost basis at the departmental level.

Finally, . . . the individual nurse is making decisions. The nurse must consider the benefits and costs of situations such as questioning a physician's order, dealing with a belligerent patient from a standpoint of acquiescence or resistance, or comforting one patient while others remain unattended.

In some cases the application of economic analysis to a specific activity will identify who should provide the service. In other instances the identification of the associated benefits and costs contain sufficient normative or nonquantifiable inputs to give ambiguous results. However, an attempt to identify the relevant benefits and costs is valuable in the efficient production of services.

If there were complete agreement about the relative values to be placed on the delivery of services by alternative providers, then the application of benefit-cost analysis would result in a specific relationship between the numbers of aides, LPNs, and RNs for each institution once the specific required nursing services were identified. However, since general agreement about who should provide what services does not exist, this approach can aid in the identification of gray areas where normative decisions will determine whether a specific service is best provided by an aide, LPN, or RN.

. . . The impact on total wages is the reason institutions are interested in substituting LPNs for RNs where possible. . . . Quantitative justification that documents that the benefits of RN staff outweigh costs is increasingly important.

HEALTH CARE AND ECONOMICS

Health care demands often have been considered infinite. Although this may be an exaggeration, in today's environment it is obvious that wants are greater than the resources available to meet them. Therefore, choices must be made between competing wants, and decisions must be made about which wants will be met and which will be left unmet. Economics provides an efficient mechanism for making those decisions.

REFERENCES

Feldstein, P.J. (1983). *Health care economics* (2d ed.). New York: John Wiley & Sons.

Fuchs, V.R. (1966). The contribution of health services to the American economy. *Milbank Memorial Fund Quarterly, 44*(2), 65–101.

Fuchs, V.R. (1974). *Who shall live? Health, economics, and social choice.* New York: Basic Books, Inc.

Nemmers, E.E. (1970). *Dictionary of economics and business.* Totowa, NJ: Littlefield, Adams & Co.

Rorem, C.R. (1982). *A quest for certainty: Essays on health care economics, 1930–1970.* Ann Arbor, MI: Health Administration Press.

Salkever, D.S. & Sorkin, A.L. (1983). Economics, health economics, and health administration. *The Journal of Health Administration Education, 1*(3), 225–263.

Schwartz, W.B. & Aaron, H.J. (1984). Rationing hospital care: Lessons from Britain. *The New England Journal of Medicine, 310*(1), 52–56.

Ward, R.A. (1975). *The economics of health resources.* Reading, MA: Addison-Wesley Publishing Company.

The first wealth is health.
— Ralph Waldo Emerson

Katharine R. Levit / Helen C. Lazenby / Cathy A. Cowan / Suzanne W. Letsch

National Health Expenditures

HIGHLIGHTS

Health care expenditures reached $666.2 billion in 1990. During the last three decades, health care expenditures grew at a substantially faster pace than did the overall economy, consuming an increasing percentage of gross national product (GNP). Following are several highlights from the 1990 numbers:

- National health expenditures (NHE) rose 10.5 percent from 1989 to 1990, approximately the same growth rate as for the prior 2 years.
- In 1990, NHE absorbed 12.2 percent of GNP, compared with 11.6 percent for the preceding year. The abnormally high increase in the share of GNP spent for health care in 1990, the second largest jump since 1960, is the result of a slowdown in the general economy rather than an acceleration in the growth of health care costs.
- Per capita expenditures of $2,566 in 1990 were almost 1.5 times as great as expenditures 10 years earlier (table 1). Personal health care expenditures accounted for 88 percent of that amount, or $2,255 per person.
- In 1990, spending for hospital services returned to the double-digit growth experienced in 1982 and earlier, prior to the advent of the prospective payment system (PPS). Expenditures for this category increased 10.1 percent from 1989 to $256.0 billion in 1990. Hospital spending, 38.4 percent of total health expenditures, is the largest category in NHE (figure 1).
- Expenditures for professional services, which consist of physician services, dental services, and services of other professionals, totaled $191.3 billion for 1990, 28.7 percent of all health spending. This is an increase of 11.0 percent from 1989.

The authors are analysts at the Office of National Health Statistics, U.S. Health Care Financing Administration.

Abridged from Levit, K.R., Lazenby, H.C., Cowan, C.A., and Letsch, S.W. (1991). National health expenditures, 1990. *Health Care Financing Review* 13 (1):29–54. Used with permission.

Where It Came From   **Where It Went**

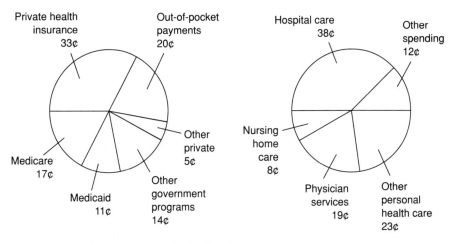

FIGURE 1   The Nation's Health Dollar: 1990

Notes: Other private includes industrial in-plant health services, nonpatient revenues, and privately financed construction. Other personal health care includes dental, other professional services, home health care, drugs and other nondurable medical products, and vision products and other durable medical products. Other spending covers program administration and the net cost of private health insurance, government public health, and research and construction.

Source: Health Care Financing Administration, Office of the Actuary: Data from the Office of National Cost Estimates.

- Public programs contributed 42.4 percent of the funding for health care, with private payments funding the other 57.6 percent. Public programs funded a larger share of NHE in 1990 than in any previous year. Medicaid was the single largest contributor to the rising public share. Medicaid payments grew 20.7 percent from 1989 through 1990, the highest growth since the mid-1970s.
- Medicaid and Medicare combined paid for 28.0 percent of NHE in 1990, up from 27.3 percent during 1989. These two programs financed 37.8 percent of hospital care and approximately one-third of physician services.
- Consumers continued paying for a little more than one-half of all health care expenditures through private health insurance and out-of-pocket payments, a share that has changed very little during the past 16 years. The private health insurance share remained relatively constant for the last 2 years, after steadily increasing since 1960. Out-of-pocket payments dropped slightly as a percent of total expenditures in 1989 and 1990.

TABLE 1   National Health Expenditures Aggregate and Per Capita Amounts, Percent Distribution, and Average Annual Percent Growth, by Source of Funds: Selected Years 1960–90

Item	1960	1970	1980	1985	1986	1987	1988	1989	1990
					Amount in billions				
National health expenditures	$27.1	$74.4	$250.1	$422.6	$454.8	$494.1	$546.0	$602.8	$666.2
Private	20.5	46.7	145.0	247.9	264.6	285.7	318.9	350.2	383.6
Public	6.7	27.7	105.2	174.8	190.2	208.4	227.1	252.6	282.6
Federal	2.9	17.7	72.0	123.6	133.1	144.0	156.7	175.0	195.4
State and local	3.7	9.9	33.2	51.2	57.2	64.4	70.5	77.6	87.3
					Number in millions				
U.S. population[1]	190.1	214.9	235.3	247.2	249.6	252.0	254.5	257.0	259.6
					Amount in billions				
Gross national product	$515	$1,015	$2,732	$4,015	$4,232	$4,516	$4,874	$5,201	$5,465
					Per capita amount				
National health expenditures	$143	$346	$1,063	$1,710	$1,822	$1,961	$2,146	$2,346	$2,566
Private	108	217	616	1,003	1,060	1,134	1,253	1,363	1,478
Public	35	129	447	707	762	827	893	983	1,089
Federal	15	83	306	500	533	571	616	681	753
State and local	20	46	141	207	229	255	277	302	336

Percent distribution

National health expenditures	100.0	100.0	100.0	100.0	100.0	100.0	100.0	100.0	100.0
Private	75.5	62.8	58.0	58.6	58.2	57.8	58.4	58.1	57.6
Public	24.5	37.2	42.0	41.4	41.8	42.2	41.6	41.9	42.4
Federal	10.7	23.9	28.8	29.2	29.3	29.1	28.7	29.0	29.3
State and local	13.8	13.3	13.3	12.1	12.6	13.0	12.9	12.9	13.1
Percent of gross national product									
National health expenditures	5.3	7.3	9.2	10.5	10.7	10.9	11.2	11.6	12.2
Average annual percent growth from previous year shown									
National health expenditures	—	10.6	12.9	11.1	7.6	8.6	10.5	10.4	10.5
Private	—	8.6	12.0	11.3	6.8	8.0	11.6	9.8	9.5
Public	—	15.3	14.3	10.7	8.8	9.5	9.0	11.2	11.9
Federal	—	19.8	15.0	11.4	7.6	8.2	8.8	11.7	11.7
State and local	—	10.2	12.8	9.0	11.8	12.6	9.5	10.1	12.5
U.S. population	—	1.2	0.9	1.0	1.0	1.0	1.0	1.0	1.0
Gross national product	—	7.0	10.4	8.0	5.4	6.7	7.9	6.7	5.1

[1]July 1 Social Security area population estimates.

Note: Numbers and percents may not add to totals because of rounding.

Source: Health Care Financing Administration, Office of the Actuary: Data from the Office of National Health Statistics.

TABLE 2   Personal Health Care Expenditures in Current Dollars by Type of Spending: Selected Years 1960–90

Type of spending	1960	1970	1980	1982	1990
	Current dollars in billions				
Personal health care	$23.9	$64.9	$219.4	$286.4	$585.3
Hospital care	9.3	27.9	102.4	135.9	256.0
Physician services	5.3	13.6	41.9	53.8	125.7
Dental services	2.0	4.7	14.4	18.4	34.0
Other professional services and home health care	0.6	1.7	10.0	14.0	38.5
Drugs and other medical non-durables	4.2	8.8	21.6	27.6	54.6
Vision products and other medical durables	0.8	2.0	4.6	5.1	12.1
Nursing home care	1.0	4.9	20.0	26.1	53.1
Other personal health care	0.7	1.4	4.6	5.6	11.3

Source: Health Care Financing Administration, Office of the Actuary: Data from the Office of National Health Statistics.

Health care costs continue to rise faster than GNP, a measure of total output of the United States. Despite an increasing share of GNP devoted to health care, a large and increasing number of people (33.4 million in 1989) remain uninsured by private health insurance or by public programs; additional persons are underinsured. Without sufficient insurance coverage, many Americans find access to the health care system limited for many services.

Extensive debate on various proposals that attempt to address the questions of access and rising health care costs is under way. The NHE estimates provide a backdrop for understanding health care financing issues and the factors that account for cost increases during the past three decades. . . .

NATIONAL HEALTH EXPENDITURES

NHE reached a level of $666.2 billion in 1990. Spending grew 10.5 percent, the third consecutive year of similar growth. In 1990, health expenditures absorbed 12.2 percent of GNP, compared with 11.6 percent of GNP in 1989. The 0.6-percentage-point change in the ratio from 1989 to 1990 was the largest increase since 1982 and the second largest increase since 1960. The increase in the proportion of the nation's output going for health care can be attributed to rising health care costs and, more importantly, to the recession that began at the end of 1990. As GNP growth slowed in 1990 and health care cost growth remained strong, health care consumed an even greater incremental share of GNP than in the recent past.

In the United States, the average expenditure per person for health care reached $2,566 during 1990, an increase of 9.4 percent from 1989. Public expenditures accounted for $1,089 per capita (42.4 percent of the total expenditures for health care), and private funds paid for the remaining $1,478 (57.6 percent).

NHE is divided into two broad categories. The first category, health services and supplies (expenditures related to current health care), increased 10.5 percent to $643.4 billion in 1990, accounting for 96.6 percent of health expenditures. Health services and supplies, in turn, consist of personal health care (the direct provision of care), program administration and the net cost of private health insurance, and government public health activities.

The second category, research and construction of medical facilities (expenditures related to future health care), accounted for 3.4 percent of total expenditures, or $22.8 billion.

PERSONAL HEALTH CARE EXPENDITURES

Personal health care expenditures (PHCE) reached $585.3 billion in 1990, accounting for 87.9 percent of all NHE. PHCE includes all spending for health services received by individuals and health products purchased in retail outlets. The proportion of NHE that is PHCE has been fairly constant since 1960. The amount spent per person averaged $2,255 in 1990. Spending for personal health care increased 10.5 percent from 1989 to 1990. This rate of growth is equal to growth in NHE for the same period and about the same as the average growth in PHCE for the 1980s.

The factors that cause growth in PHCE have changed during the past three decades. Factors affecting growth are economywide inflation, medical price inflation in excess of economywide inflation, population, and all other factors. Other factors include any increases in use and intensity of health care services delivered per capita. The average annual growth in PHCE from 1960 to 1970 was 10.5 percent. One-half of this growth was caused by increases in use and intensity of health care services (figure 2), primarily as a result of the implementation of the Medicare and Medicaid programs that increased access to health care by the elderly and poor beginning in 1966. Increases in population caused a larger portion (12 percent) of this increase than in later decades as the last spurt in the postwar baby boom occurred in the early 1960s.

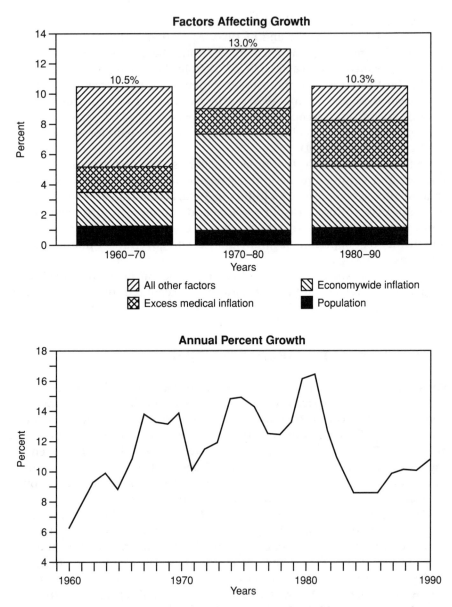

FIGURE 2 Annual Percent Growth in Personal Health Care Expenditures (PHCE) and Factors Affecting Average Annual Growth in PHCE for Selected Periods: 1960–90

Source: Health Care Financing Administration, Office of the Actuary: Data from the Office of National Health Statistics.

During the period 1970–80, growth in PHCE was the highest, averaging 13.0 percent per year. The entire economy experienced high inflation causing one-half of this growth. Although population growth during this period was stable, the share of growth attributable to population increases was the lowest in three decades because population growth was small relative to the large growth in PHCE.

During the 1980s, economywide inflation remained a major factor, responsible for nearly one-half of the growth in PHCE. PHCE grew at an average annual rate of 10.3 percent, somewhat lower than it had in the 1970s. Increases in medical-specific prices affected health expenditures more during the 1980s than in the previous two decades. Medical price inflation in excess of economywide inflation caused 22 percent of the growth. Excess medical inflation caused 16 percent of the growth in the 1960s and only 12 percent in the 1970s.

During the last three decades, the components of personal health care have grown at different rates, changing the distribution among the different types of spending. In the 1960s and 1970s, spending for hospital care grew more rapidly than spending for other types of care. As a result, hospital care as a share of total PHCE increased. During the 1980s, cost-containment efforts of public and private insurers were focused on hospital care spending. These efforts were effective in slowing the growth of hospital spending and, as a result, its share of PHCE decreased. At the same time, expenditures for physician services were growing more rapidly than other types of spending. In 1980, 19.1 percent of PHCE was for physician services. By 1990, this share rose to 21.5 percent. In the past 30 years, expenditures for drugs and other medical nondurables have not grown as rapidly as other types of health care spending, causing drugs and medical nondurables' share of PHCE to decrease by one-half from 17.8 percent in 1960 to 9.3 percent in 1990. . . .

HOME HEALTH CARE

The NHE category of home health care includes expenditures for services and supplies furnished by non-facility-based home health agencies (HHAs). Spending for home health care included in NHE reached $6.9 billion in 1990. An additional $1.6 billion, not included in the NHE home health care category, was spent for care furnished by facility-based (primarily hospital-based) HHAs (included with hospital care in this article). Including the hospital share, $8.5 billion was spent for home health care services in 1990 (figure 3).

Spending for home health care grew faster than spending for any other category of personal health care in 1989 and in 1990. Growth in spending for home health care increased 22.5 percent in 1990, almost as fast as the

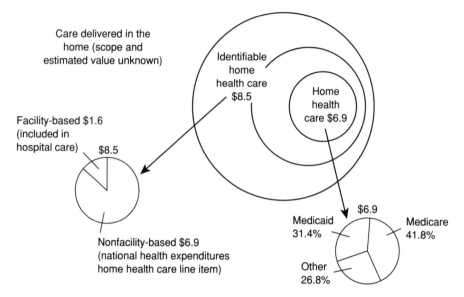

FIGURE 3   Scope and Source of Funds for Home Health Care Spending[1]: 1990

[1]Amounts shown are billions of dollars.

Source: Health Care Financing Administration, Office of the Actuary: Data from the Office of National Statistics.

24.9 percent growth in 1989. After 4 years of slower growth, spending for home health care accelerated in 1989 primarily because of increased funding by the Medicare and Medicaid programs. Medicare clarified its home health care coverage criteria in 1988 and fewer of these claims are being denied.

Public sources financed three-fourths of the home health care services described here. More than one-half of public spending was paid by Medicare and almost all of the residual by Medicaid. Out-of-pocket payments accounted for 12.1 percent of home health care spending and the residual private share, 14.4 percent, was split between private health insurance and non-patient revenue.

The home health care segment of NHE measures a portion of the nation's annual expenditures for medical care services delivered in the home. These estimates are constructed from information reported to the Health Care Financing Administration (HCFA) by HHAs participating in the Medicare and Medicaid programs. A broader definition of home health care would include services delivered by facility-based agencies (counted in the NHE hospital category) and by non-Medicare providers, unpaid caregivers, and services currently beyond the scope of NHE. . . .

MEDICARE

Medicare, a federal insurance program created by Title XVIII of the Social Security Act of 1965, was originally designed to protect people 65 years of age or over from the high cost of health care. In 1972, the program was expanded to cover permanently disabled workers eligible for old age, survivors, and disability insurance benefits and their dependents, as well as people with end stage renal disease.

Medicare has two parts, each with its own trust fund. The hospital insurance (HI) program pays for inpatient hospital services, post-hospital skilled nursing services, home health care services, and hospice care. The supplementary medical insurance (SMI) program covers physician services, outpatient hospital services and therapy, and a few other services.

Unlike other federal health programs, Medicare is not financed solely by general revenue (appropriations from general tax receipts). In 1990, 89 percent of the income for the HI program came from a 1.45-percent payroll tax levied on employers and on employees for the first $51,300 of wages. (Self-employed people were required to contribute 2.9 percent, the equivalent of both the employer's and the employee's share of the HI tax.)

The SMI program was financed by monthly premium payments of $28.60 per enrollee in 1990 and by general revenue. The general revenue share of SMI receipts grew from about 50 percent in the early 1970s to approximately 70 percent in 1980 and later. In 1990, the general revenue share accounted for 72 percent of SMI program income.

More than 34 million aged and disabled people were enrolled in Medicare on July 1, 1990. The program spent $108.9 billion in personal health care (benefit) payments for expenses incurred in 1990 by the 26.6 million enrollees who received benefits. Growth in Medicare spending for personal health care slowed to 8.6 percent in 1990 from the 13.4 percent growth experienced in 1989.

During the past two decades, Medicare has accounted for increasing shares of spending for personal health care. In 1990, Medicare financed 45.0 percent of the public share of PHCE and 18.6 percent of total spending for personal health care. From 1970 to 1980, these shares grew from 32.2 percent to 41.8 percent of the public share and 11.1 percent to 16.6 percent of total spending for personal health care.

Almost 63 percent of Medicare benefits were for hospital care and another 27.5 percent for physician services in 1990. Prior to implementation of various hospital cost-containment measures starting in 1983, the distribution of Medicare spending was relatively stable at approximately 72 percent for hospital care and 22 percent for physician services.

Medicare expenditures for hospital care reached $68.3 billion in 1990, an increase of 9.9 percent from 1989. Medicare's PPS, other cost-containment measures, and a slowdown in growth of general and medical prices caused growth in Medicare spending for hospital care to decelerate from a high of 21.4 percent in 1980 to a low of 5.1 percent in 1986. Since then, growth in Medicare spending for hospital care services including inpatient, outpatient, and hospital-based HHA services has accelerated, almost returning to the double digits observed through the early-1980s. Current efforts to control the growth in Medicare spending for hospital care include reductions in payments for outpatient hospital services.

Medicare spending for physician services increased 9.5 percent from 1989, reaching $30.0 billion in 1990. Medicare's share of total spending for physician services grew from 11.8 percent in 1970 to 19.0 percent in 1980 and 23.9 percent in 1990. Efforts to restrain the growth in spending for physician services included incentives to encourage physician participation in the Medicare program, a temporary freeze on physician fees for Medicare services, reductions in payments to certain physicians, and reductions in payments for diagnostic laboratory tests and some overpriced surgical procedures.

The federal government is currently attempting to control the growth in Medicare spending for physician services through reductions in Medicare payments for additional overpriced procedures, volume performance standards, and other restrictions that limit the growth of Medicare payments to physicians, and increased beneficiary cost-sharing through higher Part B deductibles. Fee schedules based on resource-based relative value scales are scheduled to be phased in over a 3-year period starting in 1992.

Medicare paid $2.5 billion for skilled nursing facility care in 1990, 35 percent less than in 1989. Provisions of the Medicare Catastrophic Coverage Act of 1988 that affected the Medicare nursing home benefit became effective in 1989. In December 1989, the Act was repealed, but Medicare beneficiaries who were entitled to nursing home benefits under the less restrictive provisions of the Act continued to receive benefits. Effects of the Act lingered but are now diminishing. As a result, Medicare's share of total spending for nursing home care declined from 8.0 percent in 1989 to 4.7 percent in 1990. This compares with Medicare's share of total spending for nursing home care of 5.0 percent in 1970 and 2.1 percent in 1980.

Because Medicare clarified its conditions for payment in 1988, it seems likely that Medicare will maintain its current share of total spending for nursing home care at 4–5 percent.

MEDICAID

Medicaid spent $71.3 billion of combined federal and state funds for personal health care in 1990. Growth in program spending for personal health care accelerated from 13.6 percent in 1989 to 20.6 percent in 1990, the fastest annual rate of growth in Medicaid spending since 1975. As a result, Medicaid's share of PHCE grew from 11.2 percent in 1989 to 12.2 percent in 1990.

Medicaid expenditures are largely institutional, with 39.9 percent spent on hospital care and 33.8 percent spent on nursing home care in 1990. Medicaid continues to be the largest third-party payer of long-term care expenditures, financing 45.4 percent of nursing home care in 1990. Growth in Medicaid benefit expenditures accelerated in 1990 for almost all categories of service. In 1990, growth in Medicaid spending accelerated from 14.5 percent in 1989 to 24.1 percent for hospitals, and from 8.6 percent to 17.0 percent for nursing homes.

Medicaid is funded jointly by federal and state and local governments. The federal government sets minimum requirements for eligibility and services, allowing state governments considerable flexibility in designing the total scope of the program within the constraints of the state budgetary process. The federal government requires that all people receiving income benefits under the Supplementary Security Income (SSI) program (covering aged, blind, and disabled individuals) and families qualifying for Aid to Families with Dependent Children (AFDC) automatically qualify for Medicaid benefits. Certain individuals (pregnant women, children under age 6, Medicare enrollees, and Social Security Title IV-E recipients of foster care and adoption assistance) with income too high to qualify for SSI or AFDC cash benefits are also mandatorily eligible for Medicaid. Mandatory coverage of certain children ages 7–18 will be phased in as children born after September 30, 1983, attain age 7. State governments may, at their option, extend the program to cover "medically indigent" individuals or families, recipients of state supplementary payments, and other people with income or resources below specified levels.

Aged and disabled Medicare enrollees with incomes below certain levels were mandatorily covered by Medicaid under the Medicare Catastrophic Coverage Act of 1988. These Medicaid recipients are not eligible for full Medicaid benefits; Medicaid is required to pay only the Medicare premiums, deductibles, and coinsurance amounts. Legislation in 1989 required Medicaid to pay a portion of the Medicare HI premium for certain low-income disabled people. These are Medicare enrollees who qualified for Medicare because they were disabled but who, through rehabilitation and retraining, were able to return to work. Previously, after a specified number of months, these enrollees would have lost their eligibility for Medicare coverage. So that these working disabled people are not penalized for returning to work, they are allowed to retain Medicare coverage by paying the monthly HI and SMI premiums. (Medicaid is not required to pay the SMI premium.)

The federal government also defines minimum services that must be provided to all or specified groups of Medicaid recipients. These services include inpatient and outpatient hospital services; physician care; rural health clinic services; laboratory and X-ray services; nursing home and home health care; and services of selected other health professionals. States may elect to provide additional services such as prescribed drugs, eyeglasses, dental care, and ICFs/MR.

Through state "buy-in" agreements, Medicaid purchases Medicare supplementary medical insurance (Part B) coverage for people who are eligible for both programs. For these "dual-eligibles," Medicare is the primary payer for Medicare-covered services, and Medicaid pays deductibles and coinsurance amounts and provides additional Medicaid-covered health care services. To avoid double counting, the Medicaid estimates presented here do not include the $1.1 billion paid to Medicare by Medicaid in 1990 for buy-in premiums. Therefore, actual Medicaid program expenditures were $72.5 billion in 1990.

Although more than two-thirds of Medicaid recipients in fiscal year 1990 qualified because they were members of an AFDC family, they consumed only one-fourth of program benefits. Conversely, the aged, blind, and disabled, who represent less than one-third of Medicaid recipients, consumed nearly three-fourths of Medicaid benefits.

In fiscal year 1990, there were 25.3 million people who received some type of Medicaid benefit. The number of Medicaid recipients has increased rapidly in recent years. In fiscal year 1990, an additional 1.7 million people received Medicaid benefits. With recent legislation phasing in various expansions to the Medicaid program and limited revenues available to finance the program, states are being pressured to control program costs (*The Nation's Health*, 1991). Tactics in use or proposed by some states include reallocation of available funds from high-cost services provided to selected recipients to lower cost services furnished to broader groups of recipients (Mayer and Kimball, 1991), creative techniques to generate additional financing such as provider-specific taxes and "voluntary donations" from hospitals and physicians (Kimball, 1991) and overall spending cuts. . . .

BIBLIOGRAPHY

American Hospital Association: *Hospital Statistics: A Comprehensive Summary of U.S. Hospitals, 1990–1991.* Chicago, 1990.

American Medical Association: *Socioeconomic Characteristics of Medical Practice, 1990–1991.* Chicago, 1991.

Kimball, M.C.: States outfox feds for Medicaid cash. *HealthWeek* 5(10): 1.59, May 20, 1991.

Lakin, K.C., Prouty, R.W., White, C.C., et al.: *Intermediate Care Facilities for Persons with Mental Retardation (ICFs-MR): Program Utilization and Resident Characteristics.* Center for Residential and Community Services, University of Minnesota. Minneapolis, Mar. 1990.

Lazenby, H.C., and Letsch, S.W.: National health expenditures, 1989. *Health Care Financing Review* 12(2): 1–26. HCFA Pub. No. 03316. Office of Research and Demonstrations, Health Care Financing Administration. Washington. U.S. Government Printing Office, Winter 1991.

Letsch, S.W., Maple, B.M., Cowan, C.A., and Donham, C.S.: Health Care Indicators, *Health Care Financing Review* 13(1):129–153. HCFA Pub. No. 03321. Office of Research and Demonstrations, Health Care Financing Administration. Washington, U.S. Government Printing Office, Fall 1991.

Levit, K.R., and Cowan, C.A.: The burden of health care costs: Business, households, and governments. *Health Care Financing Review* 12(2): 127–137. HCFA Pub. No. 03298. Office of Research and Demonstrations, Health Care Financing Administration. Washington. U.S. Government Printing Office, Winter 1990.

Mayer, D., and Kimball, M.C.: Ore. commission OKs Medicaid pecking order. *HealthWeek* 5(4):1,36, Feb. 25, 1991.

Office of National Cost Estimates: Revisions to the national health accounts and methodology. *Health Care Financing Review* 11(4):42–54. HCFA Pub. No. 03298. Office of Research and Demonstrations, Health Care Financing Administration. Washington, U.S. Government Printing Office, Summer 1990.

The Nation's Health: Outlays for Medicaid Mandates Strapping Budgets, say States. 21(2):5. American Public Health Association, Washington, Feb. 1991.

U.S. Bureau of the Census: *Services Annual Survey.* U.S. Department of Commerce. Washington, U.S. Government Printing Office, 1990.

The quality of a health *care system is truly measured not by what it spends or the number of sophisticated procedures it performs, but how it enhances the potential of the population to fulfill its personal and social choices and the extent to which it limits suffering.*
— David Mechanic

George J. Schieber / Jean-Pierre Poullier /
Leslie M. Greenwald

U.S. Health Expenditure Performance: An International Comparison and Data Update

In this article, we examine expenditure trends and the economic performance of the health systems of the 24 Organization for Economic Cooperation and Development (OECD) countries with special emphasis on 6:
Canada, France, Germany (the former Federal Republic of Germany), Japan, the United Kingdom, and the United States. . . .

EXPENDITURE PERFORMANCE IN 24 COUNTRIES

. . . In 1980, the share of health in gross domestic product (GDP) averaged
7.0 percent for the OECD countries, ranging from 4.0 in Turkey to 9.4 in
Sweden. The United States and Ireland had the second-highest shares, at
9.2 percent. In 1990, the average had increased to 7.6 percent, but the
range widened from 4.0 in Turkey to 12.1 in the United States. Most
countries have stabilized their health-to-GDP ratios, as evidenced by the
fact that the average ratio has barely changed since 1983. The dispersion in
the health-to-GDP ratio, as measured by the coefficient of variation (i.e.,
the standard deviation divided by the mean), has been relatively stable,
0.19 in 1980 and 0.20 in 1990.

The United States exhibits the largest absolute growth in its health-to-
GDP ratio (table 1). The U.S. ratio has increased by 2.9 percentage points
since 1980, compared with an average OECD increase of 0.6 percentage
points. Iceland, which had the second-largest absolute increase, had an
increase of 2.1 percentage points. The U.S. ratio grew at 2.7 percent a year
(second only to Iceland), compared with an OECD average of 0.8-percent
growth.

The authors are analysts at the U.S. Health Care Financing Administration.

Abridged from Shieber, G.J., Poullier, J-P., and Greenwald, L.M. (1992). U.S. health
expenditure performance: An international comparison and data update. *Health Care
Financing Review* 13(4):1–17. Used with permission.

TABLE 1 Total Health Expenditures as a Percent of Gross Domestic Product for 24 Organization for Economic Cooperation and Development (OECD) Countries: 1980–90

Country	1980	1981	1982	1983	1984	1985	1986	1987	1988	1989	1990	Compound growth rate[1]
Australia	7.3	7.5	7.7	7.7	7.7	7.7	8.0	7.8	7.7	7.7	8.2	1.1
Austria	7.9	8.2	8.0	8.0	7.9	8.1	8.3	8.4	8.4	8.4	8.4	0.6
Belgium	6.7	7.3	7.4	7.5	7.4	7.4	7.4	7.5	7.5	7.4	7.5	1.2
Canada	7.4	7.5	8.4	8.6	8.5	8.5	8.8	8.8	8.7	8.8	9.3	2.3
Denmark	6.8	6.8	6.8	6.6	6.4	6.3	6.0	6.3	6.5	6.4	6.3	−0.8
Finland	6.5	6.6	6.7	6.9	6.9	7.2	7.4	7.4	7.2	7.2	7.8	1.9
France	7.6	7.9	8.0	8.2	8.5	8.5	8.5	8.5	8.6	8.7	8.8	1.6
Germany	8.4	8.7	8.6	8.5	8.7	8.7	8.7	8.7	8.9	8.2	8.1	−0.4
Greece	4.3	4.5	4.4	4.6	4.5	4.9	5.4	5.2	5.0	5.3	5.5	2.4
Iceland	6.5	6.6	6.9	7.6	7.0	7.1	7.8	7.9	8.5	8.7	8.6	2.9
Ireland	9.2	8.8	8.4	8.5	8.2	8.2	8.1	7.9	7.3	6.9	7.0	−2.6
Italy	6.9	6.7	6.9	7.0	6.8	7.0	6.9	7.4	7.6	7.6	7.7	1.2
Japan	6.4	6.6	6.8	6.8	6.6	6.5	6.6	6.7	6.6	6.6	6.5	0.1
Luxembourg	6.8	7.1	6.9	6.8	6.6	6.8	6.7	7.3	7.2	6.9	7.2	0.5
Netherlands	8.0	8.2	8.4	8.4	8.1	8.0	8.1	8.3	8.2	8.1	8.2	0.2
New Zealand	7.2	6.9	6.7	6.6	6.2	6.6	6.8	7.3	7.3	7.3	7.4	0.2
Norway	6.6	6.6	6.8	6.8	6.5	6.4	7.1	7.4	7.7	7.4	7.4	1.1
Portugal	5.9	6.4	6.3	6.2	6.3	7.0	6.6	6.8	7.1	7.2	6.7	1.2
Spain	5.6	5.8	5.9	6.0	5.8	5.7	5.6	5.7	6.0	6.3	6.6	1.7
Sweden	9.4	9.5	9.7	9.6	9.4	8.8	8.5	8.6	8.6	8.6	8.6	−0.9
Switzerland	7.3	7.3	7.5	7.8	7.8	7.6	7.6	7.7	7.8	7.8	7.7	0.5
Turkey	4.0	4.4	3.6	3.6	3.5	2.8	3.5	3.6	3.8	3.9	4.0	0.0
United Kingdom	5.8	6.0	5.9	6.1	6.1	6.0	6.0	6.1	6.1	6.1	6.2	0.7
United States	9.2	9.6	10.4	10.5	10.3	10.5	10.7	10.9	11.1	11.5	12.1	2.7
OECD average	7.0	7.2	7.2	7.3	7.2	7.2	7.3	7.4	7.5	7.5	7.6	0.8

[1]Compound growth rate expressed as a percentage point.

Source: Tables 1 and 33 of the Appendix to the original article.

The public share of total health spending for 1980–90 (table 2) has been fairly stable since the mid-1970s. In 1980, the public share ranged from 27 percent in Turkey to 98 percent in Norway, with an OECD average of 76 percent. The United States, with a ratio of 42 percent, was the second lowest. In 1990, the average ratio for the OECD was 74 percent, ranging from 36 percent in Turkey to 95 percent in Norway. Once again, the United States, at 42 percent, has the second-lowest ratio and is the only country other than Turkey with a ratio below 60 percent. . . .

PERFORMANCE OF SIX MAJOR COUNTRIES

. . . The expenditure performance of the U.S. health sector is compared with the health sector performances of Canada, France, Germany, Japan, and the United Kingdom on the basis of . . . level and rate of growth in the health-to-GDP ratio; growth in nominal GDP and nominal total health spending; growth in nominal and real (health deflator-adjusted) per capita health spending; growth in real (GDP deflator-adjusted) per capita health spending; levels and rates of growth of per capita health spending in U.S. dollars; growth in nominal and real per capita GDP; levels and rates of growth in per capita GDP in U.S. dollars; growth in health care and overall prices (e.g., GDP deflator), as well as excess health care inflation (i.e., rate of growth in health care prices relative to the rate of growth in the GDP deflator); and growth in population.

. . . The comparative performance of each country is discussed in turn, and where rankings are mentioned, we are referring to a nation's rank within these 6 countries. . . .

Canada

The Canadian system has been characterized as a provincial government health insurance model, in which each of the 10 provinces runs its own health system under general federal rules and with a fixed federal contribution. Entitlement to benefits is linked to residency, and the system is financed through general taxation. Private insurance is prohibited from covering the same benefits covered by the public system. However, more than 60 percent of Canadians are covered by complementary private policies. Seventy-three percent of all health expenditures are public, and an estimated 20 percent of health care expenditures are paid out of pocket. Hospitals are funded on the basis of global budgets, and physicians in both inpatient and outpatient settings are paid on a negotiated fee-for-service basis. The systems vary somewhat from province to province, and certain provinces such as Quebec have established global budgets for physician services. The federal government share of spending has progres-

TABLE 2 Public Health Expenditures as a Percent of Total Health Expenditures for 24 Organization for Economic Cooperation and Development (OECD) Countries: 1980–90

Country	1980	1981	1982	1983	1984	1985	1986	1987	1988	1989	1990
Australia	63	62	61	65	72	72	71	70	69	69	68
Austria	69	70	68	67	66	67	68	67	66	67	67
Belgium	83	80	86	83	83	82	81	83	83	83	83
Canada	75	76	76	76	75	75	74	74	74	73	73
Denmark	85	85	85	85	85	84	85	84	84	83	83
Finland	79	80	80	79	79	79	79	80	79	80	81
France	79	79	79	78	77	77	76	76	75	75	74
Germany	75	75	75	73	73	74	73	74	73	73	73
Greece	82	84	91	88	88	81	81	80	83	76	76
Iceland	88	89	89	90	87	91	87	87	87	87	87
Ireland	82	83	82	80	78	77	76	73	73	73	75
Italy	81	79	79	79	78	77	76	78	78	77	76
Japan	71	70	70	72	72	73	73	73	72	71	72
Luxembourg	93	93	93	89	89	89	89	92	92	91	91
Netherlands	75	75	76	75	76	75	72	74	73	72	71
New Zealand	84	88	84	86	86	85	86	85	85	82	82
Norway	98	98	97	98	97	96	96	98	96	96	95
Portugal	72	71	62	56	55	56	58	58	58	58	62
Spain	80	79	79	84	82	81	79	78	78	78	78
Sweden	93	92	92	92	92	90	90	90	89	89	90
Switzerland	68	68	68	69	68	69	69	67	68	68	68
Turkey	27	—	—	—	41	50	42	40	38	37	36
United Kingdom	90	89	88	88	87	87	86	86	85	85	84
United States	42	42	41	41	41	41	42	42	42	42	42
OECD average	76	79	78	78	76	76	75	75	75	74	74

Source: Tables 1 and 2 of the Appendix to the original article.

sively declined from the historic 50-percent share of all costs to 38 percent in 1990. The delivery system is composed largely of nonprofit community hospitals and self-employed physicians. Only about 5 percent of Canadian hospital beds are not public; private hospitals do not participate in the public insurance program (Iglehart, 1986; Neuschler, 1990).

. . . Canada's health-to-GDP ratio increased sharply from 7.4 percent in 1980 to 9.3 in 1990; the rate of growth was second only to that of the United States. Canadian nominal health expenditures have grown faster relative to GDP than in the other five countries, with the exception of the United States.

France

The French health care system is based on the social insurance or Bismarck model. Virtually the entire population is covered by a statutorily based compulsory health insurance plan financed through the social security system. There are three major programs and several smaller ones (although the principal one, Caisse Nationale d'Assurance Maladie des Travailleurs Salaries, covers about 70 percent of the population) that are quasi-autonomous nongovernmental bodies. The system is financed through employee and employer payroll tax contributions. There is significant cost sharing and more than 80 percent of the population supplements their public benefits by purchasing insurance from private nonprofit mutuels. About 2 percent of the population has private commercial insurance.

The public share of total health spending is 74 percent, and about 17 percent of expenditures represent direct out-of-pocket payments. Physicians practicing in public hospitals are salaried, but physicians in private hospitals and in ambulatory care settings are typically paid on a negotiated fee-for-service basis. Public hospitals are paid by means of prospective global budgets, and private hospitals are paid on the basis of negotiated per diem payment rates. In terms of the delivery system, about 65 percent of hospital beds are public, with the remaining 35 percent private (and equally divided between profit and nonprofit). Ambulatory care physicians and those practicing in private hospitals are generally self-employed, while those practicing in municipal health centers and public hospitals are salaried employees (Organization for Economic Cooperation and Development, 1992; Schneider et al., 1992; Glaser, 1991; U.S. General Accounting Office, 1991).

. . . France's health-to-GDP ratio increased from 7.6 percent in 1980 to 8.8 percent in 1990 and exhibited the third-highest rate of growth after the United States and Canada. France (like the United States and Canada) demonstrated nominal health spending growth that significantly exceeded growth in GDP.

Germany

The German health care system is also based on the social insurance model. Virtually the entire population is covered by statutory sickness funds and private insurance. There are some 1,200 sickness funds that cover about 88 percent of the population. These sickness funds are financed through payroll-based contributions by the employee and employer. About 9 percent of sickness fund members purchase complementary private insurance. Another 10 percent of the population chooses not to participate in the public system and is fully covered by private insurance. Seventy-three percent of all health expenditures are public, and about 11 percent are direct out-of-pocket payments.

Ambulatory and inpatient care are completely separate, and German hospitals generally do not have outpatient departments. Ambulatory care physicians are paid on the basis of fee schedules negotiated between the organizations of sickness funds and the organizations of physicians. There is a separate fee schedule for private patients that uses the same relative value scale. Hospitals are paid on the basis of negotiated per diem payments that include the physician's remuneration, except for private patients, for whom private insurers make separate fee-for-service payments for inpatient physician services. Individual hospitals negotiate payment rates with the sickness funds.

With regard to the delivery system, public (federal, state, and local) hospitals account for about 51 percent of the beds; private voluntary hospitals, often run by religious organizations, account for 35 percent of the beds; and private for-profit hospitals, generally owned by physicians, account for 14 percent of the beds. Ambulatory care physicians are generally self-employed professionals, and most hospital-based physicians are salaried employees of the hospital (Schneider, 1991, 1992; Hurst, 1991; Wicks, 1992).

. . . Germany's health-to-GDP ratio declined over the 1980–90 period, from 8.4 percent in 1980 to 8.1 percent in 1990. Germany was the only country of the six examined in which growth in nominal health spending did not exceed growth in the overall economy.

Japan

Japan's health care financing is also based on the social insurance model and, in particular, on the German health care system. The entire population is covered by three general schemes: Employee Health Insurance, Community Health Insurance, and Health and Medical Services for the Aged. About 62 percent of the population receives coverage through some 1,800 employer-sponsored plans. Small businesses, the self-employed, and farmers are covered through Community Health Insurance, which is administered by a conglomeration of local governmental and private bodies. The elderly are covered by a separate plan that largely pools funds from the other plans.

The system is financed through employer and employee income-related premiums. There are different levels of public subsidization of the three different schemes. Limited private insurance exists for supplemental coverage. Public expenditures account for 72 percent of total health spending, while out-of-pocket expenses account for about 12 percent. Physicians and hospitals are paid on the basis of national negotiated fee schedules. Physicians practicing in public hospitals are salaried, while those practicing in physician-owned clinics and private hospitals are reimbursed on a fee-for-service basis. Physicians prescribe and dispense pharmaceuticals. About 80 percent of Japan's hospitals are privately operated (and often physician-owned), with the remaining 20 percent being public. For-profit hospitals are prohibited (Ikegami, 1991; Iglehart, 1988; U.S. General Accounting Office, 1991; Powell and Anesaki, 1990).

. . . Japan's health-to-GDP ratio remained relatively stable, increasing slightly from 6.4 percent in 1980 to 6.5 percent in 1990. In both 1980 and 1990, Japan consistently had the second-lowest health-to-GDP ratio behind the United Kingdom. Over this 10-year period, Japan's nominal health spending increased at about the same rate as nominal GDP.

United Kingdom

The United Kingdom employs the National Health Service or Beveridge model to finance and deliver health care. The entire population is covered under a system that is financed mainly from general taxation. There is minimal cost sharing. Some 15 percent of the population buys private insurance either as a supplement to the public system or as an alternative. Eighty-four percent of all health spending is public and about 4 percent of all spending represents direct out-of-pocket payments. Services are organized and managed by regional and local public authorities. General practitioners serve as gatekeepers and are reimbursed on the basis of a combination of capitation payments, fees, and other allowances. Hospitals receive global budgets from district health authorities, and hospital-based physicians are salaried. Private insurance reimburses both physicians and hospitals on a fee-for-service basis.

With regard to the delivery system, self-employed general practitioners are considered independent contractors, and salaried hospital-based physicians are public employees. Ninety percent of the United Kingdom's hospital beds are public and generally owned by the National Health Service. As of 1991, it became possible for large physician practices to become "budget holders," receiving a larger capitation payment and being placed at risk for a defined list of inpatient and outpatient services. Similarly, individual hospitals may become "self-governing trust hospitals," whereby they can compete for patients and sell their services (Organization for Economic Cooperation and Development, to be published; Schneider, 1992; Day and Klein, 1991).

. . . The United Kingdom consistently had the lowest-ranking health-to-GDP ratio, devoting 5.8 percent in 1980 and 6.2 percent in 1990. Nominal health spending grew at 9.8 percent, increasing only slightly faster than GDP at 9.0 percent, giving the United Kingdom the third-lowest differential in growth between health and GDP after Germany and Japan.

United States

The U.S. health care financing system is based on the consumer sovereignty or private insurance model. About three-quarters of the population is covered by private insurance obtained through employers or individually purchased. Nineteen percent of the population is covered by public programs, while some 14 percent of the population has no coverage. These percentages total more than 100 percent because 13 percent of the population has multiple health insurance coverage (e.g., public and private coverage). There are more than 1,000 private insurance companies. Employer-based health insurance is tax-subsidized, as health insurance premiums are a tax-deductible business expense, but are not taxed as employee compensation. Benefits, premiums, and provider reimbursement methods differ among private insurance plans and differ among public programs as well. Public spending accounts for 42 percent of total health expenditures, and direct out-of-pocket payments account for 20 percent.

Physicians, providing both ambulatory and inpatient care, are generally reimbursed on a fee-for-service basis, and payment rates vary among insurers. Hospitals are paid on the basis of charges, costs, negotiated rates, or diagnosis-related groups, depending on the patient's insurer. There are no overall global budgets or expenditure limits.

There are some 6,700 hospitals in the United States: 340 federal hospitals, 880 specialty hospitals, and 5,500 community hospitals. Of the community hospitals, 27 percent are public; 59 percent are private nonprofit; and 14 percent are private for-profit. Physicians are generally self-employed professionals (Levit et al., 1991; DeLew, Greenberg, and Kinchen, 1992).

The United States had the highest health-to-GDP ratio in both 1980 and 1990 and also the fastest rate of growth. The health-to-GDP ratio increased from 9.2 percent in 1980 to 12.1 percent in 1990, for a 2.7-percent annual rate of growth. This rate of increase far exceeded the 2.3-percent rate of growth in Canada, the second-fastest growing country, as well as the 1.6-percent rate for France, the third-fastest. This rapid growth in the health-to-GDP ratio is primarily the result of the substantially faster rate of growth in U.S. health spending relative to GDP. . . .

CONCLUSION

By virtually all measures, U.S. health spending is the highest in the world. Over the past 10 years, whether in absolute dollar terms or relative to its GDP, U.S. health care expenditures have increased faster than spending in other countries, and the gap between the United States and other major industrialized countries has increased. The opportunity costs of U.S. health expenditure growth are the largest of the six major countries. Excess health care inflation in the United States exceeds excess health care inflation in other major countries. Health spending relative to GDP is increasing more rapidly in the United States than in other countries.

Although one cannot draw definitive conclusions about overall health sector performance in the absence of better measures of underlying morbidity and outcomes, the cost-containment measures of the past have done little to slow the growth of U.S. health care expenditures. This is not surprising because virtually all incentives (e.g., tax subsidies, fee-for-service reimbursement, non-price competition among providers, consumer expectations, malpractice risks) promote increased spending. In a system in which no one is in charge—neither empowered consumers nor powerful regulatory bodies—and in which major new technological breakthroughs abound, it is not surprising that costs are out of control while millions of people lack insurance coverage. Moreover, unlike other countries, the United States has not found an equitable way to spread over its entire population the costs of insuring its health risks.

For health care reform to succeed, the United States must solve at least three problems that have been dealt with by the other major industrialized countries:

- The poor and disadvantaged must be provided with health services, health insurance, or the financial means to purchase health insurance.
- For the non-poor, a mechanism must be found to pool health risks while reforming private health insurance (e.g., having guaranteed issue, eliminating preexisting conditions and nonrenewability clauses).
- Mechanisms must be found to control costs.

All other major industrialized countries cover their entire populations either through guaranteed entitlement or as an earned right. There are special provisions to cover the poor and disadvantaged and those outside the labor force. All the major U.S. reform bills deal with this problem either through tax credits or direct entitlement. However, underlying all these reforms is the need for the United States to find a way to finance this enhanced coverage. Other countries have been willing to accept higher aggregate tax burdens (Organization for Economic Cooperation and Development, 1990). What will emerge from the current U.S. debate is unclear (Enthoven, 1992; Reinhart, 1992), although the financing mechanisms under discussion include: higher taxes, administrative efficiencies, insurance market reform, coordinated care, managed competition, all-payer rate-setting, expenditure limits, cost-sharing, beneficiary premiums, reduction of tax subsidies, effectiveness research, and medical malpractice reform.

Other countries have dealt with pooling health risks in a more equitable manner either through universal entitlement to a single system or by forcing financial transfers across sickness funds to adjust for differential risk selection. For example, in the United Kingdom, everyone is guaranteed access to the National Health Service. In both Germany and Japan, interfund transfers are required to adjust for the favorable health risk selection of some plans over others. Ability to pay is dealt with either through a progressive national tax structure as in the United Kingdom or through subsidies by social assistance programs and local governments as in Germany and Japan. Making the plausible assumption that private health insurance will remain the principal form of health insurance for the non-poor and non-aged in the United States, it is essential to develop policies that either prohibit or counteract the mechanisms used to achieve favorable risk selection (Light, 1992).

Perhaps most difficult is the need to control costs. Other major industrialized countries have tended to rely on regulatory mechanisms such as expenditure caps, global budgets for hospitals, salary and capitation payments for physicians, and health planning. Nevertheless, these countries have also learned that capping spending does not necessarily lead to efficient provision or consumption within the cap. As a result, numerous countries are attempting to eliminate micro-inefficiencies by experimenting with diagnosis-related groups and other market-oriented payment incentives.

Effective cost-containment is a necessary condition for health care reform. Successful cost-containment in this country will require a fundamental commitment to a major market-oriented and/or serious regulatory approach. As Altman and Rodwin (1988) have argued, the halfway measures of the past have not worked. The basic questions are: Do Americans and their elected representatives have the desire and political will to change a worsening status quo? Are Americans interested in value for money and equity? Is there a willingness to redistribute income in the current social and economic climate? These are important questions to ponder as the Unites States approaches the twenty-first century with the prospect of a $1.6 trillion health sector consuming one out of every six dollars of total output.

BIBLIOGRAPHY

Altman, S.H., and Rodwin, M.A.: Halfway Competitive Markets and Ineffective Regulation: The American Health Care System. *Journal of Health Politics, Policy and Law* 13(2):323–339, Summer 1988.

Barer, M.L., Welch, W.P., and Antioch, L.: Canadian/U.S. Health Care: Reflections on the HIAA's Analysis. *Health Affairs* 10(3):229–236, Fall 1991.

Day, P., and Klein, R.: Britain's Health Care Experiment. *Health Affairs* 10(3):39–59, Fall 1991.

DeLew, N., Greenberg, G., and Kinchen, K.: A layman's guide to the U.S. health care system. *Health Care Financing Review.* Office of Research and Demonstrations, Health Care Financing Administration. Washington. U.S. Government Printing Office. 1992.

Enthoven, A.C.: Commentary: Measuring the Candidates on Health Care. *New England Journal of Medicine* 327(11):807–809, Sept. 10, 1992.

Glaser, W.A.: *Health Insurance in Practice.* San Francisco. Jossey-Bass, 1991.

Hurst, J.: Reform of health care in Germany. *Health Care Financing Review* 12(3):73–86. HCFA Pub. No. 03317. Office of Research and Demonstrations, Health Care Financing Administration. Washington. U.S. Government Printing Office, Spring 1991.

Iglehart, J.K.: Canada's Health Care System. *New England Journal of Medicine* 315(4):202–208, 315(12):778–784, and 315(25):1608–1610, July 17, Sept. 18, and Dec. 18, 1986.

Iglehart, J.K.: Japan's Medical Care System. *New England Journal of Medicine* 319(12):807–812 and 319(17):1166–1172, Sept. 22 and Oct. 27, 1988.

Ikegami, N.: Japanese Health Care: Low Cost Through Regulated Fees. *Health Affairs* 10(3):87–109, Fall 1991.

Levit, K., Lazenby, H., Cowan, C., and Letsch, S.: National Health Expenditures, 1990. *Health Care Financing Review* 13(1):29–54. HCFA Pub. No. 03321. Office of Research and Demonstrations, Health Care Financing Administration. Washington. U.S. Government Printing Office, Fall 1991.

Light, D.W.: The practice and ethics of risk-rated health insurance. *Journal of the American Medical Association* 267(18):2503–2506, May 13, 1992.

Neuschler, E.: *Canadian Health Care: The Implications of Public Insurance.* Washington. Health Insurance Association of America, 1990.

Organization for Economic Cooperation and Development: *Measuring Health Care.* Paris. 1985.

Organization for Economic Cooperation and Development: *Revenue Statistics of OECD Member Countries, 1965–1989.* Paris, 1990.

Organization for Economic Cooperation and Development: *National Accounts, 1992.* Vol. I, Part VIII. Paris, 1992a.

Organization for Economic Cooperation and Development: *OECD Health Systems: Facts and Trends.* Paris, 1992b.

Organization for Economic Cooperation and Development: *The Reform of Health Care: A Comparative Analysis of Seven OECD Countries.* Paris, 1992.

Poullier, J.-P.: Health data file: Overview and methodology. *Health Care Financing Review* Annual Supplement 1989. Pp. 111–118. HCFA Pub. No. 03291. Office of Research and Demonstrations, Health Care Financing Administration. Washington. U.S. Government Printing Office, Dec. 1989.

Powell, M., and Anesaki, M.: *Health Care in Japan.* London and New York. Routledge, 1990.

Reinhart, U.E.: Commentary: Politics and the Health Care System. *New*

England Journal of Medicine 327(11): 809–811, Sept. 10, 1992.

Schieber, G.J.: Health care expenditures in major industrialized countries, 1960–87. *Health Care Financing Review* 11(4):159–167. HCFA Pub. No. 03298. Office of Research and Demonstrations, Health Care Financing Administration. Washington. U.S. Government Printing Office, Summer 1990.

Schieber, G.J., and Poullier, J.-P.: Overview of international comparisons of health care expenditures. *Health Care Financing Review* Annual Supplement 1989:1–7. HCFA Pub. No. 03291. Office of Research and Demonstrations, Health Care Financing Administration. Washington. U.S. Government Printing Office, Dec. 1989.

Schieber, G.J., and Poullier, J.-P.: International Health Spending: Issues and Trends. *Health Affairs* 10(1): 106–116, Spring 1991.

Schieber, G.J., Poullier, J.-P., and Greenwald, L.M.: Health Care Systems in Twenty-four Countries. *Health Affairs* 10(3):22–38, Fall 1991.

Schneider, M.: Health care cost containment in the Federal Republic of Germany. *Health Care Financing Review* 12(3):87–101. HCFA Pub. No. 03317. Office of Research and Demonstrations, Health Care Financing Administration. Washington. U.S. Government Printing Office, Spring 1991.

Schneider, M., et al.: Health care in the EC member states. *Health Policy* 20(1–2):1–251, Feb. 1992.

U.S. General Accounting Office: *Health Care Spending Control: The Experience of France, Germany, and Japan.* Gaithersburg, MD. Nov. 1991.

Wicks, E.K.: *German Health Care: Financing, Administration, and Coverage.* Washington. Health Insurance Association of America, 1992.

Modern science and modern biomedicine in the hands of sensitive and dedicated practitioners have given us immense gifts of comfort, life, and health. *The technologies have also made possible the perpetration of hideous monstrosities; the threat of nuclear war has not yet receded.*
— Margaret Stacey

Daniel R. Waldo / Sally T. Sonnefeld / Jeffrey A. Lemieux /
David R. McKusick

Health Spending Through 2030: Three Scenarios

Rising health expenditures continue to challenge traditional means of paying for health care. In 1990, health expenditures reached $666.2 billion and accounted for 12.2 percent of gross national product (GNP), up from 11.6 percent in 1989. Health expenditures increased more than twice as fast as did the general economy in 1990, as measured by GNP, and continues to grow: A projection for 1991 suggests that the health spending ratio will reach 13.1 percent. This rather sharp increase in health spending relative to GNP is due more to deceleration of GNP than to acceleration of health spending, but this is scant consolation to those faced with rising health bills and shrinking resources.

Recent changes in Financial Accounting Standards Board (FASB) regulations regarding retiree health costs and trustees' recommendations concerning the Medicare trust funds have spurred interest in long-range estimates of health spending. To that end, we have developed three scenarios describing health expenditures over the next forty years. For our main case—our "middle scenario"—we prepared a plausible extrapolation of long-term trends that is consistent with government projections of Medicare and Medicaid spending. In this middle scenario, spending for health reaches 26.1 percent of GNP by the year 2030. In another scenario, we followed the basic pattern of the middle scenario but allowed growth rates to stay somewhat higher. In this case, health expenditures reach 43.7 percent of GNP by 2030. In a third scenario, we severely curtailed trends in consumption per capita beginning in 1992 and discovered that this leads to a health-to-GNP ratio of 14.4 percent by 2030. These projections highlight the momentum of the health care system and suggest that if reform is to have a significant impact on future levels of health spending, the United States will need to adopt that reform sooner rather than later.

The authors are analysts at the Office of National Health Statistics, U.S. Health Care Financing Administration.

Abridged from Waldo, D.R., Sonnefeld, S.T., Lemieux, J.A., and McKusick, D.R. (1991). Health spending through 2030: Three scenarios. *Health Affairs* 10(4):230–242. Used with permission from Project HOPE.

THE MODEL

The model we used to quantify the scenarios is actuarial in nature, in that it relies on trend analysis rather than on econometric fitting of dependent to independent variables, and consists of a series of identities, the factors of which are projected and reconciled.[1] It explicitly incorporates the effects over time of change in the age/sex composition of the population, using factors that describe the effects of that change on use per capita and "intensity" per unit of use.

The scenarios incorporate several exogenous factors. Each takes as given the intermediate (Alternative II) population estimates and macro-economic assumptions used by the federal government to prepare the Medicare and Social Security trust fund reports. In the trustees' assumptions, the U.S. population grows slowly and ages rapidly. The increase in the population over the next forty years is projected to diminish from its current rate of 1 percent per year to 0.3 percent per year by the year 2030, averaging 0.6 percent per year over the 40-year span. However, the population age 65 and older is projected to grow at an average annual rate of 1.9 percent, and that under age 65, 0.4 percent. Consequently, the proportion of the population age 65 and older is projected to grow from 12.3 percent in 1990 to 20.4 percent in 2030.

This change has two effects. First, population-driven demand for health care will increase faster than the 0.6 percent growth of the population. People age 65 and older currently spend four times as much for health care as do those under age 65; the difference in consumption is particularly pronounced for nursing home, home health, and hospital care.[2] Our model tells us that health spending in the year 2000 will be 5 percent higher than it was in 1990 simply as a result of changes in the age/sex composition of the population. Solely as a result of these changes, spending in 2010 will be 10 percent higher than in 1990; in 2020, 17 percent higher; and in 2030, 27 percent higher.[3]

The second effect of demographic change is on financing. Government programs, such as Medicare, that depend on workers for funds will be increasingly strained in the future. Today, there are 3.4 covered workers for every Medicare beneficiary in the nation, but that ratio will fall to 2 workers per beneficiary by 2030. Consequently, each worker's burden of support for existing programs will increase by more than half.

Change in the composition of the population also is reflected in the projections of real GNP growth. Over the past decade, real GNP (the value of production of goods and services in the economy, adjusted for price inflation) has increased an average of 2.7 percent per year. In the coming decade, it is projected to average 2.1 percent per year; over the whole 40-year projection period, reacting to a more slowly growing work force, average annual growth is projected to be 1.7 percent.

We assume little change in the general rate of inflation over the next 40 years. As measured by the GNP implicit price deflator, inflation is assumed to stabilize at 4 percent, quite close to the 1990 rate of 4.1 percent and the 1980–1990 average of 4.4 percent per year.

Some limitations imposed by exogenous macroeconomic assumptions, by definition, do not vary from scenario to scenario. The health sector and the rest of the economy affect each other in several ways. Our model incorporates "global" pressures on the health sector, but not the reverse pressures.[4] First, the delivery of health care services tends to be characterized by slow labor productivity growth (as is true of almost all service industries). In a long-range projection, the greater the production of health care (or any service), the lower is average productivity and (by consequence) real GNP per person. This phenomenon is neither good nor bad; it merely reflects the types of goods and services consumers purchase. However, it results in a correlation between long-run trends in health care expenditure and those of general economic activity. Second, there is a correlation between illness and health expenditure, between illness and productivity, and thus between health expenditure and productivity (independent of that discussed above). We assume, however, that raising health expenditures will not affect health status enough to raise overall productivity or survival rates, nor will lowering health expenditures achieve the reverse. The effects of these limitations vary across the scenario. In the case of the middle scenario, the effects probably are minimal; the further one diverges from the trustees' basic assumptions, the more pronounced the effects will be.

THE MIDDLE SCENARIO

Our middle scenario is an "envelope" for plausible projections of government outlays under Medicare and Medicaid. It is tied to the assumptions and conclusions of the Medicare trustees' reports for 1991, and projected values of hospital insurance (Medicare Part A) and supplementary medical insurance (Medicare Part B) benefits are built into the projection model. The scenario is predicated on "current law"; that is, we assume that current programs, regulations, and practices continue—that there are no shocks to the economy, no technological breakthroughs, and no reforms of the health care delivery and financing systems, except that the Medicare trust fund is allowed to borrow to meet its obligations. This scenario also incorporates constraints imposed by physician supply: projections of the numbers of physicians and dentists, made by the Health Resources and Services Administration, have been used to project expenditures for the services of those professionals.

Given these assumptions, our middle scenario shows health spending rising to 16.4 percent of GNP by the year 2000 and 26.1 percent of GNP by 2030. In this scenario, hospital care and physician services account for an increasing share of the health dollar. Expenditures for nursing home care also grow more rapidly than total spending, although the real surge in demand for that care does not begin until after 2015, when the postwar baby-boom cohorts begin to reach age 70 (exhibit 1).

Over the next 40 years, private funds are projected to account for a smaller share of total spending, while Medicare picks up a larger share. The aging of the population means that more of the population is eligible for Medicare benefits, and Medicare is projected to account for a quarter of all health spending by 2030 (provided that it is fully funded). Medicaid is also expected to pay for a larger share of health care. This is due less to the size of the program itself than to the increased use of nursing home care: Medicaid accounts for almost 45 cents of every dollar of nursing home revenue. The flip side of these phenomena is a reduction of the private share of health expenditures. When people become eligible for Medicare, that program assumes responsibility for much of the health care previously covered by private health insurance; typically, beneficiaries convert their private insurance to Medigap policies. As a result, both the private insurance share of spending and the out-of-pocket share of spending are expected to fall. We note also that the notion of current law projections presumes that funds will be made available to the various channels of payment, be it through higher taxes, lower wages (in the case of employer-sponsored insurance), or whatever means.

The $13 trillion spent for health care by the year 2030 reflects a great deal of price inflation. Over the next 40 years, total expenditure is projected to grow an average of 7.7 percent per year. The price of health goods and services, measured by the implicit price deflator for health, is projected to grow 4.8 percent, compared with a 4 percent increase in the general economywide price level.[5] The U.S. population will grow by 0.6 percent implying a 2.2 percent per capita increase in consumption of (constant dollar expenditure for) health goods and services.

HIGH-SIDE SCENARIO

Our middle scenario might reasonably come to pass if current laws and practices continue over the next 40 years. However, only a little additional growth above that of the middle scenario paints a significantly more depressing picture. Our "high-side" scenario is similar to the middle scenario, in that the future trends in use and price are consistent with those of the past. It differs from the middle scenario in that the ultimate growth rates (the rates at which growth eventually stabilizes) are somewhat higher. Under these assumptions, health spending reaches 43.7 percent of GNP by the year 2030. This higher level of spending is attributable both to greater health price inflation and to more consumption of health goods and services. Divergence from the middle scenario is shown in exhibit 2.

EXHIBIT 1   National Health Expenditures, by Type of Service, Middle Scenario, Selected Calendar Years 1980–2030

Spending Category	1980	1990[a]	2000[a]	2010[a]	2020[a]	2030[a]
National health expenditures[b]	$249.1	$670.9	$1,615.9	$3,369.6	$6,801.9	$13,199.3
Personal health care	218.3	589.3	1,456.0	3,056.5	6,211.6	12,133.2
Hospital care	102.4	257.7	654.2	1,427.0	3,019.2	5,857.2
Physician services	41.9	132.7	360.5	761.3	1,524.8	2,923.1
Nursing home care	20.0	53.6	130.8	278.8	579.4	1,345.2
Other personal health care	54.1	145.3	310.5	589.5	1,088.1	2,007.7
Other national health expenditures	30.7	81.7	159.9	313.0	590.3	1,066.1
Gross national product[b]	$2,732	$5,463	$9,865	$17,528	$30,010	$50,669
Health spending as percent of GNP	9.1%	12.3%	16.4%	19.2%	22.7%	26.1%
Percent Distribution[b]						
National health expenditures	100.0%	100.0%	100.0%	100.0%	100.0%	100.0%
Personal health care	87.7	87.8	90.1	90.7	91.3	91.9
Hospital care	41.1	38.4	40.5	42.4	44.4	44.4
Physician services	16.8	19.8	22.3	22.6	22.4	22.1

Nursing home care	8.0	8.0	8.1	8.3	8.5	10.2
Other personal health care	21.7	21.7	19.2	17.5	16.0	15.2
Other national health expenditures	12.3	12.2	9.9	9.3	8.7	8.1

Annual Percent Change During Decade

National health expenditures	12.8%	10.4%	9.2%	7.6%	7.3%	6.9%
Personal health care	12.9	10.4	9.5	7.7	7.3	6.9
Hospital care	13.9	9.7	9.8	8.1	7.8	6.9
Physician services	11.9	12.2	10.5	7.8	7.2	6.7
Nursing home care	15.2	10.4	9.3	7.9	7.6	8.8
Other personal health care	11.3	10.4	7.9	6.6	6.3	6.3
Other national health expenditures	12.5	10.3	7.0	6.9	6.5	6.1

[a]Projected.
[b]Billions of dollars.
Source: Health Care Financing Administration, Office of the Actuary, data from the Office of National Health Statistics.

EXHIBIT 2   National Health Expeditures, by Type of Service, High-Side Scenario, Selected Calendar Years 1980–2030

Spending Category	1980	1990ᵃ	2000ᵃ	2010ᵃ	2020ᵃ	2030ᵃ
National health expendituresᵇ	$249.1	$670.9	$1,714.6	$4,032.7	$9,450.0	$22,143.7
Personal health care	218.3	589.3	1,549.3	3,682.3	8,707.6	20,600.7
Hospital care	102.4	257.7	704.1	1,736.9	4,306.1	10,419.7
Physician services	41.9	132.7	373.5	872.6	1,978.0	4,399.4
Nursing home care	20.0	53.6	137.5	333.5	787.4	2,089.7
Other personal health care	54.1	145.3	334.2	739.3	1,636.1	3,691.9
Other national health expenditures	30.7	81.7	165.3	350.4	742.4	1,543.0
Gross national productᵇ	$2,732	$5,463	$9,865	$17,528	$30,010	$50,669
Health spending as percent of GNP	9.1%	12.3%	17.4%	23.0%	31.5%	43.7%
Percent Distribution						
National health expenditures	100.0%	100.0%	100.0%	100.0%	100.0%	100.0%
Personal health care	87.7	87.8	90.4	91.3	92.1	93.0
Hospital care	41.1	38.4	41.1	43.1	45.6	47.1
Physician services	16.8	19.8	21.8	21.6	20.9	19.9
Nursing home care	8.0	8.0	8.0	8.3	8.3	9.4
Other personal health care	21.7	21.7	19.5	18.3	17.3	16.7
Other national health expenditures	12.3	12.2	9.6	8.7	7.9	7.0

Annual Percent Change During Decade

National health expenditures	12.8%	10.4%	9.8%	8.9%	8.9%	8.9%
Personal health care	12.9	10.4	10.1	9.0	9.0	9.0
Hospital care	13.9	9.7	10.6	9.4	9.5	9.2
Physician services	11.9	12.2	10.9	8.9	8.5	8.3
Nursing home care	15.2	10.4	9.9	9.3	9.0	10.3
Other personal health care	11.3	10.4	8.7	8.3	8.3	8.5
Other national health expenditures	12.5	10.3	7.3	7.8	7.8	7.6

Percent of Middle Scenario Level

National health expenditures	100.0%	100.0%	106.1%	119.7%	138.9%	167.8%
Personal health care	100.0	100.0	106.4	120.5	140.2	169.8
Hospital care	100.0	100.0	107.6	121.7	142.6	177.9
Physician services	100.0	100.0	103.6	114.6	129.7	150.5
Nursing home care	100.0	100.0	105.2	119.6	135.9	155.3
Other personal health care	100.0	100.0	107.6	125.4	150.4	183.9
Other national health expenditures	100.0	100.0	103.4	111.9	125.8	144.7

[a]Projected.
[b]Billions of dollars.
Sources: Health Care Financing Administration, Office of the Actuary, data from the Office of National Health Statistics.

EXHIBIT 3 National Health Expenditures, by Type of Service, "Draconian" Scenario Beginning in 1992, Selected Calendar Years 1980–2030

Spending Category	1980	1990[a]	2000[a]	2010[a]	2020[a]	2030[a]
National health expenditures[b]	$249.1	$670.9	$1,288.4	$2,333.8	$4,115.3	$7,286.5
Personal health care	218.3	589.3	1,148.1	2,089.4	3,599.9	6,582.8
Hospital care	102.4	257.7	510.1	940.0	1,703.4	3,054.3
Physician services	41.9	132.7	264.1	482.0	844.8	1,444.4
Nursing home care	20.0	53.6	116.9	227.4	418.3	861.4
Other personal health care	54.1	145.3	257.0	440.1	733.4	1,222.7
Other national health expenditures	30.7	81.7	140.4	244.4	415.4	703.7
Gross national product[b]	$2,732	$5,463	$9,865	$17,528	$30,010	$50,669
Health spending as percent of GNP	9.1%	12.3%	13.1%	13.3%	13.7%	14.4%
Percent Distribution						
National health expenditures	100.0%	100.0%	100.0%	100.0%	100.0%	100.0%
Personal health care	87.7	87.8	89.1	89.5	89.9	90.3
Hospital care	41.1	38.4	39.6	40.3	41.4	41.9
Physician services	16.8	19.8	20.5	20.7	20.5	19.8
Nursing home care	8.0	8.0	9.1	9.7	10.2	11.8
Other personal health care	21.7	21.7	19.9	18.9	17.8	16.8
Other national health expenditures	12.3	12.2	10.9	10.5	10.1	9.7

Annual Percent Change During Decade

	12.8%	10.4%	6.7%	6.1%	5.8%	5.9%
National health expenditures	12.8%	10.4%	6.7%	6.1%	5.8%	5.9%
Personal health care	12.9	10.4	6.9	6.2	5.9	5.9
Hospital care	13.9	9.7	7.1	6.3	6.1	6.0
Physician services	11.9	12.2	7.1	6.2	5.8	5.5
Nursing home care	15.2	10.4	8.1	6.9	6.3	7.5
Other personal health care	11.3	10.4	5.9	5.5	5.2	5.2
Other national health expenditures	12.5	10.3	5.6	5.7	5.4	5.4

Percent of Middle Scenario Level

	100.0%	100.0%	79.7%	69.3%	60.5%	55.2%
National health expenditures	100.0%	100.0%	79.7%	69.3%	60.5%	55.2%
Personal health care	100.0	100.0	78.9	68.4	59.6	54.3
Hospital care	100.0	100.0	78.0	65.9	56.4	52.1
Physician services	100.0	100.0	73.3	63.3	55.4	49.4
Nursing home care	100.0	100.0	89.4	81.6	72.2	64.0
Other personal health care	100.0	100.0	82.8	74.7	67.4	60.9
Other national health expenditures	100.0	100.0	87.8	78.1	70.4	66.0

[a]Projected.
[b]Billions of dollars.

Source: Health Care Financing Administration, Office of the Actuary, data from the Office of National Health Statistics.

Two important points emerge from this scenario. First, its main usefulness it to show that current trends could lead to breathtaking levels of
health expenditure down the road; even in this scenario, the ultimate rates
of growth are lower than those of the recent past. Second, the comparison
of health expenditure with GNP in this scenario is not entirely appropriate; the GNP figure would almost certainly be lower if the level of health
spending reached that of the high-side scenario.

'DRACONIAN' SCENARIO

To illustrate the momentum of the health care financing system, we have
also modeled a scenario of extreme restrictions. In this scenario, a massive
(and immediately effective) reform of the system takes place, with the
result that health care prices rise no faster than the GNP deflator, rather
than at higher rates as in the past. Further, change in consumption (or
constant dollar expenditure) per capita is limited to change in real GNP
per capita compounded by the effects of changes in the age/sex composition of the population or the change modeled in the middle scenario,
whichever is less.

If the draconian scenario were to occur, health expenditures would
still rise as a percentage of GNP, but only to the extent that the population
ages. Assuming that the draconian measures began in 1992, spending for
health would still be 13.1 percent of GNP by the year 2000—the same as in
1991—and would hit 14.4 percent by 2030 (exhibit 3).

This scenario is highly implausible but quite instructive. It is implausible because there is virtually no chance of creating and implementing the
type of system reform it depicts by the beginning of 1992. It is instructive
because it shows the momentum of the health care system and how an
increase in the share of GNP going to health is almost inevitable. Further,
the scenario can be manipulated to show how delays in reform can affect
long-range expenditures. If the draconian measures are not implemented
until 1996, health expenditures as a percentage of GNP rise to 16.2 percent
by 2030 instead of 14.4 percent. If the measures are delayed until 2000, the
health-to-GNP ratio rises more sharply, to 17.6 percent by 2030.

SUMMARY

Growth in health spending as a percentage of GNP stems from changes in
income, the introduction of new services and technologies, and changes in
the social and demographic characteristics of the population. It is facilitated
by third-party reimbursement, by market failures that make it difficult for
consumers to assess the benefits and costs of their buying decisions, and by

payment mechanisms that encourage an oversupply of providers. Assuming that current laws and practices continue over the next 40 years, we might reasonably expect health spending to reach a quarter of our nation's GNP. The scenario in which this occurs presumes a sort of Gompertz curve argument for attenuated growth over time and argues that some recent growth has resulted from shocks to the system (such as the response of hospital outpatient services to limitations on inpatient care). Yet it does not take much stretching to find a scenario in which health expenditures reach almost half of GNP by 2030. Such a scenario requires ultimate growth rates only slightly higher than in the first case.

Even with drastic restrictions of use and relative prices, health spending will consume a greater proportion of GNP by 2030 than it does today. Since it is easier to not expand spending than it is to actually cut spending, the logical conclusion of this exercise is that if we want to affect the long-run proportion of our income spent on health, the sooner we act, the better.

NOTES

1. See S.T. Sonnefeld et al., Projections of health care spending through the year 2000, *Health Care Financing Review* (Fall 1991): 1–28; R.A. Arnett et al., Projections of health care spending to 1990, *Health Care Financing Review* (Spring 1986): 1–36; and Division of National Cost Estimates, National health expenditures, 1986–2000, *Health Care Financing Review* (Summer 1987): 1–36.

2. D.R. Waldo et al., Health expenditures by age group, 1977 and 1987, *Health Care Financing Review* (Summer 1989): 111–120. Note that the tables on pages 115 and 117 of the *Review* are mislabeled; correctly titled, they cover the population ages 19 to 64 and 65 and older.

3. To make these comparisons, expenditures per capita were estimated by five-year age cohort and sex, using data from the 1977 National Medical Care Expenditure Survey, the Hospital Discharge Survey, and other surveys of health care use and expenditure. These per capita figures were applied to the populations of the various years, and the resulting average per capita figures were compared.

4. The authors are working with the University of Maryland's Inforum project to model the effects of health spending growth on the rest of the economy; this work is not yet finished.

5. The implicit price deflator for health spending is found as the ratio of current dollar and constant dollar expenditure. Current dollar expenditure during a year is consumption measured in that year's dollars; constant dollar expenditure is consumption measured as though prices were unchanged from 1982. Economywide inflation is measured by the GNP implicit price deflator.

2

Health Care Market

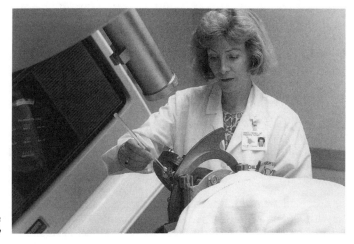

*Nurse researcher in
hospital surgical lab*

Carroll L. Estes / Charlene Harrington / Solomon Davis

The Medical-Industrial Complex

The concept of the medical-industrial complex was first introduced in the 1971 book, *The American Health Empire* (Ehrenreich and Ehrenreich 1971) by Health-PAC. The medical-industrial complex (MIC) refers to the health industry, which is comprised of the multibillion dollar congeries of enterprises including doctors, hospitals, nursing homes, insurance companies, drug manufacturers, hospital supply and equipment companies, real estate and construction businesses, health systems consulting and accounting firms, and banks. As employed by the Ehrenreichs, the concept conveys the idea that an important (if not the primary) function of the health care system in the United States is business, that is, to make profits, with two other secondary functions of research and education.

Since that time, a number of authors have examined the medical-industrial complex: Navarro (1976, pp. 76, 80), Relman (1980), Waitzkin (1983), Estes et al. (1984), Wohl (1984), McKinlay and Stoeckle (1988), and Salmon (1990). Himmelstein and Woolhandler (1990) argue that health care facilitates profit making by (1) improving the productivity (health) of workers; (2) ideologically ensuring the social stability needed to support production and profit; and (3) providing major opportunities for investment and profit (p. 16). The last function, profit, is now "the driving force," as health care has fully "come into the age of capitalist production" (p. 17).

Arnold Relman (1980), Harvard medical professor and editor of the *New England Journal of Medicine,* was the first physician to employ the concept, observing that recent developments in health care, particularly the cor-

---

Carroll L. Estes, Ph.D., is Director of the Institute for Health & Aging, and Professor, Department of Social and Behavioral Sciences, School of Nursing at the University of California, San Francisco.

Charlene Harrington, Ph.D., R.N., F.A.A.N., is Associate Director of the Institute for Health & Aging, and Professor and Chair of the Department of Social and Behavioral Sciences, School of Nursing at the University of California, San Francisco.

Solomon Davis, Ph.D., is Assistant Professor of Sociology at Hampton University, Hampton, Virginia.

From Estes, C.L., Harrington, C., and Davis, S. (1982). The medical-industrial complex. In Edgar F. Borgatta, Editor-in-Chief, and Marie L. Borgotta, *The Encyclopedia of Sociology,* Vol. 3 (pp. 1243–1254). Copyright © 1982 by Edgar F. Borgatta and Marie L. Borgatta. Reprinted with permission of Macmillan Publishing Company.

poratization of medicine, are a challenge to physician authority, autonomy, and even legitimacy for the doctors who become health care industry owners. Ginzberg (1988), Gray (1983; Gray and McNerney 1986), and others (Starr 1982; Estes et al. 1984; Light 1986; Himmelstein and Woolhandler 1990; Bodenheimer 1990; Bergthold 1990) have written about the monetarization, corporatization, and proprietarization of "health" care. By the mid-1980s, the author of a book appearing with the title *The Medical Industrial Complex* (Wohl 1984) did not see the need to define it but, rather, began with "the story of the explosive growth of . . . corporate medicine" and focused on "medical moguls" and monopoly and prescription for profit.

The health-care industry has not only contributed to improvements in the health status of the population and protected a plurality of vested interests but also strengthened and preserved the private sector. In U.S. society, the medical-industrial complex functions economically as a source of growth, accumulation of profit, investment opportunity, and employment (Estes et al. 1984). It also contributes to the human capital needed for productivity and profit, an able-bodied work force whose work is not sapped by illness (Rodberg and Stevenson 1977).

STRUCTURE OF THE HEALTH-CARE INDUSTRY

Industry Components

Today's medical-industrial complex consists of more than a dozen major components: hospitals; nursing homes; physicians (salaried and fee-for-service); home health agencies; supply and equipment manufacturers; drug companies; insurance companies; new managed-care organizations (HMOs, PPOs, IPAs); specialized centers (urgi, surgi, dialysis); hospices; nurses and all other health-care workers; administrators, marketers, lawyers, planners; and research organizations. In addition to these entities, thousands of other organizations are springing up in long-term care (e.g., case management, respite care, homemaker/chore, independent living centers) and other services for the disabled and aging including social services that have incorporated health-care components such as senior centers (Estes and Wood 1986; Wood and Estes 1988).

Changes in the Structure of the Industry

There were a number of significant changes in the structure of the health-care industry during the 1970s and 1980s, including (1) rapid growth and consolidation of the industry into larger organizations; (2) horizontal integration; (3) vertical integration; (4) change in ownership from government to private nonprofit and for-profit organizations; and (5) diversification and corporate restructuring (Starr 1982; McKinlay and Stoeckle 1988;

White 1990). These changes occurred across the different sectors, which are dominated by large hospital and insurance/managed care organizations.

Rapid Growth and Consolidation

Health care has long been moved from its cottage industry stage with small individual hospitals and solo physician practitioners to large corporate enterprises. The types of health-care corporations are diverse and growing in terms of size and complexity. Hospitals are the largest sector of the health-care industry, accounting for 43 percent of total personal health expenditures (U.S. Department of Commerce [U.S. DOC] 1990). While the growth rate in hospital expenditures was increasing rapidly, the number of community hospitals actually declined from 5,746 in 1972 to 5,533 in 1988 (−3.6%) (American Hospital Association [AHA] 1989) (table 1). In 1986 alone, 71 hospitals closed, nearly twice the average annual rate for the previous five-year period. These reductions were primarily in small rural hospitals (AHA 1987). The number of hospital beds also began to decline to 947,000 in 1988 (AHA 1989).

As hospitals are reducing in numbers, they are increasing in size, from an average of 167 to 171 beds between 1978 and 1988 (AHA 1989). The decline in growth in the hospital sector has been accompanied by a decline in average occupancy rates from 74 percent in 1978 to 66 percent, a 9 percent decline in admissions, and a 13 percent decrease in inpatient days during the 1978–1988 period (AHA 1989). Although the community hospitals are declining, the number of specialty hospitals, especially psychiat-

TABLE 1   Community Hospitals and Beds by Ownership, 1970, 1980, and 1987

Type of Ownership	1972		1978		1988	
	Hospitals	Beds	Hospitals	Beds	Hospitals	Beds
Nonprofit	3,301	617,000	3,339	683,000	3,242	668,000
	(57%)	(70%)	(57%)	(70%)	(59%)	(71%)
Proprietary	738	57,000	732	81,000	790	104,000
	(13%)	(7%)	(13%)	(8%)	(14%)	(11%)
Government	1,707	205,000	1,778	211,000	1,501	175,000
	(30%)	(23%)	(30%)	(22%)	(27%)	(18%)
Total	5,746	879,000	5,851	975,000	5,533	947,000

Note: Excludes federal, psychiatric, tuberculosis, and other hospitals.

Source: Adapted from American Hospital Association. *Hospital Statistics, 1989–90 Edition.* Chicago: AHA, 1989.

ric facilities, has been growing rapidly. Between 1987 and 1988 alone, 47 new investor-owned psychiatric hospitals opened, for a total of 545, and 13 new rehabilitation hospitals with over 1,600 beds were under construction (U.S. DOC 1990).

Nursing homes represent 9 percent of total U.S. health-care expenditures. Nursing homes grew rapidly in numbers of facilities and beds after the passage of Medicaid and Medicare legislation. In 1985, there were approximately 19,000 facilities in the United States providing care for 1.5 million residents (U.S. National Center for Health Statistics 1989). More recently, their overall growth has leveled off, so that growth is not keeping pace with the aging of the population (Harrington, Swan, and Grant 1988).

Home health-care agencies have also grown rapidly since the introduction of Medicare and Medicaid in 1965. In 1980 there were an estimated 16 million home health-care visits provided to 726,000 individuals (U.S. DOC 1990). By 1988, an estimated 37 million visits were provided to 1.3 million individuals by about 11,000 home health-care agencies (U.S. DOC 1990). Expenditures for these services were climbing about 20 percent per year in the latter 1980s (U.S. DOC 1990).

Relatively new and influential corporate forces in the health industry are the managed-care organizations such as health maintenance organizations (HMOs), preferred provider organizations (PPOs), and independent practice associations (IPAs). There has been a large growth in HMOs, which provide health-care services on the basis of fixed monthly charges per enrollee. In 1984 there were only 337 HMOs with 17 million enrollees. By 1988 there were 31 million members enrolled in 643 HMOs (InterStudy 1989). By 1989 there were somewhat fewer HMOs, but enrollment was expected to reach 33 million (U.S. DOC 1990). There have been a number of mergers and acquisitions among HMOs, and some nonprofit HMO corporations have established profit-making operations (Salmon 1990). HMOs have rapidly become national firms, so that, by 1988, 49 percent of all HMOs were national firms, with 59 percent of the total HMO enrollment in the United States (Shadle and Hunter 1988).

PPOs are modified HMOs that provide health care for lower costs when the enrollee uses participating providers who are paid on the basis of negotiated or discount rates (U.S. DOC 1990). In 1988 there were about 620 PPOs with about 36 million members. The total number of enrollees in HMOs and PPOs (managed-care programs) was estimated to be 25 percent of the population in the late 1980s, compared with only 3 percent in 1970 (U.S. DOC 1990).

Private health insurance companies are also one of the largest sectors of the health industry. The United States has over 1,000 for-profit, commercial health insurers and 85 Blue Cross and Blue Shield plans (Feldstein 1988). These private insurance organizations, along with HMOs, PPOs, and other third-party payers, paid for 32 percent ($175 billion out of $540 billion) of the total expenditures in 1988 (U.S. Office of National Cost Estimates [U.S. ONCE] 1990).

Physician practice patterns changed rapidly in the 1970s and 1980s, moving toward larger partnerships and group practices. In 1969 18 percent of physicians were in group practices (with three or more physicians), compared with 28 percent in 1984 (Andersen and Mullner 1989). It is estimated that about 75 percent of all practicing physicians are part of at least one qualified health management organization (U.S. DOC 1990). Thus, physicians are moving toward larger and more complex forms of group practice. In addition, physicians are actively involved in the ownership and operation of many of the newer forms of HMOs, PPOs, IPAs, and other types of corporate health care activities (Relman 1980; Iglehart 1989).

Horizontal Integration

The major changes in corporate arrangements have been the development of multiorganizational systems through horizontal integration. The formation of multihospital systems has grown tremendously within the industry. Ermann and Gabel (1984) estimated there were 202 multihospital systems controlling 1,405 hospitals and 293,000 beds in 1975 (or 24 percent of the hospitals and 31 percent of all beds). In 1988, there were 303 multihospital systems controlling 438,433 beds (table 2). Thus, in 1988 such multihospital systems controlled 38 percent of all hospitals and 35 percent of all hospital beds. This represents a 50 percent increase in the number of multihospital systems between 1975 and 1988.

Multihospital corporations are becoming consolidated, with large companies controlling the largest share of the overall hospital market. In 1986 the five largest nonprofit hospital systems controlled about 13 percent of the hospitals and 17 percent of the nonprofit beds, while the five largest for-profit systems controlled 57 percent of the for-profit hospitals and 71 percent of the for-profit beds (White 1990). Most of the recent increase in these systems has been the result of purchasing or leasing existing facilities and mergers of organizations, rather than of construction of new facilities.

Vertical Integration

Vertical integration involves the development of organizations with different levels and types of organization and services. One such type of integration has involved the linkage of hospitals and health maintenance organizations and/or insurance companies. For example, National Medical Enterprises owns hospitals, nursing homes, psychiatric hospitals, re-

TABLE 2 Hospitals and Beds in Multihospital Health Care Systems, by Type
of Ownership and Control

	Total Not-for-Profit		Investor-Owned		All Systems	
Type of Ownership	*Hospitals*	*Beds*	*Hospitals*	*Beds*	*Hospitals*	*Beds*
Owned, leased	1,135	266,906	865	114,090	2,000	380,996
or Sponsored	(44%)	(61%)	(34%)	(26%)	(78%)	(87%)
Contracted-	254	25,724	318	31,713	571	57,437
managed	(10%)	(6%)	(12%)	(7%)	(22%)	(13%)
Total	1,389	292,630	1,183	145,803	2,572	438,433
	(54%)	(67%)	(46%)	(33%)	(100%)	(100%)

Source: Adapted from American Hospital Association. *Hospital Statistics, 1989–90 Edition.* Chicago: AHA 1989 Table 3 B3.

covery centers, and rehabilitation hospitals (Federation of American Health Systems [FAHS] 1990). Academic medical center hospitals have relationships with proprietary hospital firms (seventeen in 1985), according to Berliner and Burlage (1990, p. 97). Many of the major investor-owned health-care corporations are diversified, with many different types of health-care operations.

Changes in Ownership

During the 1970s and 1980s the organizational side of health care witnessed a surge in the growth of for-profit health-care delivery corporations, initially hospitals and later extending to other types of health organizations. The ownership of hospitals shifted from public to nonprofit and for-profit organizations (see table 1). The percentage of government-owned community hospitals dropped from 30 percent of the total community hospitals in 1972 to 27 percent in 1988, but the percentage of total beds declined from 23 percent to 18 percent between 1972 and 1988 (AHA 1989). In contrast, the percentage of proprietary facilities increased from 13 percent to 14 percent, and the percentage of beds increased from 7 percent to 11 percent, of the total during the 1972–1988 period. The percentage of total U.S. hospitals owned by nonprofit corporations increased from 57 percent to 59 percent during the period, while the percentage of beds was 70 percent in 1972 and 71 percent in 1988 (AHA 1989). While these changes reflected only modest overall shifts, recent growth within multihospital systems was largely proprietary (White 1990). Of the total 303 multihospital systems in 1988, investor-owned systems controlled 46 percent of the hospitals and 33 percent of the beds, compared with nonprofit facilities (AHA 1987).

Multinational health enterprises are an increasingly important part of the medical-industrial complex, with investor-owned and investor-operated companies active not only in the United States but also in many foreign countries. In 1990 a report showed 97 companies reporting ownership or operation of 1,492 hospitals with 182,644 beds in the United States and 100 hospitals with 11,974 beds in foreign countries (FAHS 1990). The four largest for-profit chains owned two-thirds of the foreign hospitals (Berliner and Regan 1990). The effects of these developments in foreign countries and the profit-potential of these operations are not clearly understood (Berliner and Regan 1990).

Nursing homes have the largest share of proprietary ownership in the health field (except for the drug and supply industries). In 1985 some 75 percent of all nursing homes were profit-making, 20 percent were nonprofit, and 5 percent were government-run (NCHS 1989). By 1985 chains owned 41 percent of the total nursing home facilities and 49 percent of the nursing home beds (NCHS 1989).

While the largest HMO in the United States is a nonprofit corporation (Kaiser Permanente), the largest growth has been in large investor-owned HMO corporations. By 1988 a total of 84 percent of the national HMOs were for-profit, and they had 54 percent of the total national HMO enrollment, compared with the nonprofit firms (InterStudy 1989).

Investor-owned corporations have also established themselves in many other areas of health care, ranging from primary-care clinics to specialized referral centers and home health care. The number of proprietary home health corporations is increasing rapidly, while the number of traditional visiting nurse associations is declining. In 1982 it was estimated that 14 percent of the Medicare home health charges were by proprietary agencies, 26 percent by nonprofit organizations, 32 percent by visiting nurse associations, 15 percent by facility-based agencies, and 14 percent by other agencies (U.S. Department of Health and Human Services [U.S. DHHS] 1989). By 1988 proprietary agencies accounted for 34 percent of total Medicare charges, nonprofit care for 15 percent, visiting nurses for 20 percent, facility-based agencies for 25 percent, and others for 7 percent (U.S. DHHS 1989). This represents a dramatic shift in ownership structure within a six-year period. The changes brought about by the for-profit chains are more extensive than their proportionate representation among health-care providers might suggest. By force of example and direct competition, for-profit chains have encouraged many nonprofit hospitals and other health entities to combine into chains.

Diversification and Restructuring

Diversification of health-care corporations is continuing to occur. Some large hospital corporations have developed ambulatory care centers (such as Humana, which later sold its centers), while others have developed their own HMOs or insurance (Bell 1987).

By the mid-1980s, many experts expected America's health-care system to be dominated by the four largest for-profit hospital chains: Hospital Corporation of America, Humana, National Medical Enterprises, and American Medical International. Economic problems in the late 1980s resulted in some industry restructuring, by scaling down operations and spinning off substantial segments (Ginzberg 1988). For example, in 1987 the largest multiunit system, Hospital Corporation of America, sold about 25 percent of its hospitals, restructuring to stay competitive (Greene 1988). Beverly Enterprises, the nation's largest nursing home corporation, which had been profitable during the early 1980s, experienced financial difficulties in 1987 through 1989 and is in the process of restructuring its corporation (Fritz 1990; Wagner 1988).

As the restructuring of health organizations has been occurring, multihospital systems have continued to grow. In the two years between 1987 and 1989 alone, multihospital systems grew by 9 percent, although the number of total hospitals and beds increased by only 2 percent (AHA 1987; 1989). In spite of the problems of some corporations, the predictions are that corporate growth will continue, although at perhaps a slower pace than in the early 1980s (White 1990).

Financial Status and Profits

The private health sector continues to be extremely healthy financially. *Forbes*'s annual report on investor-owned health corporations shows that the overall median return-on-equity for health corporations during the previous 12 months to its publication was 18.7 percent, well above the 14.3 percent for all U.S. industries (Fritz 1990) (see table 3). The ten-year average return-on-equity was 18.7 percent for investor-owned health corporations, compared with 14.3 percent for all U.S. industries (Fritz 1990). Median health industry sales for investor-owned companies grew 8.8 percent for 1989 and at a 12.5 percent rate for the 10-year average. Earnings-per-share were 15.2 percent in the most recent 12 months, compared with 12.2 percent for the 10-year average. The earnings per share were much higher than those of 8.0 percent for all U.S. industries in the most recent 12 months in 1989 (Fritz 1990).

The *Forbes* financial reports for the largest health corporations are shown in table 3 for three different sectors of the industry: health-care services, drugs, and medical supply companies (Fritz 1990). The most profitable health-care service corporation in 1989 was Humana, which owns both hospitals and insurance companies. In 1989 its group health insurance division had almost one million members and a $4 million operating profit (Fritz 1990).

TABLE 3   Selected U.S. Health-Care Investor Corporations, 1990

Company	Profitability Growth Return on Equity		Sales		Earnings per Share		Net Income
	10-year average %	Latest 12 mos. %	10-year average %	Latest 12 mos. %	10-year average %	Latest 12 mos. %	Latest 12 mos. $ mil
Health-care services							
Humana	24.4	21.7	16.3	19.0	18.9	11.3	256
Manor Care	22.2	11.8	34.9	16.9	NA	D-P	23
National Medical	15.3	14.5	31.7	15.5	13.1	0.0	152
Universal Health	11.8	5.2	30.7a	5.5	NM	Z-P	8
Beverly Enterprises	7.1	def	34.0	3.8	NM	D-D	−118
FHP International	NA	34.9	NA	37.9	NA	31.5	25
PacifiCare Health	NA	24.6	76.2b	45.9	NA	83.0	9
United Health Care	NA	61.9	NA	−18.1	NA	D-P	10
US Healthcare	NA	13.7	61.4	29.8	NA	133.3	20
Medians	15.3	14.5	34.0	16.9	NM	83.0	
Drugs							
American Home Prods	35.0	33.7	5.1	5.8	10.9	10.0	1,005
Syntex	31.2	47.9	11.3	5.7	19.8	4.1	312
Merck	30.8	50.3	9.8	9.0	13.5	26.4	1,435
Abbott Laboratories	30.4	33.8	12.3	7.5	18.1	16.4	829
Marion Laboratories	30.0	15.1	21.7	22.0	33.6	−54.3	79
Medians	20.1	19.3	10.1	8.6	10.5	18.2	
Medical Supplies							
CR Bard	20.8	22.6	14.3	6.4	20.7	1.9	74
Medtronic	20.2	21.1	10.9	8.9	14.2	7.3	100
Hillenbrand Inds	19.2	20.5	12.8	15.7	13.0	4.3	72
Bausch & Lomb	16.8	17.1	6.4	27.4	10.2	15.3	109
Medians	14.5	17.1	10.9	8.8	10.2	3.1	
Industry Medians	18.7	18.4	12.5	8.8	10.2	15.2	
All-Industry Medians	14.3	14.4	9.3	8.5	6.4	8.0	

Note: D-D: Deficit to deficit D-P: Deficit to profit P-D: Profit to deficit def: Deficit NA: Not available NM: Not meaningful a: Nine-year average b: Eight-year average.

Source: Adapted from M. Fritz, 1990, "Health," *Forbes* January 8:180–182.

Nursing homes have traditionally been very profitable. Manor Care and National Medical Enterprises own large numbers of nursing homes. These corporations showed 11.8 percent and 14.5 percent returns on equity in 1989, and many have had a 22.2 percent return-on-equity for the previous 10-year period (Fritz 1990).

FHP International, PacifiCare Health, United HealthCare, and US Healthcare are large investor-owned HMOs showing high returns on equity and high sales (Fritz 1990). Many of the companies are now offering diversified products and showing high profit levels (Sussman 1990). Life and health insurance had a 32.7 percent earning per share in 1989 over the previous year, compared with a 10-year average of 7.1 percent per share (Clements 1990).

Because of the pluralistically financed health-care system in the United States, administrative costs are much higher than those of the national and publicly financed health-care systems of virtually all other Western industrialized nations, with the exception of South Africa (Evans et al. 1989; Himmelstein and Woolhandler 1986). According to one report, 5 percent of total U.S. expenditures ($26 billion in 1988) was spent on program administrative costs and profits for private health insurance (U.S. ONCE 1990). Evans et al. (1989) estimate these costs to be even higher, at approximately 1 percent of GNP ($40 billion in 1987), excluding many unquantified costs of negotiations, time, and organization. Administrative costs and profits in the United States for private insurance companies range from about 35 percent on individual policies to 7 to 14 percent on group plans and vary by type of plan (Feldstein 1988). The overall administrative costs for the multiple, private, third-party organizations have been estimated to be about 8 percent, whereas both the Medicare program and the Canadian national health program have overhead costs of only 2 to 3 percent (Evans et al. 1989). Thus, these private-sector financing proposals continue to support the private insurance industry and all of the overhead and profits associated with private third-party payers.

Earnings-per-share of drug companies rose by 18.2 percent between 1988 and 1989, which was up from the 10-year average of 10.5 percent (Fritz 1990). Returns-on-equity reported for drug companies increased to 19.3 percent in 1989 and were 20.1 percent on average over the previous 10 years (Fritz 1990). While earnings-per-share of medical supply companies were down in 1989 to 3.1 percent over the previous year, their 10-year median earning was 10.2 percent, and their return-on-equity for the previous 10 years was 14.5 percent (Fritz 1990). In 1989 a number of large drug company mergers occurred, particularly between U.S. firms and foreign corporations such as Genentech, Inc. and Roche Holding, Ltd. of Switzerland (Southwick 1990). Although the biotechnology industry did not show overall profits in 1989, the sales growth rates were strong, and some companies had high profit rates, such as Diagnostic Products, with a 22.3 percent earnings-per-share and a 23.6 percent return-on-equity in 1989 over the previous year (Clements 1990).

It is difficult to determine the overall revenues and profits of the medical-industrial complex. In 1965, according to the Ehrenreichs (1971), the medical-industrial complex reaped an estimated $2.5 plus billion in after-tax profits. For 1979 Arnold Relman estimated $35 to $40 billion in gross income (about 25 percent of total personal health care costs) for what he defined as the "new medical-industrial complex," or "the vast array of investor owned businesses supplying health services for a profit" (1980, p. 965). However, this estimate excludes profits of the "old medical-industrial complex . . . the businesses concerned with the manufacture and sale of drugs, medical supplies and equipment" (p. 965). As noted, the insurance industry, HMOs, PPOs, and other third-party payers had 32 percent ($175 billion) of the gross revenues for health and another 5 percent ($26 billion) for program administration and profits in the United States in 1988 (U.S. ONCE 1990).

In summary, the 1980s were a decade of rationalization for health care, with the formation of large, complex, bureaucratically interconnected units and arrangements that reached well beyond the hospital and permeated virtually all sectors of the health industry. This vertical and horizontal integration, combined with the revival of market ideologies and government policies promoting competition and deregulation, profoundly altered the shape of U.S. health-care delivery. These changes signal a fundamental transformation of American medicine and a rationalization of the system under private control (Starr 1982).

Reasons for Growth in the For-Profit Sector

In the 55-year period prior to 1965, for-profit medical enterprises were largely confined to the manufacture and sale of drugs, medical equipment, and appliances and to selling health insurance policies (Ginzberg 1988; Relman 1980). A number of factors encouraged the penetration and rapid growth of the for-profit sector in all areas of health care subsequent to 1965.

The federal government was crucial in the development of the medical-industrial complex. After World War II, the federal role expanded as Congress enacted legislation and authorized money for research, education, training, and financing of health services. The passage of Medicare and Medicaid in 1965 was pivotal in expanding the medical-industrial complex, as government became the third-party payer for health-care services (Estes et al. 1984). Public demand for health care among the aged, blind, disabled, and poor (all previously limited in access) was secure. Medicare and Medicaid provided the major sources of long-term capital financing for hospitals and contributed to the marked increase in service volume and technology, as well as to the current oversupply of physicians.

Largely with the help of Medicare's cost-based reimbursement policy (from 1965 to 1983), national expenditures for hospital care catapulted. For nursing home expenditures, Medicaid became a primary payer, with 48 percent of total payments (U.S. DOC 1990). Medicare changes that added coverage of dialysis centers (1972) and coverage for the mentally impaired (1974) also expanded the private sector. Government's share of health spending increased from 25 percent in 1965 to 42 percent in 1988 (U.S. ONCE 1990). In summary, federal financing of health care has performed the very important functions of sustaining aggregate demand through health insurance programs, protecting against financial risks, subsidizing research and guaranteeing substantial financial returns, supporting the system's infrastructure through training subsidies and capital expansion, and regulating competition through licensure and accreditation (LeRoy 1979).

In addition to government spending, third-party insurance offered by Blue Cross/Blue Shield and private commercial companies covered most of the remaining inpatient hospital expenditures and a significant proportion of physician costs. The cost-based service reimbursement by private insurers, Blue Cross, and Medicare created and sustained strong cash flows in the hospital industry (Ginzberg 1988). With public- and private-sector third-party payments covering 90 percent of all inpatient hospital expenditures, the hospital business became virtually risk-free.

Ginzberg (1988) contends the growth in for-profits after the mid-1960s was also related to the overall shortage of hospital beds and the increased demand for health services, particularly in areas of rapid population growth. The growth of for-profit health-care organizations was also further extended by Medicare payments for a return-on-equity for care provided to Medicare beneficiaries (Ginzberg 1988). Medicare also paid for interest payments and depreciation rates on properties purchased by for-profit organizations (Ginzberg 1988).

The for-profit health sector was dramatically expanded by entry into the equity market. The receptivity of Wall Street boosted the medical-industrial complex, as investors willingly raised substantial funds for new corporations and for the purchase of existing facilities and organizations during the 1980s (Ginzberg 1988). The results of these investments paid well, as shown earlier in the high profits of the major corporations.

In the 1980s, two other forces were responsible for the dramatic changes in the medical-industrial complex: a change in the ideological climate with the election of President Reagan and changes in state policies to promote privatization, rationalization, and competition in health care (Estes 1990). These changes contributed to increases in the proportion of services provided by proprietary institutions (Schlesinger, Marmor, and Smithey 1987).

While policies of the 1960s and 1970s encouraged a form of privatization built on the voluntary sector (Estes and Bergthold 1988), President Reagan shifted the direction and accelerated privatization. In the 1980s, the form of privatization was government subsidy of for-profit (rather than nonprofit) enterprise (Bergthold, Estes, and Villanueva 1990) and privatization in the form of a transfer of work from the hospital to the informal sector of home and family (Binney, Estes, and Humphers 1989). Regulatory and legislative devices were important in the health and social services. The Omnibus Reconciliation Act of 1980 and the Omnibus Budget Reconciliation Act of 1981 contributed to competition and deregulation, private contracting, and growth of for-profits in service areas that were traditionally dominated by nonprofit or public providers (e.g., home health care).

Given the long-term historical role of the private, nonprofit sector in U.S. health and social services since the earliest days of the Republic and the rapid organizational changes of the 1980s, vertical and horizontal integration have blurred boundaries between the heretofore distinct nonprofit and for-profit health-care sectors. For-profit entities have nonprofit subsidiaries, and vice versa, and conceptual and structural complexities have multiplied, rendering impossible the simple differentiation of *public* from *private.* It is noteworthy that government-initiated privatization strategies did not reduce public-sector costs.

Issues Raised by the Medical-Industrial Complex

Commodification, commercialization, proprietarization, and *monetarization* are all terms used to describe an increasingly salient dynamic in the medical-industrial complex: the potentially distorting effects of money, profit, and market rationality as a (if not the) central determining force in health care. After a decade devoted to market rhetoric, cost-containment effort, and stunning organizational rationalization, the bottom line is the complete failure of any of these to stem the swelling tide of problems of access and cost. Meanwhile, public opinion clearly favors change and a national solution that assures access regardless of ability to pay (Bodenheimer 1990), while a nascent movement for national health insurance stirs.

The rapidly growing health-care industry is creating strains on the economic system while it also is creating a financial burden on government, business, and individuals through their payments for health services. These strains are occurring simultaneously with a huge federal debt, increasing fiscal problems at all levels of government, and a sluggish and uncompetitive general economy. Responses to these strains have included cutbacks in services and reimbursements, cost shifts onto consumers, and alterations in the structure of the health-care system itself to accord better with a competitive, for-profit model.

The competition model as a prescription for the nation's health-care woes has restricted access to health care and raised questions of quality of care (Estes et al. 1984, p. 70). Cost shifting to consumers is increasingly limiting access to needed services for those with less ability to pay.

The juxtaposition of the commercial ethos familiar in fast-food chains with health care collides with traditional images of medicine as the embodiment of humane service. Investor-owned health-care enterprises have elicited a number of specific criticisms. It has been argued that commercial considerations can undermine the responsibility of doctors toward their patients and lead to unnecessary tests and procedures and, given other financial incentives, to inadequate treatment (Relman 1980). The interrelationships among physicians and the private health-care sector, particularly for-profit corporations, raises many issues about the effects on quality of care and health-care utilization and expenditures. Many have argued that the potential for abuse, exploitation, unethical practices, and disregard of fiduciary responsibilities to patients is pervasive (Iglehart 1989). Legislation has even been introduced in Congress that would prohibit physicians from referring patients to entities in which they hold a financial interest and from receiving compensation from entities to which they refer patients (Iglehart 1989).

Critics of for-profits argue that such ownership drives up the cost of health care, reduces quality, neglects teaching and research, and excludes those who cannot pay for treatment. Opponents of the market model for health care reflect diverse interests, including members of the medical profession seeking to preserve their professional autonomy, advocates for access to health care for the poor and uninsured, those concerned about the impact of profit seeking on quality of care, and many others. As government and business attempt to restrain health-care spending, cutting into profits and forcing cost reductions, these concerns intensify (Light 1986).

Issues for sociological investigation include the systematic identification of the ways in which the new commercial practices and organization of health care affect health-care delivery. Organizational studies are needed to disentangle the effects of organizational characteristics (e.g., tax status and system affiliation) on the outcomes of equity, access, utilization, cost, and quality of care. Further, the effects on provider–patient interactions of these structural and normative changes in health care require investigation. A general sociological theory of the professions will emerge from understanding the ways in which the dominant medical profession responds to present restructuring of health care and accompanying challenges to its ability to control the substance of its own work, erosions in its monopoly over medical knowledge, diminishing authority over patients resulting from health policy changes, major technological and economic developments, and changes in the medical-industrial complex.

REFERENCES

American Hospital Association 1987 *Hospital Statistics, 1987.* Chicago: AHA.
——— 1989 *Hospital Statistics, 1989–90.* Chicago: AHA.

Andersen, Ronald M., and Ross M. Mullner 1989 "Trends in the Organization of Health Services." In H. E. Freeman and S. Levine, eds., *Handbook of Medical Sociology,* 4th ed.,

144–165. Englewood Cliffs, N.J.: Prentice Hall.

Bell, Colin 1987 Multi-Unit Providers. *Modern Healthcare* 17(12):37–58.

Bergthold, Linda A. 1990 "Business and the Pushcart Vendors in an Age of Supermarkets." In J. W. Salmon, ed., *The Corporate Transformation of Health Care: Issues and Directions.* Amityville, N.Y.: Baywood.

———, Carroll L. Estes, and A. Villanueva 1990 "Public Light and Private Dark: The Privatization of Home Health Services for the Elderly in the United States." *Home Health Services Quarterly* 11:7–33.

Berliner, Howard S., and R. K. Burlage 1990 "Proprietary Hospital Chains and Academic Medical Centers." In J. W. Salmon, ed., *The Corporate Transformation of Health Care: Issues and Directions.* Amityville, N.Y.: Baywood.

Berliner, Howard W., and C. Regan 1990 "Multi-National Operations of U.S. For-Profit Hospital Chains: Trends and Implications." In J. W. Salmon, ed., *The Corporate Transformation of Health Care: Issues and Directions.* Amityville, N.Y.: Baywood.

Binney, Elizabeth A., Carroll L. Estes, and Susan E. Humphers 1989 Informalization and Community Care for the Elderly. Unpublished manuscript, University of California, San Francisco.

Bodenheimer, Thomas 1990 "Should We Abolish the Private Health Insurance Industry?" *International Journal of Health Services* 20:199–220.

Clements, J. 1990 "Insurance." *Forbes* January 8:184–186.

Ehrenreich, Barbara, and John Ehrenreich 1971 *The American Health Empire: Power, Profits and Politics.* New York: Vintage.

Ermann, Dan, and Jon Gabel 1984 "Multihospital Systems: Issues and Empirical Findings." *Health Affairs* 3:50–64.

Estes, Carroll L. 1990 "The Reagan Legacy: Privatization, the Welfare State and Aging." In J. Quadagno and J. Myles, eds., *Aging and the*

Welfare State. Philadelphia: Temple University Press.

———, and Linda A. Bergthold 1988 "The Unraveling of the Nonprofit Service Sector in the U.S." In J. I. Nelson, ed., *The Service Economy.* (special issue of *International Journal of Sociology and Social Policy*) 9:18–33.

———, Lenore E. Gerard, Jane Sprague Zones, and James H. Swan 1984 *Political Economy, Health, and Aging.* Boston: Little, Brown.

———, and Juanita B. Wood 1986 "The Nonprofit Sector and Community-based Care for the Elderly in the U.S.: A Disappearing Resource?" *Social Science and Medicine* 23:1261–1266.

Evans, Robert G., J. Lomas, M. L. Barer, R. J. Labelle, C. Fooks, G. L. Stoddart, G. M. Anderson, D. Feeny, A. Gafni, and G. W. Torrance 1989 "Controlling Health Expenditures: The Canadian Reality." *New England Journal of Medicine* 320:571–577.

Federation of American Health Systems 1990 *1990 Directory.* Little Rock, Ark.: FAHS Review.

Feldstein, Paul J. 1988 *Health Care Economics.* New York: Wiley.

Fritz, M. 1990 "Health." *Forbes* (January 8):180–182.

Ginzberg, Eli 1988 "For-Profit Medicine: A Reassessment." *New England Journal of Medicine* 319:757–761.

Gray, Bradford H., ed. 1983 *The New Health Care For-Profit.* Washington, D.C.: National Academy Press.

———, and Walter J. McNerney 1986 "For-Profit Enterprise in Health Care: The Institute of Medicine Study." *New England Journal of Medicine* 314:1523–1528.

Greene, J. 1988 "Multihospital Systems: Systems Went Back to Basics in 1987, Restructuring to Stay Competitive." *Modern Healthcare* 18:45–117.

Harrington, Charlene, James H. Swan, and Leslie A. Grant 1988 "Nursing Home Bed Capacity in the States, 1978–86." *Health Care Financing Review* 9:81–111.

Himmelstein, David U., and Steffie

Woolhandler 1986 "Cost Without Benefit: Administrative Waste in the U.S. *New England Journal of Medicine* 314:440–441.

——1990 "The Corporate Compromise: A Marxist View of Health Policy." *Monthly Review* (May):14–29.

Iglehart, John K. 1989 "The Debate over Physician Ownership of Health Care Facilities." *New England Journal of Medicine* 321:198–204.

InterStudy. 1989 "Findings on Open-Ended HMOs Reports by Inter-Study." *InterStudy Press Release* March 7. Excelsior, MN.: InterStudy.

LeRoy, Lauren 1979 The Political Economy of U.S. Federal Health Policy: A Closer Look at Medicare. Unpublished manuscript, University of California, San Francisco.

Light, Donald W. 1986 "Corporate Medicine for Profit." *Scientific American* 255:38–45.

McKinlay, John B., and John D. Stoeckle 1988 "Corporatization and the Social Transformation of Doctoring." In J. W. Salmon, ed., *The Corporate Transformation of Health Care: Issues and Directions.* Amityville, N.Y.: Baywood.

Navarro, Vicente 1976 *Medicine under Capitalism.* New York: Prodist.

Relman, Arnold S. 1980 "The New Medical-Industrial Complex." *New England Journal of Medicine* 303:963–970.

Rodberg, L., and G. Stevenson 1977 "The Health Care Industry in Advanced Capitalism." *Review of Radical Political Economics* 9:104–115.

Salmon, J. Warren 1990 "Profit and Health Care: Trends in Corporatization and Proprietarization." In J. W. Salmon, ed., *The Corporate Transformation of Health Care: Issues and Directions.* Amityville, N.Y.: Baywood.

Schlesinger, Mark, Theodore R. Marmor, and Richard Smithey 1987 "Nonprofit and For-Profit Medical Care: Shifting Roles and Implications for Health Policy." *Journal of Health Politics and Law* 12(3):427–457.

Shadle, M., and M. M. Hunter 1988 *National HMO Firms 1988.* Excelsior, MN: InterStudy.

Southwick, Karen 1990 "More Merger Mania among Drugmakers." *Healthweek* 4:1, 51.

Starr, Paul 1982 *The Social Transformation of American Medicine.* New York, N.Y.: Basic Books.

Sussman, David 1990 "HMOs Are Still Riding a Wave of Profitability." *Healthweek* 4:12.

U.S. Department of Commerce, International Trade Administration (1990) "Health and Medical Services." *U.S. Industrial Outlook 1990.* Washington, D.C.: U.S. DOC.

U.S. Department of Health and Human Services 1989 *Health United States, 1989.* DHHS 90-1232. Hyattsville, Md.: U.S. DHHS.

U.S. Office of National Cost Estimates (U.S. ONCE) 1990 "National Health Expenditures, 1988." *Health Care Financing Review* 11:1–41.

U.S. National Center for Health Statistics [U.S. NCHS], Hing, E., Sekscenski, E. and Strahan, G. 1989 National Nursing Home Survey: 1985 Summary for the United States. *Vital and Health Statistics* Series 13 Hyattsville, Md.: Public Health Service.

Wagner, L. 1988 "Nursing Homes Buffeted by Troubles." *Modern Healthcare* 33–42.

Waitzkin, Howard 1983 *The Second Sickness: Contradictions of Capitalist Health Care.* New York: Free Press.

White, William D. 1990 "The 'Corporatization' of U.S. Hospitals: What Can We Learn from the Nineteenth Century Industrial Experience?" *International Journal of Health Services* 20:85–113.

Wohl, Stanley 1984 *The Medical Industrial Complex.* New York: Harmony.

Wood, Juanita B., and Carroll L. Estes 1988 The Medicalization of Community Services for the Elderly. *Health and Social Work* 13(1):35–43.

Arnold S. Relman

What Market Values Are Doing to Medicine

From its earliest origins the profession of medicine has steadfastly held that physicians' responsibility to their patients takes precedence over their own economic interests. Thus the oath of Hippocrates enjoins physicians to serve only "for the benefit of the sick," and the oft-recited prayer attributed to Moses Maimonides, a revered physician of the twelfth century, asks God not to allow "thirst for profit" or "ambition for renown" to interfere with the physician's practice of his [sic] profession. In modern times this theme has figured prominently in many medical codes of ethics. The International Code of the World Medical Organization, for example, says that "a doctor must practice his profession uninfluenced by motives of profit." And in 1957, in its newly revised Principles of Medical Ethics, the American Medical Association declared that "the principal objective of the medical profession is to render service to humanity." It went on to say, "In the practice of medicine a physician should limit the source of his professional income to medical services actually rendered by him, or under his supervision, to his patients."

Such lofty pronouncements notwithstanding, the medical profession has never been immune to knavery and profiteering. And, particularly in the days before biomedical science began to establish a rational basis for the practice of medicine, the profession has had its share of charlatans and quacks. Still, the highest aspiration of the medical profession—sometimes honored in the breach, to be sure—has always been to serve the needs of the sick. And that has been the basis of a de facto contract between modern society and the profession.

What are the terms of this contract? In this country, state governments grant physicians a licensed monopoly to practice their profession and allow them considerable autonomy in setting their educational and professional standards and their working conditions. The professional education

Arnold S. Relman, M.D., is Editor-in-Chief Emeritus of the *New England Journal of Medicine,* Waltham, Massachusetts, and Professor of Medicine and Social Medicine at Harvard Medical School.

Abridged from Relman, A.S. (1992). What market values are doing to medicine. *The Atlantic Monthly* 269(3):99–106. Used with permission.

of physicians is heavily subsidized, because tuition, even in the private medical schools, does not nearly cover the costs of educating medical students. Furthermore, the information, tools, and techniques that physicians use to practice their profession are usually developed through publicly supported research. Finally, hospitals provide physicians with the facilities and personnel and often even the specialized equipment they need to treat their hospitalized patients, thus relieving doctors of many of the kinds of overhead costs that businessmen [sic] must pay. Physicians have enjoyed a privileged position in our society, virtually assuring them of high social status and a good living. They have been accorded these privileges in the expectation that they will remain competent and trustworthy and will faithfully discharge the fiduciary responsibility to patients proclaimed in their ethical codes.

THE DISTINCTIONS BETWEEN MEDICAL PRACTICE AND COMMERCE

Now, if this description of a contract between society and the medical profession is even approximately correct, then clearly there are important distinctions to be made between what society has a right to expect of practicing physicians and what it expects of people in business. Both are expected to earn their living from their occupation, but the relation between physicians and patients is supposed to be quite different from that between businessmen and customers. Patients depend on their physicians to be altruistic and committed in advising them on their health-care needs and providing necessary medical services. Most patients do not have the expertise to evaluate their own need for medical care. The quality of life and sometimes life itself are at stake, and price is of relatively little importance, not only because of the unique value of the services rendered but also because patients usually do not pay out of pocket for services at the time they are received. Although most physicians are paid (usually by the government or an insurance company) for each service they provide, the assumption is that they are acting in the best interests of patients rather than of themselves. A fact that underscores the centrality of the patient's interests is that advertising and marketing in medical practice were until very recently considered unethical.

In contrast, in a commerical market multiple providers of goods and services try to induce customers to buy. That's the whole point. Competing with one another, businesses rely heavily on marketing and advertising to generate demand for services or products, regardless of whether they are needed, because each provider's primary concern is to increase his sales and thereby maximize his income. Although commercial vendors have an obligation to produce a good product and advertise it without deception, they have no responsibility to consider the consumer's interests—to advise the consumer which product, if any, is really needed, or to worry about those who cannot afford to buy any of the vendors' products. Markets may be effective mechanisms for distributing goods and services according to consumers' desires and ability to pay, but they have no interest in consumers' needs, or in achieving universal access.

In a commercial market, consumers are expected to fend for themselves in judging what they can afford and want to buy. *"Caveat emptor"* is the rule. According to classical market theory, when well-informed consumers and competing suppliers are free to seek their own objectives, the best interests of both groups are likely to be served. Thus, in commerce, market competition is relied upon to protect the interests of consumers. This is quite different from the situation in health care, where the provider of services protects the patient's interests by acting as advocate and counselor. Unlike the independent shoppers envisioned by market theory, sick and worried patients cannot adequately look after their own interests, nor do they usually want to. Personal medical service does not come in standardized packages and in different grades for the consumer's comparison and selection. Moreover, a sick patient often does not have the option of deferring his purchase of medical care or shopping around for the best buy. A patient with seizures and severe headaches who is told that he has a brain tumor requiring surgery, or a patient with intractable angina and high-grade obstruction of a coronary artery who is advised to have a coronary bypass, does not look for the "best buy" or consider whether he really needs "top-of-the-line" surgical quality. If he does not trust the judgment and competence of the first surgeon he consults, he may seek the opinion of another, but he will very shortly have to trust someone to act as his beneficent counselor, and he will surely want the best care available, regardless of how much or how little his insurance will pay the doctor.

Some skeptics have always looked askance at the physician's double role as purveyor of services and patients' advocate. They have questioned whether doctors paid on a fee-for-service basis can really give advice to patients that is free of economic self-interest. One of the most caustic critiques of private fee-for-service medical practice was written early in this century by George Bernard Shaw, in his preface to *The Doctor's Dilemma*. It begins,

> It is not the fault of our doctors that the medical service of the community, as at present provided for, is a murderous absurdity. That any sane nation, having observed that you could provide for the supply of bread by giving bakers a pecuniary interest in baking for you, should go on to give a surgeon a pecuniary interest in cutting off your leg, is enough to make one despair of political humanity. But that is precisely what we have done. And the more appalling the mutilation, the more the mutilator is paid. . . .

> Scandalized voices murmur that . . . operations are necessary. They may be. It may also be necessary to hang a man or pull down a house. But we take good care not to make the hangman and the housebreaker the judges of that. If we did, no man's neck would be safe and no man's house stable.

Some contemporary defenders of fee-for-service evidently see no need to answer attacks like Shaw's. They reject the distinctions I have drawn between business and medical practice, claiming that medicine is just another market—admittedly with more imperfections than most, but a market nevertheless. They profess not to see much difference between medical care and any other important economic commodity, such as food, clothing, or housing. Such critics dismiss the notion of a de facto social contract in medical care. They assert that physicians and private hospitals owe nothing to society and should be free to sell or otherwise dispose of their services in any lawful manner they choose.

THE MEDICAL-INDUSTRIAL COMPLEX

Until recently such views had little influence. Most people considered medical care to be a social good, not a commodity, and physicians usually acted as if they agreed. Physicians were not impervious to economic pressures, but the pressures were relatively weak and the tradition of professionalism was relatively strong.

This situation is now rapidly changing. In the past two decades or so health care has become commercialized as never before, and professionalism in medicine seems to be giving way to entrepreneurialism. The health-care system is now widely regarded as an industry, and medical practice as a competitive business. . . .

EFFECTS ON PROVIDERS

This corporatization of health care, coupled with increasingly hostile and cost-conscious policies by private insurance companies and government, has had a powerful and pervasive effect on the attitudes of health-care providers—including those in the not-for-profit sector. Not-for-profit, nonpublic hospitals ("voluntary hospitals"), which constitute more than three quarters of the nonpublic acute-care general hospitals in the country, originally were philanthropic social institutions, with the primary mission of serving the health-care needs of their communities. Now, forced to compete with investor-owned hospitals and a rapidly growing number of for-profit ambulatory facilities, and struggling to maintain their economic viability in the face of sharp reductions in third-party payments, they increasingly see themselves as beleaguered businesses, and they act accordingly. Altruistic concerns are being distorted in many voluntary hospitals by a concern for the bottom line. Management decisions are now often based more on considerations of profit than on the health needs of the community. Many voluntary hospitals seek to avoid or to limit services to the poor. They actively promote their profitable services to insured patients, they advertise themselves, they establish health-related businesses, and they make deals with physicians to generate more revenue. Avoiding uninsured patients simply adds to the problems of our underserved indigent population and widens the gap in medical care between rich and poor. Promoting elective care for insured patients leads to overuse of medical services and runs up the national health-care bill.

Physicians are reacting similarly as they struggle to maintain their income in an increasingly competitive economic climate. Like hospitals, practicing physicians have begun to use advertising, marketing, and public-relations techniques to attract more patients. Until recently most medical professional societies considered self-promotion of this kind to be unethical, but attitudes have changed; now competition among physicians is viewed as a necessary, even beneficial, feature of the new medical marketplace.

Many financially attractive opportunities now exist for physicians to invest in health-care facilities to which they can then refer their patients, and a growing number of doctors have become limited partners in such enterprises—for example, for-profit diagnostic laboratories and MRI centers, to which they refer their patients but over which they can exercise no professional supervision. Surgeons invest in ambulatory-surgery facilities that are owned and managed by businesses or hospitals, and in which they perform surgery on their patients. Thus they both are paid for their professional services and share in the profits resulting from the referral of their patients to a particular facility. A recent study in Florida revealed that approximately 40 percent of all physicians practicing in that state had financial interests in facilities to which they referred patients. The AMA, however, estimates that nationwide the figure is about 10 percent.

In other kinds of entrepreneurial arrangements, office-based practitioners make deals with wholesalers of prescription drugs and sell those drugs to their patients at a profit, or buy prostheses from manufacturers at reduced rates and sell them at a profit—in addition to the fees they receive for implanting the prostheses. In entering into these and similar business arrangements, physicians are trading on their patients' trust. This is a clear violation of the traditional ethical rule against earning professional income by referring patients to others or by investing in the goods and services recommended to patients. Such arrangements create conflicts of interest that go far beyond the economic conflict of interest in the fee-for-service system, and they blur the distinction between business and the medical profession.

Not only practitioners but also physicians doing clinical research at teaching hospitals are joining the entrepreneurial trend. Manufacturers of new drugs, devices, and clinical tests are entering into financial arrangements with clinicians engaged in testing their products—and the results of those studies may have an important effect on the commercial success of the product. Clinical investigators may own equity interest in the company that produces the product or may serve as paid consultants and scientific advisers, thus calling into question their ability to act as rigorously impartial evaluators. Harvard Medical School has wisely taken a stand against such arrangements, but unfortunately this obvious conflict of interest has so far been ignored, or at least tolerated, in many other institutions.

Business arrangements of this kind are also common in postgraduate education. Respected academic clinicians are frequently hired by drug firms to give lectures or write articles about the manufacturers' new products. The assumption, of course, is that these experts are expressing honest and dispassionate opinions about the relative merits of competing products, but such an assumption is strained by the realization that an expert is being handsomely paid by the manufacturer of one particular product in a market that is often highly competitive.

Similarly, drug manufacturers offer inducements to practicing physicians to attend seminars at which their products are touted, and even to institute treatment with a particular drug. In the former case the ostensible justification is furtherance of postgraduate education; in the latter it is the gathering of post-marketing information about a new drug. The embarrassing transparency of these subterfuges has recently caused pharmaceutical manufacturers to agree with the AMA that such practices should be curtailed.

In short, at every turn in the road physicians both in practice and in academic institutions are being attracted by financial arrangements that can compromise their professional independence.

ANTITRUST MEDICINE

The courts have significantly contributed to the change in atmosphere. For many years the legal and medical professions enjoyed immunity from antitrust law because it was generally believed that they were not engaged in the kind of commercial activity that the Sherman Act and the Federal Trade Commission Act were designed to regulate. In 1975 the Supreme Court ended this immunity (*Goldfarb* v. *Virginia State Bar*). It decided that the reach of antitrust law extended to the professions. Since then numerous legal actions have been taken against individual physicians or physicians' organizations to curb what government has perceived to be "anti-competitive" practices. Thus the courts and the Federal Trade Commission have prevented medical societies in recent years from prohibiting commercial advertising or marketing and from taking any action that might influence professional fees or legal business ventures by physicians.

Concerns about possible antitrust liability have caused the AMA to retreat from many of the anti-commercial recommendations in its 1957 code of ethics. The latest revisions of the ethical code say that advertising is permissible so long as it is not deceptive. Investments in health-care facilities are also permissible, provided that they are allowed by law and disclosed to patients, and provided also that they do not interfere with the physician's primary duty to his or her patients. Reflecting the new economic spirit, a statement has been added that competition is "not only ethical but is encouraged." Indeed, the AMA goes even further, declaring that "ethical medical practice thrives best under free market conditions when prospective patients have adequate information and opportunity to choose freely between and among competing physicians and alternate systems of medical care." Thus an earlier forthright stand by organized medicine against the commercialization of medical practice has now been replaced by an uneasy ambivalence.

Very recently, however, the AMA seems to have reconsidered its position, at least with respect to some kinds of entrepreneurial activity. At its last meeting it adopted a resolution advising physicians not to refer patients to an outside facility in which the physician has an ownership interest—except when the facility was built in response to a demonstrated need and alternative financing for its construction was not available. It remains to be seen whether this advice will be heeded and whether the AMA will take a similar position on other commercial practices. It will also be interesting to see what response this modest stand in defense of professional ethics will elicit from the Federal Trade Commission.

THE GOVERNMENT'S RESPONSE

Government policy has also been ambivalent. The Reagan and Bush Administrations have staunchly supported competition and free markets in medicine under the delusion that this is a way to limit expenditures. The White House has therefore supported the Federal Trade Commission's antitrust policies and until recently has resisted all proposals for curbing entrepreneurial initiatives in health care. But expenditures are not likely to be limited in a market lacking the restraints ordinarily imposed by cost-conscious consumers who must pay for what they want and can afford. And if the competing providers in such a market have great power to determine what is to be purchased, then their competition inevitably drives up expenditures and the total size of the market. In business, success is measured in terms of increasing sales volume and revenues—the last thing we want to see in the health-care system. Despite its preference for market mechanisms, however, the Bush Administration recently abandoned ideology and supported legislation to regulate physicians' fees and to prevent physicians from referring their Medicare patients to diagnostic laboratories in which they have a financial interest. Regulations and new legislation to provide even stricter limits on physicians' investments in health-care facilities are currently under consideration in several states—not for ethical reasons but simply as measures to limit health-care spending. Clearly, cost control is now the highest priority in public policy.

Despite its recent willingness to intervene in limited ways to control costs generated by some of the entrepreneurial activities of physicians, the government has as yet shown little interest in interfering with the spreading commercialization of our health-care system. That should not be surprising, because private enterprise is now widely heralded as the answer to most economic problems. We hear much these days about the privatization of schools, highways, airports, jails, national parks, the postal service, and many other aspects of our society—and by this is meant not simply removal from government control but transfer to investor ownership. Business, it is said, can do a much better job of running most of these things than government, so why not turn them over to private enterprise? I do not want to debate this general proposition here, but medical care, I suggest, is in many ways uniquely unsuited to private enterprise. It is an essential social service, requiring the involvement of the community and the commitment of health-care professionals. It flourishes best in the private sector but it needs public support, and it cannot meet its responsibilities to society if it is dominated by business interests.

WHY SHOULD THE PUBLIC CARE?

If government is not concerned about the loss of social and professional values in our health-care system, should the American public care? I think it must. The quality and effectiveness of our medical care depend critically on the values and the behavior of its providers. If health care is not a business, then we should encourage our physicians to stand by their traditional fiduciary obligations, and we should enable, if not require, our voluntary hospitals to honor their commitments to the community.

If most of our physicians become entrepreneurs and most of our hospitals and health-care facilities become businesses, paying patients will get more care than they need and poor patients will get less. In a commercialized system the cost of health care will continue to escalate and yet we will not be assured of getting the kind of care we really need. In such a system we will no longer be able to trust our physicians, because the bond of fiduciary responsibility will have been broken. To control costs, government will be driven to adopt increasingly stringent regulations. Ultimately health care will have to be regulated like a public utility, and much greater constraints will be placed on physicians and hospitals than are now in place or even contemplated.

Our health-care system is inequitable, inefficient, and too expensive. It badly needs reform. The task will be arduous and the solution is far from clear, but I believe that the first step must be to gain a firm consensus on what we value in health care and what kind of a medical profession we want. The medical profession has held a privileged position in American society, based on the expectation that it will serve society's needs first of all. How can it hope to continue in that position if it loses the trust of the public? We cannot expect to solve our health-care problems unless we can count on the basic altruism of the profession and its sense of responsibility to patients and the general public welfare. American society and the medical profession need to reaffirm their de facto contract, because they will have to depend on each other as the United States painfully gropes its way toward a better system of health care.

Physicians have the power to make health-care reform possible. They know the system better than anyone, and if they want to, they can use its resources more prudently than they do now without any loss of medical effectiveness. It is primarily their decisions that determine what medical services will be provided in each case, and therefore what the aggregate expenditure for health care will be. If physicians remain free of conflicting economic ties, and if they act in a truly professional manner, medical facilities will probably be used more appropriately, regardless of their ownership or organization. In any case, no proposed reforms in the health-care system can ultimately be successful without a properly motivated medical profession. But if physicians continue to allow themselves to be drawn along the path of private entrepreneurship, they will increasingly be seen as self-interested businessmen and will lose many of the privileges they now enjoy as fiduciaries and trusted professionals. They will also lose the opportunity to play a constructive role in shaping the major reforms that are surely coming.

The medical profession is not likely to change its direction without help. The incentives that now encourage—indeed, in many cases require—physicians to act primarily as businessmen will have to be changed, and probably so will the configurations in which most physicians practice. In my opinion, a greater reliance on group practice and more emphasis on medical insurance that prepays providers at a fixed annual rate offer the best chance of solving the economic problems of health care, because these arrangements put physicians in the most favorable position to act as prudent advocates for their patients, rather than as entrepreneurial vendors of services. However, regardless of what structural changes in the health-care system are ultimately adopted, physicians hold the key. The sooner they join with government and the public in reaffirming the medical profession's ethical contract with society, the easier will be the task of reform and the greater the chance of its success.

The relations [of production] do not only include the production of goods and services, but they also include the production of health and disease and above all the production of knowledge.
— Ronald Frankenberg

Steffie Woolhandler / David U. Himmelstein

The Deteriorating Administrative Efficiency of the U.S. Health Care System

Medicine is increasingly a spectator sport. Doctors, patients, and nurses perform before an enlarging audience of utilization reviewers, efficiency experts, and cost managers (figure 1). A cynic viewing the uninflected curve of rising health care spending might wonder whether the cost-containment experts cost more than they contain; one is reminded of the Chinese proverb "There is no use going to bed early to save candles if the result is twins."

In 1983 the proportion of health care spending consumed by administrative costs in the United States was 60 percent higher than in Canada and 97 percent higher than in Britain.[2] Recent U.S. health policies have increased bureaucratic burdens and curtailed access to care. Yet they have failed to contain overall costs. This study updates and expands estimates of the costs of health administration in North America through 1987.[2] The results demonstrate that the bureaucratic profligacy of the U.S. health care system has increased sharply, while in Canada the proportion of spending on health care consumed by administration has declined.

METHODS

We examined four components of administrative costs in the United States and Canada: insurance overhead, hospital administration, nursing home administration, and physicians' overhead and billing expenses (table 1).

Steffie Woolhandler, M.D., M.P.H., is Staff Physician and Director of Inpatient Services of the Division of Social and Community Medicine, Department of Medicine at Cambridge Hospital and is Assistant Professor at Harvard Medical School. David U. Himmelstein, M.D., is Staff Physician and Chief of the Division of Social and Community Medicine, Department of Medicine at Cambridge Hospital and is Associate Professor at Harvard Medical School.

Abridged from Woolhandler, S., and Himmelstein, D.U. (1991). The deteriorating administrative efficiency of the U.S. health care system. *N Engl J Med* 324(18):1253–1258. Used with permission from *The New England Journal of Medicine*.

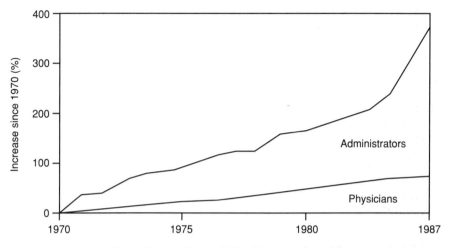

FIGURE 1.   Growth in the Numbers of Physicians and Health Care Administrators from 1970 to 1987

The data are from *Statistical Abstract of the United States* for these years (Table 64-2, 109th edition). Because of a modification in the Bureau of the Census' definition of "health administrators," the change between 1982 and 1983 is interpolated rather than actual.

All estimates are for fiscal year 1987, the most recent year for which complete data were available. Costs are reported in 1987 U.S. dollars, based on the 1987 exchange rate of $1.33 (Canadian) = $1 (U.S.); calculations of per capita spending were based on populations of 243,934,000 in the United States and 25,652,000 in Canada. . . .[4-6]

Only indirect or incomplete information is available on the billing costs of Canadian and U.S. physicians. We therefore used two different methods to estimate these costs, one based on physicians' reports of their professional expenses and the other on the numbers of employees in physicians' offices. The expense-based method (Method 1) probably overestimates the actual difference in billing costs between the two nations, whereas the personnel-based approach (Method 2) may underestimate the difference. . . .[14]

Finally, to evaluate trends over time, we recalculated the 1987 figures to maintain strict comparability with the less detailed and less complete data for 1983.[2] As in our earlier paper,[2] we estimated physicians' billing and overhead costs by the expense-based method (Method 1). However, we excluded the cost of physicians' time spent on billing because comparable data were unavailable for 1983. In keeping with our earlier method, we included malpractice costs in physicians' overhead expenses but corrected for increases over time in these costs.[11,12,16] For each country we took average total professional expenses in 1987, subtracted the average 1987

TABLE 1   Cost of Health Care Administration in the United States and Canada, 1987

Cost Category	Spending per Capita[a] U.S.	Canada
Insurance administration	106	17
Hospital administration	162	50
Nursing home administration	26	9
Physicians' overhead and billing expenses		
Expense-based estimate	203	80
Personnel-based estimate	106	41
Total costs of health care administration[†]		
High estimate	497	156
Low estimate	400	117

[a]All costs are expressed in U.S. dollars.

[†]The high estimate incorporates physicians' administrative costs derived by the expense-based method, and the low estimate costs derived by the personnel-based method.

malpractice premium, then added the average 1983 malpractice premium (all expressed as a percentage of gross income). The 1983 figures were converted to 1987 dollars with use of the gross-domestic-product price index for each country.[17]

RESULTS

Insurance Overhead

In 1987 private insurance firms in the United States retained $18.7 billion for administration and profits out of total premium revenues of $157.8 billion.[3] Their average overhead costs (11.9 percent of premiums) were considerably higher than the 3.2 percent administrative costs of government health programs such as Medicare and Medicaid ($6.6 billion out of total expenditures of $207.3 billion).[3] Together, administration of private and public insurance programs consumed 5.1 percent of the $500.3 billion spent for health care, or $106 per capita.

The overhead costs for Canada's provincial insurance plans amounted to $235 million (0.9 percent) of the $26.57 billion spent by the plans[17] (and Health Information Division, Health and Welfare Canada: personal communication). The administrative costs of Canadian private insurers averaged 10.9 percent of premiums ($200 million of the $1.83 billion spent for such coverage) (Health Information Division, Health and Welfare Canada:

personal communication). Total administrative costs for Canadian health insurance consumed 1.2 percent of health care spending, or $17 per capita.

Hospital Administration

Hospital administration represented 20.2 percent of hospital costs in California in 1987–1988.[18] Extrapolating this figure to the total U.S. hospital expenditures of $194.7 billion in 1987[2] yielded an estimate of $39.3 billion, or $162 per capita, consumed by hospital administration. In Canada, hospital administration cost $1.27 billion, amounting to 9.0 percent of total hospital expenditures of $14.14 billion (Health Information Division, Health and Welfare Canada: personal communication), or $50 per capita.

Nursing Home Administration

The administrative costs in California's nursing homes accounted for 15.8 percent of total revenues in 1987–1988.[19] On the basis of this figure, we estimate that administration cost $6.4 billion of the $40.6 billion spent nationally for nursing home care,[3] or $26 per capita. Canadian nursing homes spent $231 million on administration in 1987–1988, amounting to 13.7 percent of the total expenditures of $1.69 billion (Statistics Canada, Canadian Center for Health Information: personal communication), or $9 per capita.

Physicians' Billing Expense

Method 1.   When calculated according to Method 1, U.S. physicians' overhead and billing expenses, excluding malpractice premiums, made up 43.7 percent of their gross professional income[12]—$44.9 billion of the $102.7 billion spent for physicians' services.[3] In addition, physicians spent an average of six minutes on each Medicare and Blue Shield claim.[13] Assuming that the time required to bill other insurers was similar, the average physician spent about 134.4 hours per year (4.4 percent of his or her total professional activity) on billing; this time had a total value of $4.5 billion. Thus, the total value of U.S. physicians' billing and overhead was $49.4 billion, or $203 per capita.

Canadian physicians' professional expenses, excluding malpractice premiums, amounted to $1.99 billion, or 34.4 percent of their gross income (Rehmer L: personal communication). According to the director of professional affairs of the Ontario Medical Association, "The commitment of time to billing . . . is trivial and can be measured in seconds [per claim]" (Peachey D: personal communication). Assuming that the average physician spends 1 percent of his or her professional time on billing, with a total value of $58 million annually, the total cost of physicians' billing and overhead was $2.04 billion, or $80 per capita.

Method 2. The average office-based physician in the United States employed 1.47 clerical and managerial workers (Himmelstein DU, Woolhandler S: unpublished data), at an annual cost of $51,564 per physician, for a total of $20.0 billion. As calculated above (Method 1), the time physicians spent on billing was valued at $4.5 billion. In addition, 13.9 percent of physicians contracted with outside billing firms, at an average annual cost of $23,196 each,[13] for a total of $1.3 billion. Physicians' total billing and clerical expenses amounted to $25.8 billion, or $106 per capita.

The average office-based general practitioner in Quebec employed 0.733 receptionists and secretaries[15] at an annual cost of $25,655 per physician, for a total of $1.0 billion for Canadian physicians. In addition, the time physicians spent on billing was valued at $58 million. Physicians' total billing and clerical expenses were thus $1.06 billion, or $41 per capita.

Total Costs of Administration

Table 1 summarizes the per capita costs of health care administration in the United States and Canada, including physicians' billing and overhead costs as calculated by the two different methods. Overall expenditures for health care administration in the United States totaled $96.8 billion to $120.4 billion ($400 to $497 per capita), accounting for 19.3 to 24.1 percent of the $500.3 billion spent for health care. Canadians spent $3.00 billion to $3.98 billion for health care administration ($117 to $156 per capita), amounting to 8.4 to 11.1 percent of the $35.9 billion spent for health care. The difference of $283 to $341 in the per capita cost of health care administration and billing accounted for 43.5 to 52.5 percent of the total difference in health spending between the two nations. If U.S. health care administration had been as efficient as Canada's $69.0 to $83.2 billion (13.8 to 16.6 percent of total spending on health care) would have been saved in 1987.

The difference between the United States and Canada in billing and administrative costs has markedly increased since 1983.[2] Insurance overhead in the United States has risen from 4.4 percent to 5.1 percent of total health care spending, whereas insurance overhead in Canada has declined from 2.5 percent to 1.2 percent.[2] Hospital administrative costs have risen from 18.3 percent to 20.2 percent of total hospital spending in the United States, whereas in Canada these costs have climbed slightly from 8.0 percent to 9.0 percent.[2] Administrative expenses in U.S. nursing homes rose from 14.4 percent to 15.8 percent of costs, whereas administration's share of total costs rose from 10.5 to 13.7 percent in Canada.[2] Physicians' professional expenses (excluding malpractice premiums) have increased from 41.4 percent to 43.8 percent of gross income in the United States, whereas the Canadian figure declined from 35.5 percent to 34.4 percent.[2]

When we recalculated the 1987 figures to maintain comparability with the less complete 1983 data, we found that U.S. administrative costs rose from 21.9 percent to 23.9 percent of health care spending between 1983 and 1987, whereas in Canada administrative costs declined from 13.7 percent to 11.0 percent.[2] After adjustment for inflation, the divergence was even more striking. The costs of the health care bureaucracy in the United States rose by $32.2 billion (37 percent) between 1983 and 1987, an increase of $118 per capita. Administrative costs in the Canadian health care system fell by $161 million during this period, a decrease of $6 per capita.

DISCUSSION

Most of our analysis is based on well-substantiated data, although in some areas reliable figures are sparse. The comparability of the data on hospital administrative costs in Canada and the United States is uncertain. However, we relied on detailed budgetary categories that appeared closely matched in the two nations. Although data on the administrative costs of health maintenance organizations are limited, they do not appear to differ substantially from those in the U.S. fee-for-service sector.[20–22]

Both of our methods for estimating physicians' billing costs are imprecise. The expense-based method (Method 1) may overstate the difference between the United States and Canada, since it assumes that the entire discrepancy in the proportion of income devoted to professional expenses was accounted for by malpractice premiums, billing, and administration. The personnel-based method (Method 2) may understate the difference because it assumes that aides and other clinical personnel employed in physicians' offices performed no activities related to billing, that the total annual cost per clerical worker was no less in Canada than in the United States, and that Canadian billing operations have not been streamlined since 1977 despite computerization. An official of the Ontario Medical Association estimates that electronic claims submission and reconciliation takes about one sixth as much staff time as paper-based billing (Peachey D: personal communication).

In the United States, clerical and managerial staff accounted for 59.5 percent of the nonphysician employees in doctors' offices in 1988, and 74,700 more were added over the ensuing two years (Himmelstein DU, Woolhandler S: unpublished data). In contrast, technicians and technologists accounted for only 7.3 percent of nonphysician office workers in 1988 and for only 5.7 percent in 1990 (Himmelstein DU, Woolhandler S: unpublished data). In 1988, the staff in a typical U.S. physician's office spent about one hour on each Blue Shield or Medicare claim,[13] at least 20 times more than in Ontario (Peachey D: personal communication; Weinkauf D: personal communication). In a typical practice in Canada, "One person does all the billing, bookkeeping and typing . . . for 8 physicians."[23]

Our estimates omit the administrative costs of union and employer health-benefit programs and the administrative work done by hospital nurses and other nonphysician clinical personnel—all probably greater in the United States than in Canada. Moreover, patients in the United States spend far more time (and anguish) on insurance paperwork than do Canadians; these costs are not reflected in our figures. On the other hand, some argue that funding health services through taxes, as in Canada, erodes productivity throughout the economy by discouraging work and investment—the so-called dead-weight loss.[24] Within the range of tax rates in North America, however, the magnitude, and even existence, of this dead-weight loss is controversial.[25]

The United States spent 37 percent more in real dollars on health administration in 1987 than in 1983.[2] The recent quest for efficiency has apparently amplified inefficiency. Cost-containment programs predicated on stringent scrutiny of the clinical encounter have required an army of bureaucrats to eliminate modest amounts of unnecessary care. Each piece of medical terrain is meticulously inspected except that beneath the inspectors' feet. Paradoxically, the cost-management industry is among the fastest-growing segments of the health care economy and is expected to generate $7 billion in revenues by 1993.[26] The focus on micromanagement has obscured the fundamentally inefficient structure required to implement such policies. In contrast, Canada has evolved simple mechanisms to enforce an overall budget, but it allows doctors and patients wide latitude in deciding how the funds are spent. Reducing our administrative costs to Canadian levels would save enough money to fund coverage for all uninsured and underinsured Americans.[27] Universal comprehensive coverage under a single, publicly administered insurance program is the sine qua non of such administrative simplification.

The fragmented and complex payment structure of the U.S. health care system is inherently less efficient than the Canadian single-payer system. The existence of numerous insurers necessitates determinations of eligibility that would be superfluous if everyone were covered under a single, comprehensive program. Rather than a single claims-processing apparatus in each region, there are hundreds. Fragmentation also reduces the size of the insured group, limiting savings from economies of scale. Insurance overhead for U.S. employee groups with fewer than 5 members is 40 percent of premiums but falls to 5.5 percent for groups of more than 10,000.[28] Competition among insurers leads to marketing and cost shifting, which benefit the individual insurance firm but raise systemwide costs.

A lack of comprehensiveness in coverage also drives up administrative costs. Copayments, deductibles, and exclusions are expensive to enforce and lead many enrollees to purchase secondary "Medigap" policies. The secondary insurers maintain redundant and expensive bureaucracies.[29]

The efficiency of U.S. health care is further compromised by the extensive participation of private insurance firms whose overhead consumes 11.9 percent of premiums, as compared with 3.2 percent in U.S. public programs.[3] Even the "public" figure reflects the inefficiency of the private firms that process claims for Medicare for an average of $2.74 per claim,[30] whereas Ontario's Ministry of Health processes claims for $0.41 each (Davis J: personal communication). Moreover, the inefficiency of private insurers is not unique to the United States. The small private-insurance sectors of Canada, the United Kingdom, and Germany have overheads of 10.9 percent, 16 percent, and 15.7 percent, respectively.[31,32] A major advantage of public programs in terms of efficiency is their use of existing tax-collection structures, obviating the need for a redundant bureaucracy to collect money for health services. Thus, the overhead in Germany's premium-based, quasi-public sickness funds is between 4.6 percent[33] and 4.8 percent (Kuhn H: personal communication)—considerably higher than the overhead in tax-funded systems.

The scale of waste among private carriers is illustrated by Blue Cross/Blue Shield of Massachusetts, which covers 2.7 million subscribers and employs 6,682 workers[34]—more than work for all of Canada's provincial health plans, which together cover more than 25 million people[7–10] (and Davis J: personal communication; Cunningham D: personal communication); 435 provincial employees administer the coverage for more than 3 million people in British Columbia (Cunningham D: personal communication).

The existence of multiple payers in the United States also imposes bureaucratic costs on health care providers. Hospitals must bill several insurance programs with varying and voluminous regulations on coverage, eligibility, and documentation. Moreover, billing on a per-patient basis requires an extensive internal accounting apparatus for attributing costs and charges to individual patients and insurers. In contrast, Canada's single-payer system funds hospitals through global budgets, eliminating almost all hospital billing. The striking administrative efficiency of the Shriners' hospitals in the United States, which bill neither patients nor third parties and devote only 2 percent of their revenues to administration,[35] suggests that payment mechanisms rather than cultural or political milieus determine administrative costs. Here, too, the European experience parallels North America's. British hospitals that are assigned global budgets devote 6.9 percent of spending to administration,[36] but those paid on a per-patient basis (such as Humana's Wellington Hospital in London) spend 18 percent.[37]

The synchronous growth of bureaucratic profligacy and unmet health needs is reminiscent of Dickens' somber tale of six poor travelers who were relegated to outbuildings when the hostel built for them was fully occupied by its charitable administrators.

I found, too, that about a thirtieth part of the annual revenue was now expended on the purposes commemorated in the inscription over the door; the rest being handsomely laid out in Chancery, law expenses, collectorship, receivership, poundage, and other appendages of management, highly complimentary to the importance of the six Poor Travellers.[38]

The house of medicine is host to a growing array of specialists in fields unconnected to healing. At its present rate of growth, administration will consume a third of spending on health care 12 years hence, and half of the health care budget in the year 2020.

BIBLIOGRAPHY

1. Bureau of the Census. Statistical abstract of the United States. 102nd–109th eds. Washington, D.C.: Government Printing Office, 1981–1989.

2. Himmelstein DU, Woolhandler S. Cost without benefit: administrative waste in U.S. health care. N Engl J Med 1986;314:441–5.

3. Letsch SW, Levit KR, Waldo DR. National health expenditures, 1987. Health Care Financ Rev 1988; 10(2):109–22.

4. American Hospital Association. Hospital statistics: 1984 ed. Chicago, American Hospital Association, 1984.

5. *Idem.* Hospital statistics: 1988 ed. Chicago: American Hospital Association, 1988.

6. Hospital statistics 1986–1987. Toronto. Queen's Printer, 1987.

7. Ontario Ministry of Health. Annual report 1988–89. Kingston, Ontario Ministry of Health, 1989.

8. Regie de L'assurance-maladie du Quebec. Rapport Annuel 1986–1987. Quebec: Government of Quebec, 1987:30.

9. Saskatchewan Medical Care Insurance Commission. Annual report 1985–86. Regina: Government of Saskatchewan, 1986.

10. Nova Scotia Medical Services Insurance. Annual statistical tables: fiscal year 1985–86. Halifax: Government of Nova Scotia, 1986:3.

11. Canadian Medical Protective Association (CMPA) membership fees, 1971–1990. Toronto: Canadian Medical Association, 1989.

12. Gonzalez ML, Emmons DW, eds. Socioeconomic characteristics of medical practice 1989. Chicago: American Medical Association, 1989.

13. AMA Center for Health Policy Research. The administrative burden of health insurance on physicians. SMS Report 1989; 3(2):2–4.

14. Bureau of the Census. Current population survey, March 1988: technical documentation. Washington, D.C.: Department of Commerce, 1988.

15. Berry C, Brewster JA, Held PJ, Kehrer BH, Manheim LM, Reinhardt U. A study of the responses

of Canadian physicians to the introduction of universal medical care insurance: the first five years in Quebec. Princeton, N.J.: Mathematica Policy Research, 1978.

16. Reynolds RA, Abram JB, eds. Socioeconomic characteristics of medical practice 1983. Chicago American Medical Association, 1983.

17. Poullier J-P. Compendium: health care expenditure and other data. Health Care Financ Rev 1989; 11: Suppl.111−94.

18. Aggregate hospital financial data for California report periods ending June 30, 1987−June 29, 1988. Sacramento California Health Facilities Commission, 1989.

19. Aggregate long-term care facility financial data: report periods ending December 31, 1987−December 30, 1988. Sacramento, California Health Facilities Commission, 1989.

20. PHS will be challenged to maintain unbroken streak of profitability. Mod Healthcare 1989;19(31): 32−4.

21. Kenkel PJ. Improving managed care's management. Mod Healthcare 1990;20(19):27−34.

22. *Idem.* Medicaid HMOs struggle for viability: federal plan aims to ease the burden. Mod Healthcare 1990; 20(16):32.

23. Gerber PC. What your life would be like under a Canadian-type NHI. Physician's Manage 1990; 30(5):32−9

24. Ballad CA, Shoven JB. Wholley J. The total welfare costs of the U.S. tax system: a general equilibrium approach. Natl Tax J 1985; 38: 125−40.

25. MacEwan A, Campen J. Crisis, contradiction, and conservative controversies in contemporary U.S. capitalism. Rev Radical Polit Econ 1982; 14(3):1−22.

26. Cost-management industry grew in 1988. Mod Healthcare 1989; 19(33): 64.

27. Woolhandler S, Himmelstein DU. Free care: a quantitative analysis of health and cost effects of a national health program for the United States. Int J Health Serv 1988; 18:393−9.

28. Congressional Research Service, Library of Congress. Cost and effects of extending health insurance coverage. Washington, D.C.: Government Printing Office, 1988. (Education and Labor serial number 100-EE.)

29. Statement of Janet L. Shikles, Director, Health Financing and Policy Issues. Human Resources Division, General Accounting Office, before the Subcommittee of Health. Committee on Ways and Means, U.S. House of Representatives, March 13, 1990. Washington, D.C.: Government Printing Office, 1990. (SUDOC no. GAO/T-HRD-90-16.)

30. Statement of Janet L. Shikles, Director, Health Financing and Policy Issues. Human Resources Division, General Accounting Office, before the Subcommittee on Health. Committee on Ways and Means, U.S. House of Representatives, June 14, 1990. Washington, D.C.: Government Printing Office, 1990. (SUDOC no. GAO, T-HRD-90-42.)

31. Vayda E. Private practice in the United Kingdom: a growing concern J. Public Health Policy 1989; 10:359−76.

32. Verband der privaten Krankenversicherung e. V Dic private Krankenversicherung. Zahlenbericht 1988−1989.

33. Die gesetzliche Krankenversicherung in der Bundesrepublik Deutschland im Jahre 1988. Bonn, Germany: Bundesministerium für Arbeit und Sozialordnung, 1989.

34. Blue Cross/Blue Shield corporate report. Boston: Blue Cross/Blue Shield of Massachusetts, May 1990.

35. Guest DB. Health care policies in the United States: can the "American Way" succeed? Lancet 1985; 2:997–1000.

36. Compendium of health statistics. London: Office of Health Economics, 1984.

37. Parker P. A free market in health care. Lancet 1988; 1:1210–4.

38. Dickens C. Seven poor travellers. In: Dickens the Younger C, ed. Stories from the Christmas numbers of "Household Words" and "All the Year Round" 1852–1867. New York: Macmillan, 1896.

Allowing . . . health *and long-term care problems to persist not only deprives millions of Americans of what they ought to be able to have . . . it diminishes our economy . . . [and] the United States of America.*
— John D. Rockefeller

3

Private Insurance and Managed Care

Boston skyline with prominent insurance buildings

Stuart H. Altman / Marc A. Rodwin

Halfway Competitive Markets and Ineffective Regulation: The American Health Care System

A decade ago there was a perceived need to control medical care spending, which was increasing at a rate one-third faster than the gross national product (Waldo, Lent, and Lazenby 1986). There was a consensus among health care analysts that this spending did not provide equivalent benefits. Experiments with capitated forms of financing delivery of medical services, such as health maintenance organizations (HMOs), had shown that the use of resources (principally hospitals) could be reduced and personnel used more efficiently with no apparent ill effects on patient care (Enthoven 1978). In addition, sociological and other studies of health suggested that public health measures, personal lifestyles, and social and environmental conditions were in many respects more significant determinants of aggregate health than use of medical services.

At the time, Altman and Weiner (1978) characterized the use of regulation to contain medical inflation and real growth in the medical sector as a "second-best" alternative, one that was necessary—if not desirable—because of the nature of medical care and the way it was financed. Regulation was needed because market forces could have only a marginal impact on medical spending at best. The ineffectiveness of market forces was due to the existence of extensive insurance coverage, which made patients largely unresponsive to costs and to government subsidies of insurance and medical education; this in turn artificially increased the demand as well as the supply of medical services. Other factors also made sole reliance on market mechanisms inappropriate. Patients do not behave like ordinary consumers; they depend on physicians to make crucial choices.

Stuart H. Altman, Ph.D., is Dean of Florence Heller School for Advanced Studies in Social Welfare at Brandeis University.

Marc A. Rodwin, Ph.D., is Associate Professor, School of Public and Environmental Affairs at Indiana University.

Abridged from Altman, S.H., and Rodwin, M.A. (1988). Halfway competitive markets and ineffective regulation: The American health care system. *Journal of Health Politics, Policy and Law* 13(2):323–339. Copyright 1988, Duke University Press. Reprinted with permission of the publisher.

And physicians, because of their training and their role as patient advocates, tend to do as much as possible for their patients. While much has changed in the medical care sector, these characteristics have not.

A factor present a decade ago, which has since changed, is that organized buyers of medical services (such as commercial insurance companies and Blue Cross and Blue Shield plans) either lacked sufficient market power to require hospitals and physicians to limit their costs or did not use it. With no significant checks, these institutional and organizational arrangements promoted extraordinary growth in the medical sector and corresponding increases in expenditures. However, neither planning nor regulation as typically practiced were very successful in controlling the expanding medical care sector in the face of strong opposing incentives for key actors to continue their existing behavior. Since 1977, even these modest attempts at regulation have been sharply cut back. Several states that had rate-setting programs have eliminated them; others, including New York, have made them less restrictive.

In the last decade incentives, markets, and competition have been used more often than regulation. For example, private insurers, in part pushed by their large corporate clients, have used a variety of means (including some reduction in medical insurance coverage) to effect change in the medical care market. These changes have been significant and have generally increased efficiency. Yet despite the increased use of market forces, the medical care sector is still not a competitive market—rather, it is characterized by "halfway" markets. Government shapes the context within which markets function, both by supporting them and by keeping them under rein. While the delivery of medical care is overwhelmingly private, government at all levels directly finances more than 40 percent of this care and indirectly subsidizes the rest through various tax incentives. Government also structures market activity through various forms of regulation—some that promote and others that constrain or halt the market's activities. Government's involvement in medical markets is so ubiquitous that much of it is taken for granted, even by advocates of market competition.

The halfway character of medical markets and regulation reflects our indecisiveness about two approaches to social policy. Government regulation and competitive markets are alternative ways to allocate medical services, control cost and quality, and choose social priorities. Each method has its loyal adherents. Those who favor competitive markets believe that liberty and the public good flow from private sector and individual initiatives with decentralized decision making and a limited role for government. Those who favor tighter government control believe that liberty and the public good stem from democratic control and collective self-determination (Vladeck 1981). However, because of the nature of the American political system and the special characteristics of the medical care sector, neither of these approaches has been able to prevail. We seem to lack the political will to have either a competitive market system or an effective government regulatory approach. Instead, we vacillate between the two approaches. We allow some markets to exist, but insist that the government structure and monitor their performance. If the market does not provide a solution acceptable to powerful interest groups, political pressure is brought to bear for government to do something—and it often does.

There is no doubt that government intervention limits market activities. If we view efforts individually and consider only the short run, regulation often distorts markets. But viewed in a larger, longer-run context, regulation can often promote and foster markets. For example, licensing professionals reduces consumer uncertainty over the quality and nature of medical service. Consumers can assume that the practitioner is competent, which lowers their information costs. This assurance makes patients more willing to avail themselves of medical services, particularly in new or unknown areas. In this respect licensing, and many other seemingly restrictive regulations, promotes markets. To the extent that regulations limit choice, they are like budgets that allow market activity but make it subject to constraints. Such restrictions on particular market activities preserve the institution of the market.

However, two of the most sought-after features of markets—competition that reduces price and budget constraints that control spending—are notably absent or diminished in medical markets. Regulations that raise minimum standards contribute to the lack of price competition. But there are more fundamental distortions that prevent the optimum functioning of medical markets. Many people believe that medical care is a special service that should be allocated largely based on need (Fein 1986). The uncertainty and risk of many medical problems prompt patients to demand extra precautions in diagnosis and treatment, and the physician's ethic promotes the same tendency. Given the complexity and ambiguity of medicine, it is always possible to expend further resources in precaution, diagnosis, or treatment. Further, the presence of extensive insurance makes patients and providers much less sensitive to prices. Therefore, there is rarely a reduction in the demand for medical services when prices rise; neither do providers lower their prices when faced with greater competition.

These characteristics of the halfway competitive markets and ineffective regulation in medical care have fueled the growth of medical expenditures, which continue to grow at rates that far exceed the growth in national income. In this evaluation we will elaborate on why neither increased competition nor conventional government regulation can succeed in controlling medical care spending. Although tough budget regulation can control spending, it would force the country to face many difficult distributive choices and to incur substantial social costs—choices and costs which the country has preferred to avoid (Blendon and Altman 1987).

THE LIMITED EFFECTS OF INCREASED COMPETITION IN CONTROLLING MEDICAL CARE SPENDING

In the last decade the public and private sectors have employed three market approaches to controlling medical care spending (Meyer 1983). One strategy focused on the role of consumers, increasing the prices they pay and their choice of insurance policies. Another strategy relied on HMOs and other alternative delivery systems that compete with traditional providers. A third strategy used the market power of organized purchasers of medical services to demand more favorable payment arrangements. . . .

Competition and Market Reforms in Perspective

Although the growth of market competition has brought and will continue to bring a measure of increased efficiency in the delivery of medical care, spending will not be substantially reduced. Due to the halfway nature of markets that exist in the medical care sector, increased competition will not produce savings as great as those that are realized when market competition is more robust. Markets sometimes force producers to compete over price, but most often they compete in other ways. Moreover, efficiency gains in the provision of medical care do not always result in reduced spending for purchasers.

An important limitation of all the market competition strategies used to control spending is that there are many significant forces increasing expenditures other than the inefficient use of medical services (Schwartz 1987). These forces are unaffected by any efficiency gains produced by market competition. Among these cost-generating forces are a growing population; the increasing size of the oldest age cohort, which uses more medical services and long-term care; the increasing medicalization of social problems; and, in the future, the growing AIDS epidemic.

. . . Medical care spending has not abated during the last decade. . . . In the period 1976–1987, medical care spending increased by almost 80 percent above the level of inflation. This growth also far exceeded the growth in the country's national income (as measured by GNP). In 1976, medical care spending stood at 8.5 percent of GNP; by 1987, it had grown to 11.2 percent. The . . . rate of growth in real spending . . . was relatively stable from 1979 to 1983. In 1984, there was a small but noticeable decline in the growth rate, reflecting in part the impact of the more aggressive behavior of private payers and the federal government. However, the cumulative growth rate resumed its pre-1982 level in 1985 and continues to follow that pattern today.

A similar picture emerges from an analysis of the spending levels for hospital care. Prior to 1983 and the start of the Medicare prospective payment system (PPS) and many of the prudent purchaser programs of private corporations and insurers, total revenues (spending) for all hospital services were increasing at a rate of 7.3 percent after adjusting for inflation. This was the average annual rate during the 1976–1982 period. On a per admission basis, the annual average growth in spending was 5.2 percent. The first three years after 1982 were marked by a significant downturn in the growth in total spending for all hospital care, particularly 1984 and 1985. But in 1986 this downturn was reversed, and in the last two years spending levels appear to be close to pre-PPS levels. Much of the reduction was the result of a drop in hospital inpatient admissions, as can be seen by the relative stability in the growth in spending per admission and the sizable increases in the growth in real spending for hospital outpatient care.

REGULATION AS A STRATEGY FOR
CONTROLLING SPENDING

. . . Market processes alone have not and cannot bring about substantial control over medical care spending in the current American economic and political environment. Will government regulation do any better? We do not think it likely. This is because our halfway markets in medical care limit the effectiveness of regulation as well as competition. As a general rule, we have not allowed our regulatory system sufficient authority over the levers of spending to be effective in controlling total medical expenditures.

Health Planning and Regulation

The regulatory approach of the 1970s was implemented by a network of planning bodies called health systems agencies (HSAs) which were established by federal legislation. Their aim was to control the formation of expensive new capital projects, such as the building or renovation of a hospital and the purchase of new equipment costing more than $150,000. No new major hospital expansion or capital expenditures were permitted without a state-approved certificate of need.

From the beginning, HSAs were severely constrained by their lack of direct control over hospital reimbursement and the state regulatory apparatus. At the state government level, HSAs had to contend with organized opposition from hospitals and other providers that had more resources and better trained staffs and that were waging a single battle while each HSA fought many. In contrast to the concentrated interests of providers, the HSAs represented the diffuse interests of consumers and HSA board members, who were unaccountable to the public (Marmor and Marone 1980). The combination of these factors tilted the outcome of political fights against effective regulation.

Conflicts over the goals of health planning also make it difficult to control spending. HSAs had a broad planning agenda. Some groups wanted to control costs; others wanted to improve access to medical care; still others wanted to expand and improve institutions. The multiplicity of goals made the pursuit of spending control difficult and gave additional ammunition to providers who opposed controls. Providers could always reasonably argue that important goals were being thwarted by regulation and then find ways to get around the most restrictive provisions.

The closest the federal government came to giving any public agency control over the reimbursement of medical care institutions was during the period of the economic stabilization program (ESP) from 1971 to 1974. Even then the control was over what hospitals and physicians could charge for their services, not what they could spend. Nevertheless, ESP was successful in limiting spending for hospital care. Just prior to the ESP period, hospital costs per admission grew by 11.2 percent; during ESP the growth rate slowed to 8.5 percent. After Congress ended the control program in 1974, hospital and total medical care spending returned to pre-ESP levels (Altman and Eichenholz 1976).

Regulations that Increase Costs

Not only did government regulations established in the 1970s fail to control spending effectively, but they also often contributed to increased costs by raising standards, by ensuring quality and safety, or by promoting social justice. The attentive public responded to this kind of regulation—which is often beneficial—not only by accepting it, but by clamoring for more.

The extent of such regulation is enormous. State laws require insurers to maintain a minimum amount of reserves to pay beneficiaries. They can also prohibit the sale of any policy that does not have rate structures, benefit packages, and prices they approve. For example, medical insurance for a particular disease (such as cancer) is often disallowed on the grounds that it takes advantage of people's fears and does not provide useful protection. States license physicians, nurses, and other practitioners, and government funding for education helps regulate entry into these professions. Rules of legal liability require negligent practitioners and institutions to pay damages. Medical experimentation must conform to a special review process. Hospitals must afford doctors procedural due process before terminating their privileges. And new drug and medical devices must be approved by the Food and Drug Administration before they can be marketed.

A host of other regulations are directed not just to the medical sector but to all business. For example, the employment relationship is bound by rules protecting collective bargaining, providing unemployment benefits, establishing minimum wages and maximum hours of work, and prohibiting child labor and preferential treatment on the basis of race or sex. Also, just as other businesses do, medical providers must comply with laws governing commerce (such as the Uniform Commercial Code), property law, and laws regarding the sale of securities, insolvency, and the rights and obligations of the business owners.

Rate-setting Regulation

Government regulation failed to control spending in the 1970s not because regulation can never work but because the form of regulation used did not account for or use financial incentives and because there was insufficient political consensus for enforcing effective regulation (e.g., rate setting). Yet there is evidence that rate setting can be effective in controlling hospital spending. In a comparison of medical expenditures from 1976 to 1984 between six rate-controlled states and the rest of the nation, Schramm et al. (1986) reported that there was an 87 percent larger increase in expenses per hospital admission in unregulated states than in regulated states. If savings are calculated by the reduction in inflation from the national average, the six states saved approximately $8 billion. The annual per capita hospital expenses in the six rate-control states showed increases of 33 percent for the period 1972–1976, while the growth rate in the nonregulated states was 38 percent.

New York State in particular has demonstrated that when a political body really faces a serious fiscal crisis it can create and administer an effective medical care spending control program (Schramm 1986). For several years, New York brought down the growth rate of medical care spending. But without the spur of its fiscal crisis, it is doubtful that even New York would have been able to muster the political consensus required to implement such a program.

Prospective Payment as Partial Budget Regulation

One innovative form of budget regulation is Medicare's prospective payment system, which uses financial incentives and allows providers latitude in managing their resources. However, the driving force of PPS is not consumer choice but government, which manipulates reimbursement to get hospitals to change their practice patterns. PPS is closer to an administrative price scheme than to either price control or a competitive market (Ginsburg 1987). Under PPS, government establishes a payment rate for each diagnosis-related group (DRG), leaving the hospital and physician to decide how to manage resources. Hospitals therefore have a financial incentive to use resources in a more parsimonious manner.

PPS has produced significant short-run improvements in medical practice and utilization. Hospitals have developed management information systems, evaluated their expenditure patterns more carefully, economized in their use of resources, and shortened the average length of patient stay. Numerous procedures that were performed in hospitals in the past are now done on an outpatient basis, a change that health planners advocated for years without success. But while this system has produced reductions in the spending rate for inhospital care, much of these savings have been used to finance more outpatient and home health care. Further, the most recent data show that even hospital inpatient costs are beginning to approach pre-PPS levels.

PPS is a prime example of regulation that makes use of incentives and market process, and it has made progress toward controlling hospital costs and changing institutional behavior. But PPS does not control reimbursement for procedures performed outside hospitals. The combination of prospectively setting hospital reimbursement rates and reimbursing outpatient care on the basis of customary, prevailing, and reasonable fees has created what might be called the "squeezed balloon" effect. By squeezing spending on inpatient care, the system has created a bulge in spending at the opposite end—outpatient and home care. Though PPS has produced change, it can only have a limited impact on total medical expenditures because it only affects part of the system.

BUDGET REGULATION: AN EFFECTIVE SOLUTION?

Since the use of both increased market competition and conventional government regulation have had only limited success in controlling medical care spending, what is to be done?

Spending for medical services can be controlled in three ways (Fuchs 1986). One approach is to improve efficiency in the provision and allocation of services. A second approach is to reduce the prices paid for the materials and services used in medical care, which implies paying producers and providers less. A third approach is to reduce the volume of services provided or to shift the balance from high-cost to low-cost services. Both regulatory tools and market mechanisms can be used to implement these three strategies. But given the halfway markets in medical care, without some kind of systemwide control the use of market mechanisms and/or regulation is unlikely to be more effective than it has been in the past.

Is there a point in the spending spiral where medical costs will become so large that payers of care—both public and private—will stand up to the political pressures of providers and patients and demand effective cost control? It almost happened in the early 1980s, and there were some real changes in the delivery system. But several years of reduced general inflation and high corporate earnings have blunted the aggressive behavior of payers. There are indications that the rate of growth of medical spending is returning to pre-1982 levels. Insurance premiums are again rising by 10 to 20 percent (Medical Benefits 1987). The percentage of GNP going to medical care has risen from 10.5 percent in 1982 to 11.2 percent in 1987, and unofficial estimates for 1988 predict that it will approach 11.5 percent, or over $550 billion (ProPAC 1988).

There is no question that budget regulation can control spending. The experiences of Canada and Britain suggest that it can produce dramatic results (Evans 1987). The issue is whether we are willing to accept the negative consequences entailed—and "we" means everybody. Access to care would be limited somewhat for most Americans, although those who use the system the most (the elderly and the poor) will be most vulnerable. Such limitations could be across the board or focused on certain high-cost technologies, particularly those that are used during the last months of life. Quality of care might also suffer. In Canada, strict budgets did not produce measurable harmful reductions in services because they were able to focus these efforts on limiting the amount paid to providers. But our provider groups are politically much stronger, and therefore reduced spending is unlikely to be borne by them alone.

The strongest impetus for controlling spending in the Canadian system was the federal government's decision to limit its contribution to each province. This decision forced provinces to absorb the full impact of increases in spending beyond a tight predetermined level. With this political backbone in place, the provinces became much tougher in imposing restrictions on their physicians and hospitals. But in the United States, the political situation will almost certainly differ. In spite of the studies suggesting that it is possible to substantially reduce medical spending with no negative impact on the quality of care (Eddy 1987), it is likely that even small reductions would be opposed due to perceived (as opposed to technically measured) quality deterioration. Even though independent assessments have not turned up many examples of serious reductions in the quality of care under PPS, consumers and providers have voiced serious concerns. These concerns have been enough to cause Congress to legislate important changes in the PPS system and to threaten even more far-reaching changes. Under a budget control system, Medicare and Medicaid beneficiaries would become "quality-of-care" watchdogs that would pressure legislators and the executive branch to provide what they (and their medical care providers) believe is a decent level of quality. This will require funding and could undermine budget control regulation in the most direct manner—by increasing the budget.

Both the major virtue and the major drawback of budget regulation is that it forces explicit choices about the allocation of resources and consideration of social priorities. This is a virtue because it brings to light choices that otherwise are not seen or are intentionally avoided; it is a drawback because facing such choices is a difficult and painful process. There may be no generally agreed-upon goals, or such goals may be sufficiently vague and ambiguous that translating them into specific policies and funding decisions is inherently controversial. This is the stuff from which political conflict is kindled.

Over the past two decades the United States has undertaken numerous regulatory and market-oriented programs to limit spending, but these have been partial and fragmented. Often, just as the programs have verged on becoming effective, groups that would be adversely affected have exerted political pressure to protect their interests in ways that undermine the program. Economically and politically we want to have our cake and eat it, too. Thus we allow a political stalemate to support halfway competitive markets and to produce ineffective regulation in medical care.

However, increased spending is not inevitable, and we do not need to accept a totally governmental regulatory system to bring about a balanced rate of spending. We believe that it is possible to structure a system that permits many of the advantages of competition to remain but overlays competitive markets with a tougher, more effective regulatory system. One might have expected the current level of spending already to have forced such difficult social choices. But so far the nation has either avoided the tough trade-offs required or decided that the benefits of open-ended medical spending outweigh the social costs of its control. It is not clear that we really want to control spending. At the moment, spending 15 percent of the GNP for medical care by the year 2000 is clearly a possibility.

BIBLIOGRAPHY

Altman, S., and J. Eichenholz. 1976. Inflation in the Health Industry: Causes and Cures. In *Health: A Victim or Cause of Inflation,* ed. M. Zubkoff. New York: Prodist.

Altman, S., and S. Weiner. 1978. Regulation as a Second Best. In *Competition in the Health Care Sector: Past, Present, and Future,* ed. Warren Greenberg. Germantown, MD: Aspen Systems.

Blendon, R., and D. Altman. 1987.

Public Opinion and Health Care Costs. In *Health Care and Its Costs,* ed. C. Schramm. New York: W. W. Norton.

Butler, L., H. Luft, and H. Lipton. 1987. *Medical Life on the Western Frontier: A Closer Look at the Competitive Impact of Prepaid Medical Plans in California.* Berkeley: Institute for Governmental Studies, University of California.

Crosier, D. 1983. Data Watch: National

Medical Care Spending. *Health Affairs* 2: 1–30.

Enthoven, A. 1978. *Health Plan: The Only Practical Solution to the Soaring Cost of Medicare.* Reading, MA: Addison-Wesley.

Etheridge, L. 1986. Ethics and the New Insurance Market. Inquiry 23: 305–15.

Eddy, D. 1987. The Quality of Medical Evidence and Medical Practice. Paper prepared for the National Leadership Commission on Health Care, Washington, DC, June.

Evans, R. 1987. Finding the Levers, Finding the Courage: Lessons from Cost Containment in North America. *Journal of Health Politics, Policy and Law* 11: 585–615.

Fein, R. 1986. *Medicare, Medicaid Costs: The Search for a Health Insurance Policy.* Cambridge, MA: Harvard University Press.

Feldman, R., B. Dowd, D. McCann, and A. Johnson. 1986. The Competitive Impact of Health Maintenance Organizations on Hospital Finances: An Exploratory Study. Journal of Health Politics, Policy and Law 10: 675–97.

Fuchs, V. 1986. Has Cost Containment Gone Too Far? *Milbank Memorial Fund Quarterly* 64:479–88.

Gertman, P. 1987. Unpublished Estimates. Lexington, MA: Health Data Institute.

Gibson, R., and D. Waldo. 1984. National Health Expenditures, 1983. *Health Care Financing Review* 6: 1–30.

Ginsburg, P. 1987. Medicare's Prospective Payment System: The Expectations and the Realities. *Inquiry* 24 (2): 187–88.

Goldberg, V. 1976. Regulation and Administration Contracts. *Bell Journal of Economics* 7: 426–48.

Hewitt Associates. 1984. Comparing Practices in Health Care Cost Management. Lincolnshire, IL: Hewitt Associates.

Johnson, A., and D. Aquilina. 1986. The Competitive Impact of Health Maintenance Organizations and

Competition on Hospitals in Minneapolis/St. Paul. *Journal of Health Politics, Policy and Law* 10: 659–97.

Luft, H. 1984. How Do HMOs Achieve Their Savings? Rhetoric and Evidence. *New England Journal of Medicine* 298(6): 1136–43.

———. 1985. HMOs: Friends or Foes? *Business and Health* 3: 5–9.

Luft, H., S. Maerki, and J. Trauner. 1986. The Competitive Effects of Health Maintenance Organizations: Another Look at the Evidence from Hawaii, Rochester, and Minneapolis/St. Paul. *Journal of Health Politics, Policy and Law* 10: 625–58.

Manning, W., Arleen Leibowitz, George A. Goldberg, William H. Rogers, and Joseph Newhouse. 1984. A Controlled Trial of the Effects of Prepaid Group Practices on Use of Services. *New England Journal of Medicine* 310(23):1505–10.

Marmor, T., and J. Marone. 1980. Representing Consumers' Interests: Imbalanced Markets, Health Planning and HSAs. *Milbank Memorial Fund Quarterly* 58(1): 125–65.

Medical Benefits. 1987. Health Insurance Rates Keep Climbing. (Reprinted from *Business Insurance.*) 15 September, p. 4.

Merrill, J., and C. McLaughlin. 1986. Competition versus Regulation: Some Empirical Evidence. *Journal of Health Politics, Policy and Law* 10: 613–23.

Meyer, J., ed. 1983. *Market Reform in Health Care.* Washington, DC: American Enterprise Institute.

Newhouse, J., Carl N. Morris, Larry L. Orr, et al. 1981. Some Interim Results from a Controlled Trial of Cost Sharing in Health Insurance. *New England Journal of Medicine* 305 (25) 1501–1507.

Prospective Payment Assessment Commission. 1988. Impact of the Prospective Payment System on the American Healthcare System. Unpublished draft. Washington, DC: ProPAC.

Schramm, C., Steven C. Renn, and Brian Biles. 1986. New Perspectives on State Rate Setting. Health Affairs 5: 22–33.

Schwartz, W. 1987. The Inevitable Failure of Current Cost-Containment Strategies: Why They Can Provide Only Temporary Relief. *Journal of the American Medical Association* 257(2): 220–24.

Sullivan, S., and P. Ehrenhaft. 1984. *Managing Health Care Costs: Private Sector Initiatives.* Washington, DC: American Enterprise Institute.

Sykvetta, M., and J. Swartz. 1986. *The Uninsured and Uncompensated Care.* Washington, DC: National Health Policy Forum, George Washington University.

Vladeck, B. 1981. The Market vs. Regulation: The Case for Regulation. *Milbank Memorial Fund Quarterly* 59: 209–23.

Waldo, D., K. Lent, and H. Lazenby. 1986. National Health Expenditures, 1985. *Health Care Financing Review* 8: 1–21.

Wallack, S. 1981. Federal Health Professional Training Programs: The History and Impact. In *Federal Health Programs: Problems and Prospects,* ed. S. Altman and H. Sapolsky. Lexington, MA: Lexington Books.

Wilensky, G., and L. Rossiter. 1986. Patient Self-Selection in HMOs. *Health Affairs* 5: 66–80.

For-profit health care . . . and the resultant corporatization of the "not-for-profit" firms is removing health *care from those Americans most in need.*
— D. G. Whiteis and J. W. Salmon

Donald W. Light

The Practice and Ethics of Risk-rated Health Insurance

The foundation of private American health insurance is risk rating, the practice of setting premiums and other terms of policies for groups and individuals according to the age, sex, occupation, health status, and health risks of policyholders. Through competition, risk rating should give policyholders the best value for their money and also be the most fair. However, with half of all expenses incurred by 5% of the population and 70% of all expenses incurred by 10% of the population, risk rating can be both highly profitable and highly injurious to its victims.

This article describes a number of disturbing practices that throw into question the alleged merits of competitive risk-rated health insurance. It describes the techniques of risk rating that lead to a growing number of uncovered medical conditions and unpaid medical bills. It then examines the moral justification that underlies risk rating and shows how not being thy brother's keeper may be actuarially fair but is morally unfair. Few of these issues or practices are addressed by the leading proposals for universal health insurance. My purpose here is to present a policy issue and a position to foster debate. Comprehensiveness is not possible within the short span of this article.

THE PRACTICES AND CONSEQUENCES
OF RISK RATING

Risk-based insurance comes in several forms that can be classified as direct or indirect risk rating.

Donald W. Light, Ph.D., is Professor in the Division of Social and Behavioral Medicine, Department of Psychiatry at the University of Medicine and Dentistry of New Jersey, Camden, New Jersey.

Abridged from Light, D.W. (1992). The practice and ethics of risk-rated health insurance. *JAMA* 267(18):2503–2508. Copyright 1992, American Medical Association. Used with permission.

Direct Risk Rating

Direct risk rating, or *medical underwriting*, means the opposite of what it implies. It means to document the medical problems or risks people have, not to support or "underwrite" them, but to reduce coverage or add charges or deny coverage altogether. Thus, *medical underwriting* would more accurately be called *medical underinsuring*.

. . . Risk rating has proliferated to include common, often minor health problems, such as allergies, asthma, back strain, arthritis, and obesity. But exclusions and denials are also applied to costly cases involving disabilities, serious illness, and chronicity.[1]

Insurance companies also risk rate by redlining, or excluding entire industries, such as beauty shops, hotels, restaurants, trucking firms, hospitals, nursing homes, and physicians' practices.[2,3] But far more frequently insurers drop groups one by one when the bills of a few very sick members become large.

Indirect Risk Rating

A second cluster of risk-rating techniques are, strictly speaking, unrelated to risk rating or actuarial underwriting. Waiting periods, copayments, and payment ceilings are the most common forms, along with exclusion of certain procedures, tests, or drugs. The impact of these restrictions, however, is directly proportional to a policyholder's need for medical services, and the unpaid claims are likewise proportional. Thus, these de jure neutral techniques are de facto indirect forms of risk rating. They are used for a number of purposes: to reduce claims paid, to discourage sick people from abusing health insurance, and to help employers keep costs down.[4] Over the past 10 years, employers and insurers have lengthened waiting periods, increased copayments, increased exclusions for various procedures or drugs, and capped payment levels so that subscribers pay the entire balance of the bill.

The Inverse Coverage Law

In these ways, risk rating leads to the inverse coverage law: the more people need coverage, the less coverage they are likely to get or the more they are likely to pay for what they get. Risk rating systematically discriminates against disadvantaged minorities, older workers, and those with chronic conditions, and against groups that include such individuals.[5-7] It is important to realize that "high risk" and "uninsurability" are not categories in nature but products of risk rating. They result in the threat of sudden downward mobility through medical impoverishment that can strike at any time or the outlay of large sums for high premiums, deductibles, copayments, and exclusions. As of 1984, about 56 million Americans, or a quarter of the nonelderly population, were estimated to have inadequate coverage to pay the bills for major medical expenses.[8] About 81 million people under the age of 65 have chronic problems that self-insured employers can drop. . . .[9-14]

Inaccurate Risk Rating

Exacerbating the consequences of risk rating are inaccurate or manipulative uses. Although we commonly assume that premium increases and other forms of risk rating accurately reflect risk rating, evidence to the contrary keeps appearing.[15] Yet no state insurance department or other independent reviewer holds insurance companies accountable for their risk rating, and therefore little rigorous evidence exists. . . .[16-24]

Spiral of Discrimination

With increasing acceleration in the 1980s and 1990s, competition among risk-based insurance companies has driven them to risk rate more and to use allegedly neutral cost containment protocols to reduce the claims paid to people who most need medical services. The spiral of competitive risk rating has added four techniques, which could be called *policy churning, within-group underwriting, renewal underwriting,* and *selective marketing.*

In policy churning, employers switch policies just as the waiting periods end and the medical expenses of employees with medical problems start to push premiums up.[19] As a result, employees with preexisting conditions continue to be uncovered. . . .

Within-group underwriting reflects the breakdown of uniform group rates as a tradition that has allowed those at risk and with chronic problems nevertheless to have access to health care. Until now, such people were protected as employees of a group policy, because there was no risk rating within groups. Granted, their medical problems or risks raised the overall group rate (a disincentive for most small employers to employ handicapped or high-risk people); but at least they were not singled out for "special" treatment. Now that barrier is breaking down. . . .[25]

In renewal underwriting, anyone who has contracted a new costly medical condition during a policy year will have that condition added to those previously excluded from coverage when the policy is renewed.[3,26] This, together with the above two techniques, leaves no safe haven.

Selective marketing consists of identifying groups with lower risks and concentrating sales efforts on signing them up. Conversely, selective marketing involves not responding to inquiries from higher-risk groups.

Even under community-rated universal insurance, selective marketing can be a powerful tool for lowering the risk of one's portfolio of policies. From an insurance company's point of view, selective marketing and the other forms of risk rating are natural and necessary. For the task of insurance as a business (rather than as a social institution) is to maximize sales while minimizing claims and maximizing profits. In sum, those supporting risk-based insurance should be clear about what they are supporting, its consequences, and the medical outcasts it creates.

Techniques to Reduce Bills Paid

Direct and indirect forms of risk rating still leave insurance companies with millions of claims for medical services that have to be paid. Under the pressure of competition, techniques for reducing the number of medical bills paid seem to be increasing, although it is impossible to gather reliable data and no one monitors actual claims practices. . . .

Perhaps most prevalent have been changes in policies to shift expenses for claims back to subscribers by increasing copayments, deductibles, and limitations of coverage for dependents or for classes of procedures. . . .

Besides elaborate rules for claims eligibility, an increasing number of insurance companies seem to practice claims harassment, with employers as consenting partners. . . .[27]

Some patients with health problems report the technique of *exclusion by association,* another practice on which no systematic data are collected by commissioners of health insurance. In exclusion by association, insurers state that a certain medical problem is caused by another whose coverage is excluded. . . .

All of these techniques save insurance companies money. At the least they delay payment, which increases investment income, and at the most they make claimants give up and go away—a highly profitable outcome.

Consequences

The practices described fall most heavily on disadvantaged minorities, older workers, and those with chronic conditions, and against groups that include such individuals. Although, strictly speaking, only some of these practices involve direct risk rating, the others also harm those with medical problems or higher risks more than those with lower risks. The practices of risk rating contribute to a new and growing kind of poverty—medical poverty—which can occur any time that serious illness strikes and produces uncovered bills. The impact on physicians and hospitals is also great. A study of all unpaid hospital bills in a large midwestern sample found that 46.8% came from patients *with* health insurance. . . .[28–34]

THE ETHIC OF RISK-BASED INSURANCE

. . . Whether insurance officers think of risk-rated health insurance in moral terms or just as smart economics, the practice of risk rating embodies the notion that it is unjust to force one person or group to pay for the needs or burdens of another. A libertarian ethic holds that such coercion reduces the liberty of the first person or group.[42–44] If people choose to help pay for someone else's health care, that is fine. But to impose a common premium on everyone, for example, is to take money from healthier people to pay for the care of less healthy people.

This ethical stance toward health insurance has wide support in the United States and reflects its individualistic culture of "every man for himself" and "look out for number one." The realities of the stance that we have described, however, might make even a libertarian shrink from the consequences. A libertarian ethic also underlies insurance theory and the insurance industry. . . .[45,46]

Some Arguments for Risk Rating

Advocates of risk rating argue that it makes insurance more affordable and therefore makes health care more accessible. Even at face value this argument is weak. Risk-rated insurance for a population per se costs no less than community-rated insurance; it merely shifts costs from the healthy to those at risk or sick. Since most medical costs are incurred by a small percentage of rather sick people, it is a matter of raising their premiums a lot in order to decrease everyone else's premiums a little.

Thus, risk rating makes insurance less affordable to those who need it most and thereby decreases both access to medical services and their quality if obtained.[47] It also means more unpaid medical bills. For whether the high-risk person or group cannot afford insurance because the premium is too high or the coverage is incomplete, precisely those who use the most medical treatment have the least ability to pay for it.

Risk-based insurance is less affordable to everyone else as well because it drives up overall costs.[48] First, insurers incur the considerable costs of designing thousands of different policies, rating tens of thousands of different groups, and marketing these thousands of differences by hundreds of companies in an effort to persuade buyers that their policy and terms are the best. Second, buyers have added costs assessing competing policies, choosing one policy, and then (in most cases) trying to figure out why their health insurance costs are still rising at rates two to three times inflation. Third, competitive risk rating pits each company or group against the others and prevents the formation of a unified structure for budgeting and coordinating medical expenditures. Even when a given company manages its own costs well, it cannot manage systemic sources of increase, and it largely prompts providers to shift costs over to other policyholding groups that manage their health costs less well. It is this inflationary side effect of risk rating that leads employers to drop coverage for more and more low-income workers. . . .[49,50]

Advocates of risk-based insurance also maintain that it is "natural," because if everyone were charged equally, lower-risk people or firms would seek an insurer to cover them for less and create the very risk-based market one was trying to avoid by starting out with an "unnatural" community rate. This argument lies behind why most firms think they can beat the area-wide average and pay less for the same coverage. In practice, however, it is more difficult for this "natural" outcome to be achieved. The people or firms involved would have to know their actual risks, which often they do not, and the policies offered to them would have to accurately reflect the differences among their risks. Even then, of course, half of them would lose, because by definition half are above the median if we assume high-risk cases to be equally distributed. In addition, many of those below the median would find their savings erased by the higher costs of a competitive risk-rated market and by the lack of controls over the rise of overall expenditures.

Actuarial vs. Moral Fairness

When insurers state that underwriting is fair because low-risk people should not have to share the burdens of high-risk people, they are consciously or unconsciously assuming that the purpose of the health insurance market in society is to allow those who are younger, more affluent, constitutionally more sound, and healthier to pursue their advantage of lower risk over those who are older, poorer, constitutionally less sound, and less healthy. As Norman Daniels has observed, "This assumption is far from morally neutral."[51(p502)] However, if we believe justice should center on equality of opportunity,[52] then the question is what are the foundations or preconditions for the just distribution of opportunity, and which individual differences, particularly disabilities, should be allowed to affect the distribution of opportunities, liberties, and rights?

Our society has decided that race, sex, physical handicaps, and in some cases, age shall not be so used for employment and access to many facilities and resources, though the law is more ambivalent about equal access to health care.[4(ch3)] We are thus at a point of transition and contradiction in which laws require sweeping access to facilities for the handicapped while extensive discrimination is still allowed in health insurance, thus limiting their access to medical services. Following Daniels,[53] I contend that in a just society, differences in health and health risk should not be used as a basis for distributing opportunities. In addition, avoidable or treatable pain and suffering should not be condoned.

A morally fair system therefore requires access to services that can minimize disadvantages and suffering due to illness, as the President's Commission on Ethics in Medicine concluded.[54] Thus, actuarial fairness is morally unfair, because it reduces access to life opportunities and increases suffering for those disadvantaged by risk, pain, and illness. This does not mean that differences in capacity due to health will not exist. Inequalities of many kinds exist in all societies. The point is to minimize the disadvantages of ill health and reject any system of financing or organization that deliberately capitalizes on those disadvantages. (The issue of differential insurance policies or rates for self-induced risks requires a separate article, which would conclude that little evidence exists that such rates are effective and that such risk rating leads to a tangle of problems about where to draw lines and how to monitor them.)

The medical profession, its various associations, and policymakers in general need to think through their moral stand on risk-rated health insurance. In deciding what kind of universal health insurance to support, one needs to examine carefully how different proposals address various forms of risk rating described in these pages.

Of particular importance are indirect forms of risk rating left unaddressed by legislation that eliminates direct risk rating; for insurance pools or companies, especially if they are competing for profit, have a natural and strong motive to use selective marketing, benefits design, and the various techniques to reduce or delay claims paid so that they avoid or drive away the small percent of people who run up a large percent of all medical bills. In the meantime, the medical profession and the public can expect more medical bills to be uncovered as competitive risk rating accelerates the spiral of discrimination and exclusion.

REFERENCES

1. US Office of Technology Assistance. *AIDS and Health Insurance.* Washington, DC: US Office of Technology Assistance; 1988.

2. *Promoting Health Insurance in the Workplace: State and Local Initiatives to Increase Private Coverage.* Chicago, Ill: American Hospital Association; 1988.

3. US General Accounting Office. *Health Insurance: Cost Increases Lead to Coverage Limitations and Cost Shifting.* Washington, DC: US General Accounting Office; 1990. Publication HRD-90-68.

4. Congressional Research Service. *Health Insurance and the Uninsured: Background Data and Analysis.* Washington, DC: Congressional Research Service; 1988. Publication 85-568.

5. Trevino FM, Moyer ME, Valdez RB, Stroup-Benham CA. Health insurance coverage and utilization of health services by Mexican Americans, mainland Puerto Ricans, and Cuban Americans. *JAMA.* 1991;265:233–237.

6. Wenneker MB, Epstein AM. Racial inequalities in the use of

procedures for patients with ischemic heart disease in Massachusetts. *JAMA.* 1989;261:253–257.

7. Short PF. *National Medical Expenditures Survey: Estimates of the Uninsured Population: Calendar Year 1987: Data Summary 2.* Rockville, Md: National Center for Health Services Research and Health Care Technology Assessment; 1990.

8. Farley P. Who are the underinsured? *Milbank Q.* 1985;63:476–503.

9. Freudenheim M. Employers winning wide leeway to cut medical insurance benefits. *New York Times.* March 29, 1992:1, 24.

10. Rothstein MA. *Medical Screening and the Employee Health Cost Crisis.* Washington, DC: Bureau of National Affairs; 1989.

11. Nelkin D, Tancredi L. *Dangerous Diagnostics.* New York, NY: Basic Books Inc Publishers; 1989.

12. Stone D. At risk in the welfare state. *Social Res.* 1989;56:591–633.

13. Hunt M. The total gene screen. *New York Times Magazine.* January 19, 1986;33, 38, 55–60.

14. Waldholz M. The diagnostic power of genetics is posing hard medical choices: ability to detect conditions but not to treat them may increase abortions. *Wall Street J.* February 18, 1986:1.

15. Neil RAW, Mant D. Cholesterol screening and life assurance. *BMJ.* 1991;302:891–893.

16. Cotton P. Preexisting conditions 'hold Americans hostage' to employers and insurance. *JAMA. 1991;265:2451–2453.*

17. Beebe J, Lubtiz J, Eggers P. Using prior utilization to determine payments for Medicare enrollees in health maintenance organizations. *Health Care Finan Rev.* 1985; 6:27–37.

18. Lubtiz J. Health status adjustments for Medicare capitation. *Inquiry.* 1987;24:362–375.

19. Nadel MY. *Health Insurance: Availability and Adequacy for Small Businesses.* Testimony before the Subcommittee on Antitrust, Monopolies and Business Rights, Committee on the Judiciary, US Senate. US General Accounting Office publication GAO/T-HRD-90-33; June 5, 1990.

20. *Community Rate Schedules and Development.* Newark, NJ: Blue Cross and Blue Shield of New Jersey, Inc; March 28, 1990.

21. *The Public Advocate vs Blue Cross and Blue Shield of New Jersey.* NJ Super Ct App Div A-2232-89T1.

22. Light DW. NJ citizens stop Blue Cross discrimination. *Health/PAC Bull.* Winter 1990:34–35.

23. Mondics C. Anger grows over Blue Cross rate hike. *Bergen Rec.* March 13, 1992:1.

24. Heidorn R Jr. State tries to deal with insurance fiasco. *Philadelphia Inquirer.* March 29, 1992:B1, B3.

25. *Indemnity Plans: Costs, Design, and Funding.* Princeton, NJ: Foster Higgins; 1990.

26. Kolata G. New insurance practice: dividing sick from well. *New York Times* March 4, 1992:A1, A15.

27. Grumet GW. Health care rationing through inconvenience: the third party's secret weapon. *N Engl J Med.* 1989;321:607–611.

28. Saywell RM Jr, Zollinger TW, Chu OK, MacBeth CA, Sechrist ME. Hospital and patient characteristics on uncompensated hospital care: policy implications. *J Health Polit Policy Law.* 1989;14(2):287–307.

29. Blendon RJ, Leitman R, Morrison I, Donelan K. Satisfaction with health systems in ten nations. *Health Aff.* 1990;9:185–192.

30. Harvey LK. *American Medical Association Survey of Public and Physicians' Opinions on Health Care Issues.* Chicago, Ill.: American Medical Association; 1990.

31. Harvey LK. *American Medical Association Survey of Public and Physicians' Opinions on Health Care Issues.* Chicago, Ill: American Medical Association; 1991.

32. McQueen M. Voters, sick of the current health-care system, want federal government to prescribe remedy. *Wall Street J.* June 28, 1991:A14.

33. US House of Representatives, Select Committee on Aging. *Abuses in the Sale of Health Insurance to the Elderly in Supplementation of Medicare: A National Scandal.* Washington, DC.: US House of Representatives Select Committee on Aging; 1978. US Dept of Health, Education, and Welfare publication 052-070-04742-9.

34. McCall N, Rice T, Hall A. The effect of state regulations on the quality and sale of insurance policies to Medicare beneficiaries. *J Health Polit Policy Law.* 1987;12:53–76.

[See original article for Notes 35–41.]

42. Schramm CJ. Insurers advocate HIV testing. *AIDS Patient Care.* February 1988:4–6.

43. Reproduced in Stone DA. AIDS and the moral economy of insurance. *Am Prospect.* 1990;No. 1:62–74.

44. Nozick R. *Anarchy, State and Utopia.* Oxford, England: Blackwell Scientific Publications Inc; 1974.

45. Clifford HA, Iuculano RP. AIDS and insurance: the rationale for AIDS-related testing. *Harvard Law Rev.* 1987;99:727–751.

46. Wright R. The end of insurance. *New Republic.* July 9/16, 1990:26.

47. Hadley J, Steinberg EP, Feder J. Comparison of uninsured and privately insured hospital patients: condition on admission, resource use, and outcome. *JAMA.* 1991; 265:374–379.

48. US Government Accounting Office. *Canadian Health Insurance: Lessons for the United States.* Washington, DC: US General Accounting Office; 1991. Publication GAO/HRD-91-90.

49. Kronick R. Health insurance, 1979–1989: the frayed connection between employment and insurance. *Inquiry.* 1991;28:318–322.

50. US Dept of Commerce. *US Industrial Outlook 1991: Health and Medical Services.* Washington, DC: US Dept of Commerce; 1991.

51. Daniels N. Insurability and the HIV epidemic: ethical issues in underwriting. *Milbank Q.* 1990; 68:497–525.

52. Rawls J. *A Theory of Justice.* Oxford, England: Oxford University Press; 1989.

53. Daniels N. *Just Health Care.* Cambridge, England: Cambridge University Press; 1985.

54. President's Commission for the Study of Ethical Problems in Medicine and Behavioral Research. *Securing Access to Health Care.* Washington, DC: President's Commission for the Study of Ethical Problems in Medicine and Behavioral Research; 1983:4–5.

The societal and cultural responses to disease create a second illness in addition to the original affliction . . . the layers of stigma, rejection, fear, and exclusion that attach to particularly dreaded diseases . . . [and] force the patient, now twice victimized, further into the cage of his or her illness, shunned, silenced, and shamed in addition to being very sick.

— N. Scheper-Hughes and M. M. Lock

Ellen M. Morrison / Harold S. Luft

Health Maintenance Organization Environments in the 1980s and Beyond

INTRODUCTION

Organizations that combine the financing and delivery of health care (prepaid health plans) were in existence before the turn of the century. However, prior to the 1970s, prepaid health plans were few in number, small in size, and often struggled with organized medical groups and with public and legal opinions. When the term health maintenance organization was coined, followed by HMO-enabling legislation at the Federal level in 1973 and by grants and loans to new HMOs, prepaid health plans took a leap in legitimacy. These plans, representing a dramatic alternative to fee-for-service medicine, were envisioned by some analysts as agents of change that would introduce competition into the health care industry. HMOs were predicted to cover 40 million persons and to be available to 90 percent of the entire U.S. population by the late 1970s (Falkson, 1980). That prediction wildly overestimated both the pace and the form of HMO growth in the years to follow.

Today, 17 years after the passage of the HMO Act of 1973, these organizations cover approximately 15 percent of the total U.S. population and their availability and popularity are distributed unevenly across geographical areas and segments of the population. HMOs are often not available to the poor, the elderly, rural residents, and employees of small businesses, and they are not universally popular among individuals who have the option of enrolling (Langwell et al., 1987; Freund and Neuschler, 1986, Feldman, Kralewski, and Dowd, 1989; Gruber, Shadle, and Polich, 1988; Ginsburg, Hosek, and Marquis, 1987; Welch and Frank, 1986). Many of

Ellen M. Morrison, Ph.D., is a Research Fellow at the Institute for the Future, Menlo Park, California.

Harold S. Luft, Ph.D., is Professor of Health Economics and Acting Director of the Institute for Health Policy Studies at the University of California, San Francisco.

Abridged from Morrison, E. M., and Luft, H. S. (1990) Health maintenance organization environments in the 1980s and beyond. *Health Care Financing Review* 12 (1):81–90. Used with permission.

the small prepaid plans that received Federal start up monies in the mid-1970s failed outright, while many others lingered only long enough to be subsumed by larger HMOs or insurance companies (Strumpf and Garramore, 1976; Kohrman, 1986a).

Even though HMO growth has fallen considerably short of expectations, HMOs have been significant agents of change. Specifically, physicians, employers, consumers, and entrepreneurs have reacted to and acted on the original HMO concept. In so doing, they have tailored HMOs into diverse organizational forms and have evoked competitive organizational responses from indemnity carriers. Now second and third generation alternative delivery systems present considerable competitive threat to the stability of established traditional HMOs.

The 1980s provided rapid and dramatic change for the health care industry. Regulatory and competitive pressures, in addition to rising costs and developing technologies pushed providers, payers, and consumers into new behaviors. Providers behaved more defensively and payers more aggressively, while consumers carried the burden of decreased public and private payer willingness to pay for health care services. HMOs, promoted a decade earlier as alternatives to fee-for-service medicine, faced increased competition from one another and from new alternatives. As we enter the 1990s, the effectiveness and efficiency with which these organizations serve both private and public enrollees are still at issue. . . .

INTENSIFIED COMPETITION

Sensitivity in the early 1980s by public and private payers to dramatically rising health care costs resulted in increased pressure on traditional providers to contain costs and on consumers to share more of the costs (Juffer, 1982; *Business Week,* 1983). Rising costs caused increased interest in HMOs for their cost-containment potential (owing, for the most part, to their lower rates of hospitalization), even among employers who had previously avoided HMO involvement. Many employers for the first time began offering, and advocating, these organizations to their employees (Sapolsky et al., 1981; Anderson et al., 1985). Employees were not attracted, however, in large numbers to Staff or General Model HMOs with restricted choices of physicians and hospitals (Louis Harris and Associates, 1980; Appel and Aquilina, 1982). Community physicians rejected the restrictions on their referral networks inherent in HMOs. HMOs had particular difficulties gaining enrollees and physician support in communities with a high proportion of solo practice physicians and consumers with established physician relationships (Boehm, 1976). HMO advocates responded by developing independent practice association (IPA) HMOs. In IPAs, patients can select from a list of community physicians whose participation in these plans represent a small percentage of their overall practice. This model allows patients more choice in selecting a physician. Physicians are allowed a wider network in which to refer patients than in traditional HMOs. IPAs require far less capital investment than do staff model plans because plan physicians continue to practice in their own offices. Popularity among consumers and low start-up costs resulted in IPA models becoming the fastest growing plan type. From 1980 through 1985, the number of IPAs increased from 97 to 181 plans or 87 percent, whereas other HMO models increased from 132 to 162 plans or only 17 percent (*InterStudy,* 1985).

The success of IPA models increased experimentation with varying levels of consumer and physician choice that eventually led to the introduction of preferred provider organizations (PPOs). PPOs, in general, offer the consumer a choice of full (HMO-like) coverage of ambulatory and inpatient care with a selected panel of providers combined with a limited (indemnity-like) range of coverage for out-of-plan use (Gabel et al., 1986). These plans are not regulated by the Federal HMO Act or by any State HMO mandates and are not required to offer the broad range of services or the community premium ratings mandated for federally qualified HMOs. Consumers typically enroll in the indemnity plan and are able to decide whether to use providers in or out of the plan (preferred providers) at the time of service. Enrollment counts, therefore, are very difficult to estimate, but plans have been growing steadily in physician, employer, and insurer participation.

The enhancement in consumer choice allowed by IPAs and PPOs mimics the freedom of choice—or, what Feldman, Kralewski, and Dowd (1989) describe as, the freedom of "self-refer to a specialist"—found in traditional fee-for-service medicine. Overcoming the obstacles of restricted choice to consumer and physician acceptance has helped alternative delivery systems expand rapidly and consequently has resulted in reduced market share for indemnity carriers and Blue Cross and Blue Shield (BC/BS) plans (Traska, 1987a). In some markets the fee-for-service sector has responded by introducing utilization review and stringent cost-containment efforts (sometimes referred to as managed fee-for-service), as well as PPOs or more limited coverage, in order to be price competitive with prepaid plans.

The next step along the line of HMO evolution appears to be the introduction of "open-ended" or "hybrid" plans by established staff and group models, i.e., plans that offer consumers a choice of Staff, Network, IPA, and PPO options. Some plans have joint ventures with insurance companies to add an indemnity component, thereby becoming triple option plans (HMO, PPO, and indemnity). Joint ventures (with insurance companies) and subsidiaries that offer the full range of coverage and provider choice with varying degrees of associated premium and out-of-pocket costs make it even more difficult to distinguish between the organizations we used to know as HMOs and fee-for-service practices. Feldman, Kralewski, and Dowd (1989), in studying the changes in the mature HMO market of Minneapolis-St. Paul, conclude that the diversity within both fee-for-service and prepaid plans has blurred the distinctions between health plan types, thereby creating more of a continuum rather than separate categories. . . .

Open-ended and hybrid plans introduced by established HMOs serve to protect or to prevent erosion of the plans' market share and appear to be diverting consumer interest away from traditional plans. Hybrid plans are also being introduced by traditional fee-for-service providers and are influencing the loyalties of even established HMO members (Kenkel, 1988b; Oberman, 1988). . . . Nationally, enrollment in open-ended plans grew from 250,000 in 1986 to 702,648 by July of 1989. Enrollment in traditional HMOs, i.e. Staff, Group, and IPA models, has continued to increase overall, reaching 30.5 million by July 1989, but the pace of growth has slowed, with losses in some states offsetting gains in others (Traska, 1988a).

Increasing membership rolls, however, have not guaranteed financial stability. In 1987, the HMO industry as a whole lost $692 million. Nearly three-fourths (179) of the 243 plans surveyed by National Underwriter lost money during the year (Kenkel, 1988b).

Competition from alternative plans is not the only reason for the HMO depression in growth. According to Gruber, Shadle, and Polich (1988), three factors heavily influenced the 1987 slowdown in HMO enrollment:

- Increased competition from other health care organizations and products (e.g., PPOs and triple option plans).
- Difficulties plans faced in responding to employers' demands for experience-rated premiums.
- Purchasers' frustrations in not receiving group-specific data on cost, use, and quality.

To expand on the last point, many employers are suspicious of HMOs' ability to provide cost-effective, quality care. These employers are beginning to demand proof from HMOs that their premium increases reflect true cost increases rather than a shadowing of indemnity plan premiums, i.e., pricing premiums slightly less than competing indemnity plans, and that HMOs are not the recipients of favorable selection by young, healthy employees (Luft, Trauner, and Maerki, 1985).

The losses of 1987 were not confined to small or freestanding HMOs, for some large HMOs and HMO-hospital chains also showed financial losses (Kenkel, 1988b). This was the first year Maxicare, one of the largest for-profit, multi-state HMOs, began revealing financial difficulties (losses of $225 million on total revenues of $1.8 billion) that resulted in the resignation of its top management, legal action from physicians regarding financial practices, and eventually the plan's bankruptcy in the spring of 1989 (Kenkel, 1988a and 1988c; Gardner, 1988; Larkin, 1989).

Bankruptcy of plans all over the country appears to be in its second generation. In the mid-to-late 1970s, plans that had received Federal startup grants and loans discovered the difficulties of acquiring and maintaining Federal qualification and in managing the actuarial and service delivery components of their plans (Strumpf and Garramore, 1976). In the first generation of plan failure, many hospitals considering HMO contracts viewed small or newly established HMOs with suspicion, concerned that these plans would go belly up, leaving the hospitals with uncollectables (Anderson et al., 1985). The second generation of bankruptcies more often takes large, established plans as victims, the smaller plans being more susceptible to acquisition than to Chapter 11 (Traska, 1987b).

MARKET ENTRY, EXPANSION, AND EXIT

As with other organizations that either deliver or finance health care, HMOs describe their markets in at least two ways; geographical markets and payment markets. In the academic and popular literature on HMO market entry, expansion, and exit, generic differences have surfaced based on payment markets, i.e., private versus public sources of payment. The issues for HMOs seeking to enroll employees (private) are significantly different than those facing HMOs considering Medicare or Medicaid contracts (public).

EMPLOYEE PRIVATE MARKETS

Descriptive History

Prior to 1970, prepaid plans (later called HMOs) were developed primarily by two different groups: physican or consumer activist groups attempting to provide high-quality, comprehensive care to their communities . . . and employers attempting to provide basic health care services to their workers . . . (Uphoff and Uphoff, 1980). Plans did not select the environments in which they would operate in these early days before communities became markets. Rather, the community or the work site was a critical element in a plan's formation. The consumer-founded plans were located in their communities of origin, and employer-based plans were located near the employer's site so that workers could minimize time lost from work. . . .

The primary role of the private sector in HMO development has been that of a payer of employee health benefits. Rising health benefit costs in the private sector increased business involvement in HMOs in the early 1980s. Business promotion of HMOs was not in the form of subsidies or low-interest loans but in the form of interested customers representing blocs of potential enrollees. . . .

PUBLIC SECTOR RISK CONTRACTING

Descriptive History

Historically, the Federal Government's involvement in HMOs has been that of an employer and a payer. As an employer, its Federal Employee Health Benefit Plan has long offered HMOs as enrollment options and is the largest source of enrollees for many of these plans. The Federal Government is exempt, however, from the HMO Act. For example, Government Agencies cannot be mandated by HMOs. The major focus of Federal health care policy related to HMOs has been the Government's role as a payer, i.e., in the Medicare and Medicaid programs, and here the history is relatively brief.

Medicare

Although HMOs have had the legal ability to contract with the Federal Government to provide services to Medicare beneficiaries since the program's inception in 1965, they were not attracted to the Government's options for payment. The choices, i.e., risk contracts, cost contracts, and health care prepayment plans, were all retrospective and cost based. . . .

The turning point in Federal involvement on a grand scale was the passage of the Tax Equity and Fiscal Responsibility Act (TEFRA) of 1982, implemented in 1985. True risk contracts were authorized by TEFRA, including prospective reimbursement not later adjusted for actual cost (Gruber, Shadle, and Polich, 1988). The legislation also allows competitive medical plans, i.e., plans that do not meet the requirements to become federally qualified HMOs, to enter into risk contracts. TEFRA succeeded in dramatically boosting plan participation in risk contracts. As a result, HMO enrollment of Medicare beneficiaries increased from 262,000 in 1985 to 990,000 in April 1988 (Gruber, Shadle, and Polich, 1988). . . .

Medicaid

In contrast to its medicare role as the primary payer, the Federal Government's role in the Medicaid program is to provide support to State and locally funded and administered programs. The amount of Federal support received by each State is determined by a complex formula based on multiple factors, including the State's wealth. Individual States have the flexibility to develop programs and services, set eligibility criteria, and determine benefit levels. From the time of Medicaid's inception until 1981, States, under Section 1115 of the Social Security Act, could apply to HCFA for waivers to experiment with and to evaluate different payment and service delivery mechanisms. Under a section 1115 waiver, requirements for Medicaid programs such as eligibility definitions, statewideness and the amount, duration, and scope of services could be relaxed or waived (Freund and Hurley, 1987). Prepaid programs operating under a waiver were required to conform to Federal qualification standards and were not permitted to enroll more than 50 percent of Medicaid and Medicare beneficiaries. Even though most State Medicaid programs were familiar with the HMO concept and knew that Section 1115 waivers offered greater flexibility in risk sharing than did the Medicare contracts of the same time, i.e., prior to TEFRA of 1982, relatively few programs were in operation by 1981. Eighteen States had operational plans, but only seven had more than two. Only California with 13 operational plans and 47 percent of the total U.S. enrollment in Medicaid prepaid plans (132,079 out of 281,926) could have been considered actively involved in Medicaid prepaid contracting by 1981 (Freund and Neuschler, 1986; Freund and Hurley, 1987).

One year prior to TEFRA having opened the door to true risk contracting for Medicare, the Omnibus Budget Reconciliation Act (OBRA) of 1981, Public Law 97-35, allowed States more choices in developing alternative financing and delivery mechanisms in their Medicaid programs. OBRA permitted States to establish their own qualification standards and prepaid plans to enroll up to 75 percent Medicaid and Medicare beneficiaries. Section 1915(b) of OBRA allowed States to develop primary care management systems, select providers based on cost-effectiveness, limit freedom of choice of provider, modify payment arrangements with selected providers, and offer clients incentives to join selected provider organizations (Freund and Neuschler, 1986; Freund and Hurly, 1987).

To stimulate greater experimentation in this area, HCFA in 1982 solicited bids from States for managed care demonstration projects. Six States (California, Florida, Minnesota, Missouri, New Jersey, and New York) received waivers. The plans were implemented between June 1983 and September 1987 and differed from one another by type of enrollment (mandatory versus voluntary), organizational structure (contracts with physicians, hospitals, primary care organizations, prepaid plans, or intermediaries), eligible populations, e.g., categorically needy, medically needy, and Aid to Families with Dependent Children, participating providers, and mechanisms for provider payment. Three of the four proposed modules of the Florida plan were never implemented as demonstrations (Freund et al., 1989). The sites with the largest and the smallest enrollment (Monroe County, New York, with an estimated maximum of 41,300 and Itasca County, Minnesota, with an estimated maximum of 3,441) mandated beneficiaries to enroll in a capitated plan but allowed enrollees to choose their provider.

In addition to Medicaid competition demonstrations, following OBRA 1981, many States received Section 1915 waivers and have implemented both competitive (vountary enrollment) and noncompetitive (mandatory enrollment) plans. Neuschler and Squarrel (1985) characterize waiver plans along three dimensions: financial incentives, organizational arrangements, and recipient participation. The estimated nationwide enrollment in Medicaid prepaid plans as of June 1986 was 840,849. California still leads in terms of enrollment size, with an estimated 218,475 enrollees, but Wisconsin with 124,642 enrollees and Arizona with 119,237 enrollees have increased their enrollments at a faster pace since the passage of OBRA 1981. Arizona is particularly noteworthy because of its mandatory statewide prepaid program, Arizona Health Care Cost Containment System (AHCCCS), the State's first Medicaid program, implemented in 1982. Although there exists no single definition of managed care to which plans conform, all programs share the following characteristics:

- Limitations on freedom of choice of provider.
- Attempts to modify patient utilization patterns through the coordination of service delivery.
- Financial incentives and risk sharing to alter physician behavior and/or encourage formation of new organizational entities (Freund, 1987). . . .

CONCLUSION

The academic research and trade literature available on HMOs in this decade are extensive, however, many questions have yet to be answered and more have to be asked. In the area of competitive effects on HMOs, we are faced with dramatic changes in both fee-for-service and alternative delivery organizations in choice of provider and scope of benefits. We must find ways to classify organizations and plans that allow us to document growth and outcomes while not placing organizations in artificial categories, e.g., HMO, PPO, and fee-for-service.

In examining the determinants of market entry and exit, we have found that financial incentives, particularly a large enrollment base and tax benefits in the private sector and Federal and State payment generosity in the public sector, are key issues in determining market entry in the current environment. We know little about the factors that reduce market exit in either the private or public sector and even less about the motivating factors for entry into the Medicaid market.

BIBLIOGRAPHY

Adamache, K. W., and Rossiter, L. F.: The entry of HMOs into the Medicare market: Implications for TEFRA's mandate. *Inquiry* 23:349–364, Winter 1986.

American Medical Association Center for Health Services Research and Development, *health care issues: Physician and public attitudes.* Chicago: American Medical Association, 1979.

Anderson, O., Herold, T., Butler, B., et al.: *HMO development: Patterns and prospects.* Chicago: Pluribus Press, 1985.

Appel, G. L., and Aquilina, D.: Hospitals won't compete on price until spurred by buyers' shopping. *Modern healthcare* 108–110, Nov. 1982.

Baldwin, M. F.: HMO supporters praise HCFA's decision to terminate Medicare contract with IMC. *Modern Healthcare* 17(11):11, 1987.

Berki, S. E., and Ashcraft, M. L.: HMO enrollment: Who joins what and why. *Milbank Memorial Fund Quarterly* 58:588–632, 1980.

Birnbaum, R. W.: *Health maintenance organizations: A guide to planning and development.* New York. Spectrum Publications, 1976.

Boehm, W. F.: Prepayment group practice: An insider's viewpoint. *Chicago Medicine* 79:601–604, June 12, 1976.

Brown, L. D.: Competition and health cost containment: Cautions and conjectures. *Milbank Memorial Fund Quarterly* 59(2):145–189, 1981.

Business Week. Trying to curb health care costs at the bargaining table. 73–76, Sept. 19, 1983.

Butler, L. H., Luft, H. S., Lipton, H. L., et al.: *Medical life on the western frontier: The competitive impact of prepaid medical care plans in California.* Berkeley: California Policy Seminar, Institute of Governmental Studies, University of California, Monograph Number 6, 1980.

Christianson, J.: The impact of HMOs: Evidence and research issues. *Journal of Health Politics, Policy and Law.* 5(2):354–367, 1980.

Enthoven, A., and Kronick, R.: A consumer-choice health plan for the 1990s: Universal health insurance in a system designed to promote quality and economy, Part 1. *New England Journal of Medicine* 320(1):29–37, 1989a.

Enthoven, A., and Kronick, R.: A consumer-choice health plan for the 1990s: Universal health insurance in a system designed to promote quality and economy, Part 2. *New England Journal of Medicine* 320(2):94–101, 1989b.

Evans, R. G., et al.: Controlling health expenditures—the Canadian reality. *New England Journal of Medicine* 320:571–577, 1989.

Falkson, J. L.: *HMOs and the politics of health system reform.* Chicago. American Hospital Association, 1980.

Feldman, R., Dowd, B., McCann, D., et al.: The competitive impact of health maintenance organizations on hospital finances: An exploratory study. *Journal of Health Practices, Policy and Law* 10(4):675–697, 1986.

Feldman, R., Kralewski, J., and Dowd, B.: Health maintenance organizations: The beginning or the end? *Health Services Research* 24(2):191–211, 1989.

Freund, D. A.: Competitive health plans and alternative payment arrangements for physicians in the United States: Public sector examples. *Health Policy* 7:163–173, 1987.

Freund, D. A., and Hurley, R. E.: Managed care in Medicaid: Selected issues in program origins, design, and research. *Annual Review of Public Health* 8:137–163, 1987.

Freund, D. A., Hurley, R. E., Paul, J., et al.: Interim findings from the Medicaid competition demonstrations. *Advances in Health Economics and Health Services Research* 10:153–181, 1989.

Freund, D. A., and Neuschler, E.: Overview of Medicaid capitation and case-management initiatives. *Health Care Financing Review* 1986 Annual Supplement. HCFA Pub. No. 03225. Office of Research and Demonstrations, Health Care Financing Administration, Washington. U.S. Government Printing Office, Dec. 1986.

Gabel, J., Ermann, D., Rice, T., et al.: The emergence and future of PPOs. *Journal of Health Politics, Policy and Law* 11(2);305–322, 1986.

Galblum, T. W., and Trieger, S.: Demonstrations of alternative delivery systems under Medicare and Medicaid. *Health Care Financing Review,* Vol. 3, No. 3. HCFA Pub. No. 03295. Office of Research and Demonstrations, Health Care Financing Administration. Washington, U.S. Government Printing Office, Mar. 1982.

Gardner, E.: Maxicare slapped with restraining order. *Modern Healthcare* 18(29):4, 1988.

Group Health Association of America: *Medicare risk contracting: An assessment.* GHAA Conference. Baltimore, MD. Oct. 14–16, 1987.

Group Health Association of America: The AAPCC explained. *Research Briefs* 8 Feb. 1989.

Ginsburg, P. B., Hosek, S. D., and Marquis, S.: Who joins a PPO? *Business and Health* 36–41, Feb. 1987.

Goldberg, L. G., and Greenberg, W.: The determinants of HMO enrollment and growth. *Health Services Research* 16: 421–438, Winter 1981.

Gruber, L. R., Shadle, M., and Polich, C. L.: From movement to industry: The growth of HMOs. *Health Affairs* 7(3):197–208, Summer 1988.

Hewitt Associates: *New HMO Act amendments will result in more flexibility in employer-HMO relationships.* Special Report to Clients, 1988.

Horgan, C., Larson, M. J., and Schlesinger, M.: HMO growth and diffusion in U.S. metropolitan areas 1976–1986. Brandeis University,

Waltham, MA. Unpublished working paper, 1988.

InterStudy: HMO summary: June 1985. Excelsior, Minn. 1985.

Juffer, J.: Firms find recession a good time to reduce employee benefit costs. *Wall Street Journal* 21, Aug. 25, 1982.

Kenkel, P. J.: S & P downgrades Maxicare debt to CCC. *Modern Healthcare* 18(26):4, 1988a.

Kenkel, P. J.: Multi-unit providers survey—HMOs/PPOs. Managed-care growth continued in 1987 despite companies' poor operating results. *Modern Healthcare* 18(23):20–24, 28–34, 38, 1988b.

Kenkel, P. J.: Maxicare troubles mount. *Modern Healthcare* 18(13):5, 1988c.

Kohrman, C. H.: HMOs and PPOs in review. *Journal of Medical Practice Management* 1(4):245–248, 1986a.

Kohrman, C. H.: HMOs and PPOs in review. *Journal of Medical Practice Management* 2(1):36–37, 1986b.

Langwell, K.: Structure and performance of health maintenance organizations: A review. Cooperative Agreement No. 99-C-99169/5-02. Prepared for Health Care Financing Administration's Technical Advisory Panel on Health Maintenance Organization Research. Washington, D.C. Mathematica Policy Research, Inc., 1990.

Langwell, K., Rossiter, L., Brown, R., et al.: Early experience of health maintenance organizations under Medicare competition demonstrations. *Health Care Financing Review,* Vol. 8, No. 3, HCFA Pub No. 03237. Office of Research and Demonstrations. Health Care Financing Administration. Washington. U.S. Government Printing Office, Apr. 1987.

Larkin, H.: Provider exodus, lawsuit prompted Maxicare filing. *Hospitals* 63(9):50, 1989.

Lewis, K. A.: Private sector investment in HMOs, 1974–1980. Excelsior, Minn. *InterStudy,* Dec. 1981.

Louis Harris and Associates, Inc.: *Amer-*

ican attitudes toward health maintenance organizations. New York: Louis Harris and Associates, Inc., 1980.

Luft, H. S.: *Health maintenance organizations: Dimensions of performance.* New York. Wiley, 1981.

Luft, H. S., Trauner, J. B., and Maerki, S.: Chapter 6. Adverse selection in a large multiple option health benefits program: A case study of the California public employees retirement system. In: Scheffler R. M., Rossiter L. F., ed.: *Advances in Health Economics and Health Services Research.* Greenwich, CT. JAI Press, 1985.

Luft, H. S., Maerki, S., and Trauner, J. B.: The competitive effects of health maintenance organizations: Another look at the evidence from Hawaii, Rochester, and Minneapolis/St. Paul. *Journal of Health Politics, Policy and Law* 10(4):625–658, 1986.

McDermott, Will and Emery.: Health Law Update 5(24), Oct. 21, 1988.

Morrisey, M. A., and Ashby, C.S.: An empirical analysis of HMO market share. *Inquiry* 19:136–149, Summer 1982.

Neuschler, E., and Squarrel, K.: *Prepaid and managed health care in Medicaid: Overview of current initiatives.* National Governors Association, Center for Policy Research. Washington, D.C. 1985.

Nycz, G. R., Wenzel, F. J., Freisinger, R. J., et al.: Medicare risk contracting: Lessons from an unsuccessful demonstration. *Journal of the American Medical Association* 257(5):656–659, 1987.

Oberman, L.: New HMO hybrids developed as competition soars. *Hospitals* 62(18):46, 1988.

Office of Health Maintenance Organizations: *National HMO development strategy through 1988.* DHEW Pub. No. PHS 79-50111. Washington. U.S. Government Printing Office, 1979.

Office of Health Maintenance Organizations. *The health maintenance organization industry ten year report, 1973–1983.* 1984 update, 1984.

Polich, C., Iversen, L. H., and Oberg, C. N.: Risky business: An examination of TEFRA risk HMOs and their contracting experience. Excelsior, Minn. *InterStudy,* June 1988.

Ready, T.: Study faults HCFA for overpayments to some HMOs. *Health Week* 20:3, Mar. 1989.

Robinson, J. C., and Luft, H. S.: Competition and the cost of hospital care, 1972 to 1982. *Journal of the American Medical Association* 257(23): 3241–3245, 1987.

Rosenbach, M. L., Harrow, B. S., and Hurdle, S.: Physician participation in alternative health plans. *Health Care Financing Review,* Vol. 9, No. 4, HCFA Pub. No. 03265. Office of Research and Demonstrations, Health Care Financing Administration. Washington. U.S. Government Printing Office, Summer 1988.

Sapolsky, H. M., et al.: Corporate attitudes toward health care costs. *Milbank Memorial Fund Quarterly* 59(4): 551–585, 1981.

Shortell, S. M., Morrison, E. M., and Friedman, B. S.: *Strategic choices for America's hospitals: Managing change in turbulent times.* San Francisco: Jossey-Bass, 1990.

Strumpf, G. B., and Garramore, M. A.: Why some HMOs develop slowly. *Public Health Reports* 91(6):496–503, 1976.

Thomas, J. W., and Lichtenstein, R. L.: Functional health measures for adjusting health maintenance organization capitation rates. *Health Care Financing Review,* Vol. 7, No. 3, HCFA Pub. No. 03222. Office of Research and Demonstrations, Health Care Financing Administration. Washington. U.S. Government Printing Office, Apr. 1986.

Traska, M. R.: In Philadelphia, HMO-PA, blues battle for top spot. *Hospitals* 61(7):54–55, 1987a.

Traska, M. R.: HMO America's sale has financial twist to it. *Hospitals* 61(10): 47, 49, 1987b.

Traska, M. R.: Open-ended HMOs, others drive growth slowdown. *Hospitals* 62(13):36–37, 1988a.

Traska, M. R. Chicago HMO consolidation: Proceeding slowly? *Hospitals* 62(9):43, 45, 1988b.

Traska, M. R.: Medicare HMOs hit by underpayment and slower growth. *Hospitals* 62(12):37, 1988c.

Uphoff, M. J., and Uphoff, W.: *Group health: An American success story in prepaid health care.* Minneapolis, Dillon. 1980.

U.S. General Accounting Office: *Medicare issues raised by Florida health maintenance organization demonstrations.* Report to Congress, HRD-86-97, 1986.

Welch, W. P., and Frank, R. G.: The predictors of HMO enrollee populations. Results from a national sample. *Inquiry* 16–22, Spring 1986.

Wholey, D.: State regulation and the development of local HMO markets. Proposal to the National Center for Health Services Research, 1988.

Wholey, D., Christianson, J. B., and Sanchez, S. M.: The effect of State regulation on development of HMO markets. In: Libecap G, ed.: *Advances in the Study of Entrepreneurship, Innovation, and Economic Growth.* Greenwich, CT: JAI Press. To be published.

A common and often effective strategy of certain political strategists in Washington is to get those fighting on behalf of the elderly, the disabled, and the poor to fight over smaller and smaller pieces of the federal budget "pie." . . . Their strategy discourages those of us who are concerned about the health and welfare of citizens unable to share in the American dream of independence, dignity, and prosperity. This political strategy is a dangerous trap in which we would lose and must not allow ourselves to be caught.

— Gary A. Christopherson

Marsha R. Gold

HMOs and Managed Care

During the 1980s, the experience of health maintenance organizations (HMOs) altered the way in which we think of health care in the United States and began to change how it is financed and delivered. These changes also blurred the lines between HMOs and more traditional insurance products and health care delivery schemes. The challenge for the early 1990s is how to interpret these trends and what they portend for the future of the HMO industry and the role HMOs play in the U.S. health care system. . . .[1]

Data Sources

Data cited here are largely from the Group Health Association of America's (GHAA's) *National Directory of HMOs* and GHAA's Annual HMO Industry Survey. Both sources are databases on HMOs, defined here as organizations that integrate financing and delivery of health services by offering comprehensive care from an established panel of providers to an enrolled population on a capitated, prepaid basis.[2] The first includes information collected from each HMO nationwide and is used for analysis on the current composition of the HMO industry and recent trends.[3] Because GHAA data for the pre-1988 period are limited, benchmark data for earlier years are based on published analyses by InterStudy and others.[4]

Operational data on more specific aspects of HMO practice and perceptions are from GHAA's Annual HMO Industry Survey, a lengthy mail survey sent to all HMOs (including both GHAA members and nonmembers) with at least a year's operational experience.[5] Because they represent more stable structures and include almost all of the nation's HMO enrollees (and now almost all HMOs), I focus here on plans over three years old ("established plans"). In the most recent survey, covering 1990 (1989, for use and financial data), 70 percent of established plans responded, encompassing 82 percent of the total national enrollment in established plans. While response rates varied somewhat by category of plan, data are

Marsha R. Gold, Ph.D., is Senior Health Researcher at Mathematica Policy and Research in Washington, D.C. and the former Director of Research and Analysis at the Group Health Association of America.

Abridged from Gold, M.R. (1991). HMOs and managed care. *Health Affairs* 10(4):189–219. Used with permission of Project HOPE.

reasonably representative of the industry, with 60 percent or more of all plans responding in each plan-characteristics category examined. Response rates are lower for some items, such as financial data or premium information. Survey response rates for previous years were somewhat lower (63 percent in 1989 and 55 percent in 1988). Respondents have become increasingly representative of the industry over time.

CHANGES IN THE HMO INDUSTRY DURING THE 1980s

Industry Growth and Geographic Dispersion

The HMO industry grew and became increasingly visible in most areas of the country over the 1980s. HMO enrollment increased fourfold, from 9.1 million in mid-1980 to 36.5 million at the end of 1990, while the number of plans—despite some recent consolidation—more than doubled, from 236 to 569. HMOs currently enroll 15 percent of the U.S. population and over a fifth (22 percent in 1989) of residents in the 30 largest metropolitan areas. HMO penetration varies by market. HMOs include a minority of the population in most markets but have come close to achieving majority status in a few markets, most notably the San Francisco Bay area and Minneapolis-St. Paul (exhibit 1).

Regional disparities in HMO penetration lessened over the 1980s. In 1980, only 10 states had 10 or more HMOs, and only 1 (California) had as many as 1 million enrollees or more. By 1990, these figures grew to 21 and 11, respectively. The share of HMO enrollment outside of California increased from 56 percent to 73 percent. HMO penetration remains lowest in the South, but, particularly in the South Atlantic region, it steadily increased in the 1980s (exhibit 2).

The late 1980s were also a time of considerable growth in other forms of managed care. By 1990, 33 percent of all insured employees were estimated to be in either HMOs or preferred provider organizations (PPOs); a mere 18 percent were insured by plans with no utilization review features.[6] While no definitive study exists, these changes—involving adoption of what may be viewed as elements of HMO practice into traditional insurance—arguably would not have occurred without the example and competitive pressure generated by an increasingly visible HMO industry. The experience of HMOs encouraged closer attention within the larger health system to the level and appropriateness of inpatient use and to the potential benefits of integrating financing with delivery to potentially exert more influence over provider practice.

HMO enrollment statistics also reveal some cautionary notes for the industry. Most recently, HMO growth has been somewhat uneven geographically (exhibit 2). HMO growth was basically flat in the Midwest

EXHIBIT 1 HMO Market Penetration in the Largest U.S. Metropolitan Areas, in Rank Order, 1989

Metropolitan Statistical Area or Complex and State[a]	HMO Penetration Rate	Number of HMOs Serving[b]
San Francisco-Oakland-San Jose/Sacramento, CA	46%	24
Minneapolis-St. Paul, MN/WI	44	8
Milwaukee-Racine, WI	35	8
Portland-Vancouver, OR/WA	34	6
Los Angeles-Anaheim-Riverside/San Diego, CA	32	28
Boston-Lawrence-Salem, MA/NH	28	15
Denver-Boulder-Colorado Springs-Ft. Collins-Greeley, CO	26	13
Phoenix, AZ	26	11
Seattle-Tacoma, WA	24	9
Washington, DC/MD/VA/Baltimore, MD	22	21
Kansas City, MO/KS	22	11
Miami-Ft. Lauderdale, FL	21	17
Philadelphia-Wilmington-Trenton, PA/NJ/DE/MD	21	24
Detroit-Ann Arbor, MI	19	9
Columbus, OH	18	8
St. Louis, MO/IL	17	12
Chicago-Gary-Lake County, IL/IN/WI	16	25
Cleveland-Akron-Lorain, OH	16	10
Cincinnati-Hamilton, OH/KY/IN	16	8
Tampa-St. Petersburg-Clearwater, FL	12	7
Houston-Galveston-Brazoria, TX	12	8
Atlanta, GA	11	7
Dallas-Ft. Worth, TX	11	10
New York-Northern NJ-Long Island, NY/NJ/CT	11	24
San Antonio, TX	10	4
Norfolk-Virginia Beach-Newport News, VA	10	5
Pittsburgh-Beaver Valley, PA	10	7

[a] Includes 30 metropolitan statistical areas (MSAs), representing 27 areas in the statistical analysis because of consolidation among several MSAs. See source report for methods of allocating enrollment among plans serving multiple MSAs and specific limitations that may result in some small over- or understatements for particular MSAs.
[b] Some HMOs serve more than one area, particularly in New Jersey and California.

Source: Palsbo, *HMO Market Penetration in the 30 Largest Metropolitan Statistical Areas, 1989,* GHAA Research Brief 13 (revised December 1990).

EXHIBIT 2   HMO Penetration Rate and Recent Enrollment Changes, by Region, 1980–1990

	Regional Penetration				Percent Change in Enrollment		
Region	1980	1988	1989	1990	1989	1990	Annual Average 1989–1990
United States	4.0%	13.3%	14.0%	14.6%	6%	5%	6%
New England	2.4	18.8	19.6	20.9	5	7	6
Mid-Atlantic	3.4	12.0	12.7	13.8	6	9	8
South Atlantic	1.3	8.3	8.8	9.3	8	7	8
Midwest	2.8	14.0	14.1	14.0	1	−1	0
South Central	0.4	5.8	5.9	5.8	5	−1	2
Mountain[a]	3.7	14.6	15.7	14.9	11	−3	4
Pacific[b]	15.2	25.1	27.6	29.8	11	10	11

[a]Growth in 1990 may be influenced by refinement in the definition of enrollee, which may have artificially reduced apparent growth.
[b]Penetration rates exclude Guam.
Sources: GHAA's *National Directory of HMOs* database. U.S. population data from U.S. Bureau of the Census, *Statistical Abstract of the United States, 1990,* 110th ed. HMO data for 1980 from *National HMO Census, 1980,* DHHS Pub. No. (PHS)80-50159.

from 1988 to 1990; in the South Central region, growth was entirely absorbed by population growth, meaning that penetration remained constant over this period. HMOs continue to be strongest along the two U.S. coasts, despite gains elsewhere. Market strength among plans in the industry continues to vary: while 60 percent of plans gained enrollment in 1990, 39 percent lost enrollment (1 percent stayed the same). This suggests that further consolidation of HMOs is likely in the near term.

HMO penetration also remains considerably more limited in publicly financed programs than in the commercial sector for a variety of reasons, discussion of which is beyond the scope of this article. Only 6 percent of Medicare beneficiaries currently are enrolled under various Medicare HMO contracting options.[7] A similar percentage of Medicaid beneficiaries are enrolled, although penetration is considerably higher in states that have actively pursued these arrangements.[8] These patterns could change, assuming some spillover effect from the broader acceptance of HMOs in the health sector as a whole. On the other hand, the experience with public programs is not encouraging to HMOs at a time when some are advocating this approach for overall health system reform.[9] While government officials recently have tried to modify this, both Medicare and Medicaid HMO contracting practices historically have been influenced by fee-for-service practices and mind-sets; this has created barriers to HMOs' participation in these programs both in reality and because of HMOs' perceptions. Unless this is changed, an expanded HMO role under a public insurance model could be problematic.

HMO Provider Networks

Over the 1980s, HMO provider networks tapped more heavily into more traditional medical practices and settings. Over half (53 percent) of all office-based physicians were affiliated with one or more HMOs in 1990; 68 percent of all medical groups had some form of relationship with an HMO in 1988.[10] Network and independent practice association (IPA)-model plans—which base their provider networks on physicians in office-based fee-for-service practice—increased from 97 to 433 between 1980 and 1990. Their share of HMOs increased from 41 percent to 76 percent, and of enrollment from 19 percent to 58 percent, although this share has remained relatively steady since 1988. Greater HMO penetration into fee-for-service practice also occurred with the growth in enrollment in prepaid group practice–model HMOs (group and staff models). To varying extents, these plans also rely on office-based physicians to complement their more committed full-time practitioners and, more recently, to expand service areas and markets through adoption of more "mixed" models. Exhibit 3 provides more detail on the kinds of provider networks used by each type of HMO model in 1990. The data show considerable variability among HMOs that define themselves as a common model type, an important point to note in drawing any kind of general conclusion about HMOs.

By expanding their provider base and involving in their systems physicians whose predominant practice probably is fee for service, HMOs have become less distinct, when contrasted against the original prepaid group practice model. However, HMOs also have increased their impact on overall medical practice. For example, the majority of networks and IPA models have moved away from fee-for-service payment for their primary care physicians, and almost all include some financial incentives as well as utilization review and management functions encouraging cost-effective practice.[11] On the other hand, these types of dispersed and potentially less committed provider networks are inherently more difficult for an HMO to manage; thus, fee-for-service influences also have intruded more heavily into the HMO experience.

HMO Ownership

The organizations sponsoring HMOs also grew more diverse over the 1980s. In 1980, the HMO industry was mainly based around independent plans or multiplan organizations (generally nonprofit) devoted solely to the HMO business. Current HMO ownership reflects historical roots but is

EXHIBIT 3   Profile of HMO Provider Networks, by Model Type, Plans over Three Years Old, 1990

		Predominant Model			
	Total	Staff	Group	Network	IPA[a]
Other model types					
Percent yes	24%	59%	20%	49%	12%
Percent enrollment in model					
(if mixed)	27	77	68	63	74
Physicians staffing					
Total number of physicians					
per average plan[b]	1,189	399	517	1,816	1,326
Average total physicians per					
1,000 members	28.6	3.2	5.0	39.7	36.9
Average primary care physi-					
cians per 1,000 members	10.2	2.5	2.7	9.5	14.4
Average percent of primary					
care physician practice from					
that HMO[c]					
0–30 percent	66%	20%	18%	67%	88%
31–80 percent	15	17	21	25	10
81–100 percent	19	63	61	6	4
Typical HMO medical network					
Multispecialty group practice	37%	74%	84%	42%	10%
Alone	15	60	42	7	1
With others	22	14	42	35	17
Solo or partnership	29	5	3	12	45
Groups 3–7 or with solo	10	2	3	2	15
Other	24	19	10	44	23
Predominant payment method					
for primary care physicians					
Salary	15%	82%	34%	0%	1%
Capitation	56	11	66	81	59
Fee for service	28	7	0	19	40

[a]Individual practice association.
[b]From GHAA's *National Directory of HMOs* database; all plans regardless of age.
[c]Numbers do not add to 100 because of rounding.

Source: GHAA's Annual HMO Industry Survey.

considerably more consolidated and representative of the broader spectrum of health care and economic interests, which has made it more difficult at times for HMOs to maintain the unique regulatory treatment they have enjoyed in the past.

According to InterStudy, 8 national HMO firms did business in 1980 with 29 plans, or 12 percent of all HMOs. In 1990, excluding the Blue Cross/Blue Shield network, 22 corporate entities owning or managing multiple HMOs accounted for 242 HMOs, or 43 percent of all plans and 52 percent of all enrollees (exhibit 4). Of the top ten companies (which

EXHIBIT 4   Largest Multi-HMO Companies, in Order of Total Enrollment, 1990

Organization	Owned	Managed	Total	Total Enrollment
Kaiser Foundation Health Plans, Inc.	12	0	12	6,525,574
CIGNA Employer Benefits Company	42	0	42	1,573,338
United HealthCare Corporation	7	8	15	1,186,291
Aetna Health Plans	19	7	26	1,163,032
U.S. Healthcare, Inc.	8	0	8	1,105,000
Health Insurance Plan of Greater New York	4	0	4	1,075,627
Humana, Inc.	14	0	14	997,511
Prudential Health Care Plans, Inc.	27	0	27	874,306
FHP, Inc.	6	0	6	864,768
PacifiCare Health Systems	5	0	5	688,504
Senus Corporation Health Systems	4	1	5	641,863
Lincoln National Admin. Services Corp.	14	0	14	435,489
Maxicare Health Plans, Inc.	8	0	8	302,437
Coventry Corporation	3	0	3	265,500
Independent Health Association, Inc.	2	1	3	252,162
Qual-Med, Inc.	5	0	5	245,064
Metropolitan Life Insurance Company	15	0	15	236,406
Community Health Plan (CHP), Inc.	5	0	5	178,800
Principal Health Care, Inc.	7	0	7	162,030
Healthsource Management Company	4	1	5	127,071
Physician Corporation of America	3	0	3	108,756
The Travelers Health Network, Inc.	10	0	10	102,984

Notes: This list does not include the network of 82 Blue Cross/Blue Shield HMOs, which are affiliated nationally but owned and operated by individual Blue Cross/Blue Shield organizations. Together, Blue Cross/Blue Shield HMOs enroll 4.6 million members nationwide.

Source: GHAA's *National Directory of HMOs* database.

account for 44 percent of national HMO enrollment), 2—Kaiser and Health Insurance Plan (HIP) of Greater New York—represent what most regard as the traditional base of the HMO industry, 3 are commercial insurance companies, and 5 are publicly traded companies, most of which also offer other health care products. In 1990, 66 percent of HMOs were for-profit, with 47 percent of all HMO enrollees; however, there has been little change in their market share over the most recent period (1988–1990).

In 1990, insurers owned or managed 43 percent of all HMOs and enrolled 27 percent of all HMO enrollees. HMOs owned by commercial insurers represented 29 percent of all HMOs and 15 percent of all HMO enrollees; the comparable share for HMOs owned by Blue Cross/Blue Shield plans was 14 percent and 13 percent, respectively. Two-thirds (65 percent) of HMOs sponsored by commercial insurers were started in 1985 or later, compared to half of HMOs sponsored by Blue Cross/Blue Shield organizations or by HMOs and others (48 percent each). This has contributed to the diffusion of HMO concepts but also to a growing indemnity influence on HMOs, for both insurer-owned plans and their competitors.

At the same time, despite the considerable changes over the 1980s, the HMO industry still has strong roots in its past. Kaiser Foundation Health Plan remains dominant in the industry, representing 18 percent of national HMO enrollment—a share larger than either of the insurance sectors and four times the size of the second-largest HMO company. A number of the largest individual HMOs continue to be more traditional plans; in addition to the two California Kaiser plans, HIP, Group Health Cooperative of Puget Sound, Harvard Community Health Plan, and Health Alliance Plan all are among the 10 largest individual HMOs.

The HMO industry also retains many elements of a "cottage" industry. Despite the fact that 64 percent of HMO enrollees were in the largest plans (100,000 or more members) in 1990, 39 percent of HMOs had fewer than 20,000 enrollees in 1990, and 31 percent, between 20,000 and 50,000— meaning that a full 70 percent of all HMOs (versus 88 percent in 1980) continue to be reasonably small. Some smaller plans with neither a strong community or market niche nor strong company affiliation may find it difficult to respond to current environmental pressures, another reason why further consolidation in the HMO industry is likely.

Problems with Growth

The rapid growth of HMOs in the 1980s caused some short-term problems, which appear to be resolving as the industry matures. Growth was stronger from mid-1984 to mid-1987; the number of plans increased from 306 to an all-time high of 662, and enrollment essentially doubled, from 15 to 29 million. The result was that half of all HMOs were under three years old in 1987.

The financial effects of these patterns were predictable. New plans aimed to succeed by growing rapidly, leading to considerable price competition beneath that required to cover expenses. As with any business, some sponsors proved better managers than others, some plans proved better situated in the market than others, and profitability was eroded by start-up costs. In 1987, only 38 percent of established plan and 13 percent of new plans were profitable, with the industry losing an estimated $1 billion, before taxes, on an estimated revenue base of 24.9 billion. Seventy-six, mostly small HMOs (median enrollment was 3,650), ceased operations between the end of 1987 and mid-1990; 61 merged or consolidated with other HMOs.[12]

There are signs that the HMO industry has matured and is in considerably stronger shape entering the 1990s. The recent consolidation of the HMO industry caused short-term dislocations but also increased the share of stronger, more competitive plans. In 1989, 66 percent of established plans (and 46 percent of new plans) were profitable; the HMO industry as a whole gained an estimated $0.23 billion, before taxes, on $38.3 billion in revenue. While this 0.6 percent gain is low in relation to optimum margins, it stands in stark contrast to aggregate losses of about -4.2 percent in both 1988 and 1987. Furthermore, improvements in financial performance appear to extend beyond profitability measures into operational performance; values for 9 of the 10 solvency surveillance indicators (developed by the National Association of HMO Regulators for monitoring HMO financial performance) improved from 1988 to 1989 (exhibit 5). Preliminary data suggest that financial improvements have continued in 1990, with fewer than 85 percent of established plans profitable, although some continue to have financial difficulties.[13]

HMOs attribute their improved financial condition about equally to increased revenues (largely through premium increases) and to improved cost controls (improved utilization review, more efficient administration, and renegotiated provider contracts). The duality of HMO responses reflects both the influence of overall inflationary forces on HMOs and the ability of HMOs to influence these costs through their organization and incentives. Among the 110 HMOs providing financial data for 1987–1989, the 2-year average increase in revenues per member per month was 26 percent, while the average increase in expenses was 21 percent.

The HMO rate increase profile over the late 1980s presents a mixed picture. The Health Insurance Association of America's (HIAA's) Employer Survey results show that HMO premium increases appear to have been below those of indemnity plans over the most recent time period.[14] However, HMOs did increase their premiums substantially over this period, generating concerns among some purchasers and policymakers. According to GHAA data, HMO premium increases averaged 11–12 percent in 1988, and 17–18 percent in both 1989 and 1990; preliminary data for

EXHIBIT 5   Trends in Solvency Surveillance Indicators and Selected Other Measures, HMO Plans over Three Years Old, 1988–1989[a]

Indicator	Sample Size	1988	1989	Significance
Net profit margin	128	−0.0133	0.0160	.000[b]
Tangible net worth	124	$7,432,241	$9,829,060	.000[b]
Current ratio	124	0.9454	1.0135	.017[b]
Health care expense ratio	129	0.9127	0.8951	.004[b]
Administrative expense ratio	130	0.1209	0.1139	.013[b]
Tangible asset financing ratio	121	0.9107	0.8167	.000[b]
Enrollment level	134	129,406	135,832	.038[b]
Premium receivable turnover	124	0.6957	0.6273	.026[b]
Cash flow to total debt	113	0.0375	0.1702	.000[b]
Days claims and IBNR payable[c]	122	46.58	46.99	.778
Other measures				
Equity per member	125	$37.66	$65.51	.000[b]
Assets per member	126	$281.14	$330.50	.000[b]

[a]Includes all plans over three years old in 1988 that also reported in 1989.
[b]Significant at the $p<.05$ level.
[c]Incurred but not reported.
Source: GHAA's Annual HMO Industry Survey.

1991 indicate a moderation, with increases averaging about 12 percent.[15] The slower growth rates for the HMO industry over the late 1980s (enrollment grew 6.4 percent in 1989 and 4.9 percent in 1990) may reflect an emphasis among HMOs toward solidifying their revenue base and enhancing their delivery systems to strengthen provider networks and internal systems to better absorb growth and restrain costs. To the extent that this has occurred, HMOs should be in a stronger position to expand over the 1990s.

TRENDS IN HMO PRODUCTS AND PRACTICES

Employer Influences

Arguably the most significant influence on the HMO industry today is employers, who are responding to rapid escalation in health costs. Employers, particularly larger ones, have become more involved purchasers, actively engaged in assessing the value of each benefit option and in designing the overall mix and integration of their total benefit package. This has created an opportunity for HMOs but also has increased the demands upon them. In 1990, three-quarters or more of HMOs had requests from employers for data on utilization, demographics, quality of care, costs, finances, and consumer satisfaction. Employers also have become more assertive in influencing the structure of HMOs.

EXHIBIT 6   HMO Perceptions of Employer Pressures in Selected Areas, Plans over Three Years Old, 1988–1990

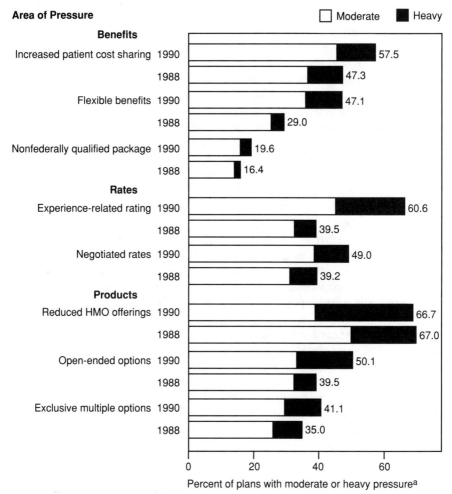

aOther choices were "limited pressure" or "none."
Source: GHAA's Annual HMO Industry Survey.

Exhibit 6 shows HMOs' perceptions of how these employer concerns translate into selected concerns with respect to the HMO benefit package, HMO rating practices, and the employer's overall health benefits design. I contrast perceptions in 1990 with those of 1988 and discuss them along with the HMO response in the sections that follow.[16]

HMO Benefit Packages

Experienced with indemnity plans, employers tend to regard employee cost sharing as an important tool for controlling costs.[17] Fifty-eight percent of HMOs perceived moderate to heavy pressure from employers to increase patient cost sharing in their benefit package in 1990, up from 47 percent in 1988. While HMOs have responded to some extent, major changes have not yet occurred in the most commonly offered HMO benefit packages.

Traditionally, HMOs have stressed comprehensive benefits with limited out-of-pocket costs, perceiving themselves as prepayment and insurance entities and relying on systems design rather than cost sharing to control costs. Hence, growth in HMO enrollment should have restrained growth in out-of-pocket spending and cost sharing in the health system as a whole, even if one makes no assumptions about spillover effects.

While HMOs have increased cost sharing to some extent, first-dollar coverage continued to be the pattern in 1990. The best-selling benefit package of most HMOs (which 66 percent of an HMO's enrollees purchase, on average) relies, where cost sharing is used, on fixed-dollar copayments rather than on the deductibles or coinsurance common in indemnity plans. The most common HMO copayment for primary care visits was five dollars in 1990; under a quarter of plans (23 percent) had cost sharing for hospitalizations, with only 14 percent of HMO enrollees in such plans, since larger plans were less likely to apply cost-sharing requirements. Seventy-two percent of plans (with 56 percent of enrollees) charged copayments for primary care visits in 1990 (fewer for preventive services such as prenatal care), up from 48 percent in 1988 and 60 percent in 1989; there also was some growth in cost sharing for hospital services. Although 35 to 44 percent of plans increased average cost sharing in their best-selling benefit package in each of 1988, 1989, and 1990, 32 percent reported no net increase in cost sharing in any of the three years. Possibly some HMOs are responding to employer pressures through the development of alternative, less comprehensive packages (84 percent offered at least one less comprehensive package; 47 percent at least one more comprehensive package), but overall HMO benefits continued to be comprehensive in 1990 and to depart considerably from the structure of indemnity plans. Because this is an important selling feature for HMOs, major change in this area seems unlikely.

HMO Rating Practices

Employers are more closely scrutinizing the rates they pay HMOs and the methods by which these rates are set. Over half of all HMOs (more than in 1988) perceived moderate to heavy employer pressure for experience-related rating or negotiated rates; a larger share of HMOs characterized such pressure as heavy rather than moderate in 1990 than in 1988. The evidence suggests that employers increasingly are concerned with negotiating rates consistent with the anticipated cost experience of their employees (and dependents).

Traditionally, HMOs have used standard community rating, with no adjustment for the characteristics of particular employer groups, as these might bear on anticipated health care costs (that is, no group-specific rating). This is based at least in part on the notion that risk is best pooled over all enrollees to encourage affordable coverage for expenses that vary widely across a population. However, many employers believe this results in inappropriate cross-subsidies. Federally qualified HMOs were provided additional flexibility to respond to marketplace pressures in the 1988 amendments to the federal HMO Act through the allowance for "adjusted community rating," in which prospective group-specific rating was allowed, with restrictions to encourage affordable rates for small groups (100 employees or fewer) whose rates cannot depart by more than 110 percent from the community rate. (Prior to this, HMOs could partially address employer concerns by using community rating by class, in which separate planwide rates are established by demographic factors associated with costs, such as age and sex.) Nonfederally qualified HMOs are not subject to these restrictions, though they may be constrained by state law.

HMOs appear to be moving to meet employers' demands for group-specific rating, but most are using methods that retain the prospective nature of HMO rating, which many regard as providing the critical risk-bearing incentives needed for HMO success. Most also continue to use methods that encourage affordable coverage for small employer groups. In 1990, 56 percent of HMOs used some rating method involving an explicit adjustment for employer group experience. Indemnity experience–based rating typically involves a retrospective adjustment in rates for previous shortfalls or overestimates; under 10 percent of all HMOs used such adjustments. Because the larger and older HMOs tend to rely more heavily on traditional HMO rating methods, 90 percent of HMO enrollees in 1990 were rated using the three community rating methods permissible under the federal HMO Act (exhibit 7). Despite changes that move HMO rating closer to that of traditional insurers, HMO rating retained distinctive characteristics in 1990. Most notably, HMO rating is prospective and pays closer attention to equity considerations inherent in such issues as small groups or higher-cost accounts. Federal and state policy may play a large

EXHIBIT 7   Distribution of All HMO Enrollees, by Rating Method Used, Plans over Three Years Old, 1990

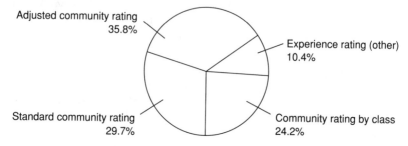

Adjusted community rating
35.8%

Experience rating (other)
10.4%

Standard community rating
29.7%

Community rating by class
24.2%

Notes: Plans that responded to this survey item account for 26.2 million enrollees.
Source: GHAA's Annual HMO Industry Survey.

role in determining whether HMOs keep their distinctive policies. The Blue Cross/Blue Shield historical experience suggests that it is difficult for a single payer to maintain community rating practices if others do not, because of adverse selection effects.

Benefit Package Design

HMOs' perceptions confirm employers' more active involvement in the design of their health benefit programs. Two-thirds of HMOs perceived moderate to heavy pressure from employers to reduce the number of HMO options offered to employees in 1990. This percentage remained unchanged from 1988, but it included more plans perceiving heavier pressure. This does not necessarily mean that employers are less committed to HMOs in general, but it does suggest that many are becoming more selective in their offerings. The number of HMO plans grew rapidly over the 1980s; many employers appear to want to streamline the number of options they offer, based on the perception that numerous choices increase administrative burden, confuse employees, reduce employer purchasing power, and add to risk segmentation.

This has increased employers' interest in newer products oriented to this need. Between 1988 and 1990, employers showed greater interest in open-ended HMO products (under which an employee is enrolled in the HMO but may self-refer to providers outside the network, typically with cost sharing equivalent to traditional insurance products) and in exclusive multiple options (under which an HMO is part of an entity offering employers the ability to substitute a total replacement product for their current health benefits). Although these insurance products have not been tested over time, employers are interested in them for their ability to blend managed care features with the broader provider choice of traditional indemnity products, thus allowing employers to simplify their benefit offerings.

HMOs have not responded consistently to these pressures, and trends are somewhat unclear. To address the needs of national accounts or employers wishing to offer HMO options under a single umbrella, 42 percent of HMOs in 1990 had or were in the process of implementing agreements with other HMOs. In 1990, just under half (46 percent) of HMOs offered one or more of five types of diversified options. HMOs owned by commercial insurance companies were considerably more likely to offer diversified options than other HMOs (exhibit 8). By model type, IPAs were most likely to offer diversified options (58 percent) and group models least likely (18 percent). An HMO's structure and legal basis of incorporation make it easier for some plans to diversify than others.

The most noticeable trend has been in the growth of open-ended HMO products, up to 20 percent of plans in early 1990 from 16 percent in 1989. As noted, these options allow HMO enrollees to self-refer to providers outside the HMO network with cost-sharing requirements. Thirty-six percent of all HMOs in GHAA's *National Directory of HMOs* for 1991 offered such an option; sample GHAA surveys also indicate considerable recent growth.[18] It is unclear whether these products will serve as a permanent

EXHIBIT 8   Percentage of HMOs with Various Diversification Options, by Ownership and Model, Plans over Three Years Old, 1990

		Ownership			Model			
Option	All Plans	Commer-cial Insurers	Blue Cross/ Blue Shield	All others	Staff	Group	Network	IPA[a]
Any of five specified options	46%	72%	29%	40%	34%	18%	39%	58%
Open-ended option	20	39	10	16	25	9	7	26
PPO option[b]	27	61	10	18	21	13	22	34
Indemnity option	24	66	8	12	16	11	17	32
Exclusive mul-tiple option	16	47	10	6	11	7	11	21
Employer self-insured option	25	49	16	18	16	7	11	35

[a]Individual practice association.
[b]Preferred provider organization.

Source: GHAA's Annual HMO Industry Survey.

feature of the health care landscape or more as a midway station to growing enrollment in more traditional HMO plans. Evidence on the performance of these kinds of options is limited; they have the previously noted attractive features but also draw more heavily on traditional insurance features and probably are more costly, depending upon out-of-plan use, than traditional HMO coverage.

This may explain why some HMOs are moving cautiously to expand these options; only 3.4 percent of HMO enrollees were in such options at the start of 1991.[19] Some HMOs are proceeding rapidly to develop these options, while others are uncertain about how these options would affect their long-term position. In a cost-containment environment, employers are concerned with both HMO cost-effectiveness and total health care costs—which also are influenced by the ability to attract individuals currently enrolled in indemnity or more loosely managed products into more tightly managed situations. HMOs differ in their philosophies, structure, market niche, and perspective on the importance of enrollment growth; it therefore seems likely that their responses to these pressures will continue to differ considerably, absent any overwhelming pressure from the environment to require broad-based change.

TRENDS AND FUTURE IMPLICATIONS

The HMO industry expanded considerably in the 1980s, resulting in a more geographically dispersed base and a more diversified industry and set of HMO sponsors. Even though most HMOs remain small and many are independent, the majority of enrollees are either in the largest plans or in plans sponsored by multi-HMO companies. Further consolidation is likely over the next several years, given the variability in both financial performance and market position across the industry.

Despite the industry's internal diversity, HMOs continue to claim certain unique properties: their absorption of prospective risk, comprehensive benefits, and integrated delivery systems with provider incentives for efficiency. At the same time, some of these distinctions have become more difficult to articulate, given the growth of other products—encouraged by HMO growth—that also use provider networks and enhanced coverage for primary care. HMOs' response to marketplace pressures by offering diversified products further blurs traditional distinctions.

With the growth of managed care, it has become virtually impossible to consider the future role of HMOs without simultaneously considering the complete spectrum of so-termed managed care products in which HMOs have become embedded. In considering trends, one can emphasize either the similarities or the differences between HMOs and the rest of the health care system. There clearly is a continuum of managed care products differentiated by varying degrees of management and health systems integration.[20] HMOs have served to encourage change in the organization and performance of traditional practice but may have sacrificed some uniqueness in the process. On the other hand, the overwhelming majority of the U.S. population continues to be enrolled in traditional insurance plans that overlay utilization review and guideline development over an essentially fee-for-service system. HIAA defines managed care as

> health care systems that integrate the financing and delivery of appropriate health care services to covered individuals by arrangement with selected providers to furnish a comprehensive set of health care services, explicit standards for selection of health care providers, formal programs for ongoing quality assurance and utilization review and significant financial incentives for members to use providers and procedures associated with the plan.[21]

Yet, it is unclear whether all these features (which also are part of HMO design) currently are included in many of the newer and less highly regulated managed-care organizations. The definition also excludes capitated payment and provider risk sharing, which are an important part of conceptual HMO design, as well as the integrated medical facilities some HMOs use (in particular, prepaid group practices).

Since there are many unpredictable factors, it is problematic to predict now how distinctive or important HMOs will be in the future, although many views exist. HMOs—acknowledging their internal diversity—could remain a distinctive minority player serving as an example. HMOs could become the dominant player if the further development of managed-care organizations leads to adoption of more HMO features in the search for cost-effectiveness. Or, with the traditional disjointed incrementalism of U.S. policy, a managed-care continuum of continuing pluralism could remain, in which the term *HMO* may or may not continue to be used. Which of these occurs could be influenced heavily by the current interest in health systems reform and universal coverage systems at both the federal and state levels. For the HMO industry, this creates a critical challenge to articulate effectively both the organizational form and its merits, including addressing the diverse issues that have been raised.

From a policy perspective, it probably is of less immediate relevance to predict the future than to influence it. In this regard, it is increasingly important to recognize the variability in current forms of "managed care," including variability within organizations of the same label. From my perspective, policymakers might be better served if the term *managed care* were dropped or at least deemphasized in favor of a conceptual framework to define better the key elements present in or absent from managed care plans or organizations on any point on any continuum. This could encourage greater clarity and content in the policy debates concerning managed care, better understanding of current trends, and an improved ability to interpret the meaning of any research and analysis on the effectiveness of various kinds of plans or organizations.

To accomplish this, statistical systems will need to provide a better empirical basis for assessing the extent of inclusion of these elements in the various managed care organizations or products. The current fragmentation of data collection and regulatory responsibilities for managed care plans impedes the ability to collect such data, even if consensus existed on what to collect. These difficulties are compounded because current national databases and reports, such as those produced by the Bureau of Labor Statistics and the National Center for Health Statistics, were developed in an earlier environment; they do not provide good measures of the managed care plans that now exist, the kinds of "insurance" coverage people have, or the features present in any plan. A thorough review of the existing national statistics to determine what new databases or modifications in current databases may be desirable given the needs created by the growth of managed care is well overdue.

The analysis and perspectives expressed in this article are those of the author and do not necessarily reflect those of the Group Health Association of America (GHAA) or its member plans. A number of GHAA staff contributed to the data analysis presented here. Dennis Hodges, a research associate at GHAA, is project manager for GHAA's Annual HMO Industry Survey and prepared much of the analysis from this source, including industrywide estimates of revenues and expenses. Susan Jelley Palsbo, a senior research associate at GHAA, provided the analysis of changes in financial performance and of statewide market penetration. Kevin Camerlo, research data coordinator, prepared statistics from GHAA's National Directory of HMOs database and assisted in overall data collection and analysis. Ingrid Reeves, Pamela Kalen, and Regina Cole of GHAA's Membership and Planning Department are responsible for developing GHAA's National Directory of HMOs database.

NOTES

1. For a benchmark and a more detailed look at these issues, see M. Gold and D. Hodges, "Health Maintenance Organizations in 1988," *Health Affairs* (Winter 1989):125–138.

2. A review of HMO history and design is included in M. Gold, "Health Maintenance Organizations: Structure, Performance, and Current Issues for Health Benefits Design," *Journal of Occupational Health* (March 1991): 228–296.

3. Data collection methods and definitions are described in Group Health Association of America, Research and Analysis Department, *Patterns in HMO Enrollment*, 1991 ed. (Washington, D.C.: GHAA, June 1991). A member was defined as an individual who has

been enrolled as a subscriber or an eligible dependent of a subscriber and for whom the HMO has accepted the responsibility for the provision of basic health services. Plans were asked to exclude PPO enrollment. The definition would include enrollees in "open-ended HMO options" but exclude those in point-of-service options where the HMO merely "rents" its delivery system to another entity operating the insurance plan.

4. July 1980 statistics were collected by the Office of Health Maintenance Organizations, *National HMO Census, 1980,* DHHS Pub. no. (PHS)80-50159 (1980). For historical trends, see L.R. Gruber, M. Shadle, and C.L. Polich, "From Movement to Industry: The Growth of Managed Care," *Health Affairs* (Summer 1988): 197–208.

5. Methods used to collect these data are further described in GHAA, *HMO Industry Profile,* 1991 ed. (Washington, D.C.: GHAA, 1991 [in three volumes]). Methods for collection have been essentially unchanged over time; prior years' editions review response rates as well as relevant statistics for the covered period.

6. C. Sullivan and T. Rice, "The Health Insurance Picture in 1990," *Health Affairs* (Summer 1991): 104–115.

7. Health Care Financing Administration, *Monthly Report, Medicare Prepaid Plans* (July 1991).

8. HCFA, Medical Bureau, "National Summary of Managed Care Plans and Enrollment" (Health Care Financing Administration, 1 May 1991).

9. GHAA, *Cautions for Prepaid Organized Health Care under a National Health System: Lessons from Canada* (Washington, D.C.: GHAA, February 1990).

10. J. Norman, "The Flowering of Managed Care," *Medical Economics* (5 March 1990): 89–105; and P.L. Havelicek, *Medical Groups in the United States: A Survey of Practice Characteristics,* 1990 ed. (Chicago: American Medical Association, 1990).

11. M. Gold and I. Reeves, "Preliminary Results of the GHAA/BC-BS Survey of Physician Incentives in Health Maintenance Organizations," *Research Brief* 1 (Washington, D.C.: GHAA, November 1987).

12. N. Kraus, M. Porter, and P. Ball, *Managed Care: A Decade in Review, 1980–1990* (Excelsior, Minn.: InterStudy, 1991), 63–64.

13. Unpublished preliminary 1991 estimates from GHAA's Annual HMO Industry Survey.

14. J. Gabel, et al., "Employer-Sponsored Health Insurance, 1989," *Health Affairs* (Fall 1990): 161–175; 1990 comparisons by type of plan are not yet available.

15. Unpublished preliminary 1991 estimates from GHAA's Annual HMO Industry Survey.

16. For more extensive conceptual discussion of employer concerns on such issues as selection, rating, and cost control, see Gold, "HMOs: Structure, Performance, and Current Issues for Health Benefits Design."

17. "*Business and Health*'s 1990 National Executive Poll on Health Care Costs and Benefits," *Business and Health* (April 1990): 24–38.

18. M. Gold and D. Hodges, *HMO Market Position Report* (Results of an October 1990 Member Plan Survey) (Washington, D.C.: GHAA, November 1990).

19. M.J. Porter, et al., *The InterStudy Competitive Edge* 1, no. 1 (Excelsior, Minn.: InterStudy, 1991).

20. For a discussion of the continuum of managed care, see R. Feldman, J. Kralewski, and B. Dowd, "Health Maintenance Organizations: The Beginning or the End," *Health Services Research* (June 1989): 191–211. This article also contains a good discussion of defining managed care and researching its effects.

21. Health Insurance Association of America, *Source Book of Health Insurance Data, 1990* (Washington, D.C.: HIAA, 1990), 118.

I view health care . . . *in this country as a house of cards . . . this house of cards cannot stand.*
— Deborah Steelman

Part II

Structure of the U.S. Health Care Delivery System

Hospitals remain at the center of the current health care system in the United States. They employ the majority of health workers and account for the greatest proportion of expenditures compared with other service providers. Because of high hospital costs, this sector was targeted for cost controls in the early 1980s through a prospective payment system (PPS) under Medicare. As a result, hospitals have changed their structure by systematic consolidation and integration with other health care providers. Many small rural hospitals have closed or are on the verge of closing. These payment controls had an impact, but the current growth in expenditures for hospital care indicates that initially the PPS has had little long-term effect on stemming hospital costs. In part, this result is because the system fails to regulate what hospitals can charge; it only regulates what Medicare and Medicaid can be charged. This effort to control inpatient services without controlling the cost of outpatient services and surgical procedures contributes to a shift in service location and a general inflation in volume and cost of both.

The growth of the for-profit sector in health care raises important questions. One is whether for-profit and nonprofit organizations differ. The evidence suggests that although for-profit and nonprofit health organizations are increasingly similar in function, there are important differences in the amount of indigent care they provide. As long as people view hospital care as a commodity and a business, whether the corporations are for-profit or nonprofit, growth in cost and rationing of services will continue.

The nursing home industry is notorious for facilities that provide poor quality of care and increase costs to consumers. Government's effort to regulate quality has not been effective in improving overall standards of care or in eliminating unhealthy facilities. The industry is characterized as underfunded and somewhat unscrupulous due to its dominant profit-making orientation. Nursing care is the key service element in long-term care organizations and is highly effective when nurses receive adequate wages and benefits, and there is a sufficient staff level and professional training, as in teaching nursing home projects. Where nursing staff does not have appropriate training or working conditions, nursing home patients frequently receive inadequate care. When acute conditions develop, patients may be sent unnecessarily to hospitals for treatment.

One major problem is the inadequate Medicaid nursing home reimbursement rate. On the other hand, rate increases often are not translated into better staffing or patient care, but instead result in higher profits and administrative overhead for nursing homes. However, the federal government, as the major purchaser of nursing home services through Medicaid, has a conflict of interest between quality and cost in regulating the nursing home industry. Government's primary effort is to keep prices low, which directly causes poor care.

Home care has its own problems with quality, access, and cost. Intermittent visits by nurses, paid for under Medicare and Medicaid, are costly and inadequate for many people with serious problems or long-term chronic care needs. The limited Medicaid and Medicare coverage for home-based services also creates financial access problems for those who need home care. Again, the federal government, as the major purchaser of home health services, attempts to keep prices and wages low, resulting in an unstable labor market and poor quality of care.

The implementation of hospital prospective payment systems encourages early discharge from hospitals and a shift of care from hospitals to informal caregivers—friends or family members—and formal home care programs. This approach jeopardizes the health and safety of individuals when adequate informal or formal community care services are not available. Nevertheless, sick people overwhelmingly prefer care at home to nursing home or hospital care. Unfortunately, most studies do not show great success in home care cost-effectiveness, in part because current services are so limited. The home care service system needs restructuring with greater specificity of what the health outcomes should be for patients in the community with acute and chronic illnesses.

Health professionals are facing great challenges. Physicians, who have traditionally dominated the health care system and the practices of other health professionals, may be losing some of their control. As more physicians become employees of or contractors to health maintenance organizations and preferred provider organizations, they have less autonomy in and control of their practice patterns. In addition, under legislation sponsored by the Physician Payment Review Commission and passed by Congress in 1989, their fees are being set by Medicare. The new fee schedules, which will be fully implemented by 1995, reduce the variation in fees and attempt to correct past inequities by increasing payment levels for family practice physicians and lowering the levels for some specialists.

Practice patterns for nursing also are changing dramatically. Most nurses are still employed by hospitals that are subject to cyclical shortages induced by a growing demand for services and historically low wages. Nurses in advanced practice (nursing practitioners and clinical nurse specialists) are moving toward independent practice. Studies demonstrate the cost-effectiveness of using advanced practice nurses and the fact that nurses can provide primary care services of high quality for a lower cost than can physicians. Being able to reimburse nurses has begun to allow for more independent practice and should improve the quality of care by improving access. For example, nurse practitioners in nursing homes are now able to bill Medicare for services separately from physicians. These changes, however, are opposed by physician organizations that do not want to relinquish control over medical care, and yet are frequently unwilling to provide primary health care services for millions of people, particularly those in vulnerable population groups.

Part II focuses on the structure of the U.S. health care delivery system from organizational and professional perspectives. Trends in the supply of and demand for hospital, nursing home, home care, and community-based services are presented. Chapter 4 examines the restructuring of hospitals into increasingly large and competitive for-profit health care organizations and reviews the debate over the impact of these trends. Chapter 5 examines nursing homes, which are already largely private for-profit organizations, and the growing regulatory, political, and clinical pressures to improve quality, access, and cost efficiency. Nursing home conditions that contribute to poor nursing care and the inappropriate use of hospitals also are described. The issues of costs, payment rates, and profits are analyzed to help explain the behavior of nursing home organizations and their impact on residents and their families.

Chapter 6 examines the growing demand for home and community-based long-term care services, the expansion of community organizations as a response, and resultant questions of how to measure the outcomes of community services on clients and how to control costs. Chapter 7 addresses the physician labor market and the historic domination of physicians over decision-making processes and management practices in health care delivery. The debate about the consequences of physicians being organized into large medical practices and becoming employees of health organizations is presented. Physician practice patterns and the excess supply of specialists are identified as major contributors to high costs and sometimes inappropriate services. New reimbursement policies and educational reforms under consideration to address these problems are outlined. Chapter 8 treats the nursing labor market, its tie to the physician labor market, and changing trends in hospital practice where the majority of nurses are employed. Analysis demonstrates that nursing services as substitutes for physician services are of high quality and can lower costs. The chapter also describes the growing recognition, by both policymakers and the public, of nurses' important role in providing traditional nursing care as well as additional primary care services in a wide variety of health care settings.

4

Hospitals

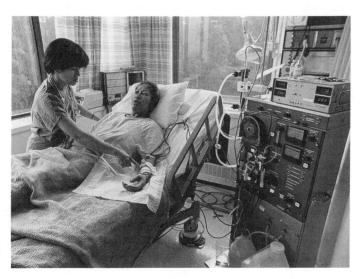

*Increasingly
expensive high-tech
hospital care*

Kathy Hull / American Hospital Association

Hospital Trends

U.S. REGISTERED HOSPITALS

The Broader Environment

As institutions serving virtually all segments of society, U.S. hospitals are directly affected by broad social, economic, demographic and political trends, as well as by specific developments in health care policy. In 1991, the United States asserted its power abroad but experienced continuing economic weakness at home. In the aftermath of the Persian Gulf War, the national mood gradually shifted, as Americans started paying more attention to the economy and other domestic concerns. Over the course of the year, health care reform emerged as one of the most pressing issues on the domestic agenda.

The U.S. Economy.   Economic conditions soured in 1991. By all important measures, the U.S. economy was weaker than in 1990. Although the economy did pull itself out of recession after the first quarter, growth was anemic during the remainder of the year. Adjusted for inflation, the nation's Gross Domestic Product (GDP) declined 1.2 percent in 1991.[1] The unemployment problem worsened, reaching an annual level of 6.7 percent.[2] Higher unemployment meant more poverty and a larger uninsured population. This, in turn, likely increased the financial strains on many hospitals in the form of a higher volume of uncompensated care.

Total industrial production fell, and business operated at roughly 79 percent of capacity. Productivity gains were negligible, and business expenditures for new plant and equipment declined.[3] In this austere business climate, employers stepped up efforts to hold the line on costs, including spending on employees' health care benefits.

Kathy Hull is a Research Analyst at the American Hospital Association. The American Hospital Association (AHA), representing almost 55,000 individuals and health care institutions, including hospitals, health care systems, and pre- and post-acute health care delivery organizations, publishes annual hospital statistics and guides to the health care field based on AHA research data.

Abridged from Hull, K., and American Hospital Association. (1993). Hospital trends. *Hospital Statistics, 1992–93 Edition* (pp. xxxiii–lii). Chicago, IL: American Hospital Association. Used with permission.

At the individual level, the economic gloom translated into a 1.3 percent decline in real per capita disposable income, the largest drop in 10 years.

Average gross weekly earnings fell for the fifth consecutive year, and personal consumption expenditures declined slightly.[4]

Lenders also became more conservative, and hospitals—like individuals and businesses generally—experienced a "credit crunch." Interest rates plunged to historic lows, but banks adopted more conservative lending practices to minimize their exposure in economically uncertain times. Loans by commercial banks to individuals fell $16 billion, while loans to commercial and industrial borrowers plunged $25 billion.[5]

Health Care Spending.   Despite the sluggish economy, health care spending was projected to continue to grow at a rate above general inflation in 1991. Preliminary government projections put 1991 national health expenditures at $738 billion, roughly 10 percent higher than 1990.[6] In addition, health spending was projected to continue to grow as a portion of the overall economy, exceeding 13 percent of Gross National Product (GNP) in 1991.[7]

Hospital care is the single largest category in national health spending, representing roughly 38 percent of the total. However, hospitals' share of total health spending has declined somewhat since 1980, while the share for physician services and other personal health care services has increased.[8] This is the result of slower growth in hospital spending than in overall health spending since the early 1980s.[9]

Rapidly rising health costs are a primary reason for the growing public scrutiny of the U.S. health care system and for claims that the country faces a "health care crisis." By the year 2000, national health spending is projected to increase to over $1.6 trillion, representing per capita spending of $5,712 (more than double the 1991 per capita amount) and accounting for over 16 percent of GNP.[10] Such projections raise legitimate concerns about the impact of health care costs on both individual pocketbooks and national competitiveness in an increasingly inter-dependent global economy.

Cost Control Efforts.   Both private and public payers stepped up their cost control efforts in 1991. Major strategies of private payers included increased use of managed care options such as HMOs and PPOs, and shifting of more costs to insured individuals through cost-sharing increases. HMOs captured 28 percent of the market for employer-sponsored health plans (compared to 20 percent in 1990), and the market share of PPOs was 15 percent (up from 13 percent in 1990). Traditional indemnity plans with no managed care features held only 5 percent market share in 1991, whereas these plans accounted for 41 percent of the market just four years earlier.[11]

Cost-sharing increases imposed on insured individuals included higher contributions toward monthly premiums, higher deductibles, and higher out-of-pocket maximums. A recent survey of over 2,000 employers found that over half of the employers required employees to share the cost of health insurance premiums, and individuals' share of premiums rose 13 percent between 1990 and 1991. In addition, the average deductible amount increased from $150 to $200, and out-of-pocket maximums for both individuals and families rose slightly.[12]

Public payers also tried to rein in their health costs, as fiscal problems deepened at all levels of government. Health spending has taken an increasingly large bite out of government revenues: health spending accounted for 8.5 percent of all federal spending in 1970 but rose steadily to 15.3 percent in 1990; at the state and local level, health spending increased from 7.4 percent of all government spending in 1970 to 11.4 percent in 1990.[13]

At the federal level, cost control efforts have focused on the Medicare program. Since the implementation of the prospective payment system (PPS) for inpatient Medicare services in 1984, Medicare payments to hospitals have increasingly failed to keep pace with the cost increases faced by hospitals. In recent years, many hospitals have been losing money on Medicare patients. The projected 1991 aggregate PPS margin is −8.9 percent, compared to −3.4 percent in 1990. Over 60 percent of hospitals lost money on Medicare patients in 1991. In addition, the Omnibus Budget Reconciliation Act of 1990 stipulated cuts of $2 billion in Medicare payments to hospitals in Federal Fiscal Year (FFY) 1991, and total cuts in hospital payments of $16.3 billion in FFY 1991–95.

States are also looking for ways to control health spending. Medicaid is now the fastest-growing portion of many state budgets, because of the growing number of poor and eligibility expansions recently mandated by Congress. But as most states confront serious budget crises of their own, Medicaid payments to providers continue to be inadequate. In 1990, Medicaid reimbursements covered an average of only 80 cents of every dollar in Medicaid services delivered by community hospitals.

The position of the states will be further weakened as a result of the 1991 passage of a federal law, effective in October 1992, limiting the use of "voluntary contributions" and provider-specific taxes to supplement the state and local portion of Medicaid funding. Under these arrangements, hospitals and other entities make payments toward state Medicaid funding. These payments can then be matched by federal Medicaid dollars and returned to health care providers in the form of higher Medicaid reimbursement levels. Constrained in their ability to use such arrangements to supplement state Medicaid funding, states are likely to have even greater difficulty making adequate reimbursements for Medicaid services in the future. The financial implications for hospitals, especially those with relatively high Medicaid caseloads, are quite bleak.

Despite the growing cost-control efforts of both public and private payers, community hospitals were able to maintain an aggregate total net margin of 4.3 percent in 1991. While total margin was positive in the aggregate, approximately 25 percent of hospitals had negative total margins. Aggregate net patient margin, moreover, stood at −3.5 percent in 1991, indicating that patient revenues continue to fall short of covering hospitals' full expenses.

The U.S. Population.   The U.S. population climbed to over 253 million people by the end of 1991,[14] and is projected to grow by approximately 7 percent during the 1990s. The highest growth will be in the South and West, as more people migrate to these regions from the Midwest and Northeast.[15]

The elderly (age 65 and over) are projected to comprise a growing percentage of the overall population in the years ahead. This trend has already begun but will become most pronounced after the year 2010, as the Baby Boom generation starts to grow older. The elderly population is projected to grow to approximately 35 million (13 percent of the total population) by the year 2000, and then shoot up to 52 million (almost 18 percent of the total) by 2020. By 2030, over one in five Americans will be elderly. In addition, the very old (those age 85 and over) will make up a growing proportion of the elderly.[16]

The aging of the population has profound implications for hospitals and the health care system in general. The elderly are admitted to hospitals more frequently (in relative terms), and average longer lengths of stay. Other health care delivery arrangements—such as long-term care and home health care—will need to develop and expand to meet the needs of the elderly. And the open question of how to finance the care of an expanding elderly population will demand an answer in the very near future. The Federal Hospital Insurance Trust Fund, which pays for the hospital portion of Medicare, is projected to be depleted by the year 2002.[17]

The proportion of the U.S. population living in poverty grew to 14.2 percent in 1991. A total of 35.7 million people were poor, an increase of 2.1 million over 1990.[18] The 1991 poverty rate was the highest since the recession of the early 1980s. Increasing poverty brings more uncompensated care to the hospital doorstep, since Medicaid no longer functions adequately as a health insurance program for the poor. The proportion of poor and near-poor covered by Medicaid has declined steadily since the 1970s, falling from 63 percent in 1975 to under 40 percent in 1990.[19]

Access to Health Care.   Along with rising health care costs, access to health care—and more specifically the growth of the uninsured population—is a key concern in the growing public debate about health care. The U.S. Census Bureau estimated that 35.4 million Americans—approximately 14 percent of the population—lacked any health insurance coverage during 1991, an increase of almost 1 million people over 1990.[20]

While higher poverty and unemployment partly explain the growth of the uninsured population, they are not the only contributing factors. An independent analysis of the 1990 Census Bureau health insurance data revealed that 85 percent of the uninsured lived in families headed by workers (and over 50 percent lived in families headed by full-time year-round workers). In addition, 45 percent of the uninsured lived in families with annual incomes of $20,000 or more.[21] Other factors influencing the growth of the uninsured population are the growing difficulty for some employers (especially small businesses) of affording health benefits for employees, the prohibitive cost of individual insurance, and the medical underwriting practices of some insurance companies, which make it difficult for people with complex medical histories to obtain coverage.

Beyond the issue of health insurance, other obstacles prevent many Americans from obtaining timely and appropriate access to health care. These include shortages of health providers in some local areas (particularly many rural areas), social or cultural barriers, such as language barriers, and lack of access to needed ancillary services, such as transportation and affordable child care.

Health Care in National Politics.   Spurred by the growing problems of costs and access, health care rose to prominence as a national political issue in 1991. Poll results reflected the growing public concern. Over 70 percent of respondents in two separate polls named health care as one of several important voting issues.[22] One in five respondents in one poll said their household had been seriously hurt by medical bills,[23] and less than one third of respondents in a second poll were confident that their future major health care costs would be taken care of.[24]

In a November special election to fill a vacant U.S. Senate seat in Pennsylvania, underdog Harris Wofford pulled out a surprise victory over former U.S. Attorney General Richard Thornburgh. Since Wofford had made health care reform a cornerstone of his campaign message, his win was widely interpreted as a harbinger of the health care issue's importance in the upcoming presidential elections.

The growing public awareness of the health care issue was accompanied by a spate of health care reform proposals. By the end of 1991, over 40 serious reform proposals had been put forward by a range of groups and individuals, including members of Congress, health care associations, physician groups, business groups, labor unions, and academics. Most reform proposals fell into one of three main categories: marketplace approaches, which rely on tax subsidies to expand insurance coverage; single-payer plans, which adopt the main features of Canada's government-financed system; and "play or pay" proposals, which require employers to offer coverage to employees or pay into a government plan.

Regulatory Developments. Several major regulatory developments related to Medicare occurred during 1991, with significant immediate and long-term implications for U.S. hospitals. These included publication of the final rule for Medicare's new reimbursement system for physician services, a new Medicare payment system for inpatient capital costs, and implementation of geographic reclassification for PPS hospitals.

In 1991, the federal government completed preparations to move to a new physician payment system for Medicare, implementing legislation passed two years earlier. Effective at the start of 1992, Medicare's reasonable charge payment system for physician services would be replaced with a national fee schedule, adjusted for geographic variations and phased in over a five-year transition period. The new prospective fee schedule was derived from a resource-based relative value scale (RBRVS) that attempts to gauge the value of the resources required to deliver specific services. The overall effect of using RBRVS will be an increase in fees for primary care services and a dramatic reduction in fees for procedures and specialists' services.

Based on the regulations published in 1991, hospitals could expect both direct and indirect effects from the implementation of physician payment reform. Hospitals will be directly affected because some of their Medicare revenue, such as reimbursements to physicians who are hospital employees, will be paid under the fee schedule. Hospitals will also be affected indirectly to the extent that the new payment system causes changes in physician behavior and influences physician-hospital relationships, although these impacts are more difficult to predict.

Final regulations for a new payment system for inpatient capital costs were also published in 1991, and took effect on October 1 of that year. These regulations eliminated the pass-through payment system for inpatient capital costs and replaced it with a prospective payment system based on national average capital costs per case, phased in over a 10-year period. While provisions for the transition period were designed to accommodate current hospital capital structures and minimize the short-term impacts on hospitals, use of national averages as a basis for capital payments will have the long-term effect of redistributing capital payments among hospitals. In the years ahead, the new payment system will significantly influence hospitals' decisions regarding capital expenditures and financing.

A third major development under Medicare was the implementation of geographic reclassification, a process that allows hospitals to request a change in how they are classified under Medicare's inpatient prospective payment system (PPS). Geographic classification determines a hospital's wage index and thus affects payment levels under PPS. In applications to be reclassified, submitted annually, hospitals attempt to demonstrate that their existing classification is not appropriate. A higher-than-expected number of hospitals obtained reclassification for Federal Fiscal Year 1992 (effective October 1, 1991). Although intended to improve the fairness of PPS payments, the geographic reclassification process raises concerns about the stability and predictability of PPS payment levels to hospitals from one year to the next.

U.S. COMMUNITY HOSPITALS

In the previous section, environmental factors influencing the nation's hospitals were reviewed. . . . The focus now shifts to an analysis of specific hospital performance trends among U.S. community hospitals in 1991.

Community hospitals include institutions that are nonfederal, short-term, general and other special hospitals whose facilities are open to the public. Not included in the community hospital category are hospital units of institutions, long-term hospitals, psychiatric hospitals, and alcoholism and chemical dependency facilities.

Distribution Trends

The total number of U.S. community hospitals has been declining since 1977, and at a faster relative pace since 1985. Reductions in the number of hospitals occur as hospitals close, merge, or are acquired by other facilities. In 1991, 45 community hospitals closed, down from the 50 reported closures in 1990. Since 1981, 558 community hospitals have closed, ceasing to provide inpatient acute care services.[25] In the same period, many hospitals merged with or were acquired by other hospitals, resulting in fewer hospitals after these transactions were concluded. Each year, reductions in the number of hospitals are offset in part by new hospital openings as well as facility reopenings. In 1991, the total number of community hospitals fell by 42 (see table 1). This 0.8 percent decline was slightly smaller than the annual decreases in excess of 1 percent seen in 1987 through 1990.

Urban and Rural Hospitals.   Declines in the number of community hospitals over the past decade have been sharper among rural hospitals than among urban hospitals. Between 1981 and 1991, the total number of community hospitals fell by 8.1 percent. During this time period, however, the number of urban community hospitals fell by only 4.2 percent, while the number of rural community hospitals plunged 12.4 percent. The number of urban community hospitals was almost unchanged between 1990 and

TABLE 1   Selected Measures in Community Hospitals, 1981 and 1990–91

Measure	Year			Percent Change*	
	1981	*1990*	*1991*	*1981–91*	*1990–91*
Hospitals	5,813	5,384	5,342	−8.1	−0.8
Beds (000s)	1,003	927	924	−7.9	−0.4
Average number of beds per hospital	173	172	173	0.2	0.4
Admissions (000s)	36,438	31,181	31,064	−14.7	−0.4
Average daily census (000s)	763	619	611	−19.9	−1.3
Average length of stay, days	7.6	7.2	7.2	−6.1	−1.0
Inpatient days (000s)	278,406	225,972	222,858	−20.0	−1.4
Occupancy percent	76.0	66.8	66.1	−13.1	−1.0
Surgical operations (000s)	19,236	21,915	22,405	16.5	2.2
Bassinets (000s)[a]	77	68	67	−11.9	−1.4
Births (000s)[a]	3,465	3,958	3,965	14.4	0.2
Outpatient visits (000s)[b]	202,768	301,329	322,048	58.8	6.9

[a]Based only on hospitals reporting newborn data.
[b]Based only on hospitals reporting outpatient visits.
*Percent changes are based on actual figures, not rounded.

1991, falling only 0.1 percent. The number of rural hospitals, by contrast, decreased 1.6 percent.

Bed Size.   Over the past decade, the number of hospitals in all bed-size categories declined, with the exception of the 200–299 bed category, in which the number of hospitals increased by 3.3 percent. Between 1981 and 1991, the number of hospitals in the following bed-size categories declined by more than 10 percent: 50–99 beds, 400–499 beds, and 500 or more beds. All bed-size categories, except 200–299 beds, saw declines of over 5 percent during this 10-year period.

Fluctuations by Regions.   Regional data show a disproportionate reduction in the number of hospitals in certain areas of the country. In the Pacific and West South Central Census divisions, the number of community hospitals decreased by over 10 percent between 1981 and 1991. The New England, Middle Atlantic, East North Central, East South Central, and West North Central divisions lost between 6 and 10 percent of their hospitals in the same period. Relative declines were smallest in the South Atlantic and Mountain divisions, where the number of hospitals fell by less than 4 percent.

Staffed Beds.   According to the data, the number of community hospital beds set up and staffed for use has been declining since 1984. The reduction in staffed beds comes in response to declines in the number of hospital admissions and in the average length of hospital stays. The number of beds in United States community hospitals peaked in 1983 at slightly over one million. The largest declines in staffed beds occurred in 1985 through 1989, with the reduction in beds leveling off somewhat in 1990 and 1991. The number of staffed beds declined 0.4 percent between 1990 and 1991, after a 0.6 percent annual decline in 1990. The decrease in staffed beds in 1991 was the smallest reduction, in both absolute and relative terms, since the number of beds began falling seven years earlier.

Like declines in the number of community hospitals, declines in staffed beds have been disproportionately concentrated in rural hospitals. Staffed beds in all community hospitals declined by 7.9 percent between 1981 and 1991. Urban hospital beds fell by 5.9 percent during this period, while the number of rural beds declined by over 14 percent. By bed-size category, the largest relative declines in staffed beds occurred in the following groups: 50–99 beds, 400–499 beds, and 500 or more beds.

Financial Trends

Expenses.   Hospital financial trends have been affected by changes in hospital reimbursement policies, medical practice patterns, and medical technology. Between 1983 and 1986 hospital expense growth averaged 8 percent annually. In the past several years, however, expenses have begun to rise more rapidly.

Community hospital expenses rose 10.6 percent in 1988, 9.6 percent in 1989, and 10.2 percent in 1990. In 1991, community hospital expense growth rose slightly, to 10.5 percent. Urban hospital expenses grew at a 10.5 percent rate in 1991, while rural hospital expenses rose 10.1 percent.

Payroll (wages and salaries) and employee benefits accounted for almost 55 percent of total community hospital expenses in 1991. Another third (32.7 percent) of hospital expenses were for medical supplies, pharmaceuticals, utilities, food, housekeeping supplies, and administrative costs. The remainder of hospital expenses were capital costs (interest and depreciation on a hospital's facilities and equipment) and fees paid for contracted professional and administrative services.

Revenue.   Growth in total community hospital revenue generally parallels the trend in total expense growth. After 1983, revenue growth was reduced to an average annual rate of about 8 percent for a period of several years. In 1991, total revenue increased 11.0 percent, up from the 10.7 percent growth reported in 1990. Net patient revenue, the revenue hospi-

TABLE 2   Total Expenditures of Community Hospitals, 1990–91

	Total Expenditures (millions)[a]		Percent Change	Average Expenditure per Hospital (millions)
	1990	1991		1991
Total community hospitals	$203,693	$225,023	10.5	$ 42
Urban community hospitals	177,480	196,154	10.5	67
Rural community hospitals	26,213	28,869	10.1	12
Bed-size category				
6–24 beds	473	532	12.5	2
25–49	4,012	4,581	14.2	5
50–99	12,590	13,946	10.8	11
100–199	33,282	37,050	11.3	28
200–299	38,698	42,643	10.2	58
300–399	33,137	36,442	10.0	92
400–499	25,297	27,609	9.1	124
500 or more	56,205	62,221	10.7	221

[a]Figures have been rounded to the nearest million; therefore, entries in vertical columns will not necessarily add to the totals given.

tals actually receive for the care provided to patients, rose 11.1 percent in 1991, compared to 10.5 percent in 1990 (see table 2).

Payer Sources.   Gross patient revenue reflects the amount hospitals would receive if all patients paid at full "retail" charges.[26] Gross patient revenue is not used to evaluate hospitals' financial position, but can indicate the level of services rendered and provide revenue source information. In 1991, Medicare represented approximately 40 percent of the total community hospital gross patient revenue while Medicaid represented 12 percent. Third-party payers accounted for 35 percent, and patients who pay for hospital services themselves or from other government and nongovernment sources accounted for 13 percent.

Utilization Trends

The data shows that trends in the utilization of hospital services over the past decade have been characterized by declines in all measures of inpatient utilization and strong growth in the use of hospital outpatient services. It follows that much hospital care that would have required an inpatient stay 10 years ago, is now routinely delivered in the outpatient setting.

Admissions.   Total admissions in community hospitals decreased 14.4 percent between 1981 to 1991. Declines in admissions were sharpest from 1984 through 1987, but have leveled off in the past several years. Relative declines in admissions were much larger among rural hospitals than among their urban counterparts. Admissions stood at 31.1 million in 1991, a modest 0.4 percent decrease from 1990. Admissions to urban community hospitals were virtually unchanged between 1990 and 1991, rising 0.1 percent, while admissions to rural community hospitals fell 2.4 percent.

Average Length of Stay.   In 1991, the average length of stay for patients admitted to community hospitals was 7.17 days, down somewhat from the average stay of 7.25 days in 1990. Ten years earlier, the length of stay was 7.6 days. Since 1984, in which the average length of stay was 7.3 days, length of stay has stabilized. The decline in length of stay from the early 1980s coincides with the beginning of Medicare prospective payment for inpatient services, and likely reflects hospitals' response to the payment system's incentives.

Inpatient Days.   Total inpatient days in community hospitals decreased by 1.4 percent in 1991, the largest relative decline in five years. Inpatient days have declined dramatically over the past 10 years. While the decline began in 1982, the largest drops occurred in 1984 and 1985 after implementation of Medicare prospective payment, when admissions and lengths of stay fell sharply. Between 1981 and 1991, total inpatient days declined by 20 percent, as a result of declining admissions and shorter hospital stays.

Hospital occupancy rates have also declined, in both urban and rural hospitals. The aggregate occupancy rate for community hospitals was 66.1 percent in 1991, down from 76.0 percent in 1981. Occupancy tends to rise with hospital size, ranging from 32.6 percent in 1991 among hospitals with 6–24 beds to 77.0 percent among those with 500 or more beds.

Changes in Outpatient Activity

While hospital reimbursement policies and technological advances have contributed to the decrease in inpatient use, they have caused outpatient hospital utilization to rise rapidly. In 1991, community hospitals reported 322 million outpatient visits, a 6.9 percent increase over 1990.

The increase in outpatient surgical procedures has been a major factor in the rapid growth in outpatient visits in both urban and rural hospitals. In 1981, less than one fifth of all surgeries performed in community hospitals were done on an outpatient basis. By 1990, that proportion had risen to over half. In 1991, outpatient surgeries accounted for 52.3 percent of all surgeries performed in community hospitals. The number of inpatient surgeries performed in community hospitals declined 1.4 percent between 1990 and 1991, while the number of outpatient surgeries increased 5.8 percent. Almost all U.S. community hospitals, regardless of size or location, now provide some type of ambulatory surgical service. As the number of noninvasive surgical methods increases, so will the proportion of all surgeries performed in the outpatient setting.

Trends in Services

As a result of technological innovations and the growth in outpatient treatment, hospitals are offering a wider range of services to patients than in the past.

Outpatient Services.   The number and variety of outpatient services available in community hospitals have mushroomed in recent years. In 1984, roughly 50 percent of all community hospitals had outpatient departments; by 1991, that proportion had risen to 86.7 percent.

Outpatient rehabilitation services have grown significantly. In 1984, 1,939 hospitals reported offering outpatient rehabilitation. By 1991, that figure increased to 2,604 reporting hospitals. As a result, over half (52.3 percent) of all community hospitals now provide these services. Home health care has also experienced substantial growth. Home health services were available from approximately 36 percent of all community hospitals in 1991, compared to 22 percent in 1984. Another growth area in outpatient hospital care is alcohol and chemical dependency treatment. In 1991, approximately one-fifth of reporting hospitals provided treatment for alcohol and drug abuse problems on an outpatient basis, up from 14.4 percent in 1984 (see table 3).

Long-term Care Services.   Responding to the growth in the over-age-65 population and the number of children and disabled adults requiring long-term nonacute care, hospitals have expanded their long-term care services. A growing number of hospitals have separate long-term care units within the hospital providing physician services and continuous professional nursing supervision to patients not requiring acute care. In 1991, hospitals had more skilled nursing units and other long-term care units than 10 years earlier. The number of hospitals reported skilled nursing units nearly doubled between 1981 and 1991, and the number of hospitals with other long-term care units increased by over 50 percent (figure 1). In 1991, 23.3 percent of reporting hospitals had skilled nursing units, compared to only 11.1 percent 10 years earlier.

TABLE 3   Trends in Selected Services of Community Hospitals, 1984 and
1990–91 (Number/Percentage of Reporting Hospitals with Selected Services)

	1984		1990		1991	
	No. of Hospitals	Percent	No. of Hospitals	Percent	No. of Hospitals	Percent
Ambulatory surgery	4,836	90.7	4,788	94.7	4,708	94.6
Birthing rooms	2,449	45.9	3,292	65.1	3,294	66.2
Emergency department	5,064	95.0	4,728	93.5	4,627	93.0
Family planning/ reproductive health	584	11.0	2,129	42.1	2,152	43.3
Home health care	1,167	21.9	1,801	35.6	1,798	36.1
Hospice	578	10.8	817	16.2	825	16.6
Neonatal ICU	557	10.4	724	14.3	740	14.9
Occupational therapy	2,140	40.1	2,510	49.6	2,595	52.2
Outpatient alcoholism/ chemical dependency	767	14.4	1,035	20.5	1,042	20.9
Outpatient department	2,634	49.4	4,309	85.2	4,311	86.7
Outpatient rehabilitation	1,939	36.4	2,606	51.5	2,604	52.3
Trauma care	938	17.6	651	12.9	667	13.4
Number of hospitals reporting	5,331		5,056		4,975	

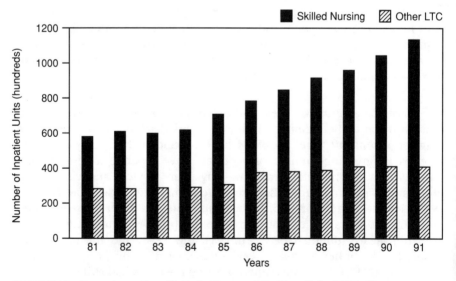

FIGURE 1   Long-term Care Units in Community Hospitals, 1981–91

Geriatric Services.   Hospitals have also developed a wide range of services and programs to meet the needs of older adults in their communities. Eight such services are surveyed (see table 4).

The proportion of community hospitals offering some type of geriatric services has remained relatively stable, rising from 60.8 percent reporting hospitals in 1990 to 62.1 percent in 1991.

All program types within geriatric services showed some growth between 1990 and 1991. The two most frequently reported service offerings are emergency response systems and senior membership programs. . . .

AIDS-Related Services.   Over 230,000 Americans have been diagnosed with acquired immune deficiency syndrome (AIDS) since the disease emerged in the early 1980s, and an estimated one million Americans are now infected with the human immunodeficiency virus (HIV) that causes AIDS.

While the rate of new AIDS cases has slowed in recent years, the disease has spread to virtually all segments of the population and all areas of the country, including rural and smaller urban areas. The disease is spreading most rapidly among women, children, and intravenous drug users and their sexual partners. In addition, racial minorities are disproportionately affected by the HIV virus.

Hospitals play a critical role in the care of people with AIDS and HIV

TABLE 4   Trends in Selected Geriatric Services of Community Hospitals, 1990–91 (Number/Percentage of Reporting Hospitals with Selected Services)

	1990		*1991*	
	No. of Hospitals	*Percent*	*No. of Hospitals*	*Percent*
Adult day care program	321	6.3	332	6.7
Alzheimer's diagnostic/ assessment services	395	7.8	431	8.7
Comprehensive geriatric assessment	918	18.2	924	18.6
Emergency response system	1,776	35.1	1,835	36.9
Geriatric acute care unit	508	10.0	504	10.1
Geriatric clinics	320	6.3	343	6.9
Respite care	841	16.6	839	16.9
Senior membership program	1,142	22.6	1,157	23.3
Geriatric services	3,072	60.8	3,091	62.1
Number of hospitals reporting	5,056		4,975	

infection. When the initial cases of AIDS were diagnosed, the disease was treated primarily on an inpatient basis. Although some inpatient care is still typically required, especially during the last stages of the disease, more care is being provided on an outpatient basis now. The health care needs of people with HIV and AIDS are also being addressed through other community resources, including home health care and hospice arrangements. Through discharge planning and case management programs, hospitals can coordinate these outpatient services for patients with HIV and AIDS.

The lifetime cost of medical care for a person with AIDS has been estimated at $85,333. Medical care costs for people with AIDS and HIV are thought to be rising as a result of increased longevity and the introduction of expensive drug therapies. In 1991, the cost of medical care for all people with HIV was estimated at $5.8 billion, and this figure is expected to rise to $10.4 billion by 1994.[27] As the medical costs associated with HIV and AIDS continue to rise, additional funding will be necessary to ease the financial burden on hospitals treating large numbers of AIDS patients.

Since 1988, the AHA Annual Survey of Hospitals has collected information on the specific types of hospital-based services available for AIDS patients. In 1991, 69.5 percent of reporting hospitals provided general inpatient care for AIDS patients, up from 67.5 percent in 1990. Some 6.1 percent of hospitals offered specialized outpatient programs for AIDS patients in 1991, compared to 5.7 percent in 1990. The proportion of hospitals reporting a specialized AIDS unit remained constant at 2.2 percent between 1990 and 1991. Hospital-based services for AIDS patients are likely to continue to change as a range of new drug therapies advances the treatment of AIDS. Also, with the number of patients with AIDS continuing to rise, hospitals are aggressively implementing more effective strategies to prevent AIDS transmission between hospital patients and their caregivers.

Evolving Medical Technologies

Technological advances have significantly influenced the number of services available in community hospitals. One of the most noteworthy developments in medical technology is the growth in outpatient applications. Many new procedures and techniques are available in outpatient settings. Less invasive procedures made possible by advances in radiology and surgery have made diagnosis and treatment of disease less traumatic for patients and have allowed more care to be provided on an outpatient basis. The 1990s are likely to bring an increase in cancer care being treated on an outpatient basis. The growing need for around-the-clock, ambulatory cancer care will reinforce the trend toward the establishment of outpatient cancer centers supported by home health services, including home infusion therapy. In addition, many nonhospital outpatient centers offer access to diagnostic and therapeutic services, including cardiac catheterization, magnetic resonance imaging (MRI), mammography, computerized tomography (CT), ultrasound, nuclear medicine, and extracorporeal shock wave lithotripsy (ESWL).

The AHA Annual Survey of Hospitals gathers information on the number of hospitals providing services involving selected medical technologies such as MRI or CT scans, rather than the number of devices in hospitals. For example, data for 1991 show 1,036 community hospitals offering MRI services. This figure does not reflect those facilities owning more than one device, nor hospitals offering a particular service on site, but sharing the use of a mobile device. In addition, because MRI services (and others) are now available in many nonhospital settings, the number of hospitals offering these services represent only a portion of the number of MRI units now available in the United States (see table 5).

Diagnostic and Therapeutic Technologies.   Several major new diagnostic and therapeutic technologies have gained widespread use in community hospitals over the past five to ten years. In 1984, 2,555 community

TABLE 5   Trends in Selected Medical Technologies Provided by Community Hospitals, 1984 and 1990–91 (Number/Percentage of Reporting Hospitals with Selected Medical Technology)

	1984		1990		1991	
	No. of Hospitals	Percent	No. of Hospitals	Percent	No. of Hospitals	Percent
Angioplasty	—	—	1,040	20.6	1,018	20.5
Cardiac catheterization	942	17.7	1,390	27.5	1,457	29.3
Cardiac rehabilitation	—	—	2,024	40.0	2,228	44.8
CT scanner	2,555	47.9	3,544	70.1	3,633	73.0
Lithotripsy (ESWL)	—	—	319	6.3	370	7.4
Magnetic resonance imaging (MRI)	166	3.1	919	18.2	1,036	20.8
Megavoltage radiation therapy	898	16.8	994	19.7	969	19.5
Non-invasive cardiac assessment	—	—	2,748	54.4	3,033	61.0
Open-heart surgery	631	11.8	847	16.8	867	17.4
Organ transplantation	244	4.6	526	10.4	555	11.2
Single photon emission computerized tomography (SPECT)	—	—	934	18.5	1,155	23.2
Number of hospitals reporting	5,331		5,056		4,975	

hospitals reported CT scanner services; by 1991, that figure had grown to 3,633, an increase of 42 percent. Another diagnostic technology, MRI, has shown a steady increase in use since its introduction, with 20.8 percent of community hospitals reported MRI services in 1991.

Recognition of the importance of chemical and metabolic information for the early and effective treatment of disease will foster the growth of nuclear medicine in the years ahead. Specifically, the 1990s should see increased use of single photon emission computerized tomography (SPECT) for cardiac and brain imaging. In 1991, 23.2 percent of reporting hospitals provided SPECT services, up from 18.5 percent in 1990.

Personnel Trends

Changes in Staffing Levels.   Hospitals employed 3.5 million full-time equivalent (FTE) employees in 1991, an increase of 3.4 percent over the 1990 level. Trends in hospitals' use of FTEs have been variable over the past decade, as the number of FTEs rose through 1982, declined in 1983 through 1985 during the initial years of Medicare prospective payment, then increased moderately through the late 1980s and early 1990s.

Average Salary and Benefits.   Average compensation (salary and benefits) for community hospital employees has maintained a fairly steady growth trend. The average annual salary for a community hospital employee in 1991 was $28,305, compared to $26,590 in 1990, representing salary growth of 6.4 percent. Community hospitals provided an average of $5,946 in fringe benefits per employee in 1991, an 11.8 percent increase over the average benefits package provided in 1990.

U.S. NONCOMMUNITY HOSPITALS

The AHA reports data for noncommunity hospitals separately, as these hospitals generally care for patients requiring longer hospital stays.

The noncommunity hospital category includes psychiatric hospitals, hospitals for tuberculosis and other respiratory diseases, chronic disease hospitals, institutions for the mentally retarded, alcoholism and chemical dependency hospitals, and other long-term hospitals and hospital units, including the various armed services hospitals, veterans' hospitals, and Native American Health Service facilities.

The total number of noncommunity hospitals was 1,292 in 1991, up slightly from 1990. Between 1981 and 1991, the total number of non-community hospitals increased 15.4 percent. The number of noncommunity hospitals began rising in 1983, following several decades of declines. Psychiatric hospitals have led the increase in noncommunity hospitals, as their numbers rose 45.7 percent between 1981 and 1991. The number of nonfederal psychiatric hospitals rose 5.7 percent between 1990 and 1991, from 757 to 800 hospitals. Nonfederal psychiatric hospitals accounted for almost two thirds of all noncommunity hospitals in 1991.

As with community hospitals, the number of noncommunity hospital beds has been decreasing. Beds in noncommunity hospitals totaled 277,480 in 1991, a 22.5 percent reduction compared to 1981. Admissions to noncommunity hospitals declined 8.4 percent between 1981 and 1991, despite increasing admissions in nonfederal psychiatric hospitals.

Nonfederal Psychiatric Hospitals

Trends for psychiatric hospitals in the past decade have run counter to some of the trends among other noncommunity hospitals and are influencing the aggregate noncommunity hospital statistics. For example, admissions to psychiatric hospitals increased 32.7 percent between 1981 and 1991. In addition, the number of psychiatric hospitals increased significantly during that time period, while the number of hospitals within all other categories of noncommunity hospitals decreased.

Similar to trends in other hospitals, the number of psychiatric hospital beds declined 24.1 percent between 1981 and 1991. The average length of stay in psychiatric hospitals has also decreased significantly, falling from 114 days in 1981 to 61 days in 1991, a 46.5 percent reduction.

Federal Hospitals

The next largest category of noncommunity hospitals is federal hospitals, which are owned and operated by the federal government. Federal hospitals have experienced a modest decline in number, from 348 in 1981 to 334 in 1991. During the same period, the number of beds in federal hospitals declined 16.4 percent, and admissions fell 18.4 percent to approximately 1.7 million. The average length of stay in federal hospitals has gone down only slightly, from 16 days in 1981 to 15 days in 1991.

NOTES

1. Council of Economic Advisers. *Economic Indicators,* July 1992. Washington: U.S. Government Printing Office, 1992.

2. Ibid.

3. Ibid.

4. Ibid.

5. Ibid.

6. Sonnefeld, Sally T., Daniel R. Waldo, Jeffrey A. Lemieux, and David R. McKusick. "Projections of national health expenditures through the year 2000." *Health Care Financing Review* 13:1 (Fall 1991).

7. Ibid. While GDP has now been adopted as the primary measure of U.S. production, GNP was still being used when these projections were made.

8. Levit, Katharine R., Helen C. Lazenby, Cathy A. Cowan, and Suzanne W. Letsch. "National health expenditures, 1990." *Health Care Financing Review* 13:1 (Fall 1991).

9. Ibid.

10. Sonnefeld et al.

11. Health Insurance Association of America. HIAA Employer Surveys, 1987 through 1991 (unpublished data). Note: PPO figure for 1991 includes PPO riders to indemnity plans.

12. A. Foster Higgins & Co., Inc. *1991 Health Care Benefits Survey, Report 1 (Indemnity Plans: Cost, Design, and Funding)*. Princeton: A. Foster Higgins & Co., Inc., 1992.

13. Levit et al.

14. U.S. Bureau of the Census, Current Population Reports, Series P-25, No. 1089, *Estimates of the Population of the United States to June 1, 1992*. Washington, D.C.: U.S. Government Printing Office, 1992.

15. U.S. Bureau of the Census, Current Population Reports, Series P-25, No. 1053, *Projections of the Population of States by Age, Sex, and Race: 1989 to 2010*. Washington, D.C.: U.S. Government Printing Office, 1990.

16. U.S. Bureau of the Census, Current Population Reports, Series P-25, No. 1018, *Projections of the Population of the United States, by Age, Sex, and Race: 1988 to 2080*, by Gregory Spencer. Washington, D.C.: U.S. Government Printing Office, 1989. All projections cited in the text are taken from the "middle series" projections.

17. The Board of Trustees, Federal Hospital Insurance Trust Fund. *1992 Annual Report of the Board of Trustees of the Federal Hospital Insurance Trust Fund*. April 1992.

18. U.S. Bureau of the Census, Current Population Reports, Series P-60, No. 181, *Poverty in the United States: 1991*. Washington, D.C.: U.S. Government Printing Office, 1992, p. vii.

19. U.S. Bureau of the Census and Robert Wood Johnson Foundation, published in *Digest of National Health Care Use and Expense Indicators* (Chicago: American Hospital Association, June 1992). The "near-poor" are those with incomes between the federal poverty level and 125 percent of the poverty level.

20. U.S. Bureau of the Census, *Poverty in the United States: 1991*, p. 149.

21. Foley, Jill. "Sources of Health Insurance and Characteristics of the Uninsured." Washington, D.C.: Employee Benefit Research Institute, 1992.

22. Blendon, Robert J. and Ulrike S. Szalay. "Health Care Reform: A Public Opinion Update." Boston: Harvard School of Public Health, 1992. Results of CBS/New York Times poll (August 1991) and ABC/Washington Post poll (December 1991).

23. Ibid, CBS/New York Times poll.

24. Ibid, ABC/Washington Post poll.

25. This number is the sum of hospitals that were reported to have closed as of the end of December of each year. Some of these facilities may have reopened in a later calendar year. In addition, while no longer acute care facilities, hospitals reported closed may continue to provide other health care services.

26. See "Revenue" under the "Definition of Terms" section, page xxiii.

27. Hellinger, Fred J. "Forecasting the Medical Care Costs of the HIV Epidemic: 1991–1994." *Inquiry* 28: 213–225 (Fall 1991).

Medicare and the American Health Care System

The financial status of hospitals is determined by their expenses and the payments they receive from third-party payers and other sources. Payments and expenses, in turn, are determined by many factors, including the types of services hospitals provide and how efficiently they provide them; the number and types of patients using hospital care; the way state and federal government, private insurers, and others pay for hospital services; and other aspects of the environment in which hospitals operate. In this article, the financial condition of the hospital industry is examined, focusing on the role of prospective payment and including data on hospitals' overall financial status. . . .

HOSPITAL FINANCIAL CONDITION UNDER PPS

The amount and distribution of the Medicare prospective payment system (PPS) payments are major policy issues with important consequences for both hospitals and Medicare beneficiaries. Each year, changes in the Medicare program lead to changes in the amount and distribution of payments. These changes, in combination with the trend in operating costs, determine the financial performance of hospitals under PPS.

PPS Payments to Hospitals

Under PPS, each hospital receives a fixed payment rate per discharge for each type of case. Types of cases are defined by the diagnosis-related groups (DRG) patient classification system. A hospital's basic payment rate for each DRG is based on a national standardized payment amount,

The Prospective Payment Assessment Commission (ProPAC) was established by Congress in 1983 to report to the Congress and make recommendations to the Secretary of Health and Human Services on various aspects of the Medicare diagnosis-related groups payment program for hospital services.

Abridged from Prospective Payment Assessment Commission (1991). *Medicare and the American health care system* (pp. 41–85). Washington, D.C.: The Commission. Used with permission.

which differs according to the hospital's location in a large urban area (a metropolitan statistical area, or MSA, with a population of more than 1 million); an other urban area (an MSA with a population of 1 million or fewer); or a rural area (outside of any MSA).

To account for variation in wage rates across areas, the labor cost portion of the hospital's standardized payment amount (about 70 percent of the total) is adjusted by a wage index for the hospital's area. The wage index measures the relative level of wage rates for hospital workers in each urban or statewide rural area compared with the national average level of hospital wages. The hospital's wage-adjusted standardized amount is then multiplied by the national relative weight for each DRG to obtain the hospital's basic DRG payment rate for that type of case. Each DRG weight measures the relative costliness of treating an average case in the DRG compared with the national average cost of care for all PPS cases.

Given this design, the average basic DRG payment rate a hospital receives reflects its location, the level of local wage rates, and the mix of Medicare cases it admits for inpatient care. This is part of the explanation of why urban hospitals tend to have higher payments per discharge than rural hospitals. Urban hospitals start with higher standardized payment amounts, based on historical and continuing differences in their costs per discharge. Moreover, urban hospitals tend to be located in labor market areas that have higher wage rates, and they are likely to treat a more complex and costly mix of Medicare patients.

Aside from basic DRG payments, a hospital will receive additional payments under PPS if it operates graduate medical education programs (for the training of interns and residents), serves a disproportionate share of low-income patients, or treats patients with unusually long stays or extraordinarily high costs (outlier cases). This is the other source of higher payments for urban hospitals. These hospitals are far more likely than rural hospitals to train interns and residents. Further, urban hospitals are more likely to qualify for additional payments for serving a disproportionate share of low-income patients, and they are also more likely to treat outlier cases.

In fiscal year 1991, hospitals will receive an estimated $53.2 billion in PPS payments. Of that amount, $47.8 billion will be paid from the Medicare Hospital Insurance (Part A) Trust Fund. The remaining $5.4 billion will be paid by beneficiaries through Medicare cost-sharing requirements (inpatient deductibles and copayments). . . .[1]

Indirect Medical Education and Disproportionate Share Payments.   In fiscal year 1991, indirect medical education (IME) and disproportionate share (DSH) payments are expected to account for 9.6 percent of all PPS payments, or about $5.1 billion. The IME adjustment is intended to recognize hospitals' indirect costs of operating approved graduate medical education programs. Teaching hospitals are thought to offer a wider range of services and technologies, treat patients who are more severely ill, and generally provide care in a different way than other hospitals. Therefore, they tend to produce a greater volume and a more expensive mix of services per case. . . .

Outlier Payments.   Outlier payments are intended to protect hospitals from the risk of financial losses due to cases with exceptionally long stays or high costs. They are also designed to mitigate the incentive to avoid or inappropriately treat patients who are likely to become unusually costly. In fiscal year 1991, payments for outliers are expected to account for about 5.6 percent of total PPS payments, or almost $3 billion. . . .

The Effects of Payment Policy Changes

Before the beginning of prospective payment in fiscal year 1984, hospitals were paid on the basis of the costs they actually incurred in providing services to Medicare beneficiaries. Under this method, payments to hospitals were unevenly distributed because of differences in hospital characteristics and costliness. Teaching hospitals, for instance, have historically received a disproportionate share of payments because they are generally large hospitals with a high volume of Medicare discharges and high costs per case.

By paying hospitals on the basis of a fixed payment rate for each DRG, PPS has removed the direct connection between the costs of the individual hospital and its Medicare payments. This connection has been replaced with adjustments designed to recognize the impact of certain factors that affect a hospital's cost but are beyond its control, such as local market conditions and the mix of patients it treats.

As is noted later, the distribution of Medicare payments among hospitals changed substantially in the first year of PPS. In addition, changes in hospital behavior and other factors resulted in marked changes in the level and distribution of Medicare operating costs per case. The combination of these changes resulted immediately in large disparities in financial performance among hospitals under PPS.

Congress responded by enacting a series of policy changes that were intended to mitigate the perceived inequities in payments under the initial design of PPS. For example, the IME adjustment was reduced and the DSH adjustment added beginning in fiscal year 1986. Similarly, Congress has mandated separate update factors for rural hospitals, hospitals located in large urban areas, and those located in other urban areas each year beginning in fiscal year 1988. These changes in policy have affected the level and distribution of PPS payments among hospitals, generally as Congress intended.

Other changes in the distribution of payments have occurred when specific elements of the payment system have been updated to reflect new data. Elements of PPS that are subject to periodic updating include the area wage index, the DRG classification system and weights, and the outlier thresholds.

With Medicare payments no longer tied to each hospital's actual costs, hospitals are more vulnerable to the effects of policy decisions. The following discussion focuses on the impact of payment policy changes adopted after the first year of PPS. The impact on payments is measured relative to the policy in effect during the first PPS year. However, under the transition policy adopted in implementing PPS, payments in the first through fourth years were based on a changing blend of hospital-specific, regional, and national rates. To isolate the impact of policy changes from the effects of the transition, the estimates presented here reflect the impact of policy changes on the national payment rates only. Moreover, the policies in effect at the end of each fiscal year (including any policies adopted during the year) are treated as if they were in effect throughout the year. Although this approach does not measure the actual changes in payments that occurred, it gives a better picture of the ultimate impact of each policy change once it is fully implemented.

It is also important to note that changes in payments are attributable both to policy decisions and to other factors that are not directly affected by these decisions. Other significant factors include changes in the distribution of Medicare discharges among hospital groups and rapid but uneven increases in the complexity and costliness of the mix of Medicare patients admitted for care (case mix).

Although the volume of Medicare discharges from PPS hospitals has declined only a small amount since 1983, this volume has declined substantially for both small urban and small rural hospitals. At the same time, important changes in medical technology permitted a major shift in the site of care toward much greater use of outpatient services. Moreover, the kinds of Medicare cases affected by the shift from inpatient to outpatient care have tended to be cases that generally would have required relatively short inpatient stays and incurred relatively low costs, if admitted for care. Consequently, the Medicare case-mix index, which measures the expected costliness of a hospital's Medicare inpatient cases, has increased rapidly since PPS began. However, the rate of increase of the case-mix index (CMI) among hospital groups has been uneven.

Changes in CMI directly affect PPS payments to hospitals. The effects of CMI change on payments can be isolated from the effects of changes in PPS policy by examining the rate of increase in average PPS payments per case while holding case mix constant. . . .

Cumulative Effects of Payment Policy.   The PPS update factor and other payment policy decisions made between the first and eighth years of PPS have increased per-case PPS payments by a cumulative 24.7 percent. However, rural hospitals have benefited from these decisions substantially more than urban hospitals, with a cumulative increase that is almost 10 percentage points higher (30.7 percent compared with 21.0 percent). Small rural hospitals have been helped much more than large hospitals in any location, while urban hospitals with fewer than 100 beds have fared worse than most other groups.

Disproportionate share hospitals located in large urban areas also have experienced substantial increases in payments under the policy changes implemented since PPS began. However, the IME adjustment was reduced in fiscal year 1986, primarily in reaction to the effects of the large IME adjustment received by teaching hospitals in the first year of PPS. Consequently, policy changes adopted since the first year of PPS have provided a relatively low cumulative increase in payments for major teaching hospitals, despite the large overlap between teaching activity and service to low-income patients.

Historically, much of the policy debate each year focuses on the size of the PPS update factor, although other payment policy decisions attract attention as well. However, the rate of increase in the CMI is about equally important in determining the overall increase in per-case PPS payments. In addition, the distribution of case-mix change is often quite different from the pattern of payment policy effects. For example, rural hospitals had a relatively large increase in payments per case due to policy effects, but their increase in payments due to CMI change was well below average. Consequently, the cumulative effect of policy and CMI change is only three percentage points higher for rural than for urban hospitals. The trend and pattern of CMI changes are described in more detail below.

Case-Mix Index Change.   The CMI is the average DRG weight for all cases paid under PPS. It measures the relative costliness of the patients treated in each hospital or group of hospitals. However, an increase in the CMI may result from either changes in patient resource use or refinement of medical record documentation and coding practices. Changes in patient resource use may be due to treating patients who are more severely ill or to providing more complex services. These reflect real changes in the costliness of treatment. Refinement of medical record documentation and coding practices, on the other hand, may result in higher payment but does not reflect changes in treatment costs.

The CMI has increased each year since the implementation of PPS. The CMI for all hospitals was 1.048 in 1981 (pre-PPS) and increased to 1.319 by fiscal year 1989. Between fiscal years 1984 and 1989, the CMI increased at an average annual rate of 3.2 percent. From 1988 to 1989, the increase was 2.8 percent.

The largest single-year increase in the CMI occurred in the first year of PPS. This increase coincided with the introduction of financial incentives to improve coding completeness and accuracy, and with large shifts of patients to outpatient settings. Another major increase occurred in fiscal year 1988, when changes in the structure of several DRGs provided hospitals with new incentives for more complete coding. . . .

Changes in PPS Discharges.   Medicare discharges from PPS hospitals decreased dramatically during the first few years of PPS. The drop in discharges was much greater for rural than urban hospitals, and the declines were largest for the smallest rural and smallest urban hospitals. Discharges also declined less in major teaching hospitals than in other hospitals. By the fifth year of PPS, however, discharges had begun to increase. During the sixth year, total PPS discharges rose by 1.1 percent, still substantially less than the annual increase in Medicare enrollment.

Changes in Operating Costs per Discharge.   Except for the first year of PPS, operating costs per discharge have grown at a fairly constant rate, between 9.0 percent and 10.6 percent per year. In the first year, operating costs per discharge grew by only 1.9 percent. The increase in the sixth year was 9.7 percent. The cumulative growth in operating costs per discharge under PPS is projected to be almost 95 percent by the eighth year. This increase has far exceeded that in the PPS market basket (the index of the cost of inputs used to produce care for Medicare patients), although it slowed somewhat relative to the market basket in the sixth year. The increase in operating costs per discharge has been more than twice the 41 percent increase in the market basket through the eighth year of PPS.

The pattern of change in operating costs per discharge varies slightly across the different hospital groups. Sole community hospitals consistently had lower than average cost per case increases in each of the first six years of PPS. Through the first four years, major teaching hospitals also had slower growth in costs per case. In the sixth year, rural hospitals with 200 or more beds and rural referral centers had the fastest growth in per-case costs, over 11 percent, and rural hospitals with fewer than 50 beds had the slowest growth, about 5 percent.

Changes in Payments per Discharge.   Payments per discharge increased by 18.5 percent in the first year of PPS and 10.3 percent in the second year. In the third year, they grew by only 3.2 percent, but they have since accelerated. In the fourth through sixth years, the increase in payments per discharge has been between 5.0 percent and 5.7 percent. PPS payments per discharge have grown much more rapidly than the update factor in every year. This is primarily due to CMI increases, as discussed above. In the first eight years of PPS, the update factor has increased payment rates by a cumulative 28 percent. Total PPS payments per discharge, however, have risen an estimated 80 percent.

There has been considerably more variation across hospital groups in PPS payments per case than in costs per case. During the first year of PPS, urban hospitals had a substantially higher per-case payment increase than rural hospitals, 19.8 percent compared with 11.6 percent. More recently, however, rural hospitals have had larger increases in payments than urban hospitals. This reflects payment policy changes as discussed above. . . .

Summary.   Payment variables, which are intended to correct for circumstances beyond the hospital's control, influence but do not completely determine performance under PPS. Teaching hospitals and hospitals that receive DSH payments are more likely to be winners under PPS. However, a number of hospitals that do not offer teaching programs and do not receive DSH payments are also successful under PPS. Moreover, there are hospitals that receive IME and DSH payments that are losers under PPS. The case-mix index and the wage index appear to have no consistent effect.

Winners are hospitals that reduced length of stay, controlled labor costs in relation to others in their market area or state, and offered more services to attract patients. At least in urban areas, winning hospitals also used less expensive mixes of labor. For rural hospitals, winning depended on slowing the decline in admissions and improving their share of area admissions. These factors are generally within the hospital's control, suggesting that hospitals can influence their own performance under PPS, at least to some extent, through good management. . . .

UNCOMPENSATED CARE

Uncompensated care costs, encompassing both charity care and bad debts, can have a substantial deleterious effect on hospital financial condition. Most nonpaying patients have no health insurance, while some have inadequate insurance and others, including some Medicare patients, are unable to pay required coinsurance payments.

The Trend in Uncompensated Care

Hospital uncompensated care costs have grown steadily throughout the 1980s. Before PPS, hospitals devoted about 5 percent of their resources to providing uncompensated care. However, overall cost growth slowed with the introduction of PPS, while the amount of uncompensated care provided accelerated. By 1986, uncompensated care accounted for 6.4 percent of total costs. The situation has improved slightly since that time, suggesting that expanded eligibility for Medicaid and other charity care programs in some states may have had a beneficial effect.

The financial impact of uncompensated care has been exacerbated by the failure of subsidies from state and local governments, which offset uncompensated care losses, to keep pace with hospital cost inflation. Increases in these subsidies lagged behind rising uncompensated care costs in the years preceding PPS, primarily because local governments were having to contend with double-digit growth in overall hospital costs. In 1984, conversely, there was a large increase in subsidy payments, made possible at least in part by a dramatic decline in overall hospital cost inflation in response to PPS. Further, state and local governments were able to keep up with the trend in total costs through 1987. But by 1989, as recessionary pressures began affecting government expenditures and tax receipts, operating subsidy payments from tax appropriations actually declined. Federally mandated expansions in Medicaid eligibility may have at least slightly reduced the need for subsidy payments to cover uncompensated care costs during this period.

The Distribution of Uncompensated Care Costs

Uncompensated care has traditionally been associated with large, inner-city teaching hospitals and with publicly owned institutions. But over the last decade, the problem has increasingly affected the entire industry. Most important, uncompensated care is not only an urban problem. After offsetting government operating subsidies, uncompensated care commands the same proportion of hospital resources in rural areas as in urban areas. Public hospitals continue to provide the most uncompensated care, but the proportion of all unpaid care costs net of subsidy borne by these hospitals has declined from 24 percent in 1980 to 17 percent in 1989. Similarly, the proportion provided by major teaching hospitals has decreased from 22 percent to 18 percent, and the proportion for hospitals located in the central city portion of large metropolitan areas has fallen from 72 percent to 67 percent.

A number of factors may have contributed to the spread of the uncompensated care burden beyond public, major teaching, and inner-city hospitals. Public hospitals have been under increasing financial pressure in recent years. Many have had to downsize and are operating at virtual capacity, which may have prevented some uninsured patients from being able to seek care at these hospitals. There also have been expanded rules requiring all hospitals to treat emergency patients regardless of their ability to pay. This may have prompted some private hospitals to cut down on their economic transfers to public hospitals. In addition, the 1980s have seen a major shift in population from central cities to suburban areas. This has included some low-income and uninsured people, who then might be expected to seek care at suburban hospitals. Finally, an increasing proportion of uncompensated care losses is coming from patients who have insurance, but cannot afford ever-larger deductibles and coinsurance payments. These patients can be found in community hospitals everywhere.

While charity care and bad debts have become a significant financial burden for a greater number and variety of hospitals, the amount of uncompensated care provided by individual hospitals varies within all of the standard hospital groups. There is substantial variation in the proportion of hospital resources devoted to uncompensated care in both urban and rural areas, among regions of the country, and among specific large cities and metropolitan areas. The distribution is equally widespread among both teaching and nonteaching hospitals, and even among government hospitals. This tremendous diversity complicates the task of addressing uncompensated care in payment policy.

Although a hospital's uncompensated care burden is an important determinant of its overall financial position, the Commission believes that it is not the only significant payment factor. Medicaid payment shortfalls, while less in aggregate than uncompensated care losses, have risen dramatically during the 1980s. These losses, along with uncompensated care costs, put downward pressure on hospital profit margins. Another factor regarded as important in explaining differences in financial performance is the degree to which hospitals can generate revenues from privately insured patients through payments that are higher than costs. This practice has been called cost shifting. The Prospective Payment Assessment Commission (ProPAC) is planning a comprehensive study of cost shifting to nongovernment payers, including the role of uncompensated care costs and Medicaid payment shortfalls, in the coming year. . . .

CONCLUSION

More data on hospital financial performance are available than ever before. Yet even with these data, which raise many new questions as others are answered, it remains difficult to assess the effects of PPS.

The information presented here and the questions it raises underscore the complexity of health policy decision making. In the case of PPS, Medicare has a responsibility to pay hospitals adequately and fairly for the services they provide to beneficiaries, while encouraging both the optimal quality of care and the efficient provision of services. At the same time, Medicare is usually not the dominant source of hospital payment. Understanding how Medicare and other sources of payment interact to affect both costs and revenues is critical to the development of hospital payment policy. These interactions affect both the availability and quality of hospital care, not only for Medicare beneficiaries but for all Americans.

In accordance with the expanded scope of responsibilities given to the Commission in OBRA 1990, ProPAC will devote a greater portion of its resources to analyzing issues of overall financial status. This continues to include measuring total margins and other financial indicators relating to both operating and capital costs. But it also encompasses expanded analysis of other providers such as skilled nursing facilities, home health agencies, and ambulatory surgery centers. In addition, the Commission will examine the relationship among the Medicare program, the Medicaid program, uncompensated care, and commercial payers. These analyses will help to strike an appropriate balance between the objectives of PPS payment and the broader implications of PPS and other Medicare payment decisions for hospitals and other providers, as well as the patients they treat.

NOTE

1. These figures are based on unpublished estimates prepared by the Congressional Budget Office in February 1991. Estimates provided by the Office of the Actuary, Health Care Financing Administration, are similar.

Health *involves body, mind and spirit . . . an idea that stretches back
into antiquity . . . Considering how modern understanding of those
parts of the human condition are divided among so many different
specialists, it is small wonder that we know so little about
health. . . .*
— Eric Cassell

Bradford H. Gray

The Performance of For-Profit and Nonprofit Health Care Organizations

. . . The hospital field embodies most of the issues involved in the increasing profit orientation of the health care system. Also worth noting is the fact that developments in the hospital field have produced criticism not only of for-profit ownership (criticisms, incidentally, that are very similar to those made of other types of for-profit health care organizations) but also of the *nonprofits*—pertaining both to social responsibility and to justifications for tax exemptions. More so among hospitals than other types of health care organizations, the comparative behavior of for-profit and nonprofit organizations has public policy implications for *both* sectors.

This article focuses on comparative evidence about the performance of for-profit and nonprofit hospitals and the implications of changing economic conditions in the industry. . . .

DIFFERENCES ASSOCIATED WITH PROPERTY RIGHTS

. . . Three different arguments about the comparative behavior of for-profit and nonprofit health care organizations are that for-profit ownership is worse in some respects, that it is better, or that type of ownership makes little real difference. The first two arguments rest on a key distinction between the two types: the presence in for-profit organizations, as opposed to nonprofit organizations, of owners who have a property right to their share of the organization's profits.

To critics this means that for-profit providers of health care will tend to respond poorly in some crucial situations, such as when a patient who

Bradford H. Gray, Ph.D., is Professor Adjunct of Research and Public Health and Sociology Director at the Institution for Social and Policy Studies, Yale University, and Director of the Yale Program on Nonprofit Organizations.

Abridged from Gray, B.H. (1991). Performance of for-profit and nonprofit health care organizations. In Bradford H. Gray, *Profit Motive and Patient Care: The Changing Accountability of Doctors and Hospitals*. Cambridge, MA: Harvard University Press. Copyright © 1991 by the Twentieth Century Fund. Reprinted by permission of the publisher.

lacks the means to pay requires care, when there is a need in the community for a service that cannot be provided profitably, or when decisions must be made whether to invest in activities such as clinical research and education that are substantially public goods.[1] The advocates of for-profit health care argue that socially responsible behavior is not limited to any one type of institution,[2] and that the owners' interest in the profits of for-profit organizations provides incentives that make these organizations more efficient than nonprofits.[3]

The question of who is entitled to any income generated by the organization may not, however, be as crucial in shaping organizational behavior as is the environment in which the organization operates. As Paul DiMaggio and Walter W. Powell have observed, organizations in the same field tend to take on a degree of similarity (isomorphism).[4] This occurs because organizations in the same field may face similar competitive conditions, because they may have to meet common requirements (for example, accreditation or certification), and because of imitation.

There are reasons, therefore, to predict either differences or similarities in the behavior of for-profit and nonprofit organizations, differences that could affect patients, physicians, payers, and public policy. . . .

HOSPITALS AND THE COST QUESTION

The comparative economic behavior of for-profit and nonprofit hospitals has been more extensively studied than any other aspect of their activity. Research on the theoretically interesting question of whether for-profits are indeed more efficient than nonprofits has produced answers that range from equivocal to negative. Research making the more practical comparison of the direct cost to purchasers of care shows clearly that it has cost more to buy hospital services from for-profit hospitals than from nonprofit hospitals. . . .

Cost to the Payer

. . . Even if there are good methodological reasons for researchers who are interested in the efficiency hypothesis to "adjust" the nonprofits' expenses upward to compensate for the effects of taxes not paid and charitable contributions received, and to adjust the for-profits' expenses downward to correct for the distorting effects of their high capital expenses, those adjustments are irrelevant to the payer. Payers' expenditures until recent years were based either on their reimbursing hospitals on the basis of conventionally accounted-for costs, as with Medicare's cost-based reimbursement, or on their paying the hospital's charges for services it provided.

Six studies of hospital prices (that is, of the cost to the payer) . . . found that the cost to payers that reimbursed hospitals for allowable costs was from 8 to 15 percent higher in investor-owned chain hospitals than in nonprofit hospitals. These higher costs stemmed not only from the previously mentioned factors (for example, the for-profits' acquisition patterns), but also from the Medicare reimbursement formula that included a return-on-equity payment only for for-profit institutions. As a result of this formula, for example, the Congressional Budget Office projected Medicare capital reimbursement *per bed* in fiscal 1984 at $7,170 in for-profit hospitals (of which $3,410 was the return-on-equity payment), compared to $3,360 in nonprofit hospitals and $2,230 in public hospitals.[5]

It might be assumed that Medicare's move from a cost-based system based on price (per case) would have hurt the for-profits, with their higher accounting costs, or that in any case the question of comparative cost to that particular payer would no longer be an issue. Available evidence suggests, however, that the earlier picture regarding comparative costs to Medicare may not have changed. Despite their higher historical costs, for-profit hospitals initially had higher profits under the prospective payment system than did nonprofits.[6] The reasons for this probably include the following: (1) artifacts of the period of transition from cost-based to prospective payment and the fact that investor-owned hospitals were concentrated in parts of the country were average lengths of hospital stay were comparatively short even prior to the new system; and (2) the fact that capital costs—a major source of revenues for for-profit hospitals in Medicare's ostensibly cost-based system—continued to be paid under the old cost-based system. Thus, it seems likely that Medicare's cost of purchasing care continues to be higher in for-profit hospitals than in comparable nonprofit hospitals, although no new studies have as yet been done.

For purchasers who pay billed charges, their cost disadvantage in buying services from an investor-owned hospital has been even more pronounced because investor-owned hospitals have higher markups than nonprofit hospitals.[7] Studies found the price per admission for charge-paying patients to be from 17 to 24 percent higher in investor-owned hospitals than in nonprofit hospitals.[8] On a per-day basis the difference was even more dramatic, with charges 23 to 29 percent higher in investor-owned hospitals than in nonprofits.[9] It is not known how growing competitive pressures in the 1980s affected these price differences.

Thus, available evidence does not support the notion that for-profit hospitals are more efficient than nonprofits, and there is strong evidence that from the purchaser's standpoint, for-profit hospitals have been substantially more expensive. It is worth noting here, however, that data about comparative costs in hospitals cannot be generalized to other types of health care organizations. . . .

THE QUALITY-OF-CARE QUESTION

Is the quality of care better or worse in for-profit than in nonprofit institutions? Although clear theoretical reasons can be offered to support the expectation that for-profits would be more efficient or would provide less charity care, it is less clear why people expect a difference between for-profits and nonprofits in quality of care.

One answer to why profit status might affect quality has been offered by Burton A. Weisbrod and Mark Schlesinger, who observe that there are aspects of quality that the market can detect and aspects that it cannot.[10] For-profit organizations, they hypothesize, may perform better than the nonprofits with regard to the tangible aspects of quality care but worse on those aspects of care in which quality is more subtle and, thus, difficult for the recipient to evaluate. This intriguing hypothesis faces two difficulties, however. First, testing it would require that researchers find measures of quality that the market cannot detect; if such measures were readily available, presumably the market would be making use of them. Second, in hospitals the most direct customers are physicians, and they *do* have the ability to assess the quality of hospital services. If physicians act in the best interests of their patients, there would seem to be little competitive advantage accruing to hospitals that reduce quality in ways that are unacceptable to physicians.

This may explain why studies have generally found no substantial differences in quality of care between investor-owned and nonprofit hospitals. Two early studies of malpractice cases in the 1970s found no evidence of any overrepresentation of for-profit hospitals.[11] The Institute of Medicine examined a much larger body of evidence on such indicators of quality as hospital accreditation, board certification of staff physicians, numbers of nursing personnel, and mortality from several elective surgical procedures. Differences were small and did not consistently favor either ownership form; the IOM committee concluded that there is "no overall pattern of either inferior or superior quality in investor-owned chain hospitals as compared to not-for-profit hospitals."[12]

The rise of the investor-owned hospital companies may actually have improved quality in the hospitals they acquired. Some hospitals were available for acquisition because of their unsound financial situation, a factor that could detract from quality.[13] Many hospitals purchased by investor-owned companies were subsequently renovated or replaced. Also, most hospitals that were bought by these companies had previously been independent proprietaries, which were often undercapitalized and did not have to compete for the patients of their physician-owners.[14] Accreditation rates are much lower among proprietary hospitals than hospitals owned by investor-owned chains.[15]

The incentives in the era of cost-based and charge-based payment systems gave hospitals no reason to compromise on quality, particularly since they were competing for the allegiance of admitting physicians. But with Medicare shifting to a per-case payment system, and with competition growing among hospitals for the business of charge-paying purchasers of care, hospitals have been given powerful incentives to cut costs. Might the new incentives be so powerful—particularly at for-profit hospitals—as to overwhelm the factors that encourage high quality (scruples, fear of liability, the continuing need to satisfy physicians)? . . .

It is clear that continued improvement is needed in the measurement of quality of care, and additional analyses of ownership-related differences in quality are called for. Past absence of differences cannot be projected into the future with confidence, particularly since the circumstances that caused them are so poorly understood.

PROVISION OF UNCOMPENSATED OR UNPROFITABLE SERVICES

As recipients and dispensers of charitable contributions and government support, hospitals have long helped fill gaps in the financing of medical services. Various estimates over the last decade have shown that 31 million to 37 million Americans lack health insurance, and hospitals that serve them often lose money in the process. Furthermore, some services offered by hospitals generate costs that exceed revenues.

The most common objection to for-profit health care is the presumed unwillingness of for-profit organizations to serve patients who cannot pay for care or to provide necessary but unprofitable services. Some critics have been content to assume that a striking contrast with nonprofit organizations exists. . . . However, nonprofit hospitals, like investor-owned hospitals, are under strong pressure to perform well economically.

The presumption that for-profit hospitals do not provide uncompensated care or unprofitable services is clearly not correct. American Hospital Association data show that the uncompensated care (bad debt plus charity) in for-profit hospitals amounts to approximately 3 or 4 percent of revenues,[16] and a national survey in the early 1980s showed that 6 percent of the patients admitted at the average for-profit hospital were uninsured.[17] In a few for-profit hospitals (3.1 percent) more than one-fifth of the patients were uninsured.[18] Documented cases of refusal to provide services to patients who need care but who lack the means to pay have not been peculiar to investor-owned hospitals and have involved only a very small proportion of them.[19]

Regarding presumed unprofitable services, there are numerous examples of for-profit hospitals' providing virtually any service that can be cited.[20] Many investor-owned hospitals have neonatal intensive care centers, and more than 90 percent of investor-owned hospitals with more than 50 beds have emergency departments. In the early 1980s even the investor-owned hospitals' lack of involvement in teaching and research activities underwent a change.[21]

Yet, a listing of the unprofitable activities of for-profit organizations should not obscure their basic for-profit purpose: to generate a return on investment. The pursuit of profit does not require—and may not be facilitated by—an attempt to make a profit on each and every service or patient. Other factors also play a role. Under some circumstances a hospital may risk civil liability or expulsion from the Medicare program if it refuses to provide urgently needed care. Moreover, hospitals' concern for their reputation and image in the community sometimes encourages behavior that cannot be justified solely on short-term economic grounds. The need to maintain good relations with the physicians who admit paying patients may sometimes make it expedient for a hospital to offer certain services that are not themselves profitable, or may make it prudent to allow a staff physician to admit a patient who lacks the means to pay. Also, a certain level of bad debt is inevitable in a business in which services often must be provided in advance of payment. Some services that a hospital offers may generate both bad debt and revenue. For example, an emergency room will inevitably bring in some bad debt, but a hospital may nevertheless find it profitable to have an emergency department because one-half of hospital admissions commonly come by that route.

For such reasons it makes little sense to analyze the behavior of for-profit hospitals by comparing them with hypothetical models of expected behavior. Comparisons with nonprofit hospitals are much more useful because the nonprofits predominate and are expected to behave in some measure as charitable institutions.[22] When comparisons are made, however, they raise as many questions about the nonprofit sector as about for-profits. This occurs, in part, because the consequences of using *national* data for such comparisons are not always recognized.

Analyses of two sources of national data on hospitals' service to patients who lack the means to pay have found differences that are surprisingly small in light of common perceptions about for-profit and nonprofit organizations. In 1982 the Office for Civil Rights in the Department of Health and Human Services (DHHS) conducted a national census of hospitals, which were asked to report admissions by payment source for a two-week period. Although nonprofit hospitals had a larger percentage of uninsured and Medicaid patients than did for-profit hospitals, the differences were small. The contrast with public hospitals makes the similarity between the for-profits and the nonprofits more striking. The other source of national data—surveys by the American Hospital Association—have shown similarly minor differences.[23] For example, in 1983 uncompensated care (bad debt and charity) in nonprofit hospitals amounted to 4.2 percent of gross patient revenues, compared to 3.1 percent in for-profit hospitals. In 1982 the difference was even smaller, and in nonmetropolitan areas for-profit hospitals reported slightly *higher* levels of uncompensated care than did nonprofits.

Figures such as these have contributed to the widespread perception in health policy circles that there is little or no difference between for-profit and nonprofit hospitals beyond their tax status. These data, however, do not actually measure the extent to which hospitals serve patients who lack the means to pay,[24] and the AHA data—voluntary and self-reported as they are—are subject to many sorts of bias. Investor-owned hospitals tended not to respond to the financial portions of the AHA survey on which uncompensated care percentages were based.

Another national study, published in 1990, showed more substantial national differences between nonprofits and for-profits. Richard Frank, David Salkever, and Fitzhugh Mullan analyzed the data on the approximately 200,000 patients who were discharged annually from the hospitals participating in the National Hospital Discharge Survey between 1979 and 1984.[25] The numbers pertain to *patients* discharged from these hospitals, rather than *dollars* from different sources of payment. In the six years covered by the study, nonprofit hospitals (reported separately for church affiliated and nonchurch affiliated) served from 3 to 4 percent more uncompensated and Medicaid patients than did the for-profits. A contrast with public hospitals is also apparent.

Because investor-owned hospitals are heavily concentrated in certain states, national comparisons of for-profit and nonprofit hospitals inevitably mean that hospitals operating under different circumstances are being compared. This is an important point, because on at least two highly relevant matters—the presence of public hospitals and the adequacy of Medicaid programs—conditions vary widely from state to state. This means that the number of poor, uninsured people who potentially depend for care on the willingness of private hospitals (whether for-profit or nonprofit) to serve them also varies from state to state. The national data about nonprofit hospitals are influenced by the fact that in many states where they are located (and where there are few if any for-profit hospitals), the overall level of uncompensated care is very low because of state mechanisms that in effect compensate hospitals for providing charity care (as in Maryland, Massachusetts, New Jersey, and New York). In many other states where nonprofits are plentiful but for-profits are not, the Medicaid program covers a comparatively high percentage of the poverty population (as in Indiana, Michigan, and Pennsylvania). Thus, the national figures on uncompensated care are substantially influenced by the nonprofit hospitals' disproportionate presence in states where there is a comparatively heavy governmental presence and where the need for uncompensated care is, accordingly, comparatively low.[26]

It should be noted that this pattern is not due to nonprofit hospitals' having selected such states as places to locate. In most instances the hospitals predated the state programs. The operative factor seems to be that investor-owned hospitals tend *not* to locate in states with a heavy regulatory environment; those states have done disproportionately more to finance care for people who lack the means to pay.

. . . Although it is undoubtedly true that a hospital's location and educational activities influence the extent of its uncompensated care, this interpretation of the data concedes a major difference between sectors—the range of types and locales of hospitals—that is directly relevant to the point that the nonprofit sector is more responsive than for-profits to local needs that cannot be met profitably.

Several other differences between for-profit and nonprofit hospitals show the latter to be more involved in activities that do not provide an economic return. Even though the investor-owned companies started becoming active in medical education and research in the 1980s, the examples either were isolated or were part of a strategy to build a regional patient care network that would provide marketing advantages. Except for a handful of examples, major teaching hospitals remain either nonprofit or public in ownership; the number of investor-owned hospitals with teaching programs remains very small.[27]

In addititon, nonprofit hospitals tend to offer a wider range of services than do investor-owned hospitals of similar size.[28] Although there are no direct data regarding the profitability of specific services at particular hospitals, the services that are less common in investor-owned hospitals include many that are often unprofitable: intensive-care nurseries, outpatient departments, family planning services, and many others. Nonprofit hospitals are more likely than investor-owned hospitals to offer outpatient services that they report to be unprofitable.[29]

. . . Schlesinger, Marmor, and Smithey offer several intriguing, if somewhat speculative, empirical generalizations. First, the type of service makes a difference in the consequences of type of ownership, in part because of the role of physicians:

> For health services in which physicians play an important role, facility ownership has little effect on quality or cost, although under some circumstances for-profit ownership may increase costs of care.
>
> In services in which professionals have a smaller role, proprietary services are less costly than those offered in nonprofit settings. For such services, however, investor-owned facilities are also disproportionately represented among the institutions offering very low quality treatment. Thus, where professional norms do not mediate the influence of ownership, there appears to be a trade-off between less costly services and a greater risk of exploitation of patients by providers interested in short-term profits.[30]

In addition, there is some evidence to suggest that the for-profit–nonprofit composition of an area of service delivery often goes through several stages. At first, services are offered in predominantly nonprofit settings (in part because reimbursement is limited or unavailable). Then demand grows and exceeds the capacity of nonprofit organizations because their ambition for expansion or their access to capital is limited. In this stage, for-profit facilities may play a leading role in expanding access to services. In later stages, as demand stabilizes, the ability of for-profits to attract capital becomes less of a factor in providing access to services, and the growing competitive situation begins to influence the behavior of nonprofits—perhaps leading them to introduce additional restrictions on access.

This analysis suggests that public policy should take account of the stage of development of a field, perhaps encouraging for-profits during the stage when demand is growing but favoring nonprofits when demand is stable.

. . . The comparative behavior of for-profit and nonprofit health care organizations is not carved in stone. Expectations for nonprofit health care organizations should rest on more than assumptions about their behavior. By the same token, criticisms should be based on a realistic assessment of their resources. Though unsatisfactory to people who want a simple, unambiguous conclusion, the evidence . . . suggests that both for-profit and nonprofit forms of ownership may serve legitimate purposes in health care.

For-profits play a particularly important role in periods of rapid increases in demand, while nonprofits do so where there are serious flaws in the operation of market mechanisms, as when adequate payment is lacking or when the market has difficulty detecting differences in quality. . . . The comparative immobility of nonprofits' capital and their ability to draw on community support are sources of stability.

On economic measures, the relative performance of for-profit and nonprofit health care organizations appears to depend on a number of circumstances—the type of service that is involved, incentives built into payment systems, the role of physicians in making decisions that affect expenditures, and market niche. There are circumstances in which nonprofit organizations clearly provide care in a more economical fashion from the payer's standpoint. Whether because of their conception of mission or the fact that they must expend surplus revenues for the purposes for which they are chartered, it appears that nonprofits behave differently from for-profits at the margin. In nursing homes, for example, they appear more likely to spend money on enhanced quality than on expansion. In hospitals they seem more inclined to respond to needs that cannot necessarily be met profitably and to forgo opportunities to increase prices.

NOTES

1. The most influential and persistent critic of for-profit health care has been Arnold S. Relman, editor of the *New England Journal of Medicine*. See Arnold S. Relman, "The New Medical-Industrial Complex," *New England Journal of Medicine*, October 23, 1980, pp. 963–969; and Arnold S. Relman and Uwe Reinhardt, "An Exchange on For-Profit Health Care," in Bradford H. Gray, ed. *For-Profit Enterprise in Health Care* (Washington, D.C.: National Academy Press, 1986), pp. 209–223.

2. Michael Bromberg, "The Medical-Industrial Complex: Our National Defense," *New England Journal of Medicine*, November 24, 1983, pp. 1314–15.

3. See, for example, Frank A. Sloan, "Property Rights in the Hospital Industry," pp. 103–141 in H. E. Frech III, *Health Care in America* (San Francisco: Pacific Research Institute for Public Policy, 1988); and Regina Herzlinger and William S. Krasker, "Who Profits from Nonprofits?" *Harvard Business Review* 65 (January–February 1987): 93–105. Of course, there are difficulties in knowing what efficiency means in health care, where products are far from standardized. For example, hospitals may differ in their costs of caring for particular kinds of patients because patients are discharged earlier in the course of their recovery from one hospital than from another. Family members may provide care in one instance that is provided in the hospital in another. From the standpoint of the purchaser, one hospital might be less costly than the other; but because the two hospitals are not providing identical sets of services, it is difficult to reach conclu-

sions about efficiency. Comparisons of the costliness of services provided by different hospitals may be influenced by such factors as differences in the severity of illness of patients, recent renovations or major capital expenditures, or location in an area where wages are comparatively high. These are all factors that researchers attempt to adjust for, with varying degrees of success, in comparing the costliness or efficiency of the services provided by different types of hospitals.

4. Paul DiMaggio and Walter W. Powell, "The Iron Cage Revisited: Institutional Isomorphism and Collective Rationality in Organizational Fields," *American Sociological Review* 82 (1983): 147–160.

5. Memorandum dated March 16, 1983, from Paul Ginsburg of Congressional Budget Office to John Kern, staff of House Ways and Means Committee.

6. This was documented in a study by the Office of the Inspector General, Department of Health and Human Services; see also Bernard Friedman and Stephen Shortell, "The Financial Performance of Selected Investor-Owned and Not-For-Profit System Hospitals before and after Medicare Prospective Payment," *Health Services Research* 23 (June 1988): 237–267.

7. Gray, *For-Profit Enterprise in Health Care*, p. 81. See also Thomas G. Rundall, Shoshanna Sofaer, and Wendy Lambert, "Uncompensated Hospital Care in California: Private and Public Hospital Responses to Competitive Market Forces," *Advances in Health Economics and Health Services Research* 9 (1988): 113–133, particularly Table 5.

8. Gray, *For-Profit Enterprise in Health Care,* p. 80.

9. Ibid.

10. Burton A. Weisbrod and Mark Schlesinger, "Public, Private, Nonprofit Ownership and the Response to Asymmetric Information: The Case of Nursing Homes," Discussion Paper no. 209, University of Wisconsin Center for Health Economics and Law, Madison, 1983.

11. Lewin and Associates examined data from Jury Verdict Research, Inc., on malpractice convictions against a sample of 345 hospitals between 1970 and 1974 and found that in the 23 cases, the percentages of nonprofit, proprietary, and investor-owned chain hospitals "approximately match[ed] the proportion of hospitals in each category in the sample as a whole." Health Services Foundation (Blue Cross), *Investor-Owned Hospitals: An Examination of Performance* (Chicago: Health Services Foundation, 1976). The National Association of Insurance Commissioners (NAIC) published data from 128 insurers on 71,782 malpractice claims closed between July 1, 1975, and December 31, 1978. *NAIC Malpractice Claims, 1975–1978* 2, no. 2 (1980). Approximately one-third of those were against hospitals. Of the 8,042 closed malpractice claims against hospitals whose ownership type was known, 11.5 percent were against for-profit hospitals, 76.9 percent were against nonprofit hospitals, and 11.6 percent were against nonfederal public hospitals. During that period approximately 8.3 percent of admissions to community hospitals were to for-profit institutions, 70.6 percent were to nonprofit hospitals, and 21.1 percent were to public hospitals. Data calculated for 1978 from American Hospital Association, *Hospital Statistics* (Chicago: American Hospital Association, 1980), p. 6, Table 1. (The NAIC data were not limited to community hospitals.) Thus, although public hospitals were sued at a rate somewhat lower than expected, there was only a slight difference between for-profit and nonprofit hospitals.

12. Bradford H. Gray and Walter J. McNerney, "For-Profit Enterprise in Health Care," *New England Journal of Medicine,* June 5, 1986, p. 1526.

13. Robert V. Pattison, "Response to Financial Incentives among Investor-Owned and Not-For-Profit Hospitals: An Analysis Based on California Data, 1978–82," in Gray, *For-Profit Enterprise in Health Care,* p. 301. A further clue about the comparatively poor economic health of acquired institutions is the finding that acquired hospitals had comparatively low occupancy rates. Ross M. Mullner and Ronald M. Andersen, "A Descriptive and Financial Ratio Analysis of Merged and Consolidated Hospitals: United States, 1980–1985," *Advances in Health Economics and Health Services Research* 7 (1987): 41–58.

14. Elizabeth W. Hoy and Bradford H. Gray, "Trends in the Growth of the Major Investor-Owned Hospital Companies," in Gray, *For-Profit Enterprise in Health Care,* pp. 250–259.

15. Gray, *For-Profit Enterprise in Health Care,* p. 129.

16. Frank A. Sloan, Joseph Valvona, and Ross Mullner, "Identifying the Issues: A Statistical Profile," in Frank A. Sloan, James F. Blumstein, and James J. Perrin, eds., *Uncompensated Hospital Care: Rights and Responsibilities* (Baltimore: Johns Hopkins University Press, 1986); Gray, *For-Profit Enterprise in Health Care,* p. 102.

17. Data from an unpublished paper by Diane Rowland based on 1981 survey by the Office for Civil Rights in the Department of Health and Human Services. See Gray, *For-Profit Enterprise in Health Care,* p. 101.

18. Ibid.

19. Office of Inspector General, *Semi-Annual Report to the Congress, October 1, 1987–March 31, 1988* (Washington, D.C.: Department of Health and Human Services, 1988), pp. 30–31. The handful of hospitals that have been publicly identified include both nonprofit and investor-owned institutions. See, for example, Sandy Lutz, "Texas Attorney General Files 'Patient Dumping' Lawsuit," *Modern Healthcare,* February 12, 1988, p. 4.

20. See Gray, *For-Profit Enterprise in Health Care,* pp. 121–126.

21. See ibid., chap. 7; Richard McK. F. Southby and Warren Greenberg, eds., *The For-Profit Hospital* (Columbus, Ohio: Battelle Press, 1986); and American Medical Association, *The Investor-Related Academic Health Center and Medical Education: An Uncertain Courtship* (Chicago: American Medical Association, 1986).

22. Comparisons with publicly owned facilities may also seem warranted because all sources of data show that they provide much higher levels of uncompensated care than do either for-profit or nonprofit hospitals. Because public hospitals are financed in part by government appropriations, however, and those appropriations depend in part on the organization's financial circumstances, it is difficult to compare the behavior of public and pri-

vate institutions, and even more difficult to interpret it.

23. Gray, *For-Profit Enterprise in Health Care,* pp. 101–102.

24. Not all uninsured patients lack the means to pay. Bad debt may not reflect volition on the hospital's part and may represent only a share (the deductibles remaining after insurance coverage) of a given patient's bill. "Charity care" figures are notoriously subject to manipulation by nonprofit hospitals seeking to discharge the "free care" obligations that came with grants under the Hill-Burton program.

25. Richard G. Frank, David S. Salkever, and Fitzhugh Mullan, "Hospital Ownership and the Care of Uninsured and Medicaid Patients: Findings from the National Hospital Discharge Survey 1979–1984," *Health Policy* 14 (1990): 1–11.

26. Lawrence S. Lewin, Timothy J. Eckels, and Dale Roenigk, *Setting the Record Straight: The Provision of Uncompensated Care by Not-For-Profit Hospitals* (Washington, D.C.: Lewin and Associates, 1988).

27. Gray, *For-Profit Enterprise in Health Care,* p. 142.

28. Ibid., pp. 121–126.

29. Stephen M. Shortell et al., "Diversification of Health Care Services: The Effects of Ownership, Environment, and Strategy," *Advances in Health Economics and Health Services Research* 7 (1987): 22–23.

30. Mark Schlesinger, Theodore R. Marmor, and Richard Smithey, "Nonprofit and For-Profit Medical Care: Shifting Roles and Implications for Health Policy," *Journal of Health Politics, Policy, and Law* 12 (Fall 1987): 450.

5

Nursing Homes

Nursing focus on resident needs and outcomes

Charlene Harrington

The Nursing Home Industry: A Structural Analysis

The poor quality of care provided in U.S. nursing homes has long been a matter of concern to consumers, professionals, and policymakers. Recently, the General Accounting Office reported that over one-third of the nation's nursing homes are operating at a substandard level, below minimum federal standards during three consecutive inspections.[1] Among the findings were evidence of untrained staff, inadequate provision of health care, unsanitary conditions, poor food, unenforced safety regulations, and many other problems.[1,2] No other segment of the health care industry has been documented to have such poor quality of care. Despite a large infusion of public funds into the nursing home industry over the past twenty-five years, investigations and exposés continue to find inadequate care and patient abuse.[1]

In 1986, the Institute of Medicine's Study on Nursing Home Regulation reported widespread quality-of-care problems and recommended the strengthening of federal regulations for nursing homes.[2] These recommendations, as well as the active efforts of many consumer advocacy and professional organizations, in 1987 resulted in Congress passing a major reform of nursing home regulation, the first significant changes since Medicare and Medicaid were adopted in 1965.[3] Congress has made enhanced regulatory efforts a priority, in spite of the costs associated with regulation, in an effort to improve quality of care and to protect residents from abuse.

This article examines the structural features of the nursing home market and the industry itself in an effort to identify factors related to poor quality of care. We argue that regulatory efforts, while essential, are not sufficient to improve the overall quality of nursing home care. Rather, efforts to develop structural reforms will be seen as necessary to make nursing home care

Charlene Harrington, Ph.D., R.N., F.A.A.N., is Associate Director of the Institute for Health & Aging, and Professor and Chair of the Department of Social and Behavioral Sciences, School of Nursing at the University of California, San Francisco.

From Harrington, C. (1991). The nursing home industry: A structural analysis. In M. Minkler and C.L. Estes, eds., *Political Economy of Aging* (pp. 153–164). Amityville, NY: Baywood Publishing Co. Used with permission of the publisher.

safe, to ensure high quality of care, to preserve the basic rights of residents, and to promote an acceptable quality of life for residents.

INCREASED DEMAND

The quality of nursing homes is receiving national attention as the demand for nursing home services is growing with the increasing numbers of individuals who are aged and chronically ill. In 1987, about 30 million Americans were age 65 and older, and this number is projected to increase to 51 million in 2020.[4] As the population ages and develops chronic illnesses, the need for long-term care, including nursing home services, increases.

The adoption of prospective payment systems for hospitals by Medicare in 1983 resulted in shortened hospital stays and increases in the demand for nursing home care. This policy change resulted in increased numbers of referrals and admissions to nursing homes from hospitals, as well as increased acuity levels of residents in nursing homes.[5] At the same time, the 1988 Health Care Financing Administration (HCFA) Medicare guidelines to the fiscal intermediaries liberalized Medicare coverage for nursing homes.[6] These changes encourage the demand for and use of nursing homes and other long-term care services.

INCREASED COMPLEXITY OF CARE

The demand for increasingly complex services in nursing homes is growing with the aging and disability level of residents. While only 4 percent of the nation's elderly are currently in nursing homes, 88 percent of nursing home residents are age 65 and older.[7] The population in nursing homes is aging so that the median age is 82.[7] The proportion of residents who were 85 years and older rose from 30 to 40 percent between 1976 and 1985[7] and is continuing to rise.

The disability level of nursing home residents is increasing. Between 1976 and 1984, the number of residents who were totally bedfast rose from about 21 to 35 percent of the discharges and the number dependent in mobility and continence increased from 35 to 45 percent.[8] The average resident has about four of six limitations in activities of daily living, and 66 percent have some type of mental impairment or disorder.[7]

As the acuity level of nursing home residents increases, medical technology formerly used only in hospitals is now being used in nursing homes. Thus, the "performance of duties" has become an even more complex task for personnel. The use of intravenous feedings and medication, ventilators, oxygen, special prosthetic equipment and devices, and other technologies has made patient care management more difficult and challenging.[9,10] The appropriate use of technology, the training and skill levels needed by nursing home personnel, and the need for emergency back-up procedures are problems caused by the use of high technology. Thus, changes in the characteristics of residents are placing greater demands on nursing home providers—demands that are frequently beyond the capacity of the current financing and delivery system.

CONSTRAINED SUPPLY

While the demand for increasingly complex nursing home care is growing, the supply of nursing home beds is not keeping pace. The 1985 National Nursing Home Survey reported approximately 19,100 facilities providing care for 1.5 million residents, including hospital-based facilities and residential facilities.[7] About 75 percent of these nursing homes were certified to provide services under Medicare and Medicaid programs. The number of beds grew rapidly after the development of Medicare and Medicaid in 1965 until the 1980s, when the growth slowed to a level below the rate of growth of the aged population.[11] As the supply of beds has been constrained (except in the Southwest), the average occupancy rate has increased to 92 percent nationally.[7] The slowing of growth is the result of complex market factors, including the high costs of capital construction, problems with the labor market, recent lowering of profit rates over previous high levels, and in some states, limits on construction by state regulations.

This limited supply and the high demand for services has created a situation in which nursing homes are able to select the residents they admit. Because they can obtain private-paying residents who can be charged higher daily rates than publicly paid residents, nursing homes prefer private clients and frequently discriminate against those who are on Medicaid.[12] Nursing homes also tend to "cream" or select the least sick patients or those for whom they can provide the most cost-effective care. In some situations, this practice reduces access for individuals with the greatest need and limits consumer choice and the competitive market for services.

HIGH COSTS

The cost of nursing home services is growing rapidly. The nation spent $49 billion on nursing home services in 1989 (8 percent of its total health expenditure) and expects to spend $54.5 billion in 1990, making this segment of the health industry third only to hospitals and physicians.[13] Although the growth in nursing home cost has slowed somewhat, the increase in 1989 was 11.2 percent over the previous year, well beyond the 5 percent rate of inflation.[13]

The growing cost of nursing home care has negative consequences for consumers and public payers. Of the total amount spent, one-half of the revenues come from public sources and one-half from out-of-pocket sources. Medicare pays for less than 2 percent of the public expenditure and Medicaid (for those with low incomes) pays most of the remainder. Because of these costs, most public policy efforts, particularly by state Medicaid programs, are focused on controlling or reducing spending.

Since private insurance for nursing home services is virtually unavailable and currently pays less than 1 percent of the cost, most individuals who require nursing home services for any extended period of time are forced to spend their life savings before they become poor enough to qualify for Medicaid services, which then pay for care. The average annual cost of $29,000 (in 1987) forces many individuals to spend their assets within thirteen weeks of admission to a nursing home.[14] The high cost of care results in inequities, with the greatest access for those with the highest income and limited access for the poor. This situation has fueled the demand for a national health care program for long-term care services.

OWNERSHIP

The nursing home industry has more proprietary ownership and chain ownership than any other segment of the health system, with the exception of the drug industry. In 1985, 75 percent of all nursing homes were profit making, 20 percent were nonprofit, and 5 percent were government owned.[7] A growing number of nursing homes are chain-owned or operated, this segment of the industry having increased its control of the total market dramatically. In 1973, the three largest chains owned 2.2 percent of the beds, but by 1982, they controlled 9.6 percent of the beds.[15] By 1985, chains owned 41 percent of the facilities and 49 percent of the nation's nursing home beds.[7]

Many U.S. for-profit health care chain corporations have become multinational, owning companies in other countries. In 1988, 11 U.S. investor-owned hospital companies owned and operated 116 hospitals with 12,560 beds in 17 foreign countries and managed another 24 hospitals with over 5,000 beds.[13] The large nursing home chains also owned many facilities in foreign countries.

Several factors have contributed to the growth in chain operations. As Hawes and Phillips note, capital reimbursement policies encourage the sale and resale of facilities, and other real estate manipulations favor more sophisticated operators.[15] Increased demand for services, constrained bed supply, high profitability, and the increased complexity required to meet federal certification standards and to obtain public reimbursement also encourage growth.

Nursing home corporations have traditionally been very profitable. For example, Beverly Enterprises had stock price gains of over 700 percent between 1978 and 1981 and National Health Enterprises of 900 percent.[15] Returns on net equity for facilities in California ranged from 58 to 154 percent in 1983 and 1984.[15]

Nursing home profits continued to grow until 1987, when some chains experienced losses. Beverly Enterprises, the largest chain with 16,000 beds, had a loss of $30.5 million in 1987 and continued to lose money through the end of the decade.[16,17] Beverly experienced losses because it incurred large debts from its aggressive expansion policies, but other nursing home chains such as Manor Care and National Medical Enterprises continued to be profitable with 14 to 17 percent returns on equity in 1989 over the previous year and 13 to 22 percentage earnings per share for the past 10-year period.[17]

Nursing home chains have primarily relied on growth through acquisition, which drove bed prices so high that earnings growth did not keep pace with the cost of expansion and which caused high debt-to-capital ratios. Many of these chains have recently been hurt by the expansion of nursing home beds in hospitals, particularly for Medicare patients. Other chains have been affected by the nursing shortage and are reportedly having to increase their wages. Even so, the industry remains profitable, although little new capital is being infused into the market at this time.

One of the major debates in research, policy, and consumer advocacy circles is whether the proprietary nature of the nursing home industry negatively affects access, costs, and quality of care. Access to services is limited to those who can pay privately because proprietary facilities provide little uncompensated care. Costs of care are driven up by the increasing demand for short-term profits.[15] The effect on quality of care has been disputed. A review of research studies on ownership and quality indicates that the preponderance of the evidence suggests the superiority of nonprofits, particularly church-related nonprofits.[15]

STAFFING AND LABOR ISSUES

The staffing and educational levels in nursing homes are low. There are only 5.1 full-time equivalent (FTE) registered nurses (RNs) per 100 patients in nursing homes in contrast with a ratio of 1 RN for every 4.5 patients in hospitals.[18] There are 7.4 FTE licensed practical nurses (LPNs) and 30.8 FTE nursing attendants per 100 patients in nursing homes.[18] Current attendant ratios are sometimes as low as 1 per 15 patients during the day, 1.25 in the evening, and 1.40 to 1.50 at night.[19] Registered nurses spend little time with nursing home residents in direct care. In a recent study, RNs in hospitals spend an average of 45 minutes per patient per day compared to less than 12 minutes for RNs in nursing homes.[20] Nearly 40 percent of the 7,402 nursing homes in the survey reported 6 minutes or less of RN time per patient per day and 60 percent reported no RN hours during the past week.[20] Staffing levels are directly associated with owner-ship, with proprietary facilities having lower staffing levels.[20]

Although the 1987 federal nursing home legislation (OBRA) required additional registered nurses, facilities are still not required to have twenty-four-hour a day registered nursing coverage and the legislation is having only a small impact on nurse staffing levels.[3] The major barrier to improved staffing is the cost to nursing homes, which in turn would necessitate rais-ing Medicaid nursing home reimbursement rates.

Not surprisingly, higher staffing levels in nursing homes have been associated with better nursing care. Spector and Takada, in a study of 2,500 nursing home residents in 80 nursing homes in Rhode Island, found that low levels of staffing in homes with very dependent residents was associated with reduced likelihood of improvement.[21] High catheter use, a low percent of residents receiving skin care, and low participation rates in organized activities were also associated with reduced outcomes, in terms of functional decline and death.[21]

Higher staffing levels could not only improve quality, but could also reduce the cost of hospitalization. A recent study of nursing home resi-dents found that 48 percent of the hospitalizations could have been avoided. Factors such as an insufficient number of adequately trained nursing staff, the inability of nursing staff to administer and monitor intravenous therapy, lack of diagnostic services, and pressure for transfer from the staff and family were found to contribute to hospitalization.[22] The investigators estimated that the 216,000 nursing home residents who are hospitalized might be treated in nursing homes, for a cost savings of $.9 billion in the United States.[22]

Wages and Benefits

Wages and benefits for nursing home employees are scandalously low. Nursing home salaries are estimated to be 20 to 40 percent below the levels for comparable positions in hospitals.[19] Nursing assistants or atten-dants, who make up 63 percent of all nursing home direct care personnel, generally work for minimum wages and few have benefits.

Low wages and benefits are directly reflected in the high turnover rates for nursing home personnel. The overall nursing personnel turnover rates in nursing homes are frequently as high as 55 to 100 percent per year.[19] A number of studies have identified poor working conditions, combined with heavy resident workloads, inadequate training and orientation, and few opportunities for advancement among the factors that contribute to high turnover rates in some facilities.[23] High registered nurse turnover is associated with decreased likelihood of functional improvement.[21] Although high turnover rates are considered undesirable in terms of quality outcomes, nursing homes, like other health facilities, have some economic incentives to encourage high turnover rates to keep wages low. Higher nursing staff turnover rates are associated with proprietary institutions.[20]

Education and Specialty Training of Staff

Nurses working in nursing homes have less education than hospital nurses. Fifty-six percent of all RNs working in nursing homes are diploma prepared nurses, and less than 3 percent have master's degrees.[18] Many nursing homes are unwilling to pay the higher wages required to attract better prepared nurses, yet evidence suggests that gerontological nursing specialists may be cost-effective.

Several geriatric nurse practitioner (GNP) demonstration projects examined the effect of GNPs in the practice setting. One evaluation, which compared 30 nursing homes employing GNPs with 30 matched control homes, found that the use of GNPs resulted in favorable changes in 2 of 8 measures of activities of daily living; 5 of 18 nursing therapies; 2 of 6 drug therapies; and 6 of 8 tracers.[24] The study also reported some reduction in hospital admissions and total days in geriatric nurse practitioner homes.[24]

The Robert Wood Johnson Teaching Nursing Home Demonstration Project was designed to bring nursing schools together with nursing homes to improve nursing education and patient care.[25] In these projects, nurse clinicians and faculty provided direct care to patients and worked as consultants and advisors to staff. The preliminary results find positive outcomes in terms of improving both the process of care and the outcomes of care.[25]

At one demonstration project, the presence of master's prepared nurses resulted in decreases in decubiti, incontinence, dependency, and use of physical restraints, catheters, psychotropic drugs, enemas, and laxatives.[26] Initial results, however, were confounded by a reversal in some of the same outcomes in subsequent years. Another study reported a gradual decline in emergency room visits, hospital admissions, infections, and falls.[27] One study related the presence of clinical specialists with a decrease in nosocomial infections and the use of pharmacologic agents.[28] Although the results of the demonstration projects appear to be positive, foundation support for the teaching nursing homes cannot fund such programs indefinitely. It is hoped that nursing homes will use the research findings to make informed changes in the types of nursing personnel they utilize.

PUBLIC INFORMATION

Public information about the quality of nursing home care, such as nursing home guides or rating systems, is also helpful in improving quality. Consumers requiring nursing home services are vulnerable and lack information on which to base informed choices about which facilities would best meet their needs. Many individuals rely on hospital discharge planners, physicians, and other health professionals for assistance in making plans and decisions regarding nursing home services. Evidence suggests that the discharge planning process is complex and not always operating effectively.[29] Discharge planners and other health professionals frequently have inadequate information on nursing homes and other long-term care provider options, particularly facts on the quality of providers. Public disclosure of administrative information, consumer guides, and rating systems are methods for assisting consumers and health professionals in making more informed decisions in the marketplace.

Expanding public information about nursing home quality may also be valuable in stimulating nursing homes to improve their services. Hospitals compete, to some extent, on the basis of the quality of their nursing services, but nursing homes have generally not done so. The lack of competition is exacerbated by the short supply of nursing homes in some areas of the country.[11] The Institute of Medicine Committee to Study Nursing Home Regulation recommended the development of nursing home rating systems based on quality indicators as one method of pressuring facilities to improve services.[2] Such approaches, which aim to give consumers and professionals greater choice in making informed decisions, are attractive but difficult to develop.

REGULATORY APPROACHES

The 1987 OBRA nursing home reform legislation was the first major legislative improvement in the federal regulation of nursing homes since 1965.[3] The legislation mandates comprehensive assessments of all nursing home residents after admission and periodically so that nursing homes can define the functional, cognitive, and affective levels of residents initially and over time. The legislation requires the development of quality indicators that are more outcome-oriented than process-oriented. Outcome measures include resident behavior, functional and mental status, and resident conditions (such as incontinence, immobility, and decubitus ulcers). More detailed and prescriptive regulations have been drafted to implement the OBRA legislation. For example, the draft regulations establish criteria for and prohibit the use of "unnecessary drugs." The OBRA legislation also requires changes in the federal survey procedures to orient them more toward the rights of residents and enforcement of the law.

The new regulation and enforcement effort should bring about substantial improvements in quality of care. The OBRA regulations appear to have had some beneficial effects already in reducing the use of physical restraints, which are used to tie nursing home residents to beds or chairs. Because the regulations do not allow the inappropriate use of restraints, a number of nursing homes are now reporting new efforts to train staff not to use such restraints and to move toward restraint-free facilities.[30]

SPECIAL INTEREST GROUP POLITICS

Three key special interest groups are involved with nursing home issues: 1) the industry, which is represented by the American Health Care Association and the American Association of Homes for the Aging; 2) the government, with interests split between quality regulators and fiscal agents who pay for services; and 3) the consumer interests, primarily represented by National Citizens' Coalition for Nursing Home Reform (NCCNHR). Both the American Medical Association and the American Nurses' Association have interests in nursing homes, but neither organization has considered these nursing home regulatory issues to be a priority. Although nursing organizations have advocated for improved nursing staff levels and wages and benefits in nursing homes, few nurses working in nursing homes are active members of major nursing organizations. This lack of representation translates into a low organizational priority on nursing home lobbying efforts when organizational resources are limited.

Unfortunately, the special interests of the three major groups are often conflicting and frequently lead to stalemate. The industry is primarily interested in minimizing government regulation of quality and access, while obtaining high government reimbursement rates with minimal strings attached to the funds. The industry wants to increase reimbursement rates substantially, but generally opposes efforts to guarantee that rate increases would be passed on to employees. While government monitoring systems, such as improved financial reporting and increased numbers of audits, could be developed to ensure greater financial accountability, the industry would fight such efforts. Because substantial amounts of public funds to nursing homes traditionally have been used to finance excessive administrative costs, high profit rates, and the expansion of chain operations, there is a legitimate distrust of the industry and an unwillingness on the part of government to spend more money.

Government is struggling to balance its interests in ensuring minimum levels of quality while at the same time controlling costs and operating under severe fiscal constraints. Consumer representatives primarily want to ensure quality and access to appropriate services through greater governmental regulation of the industry and improved enforcement efforts.

There is an unequal distribution of power between the industry and consumers. The nursing home industry is well represented by highly paid professionals with extensive organizational resources for lobbying government. Consumer groups have less funding and resources and must operate primarily through commitment and volunteer efforts, but nevertheless have a strong presence in Washington through NCCNHR. If professional groups (particularly those of nurses and physicians) would form a coalition with consumer groups and be willing to allocate resources to representing the public interest, they could shift the power base to favor consumer interests.

Consumer groups, particularly the National Citizens' Coalition for Nursing Home Reform, have worked extremely hard to have legislation passed and to develop new regulations and survey procedures.[31] Nursing home industry representatives, while generally cooperating with the new legislation, have made efforts to weaken its implementation and to use it as a means of increasing Medicaid reimbursement rates.

The current struggles between the industry and the consumers are focused on the development of new regulations and enforcement to improve the quality of regulation. Stronger support by nursing and other professional organizations would give greater weight to consumer groups in their effort to prevent the watering down of regulations by industry officials. In addition, a coalition of consumers and professionals supporting greater allocations of federal funds by Congress and the Administration to implement state survey procedures would serve to protect the public interest.

SUMMARY

The nursing home industry is growing in size and importance as a provider of long-term care. The major quality and access problems of the nursing home industry are likely to grow in magnitude as demand increases and supply is relatively inelastic. Regulatory efforts are the highest priority for improving quality of care. At the same time, renewed efforts are needed to improve wages, benefits, and staffing levels for the professionalized staff of nursing homes. This effort will entail substantial increases in public funds but is essential to the improvement of the system. Methods are needed to ensure financial accountability on the part of nursing homes. Maximum limits on nursing home administrative costs, profits, and capital expenditures are crucial. Finally, methods for reducing the trend toward proprietary ownership and the consolidation of the industry should be quickly examined in order to stimulate ownership and management by government and nonprofit corporations.

REFERENCES

1. U.S. General Accounting Office (GAO). *Medicare and Medicaid: Stronger Enforcement of Nursing Home Requirements Needed.* Report to the Chairman, Subcommittee on Health and Long-term Care, Select Committee on Aging, House of Representatives. U.S. GAO, Washington, D.C., 1987.

2. Institute of Medicine (IOM) Staff and National Research Council Staff. *Improving the Quality of Care in Nursing Homes.* National Academy Press, Washington, D.C., 1986.

3. Omnibus Budget Reconciliation Act (OBRA) of 1987. Public Law 100-203. Subtitle C: Nursing Home Reform. U.S. Government Printing Office, Washington, D.C., 1987.

4. U.S. General Accounting Office (GAO). *Long-term Care for the Elderly: Issues of Need, Access, and Cost.* Report to the Chairman, Subcommittee on Health and Long-term Care, Select Committee on Aging, House of Representatives. U.S. GAO, Washington, D.C., 1988.

5. Guterman, S., Eggers, P., Riley, G., Greene, T., and Terell, S. The first three years of Medicare prospective payment: An overview. *Health Care Fin. Rev.* 9(3): 67–77, 1988.

6. Scanlon, W. Delivery of long-term care services: Latest developments in nursing homes and housing. Commissioned paper for meeting on The Economics and Politics of Long Term Care, sponsored by the University of California, Irvine and the FHP Foundation, p. 5, 1989.

7. National Center for Health Statistics, Hing, E., Sekscenski, E., and Strahan, G. National Nursing Home Survey: 1985 Summary for the United States. *Vital and Health Statistics,* Series 13, No. 97. DHHS Pub. No. (PHS) 89-1758. U.S. Government Printing Office, Washington, D.C., 1989.

8. National Center for Health Statistics, and Sekscenski, E. Discharges from nursing homes: Preliminary data from the 1985 National Nursing Home Survey. *Advance Data from Vital and Health Statistics,* No. 142, DHHS Pub. No. (PHS) 87-1250. Public Health Service, Hyattsville, Maryland, 1987.

9. Harrington, C., and Estes, C.L. Trends in nursing homes in the post-Medicare prospective payment period. Unpublished. Institute for Health and Aging, San Francisco, California, 1989.

10. Shaughnessy, P. W., and Kramer, A. M. The increased needs of patients in nursing homes and patients receiving home health care. *New Engl. J. Med.* 322(1): 21–27, 1990.

11. Harrington, C., Swan, J. H., and Grant, L. A. Nursing home bed capacity in the states, 1978–86. *Health Care Fin. Rev.* 9(4): 81–111, 1988.

12. Phillips, C. D., and Hawes, C. *Discrimination by Nursing Homes Against Medicaid Recipients: The Potential Impact of Equal Access on the Industry's Profitability.* Research Triangle Institute, Research Triangle Park, North Carolina, 1988.

13. International Trade Administration. Health and medical services. In *U.S. Industrial Outlook 1990.* Department of Commerce, Washington, D.C., 1990.

14. U.S. Department of Health and Human Services (DHHS). Task Force on Long-term Care Policies. *Report to Congress and the Secretary: Long-term Health Care Poli-*

cies. U.S. Government Printing Office, Washington, D.C., 1987.

15. Hawes, C., and Phillips, C. D. The changing structure of the nursing home industry and the impact of ownership on quality, cost, and access. In *For-Profit Enterprise in Health Care,* edited by B. H. Gray, pp. 492–538. National Academy Press, Institute of Medicine, Washington, D.C., 1986.

16. Wagner, L. Nursing homes buffeted by troubles. *Mod. Health Care,* 18(12): 33–42, 1988.

17. Forbes. Health. *Forbes,* pp. 180–182, January 8, 1990.

18. National Center for Health Statistics, and Strahan, G. Characteristics of registered nurses in nursing homes: Preliminary data from the 1985 National Nursing Home Survey. *Advance Data from Vital and Health Statistics.* No. 152. DHHS Pub. No. (PHS) 88-1250. Public Health Service, Hyattsville, Maryland, 1988.

19. Harrington, C. Nursing home reform: Addressing critical staffing issues. *Nurs. Out.* 35(5): 208–209, 1987.

20. Jones, D., Bonito, A., Gower, S., and Williams, R. *Analysis of the Environment for the Recruitment and Retention of Registered Nurses in Nursing Homes.* U.S. Department of Health and Human Services, Washington, D.C., 1987.

21. Spector, W. D., and Takada, H. A. Characteristics of nursing homes that affect resident outcomes. Paper presented at the Gerontological Society of America, Annual Meeting, Minneapolis, Minnesota, 1989.

22. Kayser-Jones, J., Wiener, C., and Barbaccia, J. Factors contributing to the hospitalization of nursing home residents. *The Gerontologist* 29(4): 502–510, 1989.

23. Wagnild, G. A descriptive study of nurse's aide turnover in long term care facilities. *J. Long-term Care Admin.,* pp. 19–23, 1988.

24. Kane, R., Garrard, J., Skay, C., Radosevich, D., Buchanan, J., McDermott, S., Arnold, S., and Kepferle, L. Effects of a geriatric nurse practitioner on process and outcome of nursing home care. *Am. J. Pub. Health* 79(9): 1271–1277, 1989.

25. Mezey, M., Lynaugh, J., and Cartier, M. Reordering values: The teaching nursing home program. *Nursing Homes and Nursing Care: Lessons from the Teaching Nursing Homes,* pp. 11–12. Springer, New York, 1989.

26. Joel, L. and Johnson, J. Rutgers, the State University of New Jersey and Bergen Pines County Hospital. In *Teaching Nursing Homes, the Nursing Perspective,* edited by N. Small and M. Walsh. National Health Publishers, Owings Mill, Maryland, 1988.

27. Dimond, M., Johnson, M., and Hull, D. The teaching nursing home experiences, University of Utah College of Nursing and Hillhaven Convalescent Center. In *Teaching Nursing Homes, the Nursing Perspective,* edited by N. Small and M. Walsh. National Health Publishers, Owings Mill, Maryland, 1988.

28. Wykle, M., and Kaufmann, M. The teaching nursing home experiences, Case Western Reserve University, Frances Payne Bolton School of Nursing and Margaret Wagner House of the Benjamin Rose Institute. In *Teaching Nursing Homes, the Nursing Perspective,* edited by N. Small and M. Walsh. National Health Publishers, Owings Mill, Maryland, 1988.

29. Wolloch, I., Schlesinger, E., Dinerman, M., and Seaton, R. The posthospital needs and care of patients: Implications for dis-

charge planning. *Soc. Work Health Care* 12(4): 61–76, 1987.

30. Lewin, R. Nursing homes rethink tying aged as protection. *New York Times*, p. A1, December 28, 1989.

31. National Citizens' Coalition for Nursing Home Reform (NCC-NHR). *Consumer Statement of Principles for the Nursing Home Regulatory System—State Licensure and Federal Certification Programs.* NCCNHR, Washington, D.C., 1983.

[The] American health *care system . . . [is] a paradox of plenty and of want, a system where some receive the benefit of the most advanced medical technologies in the world, yet many . . . families can't get help to keep a frail parent from having to go into a nursing home.*
— Senator Dave Durenberger

J. S. Kayser-Jones / Carolyn L. Wiener /
Joseph C. Barbaccia

Factors Contributing to the Hospitalization of Nursing Home Residents

Medicare's Prospective Payment System of Diagnostic Related Groups (DRGs) provides a current example of the "balloon effect"; squeezing down costs in one area merely causes them to expand in another. By reducing the length of hospital stays, the demand for nursing home care has increased (Lyles, 1986; Older American Reports, 1985; Sager et al., 1987; U.S. Congress, General Accounting Office, 1986), as has the acuity level within nursing homes (Smith & Molzahn-Scott, 1986; Stull & Vernon, 1986). Despite the prospective payment system, the average cost of hospitalization has continued to rise. In 1986 hospital bills in the United States rose 19% (Medical Economic Digest, 1988).

An often-repeated statistic—health care's consumption of 11% of the gross national product—is usually coupled with examples of life-sustaining technologies, such as open heart surgery, organ transplant, and kidney dialysis. Overlooked is the fact that high-cost users of health care are more likely to be persons with chronic medical problems who are repeatedly admitted to the hospital (Anderson & Steinberg, 1984; Schroeder et al., 1979; Zook & Moore, 1980). Equally lost is a less dramatic statistic, one as yet unexamined by health care economists: The use of the health care dollar for the care of nursing home patients in the acute hospital.

Jeanie S. Kayser-Jones, Ph.D., R.N., F.A.A.N., is Professor, Departments of Physiological Nursing and Anthropology, School of Nursing at the University of California, San Francisco.
Carolyn L. Wiener, Ph.D., is Assistant Adjunct Professor, Department of Social and Behavioral Sciences, School of Nursing at the University of California, San Francisco.
Joseph C. Barbaccia, M.D., is Professor and Vice-Chair, Department of Family and Community Medicine, and Director, Memory Clinic and Alzheimer's Center, School of Medicine at the University of California, San Francisco.

Abridged from Kayser-Jones, J.S., Wiener, C.L., and Barbaccia, J.C. (1989). Factors contributing to the hospitalization of nursing home residents. *Gerontologist* 29(4):502–510. Copyright © 1989, The Gerontological Society of America. Used with permission.

A few studies have focused on the clinical conditions that necessitate hospitalization of nursing home patients (Irvine et al., 1984; Zimmer et al., 1988), but little is known about the social-structural (i.e., nonclinical) factors that precipitate hospitalization. This article describes the clinical conditions necessitating transfer of nursing home residents to an acute hospital. The emphasis, however, will be on the social-structural factors contributing to hospitalization.

OVERVIEW

These findings are part of a larger study that investigated the social-cultural factors and other circumstances influencing the decision-making process in the evaluation and treatment of acute illnesses in nursing homes. The study used participant observation; in-depth interviews with physicians, nursing staff, nursing home residents, and family members (100 in each category); and event analysis to gather data. Event analysis, an intensive study of a particular event, was the strategy used to study prospectively 215 acute-illness episodes in three nursing homes. Analysis of these data is underway. Reported here is an analysis of those nursing home residents who, when they became acutely ill, were transferred to an acute hospital for treatment. . . . The research was conducted over three years (1985–88) in three West Coast nursing homes, including a 1,200-bed government-owned long-term care facility (Facility A) and two proprietary nursing homes (Facility B with 135 beds, and Facility C with 182 beds).
. . . The criterion of appropriateness of transfer [from nursing home to hospital] was based on whether the acute-hospital level of care was justified by the nature of the acute illness requiring treatment (e.g., surgery for a bowel obstruction). That is, could the acute episode of illness have been treated in the nursing home (e.g., IV therapy), or was the acute-hospital setting required?

Description of Patients Who Were Transferred to the Acute Hospital

Of the 215 patients followed, 79 (36.7%) were from Facility A, 70 (32.7%) from Facility B, and 66 (30.6%) from Facility C. In Facility A, nearly two-thirds (63.4%) of the patients who became acutely ill were treated on the long-term care ward in the facility; 24% were transferred to the acute-care ward for treatment, and only 12.6% were transferred to an acute hospital. In Facilities B and C a much greater proportion of patients, 48.6% and 59% respectively, were hospitalized when an acute illness occurred.

Of the 215 patients who experienced an acute illness during the study period, 80 (37.2%) were hospitalized for treatment; 3 were transferred twice for a total of 83 transfers. Forty-seven percent of the transferees were from Facility C, 41% from Facility B, and only 12% from Facility A. Most of the transferees were readmitted to the nursing home of origin following hospitalization; a few were admitted to another nursing home, and about 20 to 30% from each facility died while at the acute-care hospital.

Fifty-three percent of the patients transferred were female and 47% male. They ranged in age from 33 to 102 years; only 6 were under the age of 60. Based on the Katz ADL instrument, the patients who were transferred were functionally very dependent; the majority (74.4%) were severely impaired; 12.8% each were none to mildly or moderately impaired (Katz et al., 1963). Their mental status as evaluated by the charge nurses was: 26% severely impaired, 44% moderately impaired, and 30% none to mild impairment.

Clinical Problems for Which Patients Were Transferred.   The illnesses for which patients were hospitalized were those that would be expected in a nursing home population (see table 1). Respiratory conditions (25%), symptoms, signs, and ill-defined conditions (18%), and genitourinary problems (12%), were the conditions most often responsible for transfer.

Since the nursing staff reported the patients' signs and symptoms to the attending physician, and based on those symptoms an order for transfer was given, patients were reclassified using only the primary sign or symptom. As shown in table 2, fever (41%) emerged as the most predominant sign or symptom followed by dyspnea, cough, and chest pain (16%). The patients who were hospitalized did not differ significantly from those who were treated in the nursing home. The only two diagnostic groups in which patients were more likely to be hospitalized were "diseases of the skin and subcutaneous tissues" (5 out of 7 patients) and "injury and poisoning" (9 out of 12 patients). The 5 patients hospitalized in the first group were residents who had developed severe and extensive decubitus ulcers, and 8 of the patients in the second group were hospitalized for fractures (femur and ankle).

Analysis of Qualitative Data

Qualitative analysis of the acute-illness episode data disclosed that in some cases social factors and structural constraints within the nursing home contributed to hospitalization of patients, as well as to the development of acute illnesses, (e.g., dehydration). To substantiate and quantify these observations, the physician on the research team analyzed each acute-illness episode and placed it in one of three categories.

Category I comprised patients whose medical condition necessitated transfer to the acute hospital, that is, the acute hospital was the appropri-

TABLE 1   Categorization of Acute-Illness Episodes by Disease Classification
($N = 215$)

International Classification of Disease Diagnosis Group		Patients Hospitalized (%) ($N = 83$)	Patients Treated in Nursing Home (%) ($N = 132$)
001–139	Infections and parasitic diseases (exclusive of infections in other categories)	1.2	3
140–239	Neoplasms	3.6	2.3
240–279	Endocrine, nutritional, and metabolic disease and immune disorders	1.2	.7
390–459	Diseases of circulatory system	11	10
460–519	Diseases of respiratory system	25	24.2
520–579	Diseases of digestive system	11	8.3
580–629	Diseases of genitourinary system	12	18.2
680–709	Diseases of skin and subcutaneous tissue	6	1.5
780–799	Signs, symptoms, and ill-defined conditions	18	26.5
800–999	Injury and poisoning	11	2.3
290–319	Mental disorders	0	1.5
710–739	Diseases of musculoskeletal system and connective tissue	0	1.5
	Total	100	100

ate level of care because of the nature of their condition. Forty-one of the transferees (49.4%), including patients with hip fractures, sepsis, or acute gastrointestinal bleeding, were placed in this group. Category II included patients whose condition did not warrant transfer to the acute hospital because their condition could have been definitively diagnosed and treated in the nursing home and did not require acute-hospital level of care. Remarkably, nearly half (48.2%) of the patients fell into this group. Category III consisted of patients who were sent to the local Veterans Administration Hospital for a routine physical exam; while there, an acute problem was diagnosed and they were hospitalized. Only two patients (2.4%) fell into this subdivision.

TABLE 2 Categorization of Acute-Illness Episodes by Primary Symptom
($N = 215$)

International Classification of Disease Symptom	Patients Hospitalized (%) ($N = 83$)	Patients Treated in Nursing Home (%) ($N = 132$)
Fever	41	43.2
Dyspnea, cough, and chest pain	16	13
Lower body skeletal pain and swelling	9.8	4.5
Acute gastrointestinal symptoms	8.4	7.5
Changes in emotional and cognitive status	6.0	10
Changes in cardiovascular status	3.6	5.2
Nausea and vomiting	3.6	0
Wounds and skin injury	2.4	3
Genitourinary symptoms	2.4	6
Decubitus ulcers and cellulitis	2.4	3.8
Anorexia and weight loss	1.0	3.8
Fall	1.0	0
Other	2.4	0
Total	100	100

Analysis of Patients in Category II

Hospitalization is costly; it is also traumatic to the patient and may lead to hospital-acquired complications that otherwise might not have occurred (Zimmer et al., 1988; Steel et al., 1981). It is therefore important to describe those patients in Category II—patients whose condition might have been handled in the nursing home and did not require acute-hospital level of care.

Seventy percent of the patients ($n = 28$) in Category II could have been treated in the nursing home if IV therapy had been available, (e.g., IV antibiotics, parenteral diuretics or IV therapy for rehydration). In an additional 15% of the cases, patients were transferred because of pressure from the family or nursing staff. The family of a dying patient, for example, felt the nursing staff could not provide adequate care and insisted their relative be hospitalized. In several cases, the nursing staff asked physicians to transfer patients who required heavy nursing care (e.g., patients with extensive decubitus ulcers). These residents were seen as difficult to care for, and in some cases the administration wanted them moved because of fear of receiving a citation from state inspectors.

Another 15% of the patients in Category II were transferred for the convenience of the physician or because of poor doctor-nurse communication. For example, two patients with nondisplaced ankle fractures were sent to the hospital, where short-leg casts were applied. The orthopedist refused to go to the nursing home because materials for casting were not readily available. In some cases, frustrated physicians hospitalized patients after having difficulty obtaining reliable information about the patient's condition from the nursing staff.

Social-Structural Factors Contributing to Hospitalization

While it is important to know which clinical conditions lead to the hospitalization of nursing home residents, it is also important to identify the social-structural factors responsible for transfer.

Analyses of data from the acute-illness episodes and participant observation disclosed that the nursing home setting shaped and structured decisions regarding transfer. The social-structural factors in the nursing home most commonly contributing to hospitalization of Category II patients were: lack of immediately available in-house support services (x-ray, laboratory, and pharmacy departments); nursing/medical issues (an insufficient number of adequately trained nursing staff, transfer for the physician's convenience, pressure from nursing staff for transfer, and poor nurse-physician communication); and family pressure for transfer. Often many of these factors interacted dynamically to influence the decision-making process.

Lack of Support Services.   Facilities B and C did not have laboratory, x-ray, or pharmacy departments. Laboratory work had to be sent out, increasing the time between the nurse's assessment of a change in the patient's condition and the physician's diagnosis and prescription of treatment. X-ray technicians had to be called in, presenting not only a time lag, but also decreasing the physician's confidence, since the quality of portable X rays was considered less accurate than those taken in a hospital radiology department. The lack of these services, therefore, precipitated hospitalization to accelerate the diagnostic process and to enhance accuracy. Conversely, for some patients who were not transferred, the delay in diagnosis increased the severity of the problem. A case in point was a woman who experienced hyperinsulinism that was not correctly assessed until five hours later, when the laboratory report showing a blood sugar of 38 mg/dl was returned. She was then immediately hospitalized and successfully treated.

Nursing/Medical Issues

Insufficient and Inadequately Trained Nursing Staff.   A large proportion (70%) of the patients could have been treated in the nursing home if the nursing staff had been able to administer IV therapy. Typically, these were patients with acute urinary or respiratory tract infections who needed IV antibiotics, or residents who needed IV fluids for rehydration. One woman with hyperinsulinism was sent to the hospital for IV glucose, and some patients were hospitalized for IV diuretics. While access to laboratory and x-ray services are necessary for treating such patients, just as important is a professional nursing staff who can monitor their response to treatment and effectively communicate with the physician.

Most of the nursing care, including the assessment of subtle changes in patients' physical and cognitive condition, was done by a small number of licensed vocational nurses (LVNs), but predominantly by nurse aides (NAs). These poorly paid, inadequately trained workers were ill equipped to deal with the large number of subacutely ill patients under their care. When the workload became too heavy, the NAs put pressure on the licensed staff, who in turn urged the physician to hospitalize residents. When physicians thought the staff was unable to care adequately for patients whose conditions were deteriorating, they transferred them to the acute hospital.

Our data further suggest that in some cases an insufficient number of adequately trained nursing staff contributed to a gradual deterioration in the patient's condition, eventually leading to hospitalization. Inadequate and irregular suctioning of semicomatose and comatose patients, for example, undoubtedly contributed to lower respiratory tract infections. One nurse stated that a 55-year-old comatose woman with a tracheostomy should have been suctioned hourly, but due to a shortage of staff, was at best suctioned once every eight hours. This same nurse confided that patients with pneumonia who were treated with antibiotics might not recover because of lack of supportive nursing care. "The coughing and deep breathing exercises, chest physical therapy, these procedures just are not done here. And they work, but they are not going to be done because we do not have enough nursing staff." In some cases, undetected fluid accumulation associated with acute congestive heart failure was not acted upon, while in other cases an unnoticed decrease in fluid intake necessitated hospitalization for rehydration therapy.

The shortage of nursing staff also contributed to nutritional problems. In Facility C, for example, one NA was responsible for feeding five to six patients simultaneously. Eating was rushed and fluid intake was not encouraged and/or recorded, resulting in the dehydration and subsequent hospitalization mentioned above. Similarly, poor nutritional intake and a staff too busy to urge the patient to eat and take adequate fluids sometimes resulted in the placement of a nasogastric tube. An NA explained, "Tube feeding is a lot easier on us. It is so frustrating when they don't eat. That's one job that takes forever. Mrs. L has been tube fed for years, and she's doing just fine." While tube feeding may be convenient for the staff, it places the patient at increased risk for aspiration pneumonia; the un-skilled, overworked staff were inattentive to positioning tube-fed patients properly.

In Facility B, one RN was responsible for the care of 135 patients on the evening and night shift. On one occasion, we observed that there were 8 patients in this facility with nasogastric tube feedings, a woman with a tracheostomy, 6 patients in a semicomatose or comatose condition, and a woman with Jakob-Creuzfeldt's disease, who was in a nearly continuous state of seizure. One RN was responsible for providing care for these 15 heavy-care patients; she also had to supervise the care of 120 other residents—an impossible task!

Convenience of the Physician.   Physicians are poorly compensated—financially and psychologically—for their treatment of nursing home pa-tients. Reimbursement rates for the one required monthly visit are low, and if a patient requires a second visit in the same month, it is often difficult and sometimes impossible to be recompensed. Physicians candidly admitted that it was more convenient to transfer the acutely ill nursing home patient to the emergency room (ER) of the acute hospital, where X rays and diagnos-tic work would be done quickly. The ER physician would help make the diagnosis, and house staff and the attending physician would follow the patient much more efficiently. Further, physicians remarked that they were better paid for hospital than for nursing home care.

The time of day and day of the week were also considered. A physi-cian with 37 patients in one nursing home remarked: "I am always trying to tailor the treatment to keep the calls down. If it is late afternoon, and the patient has a fever of 102° to 103°, I know it's either pneumonia or a urinary tract infection; if it means I'm not going to get the results of lab work, or a chest X ray, until 11 PM . . . I'd rather send them to the hospital to be evaluated." Physicians noted that they preferred to hospitalize pa-tients because ancillary services were more readily available, the quality of nursing care higher, and they would be reimbursed by Medicare for one or more daily visits.

Pressure from Nursing Staff.   Nursing home administrators encouraged the admitting nurse to screen incoming patients assiduously in an attempt to keep a full census without placing undue stress on their already over-worked staff. Since the workload increased as some residents inevitably became more disabled and dependent, directors of nursing sometimes pressed for transfer in order to keep the number of heavy-care patients as low as possible. In these cases, transfer was seen as an opportunity to extricate themselves from a patient considered burdensome. Physicians also spoke of "treating the nurse." If the nurse sounded anxious and inse-cure, the physician hospitalized the patient to avoid repeated calls. Furthermore, in an era of close surveillance by state inspectors, nursing homes sometimes urged transfer to avoid patients' dying in the nursing home; a death may attract close inspection of the chart and possible citation.

Poor Nurse-Physician Communication.   State regulations require that physicians be notified of any change in the patient's condition—whether a small bruise or a slight elevation of blood pressure or temperature. The nursing staff reported that physicians were frequently difficult to reach, often did not return calls promptly, and were sometimes irritated by phone calls reporting what they perceived as insignificant signs and symptoms. On some occasions when the physician did not return the call promptly, the staff became alarmed, dialed an emergency number, and had the patient hospitalized without a physician's order.

Additionally, the physician's decision-making process was observed to be compromised by the poor assessment and communication skills staff demonstrated when calling to report a change in the patient's condition. In such situations, physicians lost confidence in the nursing staff and hospitalized patients where they were on "home ground" with a trustworthy staff.

Pressure from Family

Families reported feeling frustrated by what they identified as inadequate nursing skills and, fearful when their relative's condition worsened, sometimes urged the physician to transfer him/her to an acute hospital. Transfers also occurred when there was uncertainty about the severity of the patient's condition. In such cases, especially if a concerned family member was present, physicians hospitalized the patient out of indecision and/or fear of litigation. An illustration is the explanation made to the researcher by one physician: "When the family is involved, it's probably safer to transfer him. He may stroke out on me; he's fragile, there could be a clot."

The Cost of Transfer

This study initially did not focus on the cost of hospitalization. It became obvious, however, that the emotional cost to patients and their families, and the financial cost to society are considerable, and our data allowed us to make an estimate of the economic cost.

Emotional Costs.   While financial costs are of great concern, no less important is the emotional cost of hospitalization. Foremost is the trauma experienced by the patient who is being transferred, often without adequate explanation, to an unfamiliar location, with unfamiliar staff and an unfamiliar physician. In some cases when patients were discharged from the hospital, their bed in the nursing home was not available. They were therefore placed in yet another strange environment, surrounded by strange caregivers.

Financial Costs.   The hospitalization of nursing patients results in the expenditure of a vast amount of money. In this study, similar to the findings of Van Buren et al. (1982) it was found that 48% (40 patients) of those transferred might have been treated in the nursing home. In California the average length of hospital stay for patients over the age of 65 is 7.4 days and the average charge per patient day is $1,127 (Office of Statewide Planning and Development, 1987). The transfer of the 40 patients in Category II, therefore, resulted in a total of 296 hospital days at $1,127 per day for a net cost of $333,592.

When using this same formula to calculate the cost of Category II transfers throughout the United States, the figure becomes astronomical. Data from the 1985 National Nursing Home Survey (Sekscenski, 1987) disclosed that 430,000 patients are discharged annually from nursing homes to general or short-stay hospitals (excluding psychiatric units). An additional 20,000 are discharged to Veterans Hospitals, for a total of 450,000 discharges. If 48% of these transfers could be avoided, 216,000 patients are perhaps being hospitalized needlessly.

The national average length of hospital stay in the United States (for the quarter ending January 1989) for patients over the age of 65 was 6.6 days, and the average cost of hospital care per day was $661.31 (American Hospital Association, 1989). Thus, the transfer of 216,000 patients annually would result in an additional 1,425,600 hospital days at a total cost of $942,763,530, an unacceptable figure in a time of escalating health care costs.

When estimating national costs, it must be noted that Medicaid reimbursement policies vary from state to state. California has a prospective class or fixed-rate reimbursement rate. That is, a single rate is paid to all facilities regardless of the acuity level; there is no financial incentive for nursing homes to keep acutely ill or heavy-care patients. (For a full discussion of Medicaid reimbursement policies, see Swan, Harrington, & Grant, 1988.) State Medicaid reimbursement rates may influence the transfer of patients to the acute hospital, and it could be argued that more transfers occur in California than in other states. With this caveat in mind, it is nevertheless clear that avoidable hospitalizations result in a large expenditure of money.

DISCUSSION

The results of this study disclosed that in 48.2% of the cases, nursing home residents were hospitalized for social-structural (i.e., lack of support services, nursing/medical issues such as an insufficient number of adequately trained nursing staff and poor nurse-physician communication, and family pressure for transfer) rather than for clinical reasons. A major question that needs to be addressed is: Can nursing homes effectively provide acute-care services to the elderly? The findings presented here are consistent with those of Zimmer et al. (1988), who, in describing an innovative program that reduced the hospitalization of acutely ill nursing home patients, emphasized that providing acute care in nursing homes is dependent upon an adequate number of skilled nursing staff, the reimbursement of phycisians for daily visits, and the availability of pharmaceutical and diagnostic services.

It is noteworthy that in Facility C only 30% of the patients who were treated in the nursing home died, while in Facility B nearly twice as many (59.3%) died. This is partially explained by the fact that Facility C seldom admitted patients who were terminally ill, and they also hospitalized a greater proportion (59%) of the patients who became acutely ill.

It is also noteworthy that in Facility A, only 12.5% of the residents who became acutely ill were hospitalized, while in Facilities B and C, 48.6% and 59% respectively of the residents who became acutely ill were transferred. This was undoubtedly due to the fact that Facility A had laboratory, x-ray, and pharmacy services and physicians on site, and an acute-care ward adequately staffed with physicians and nurses trained to provide acute-care services.

Facility A is atypical, and due to its size (1,200 beds), it can support on-site medical, diagnostic, and pharmaceutical services. Since most nursing homes are small (99 beds or less), it would not be economically feasible for them to provide support services on site. These services are generally available by contractual arrangements through commercial laboratories, pharmacies, and hospitals (Ouslander, 1988). Strengthening the professional nursing staff in nursing homes, however, is a strategy that would reduce the hospitalization of nursing home patients.

Strengthening the Professional Nursing Staff

Nursing care is the major service provided in nursing homes; yet while the average nursing home has about 41 full-time employees, less than 3 of those employees are RNs (Sirrocco, 1983). Furthermore, less than half of all skilled nursing facilities (SNFs) have an RN on duty 24 hours a day (U.S. Department of Health and Human Services, 1981). Medicare- or Medicaid-certified SNFs must have a full-time director of nursing and at least one RN on the day shift seven days a week, and a licensed nurse on duty 24 hours a day. The federal regulation, however, does not require that the licensed nurse be an RN. On evenings and nights, the charge nurse may be an RN or a licensed practical nurse (LPN). Some facilities have more professional staff than is required by federal regulation, while others meet only the minimum standard. Thus in many nursing homes LPNs are in charge of patient care, and the hands-on care is performed by the nurse aide, who typically is responsible for providing complete care for 10 to 15 patients on the day shift, 15 to 25 in the evening, and 40 to 50 during the night shift (Harrington, 1987).

It has been estimated that there are only 1.5 licensed nursing staff per 100 patients in nursing homes. By comparison, in acute-care hospitals there is one RN for every 4.5 patients (Harrington, 1987). Clearly, this dramatic reduction in professional nursing care is insufficient to meet the needs of patients who are being discharged, often in subacute conditions, from the acute- to the long-term care setting.

Given these conditions, it is not surprising that, of the identified social-structural factors contributing to hospitalization in this study, the insufficient number of adequately trained nursing staff stands out as the predominant problem. Correcting this problem would address three factors that contribute toward hospitalization: pressure for transfer from nursing home staff, poor nurse-physician communication, and pressure for transfer from families who lack confidence in the nursing staff. Ameliorating the staffing situation is essential for providing quality care to the acutely ill nursing home patient. Furthermore, without adequate nursing care, chronic conditions give rise to acute episodes of illness, and hospitalization inevitably occurs.

The problems of inadequately skilled and an insufficient number of nurses are separate but intertwined. Regarding skills, for example, staffing nursing homes with RNs capable of giving IV therapy would significantly reduce the number of hospitalizations, as was evident in Facility A. At Facility B, although the nurses were able to administer IV fluids and drugs, some physicians were unaware of this, and others questioned the nurses' ability to monitor IV therapy. At Facility C, the nursing staff did not administer IVs. Thus, many patients from Facilities B and C were hospitalized for IV therapy.

Nursing home residents are frail, very old, have multiple pathologies and physical disabilities, and many are mentally impaired. Their conditions can change rapidly; it is imperative that at least one RN be on duty 24 hours a day, seven days a week to assess patients and identify subtle changes indicative of an acute illness.

In addition to increasing the professional nursing staff, the use of the clinical nurse specialist (CNS) and the geriatric nurse practitioner (GNP) in nursing homes should be encouraged. Early studies have suggested that GNPs can improve the outcome for nursing home residents (Kane et al., 1976), and a recent study by Kane et al. (1988) found that, despite some difficulty in implementing their role in nursing homes, GNPs had a positive effect on resident outcomes. Some studies have demonstrated that

GNPs contribute to the quality of care by changing the focus from custodial to rehabilitative care (Chaffin, 1976; Gray, 1982). Recent findings from the Robert Wood Johnson Foundation Teaching Nursing Home Program (Mezey, Lynaugh, & Cartier, 1988), along with data from other demonstration projects, have shown that GNPs markedly increase the ability of nursing homes to care for acutely ill patients and those with complex problems (Mezey & Scanlon, 1989).

GNPs can play a particularly important role in the care of the acutely ill nursing home resident. In the absence of on-site physicians, the GNP could take the responsibility for ongoing patient assessment, early recognition of acute illness, and implementation of a plan of care. Further, the GNP could discuss the patient's condition with the physician to determine if: 1) the situation can be handled via telephone, 2) the patient needs to be seen by the physician, or 3) the patient needs to be hospitalized.

The reimbursement of GNPs who provide services in nursing homes has been somewhat problematic. Mezey and Scanlon (1989) suggest that reimbursing the GNP under Medicare Part B for services for which physicians are currently being reimbursed could significantly improve quality of care, and it has the potential for being cost-effective. (For a full discussion of reimbursement options see Mezey and Scanlon, 1989.) While there is some evidence that the use of GNPs is cost-effective, further studies are needed to determine cost estimates and savings.

Facility A was a nonprofit organization, while Facilities B and C were proprietary nursing homes. Given the increasing numbers of elderly and the escalating cost of health care, we in the United States must at some point decide if we can afford to sustain long-term care as a profit-making industry. If the money that is paid to the nursing home industry could be redirected to purchase additional professional services, the quality of care would surely improve.

In many states, nursing homes are not reimbursed for providing acute or subacute care (Ouslander, 1988). Numerous studies have addressed the problem of Medicaid reimbursement rates to nursing homes (Fries & Cooney, 1985; Grimaldi, 1982; Harrington & Swan, 1984; Swan, Harrington, & Grant, 1988). Medicaid reimbursement to nursing homes is a complex topic, not within the scope of this article. In view of the rising cost of health care and the increasing number of older people, however, it is imperative that a mechanism for reimbursing nursing homes for providing subacute care be developed and implemented. Ouslander (1988) has discussed several strategies, such as the establishment of a level of care and reimbursement rates somewhere between the nursing home and the acute hospital. Innovative approaches are not without potential negative consequences, as nursing homes may deliberately increase patient dependency and level of care to maximize reimbursement (Swan, Harrington, & Grant, 1988).

This study has limited generalizability because it was conducted in three facilities in one geographic area. Its strength lies in the rich qualitative data that facilitated the identification of social-structural factors contributing to hospitalization. Further studies are needed to determine under which conditions acutely ill patients can be treated successfully in nursing homes, and when patients must be hospitalized for treatment. Also necessary are studies focusing on which patients would benefit from hospitalization and how the outcomes differ for patients who are hospitalized in constrast to those who are not.

BIBLIOGRAPHY

American Hospital Association. (1989). *National Hospital Panel Survey Report.* Chicago, IL.

Anderson, G. F., & Steinberg, E. P. (1984). Hospital readmissions in the Medicare populations. *New England Journal of Medicine, 311,* 1349–1353.

Chaffin, P. (1976). Nurse practitioners: Nursing's contribution to quality care in nursing homes. *Nurse Practitioner, May–June,* 24–26.

CPHA (Commission on Professional and Hospital Activities). (1978). *International classification of diseases, 9th rev. clinical modification,* Vol. 1. Ann Arbor, MI: Edwards Brothers, Inc.

Fries, B. E., & Cooney, L. M. (1985). Resource utilization groups: A patient classification system for long-term care. *Medicare Care, 23,* 110–112.

Gray, P. L. (1982). Gerontological nurse specialist: Luxury or necessity? *American Journal of Nursing, 82,* 82–85.

Grimaldi, P. L. (1982). *Medicaid reimbursement of nursing home care.* Washington, DC: American Enterprise Institute for Public Policy Research.

Harrington, C., & Swan, J. H. (1984). Medicaid nursing home reimbursement policies, rates, and expenditures. *Health Care Financing Review,* 6(1). (HCFA Pub. No. 03176). Office of Research and Demonstrations, Health Care Financing Administra-

tion. Washington, DC: US Government Printing Office.

Harrington, C. (1987). Nursing home reform: Addressing critical staffing issues. *Nursing Outlook, 35,* 208–209.

Irvine, P., Van Buren, N., & Crossley, K. (1984). Causes for hospitalization of nursing home residents: The role of interaction *Journal of the American Geriatric Society, 32,* 103–107.

Kane, R. L., Jorgenson, L. A., Teleborg, B., & Kawahara, J. (1976). Is good nursing-home care feasible? *Journal of the American Medical Association, 235,* 516–519.

Kane, R. A., Kane, R. L., Arnold, S., Garrard, J., McDermott, S., & Kepterle, L. (1988). Geriatric nurse practitioners as nursing home employees: Implementing the role. *The Gerontologist, 28,* 469–477.

Katz, S., Ford, A. B., Moskowitz, R. W., Jackson, B. A., & Jaffee, M. W. (1963). Studies of illness in the aged—The index of ADL: A standardized measure of biological and psychosocial function. *Journal of the American Medical Association, 185,* 914–919.

Lyles, Y. M. (1986). Impact of Medicare diagnosis-related groups (DRGs) on nursing homes in the Portland, Oregon, metropolitan area. *Journal of the American Geriatric Society, 34,* 573–576.

Mezey, M., Lynaugh, J., & Cartier, M.

(Eds.). (1988). *Aging and academia: The teaching nursing home experience.* New York: Springer.

Mezey, M. D., & Scanlon, W. (1989). Reimbursement options for encouraging geriatric nurse practitioner services. In M. D. Mezey, J. E. Lynaugh, & M. M. Cartier (Eds.), *Nursing homes & nursing home care: Lessons from the teaching nursing homes.* New York: Springer.

Office of Statewide Planning and Development. (1987, Jan 1 to June 30). *Aggregate hospital discharge data summary: California hospital discharge data.* Sacramento, CA: Staff.

Ouslander, J. G. (1988). Reducing the hospitalization of nursing home residents. *Journal of the American Geriatrics Society, 36,* 171–173.

Pelto, J. P. (1970). *Anthropological research: The structure of inquiry.* New York: Harper & Row.

Sager, M. A., Leventhal, E. A., & Easterling, D. V. (1987). The impact of Medicare's prospective payment system on Wisconsin nursing homes. *Journal of the American Medical Association, 257,* 1762–1766.

Schroeder, S. A., Showstack, J. A., & Roberts, H. E. (1979). Frequency and clinical description of high-cost patients in 17 acute-care hospitals. *New England Journal of Medicine, 300,* 1306–1309.

Sekscenski, E. S. (1987, Sept. 30). [Discharges from nursing homes: Preliminary data from the 1985 national nursing home survey]. *Advance data from vital and health statistics.* No. 142. National Center for Health Statistics. DHHS Pub. No. (PHS) 87-1250. Hyattsville, MD: Public Health Service.

Sirrocco, Al. (1983, Aug. 11). [An overview of the 1980 national master facility inventory survey of nursing and related care homes]. *Advance data from vital and health statistics.* No. 91. National Center for Health Statistics. DHHS Pub. No. (PHS) 83-1250. Hyattsville, MD: Public Health Service.

Smith, D., & Molzahn-Scott, A. (1986). A comparison of nursing care requirements of patients in long-term geriatric and acute care nursing units. *Geriatric Nursing, 11,* 315–321.

Steel, K., Gertman, P. M., Crescenzi, C., & Anderson, J. (1981). Iatrogenic illness on a general medical service at a university hospital. *New England Journal of Medicine, 304,* 638–641.

Stull, M. K., & Vernon, J. A. (1986). Nursing care needs are changing in facilities with rising patient acuity. *Journal of Gerontological Nursing, 12,* 15–19.

Swan, J., Harrington, C., & Grant, L. A. (1988). State Medicaid reimbursement for nursing homes, 1978–86. *Health Care Financing Review, 9,* 3–50.

U.S. Congress, General Accounting Office. (1986). *Post hospital care: Discharge planners report increasing difficulty in placing Medicare patients* (GAO PEMD-87-567). Washington, DC: U.S. Government Printing Office.

Van Buren, C. B., Barker, W. H., Zimmer, J. G., & Williams, T. F. (1982). Acute hospitalization of nursing home patients: Characteristics, cost and potential preventability (abstract). *Gerontologist, 22,* 129.

Zimmer, J., Eggert, G., Treat, A., et al. (1988). Nursing homes as acute care providers: A pilot study of incentives to reduce hospitalizations. *Journal of the American Geriatric Society, 36,* 124–129.

Zook, C. J., & Moore, F. D. (1980). High-cost users of medical care. *New England Journal of Medicine, 302,* 966–1002.

[Zweck, Brad (Ed)]. *Older American Reports.* (1985, Aug. 2). DRGs create massive new demands on the aging network, 9(31), pp. 3, 4, 10.

Robert E. Schlenker

Nursing Home Costs, Medicaid Rates, and Profits Under Alternative Medicaid Payment Systems

OBJECTIVES AND BACKGROUND

Medicaid payment system issues continue in importance due to the rapid growth in nursing home expenditures and the major portion of those expenditures paid by Medicaid. Nursing home expenditures increased from $2.1 billion in 1965 to $35.0 billion in 1985, the main data collection year of this study. In 1985, Medicaid accounted for 42.4 percent of total nursing home expenditures (Health Care Financing Administration, Division of National Cost Estimates 1987).

This article presents cost, Medicaid payment rate, and profit findings from a larger research study of Medicaid nursing home payment systems conducted during 1983–1988 and funded by the Health Care Financing Administration (HCFA). (The overall study results are presented in Schlenker et al. 1988, and summarized in Schlenker 1991.) The major premise of the study was that the structural characteristics of a payment system strongly influence nursing home behavior and, ultimately, overall outcomes.

Payment Systems and Study States

Three major nursing home payment system types were analyzed: "case-mix," "facility-specific," and "class-rate" systems. Case-mix systems represent the newest payment approach and tie payment more directly than the other systems to patients' assessed care needs. Facility-specific systems base a nursing home's payment rate on its average costs, while class-rate

Robert E. Schlenker, Ph.D., is Associate Director of the Center for Health Services Research, and Associate Professor, School of Medicine at the University of Colorado Health Sciences Center, Denver.

Abridged from Schlenker, R.E. (1991). Nursing home costs, Medicaid rates, and profits under alternative Medicaid payment systems. *Health Services Research* 26(5):623–649. Reprinted with permission from the Hospital Research and Educational Trust.

systems pay a fixed rate per patient day regardless of costs. The performance of the case-mix systems thus was of major interest in this study. Each system type creates different financial incentives for nursing homes and, correspondingly, responses are expected to differ by payment system type.

The initial study phase involved categorizing Medicaid nursing home payment systems and then selecting representative states from each system category. The classification process focused on the Medicaid payment rate component that was most closely associated with direct patient care. This rate component typically covered nursing staff and related costs. The three payment system types and seven states selected for this study in 1984 are summarized in table 1, and discussed next.

Case-Mix Systems. As noted above, case-mix systems are relatively new, but of growing importance. The basic concept of case-mix payment is that the payment for nursing home care is based directly on patients' care needs and on state-estimated costs of providing care appropriate to those specific needs. Four states had case-mix systems at the start of this study (Illinois, Maryland, Ohio, and West Virginia) and two more (Minnesota and New York) adopted them while the study was in progress. Several other states are implementing, developing, or considering such approaches. Case-mix systems also are encouraged under the Omnibus Budget Reconciliation Act of 1987 (P.L. 100-203). In addition, four states (Kansas, Maine, Mississippi, and South Dakota) are currently involved in case-mix system development as part of the HCFA-funded Multistate Nursing Home Case Mix and Quality Demonstration.

Maryland, Ohio, and West Virginia were selected in 1984 as the study's case-mix states. Although the following descriptions point out the differences among the three state systems, their overall approaches to case-mix measurement and to translating case-mix information into payment rates are broadly similar. The approaches also set these states apart from the states representing the other two payment systems.

Maryland's patient care rate component is based on the patient's case-mix characteristics. Rates are set for four general care categories (light, moderate, heavy, and heavy-special care) based on five ADLs (activities of daily living) and three services. Separate rates also are set for ten specific services (such as turning and positioning, tube feeding, and injections). Maryland encourages nursing homes to accept heavy care patients by increasing the "profit margin" in rates paid for the heavier care patient categories. The individual ADL and service rates are determined prospectively each year (and vary according to three geographic regions) and are not tied to the costs of individual nursing homes. Nursing homes bill the state monthly for each resident's care according to these rates (these data are periodically audited by a state-contracted organization).

TABLE 1 Payment System Characteristics, by System Type and Study State

System Type and General Characteristics	Individual State Features		
	State	Case-Mix Measurement	Rate-Setting (Patient Care Component)
Case-Mix: Patient care rate component is based on patients' care needs and state-estimated costs of adequate and appropriate care.	Maryland	Four categories (based on 5 ADLs and 3 services), plus 10 special services	*Prospective, patient-specific* rates (based on needed services), independent of facility costs
	Ohio	Twenty items (5 ADLs, 9 special services, 6 rehabilitation services)	*Retrospective, facility-specific* average rates equal to the lower of actual cost per day or the case-mix–determined rate per day ceiling
	West Virginia	Fifteen items (5 ADLs, 10 special services)	*Prospective, facility-specific* average rates equal to the lower of actual cost per day or the case-mix–determined rate per day ceiling

Facility-Specific: Patient care rate component is based on the facility's past average cost per day, subject to ceilings.	Colorado	None	*Prospective, facility-specific* average rates equal to the lower of actual cost per day or the statewide ceiling; no efficiency payment for costs below the ceiling
	Florida	None	*Prospective, facility-specific* average rates equal to the lower of actual cost per day or a regional ceiling; efficiency payment for cost below ceiling if quality standards met
Class-Rate: Patient care rate component is based on patient's level of care, independent of facility costs.	Texas	None	*Prospective, patient-specific* rates by patient's Medicaid level of care (three levels)
	Utah	None	*Prospective, patient-specific* rates by patient's Medicaid level of care (three levels)

Ohio's case-mix payment methodology is facility specific and retrospective. In contrast to the Maryland approach, case-mix information is used in Ohio to set facility ceilings on reimbursement rates. Payment for patient care services is based on each facility's costs up to the case mix–determined ceiling. The case-mix ceilings are based on the state-estimated cost of 20 separate items (five ADLs, 9 special services such as injections, and 6 rehabilitation services). Patient assessments are conducted every 3 to 6 months by state personnel to determine the need for services by each nursing home's residents. Ohio's selection of the case-mix services and the service cost estimation methodology drew on West Virginia's approach and experience.

In West Virginia, rates are facility specific as in Ohio, but are set prospectively rather than retrospectively. West Virginia, like Ohio, uses case-mix information to determine facility rate ceilings. A nursing home's patient care rate component is determined from patient assessment data provided by the facility (and audited periodically by the state). The assessments are based on information for 15 services, and the state-estimated cost of providing each service (based on time studies) is used to determine the case-mix ceiling amount for each facility. The lower cost—between case-mix ceiling or actual cost (with an inflation adjustment)—becomes the facility's subsequent (prospective) patient care rate component.

Facility-Specific Systems.   At present, most states use a facility-specific payment system. The common feature of such systems is that the payment to each nursing home is linked in some way to its costs. Most such systems are prospective, so that past costs are used to set future payment rates. A HCFA survey identified 13 retrospective and 25 prospective facility-specific state systems during the study's state selection phase (Jazwiecki 1984).

Colorado and Florida were the selected facility-specific states. Although their individual features differ in detail, the two payment systems are quite similar in their overall structures.

Colorado's system is prospective and facility specific, but it does not include case mix as a factor in determining payment rates. In setting the prospective rates, costs up to ceiling amounts are allowed. In 1985, a ceiling was used for patient care and raw food costs (combined), and no efficiency incentive payments were made for costs below the ceiling. (An efficiency incentive is the payment of some portion of the difference between a ceiling and actual cost per day to facilities with costs below the ceiling.)

Florida's system is also prospective and facility specific. In determining rates, patient care costs are treated separately, with a higher ceiling than for other cost components, but case mix is not directly incorporated into the rate determination methodology. Although efficiency incentive payments are possible in the patient care rate component, they are linked to quality ratings from the Medicaid certification survey in an effort to encourage quality. Higher amounts are paid to facilities with "superior" quality ratings.

Class-Rate Systems.   In a class-rate system, nursing homes are paid a fixed amount per patient day by class or category of patient. Although class rates also can be based on nursing home characteristics such as size and geographic location, the focus in this study was on classes defined by patient characteristics, primarily the Medicaid skilled and intermediate levels of care. Class-rate systems were fairly common in the early years of Medicaid, but by the mid-1980s few states had such systems (the earlier-mentioned survey identified six class-rate states). Despite their limited current use, class-rate systems were important for this study because of the strong incentives they create for nursing homes to minimize the costs of providing care, possibly by admitting primarily light care patients or by limiting quality, or both.

Texas and Utah were selected as the study's class-rate states. Their essential features are basically the same. Although Texas implemented a case-mix payment system in 1989, during the study it used a class-rate methodology based on three levels of patient care: SNF (skilled), ICF (intermediate), and ICF-II (light intermediate). (The ICF-II category was quite rare, so that essentially two levels were in use.) Uniform statewide class rates were determined each year, with the rates based on the median plus 7 percent of statewide costs per day by level of care.

Utah's class-rate methodology also includes three levels of care: SNF, ICF-I and ICF-II. (Utah, in addition, uses separate negotiated rates for patients with extremely costly care needs.) The Utah class rates are established annually, based on negotiations between the state and the nursing home industry.

The categorization into case-mix, facility-specific, and class-rate systems was developed to highlight the major financial incentives the different payment methodologies create for nursing homes. Nursing home responses to those incentives were then hypothesized to determine overall system outcomes, as discussed next.

Hypotheses

. . . The study hypotheses . . . address expected differences across payment systems both in the levels of costs, rates, and profits, and in the associations of case mix with those variables. The major underlying assumption was that, despite each state's unique payment system features, providers' incentives and responses would be similar within a payment system category and different across categories. The null hypothesis in each instance was that no difference would be found among systems. The statistical analyses tested for alternative hypotheses in either direction.

Costs and Medicaid Rates.   The levels of (1) patient care cost per day, (2) its share of total cost, and (3) the Medicaid payment rate per day were all hypothesized to be highest for case-mix systems, lowest for class-rate systems, and between the two for facility-specific systems. The associations of case mix with both patient care costs and Medicaid payment rates also were hypothesized to be strongest in the case-mix systems, weakest in the class-rate systems, and in-between for the facility-specific systems.

The cost and rate hypotheses built on earlier studies, but added the newer case-mix approach to the facility-specific and class-rate payment system variants. (Reviews of prior relevant research include Bishop 1980b; Palmer and Cotterill 1983; Stassen and Bishop 1983; Schlenker 1986; and Hawes and Phillips 1986.) The underlying rationale for these hypotheses was that payment rates under case-mix systems were expected to respond more directly than under the other systems to differences in patient care needs. Thus, case-mix systems were expected to facilitate greater access to nursing home care by high-cost, intense case-mix Medicaid patients. The anticipated outcomes were higher expected costs and rates in those systems, and stronger associations of costs and rates with case mix.

In contrast, the fixed payments by broad level of care category under class-rate systems were expected to lead nursing homes to admit primarily light care patients within each class and to minimize the cost of their care. Rates were expected to be low in class-rate systems, both because an objective of low rates often underlies a state's decision to use a class-rate methodology, and because the low nursing home costs encouraged by class rates may reinforce a state's tendency to set low rates. These factors were expected to result in lower cost and rate levels in class-rate states, and also were expected to weaken the association of costs and rates with case mix.

Facility-specific systems were expected to be more responsive (in terms of rates) to care need and cost differences than class-rate systems but less responsive than case-mix systems. Thus, case-mix intensity and therefore cost and rate levels in facility-specific systems were hypothesized to be between those of the class-rate and case-mix systems. The association of case mix with both costs and rates in facility-specific systems also was expected to be stronger than in class-rate systems but weaker than in case-mix systems.

Profits.   Several prior studies have used the concept that nursing homes operate in two primary markets: a private pay and a Medicaid market. (See, for example, Scanlon 1980; Bishop 1980a; Cotterill 1983; and Palmer and Vogel 1983.) Conventional supply and demand forces are assumed to operate in the private pay market, while in the Medicaid market the state's buying power allows it to purchase care at a lower rate than in the private pay market, creating a situation of excess demand for Medicaid care. The

Medicaid payment system thus represents only one of several important influences on nursing home profitability. In this study, therefore, the relationships between profits and Medicaid payment system type were not expected to be as strong as those hypothesized for costs and rates.

The profit hypotheses dealt with the level of profits (measured by the profit ratio, defined further on) and with the association between case mix and profits. Specifically, profit levels were expected to be highest in class-rate systems, lowest in case-mix systems, and between the two for facility-specific systems. Further, the association between case mix and profits was hypothesized to be positive in case-mix systems and negative in class-rate systems. No strong association of case mix with profits was hypothesized for facility-specific systems.

The hypothesis on profit levels assumed that the strong class-rate incentives to minimize cost would lead to higher profits than under the other systems. In case-mix systems, rates are designed to vary with the case mix—determined costs of care, making it more difficult to achieve high profits (at least from the direct patient care portion of the payment rate). Similarly, rates in facility-specific systems are closely tied to facility costs, thereby limiting profitability.

The hypothesized positive association of profits with case mix under case-mix systems was based on concerns that such systems may encourage providers to obtain profits by keeping patients debilitated or providing them only minimal services (Smits 1984; Kane and Kane 1988). However, this hypothesis was considered to be fairly weak. For example, in some case-mix states (e.g., Ohio and West Virginia), payment rates are based on costs up to a case mix—determined ceiling. Higher payments for heavier care patients in such circumstances are unlikely to lead to higher profits since payments will be made only for the lesser between costs or the case-mix ceiling. . . .

COST, RATE, AND PROFIT LEVELS BY PAYMENT SYSTEM

Cost and Rate Levels Across Payment Systems

Descriptive cost and rate data by state for the basic and urban profit samples . . . were used to address the hypotheses on levels of costs and rates. Significance tests were not carried out due to the small sample sizes.

Average patient care cost per day (after adjustment for geographic wage rate differences) was higher in the case-mix states than in the class-rate states. The results for the facility-specific states were mixed. Florida's patient care cost per day was the highest of all study states, while Colorado's was between the averages for the case-mix and the class-rate states.

The average patient care shares (or proportions) of total cost per day were higher for the case-mix states than for the class-rate states in both samples. However, the share for the facility-specific states were higher than those for the class-rate states and for two of the three case-mix states (i.e., except Ohio).

The same general pattern was found for the Medicaid payment rate per patient day (also after geographic wage rate adjustment). The average Medicaid rates were higher for the case-mix states than for the class-rate states. For the facility-specific states, Florida's rate was the highest of all seven states, and Colorado's was between the rates of the two class-rate states (higher than the Texas rate and slightly lower than the Utah rate).

These descriptive results are consistent with the hypotheses on case-mix-class-rate system comparisons, but are relatively uninformative without the multivariate analyses. As a prelude to those analyses, the case-mix index (i.e., the average rate ratio) . . . follows the same general pattern as the cost and rate variables, suggesting that positive associations may be found between case mix and the cost and rate variables in the regression analysis.

High/Low Profit Analysis

The profit analysis included 89 urban profit nursing homes (two of the original 91 had incomplete profit data). The urban profit category was expected to be the most strongly affected by and responsive to financial and market incentives. Their overall profit (revenue:expense) ratio was 1.02, indicating that revenues exceeded expenses on average by 2 percent. Average profit ratios by payment system . . . were 1.07 for the urban profit sample case-mix and facility-specific nursing homes, and 0.91 (representing a loss) for the class-rate facilities. . . .

The high-profit groups' average revenue:expense ratios were similar for the case-mix and facility-specific systems (1.15 and 1.14), as were the low-profit ratios (0.98 and 1.00). However, both ratios were lower for the class-rate system (1.07 and .75). In fact, the low-profit class-rate group had revenues averaging only three-fourths of expenses. Clearly, these results did not support the hypothesis of higher profits under class-rate systems.

Profit Components in Case-Mix and Facility-Specific Systems.   The profit component patterns were similar for the case-mix and facility-specific systems. . . . The average Medicaid revenue and total cost per patient day variables were similar between the high- and low-profit groups. In contrast, the high-profit groups of both systems had significantly higher non-Medicaid revenue per patient day than the low-profit groups. As a result, the Medicaid revenue:cost ratios were not significantly different between the high- and low-profit groups in either system, but the non-Medicaid revenue:cost ratios were considerably higher for the high-profit than for the low-profit groups (even though the high-profit/low-profit difference was statistically significant only for the facility-specific system).

The Medicaid share was also considerably lower, on average, for high-profit compared to low-profit facilities under both systems, although the difference was statistically significant only for the case-mix system. Neither the nursing cost per patient day nor the case-mix index was significantly different between the high- and low-profit groups.

These results suggest that higher profits in these systems were obtained through a combination of (a) higher non-Medicaid revenues per (non-Medicaid) patient day, and (b) lower participation in Medicaid (i.e., lower Medicaid shares). That is, it appears that high-profit nursing homes achieved their higher profits outside the Medicaid system.

Profit Components in Class-Rate Systems.   The class-rate results differed considerably from the other two systems. The differences in Medicaid and non-Medicaid revenue per day and in the Medicaid share were not statistically significant (although the mean values of both revenue variables were higher for the high-profit group). Total cost per day, however, was significantly lower for the high-profit group, and as a result, both revenue:cost ratios were significantly higher for the high-profit group. Nursing cost per day also was significantly lower for the high-profit group, but the case-mix index was approximately the same for both groups.

Thus, profitability in the class-rate states appeared to be associated with lower overall costs, and lower nursing costs for approximately the same case mix. Whether the lower costs reflect greater efficiency or lower quality deserves further study, particularly in view of the lower nursing costs without lower case mix in the high-profit group.

THE ASSOCIATION OF CASE MIX WITH COSTS, RATES, AND PROFITS

Case Mix and Patient Care Costs

The patient care cost per day regression accounted for about two-thirds of the dependent variable variation ($R^2 = .661$). All listed variables were included in the analysis, but coefficients and significance levels are presented only for variables that were significant at the $p < .10$ level by the stepwise regression procedure. . . . A positive overall association between case mix and cost (the case-mix index coefficient is 12.307) is indicated. The case-mix interaction terms reveal a weaker case mix–cost relationship for the class-rate system (indicated by the negative class-rate coefficient of -4.482). The total case-mix effect under each payment system is the sum

TABLE 2   Case-Mix Effect

System	Case-Mix Index Coefficient (All systems)	Interaction Coefficient (Each system)	Total Case-Mix Effect by System
Case mix	12.307	—	12.307
Facility specific	12.307	—	12.307
Class rate	12.307	−4.482	7.825

of the case-mix coefficient and the relevant interaction coefficient, as in table 2.

This result is consistent with the hypothesis of a stronger case mix–cost association in the case-mix states than in the class-rate states. The results also imply that the association in facility-specific states is similar to that in the case-mix states. The only state variable to enter this equation was Ohio, with a positive coefficient. This suggests higher patient care costs in Ohio than in the other states, after controlling for the remaining variables in the equation.

The other variables to enter the equation will only be briefly mentioned. The quality indicator had a significant negative coefficient. Since a higher proportion of ulcerations is assumed to reflect lower quality, this result suggests that lower quality is associated with lower patient care cost. The nursing home beds per elderly variable was not significant, and the significant facility characteristic variables were nonprofit ownership, rural location, the percent Medicare patients (all positive coefficients), and chain affiliation (negative coefficient). The area/market and facility characteristic results generally agree with the findings of other nursing home cost studies, such as those cited earlier. The most important finding for this study was the stronger association between case-mix and patient care cost in case-mix systems (and in facility-specific systems) than in class-rate systems.

Case Mix and Medicaid Payment Rates

. . . The cost and rate regressions both revealed major differences between the case-mix and class-rate systems in the role played by case mix. In contrast, the facility-specific systems showed a strong case mix–cost association (like the case-mix systems) but a weak case mix–rate association (like the class-rate systems).

Three of the state variables had significant coefficients in the rate equation. The results implied that, compared to the other four states (Maryland, West Virginia, Colorado, and Utah), Florida had a higher Medicaid rate (positive coefficient), and Ohio and Texas had lower rates (negative coefficients), after controlling for case mix and other factors captured by the equation. The negative Ohio coefficient must be considered in conjunction with the positive coefficient for the case-mix system interaction variable. Together, the two coefficients implied a lower overall Medicaid rate in Ohio than in the other two case-mix states, but a rate that was still positively associated with case mix.

The quality variable was not significant in the equation, nor was the nursing home beds per elderly variable. The significant facility characteristics suggest that after controlling for case mix and other included factors, rural location and high-occupancy rates were associated with higher payment rates, and high participation in Medicaid was associated with lower payment rates.

Overall, the rate regression results were consistent with the hypotheses. In particular, the findings suggest a strong positive association between case mix and the Medicaid payment rate under a case-mix system, and weaker positive (and only marginally significant) associations under the facility-specific and class-rate systems.

Case Mix and Profits

. . . The only significant case-mix variable was the class-rate system interaction variable, with a negative coefficient. This implies that case mix and profits were negatively associated under class-rate systems, but were not associated under the other two systems. The only significant state variable was Texas. Its positive coefficient implies higher profits for Texas than for the other study states. However, the negative class-rate interaction coefficient denotes a lower profit ratio under the class-rate system compared to the other systems (at a given case-mix index value). Thus, within the context of lower class-rate profits, the positive Texas coefficient indicates only that the profit ratio was somewhat higher in Texas than in Utah.

The quality indicator was marginally significant (with a p-value of .099) and negative, which suggests a positive but weak association between quality and profitability that warrants further study in future work. With regard to the other significant variables, the nonprofit coefficient was negative, suggesting that lower profits were associated with nonprofit ownership. The Medicaid and Medicare variables also were significant and negative, implying that greater participation in Medicaid or Medicare was associated with lower profits. These results agree with findings of studies such as those cited earlier.

The profit regression results thus point to (a) no association between case mix and profit in case-mix and facility-specific systems, and (b) a negative association in class-rate systems. In particular, there was no evidence that under case-mix payment higher profits were obtained by facilities with more intense case mix.

DISCUSSION AND IMPLICATIONS

The main findings of these analyses were that patient care costs and Medicaid payment rates were more closely associated with case mix under case-mix systems than under the other two system types, particularly class-rate systems. Also, profits were negatively associated with case mix in class-rate systems but not associated in the other systems.

These results suggest that case mix-systems can be more effective than other systems in linking Medicaid payment to patient care needs, and also that the resulting cost structure of nursing homes is more in line with care needs in case-mix systems than in the other systems. Further, the case-mix systems may facilitate access for higher-cost Medicaid patients by avoiding the negative correlation between higher case mix and lower profits present in the class-rate systems.

The facility-specific systems shared some positive features with case-mix systems, largely because facility-specific rates are responsive to individual facility costs. However, cost differences may be due to many factors other than case mix, so that the connection of case mix to costs and rates is weaker in facility-specific systems than in case-mix systems (but stronger than in class-rate systems).

Overall, the results suggest that case-mix systems have several advantages over other nursing home payment systems. Additional analyses from the larger study supported the advantages of case-mix systems but also highlighted important caveats. In particular, both access and quality need to be studied over longer time periods, with an emphasis on tracking outcomes for patient cohorts over time. In addition, studies involving larger samples of states, facilities, and patients are needed.

The trend toward case-mix systems was noted at the outset of this article. This study examined the earlier case-mix systems, and research on the more recent systems is warranted. The newer systems usually employ the resource utilization group (RUG) patient classification methodology, which, compared to the case-mix systems covered in this study, classifies patients into broader categories and does not tie payments as directly to the provision of specific services. The evaluation of the current HCFA Multistate Case Mix and Quality Demonstration, as well as comparative longitudinal studies of states with and states without case-mix payment systems, therefore can further our understanding of nursing home payment policies and their effects.

BIBLIOGRAPHY

Alexander, J., and B. L. Lewis. "The Financial Characteristics of Hospitals under For-Profit and Nonprofit Contract Management." *Inquiry* 21, no. 3 (Fall 1984): 230–42.

Bishop, C. E. *Nursing Home Behavior under Cost-Related Reimbursement.* Waltham, MA: Brandeis University, University Health Policy Consortium, 1980a.

———. "Nursing Home Cost Studies and Reimbursement Issues." *Health Care Financing Review* 1, no. 4 (Summer 1980b): 47–64.

Cotterill, P. G. "Provider Incentives under Alternative Reimbursement Systems." In *Long-Term Care: Perspectives from Research and Demonstrations.* Edited by R. J. Vogel and H. C. Palmer. Washington, DC: U.S. Department of Health and Human Services, 1983.

Hawes, C., and C. Phillips. "The Changing Structure of the Nursing Home Industry and the Impact of Ownership on Quality, Cost and Access." In *For-Profit Enterprise in Health Care.* Edited by B. H. Gray. Washington DC: National Academy Press, 1986.

Health Care Financing Administration. Division of National Cost Estimates. Office of the Actuary. "National Health Expenditures, 1986–2000." *Health Care Financing Review* 8, no. 4 (Summer 1987): 1–36.

Jazwiecki, T. "How States Pay for Long-Term Care Facility Services under Medicaid." *Healthcare Financial Management* 38, no.4 (April 1984): 76–80.

Johnston, J. *Econometric Methods.* 2d ed. New York: McGraw-Hill, 1972.

Kane, R. A., and R. L. Kane. "Long-Term Care: Variations on a Quality Assurance Theme." *Inquiry* 25, no. 1 (Spring 1988): 132–46.

Lev, B. *Financial Statement Analysis: A New Approach.* Englewood Cliffs, NJ: Prentice-Hall, Inc., 1974.

McCaffree, K. M., S. Malhotra, and J. Wills. "Capital and the Reimbursement of the Costs of Nursing Home Services." In *Reform and Regulation in Long-Term Care.* Edited by V. LaPorte and J. Rubin. New York: Praeger, 1979.

Meigs, W. B., and R. F. Meigs. *Accounting: The Basis for Business Decisions.* 5th ed. New York: McGraw-Hill, 1981.

National Center for Health Statistics. Public Health Service. *Health, United States, 1987.* Washington, DC: Government Printing Office, 1988a.

———. *Nursing and Related Care Issues as Reported from the 1986 Inventory of Long-Term Care Places.* Huntsville, MD: 1988b.

Palmer, H. C., and P. G. Cotterill. "Studies of Nursing Home Costs." In *Long-Term Care Perspectives from Research and Demonstrations.* Edited by R. J. Vogel and H. C. Palmer. Washington, DC: U.S. Department of Health and Human Services, 1983.

Palmer, H. C., and R. J. Vogel. "Models of the Nursing Home." In *Long-Term Care: Perspectives from Research and Demonstrations.* Edited by R. J. Vogel and H. C. Palmer. Washington, DC: U.S. Department of Health and Human Services, 1983.

Scanlon, W. J. "A Theory of the Nursing Home Market." *Inquiry* 17, no. 1 (Spring 1980): 25–41.

Schlenker, R. E. "Case Mix Reimbursement for Nursing Homes." *Journal of Health Politics, Policy and Law* 11, no. 3 (Fall 1986): 445–61.

———. "Comparison of Medicaid Nursing Home Payment Systems." *Health Care Financing Review* 13, no. 1 (Fall 1991):93–109.

Schlenker, R. E., J. D. Stiles, T. Carlough, and P. A. DeVore. *A Multi-State Analysis of Medicaid Nursing Home Payment Systems. Final Report.* Vol. 1. HCFA Cooperative Agreement 18-C-98306/8. Denver, CO:

University of Colorado Health Sciences Center, Center for Health Services Research, 1988.

Smits, H. "Incentives in Case Mix Measures for Long-Term Care." *Health Care Financing Review* 6, no. 2 (Winter 1984): 53–59.

Stassen, M., and C. Bishop. *Incorporating Case Mix in Prospective Reimbursement for SNF under Medicare: Critical Review of Relavant Research*. Waltham, MA: Brandeis University Center for Health Policy Analysis and Research, 1983.

Among older people the highest priority is always health; *a close second is money. Both of these are related to what I think is the underlying issue—independence of living.*
— T. Franklin Williams

6

Home Health Care and Community-based Care

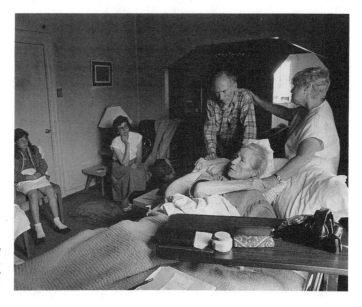

Home and community care affects extended family

Charlene Harrington

Quality, Access, and Costs: Public Policy and Home Health Care

The quality of home health services delivered by some agencies is substandard, yet the regulation of home health care quality remains underdeveloped. Access to appropriate home health care benefits for those with chronic health problems is particularly limited under current Medicare rules. These problems are occurring at a time when the demand for home health care services has increased dramatically and public expenditures for such services are increasing rapidly. National policies that ensure quality and access are needed.

Home health care refers to a combination of health care and social services provided to individuals and families in their own homes or in other community and homelike settings on a short-term or long-term basis. Such services may supplement, complement, or substitute for hospital or nursing home services.

The demand for long-term care is increasing with the dramatic growth in the aged population and the increased prevalence of chronic disease and disability in the population. The increased life expectancy is expected to nearly double the number of persons 65 years and older between 1976 and 2002, from 23 million to 45 million, and the number aged 84 and over will grow by 200 percent during the same period.[1] These changes in demography and disability are having a profound impact on the health status of the population and the demand for home health care and other health services. The demand is further increased by the general preference of the aged and disabled to have services provided, when possible, in their own homes rather than in nursing homes or institutional settings.

Charlene Harrington, Ph.D., R.N., F.A.A.N., is Associate Director of the Institute for Health & Aging, and Professor and Chair of the Department of Social and Behavioral Sciences, School of Nursing at the University of California, San Francisco.

From Harrington, C. (1988). Quality, access, and costs: public policy and home health care. *Nursing Outlook* 36:164–166. Reproduced with permission from Mosby-Year Book, Inc.

As the prospective payment system (PPS) for hospitals has been implemented, hospitals have greater incentives to discharge patients as early as possible. Home health care agencies have received a substantial increase in referrals since PPS. Anecdotal evidence shows an increase in the acuity level of the patients receiving home health care services. As patients are discharged from hospitals "quicker and sicker," the need to monitor the quality of care provided in the home increases.

Medical technology formerly used only in hospitals or nursing homes is now being used in the home, so that performance has become even more complex for home health agency personnel. The use of intravenous feedings and medication, ventilators, oxygen, and special prosthetic equipment and devices has made patient care by agencies more complex and challenging. The appropriate use of technology, the training and skill levels needed by agency personnel, emergency back-up procedures, training and supervision of family and informal caregivers all become problems when high technology is used in the home.

Nationally, the number of Medicare-certified home health care agencies grew from 3,012 in 1981 to 5,953 in 1987, a 98 percent increase.[2] Certified agencies are those that meet federal standards and therefore are eligible to receive Medicare payments for eligible individuals. There are also many unlicensed and uncertified agencies; estimates vary from another 2,400 such agencies to a number equal to the certified agencies.[3]

The largest growth in the number of certified agencies occurred between 1982 and 1986, after the 1980 Omnibus Reconciliation Act (ORA), which permitted certification of proprietary agencies in states not having licensing laws. The growth rate slowed between 1986 and 1987 to less than 0.5 percent.[3] During the last five years, the types of providers have changed dramatically. Previously, care was delivered primarily by visiting nurses' associations; now it is provided by a complex network of proprietary, chain, and hospital-based organizations.[4] By 1984, 42 percent of the nation's hospitals offered home health agency services, and this number was expected to reach 65 percent in 1986.[5] The number of proprietary agencies increased by fourfold between 1982 and 1985, to 32 percent of all agencies.[4] A growing number of home health agencies are now owned and operated by corporate chains.

Despite the rapid growth in the number of home health agencies, there are indications that the supply of home health services is not keeping up with demand. There have been reports of inappropriate, even illegal, denials of critical home health care to many sick older Americans.[6] A recent report points out that the availability of home health care services ranges from marginal to adequate across the country.[7]

Expenditures for home health care services have been growing for 20 years and are expected to continue to expand well into the future. The home health care expenditures have increased in recent years at an estimated average annual rate of 20 to 25 percent.[4] In 1982, Medicare and Medicaid paid approximately $1.8 billion for home health services. In 1986, the total expenditures were estimated to be about $4 billion, with over $2 billion paid by Medicare.[8] The total cost of home health products and services is expected to grow from $9 billion in 1985 to $16 billion by 1990.[9]

Medicaid home health care expenditures are increasing as a proportion of total Medicaid expenditures, from 1.8 percent in 1982 to 4.6 percent in 1984.[10] By 1984, Medicaid expenditures rose to over $782 million and covered some 452,500 individuals, 58.5 percent of whom were elderly.[10] States vary in the amount of the total Medicaid budget allocated for home care services and the percentage of elderly recipients. In 1984, about half of all recipients of Medicaid home health services in the United States lived in New York State.[11] Although Medicaid is still a relatively small funding source for home health services, it is growing in importance. Other public programs such as Aging and Social Services also pay for home care.

New mechanisms to control costs of home health care are under consideration by public officials and third-party payers. Some advocate case-mix reimbursement, which is used for some nursing home programs.[12,13] Other efforts to control costs have emphasized ceilings and stricter audit reviews.[14] Most of these proposals are incremental and do little to change the current fragmented fee-for-service financing and delivery system mechanisms.

Problems with quality of care delivered by home health care agencies are reported frequently. The American Bar Association recently described some of the problems in home health care identified by various officials, providers, advocates, and consumers: physical injury that may be intentional or accidental; workers' tardiness or failure to show up or spend the specified amount of time with the client; inadequate or improper performance of duties; attitudinal problems including insensitivity, disrespect, intimidation, abusiveness; and theft or financial exploitation.[3] In 1987, news reports from Florida described deaths of elderly clients related to deficiencies in home health care. The California Auditor General found 709 homemaker service providers with criminal convictions in three counties during an audit of in-home care programs (unlicensed and uncertified agencies) caring for some 11,000 needy people.[15] Reports of agencies double billing for services and fighting over patients at local emergency rooms have surfaced. Many believe these reports represent only the tip of the iceberg.

Measuring the quality of home health care is difficult and in its early stages of development. High quality of home health care in basic terms means meeting the individual's physical, medical, psychosocial, and rehabilitative needs and effectively encouraging maximum functional independence. Quality of life and the quality of care are strongly linked, but neither can be easily measured. The traditional approach to assessing the quality of health care involves structure, process, and outcome measures.[16] The process of care involves such things as the number and types of services offered. Sructural measures encompass items such as access to equipment, type of staff and organizational resources. Outcome measures may include death rates, rates of readmission to hospitals, and changes in functional status and medical condition.

Little has been done to develop outcome measures for home health care until recently. Foley developed resource utilization groups for home health.[12] Manton and Hausner recently examined case-mix for Medicare home health services and identified distinct client profiles that explained significant proportions of the differences in home health reimbursement and the number of visits.[13] In the spring of 1988, the Health Care Financing Administration began planning a new contract to develop and test outcome-based quality measures for home health care services. The goal is to develop outcome measures of health and functional status that may or may not be linked to specific diagnostic conditions, use of services, and costs. The development of outcome measures will have an important impact on shaping the nature of services and monitoring services in the future. After measures are developed, standards for minimum and desirable levels of care must be defined. Nursing can and should play a leadership role in this process.

Monitoring the delivery of care by 8,000 agencies to over 1.4 million individuals in the home setting is a difficult task. Nonetheless, because the government pays for a major portion of the services, it has a responsibility to construct mechanisms to oversee the care process and thus ensure quality. State licensure gives public permission to organizations to engage in a practice, occupation or activity otherwise unlawful, but does not necessarily assure quality. State licensing standards typically do not go beyond federal Medicare standards and are relatively weak or nonexistent. Only 32 states in 1985 required any licensure of home health agencies. Some states license only proprietary agencies.[17] The National Association for Home Care is concerned that there is no uniformity in state licensure laws or in the state implementation of federal standards.[18] NAHC further claims that there is inadequate state regulation to ensure that home health agencies are financially stable, adequately staffed, and organized so as to ensure quality care.

Agencies that receive Medicare and Medicaid payments must meet minimum federal standards for certification (Conditions for Participation), and state governments monitor these agencies for compliance with federal guidelines. These conditions cover the following 10 areas: compliance with state and local laws; organization of services and administration; requirements for professional staff; acceptance of patients, maintenance of a plan of treatment, and provision of medical supervision; provision of skilled nursing; provision of therapy; requirements for medical social services; availability of home health aide services; maintenance of clinical records; and ongoing evaluation. These regulations are primarily structural and process measures and do not define outcome measures. To certify home health agencies for Medicare, states are required to use the federal survey instrument and guidelines for annual surveys, which require routine interviews with a small number of clients. Faced with budget cutbacks, HCFA reduced its annual survey requirement to only 53 percent of the agencies. Unfortunately, because of limited financial resources and higher priorities, some states are doing little to assess the quality of care provided by these agencies. Very few home health care agencies have been "involuntarily terminated" from the Medicare program for failure to comply with the Conditions of Participation. Further, the federal government has little leverage to encourage states to be more active in enforcing certification standards.

Professional review organizations (PROs) are also charged with reviewing the appropriateness and quality of care delivered to Medicare recipients by home health care agencies. This new responsibility is in its development phase. The number of problems identified and sanctions taken by the PROs is unknown.

Accreditation is the voluntary process by which an agency or organization evaluates and recognizes an institution as meeting certain predetermined standards suggesting high quality of care. Standards have also traditionally been structural and process oriented. Currently, three professional bodies accredit home health care agencies: the Joint Commission on Accreditation of Hospitals, the National League for Nursing and the American Public Health Association (a joint body), and the National Home Caring Council.[19] The first two groups are currently revising their procedures for accreditation. Existing accreditation activities cover only a small number of the home care agencies in the nation. State and county agencies such as Aging and Social Services, which contract for home care services, generally have some mechanisms for accountability. While some agencies have developed detailed criteria and monitoring procedures, others use minimal monitoring.

Many observers argue that the home care sector of the health care industry has the least amount of external monitoring.[17,19] An American Bar Association report stated that there is no way of knowing the quality of home health care in our communities.[3] The report argued that the quality of home health care services is beyond the reach of public or professional scrutiny. Continued reports of seriously deficient providers in areas affecting patient care, e.g., coordination of patient services, implementation of a plan of treatment, conformance to physician orders, and review of clinical records, attest to the need for better regulation.

Recognizing problems in the quality of home health care and government regulation, Congress passed the first major change in Medicare home health care certification since the program was enacted. This legislation, in the Omnibus Budget Reconciliation Act of 1987 (P.L. 100-203) signed by President Reagan in December 1987, requires home health agencies to ensure specific individual patient rights, to notify state agencies of changes in ownership and management, and to set and implement home health aide training requirements for certification using competency evaluations. In addition, state agencies must conduct unannounced surveys within 15 months of the previous survey, evaluate the care for a sample of individual clients based on protocols and the patient case mix. The Secretary of HHS may appoint temporary management for an agency, terminate the certification, implement monetary penalties, and suspend Medicare payments. And finally, state agencies must maintain a toll-free hotline for complaints and must investigate such complaints.

While this legislation takes a major step toward strengthening the regulation of home care, the specific standards and policies implementing the legislation will require enormous effort. Beyond this effort, additional state and federal resources must be appropriated to carry out the regulatory requirements. Expanding state licensing to cover currently unlicensed home care agencies would be a major step toward higher quality. Even more important, a strong commitment to enforcement in the area of home health care must be developed at the federal and state levels of government.

Access to home health services is a serious problem. Medicare will pay for home health care services for those with short-term rehabilitation needs. After a limited number of visits for such services, Medicare will no longer pay for services. Many individuals with chronic health problems must then pay for their home care services directly out of pocket or spend down and become eligible for Medicaid, which covers the aged, blind, and disabled poor. . . .

Home health care is an important and rapidly growing source of formal health care. Demand for home health services is increasing and may exceed the supply of existing services and the public financing available for such services. Access needs to be improved by expanding service benefits under Medicare to cover those who are chronically ill and to add homemaker and unskilled services to those currently offered by Medicare. Defining and monitoring the quality of home health care is in early stages.

Extensive efforts and financing resources are needed to implement the new regulations. Because nurses are the primary providers of home health care services, nursing must take a leadership role in defining and assuring quality of care, appropriateness of services, and access to those services, and in promoting cost-effective delivery systems.

REFERENCES

1. Rice, D.P., and Feldman, J.J. Living longer in the United States: demographic changes and health needs of the elderly. *Milbank Mem.Fund* 61:362–396, Summer 1983.

2. Watkins, V., and Kirby, W. Health care facilities participating in Medicare and Medicaid programs, 1987. *Health Care Finance.Rev.* 9:101–105, Winter 1987.

3. American Bar Association. *The "Black Box" of Home Care Quality.* Report prepared for the House of Representatives, Washington, DC (ABA Comm. Pub. No. 99–573) Chicago, The Association, Aug. 1986.

4. Waldo, D.R., and others. National health expenditures, 1985. *Health Care Financ.Rev.* 8:1–21, Fall 1986.

5. Hospital continuing care arrangements. *Wash.Rep.Med.Health Perspectives,* March 13, 1985, p. 2.

6. U.S. Senate, Special Committee on Aging. *Crisis in Home Health Care: Greater Need, Less Care.* (Hearing; Serial No. 99-24) Washington, DC, The Senate, July 28, 1986.

7. U.S. General Accounting Office. *Posthospital Care: Discharge Planners Report Increasing Difficulty in Placing Medicare Patients.* Washington, DC, GAO, 1987.

8. U.S. Office of the Actuary, Division of National Cost Estimates. National health care expenditures,

1986–2000. *Health Care Financ.Rev.* 8:1–36, Summer 1987.

9. *Home Healthcare Products and Services: Markets in the U.S.* New York, Frost and Sullivan, 1983.

10. Holahan, J.F., and Cohen, J.W. *Medicaid: The Trade-off Between Cost Containment and Access to Care.* Washington, DC, Urban Institute Press, 1986.

11. Reif, L. Making dollars and sense of home health policy. *Nurs.Econ.* 2:382–388, Nov.–Dec. 1984.

12. Foley, W. Developing a patient classification system for home health care. *Pride Inst.J.Long Term Home Health Care* 6:22–24, Winter 1987.

13. Manton, K.G., and Hausner, T. A multidimensional approach to case-mix for home health services. *Health Care Financ.Rev.* 8:37–54, Summer 1987.

14. U.S. General Accounting Office. *Medicare: Need to Strengthen Home Health Care Payments Control and Address Unmet Needs.* (Report to Special Committee on Aging, United States Senate, Dec. 1986) Washington, DC, GAO, 1986.

15. California Auditor General. *Department of Social Services Could Reduce Costs and Improve Compliance with Regulations of In-Home Supportive Services Program.* Sacramento, The Auditor, Mar. 1987.

16. Donabedian, A. Evaluating the quality of Medicare care. *Milbank Mem.Fund Q.* 44(Suppl., Part 2):166–202, 1966.

17. Leader, S. *Home Health Benefits Under Medicare.* Washington, DC, American Association of Retired Persons, Sept. 1986.

18. The National Association for Home Care. *Toward a National Home Care Policy: Blue Print for Action.* Washington, DC, The Association, Jan. 1985.

19. Spiegel, A.D. *Home Health Care.* Ownings Mills, MD, Rynd Communications, 1983. (2nd ed. in 1987)

It is older women who are often sacrificing their livelihood, health, *and economic future to provide care, alone and unaided.*
— Tish Sommers and Laurie Shields
with the Older Women's League

Juanita B. Wood / Carroll L. Estes

The Impact of DRGs on Community-based Service Providers: Implications for the Elderly

INTRODUCTION

A number of research studies have focused on the short-term effects of the Medicare Prospective Payment System (PPS), particularly in terms of the utilization and cost of hospital services.[1-9] A limited number of studies have also focused on the effects of PPS on post-hospital care, although these have generally given primary attention to home health care and other Medicare-reimbursed services.[10-17] There has been little documentation, however, on the effects of PPS on a broader range of community-based service providers and, by extension, on the elderly population they serve. This important, but understudied, area of care is addressed here.

PPS-related early hospital discharge changed patterns of post-hospital service utilization, affecting community agencies, individuals and families.[18-26] The adequacy of the community-based service system to respond to new demands, either in the form of demand for new types of services or increased intensity of existing services, raises questions of access for the older adult population needing those services. Although this study explores DRG (diagnosis-related groups) impact from an agency perspective and records organizational changes that service providers report making, it is possible, nonetheless, to suggest some of the ways in which these organizational changes will affect clients.

Juanita B. Wood, Ph.D., is a Public Policy Analyst at the Institute for Health & Aging, and Associate Adjunct Professor, Department of Social and Behavioral Sciences, School of Nursing at the University of California, San Francisco.

Carroll L. Estes, Ph.D., is Director of the Institute for Health & Aging, and Professor, Department of Social and Behavioral Sciences, School of Nursing at the University of California, San Francisco.

From Wood, J.B., and Estes, C.L. (1990). The impact of DRGs on community-based service providers: Implications for the elderly. *American Journal of Public Health* 80(7):840–843. Copyright 1990, the American Public Health Association. Used with permission.

METHODS

The research question asks post-hospital care organizations how DRGs have affected their staffing, service provision, and the types of clients served.

Data Sources

Study data were drawn from several sources:

- Telephone survey interviews with a probability sample of seven types of service providers conducted in spring of 1986 and again in fall of 1987;
- Telephone interviews with state and local policymakers and representatives of major provider associations ("key informants") in the states studied, conducted in 1988;
- Detailed case studies and in-person interviews in two study communities;
- Secondary data obtained from a variety of sources, including the Area Resource File, Census data, and the National Nursing Home Survey of 1985.

Site Selection

Sample States.   States and SMSAs (standard metropolitan statistical areas) were selected purposively to assure some geographic variability. Each of the five states in the sample (California, Florida, Pennsylvania, Texas, and Washington) was the most populous state in its federal administrative region. They had also been identified by the regional directors of the Administration on Aging in 1976 as having the most innovative and generous aging programs in their regions. The states selected assured some diversity of socio-demographic and state economic conditions, factors that have been shown in other studies to affect expenditures and utilization of long-term care services. Our assumption is that, if we find shortfalls or gaps in these states, we would expect that the situation is likely to be as difficult or more so in smaller, less urbanized states.

Sample SMSAs.   The SMSA was selected as the geopolitical unit from which to sample provider organizations because such catchment areas better represent the referral, market and interorganizational system for long-term care services than does a single city or county. In all cases one or two of the top four largest metropolitan areas (exceeding a population of one million) in the state were included in the study: Miami and Tampa/St. Petersburg; Philadelphia and Pittsburgh; Dallas/Ft. Worth and Houston;

San Francisco/Oakland and San Diego; and Seattle. The sample represents 9 of the 11 largest metropolitan areas in the 5 sample states and 9 of the 24 largest metropolitan areas in the nation.

Provider Sample.   The sample of provider organizations was selected randomly using probability sampling techniques, and the directors of each, or their designees, were interviewed by telephone for 30 to 60 minutes. The survey instrument contained both close-ended and open-ended questions covering the topics of: organizational structure; staffing patterns; clientele; service patterns; budgetary sources; opinion questions on policy issues; and perceptions of DRG effects in specific areas. This article presents the responses to the questions on DRG impact.

The service provider sample is comprised of a total of 771 respondents, representing 7 different service providers interviewed in 1986 and again in 1987. This combined data set consists of: 178 discharge planners, 166 home health agencies, 166 nursing homes, 39 adult day care centers, 104 senior centers, 24 hospices, and 94 community mental health centers, rendering a total of 1,542 interviews.

In 1986, respondents were asked to report on events and describe organizational changes occurring between 1984 and 1986 (to tap the immediate period of DRG implementation). In 1987, respondents were asked to report on events and changes occurring between 1986 and 1987. Thus, the data collected cover the period from 1984 to 1987.

Results

Five major findings emerged from the study. . . .

- **First and Second Generation Effects.** In response to an open-ended question asking respondents to identify the policy that had the most effect or impact on their organization during the time period studied, the policies that were most frequently nominated, in rank order, were DRGs and other Medicare policies (table 1).

The types of DRG effects agencies described included increased demands as a result of earlier release of older hospital patients still needing some form of care. The other Medicare policies nominated were associated with reimbursement such as problems with fiscal intermediaries and inadequate reimbursement.

Table 1 also illustrates the lag time in reported DRG effect by different types of agencies. The "first generation" effects of DRGs (1984–86) were most immediately and directly experienced by hospital discharge planners, nursing homes, home health agencies and, to a much lesser degree,

TABLE 1 Percentage of Providers Reporting DRGs and Medicare Policies as the Most Important Policies Affecting Their Agencies

Agency Provider Type	1986*		1987**		N
	DRG	Medicare	DRG	Medicare	
	%	%	%	%	
Discharge planners	90.4	10.7	62.3	12.4	(178)
Nursing homes	28.2	12.4	24.1	13.2	(166)
Home health agencies	36.7	41.0	12.6	33.7	(166)
Community mental health	6.4	0.0	0.0	0.0	(94)
Adult day care	0.0	0.0	12.8	25.6	(39)
Hospice programs	0.0	66.7	25.0	79.2	(24)
Senior centers	0.0	0.0	0.0	0.0	(104)

*Data are for the 1984–86 time period.
**Data are for the 1986–87 time period.
Source: IHA, DRG Study. Provider Instruments, 1986, 1987. "Please tell me what policies, or interpretations of policy, have had the greatest impact on your agency in the past 12 months, and what that impact has been."

community mental health centers. In 1987, however, the percentage of these providers nominating DRGs as the most important policy affecting them declined, while adult day care centers and hospices reported being affected by DRGs for the first time.

Although the one-fourth of adult day care centers reporting DRG effects is not large, the reason given for the impact, we believe, heralds an important trend. Adult day care centers reported that they were receiving more post-hospital patients referred from home health agencies after their Medicare benefits were exhausted, but before their care needs were met. This reason also explains the dramatic increase in the percentage of day care centers that reported being affected by other Medicare policies. At present adult day care services are paid for privately or by Medicaid, but not by Medicare. These centers believe the care they are now offering should be covered by Medicare as well.

- **The "Reach" of DRG Effects.** When we calculated the percentage of all providers reporting at least one type of DRG impact, we found that all seven types of providers reported being affected by DRGs in at least one of the following ways: types of clients served, services required or provided and/or referral patterns. The percent of providers reporting one or more types of DRG impact ranged from a low of 58 percent of senior centers to a high of 98 percent of discharge planners (table not shown). This is additional evidence that DRG

effects were experienced not only by medical service providers but
also by social service providers.

- **Change in Type of Client.** Providers were asked if they experienced changes in the types of clients they serve as a result of DRGs.
  As expected, the organizations most likely to receive patients directly following hospital discharge (home health agencies, hospices, and nursing homes) more frequently reported this type of
  DRG effect. Interestingly, however, even one-third of senior centers
  reported a change in clientele linked to DRGs (table 2).

When asked to indicate *how* their clientele had changed, the predominant response across providers, was that clients were more frail, physically
sicker and/or in need of more acute care services than in the previous
study period. Overall, 60 percent reported this in 1986 and 57 percent in
1987.

- **Change in Services.** The increased tendency for clients to be
  heavier-care is also reflected in the responses to questions about
  DRG effects on services (table 3).

Discharge planners differ from other providers in that their function is
to assess and arrange for services needed by hospital patients upon discharge. Their most frequently mentioned service changes were in outpatient services and increases in the amount of discharge planning done by

TABLE 2   Percentage of Providers Reporting They Have Experienced a Change
in the Types of Clients Served

Agency Provider Type	1986*	N	1987**	N
	%		%	
Home health agencies	92.1	(165)	82.3	(164)
Hospice programs	87.5	(24)	60.9	(23)
Nursing homes	84.3	(166)	87.2	(164)
Discharge planners	71.3	(174)	70.9	(175)
Adult day care	52.6	(38)	43.2	(37)
Community mental health	30.8	(91)	40.7	(91)
Senior centers	***	***	34.0	(94)

*Data are for the 1984–86 time period.
**Data are for the 1986–87 time period.
***Question not asked of senior centers in 1986.

Source: IHA, DRG Study. Provider Instruments, 1986, 1987. "As a result of Medicare DRG
payment to hospitals in the area you serve, has your agency experienced any of the following: a) Changes in the types of clients you serve?"

TABLE 3 Percentage of Providers Reporting Changes in Services as a
Result of DRGs

Agency Provider Type	1986*	N	1987**	N
	%		%	
Home health agencies	75.5	(163)	63.4	(164)
Hospice programs	75.0	(24)	56.5	(23)
Discharge planners	68.9	(177)	—	—
Nursing homes	55.2	(165)	55.2	(165)
Adult day care	36.8	(38)	34.2	(38)
Community mental health	33.3	(90)	27.5	(91)
Senior centers	***	***	29.0	(100)

*Data are for the 1984–86 time period.
**Data are for the 1986–87 time period.
***Question not asked of that provider type that year.
Source: IHA, DRG Study. Provider Instruments, 1986, 1987. As a result of Medicare DRG
payment to hospitals in the area you serve, has your agency experienced any of the follow-
ing: b) Shifts in the kinds of services you provide?"

the hospital. For home health agencies, hospice programs, and nursing
homes, the most frequently reported shifts in service were toward: more
acute high-tech care; more skilled nursing; and more antibiotic intravenous therapy. Home health agencies reported this type of impact first
(1984–86), while nursing homes and hospices reported more shifts of this
type between 1986–87. Senior centers most frequently reported providing
increased information and referral services, and adult day care centers
reported providing more direct supervision and more rehabilitative therapy. Community mental health centers reported case management was
increased as were services for the chronically ill.

As an additional indicator of whether or not patients were being released with more medically related needs, a question was asked about
changes in the units of service required as a result of DRGs. The majority
of providers reported changes in the units of service now required by their
clientele. For both years of the survey, the reported changes were in the
direction of increased units of service required—either increases in the
number of visits or increases in the length of time of care per patient.

- **Change in Referral Ability.** A substantial percentage of agencies
  reported changes in their ability to refer clients to hospitals (table
  4). The most frequently reported change was an increased difficulty
  in referring clients from community service providers *to* hospitals
  due to stricter hospital admission policies making *both* admission
  and readmission more difficult. This problem was reported more

TABLE 4   Percentage of Agencies Reporting Changes in Ability to Refer
to Hospitals

Agency Provider Type	1986*	N	1987**	N
	%		%	
Hospice programs	58.3	(24)	40.0	(20)
Community mental health	43.3	(90)	38.6	(88)
Home health	35.7	(154)	25.5	(161)
Nursing homes	30.5	(164)	25.9	(166)
Adult day care	20.6	(34)	18.8	(32)

*Data are for the 1984–86 time period.
**Data are for the 1986–87 time period.
Source: IHA, DRG Study. Provider Instruments, 1986, 1987. "As a result of Medicare DRG
payment to hospitals in the area you serve, has your agency experienced any of the following: d) Changes in your ability to refer clients to hospitals?"

frequently in 1986 than in 1987, although a sizable proportion of
providers were still reporting difficulty in 1987.

Not all providers were queried in both 1986 and 1987 about changes
in their ability to refer to other community providers (all providers were
asked in the 1987 survey). However, of the three types of agencies for
which there are data for both 1986 and 1987, discharge planners and home
health agencies were more likely to report changes in their ability to refer
to other agencies in 1986 than in 1987. The proportion of adult day care
centers remained virtually the same both years. The direction of the
change reported was an increased difficulty in referring clients to other
community agencies

Most disturbing is the number of discharge planners who reported
changes in the direction of increased difficulty in referring their hospital
patients to other agencies for both time periods of the survey. In 1986, 31
percent of all discharge planners interviewed ($N = 178$) reported increased
referral difficulty due to fewer resources and more difficulty in gaining
admission to nursing homes. In 1987, that percentage increased slightly to
34 percent and was reported to be due to: more difficulty in obtaining
homemaker/chore services, fewer resources available in general and longer agency waiting lists.

DISCUSSION

Study data suggest that the community-based service system is becoming saturated with physically sicker, heavier-care clients filtering down

through the post-hospital community care services, affecting the service packages of both medical and social service agencies. There are three potential implications for the clients of these provider agencies:

- If the situation continues to move in the direction begun with PPS, there is likely to be a trade-off between our society's ability to meet the needs of the post-acute elderly as opposed to needs of the chronically ill elderly who have not been recently hospitalized. This could create problems of access for the chronically ill elderly residing in the community.
- Medicare coverage for services outside of the acute care setting is extremely limited. An increased need for these services can be expected to increase the already high out-of-pocket health care expenses of the elderly, creating problems of access for older persons with limited financial capacity.
- In other sections of our survey not dealing with DRGs specifically, we found that agencies were depending more on family caregivers. Increasing attention is being given to informal caregiving as a means to control costs. Insofar as possible, we expect that the informal care sector represents the "third generation" of DRG effects, as responsibility for care of the disabled and chronically ill older adults continues to shift to the informal sector.

We have examined some of the short-term effects of DRGs on a number of community agencies but we do not know how long-term these effects may be nor can we generalize our findings beyond the agencies and SMSAs studied. Continuing and more detailed research on the services and clients of providers is needed to determine if beneficiary access to both post-acute and chronic care is adequate and whether the shifts of the type we describe are occurring more generally. Our findings also need to be further validated and complemented by research on the case-mix and service-mix of organizations of the type studied here. Given the probability method of sampling and the high response rates within the sample SMSAs, however, we are confident in, and disturbed by, our results.

REFERENCES

1. Guterman S, Eggers PW, Riley G, Greene TF, Terrell SA: The first three years of Medicare prospective payment: an overview. Health Care Financ Rev 1988; 9:59–66.

2. American Society of Internal Medicine: The impact of DRGs on patient care. Washington DC: ASIM, 1984/1985.

3. Des Harnais S, Kobrinski E, Chesney J, Long R, Ament R,

Fleming S: The early effects of the prospective payment system on inpatient utilization and the quality of care. Inquiry 1987; 24: 7–16.

4. Eggers P: Prospective payment system and quality; early results and research strategy. Health Care Financ Rev Annual Supplement 1987; 29–37.

5. Heinz J: The effects of DRGs on patients. Bus Health Jul/Aug 1986; 3(8):17–20.

6. Prospective Payment Assessment Commission: Medicare prospective payment and the American health care system: report to the Congress. Washington DC: The Commission, Feb 1987.

7. Prospective Payment Assessment Commission: Medicare prospective payment and the American health care system; report to the Congress. Washington DC: The Commission, Feb 1988.

8. Schramm CJ, Gabel J: Prospective payment: some retrospective observations. (Sounding Board) N Engl J Med 1988; 318:1681–1683.

9. US Senate, Special Committee on Aging: Impact of Medicare's PPS on the quality of care received by Medicare beneficiaries. Staff report. Washington DC: US Senate, Oct 24 1985.

10. Chelimsky E: Information requirements for evaluating the impacts of Medicare prospective payment on post-hospital long-term care services. Preliminary Report to US Senate Special Committee on Aging. Washington DC: US General Accounting Office, Feb 1985.

11. Chemlinsky E: Post-hospital care: efforts to evaluate Medicare's prospective payment effects are insufficient. Report to the Chairman, U.S. Senate Special Committee on Aging. Washington DC: U.S. General Accounting Office, Jan 1986.

12. Bergthold LA: The impact of public policy on home health services for the elderly. Pride Inst J Long Term Home Care 1987; 6:12–21.

13. Neu CR, Harrington C: Posthospital care before and after the Medicare PPS. Los Angeles: RAND/UCLA Center for Health Care Financing Policy, Mar 1988.

14. Van Gelder S. Bernstein J: Home health care in the era of hospital prospective payment: some early evidence and thoughts about the future. Pride Inst J Long Term Home Health Care 1986; 5:3–11.

15. Wood JB: Public policy and the current effect on home health agencies. Home Health Care Serv Q 1984; 5:75–86.

16. Wood JB: Home care agencies and health care competition. Home Healthcare Nurse 1985; 3:22–24.

17. Wood JB: The effects of cost-containment on home health agencies. Home Health Serv Q 1985/ 1986; 6:59–78.

18. Wood JB: Estes CL, Lee PR, Fox PJ: Public policy, the private non-profit sector and the delivery of community-based long-term care services for the elderly. Year 01. San Francisco: Inst for Health Aging, University of California, 1983.

19. Wood JB, Fox PJ, Estes CL, Lee PR, Mahoney CJ: Public policy, the private nonprofit sector and the delivery of community-based long-term care services for the elderly. Year 02. San Francisco: Inst for Health Aging, University of California, 1985.

20. Wood JB. Estes CL: The "medicalization" of community services for the elderly. Health Soc Work 1988; 13:35–42.

21. Estes CL: The United States: long-term care and federal policy. Home

Health Care Serv Q 1984/1985; 5:315–328.

22. Estes CL: The politics of ageing in America. Ageing Society 1986; 6:121–134.

23. Estes CL, Wood JB: The non-profit sector and community-based care for the elderly in the US: a disappearing resource? Soc Sci Med 1986; 23:1261–1266.

24. Kinoy SK, Adamson M, Sherry S (eds): The ABCs of DRGs: How to Protect and Expand Medicare Patient's Rights. A Supplement to The Best Medicine: Organizing Local Health Care Campaigns. Washington, DC: Villers Foundation, 1988.

25. Kotelchuck R: And what about the patients? Prospective payment's impact on quality of care. Health Pac Bull 1986; 17:13–17.

26. U.S. General Accounting Office: Post-hospital care: discharge planners report increasing difficulty in placing Medicare patients. Report to the Chairman. Subcommittee on Health and Long-Term Care, U.S. House of Representatives. Washington DC: U.S. General Accounting Office, 1987.

Interviewer: How's your health right now? Respondent: My health is pretty good right now, thank God. I have arthritis in my shoulders. That hurts—it hurts like hell. I get pills for that. For my leg I get a water pill. But that's all I get. So, that's not bad for an 89-year-old woman.
— Sharon R. Kaufman

William G. Weissert

Home Care: Measuring Success

If home care for the elderly were a privately marketed product similar to movie theater tickets, there would be no need to ask, How shall we measure success? The answer would be obvious: Satisfied consumers would demand more of the product and providers would prosper. If consumers were not satisfied, demand would drop and providers would go bankrupt. But these rules of market economics apply in only a limited way when the product is a publicly subsidized social service such as health care (Pauly, 1983) where the argument has been made that the public has a stake in guaranteeing access to care for everyone (Daniels, 1985).

The success of home care (home health, homemaker, day care, respite, and other health and social services delivered at home or in the community) for the elderly may be measured in a number of ways. Employing Donabedian's (1980) perspectives on evaluating success in terms of outcome, process, and structure, a reasonable starting point is to ask, "Has home care succeeded in improving outcomes, including increased longevity, improved physical or mental functioning, or increased satisfaction or morale of the patient or informal caregiver?"

OUTCOME MEASURES OF SUCCESS

For most measures of outcome, effects have been negligible. Drawing upon evidence synthesized by Weissert, Cready, and Pawelak (1988) from the 27 home and community care demonstration projects of the past 3 decades (table 1), the accumulated results show that use of home care has not proved to be of significant measurable efficacy in helping patients live longer, function better, or experience fewer restricted activity days. Longev-

---

William G. Weissert, Ph.D., is Research Scientist at the Institute of Gerontology, and Professor of Health Services, Management and Policy at the University of Michigan, Ann Arbor.

From Weissert, W.G. (1991). Home care: measuring success. In P.R. Katz, R.L. Kane, and M.D. Mezey, eds., *Advances in Long-term Care*, Vol. 1 (pp. 186–251). Copyright 1991 by Springer Publishing Company, Inc., New York. Used by permission.

ity may sometimes be affected, but evidence was tenuous. Counting the 4 studies that examined effects in 2 discrete samples, the total number of studies reviewed was 31. Of those, 28 measured the impact of home care on survival. Half found positive and half found negative impacts. When results were significant (only 8 studies), they were usually positive. However, half (14) of the studies found no significant impacts due to home care. Some studies (6) did not report level of significance.

The effects of physical functioning appear to be negligible. Physical functioning was measured by activities of daily living (ADL), restricted activity days, and other measurements. From the total of 31 studies, 26 measured ADL functioning. About half found positive impacts due to home care. Only 7 studies found statistically significant impacts, and again, these were split almost evenly between positive (3) and negative (4) impacts. Similar patterns existed for other measures of physical functioning.

Most psychosocial outcomes, as measured by mental functioning, life satisfaction, social activities, and social interactions, were likewise rarely statistically significant. Though often the direction of findings was predominantly positive, effect sizes were usually very small and transient— lasting only 6 to 12 months despite continued use of home care (Weissert, Cready, & Pawelak, 1988).

Impacts on informal caregivers (usually measured as life satisfaction, satisfaction with patient care, or stress) were usually small and nonsignificant, but uniformly positive in direction. Performance by the informal social support network appears to have been substantially unaffected by receipt of expanded formal home care—good news for policymakers concerned that paid care would drive out unpaid care.

In short, from the perspective of outcomes, home care has achieved quite limited success—accomplishing little with respect to objective measures of patient health status, but possibly improving life satisfaction of patients and family caregivers by small transient amounts.

Why so little success in the outcomes domain? One obvious explanation is that health and medical care evaluations usually don't show much when the events studied (death, functional status change) are relatively rare in the population (Fuchs, 1974; Grannemann & Pauly, 1983; Benham & Benham, 1975; Newhouse & Friedlander, 1980; Brook et al., 1983; and DesHarnais et al., 1987). Benefits are either not produced or are missed because we have not appropriately matched patients to appropriate outcome expectations. What we need are clinically relevant subgroups of patients who might be successfully treated to ameliorate the specific health risks which they face. While home care use is nominally controlled by patient-specific care plans, both the interventions and the research have been directed to populations that are quite heterogeneous with respect to their specific risks of adverse outcome and their potential for tractability.

TABLE 1   Home and Community-based Long-term Care Demonstration
Projects, 1959–1989

Project	Interventions	Eligibility Criteria
Continuity in Care (1959–63)*	Nurse home visits	Indigent geriatric rehab. hosp. discharge
Continued Care (1963–71)*	Nurse home visits	Rehab. hosp. discharge
BRI Project Service (1964–66)*	Case management and ancillary services	Noninstitutionalized mentally impaired with no informal caregiver
Congestive Heart Failure (1964–66)*	Nurse home visits	Chronic congestive heart failure, outpatient hosp. clinic visits
BRH Home Aide (1966–69)*	Home aide visits	Geriatric rehab. hosp. discharge
Highland Heights (1970–76)	Housing	Functionally impaired or medically vulnerable
Chronic Disease (1971–76)	Interdisciplinary team home visits	Amb. care facility patient or hosp. discharge
Worcester (1973–75)*	Case management and non-Medicaid-covered home services	Noninstitutionalized and primarily receiving informal care, or institutionalized with discharge potential
Section 222 Day Care (1974–77)*	Adult day care services	In need of health care services to restore or maintain functional ability
Homemaker (1974–77)	Homemaker services	Hosp. discharge in need of health care services to restore or maintain functional ability
Health Maintenance Team (1975)*	Nonskilled nursing and nurse home visits	Chronically ill or disabled needing nonskilled care
Wisconsin CCO/ Milwaukee (1975–79)*	Case management and non-Medicaid-covered home services	At risk of institutionalization
Alarm Response (1975–80)	In-home alarm response system	Medically vulnerable or functionally impaired public housing tenant who lives alone
Georgia (1976–80)*	Case management and non-Medicaid-covered home services	Previously institutionalized nursing home applicant, or certified as Medicaid eligible for nursing home care
Triage (1976–81)	Case management and non-Medicare-covered services	Unstable condition (medical/ social problems, poor informal support, or environmental or financial problems)
Chicago (1977–80)	Interdisciplinary home visits	Homebound, ADL impaired
On Lok (1978–83)	Case management and non-Medicare-covered services	Qualified for skilled or intermediate nursing home care

Project OPEN (1978–83)*	Case management and non-Medicare-covered services	Cognitively aware with medical problem, needing function assistance
Home Health Care Team (1979–82)*	Interdisciplinary team home visits	Chronically disabled or terminally ill and homebound with informal care available
NYC Home Care (1979–84)	Case management and non-Medicare-covered services	Chronically ill with functional needs
San Diego (1979–84)	Case management and non-Medicare-covered home services	Requires assistance to remain at home, risk of institutionalization, or needs nontraditional long-term care
Florida Pentastar (1980–83)*	Case management and non-Medicaid-covered home services	Risk of institutionalization and in need of project services
Nursing Home without Walls	Case management and other non-Medicaid-	Medicaid eligible for nursing home care
Downstate (1980–83)	covered home services	
Upstate (1980–83)	Case management and other non-Medicaid-covered home services	Medicaid eligible for nursing home care
South Carolina (1980–84)*	Case management and other non-Medicaid-covered home services	Preadmission screening determined Medicaid eligible nursing home applicant
Channeling*	Case management and	2 or more ADL impairments, 3
Basic (1980–85)	limited gap-filling services	IADLs, or 1 IADL and 2 IADLs with unmet need
Financial (1980–85)	Case management and other home care services	2 or more ADL impairments, 3 IADLs, or 1 IADL and 2 IADLs with unmet need
Acute Stroke (1981–83)	Interdisciplinary team home visits	Victim of acute stroke
ACCESS		
Medicare/ Private Pay (1982–86)	Case management skilled nursing home and/or non-Medicare-covered home care services	Needs 90+ days of skilled nursing care
Medicare/ Medicaid (1982–86)	Case management skilled nursing home and/or non-Medicare-covered home care services plus non-Medicaid-covered home care services	Needs 90+ days of skilled nursing care
Post-Hospital Support (1983–85)	Case management and interdisciplinary home visits plus services for caregivers	Hosp. discharge with problem expected to last 1 yr and qualified for skilled nursing care and has informal caregiver

Note: *These studies were randomized, controlled trials; others were nonrandomly selected comparison groups.

Source: Adapted from Weissert, W.G., Cready, C.M., & Pawelak, J.E. (1988).

In other words, there is a great tendency in home care to assume that patients need pretty much the same thing and are likely to improve in pretty much the same way regardless of important differences in the specific health risks which they may face at a given point in time. Greater potential for achieving success might lie in separating the home care population into groups of individuals who face different risks (e.g., chronic physical function decline; postacute physical function rehabilitation potential; mental decline; death and family bereavement; satisfaction decline; breakdown of informal caregiver support network; hospital readmission; nursing home admission or extended stay; etc.) and treating them in accordance with ameliorating those specific risks.

Research has not yet succeeded in disaggregating the home care population into such groups. When it does, care plans can be tailored to these groups' specific needs, outcomes can be evaluated in terms of avoiding the specific health risks which they face, and resource inputs might be limited to those expected to produce the appropriate outcome. Such an approach would greatly increase statistical power in research studies and is consistent with the findings of several of the recent studies of health and medical care efficacy which have tended to show benefits only in certain subgroups facing rather immediate risks of specific adverse outcomes (Hadley, 1982; Laurie et al., 1984; Keeler et al., 1985; Ware et al., 1986), and with Wennberg's (1985) view that we need much more specific research on the effectiveness of specific medical procedures for specific types of patients.

Strategies for making this match must start with profiles of who is at risk of various adverse outcomes such as death, nursing home admission long stay, hospital admission, readmission or long stay, failure to achieve functional potential, declining life satisfaction, or caregiver burnout. Considerable work has already been done on profiling patients at risk of death, hospital admission, and nursing home entry (Boulier & Paqueo, 1988; Campbell et al., 1985; Heinemann, 1985; Branch & Jette, 1982; Cohen, Tell, & Wallack, 1986; Greenberg & Ginn, 1979; Morris, Sherwood, & Gutkin, 1988; Weissert & Cready, 1989b; Cafferata, 1987; Coulton & Frost, 1982; Evashwick et al., 1984). These tools should be used and others developed to estimate patients' risks for each type of outcome.

PROCESS MEASURES OF SUCCESS: EFFICIENCY

When home care first moved to the public agenda in the early 1970s the emphasis was not on outcomes but rather on efficiency. The claim was widely made that it would be a cost-effective substitute for nursing home care. As a consequence, the purpose of home care was to save money by serving patients more efficiently. Results on this point have been uniformly negative (Weissert, Cready, & Pawelak, 1988). While home care does provide a substitute for nursing home care for some patients, for most patients it serves as a complement to existing health care services. Most patients who use home care would not have been in a nursing home without it. Hence their additional costs of home care more than offset the savings produced by keeping a few patients out of nursing homes. Consequently, home care has not proved to be a cost-effective substitute for institutional care.

Surprisingly, cost increases have not been particularly large, however, averaging somewhere between 15 and 20% over the past three decades (Weissert & Cready, 1989a). This leads to the question: Could home care be delivered more efficiently so that it might move closer to a break-even point?

This potential appears to be worth exploring for one important reason: Most of the ways in which home care could be made more efficient appear to be traceable to better management practices which in turn might result if better data were available for management decision making.

The following formula for net costs of home care tells the story: Net costs = savings minus new spending, where savings refer to avoided nursing home and hospital care and new spending is for outpatient services and new home care services. (The value of patient benefits may also be added to the equation, but is very difficult to quantify.)

In essence this formula means that the better job home care does of targeting services to patients at high risk of long nursing home stays or hospital admission—and the better job it does of avoiding those admissions or shortening stays—the more savings are generated that can be used to offset the new costs of home care and other outpatient services used by home care patients.

Conversely, if home care patients are given cheaper home care services or fewer of them, new home care costs are reduced and therefore more limited success in generating savings from avoided inpatient care is required.

How well has home care succeeded in targeting patients at risk of long nursing home admission, avoiding those admissions as well as hospital admissions, and reducing lengths of stay? And how well has use of home care been controlled to make it as efficient as possible?

Results are mixed. Typically, among the studies reviewed, about one-fourth or one-fifth (depending upon whether or not results are weighted by study population size) of home care patients would have entered a nursing home without home care, and they would have had a length of stay of about four months, resulting in a per capita cost of $3,059. By decreasing admissions by approximately one-fourth and length of stay by about 11%, home care was able to decrease the per capita cost of nursing home care by just under a half (46%). In addition, hospital admissions are typically relatively high among home care patients, but they tend not to be much affected by home care, nor do lengths of stay drop by much. Detailed results are presented in Weissert and Cready (1989a). Therefore, while some savings are produced on these institutional use reductions, they tend to be offset by large spending on home care (Weissert & Cready, 1989a).

One of the reasons for such large home care spending appears to be a lack of consensus on home care utilization guidelines. Like all health care use, much of home care use is stochastic and defies explanation by health services researchers. By further analysis (in progress by the author and colleagues) of utilization patterns from the National Long-term Care Channeling Evaluation suggests that there is substantial room for development of clinical guidelines for utilization control, especially to decrease intensity of use after the patient and family caregiver have effectively adapted to the caregiving role. If home care suffers the same diminishing returns typical of most other inputs in life including health care (Fuchs, 1974), one might expect a systematic effort to reduce frequency, intensity and skill level of home care to decline after a few months of care. Yet patterns of home care use tend to show little of this diminishing level of use with time.

Likewise, lack of clinically relevant subgroups, discussed above as potentially important to enhanced outcomes, also are likely to be of great importance to utilization decisions. Care planners might be willing to work within a break-even budget constraint if they had the discretion and knowledge to tailor their resource spending to patients' potential to benefit.

In short, while home care has not yet been sufficiently successful in terms of efficiency to actually cost less than existing options, achievement of that goal may be closer today than it was a decade ago when home care treatment groups cost 60 to 70% more than their control groups (Weissert, Wan, Livieratos, & Katz, 1980; Weissert, Wan, Livieratos, & Pellegrino, 1980). Needed are some better clinical tools for selecting patients, including identification of those at risk of institutionalization and other adverse outcomes, and some clinically appropriate utilization control guidelines capable of achieving maximum benefit at minimum cost.

A shift in the home care cost research agenda from whether or not home care is cost-effective to how to make it cost-effective might greatly enhance its prospects for future success in the process of home care.

POLITICAL SUPPORT AND RATIONALES, QUALITY ASSURANCE MECHANISMS, AND ACCOUNTABILITY

Because it is not simply a private good, but one that must rely upon public subsidy, the ultimate measure of home care's success may have little to do with either outcomes or efficiency. If home care could garner sufficient political support to ensure a steady and adequate source of public payment, it would "succeed" in one important sense, efficiency, outcome issues not withstanding.

Yet, one must ask why that has not happened already? Why have the states or Congress not funded broad-based eligibility for home care for the aged? Current federal funding for home care comes from a variety of fragmented . . . sources including Medicare, Medicaid, Social Services Block Grant, Older American's Act, Veteran's Administration, and a variety of state and locally funded programs.

Such small fractions of the larger health care spending probably reflect more than anything else concerns over potential to exacerbate runaway budget deficits. Failure by an overwhelming vote in Congress of the Pepper bill [in 1989]—which would have extended home care to all elderly suffering dependency in at least two activities of daily living—appeared to reflect "sticker shock" at its $50 billion per year price tag.

But another reason for insufficient funding may be that home care has not succeeded in establishing a sufficiently strong rationale for itself. What is needed is a good enough reason to provide home care that society is willing to do it even at the cost of doing less about some competing worthy social goals. What comes to mind here is the floundering position in which home care finds itself when its two major claims of purpose (cost savings and improved outcomes) are substantially or wholly taken away by an overwhelmingly consistent body of research findings showing few benefits and negative savings.

Although home care advocates continue despite the contrary evidence to claim outcome and efficiency benefits, currently neither claim carries much weight among those familiar with the home care demonstration project findings, including federal budget staff, congressional committee staff, and most state Medicaid directors. There is simply no way that home care can be convincingly sold to well-informed policy analysts on the basis that it will save money. Arguing outcome benefits means citing small and transient satisfaction benefits and reduction of unmet needs without consequent change in health status.

Two alternative rationales have been less well developed. The first is that home care serves primarily not the patient but the informal (e.g., family) caregiver. Satisfaction benefits were higher among informal caregivers than patients in the recent National Long-term Care Channeling Evaluation (Kemper, 1988; Applebaum et al., 1988). Second, home care now appears to be rationed on the basis of price, irrespective of need—a notion which seems to fly in the face of the purpose of Medicare: to remove price as a barrier to equal access to health care by the elderly.

Certainly the assertion that home care in its various forms (respite, day care, homemaker aide, etc.) can take the burden off the caregiver is a point that has been made. But the notion that the real client is the informal caregiver has been advanced by few home care commentators (Hendrickson, 1988). Clearly society has an important stake in keeping the family caregiving network in place. Replacing it rather than supplementing it with formal care would be enormously expensive.

Indeed, employers have begun to recognize that workplace efficiency may be enhanced by programs which support family caregivers in the work force. Recent developments such as employer-supported family relations counselors and the American Association of Retired Persons—Travelers Insurance Company's survey of caregiving among its work force (Opinion Research Corporation, 1988) demonstrate that there is substantial potential to marshal support in the future around home care's role in freeing the employed informal caregiver from burdens which may interfere with work force productivity. The potential is enhanced by the steady increase in labor force participation among the group which has the highest potential for becoming informal caregivers—females. A recent national survey of adult day care family caregivers found that one-fourth of them were in the labor force (Weissert et al., 1990). It takes no soothsayer to anticipate that use of home care services will increase in the future as a means of freeing informal caregivers to go to work. While a true cost-effectiveness analysis from the employer's perspective might show that home care costs more than it saves in lost productivity, firms may nonetheless be forced to provide this benefit option if they are to compete successfully for top female employees. If firms want to avoid this expense, one way would be to support government subsidy of caregiver relief programs such as home care.

What makes this especially relevant is that it offers a rationale for providing home care to a subgroup of home care patients for whom improved outcomes other than caregiver relief are not relevant.

The necessity of public subsidy if equity of access is to be achieved represents another important potential rationale for public payment for home care. Preliminary . . . research by the author and colleagues suggests that among patients who are dependent in activities of daily living, use of home care increases with income. This suggests that it is currently rationed on the basis of price and ability to pay, not need. This is the opposite of the Medicare dream of equal access to health care among the aged.

No doubt this finding reflects the deliberately restrictive eligibility requirements of Medicare—the program under which most middle-class elderly would be likely to qualify. Medicare covers home care only for patients who qualify as homebound, need a skilled service, and need it only intermittently—typically for no more than three weeks. Except for incidental help with bathing, eating, and dressing of a skilled-care patient, aide services are not covered. This effectively excludes most nonacute elderly patients from eligibility for home care services under Medicare. Indeed, home care advocates have recently accused the Health Care Financing Administration of deliberately adopting a policy of more aggressive denials of home care applications (United States Senate, 1988)—a response to increased home care use following implementation of Medicare's prospective payment system for hospitals. Even the limited Medicare benefit currently authorized is thought to be less available in rural areas (United States Senate, 1988).

Again, if home care were theater tickets, few would care that it appears to be rationed on the basis of income and geography. But it is not. Instead, comparing across a subgroup with obvious commonality of need—dependency and lack of social support—price and where they live make differences in who gets care and who does not. The contemporary philosopher John Rawls would regard such a policy as unjust (Daniels, 1985) because it fails to serve the interests of this very disadvantaged social group: dependent elderly and their informal caregivers. Whether or not a sufficient number of congressmen and senators would agree remains to be seen, but in the past, equity has been a venerated rationale for public intervention.

Prospects for achieving success in obtaining broader and less fragmented public subsidy of home care on the basis of equity of access and relief of informal caregivers might be further enhanced if the suggestions made above for improved home care process were heeded: If home care were delivered efficiently, to those well-defined groups of patients or their informal caregivers most likely to benefit in specific ways, the cost might be brought down and the benefits brought up so that an argument based upon equity of access to some of society's most disadvantaged members might be persuasive.

Home care might also improve its potential for garnering political support if it were able to make a better case for assured quality of care and accountability to patients, families, and payers. At present, quality assurance in the home care field is almost entirely at the structural level—audits to determine that care was authorized and documented as having been delivered. Presentations at a recent Department of Health and Human Services (DHHS)-sponsored conference on home care quality assurance (DHHS, 1988) made it clear that few standards for measuring quality exist, few mechanisms are in place to enforce standards other than by paper review, and patients typically have little protected opportunity for redress if the quality of the care they receive is substandard. Considering that aides are typically entry-level workers, untrained or minimally trained, and unsupervised for much of their work day, the vulnerable population they serve would seem especially in need of oversight, assurance, and accountability mechanisms. Arguing the need for training of home care aides, a recent U.S. Senate (1988) report cited results of a 1987 survey by the National League for Nursing which showed that most home health aides were untrained in tasks likely to be asked of them in caring for elderly patients (e.g., 30% did not know what to do if a patient stopped breathing). Home care does not appear to have succeeded in developing the necessary structures to assure quality and accountability.

CONCLUSIONS

Home care produces minimal measurable outcome benefits; it costs more than it saves; it lacks a clear purpose in light of its minimal outcome and efficiency benefits; it is not well targeted to subgroups for whom level and mix of inputs can be weighed against expected outcome benefits; it has failed to garner sufficient political support to provide broad and unfragmented reimbursement; it lacks appropriate mechanisms for quality assurance and patient accountability guarantees; and it is available only on an inequitable basis. In these senses home care appears not to have succeeded by many of the standards which might reasonably be applied.

On the other hand, it has become more efficient and shows the potential with better management of actually breaking even or coming very close. It shows potential to benefit more patients if appropriate subgroups are served and their outcomes well specified and measured.

In turn such subgroups and their appropriate outcomes—including for example, informal caregiver relief—could provide home care with an appropriate purpose—or in the economist's argot "objective function." An additional rationale for public intervention may be available by appeal to an equity-of-access argument based upon Medicare's objectives and indications of price and geographic rationing. Its shortcomings in terms of aide training and the need for quality assurance and patient accountability mechanisms have now been recognized and are likely to see improvement efforts in the near future.

In short, home care has not yet succeeded in outcome, process, or structural goals. Its advocates need first to figure out who should get it, how much they should get, and what the care is supposed to accomplish. As this happens, it may come closer to achieving another objective: publicly subsidized equity of access to those who need it.

REFERENCES

Applebaum, R.A., Christianson, J.B., Harrigan, M., & Schore, J. (1988). The evaluation of the national long-term care demonstration: The effect of channeling on mortality, functioning, and well-being. *Health Services Research, 23,* 143–159.

Benham, L., & Benham, A. (1975). The impact of incremental medical services on health status, 1963–1970. In R. Anderson, J. Kravitz, & D.W. Anderson (Eds.), *Equity in Health Services: Empirical Analysis of Social Policy* (pp. 217–228). Cambridge, MA: Ballinger.

Boulier, B.L., & Paqueo, V.B. (1988,

May). On the theory and measurement of the determinants of mortality. *Demography, 25,* 249–263.

Branch, L., & Jette, A. (1982). A prospective study of long-term care institutionalization among the aged. *American Journal of Public Health, 72,* 1373–1379.

Brook, R.H., Ware, J.E., Rogers, W.H., Keeler, E.B., Davies, A.R., Donald, C.A., Goldberg, G.A., Lohr, K.N., Masthay, P.C., & Newhouse, J.P. (1980). Does free care improve adults' health? *New England Journal of Medicine, 309,* 1426–1433.

Cafferata, G.L. (1987). Marital status, living arrangements, and the use of health services of elderly persons. *Journal of Gerontology, 42,* 613.

Campbell, A.D., Diep, C., Reinken, J., & McCosh, L. (1985). Factors predicting mortality in a total population sample of the elderly. *J. Epidemiol Community Health, 39,* 337–342.

Cohen, M., Tell, E., & Wallack, E. (1986). Client-related risk factors of nursing home entry among elderly adults. *Journal of Gerontology, 41,* 785–792.

Coulton, C., & Frost, A.K. (1982). Use of social and health services by the elderly. *Journal of Health and Social Behavior, 23,* 330.

Daniels, N. (1985). *Just Health Care,* D.I. Wikler, (Ed.). New York: Cambridge University Press.

DesHarnais, S., Kobrinski, E., Chesney, J., Long, M., Ament, R., & Fleming, S. (1987, Spring). The early effects of the prospective payment system on inpatient utilization and the quality of care. *Inquiry,* 7–16.

Donabedian, A. (1980). *The Definition of Quality and Approaches to Its Assessment: Explorations in Quality Assessment and Monitoring, Vol. 1.* Ann Arbor, MI: Health Administration Press.

Evashwick, C., Rowe, G., Diehr, P., & Branch, L. (1984). Factors explaining the use of health care services by the elderly. *Health Services Research, 19,* 357.

Fuchs, Victor, R. (1974). *Who Shall Live?* New York: Basic Books.

Grannemann, T.W., & Pauly, M.V. (1983). *Controlling Medicaid Costs: Federalism, Competition and Choice* (Chapters 1–3, pp. 1–29). Washington DC: American Enterprise Institute.

Greenberg, J., & Ginn, A. (1979). A Multi-variate analysis of the predictors of long-term care placement. *Home Health Services Quarterly, 1,* 75–79.

Hadley, J. (1982). *More Medical Care, Better Health?* Washington, DC: The Urban Institute Press.

Heinemann, G. (1985). Negative health outcomes among the elderly: Predictors and profiles. *Research on Aging, 7,* 363–382.

Hendrickson, M.C. (1988). State tax incentives for persons giving informal care to the elderly. *Health Care Financing Review,* (Annual Supplement), 123–128.

Keeler, E.B., Brook, R.H., Goldberg, G.A., Kamberg, C.J., & Newhouse, J.P. (1985). How free care reduced hypertension in the health insurance experiment. *JAMA, 254,* 1926–1931.

Kemper, P. (1988). The evaluation of the national long-term care demonstration: Overview of the findings. *Health Services Research, 23,* 1.

Laurie, N., Ward, N.B., Shapiro, M.F., & Brook, R.H. (1984). Termination from medical—Does it affect health? *The New England Journal of Medicine, 311,* 480–484.

Morris, J.N., Sherwood, S., & Gutkin, C.E. (1988). Inst-Risk II: An approach to forecasting relative risk of future institutional placement. *Health Services Research, 23,* 511–536.

Newhouse, J.P., & Friedlander, L.J. (1980). The relationship between medical resources and measures of health: Some additional evidence. *The Journal of Human Resources, 15,* 200–218.

Opinion Research Corporation (1988). A National Survey of Caregivers. Final report for the American Association of Retired Persons and the Travelers Foundation. Washington, DC.

Pauly, M. (1983). Is medical care different? In Greenberg, W. (Ed.), *Competition in the Health Care Sector: Past, Present and Future*. Washington, DC: Federal Trade Commission, 19–27.

United States Department of Health and Human Services (1988). Report on the National Invitational Conference on Home Care Quality: Issues and Accountability, Vol. 1. Summary of Proceedings by the Office of the Assistant Secretary for Planning and Evaluation. Washington, DC.

United States Senate (1988). Home Care at the Crossroads. An information paper by the staff of the Special Committee on Aging, United States Senate. 100th Cong., 2d Sess., Serial No. 100-H. Washington, DC.

Ware, J.E., Brook, R.H., Rogers, W.H., Keeler, E.B., Davies, A.R., Sherbourne, C.D., Goldberg, G.A., Camp, P., & Newhouse, J.P. (1986, May). Comparison of health outcomes of a Health Maintenance Organization with those of fee-for-service care. *Lancet, 3,* 1017–1022.

Weissert, W.G., & Cready, C.M. (1989a). A prospective budgeting model for home and community-based long-term care. *Inquiry, 26,* 116–129.

Weissert, W.G., & Cready, C.M. (1989b, October). Toward a model for improved targeting of aged at risk of institutionalization. *Health Services Research, 24,* 485–510.

Weissert, W.G., Cready, C.M., & Pawelak, J.E. (1988). The past and future of home and community-based long-term care. *Milbank Quarterly, 66,* 309–388.

Weissert, W.G., Elston, J.M., Bolda, E.J., Zelman, W.N., Mutran, E., & Mangum, A.B. (1990). *Adult Day Care: Findings from a National Survey.* Baltimore, MD: Johns Hopkins University Press.

Weissert, W.G., Wan, T.T.H., Livieratos, B., & Pellegrino, J. (1980). Cost-effectiveness of homemaker services for the chronically ill. *Inquiry, 17,* 230–243.

Weissert, W.G., Wan, T.T.H., Livieratos, B., & Katz, S. (1980). Effects and costs of daycare services for the chronically ill: A randomized experiment. *Medical Care, 18,* 567–587.

Wennberg, J.E. (1985). On patient need, equity, supplier-induced demand, and the need to assess the outcome of common medical practices. *Medical Care, 23,* 510–520.

Health *designates a process of adaptation. It is not the result of instinct, but of autonomous and live reaction to an experienced reality. It designates the ability to adapt to changing environments, to growing up and to aging, to healing when damaged, to suffering and to the peaceful expectation of death.*

— Ivan Illich

7

Physician Labor Market

Members of a surgical research team

John B. McKinlay

The Changing Character of the Medical Profession

We are witnessing a major transformation of the health care systems of the more developed countries that is without parallel in modern times. These institutional changes have implications for the entire division of labor in health care. While there is general agreement on the fact of change, there is healthy debate over its explanation and implications, especially with respect to the evolving social position of doctors. . . .

Some of the major changes affecting the overall medical care system, its organization, and the content of services and training, are as follows:

1. The involvement of large-scale financial and industrial capital interests in the business of medicine;
2. The ever-expanding role of government at all levels, particularly through financing and regulation;
3. Technological changes in the content of care that require new plants, new equipment, different training, and new categories of workers;
4. The emergence of a new group of medical administrators (sometimes physicians) whose reference group, understandably, is the organization and whose actions (again understandably) are always in the interest of the bottom line;
5. The emergence of an apparently more knowledgeable and questioning public, which challenges traditional medical interests.
6. Evidence of the modest contribution (marginal utility) of medical care to improvement of the health status of populations (as distinct from individuals).

Other general changes could be added to this brief list. Starr (1982) has described some of the "social transformations" that are occurring in Ameri-

John B. McKinlay, Ph.D., is Vice President and Director of the New England Research Institute, Inc., Watertown, Massachusetts.

From McKinlay, J.B. (1988). The changing character of the medical profession: Introduction. *Milbank Q* 66(suppl. 2):1–9. Used with permission of The Milbank Memorial Fund.

can medicine, but their explanation and their implications, especially for health care workers, remain to be developed. . . .

MANIFESTATIONS OF CHANGE

What are some of the manifestations of these overall changes in medical care for everyday doctoring in the United States? A few illustrations should suffice. Physicians are increasingly an unhappy and disaffected group of workers. They complain more and more about bureaucratic encroachments, government interference, the crippling expense of malpractice insurance, and the effect of the threat of litigation on the content of care (defensive medicine). Medical journals regularly contain anecdotal reports from older doctors that medicine today is not like the "good old days." In discussing changes in doctoring with one medical school dean, I was told that he would not pay medical school tuition costs for his own children (although he would support their graduate training in other fields). Many physicians state openly (albeit in professional journals to their colleagues) that, if they had to do it over again, they would not pursue medicine as a career. There is evidence of the development of unionization among physicians; only about one-half of all physicians are members of the American Medical Association. The editor of, and invited commentators for, the *New England Journal of Medicine* have lamented the development of the for-profit motive and how it is eroding the ethical basis of medicine. There are complaints about a decline in real income for doctors (especially for the 50 percent or so who are fully salaried bureaucratic employees) and projections of a relative loss of earning power over the next decade.

Although still hotly argued, there are reports of an oversupply of physicians—an excess of 150,000 by the year 2000—which threatens their market position. The ratio of doctors to the United States general population is expected to reach 1 to 300 by 1990, by which time there will be 1 health worker for every 14 people in the population. These health workers are encroaching upon the traditional domain of the doctor (albeit in the name of "team work" and "specialization"). College advisors are dissuading highly talented students from choosing medicine because its job market looks so bleak. There is no disputing the fact that medical school applications have declined; students apparently fear a glutted market. Practicing doctors state that their patients do not accord them the respect that they formerly received. Patients are apparently much more assertive or demanding, and threaten to take their "business" elsewhere if the satisfaction "demanded" is not received. Caveat emptor has replaced credat emptor. As bureaucratic employees of health organizations, physicians are required to "keep the customer satisfied" (even though patients can be dissatisfied with technically competent high-quality care and satisfied with technically inadequate care). There are reports that physicians are leaving medicine to pursue more satisfying work in other fields. This brief catalogue of manifestations could be readily expanded.

OCCUPATIONAL PREROGATIVES

In my own work on modern changes in doctoring (McKinlay 1977; McKinlay and Arches 1985, 1986; McKinlay and Stoeckle 1988), in order to provide operational specificity and to facilitate the collection of useful data, I have listed seven specific occupational prerogatives that affect the relative position or power of any group of workers. They are based on earlier theoretical work and are as follows:

1. The criteria for entrance (e.g., the credentialing system and membership requirements);
2. The content of training (e.g., the scope and content of the medical curriculum);
3. Autonomy regarding the terms and content of work (e.g., the ways in which what must be done is to be accomplished);
4. The objects of labor (e.g., commodities produced or the clients served);
5. The tools of labor (e.g., machinery, biotechnology, chemical apparatus);
6. The means of labor (e.g., hospital buildings, clinic facilities, lab services); and
7. The amount and rate of remuneration for labor (e.g., wage and salary levels, fee schedules).

The extent to which there are gains and/or losses in these prerogatives (i.e., changes in the power of any occupational category) is a function of the degree of unity and cohesiveness within an occupational grouping, the stage of production associated with the sectors in which the occupation is located, and the extent to which the tasks of the occupation can be technologized. . . . The situation in the United States of small-scale fee-for-service doctoring around the turn of the century [was unlike] . . . the typical situation of bureaucratically employed doctors today. Every single occupational prerogative listed has changed, many only over the last decade or so.

LEVELS OF ANALYSIS

In approaching the changing social position of doctors it is useful to distinguish among four levels of analysis, each of which affords a different view of doctoring in the United States, and perhaps elsewhere. What sometimes appear to be diametrically opposed viewpoints become simply perspectives from different levels. The same game looks different for the spectators in the stands (the public) than it does for the players on the field (health workers) or the teams' owners in the board room, or elected league representatives who mandate changes in the rules. The four levels are:

- **The level of financial and industrial capital.** Here I refer to the activity of vast multinational institutions—both financial and industrial corporations and the individuals and interests controlling them—and how their presence in and around the medical business is profoundly changing all spheres of medical care and especially the organization and content of medical work.
- **The activities of the government (the state).** At this level we are concerned with how the vast resources of the state, subordinated as they now clearly are to the institutions and interests identified with the first level, are employed to: (a) protect and brokerage the prerogatives of these institutions; (b) ensure that medical care, as an area of investment, remains conducive to the realization of profit; and (c) shape, through partisan legislative action, the scope and content of medical work and the consumption behavior of the public with respect to medical care.
- **The level of medicine itself.** At this third level we are interested in how—within the constraining context of the partisan activities of the state on behalf of the prerogatives of financial and industrial interests—medical activity is actually conducted. This level of analysis includes, for example, research on the training and content of medical labor, managerial studies of medical organizations, positivistic accounts of the efficiency of medical practice, and epidemiological rationalizations for the existence of medicine. And, it is at this and the following fourth level that most medical care and health services research continues to be conducted.
- **The level of the public.** Here we are concerned with the vast number of people who are the potential users of, and increasingly the subjects for medicine—a category loosely termed "the public"—which may actually be incidental to medical activity itself (it could conceivably proceed without their involvement) and is presently the most vulnerable of all to the activities of those at the three other levels already distinguished.

By way of analogy, one can conceive of medical-care-related activities as *the game* among a group of highly trained players, carefully selected for the affinity of their interests with the requirements of prevailing medical institutions, that is, watched by a vast number of *spectators* (involving all of the people some of the time and, increasingly, some of the people all of the time). And surrounding this game itself, with its interested public, is *the state* (setting the rules by which the game ought to be played before the public), the presence of which ensures the legitimacy of the game and guarantees, through resources derived from spectators, that the prerogatives and interests of the owners of the park (*financial and industrial capital*) are always protected and advanced. . . .

Once one becomes aware of the magnitude of the structural changes now being forced upon the business of medicine, then the very issues selected for investigation and the levels of analysis and concepts adopted to explain them are profoundly influenced. As it is generally practiced, health services research overlooks the political and economic setting within which the medical game is currently played and, consequently, remains preoccupied with issues of relative unimportance. . . . The current preoccupation with, for example, managerial changes and the measurement of efficiency, while interesting, is likely to yield little that will enable us to understand the changing nature of the medical game and the position of participants within it (both medical care workers and a consuming public) that could result in political action, effective social policy, and change aimed at fulfilling collective needs. . . .

REFERENCES

McKinlay, J.B. 1977. The Business of Good Doctoring or Doctoring as Good Business. *International Journal of Health Services* 7(30):459–87.

McKinlay, J.B., and J. Arches, 1985. Toward the Proletarianization of Physicians. *International Journal of Health Services* 15(2):161–95.

———. 1986. Historical Changes in Doctoring. *International Journal of Health Services* 16(3):473–77.

McKinlay, J.B., and J.D. Stoeckle. 1988. Corporatization and the Social Transformation of Doctoring. *International Journal of Health Services* 18(2):191–205.

Starr, P. 1982. *The Social Transformation of American Medicine.* New York: Basic Books.

Coming to grips with the intimate conditions of their lives, when they were being born, when they were dying, watching them die, watching them get well when they were ill, has always absorbed me.
— William Carlos Williams

Vicente Navarro

Professional Dominance or Proletarianization?: Neither

One of the most important theoretical positions put forward to explain the nature of medical knowledge and practice and the organization of medicine in the United States has been the *professional-dominance* position, articulated primarily by Eliot Freidson. (Although the best-known representative of this position is Professor Freidson, many other authors have rooted their analysis of medicine in the United States in this theoretical position: Berland [1975], Illich [1976], and Arney [1982] among others. There are, of course, differences among these authors in the presentation and interpretation of professional dominance. In this article, I will focus on the main points of characterization of the professional-dominance position, best articulated, in my opinion, by Professor Freidson [1970a, 1970b, 1980, 1986].) In this position, the medical profession dominates the medical care system in the production of medical knowledge, in the division of labor in medicine, in the provision of health services, and in the organization of medicine. This dominance comes from the monopolistic control of the medical profession over the production of medical knowledge and the provision of medical services, and is reproduced by cultural, economic, and legal means. Culturally, the medical profession has been able to convince the dominant elites in our society of the value of its trade. As Freidson (1970b, 72–73) indicates, "It is essential that the dominant elite remain persuaded of the positive value or at least the harmlessness of the profession's work, so that it continues to protect it from encroachment."

While the dominant elites are those that need to be persuaded, the state is the main guarantor of the monopolistic control of the physicians' trade since it gives the medical profession its exclusive right to practice. (Freidson does not touch on the relation between the dominant elite and the

Vicente Navarro, M.D., D.M.S.A., Dr. P.H., is Professor of Health Policy, School of Hygiene and Public Health at The Johns Hopkins University, Baltimore, Maryland, and editor of the *International Journal of Health Services*.

Abridged from Navarro, V. (1988). Professional dominance or proletarianization? Neither. *Milbank Q* 66(suppl. 2):57–75. Used with permission of The Milbank Memorial Fund.

state. Thus, the source of state power is not analyzed in the professional-dominance position.)

> The foundation of medicine's control over work is thus clearly political in character, involving the aid of the state in establishing and maintaining the profession's preeminence. . . . The most strategic and treasured characteristic of the profession—its autonomy—is therefore owed to its relationship to the sovereign state from which it is not ultimately autonomous (Freidson 1970b, 23–24).

Another requirement for the reproduction of professional dominance is that the profession convince the general public of the value of its work.

> I suggested that scholarly or scientific professions may obtain and maintain a fairly secure status by virtue of winning solidly the support of a political, economic and social elite, but that such a consulting profession of medicine must, in order to win a secure status, make itself attractive to the general public which must support its members by consulting them. The contingency of the lay public was thus critical to the development of medicine as a profession (Freidson 1970b, 188).

It is important to stress that Freidson's position has remained remarkably unchanged during a time when we have witnessed enormous changes not only in the production of medical knowledge but in the individual and collective practice of medicine. In his most recent article on this topic, in which he predicts the further evolution of medicine, Freidson (1985, 32) restates that "there is no reason to believe that [in the future] medicine's position of dominance, its key position in the health care system, will change."

In this theoretical scenario, physicians and the medical profession are the dominant force that shape the nature of medicine in the United States. This position does not deny, of course, that other forces are competing with the medical profession for the power to determine the present and future course of medicine, but it does claim that the *medical profession has been, is, and will continue to be the dominant force in medicine.* . . .

DO DOCTORS CONTROL MEDICINE?

Let us focus on the basic assumptions that sustain the professional-dominance position and see the degree to which current and historical experience supports them. First, even in the lay press the perception that doctors are in charge in the institutions of medicine is changing very rapidly. As a *New York Times* article put it recently: "Doctors have lost some of their authority and independence to government officials, insurers, corporate managers and hospital administrators and they are alarmed at the trend" (Pear 1987). In the very same article, the head of a government regulatory agency is quoted as saying that "this loss of autonomy is extremely frustrating to doctors; doctors are pulling their hair out when bureaucrats like me tell them how to practice medicine" (Pear 1987). The article documents how government, insurance companies, and hospital administrators are increasingly dictating what is medically acceptable or appropriate in the treatment of patients. On the receiving end, the physicians increasingly feel that their autonomy is being forcefully challenged by nondoctors. The article concludes with the following statement from an orthopedic surgeon: "The judgment of physicians has been usurped by cookbook criteria created by people who are not doctors" (Pear 1987). Physicians themselves seem to feel that they are indeed losing control over their practice of medicine. According to a recent survey by the Association of American Medical Colleges of 500 students who scored well on admissions tests but did not apply to medical schools, 29 percent said that they had been discouraged from attending by physicians.

In the middle 1970s there were 28 applicants for every 10 places in American medical schools; in 1987, there were only 17 applicants for every 10 places. This finding is in accord with the trend in recent years: while the number of people graduating from college has not changed significantly in the last three years, the number applying to medical school has declined 22 percent in that period, from 35,944 to 28,123. Needless to say, this decline is a result of many different forces. But, it is important to note that doctors seem to be advising the young to look for other careers. This advice further illustrates doctors' frustrations.

I am, of course, aware of the argument that these data reflect mere popular and professional perceptions and may not correspond to reality. But, in the realm of power relations, perceptions are indeed important and part of reality. And, in this case, they are also indicators of a trend in which physicians are losing power to shape the practice of medicine. (For a detailed presentation of empirical evidence that shows the decline of professional dominance, see McKinlay and Arches 1985.)

Other trends also question some of Freidson's assumptions, such as high public trust in the medical profession and the subservience of other health care occupations to the medical profession. In support of the first position, Freidson (1985) quotes several polls indicating the high esteem that physicians enjoy among the population of the United States. But it is important to separate how people feel about their own doctors from how they feel about the collectivity of doctors as an organization, and how they feel about the medical system that doctors presumably dominate. Unpublished data from Louis Harris and Associates reveal that the public's confidence in medicine has fallen dramatically since the middle 1960s, from 73 percent to 39 percent (in 1985) (cited in Blendon and Altman 1987). And the degree of dissatisfaction with the system of American medicine is very high. A recent survey shows that the majority of the population of the United States is dissatisfied with the medical system in this country, and is calling for major changes (Schneider 1985).

Similarly, in the last 15 years we have witnessed an increasing number of health occupations that can practice without having their patients referred from physicians, as used to be the case. Physical therapists, for example, are able to receive patients directly in 16 states, and this number is growing.

. . . The establishment of the medical profession in the United States was not just the result of medical reformers convincing the elite—the Rockefeller Foundation—of the merits of its reforms. Medicine was not the only profession established at that time; most of the professions, as we know them today, were established then, and not all of them by the Rockefeller Foundation.

Those professions were to represent the cadre of experts supposed to carry out the rationalization of the social order under the hegemony of the capitalist class or bourgeoisie. As Kirschner (1986), a historian of professions in the United States, shows, there was a kinship between the calls for expertise as the leverage for change and the containment of social unrest, fear of revolt from below, and contempt for the working class with its strong immigrant component. Experts, rather than the populace, were supposed to guide the change. But that guidance took place within a context in which the capitalist called the shots, both outside and within the professional terrain. As Kirschner (1986) indicates, there was (and continues to be) a structural tension between democracy (popular desire to rule) and the experts, supported by the dominant establishment, as to how to direct change and society and for whose purposes.

This historical detour through the origins of the medical profession is essential to an understanding of the sociopolitical context in which the power of the professions was established and continues to be reproduced. Professional power was and is submerged in other forms of power such as class, race, gender, and other forces that shape the production of the knowledge, practice, and institutions of medicine. The power of the professions is subservient to the powerful forces such as the dominant classes that have an overwhelming influence in medicine. Needless to say, dominated classes and other dominated forces such as minorities and women can also influence the development of medicine. But the dominance of a class and the hegemony of its ideology determine the parameters within which this set of influences takes place and the realization of these influences. (For a discussion of how class power appears in medicine, see Navarro 1980, 1983. Both articles are reproduced and expanded in Navarro 1986.)

HOW OTHER SOCIAL FORCES SHAPED
WHAT DOCTORS BELIEVE, HOW THEY
PRACTICE, AND HOW THEY ARE
PAID AND ORGANIZED

In summary, whatever happens in medicine is an outcome of the resolution of internal conflicts and contradictions that occur within a matrix of class, gender, race, and other power relationships—of which professional views and interests are important but not dominant in the production of knowledge and in the practice and organization of medicine. . . .

Health and Disease

These are collective phenomena, realized individually. As phenomena, they have a material base. Disease is also a biological process with a relative autonomy. For example, although social conditions shape the nature and distribution of epidemics such as plague, the biological base of these epidemics gives them a certain autonomy in their development. The process we call disease is also perceived and interpreted by scientists according to a certain set of understandings and assumptions held not only by the scientific community but by the dominant ideology in that society. I have already indicated how the individual biological and mechanistic understanding of health and disease that dominates medical thought was based on a specific class ideology that was and continues to be hegemonic in our society. This understanding of disease continues to be reproduced today, even when nonphysicians form the majority of producers of medical knowledge. Most of the scientific breakthroughs of medicine are discovered by nonphysicians: the overwhelming number of Nobel Prizes in Medicine are awarded to nonphysicians, and most basic and laboratory research in medicine is done by nonphysicians. But the understanding of health and medicine and the priorities derived from it have not changed.

Medical Knowledge

This involves the collective set of beliefs, ideas, and knowledge in which the social thoughts of some classes, races, and gender are more dominant than those of others. It has a scientific element, owing in part to the relative autonomy of science, and an ideological element reproduced by the values, beliefs, and experiences of the scientists who work and operate in universities and social settings subject to a whole set of class, gender, race, and other forms of influences. Both elements—the scientific and the ideological—are not related in conditions of exteriority, i.e., scientific knowledge is not outside its ideological dimension. Rather, one is in the other. The history of medicine is crowded with examples of variations in the occurrence of scientific discoveries and their interpretations. Smith (1981), for example, has shown how black lung was "discovered" far earlier in the United Kingdom than in the United States, and how the interpretation of causality and symptomatology of that disease was different in both countries. As Smith indicates, the existence of a stronger labor movement in the United Kingdom explains these differences. . . .

In brief, how these two elements—the scientific and the ideological—have intermixed depends on the power relationships in society that continuously redefine the production of knowledge, i.e., what is and is not happening in medical knowledge and how it is happening.

Medical Practice

As part of social practice, medical practice has a *technical division* as well as a *social division* of labor. The former, the technical distribution of tasks in medical practice, is determined by the latter, which occurs within a well-defined set of power relationships. Thus, the different tasks carried out by the medical team (physicians, nurses, auxiliaries, and others)—the technical division of labor—are determined by the class, gender, and race relations in society—the social division of labor. None other than Florence Nightingale, the founder of nursing, spoke about the role of the nurse as one of (1) supporting the physician, equivalent to the supportive role of the wife in the family; (2) mothering the patient; and (3) mastering the auxiliaries. In essence, in medicine we witness the reproduction of the Victorian family. Today, just as the family is being redefined, the health team relationships are also being redefined. Nurses and wives are rebelling against their subordination. The increased independence of formerly dependent professions, such as physical therapists, from their past bosses is just part of that trend, which is continuing in spite of the resistance of the assumed dominant profession.

Medical Organization

Petty cottage medicine has been transformed into capitalist or corporate medicine in the same way that the dynamics of capitalism led to the change from petty commodity production to capitalist manufacture. This development has been occurring in medicine in the United States for several decades. It is important to make this observation in the light of the frequently heard remark that the corporatization of medicine and its commodification are recent phenomena due to the involvement in medicine of the "for-profit hospitals." This reductionist view of capitalist medicine ignores the dynamics in which medicine and medical services have been commodities and sources of profits for quite a long time. Indeed, the existence of the medical-industrial complex is not a reality discovered by Relman (1980) and Starr (1983); nor is this reality determined by the "for-profit hospitals." Several years before, Kelman (1971), Navarro (1976), Salmon (1977), and McKinlay (1978) described the existence of this phenomenon and predicted its further expansion. . . . It was not unexpected; it was very predictable, and those other authors did predict it. Indeed, the penetration of capitalism into the social services, including medical care, is a logical outcome of the overwhelming influence of corporate America in all areas of economic and social life. This class is the most powerful class in the Western world because of its centrality in the Western system of power. Moreover, its power is unhindered by a working class movement—such as a mass-based labor, social democratic, or socialist party—that could restrain some of its excesses. Consequently, we have an underdeveloped welfare state. The United States is the only industrialized country except South Africa that does not offer comprehensive and universal health coverage. To attribute this absence to the power of the medical profession is to overrate the power of that profession. Other countries with equally powerful medical associations have a national health program. To repeat: we do not have a national health program because we do not have a mass-based labor movement.

The primary focus on the medical profession in much of medical historiography leads to an overrepresentation of the role of the medical profession in the process of medical change. The limitation of this approach is frequently compounded by seeing history as being made by individuals rather than by social forces. . . .

Indeed, our lack of a national health program is not due primarily to opposition from the medical profession. Without minimizing the power of organized medicine, we must see that its power is limited compared with the enormous power of corporate America, unhindered by a counterbalancing force, the power of a mass-based labor movement. The power of corporate America is such that even when government responds to popular pressure and provides health benefits coverage, the way these programs are designed and operated benefits not only the population but many corporate groups—such as the insurance companies—and professional interests. And these benefits subtract from the benefits received by the population.

Needless to say, corporate America is not uniform, nor is its power omnipotent. It needs to compromise with other forces such as the medical profession. The power relationships that underlie such arrangements are changing, however, with corporate interests gaining over the professional interests. Witness, for example, the growth of private insurance companies—the main source of financial capital in the United States—taking over the dominance that Blue Cross/Blue Shield once held in the medical premium market (Navarro 1976).

PROLETARIANIZATION OF PHYSICIANS?

Thus, while the medical profession has never been the dominant force in medicine, it has nevertheless been a major force. Its power, however, has been declining for some time now. But this loss of power cannot be equated with the "proletarianization" of the medical profession. This understanding is rooted in Marx and Engels's initial understanding that with capitalist development we would witness an increased polarization of classes. According to this thesis, an increasing number of strata, including the professions, would be drawn into one of the two opposing classes: the capitalist class or owners of the means of production, and the working class, which owns only its labor power and sells it to capital. . . .

In spite of losing professional power over the material means of producing medical services (such as hospitals, medical equipment, and other resources), over the organizational forms (such as the systems of funding and organization of medical care), and even over the credentialing of their skills, physicians still retain considerable influence over these production assets, far superior to the influence that proletarians have over theirs. Moreover, professionals will not become uncredentialed skilled workers. This impossibility is a result not only of the different nature of work and the different relationships with the production assets for professionals and workers, but of the different functions that professionals and workers have in capitalist society.

As I have indicated elsewhere, medicine has a function—curing and caring—that is needed in any society. But how that needed function occurs depends on the power relationships in that society as reproduced in the knowledge, practice, and organization of medicine. As the social movements in the 1960s and 1970s showed, medicine reproduces the dominant classism, sexism, and racism in society, not only in the uses of medicine (i.e., allocation of resources), but also in the production of medicine (i.e., knowledge and practice of medicine). In other words, medicine has a needed as well as a dominating function. And the two functions are not related in conditions of exteriority; rather, one function is realized through the other. How the needed function takes place is determined by the controlling or dominating functions. (For an expansion of this point, see Navarro 1986, 241–245.)

This point is important in the light of the overabundance of authors who see medicine *primarily* as an agency of control and dominance (Illich 1976). To believe this is tantamount to believing that the popular demand for a national health program is a result of a masochistic desire for being more controlled and/or a response to an enormous false consciousness that the dominant class and the medical profession have imposed on the majority of the population. This school of thought ignores the needed function proven by the effectiveness of medical care (frequently overstated) in alleviating the damage created by disease.

On the other hand, there is the equal danger of seeing medicine as a *neutral* set of organizations, institutions, practices, and knowledge whose growth needs to be stimulated as part of "progress." This version of medicine focuses only on the needed and useful function without understanding that this function has been structured in such a way that it reproduces patterns of class, gender, and race discrimination. This "neutral" understanding of science and medicine is responsible for the unchanged professionalization of medicine in some postcapitalist societies (Navarro 1978a), with the reproduction of class, gender, and race power relationships in medicine. This reproduction of dominant relationships conflicts with the democratic force in those countries. The linkage of dominant sectors of the party with the "expert" profession can lead to a new dominant force that inhibits the full expression of the dominated forces.

Medicine has not only a needed but also a dominating function; the need to reproduce these dominant-dominated relationships, both in society and in medicine, by the state credentialing of skills and the associated allocation of privileges explains the impossibility of the profession becoming uncredentialed. The credentialing of skills is important not only to the recipients of the credentials but to the grantors of the credentials.

The term proletarianization of physicians, however, seems to indicate that the physicians can and will become proletarians after all. This is not likely to be the case. The process whereby professionals are losing autonomy is indeed a very real one, and the challenge made by "proletarianization" theorists to the professional dominance school remains unanswered, but the term and concept of "proletarianization" used by these authors does not accurately define and explain what happens in the house of medicine.

Even more important, the term can be politically misleading. Indeed, if physicians are becoming proletarianized, one could conclude that they are likely to take working-class positions and become not only allies of the working class but part of the working class itself. Historical experience shows otherwise. The medical profession and its instruments (professional associations, colleges, unions, and others) have rarely supported transformations in medicine called for by the labor movement and other progressive forces. To recognize this historical fact is not to deny that important sectors of the medical professions can play a critical role in stimulating change by supporting the demands from these progressive forces. The Socialist Medical Association in Great Britain, for example, played a very important role in showing that the British Medical Association's early opposition to the establishment of a National Health Service was based not on that association's concern for the patients' well-being (as it claimed) but rather on the defense of its economic and material interests. In the struggle for the hearts and minds of the people, a group of professionals with white coats can be very effective in showing the assumed "medical" arguments as covers for material interests. Moreover, the medical profession includes groups with clearly different interests, to which proponents of change must be sensitive. But in this diversity, certain interests will be held in common and will be different from and frequently in contradiction to the interests of labor and other progressive movements. It is this reality that the concept and terminology of proletarianization does not fully address.

Still, the specific conjuncture we are witnessing in the United States opens new possibilities for alliances with forces within the medical profession that see the commodification and corporatization of medicine as a threat to the well-being not only of the people but also of physicians.

BIBLIOGRAPHY

Arney, W.R. 1982. *Power and the Profession of Obstetrics.* Chicago: University of Chicago Press.

Berland, J.C. 1975. *Profession and Monopoly.* Berkeley: University of California Press.

Blendon, R.J., and D.E. Altman. 1987. Public Opinion and Health Care Costs. In *Health Care and Its Cost,* ed. C.J. Schramm, 49–63. New York: W. W. Norton.

Dorland's Medical Dictionary. 1968. Philadelphia: W.B. Saunders.

Engels, F. 1968. *The Conditions of the Working Class in England.* Stanford: Stanford University Press.

Flexner, A. 1910. *Medical Education in the United States and Canada.* New York: Carnegie Foundation for the Advancement of Teaching.

Fox, D. 1986. *Health Policies, Health Politics: The British and American Experience 1911–1965.* Princeton: Princeton University Press.

———. 1987. Review of Navarro, V., "Crisis, Health and Medicine." *Bulletin of the History of Medicine* 61(2):302–3.

Freidson, E. 1970a. *Professional Dominance.* New York: Atherton Press.

———. 1970b. *Profession of Medicine.* New York: Harper and Row.

———. 1980. *Doctoring Together.* Chicago: University of Chicago Press.

———. 1985. The Reorganization of the Medical Profession. *Medical Case Review* 42(1):32.

———. 1986. *Professional Powers: A Study of the Institutionalization of Formal Knowledge.* Chicago: University of Chicago Press.

Illich, I. 1976. *Medical Nemesis.* New York: Pantheon Books.

Kelman, S. 1971. Toward the Political Economy of Medical Care. *Inquiry* 8:130–38.

Kirschner, D.S. 1986. *The Paradox of Professionalism: Reform and Public Service in Urban America 1900–1940.* Westport, Conn.: Greenwood Press.

Kuhn, T. 1962. *The Structure of Scientific Revolutions.* Chicago: University of Chicago Press.

Marx, K., and F. Engels. 1948. The Communist Manifesto. In *Communist Manifesto: Socialist Landmark. An Appreciation Written for the Labour Party,* H. Laski, 120. London: George Allen and Unwin.

McKinlay, J. 1978. On the Medical-

Industrial Complex. *Monthly Review* 30(5):38–42.

McKinlay, J.B., and J. Arches. 1985. Towards the Proletarianization of Physicians. *International Journal of Health Services* 15(2):161–95.

Navarro, V. 1976. *Medicine under Capitalism.* New York: Neale Watson.

———. 1978a. *Social Security and Medicine in the USSR: A Marxist Critique.* Lexington, Mass.: Lexington Books.

———. 1978b. *Class Struggle, the State and Medicine: An Historical and Contemporary Analysis of the Medical Sector in Great Britain.* Oxford: Martin Robertson.

———. 1980. Work, Ideology and Science: The Case of Medicine. *Social Science and Medicine* 14C:191–205.

———. 1983. Radicalism, Marxism, and Medicine. *International Journal of Health Services* 13(2):179–202.

———. 1986. *Crisis, Health, and Medicine.* New York: Routledge and Kegan Paul.

———. 1989. Why Some Countries Have National Health Insurance, Others Have National Health Service, and Others Have Neither. *Social Science and Medicine* 28(9):887–898.

Oppenheimer, M. 1985. *White Collar Politics.* New York: Monthly Review Press.

Pear, R. 1987. Physicians Contend Systems of Payment Have Eroded Status. *The New York Times,* December 26.

Relman, A.S. 1980. The New Medical-Industrial Complex. *New England Journal of Medicine* 303:963–70.

Salmon, J. 1977. Monopoly Capital and the Reorganization of the Health Sector. *Review of the Radical Political Economy* 9:125–33.

Schneider, W. 1985. Public Ready for Real Change in Health Care. *National Journal* 3(23):664–65.

Smith, B.E. 1981. Black Lung: The Social Production of Disease. *International Journal of Health Services* 11(3):343–59.

Starr, P. 1983. *The Social Transformation of American Medicine.* New York: Basic Books.

Taylor, R., and A. Rieger. 1985. Medicine as a Social Science: Rudolf Virchow on the Typhus Epidemic in Upper Silesia. *International Journal of Health Services* 15(4):547–59.

Lest we all be counted sick, health *must be redefined. The so-called health professions tend to think of health as the absence of pathology, but it is not. . . . Health is the . . . ability to cope with and control one's environment to the maximum extent possible within the constraints of nature and circumstance.*
— John Gordon Freymann

Kevin Grumbach / Philip R. Lee

How Many Physicians Can We Afford?

The supply of physicians is rapidly expanding in the United States. Most studies of physician supply have focused on the issue of supply relative to a target calculated on the basis of anticipated "need" or "demand."[1-5] Vigorous debate continues about whether the increasing supply is appropriate for society's future health care needs[6-8] or is creating a physician surplus.[9-12]

In this article, we examine physician supply in the United States from a different perspective—that of costs. Rather than addressing the question "How many physicians do we need?" we explore the question "How many physicians can we afford?" As health care costs as a percent of the U.S. gross national product approach 12%, there is concern that our nation cannot continue to support such rapid growth in health care spending.[13]

Physician costs represent either expenditures or incomes, depending on whether one's vantage is that of payer or provider of care.[14] (Physician costs refer to the costs of services directly provided by physicians or persons in their employ. Although physician decisions influence other costs, e.g., those for hospitalization or prescription drugs, we follow the convention of not incorporating these associated costs into our analysis of direct physician costs.) This identity relationship can be further characterized as follows:

$$\text{Sum of Physician Expenditures}$$
$$= \text{Sum of Physician Incomes}$$
$$= \text{Number of Physicians}$$
$$\times \text{Mean Gross Income per Physician}$$

Kevin L. Grumbach, M.D., is Assistant Professor in Residence, School of Medicine, Department of Family and Community Medicine, and Institute for Health Policy Studies at the University of California, San Francisco.

Philip R. Lee, M.D., is Assistant Secretary for Health, U.S. Department of Health and Human Services, and Professor of Social Medicine, School of Medicine, and Institute for Health Policy Studies, University of California, San Francisco.

Abridged from Grumbach, K.L., and Lee, P.R. (1991). How many physicians can we afford? *JAMA* 265(18):2369–2372. Copyright 1991, American Medical Association. Used with permission.

The answer, then, to the question "How many physicians can we afford?" depends on how much society is willing to spend overall for physician services and on how much each individual physician earns.

To explore the cost implications of changing physician supply and income, we reviewed recent trends in physician income, as well as projections of future physician supply, to estimate physician costs in the year 2000 under several scenarios. We also analyze how some of the individual components of the income and supply factors—physician net income and practice expenses (overhead) as components of gross income, and the specialist-generalist mix as a feature of physician supply—may influence future costs.

Estimating costs is different from appraising value. Although we offer suggestions of what physician services may cost in the year 2000, we do not attempt to address whether the increases in expenditures will be "worth it" in terms of potentially purchasing improvements in the quality of our nation's health.

METHODS

We used data provided by the American Medical Association (AMA) for both income and supply. We designated 1986 as our base year. We restricted our analysis to all nonfederal, nonosteopathic physicians active in patient care, excluding those in postgraduate training (interns, residents, and fellows). (Although the AMA provides income data for physicians with MD degrees, no such detailed information on incomes is available for physicians with DO degrees.) The physicians included in our analysis generate the bulk—though not the entirety—of expenditures for clinical physician services.

The AMA estimates of physician supply and specialty distribution for 1986 derive from ongoing AMA monitoring programs.[15] Several sources have independently projected physician supply for the year 2000.[2-4] We used the most conservative estimate, the "best projection scenario" from the AMA Center for Health Policy Research.[4] We assumed that there would be no change in the number of fellows (7,828) and federal patient-care physicians (14,127) between 1986 and 2000 and subtracted these numbers from the AMA's best estimate of active, postresidency patient-care physicians for 2000 (506,300).

We counted all physicians who described themselves as general practitioners, family practitioners, general internists, and general pediatricians as "generalists" and all other physicians as "specialists." The generalist-specialist assignment is not dependent on board certification or on the specifics of the physician's training.

Physician income data derive from the AMA Socioeconomic Monitoring System surveys of active, nonfederal, patient-care physicians excluding interns and residents.[16] The AMA data are consistent with figures from the Health Care Financing Administration,[7] as well as with other income surveys.[17] Professional expenses are reported by the AMA only for self-employed physicians. Net incomes for all physicians surveyed are reported as "after expenses, before taxes" income. For income trends, we used the average annual real increases in net incomes and expenses for 1982 to 1987, deflating nominal rates by the consumer price index (CPI).

Projections of gross national product (GNP) and population for the year 2000 are those of the Health Care Financing Administration.[18]

RESULTS

The number of physicians is anticipated to rise from a physician-to-population ratio of 144 per 100,000 in 1986 to 176 per 100,000 in 2000 (table 1), an increase of 22%. The number of physicians actively practicing in the year 2000 will exceed by nearly 90,000 the number needed to maintain a constant physician-to-population ratio.

Table 2 provides figures for per-physician gross income (or expenditures), net income, and practice expenses. Net incomes and expenses for 1986 are those actually reported by physicians. For the year 2000, we projected incomes under three alternative scenarios.

First, under a "no growth" scenario, we simply assumed that gross incomes per physician will rise at the rate of the CPI, resulting in no increase in real (i.e., deflated) gross income between 1986 and 2000. Second, we assumed that expenditures per physician will rise at the same rate as the projected annual growth in the nation's GNP, or 2.5% per year.[18] Under this scenario, real gross income per physician will rise 41% to $335,440. Last, we projected that expenditures per physician will continue to rise according to recent trends. Between 1982 and 1987, mean real net incomes per physician rose at an average annual rate of 2.9% and expenses

TABLE 1 Physician Supply

Year	No. of Physicians*	Physician-Population Ratio
1986	359 259	144:100 000
2000		
For constant physician-population ratio	396 000	144:100 000
Actual supply projected	484 345	176:100 000

*Represents physicians actively practicing.

TABLE 2 Incomes and Expenses per Physician (in Constant 1986 Dollars)

Year	Gross Income, $	Net Income, $	Practice Expenses, $
1986 (actual)	237 900	119 500	118 400
2000			
Consumer price index	237 900	...	...
Gross national product	335 439	...	...
1982–1987 rate	449 191	178 055	271 136

at 6.1%.[16] Under this final scenario, expenditures per physician will increase 93% to $459,191 at the turn of the century. (We did not speculate about the specific rises in net incomes and practice expenses when using the CPI and GNP projections.)

Using the information in tables 1 and 2, we calculated the incremental costs associated with an expanding physician supply and with increasing expenditures per physician. We first calculated overall costs under the premise of a constant physician-to-population ratio of 144:100,000, using each of the three scenarios for growth in expenditures per physician. Overall costs for this level of supply in the year 2000 are $94 billion under the CPI scenario, $133 billion under the GNP scenario, and $178 billion under the 1982 to 1987 scenario, amounting to 1.6%, 2.2%, and 3.0%, respectively, of the projected GNP for the year 2000 (figure 1).

Next, substituting expanded physician-to-population ratio of 176:100,000 for the constant supply figure, we recalculated overall costs using the same three expenditure-per-physician scenarios. As the figure indicates, the increased physician supply is associated with an additional $21 billion in costs under the CPI scenario, $30 billion under the GNP scenario, and $40 billion under the 1982 to 1987 trend scenario, relative to year 2000 costs with the lower physician supply.

In addition to the cost implications of overall physician supply specialty distribution has important ramifications for physician expenditures. Table 3 compares the net incomes, expenses, and gross incomes of generalists and specialists. From 1982 to 1987, real net income rose faster for specialists (3.3% per year) than it did for generalists (1.9% per year).[16] The continuing divergence of incomes in this period appears to be primarily due to greater escalation of the volume and intensity of services provided by specialists rather than to differential rates of fee increases.[19] On the other hand, Medicare will fully implement the Resource-Based Relative Value Scale by the mid-1990s, which should reverse some of the discrepancies in gross incomes between specialists and generalists. Simulations by the Physician Payment Review Commission indicate that Medicare's adoption of the Resource-Based Relative Value Scale fee schedule will increase

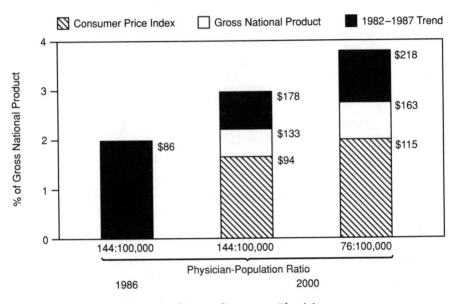

FIGURE 1   Rate of Growth of Expenditures per Physician

Physician costs, in billions of constant dollars, for 1986 and 2000. Those for the year 2000 are given (1) for a physician-population ratio held constant with that in 1986 and (2) for a ratio that reflects the actual supply of physicians projected. Details on the three scenarios depicted in the two breakdowns for the year 2000 are provided in the text.

generalists' gross incomes by an average of 5%.[20] If implemented in a "budget neutral" fashion, specialist gross incomes would decline by slightly less than 3%. (The Physician Payment Review Relative Value Scale simulations assume that the Resource-Based Relative Value Scale fee revisions do not in and of themselves immediately induce changes in the volume and mix of services.) For our year 2000 estimates, we used 1982 to 1987 trends to project growth of generalist and specialist net incomes and practice expenses and then adjusted the year 2000 projections of gross and net incomes to account for the effect of Medicare fee revisions (table 3).

In the United States, approximately 36% of practicing physicians in 1986 were generalists.[15] This specialty distribution differs considerably from that in Canada and most western European nations, where well over 50% of physicians are generalists.[21,22] Using the income data in table 3 and assuming that overall physician supply rises as projected to 176 per 100,000 population, we calculated the financial impact of redistributing 14% of the physician supply from specialists to generalists to achieve a 50:50 mix in the year 2000. A 14% redistribution would lower overall physician costs by $5 billion in the year 2000. Compared with the potential savings achieved by reducing overall physician supply, this $5 billion

TABLE 3 Incomes and Expenses per Physician (in Constant 1986 Dollars)

Year	Specialty Category	Gross Income, $	Net Income, $	Practice Expenses, $
1986	Generalist	203 400	85 000	118 400
	Specialist	257 400	139 000	118 400
2000	Generalist	405 968	134 832	271 136
	Specialist	477 015	205 879	271 136

"redistributive" saving is the equivalent of reducing the overall projected physician supply for the year 2000 by approximately 12,000 physicians under conditions of no change in specialty distribution.

COMMENT

We began by proposing that the answer to the question "How many physicians can we afford?" depends on how much society is willing to spend overall for physician services and how much each physician earns. As figure 1 indicates, physician costs could remain stable at approximately 2.0% of the GNP despite an increase in the physician-to-population ratio to 176 per 100,000 if expenditures per physician rose at the rate of the CPI. On the other hand, overall costs as a percent of GNP could rise 50% (from 2.0% to 3.0%) even without an increase in the physician-to-population ratio if recent trends in expenditures per physician continue.

The combination, however, of physician supply expanding as projected *and* expenditures per physician continuing to rise at their recent pace is a particularly volatile mixture for those concerned with health care costs. Under this scenario, payers face the prospect of physician costs as a percent of GNP nearly doubling between 1986 and 2000. The rapid expansion of physician supply in this decade will intensify the conflict between payers attempting to hold down the ceiling on expenditures per physician and physicians attempting to maintain or elevate the floor of their incomes.

Will rising physician supply on its own slow the rapid rate of inflation of expenditures per physician? According to classic market theory, an increase in physician supply should lead to a decrease in expenditures per physician.[23] Increasing competition among physicians for patients might give organized payers greater leverage to bargain discounted fees or to employ physicians on a salaried basis. Supply might outstrip demand, resulting in declining volumes of service per physician.

The simultaneous rise of supply and physician gross income in the past decade in the United States[16] and in many other nations[24,25] does not, however, instill confidence that this "inhibitory" feedback of supply on gross income will necessarily occur. Some observers have interpreted the failure of rising supply to reliably reduce costs as evidence of supplier-induced demand and physician-generated target incomes.[24–27] Others contend that recent trends merely indicate unrequited patient-initiated demand rather than market failure.[7,28] In either case, it is unlikely that payers can simply count on physician supply reaching a critical density in the year 2000 that will spontaneously alter recent trends in expenditures per physician. It also does not seem that the growing proportion of female physicians will dramatically reduce projections of the "effective" (or "full-time–equivalent") physician labor force for the year 2000.[29]

Can the course of physician supply be altered should a desire to do so exist? As one commentator has observed, health planning is like steering a tanker ship: you have to turn the rudder well in advance to change directions downstream.[30] Most of the additional physicians who will be in practice in the year 2000 are already in medical school or residency training. While some proposals have concentrated on restricting the entry of foreign medical school graduates into U.S. residency programs, the projected physician supply for the year 2000 already incorporates substantial reductions of foreign medical school graduates under existing admission policies.[4]

It may be less disruptive and more feasible to accomplish changes in physician specialty distribution than in overall supply. Our estimates suggest that redistributing the specialist-generalist mix could result in cost reductions but far fewer than those achieved by restrictions of overall supply. Adoption of the Resource-Based Relative Value Scale by third-party payers in addition to Medicare may further reduce the discrepancy between specialist and generalist incomes. Our analysis does not address how differences in practice patterns between generalists and specialists may influence nonphysician costs, such as those for hospitalization or for laboratory tests.

The rapid escalation of practice expenses presents a particular predicament for payers and physicians. If recent trends continue, the ratio of expenses to net income will rise from 0.99 to 1.52, nearly double the ratio in 1978. If payers are intent on slowing the growth in expenditures per physician, but physicians face unabated inflation of practice expenses on the order of 6% per year in real terms, physicians face the prospect of significant declines in real net income. For example, a GNP-targeted gross income of $335,439 per physician in the year 2000, combined with the projected increase of practice expenses to $271,136 per physician, would leave only $64,300 for net income in 2000, a loss of more than $50,000 in net income from 1986 (in 1986 dollars).

There is growing appreciation that the administrative costs of medical practice and health insurance in the United States are far in excess of those in other nations.[31,32] Himmelstein and Woolhandler[31] have proposed that a large proportion of practice expenses in the United States are attributable to the cumbersome and complicated payment procedures accompanying our multipayer insurance system and could be ameliorated by a uniform, national health insurance program. Greater diffusion and duplication of office-based technology may also explain a portion of American physicians' high overhead and may require stricter regulation. Malpractice insurance, while not as dominant a factor in overhead as often believed, nonetheless accounted for 12% of expenses in 1986, up from 7% in 1982.[16]

There is a paucity of information about practice expenses of physicians in health maintenance organizations, particularly large prepaid group practices. It is plausible that physicians in these settings may be spared many of the administrative expenses of fee-for-service billing, and save in other ways from efficiencies of scale. Shifts to prepaid group practice in the next decade might alter projections of practice expenses.

There is no "correct" number of physicians, any more than there is a correct amount of money to spend for health care. In this article, we have refrained from making judgments about exactly what level and quality of care we will be buying for the increasing resources that we estimate our nation will be investing in physician services in the year 2000. All costs, however, must ultimately be weighed against their benefit. Devoting more resources to physicians and physician services represents a choice, deliberate or otherwise, among alternatives for resource allocation. Well-informed choices will require careful examination of the anticipated costs and benefits of these alternatives. Physician payment policies in the 1990s will require greater attention to physician supply, specialty distribution, and practice expenses.

REFERENCES

1. Weiner JP. Forecasting physician supply: recent developments. *Health Aff.* 1989;8(4):173–179.

2. Department of Health and Human Services. *Summary Report of the Graduate Medical Education Advisory Committee to the Secretary.* Washington, DC: Dept of Health and Human Services; 1981. DHHS publication (HRA)81-651.

3. *Bureau of Health Professions: Sixth Report to the President and Congress on the State of Health Personnel in the US.* Washington, DC: Dept of Health and Human Services; 1988. DHHS publication HRS-P-OD-88-1.

4. Marder WD, Kletke PR, Silberger AB, Willke RJ. *Physician Supply and Utilization by Specialty: Trends and Projections.* Chicago, Ill: American Medical Association; 1988.

5. Iglehart JK. How many doctors do we need? *JAMA.* 1985;254:1785–1788.

6. Schwartz WB, Sloan FA, Mendelson DN. Why there will be little or no physician surplus between now and the year 2000. *N Engl J Med.* 1988;318:892–897.

7. Schwartz WB, Mendelson DN. No evidence of an emerging physician surplus. *JAMA.* 1990: 263: 557–560.

8. Harris JE. How many doctors are enough? *Health Aff.* 1986;5(4): 31–46.

9. Tarlov AR. The increasing supply of physicians, the changing structure of the health-services system, and the future practice of medicine. *N Engl J Med.* 1983; 308:1235–1244.

10. Tarlov AR. How many physicians is enough? *JAMA.* 1990;263:571–572.

11. Ginzberg E. Physician supply in the year 2000. *Health Aff.* 1989; 8(3):84–90.

12. Ginzberg E, Ostow M, eds. *The Coming Physician Surplus: In Search of a Policy.* Totowa, NJ: Rowman & Allanheld; 1984.

13. Davies NE, Felder LH. Applying brakes to the runaway American health care system. *JAMA.* 1990; 263:73–76.

14. Reinhardt UE. Resource allocation in health care: the allocation of lifestyles to providers. *Milbank Q.* 1987;65:153–176.

15. Roback G, Randolph L, Seidman B, Mead D. *Physician Characteristics and Distribution in the U. S.* Chicago, Ill: American Medical Association; 1987.

16. Gonzalez AL, Emmons DW. *Socioeconomic Characteristics of Medical Practice 1988.* Chicago, Ill: American Medical Association; 1988.

17. Owens A. Earnings make a huge breakthrough. *Med Econ.* 1990;67: 90–122.

18. Health Care Financing Administration. National health expenditures, 1986–2000. *Health Care Financing Rev.* 1987;8(4):1–36.

19. Mitchell JB, Wedig G, Cromwell J. The Medicare physician fee freeze: what really happened? *Health Aff.* 1989;8(1):21–33.

20. *Physician Payment Review Commission: Annual Report to Congress 1989.* Washington, DC: Physician Payment Review Commission; 1989.

21. Clare L, Spratley E, Schwab P, Iglehart JK. Trends in health personnel. *Health Aff.* 1987;6(4):90–103.

22. Schroeder SA. Western European responses to physician oversupply. *JAMA.* 1984;252:373–384.

23. Luft HS, Arno P. Impact of increasing physician supply. *Health Aff.* 1986;5(4):32–46.

24. Barer ML, Evans RG, Labelle RJ. Fee controls as cost control: tales from the frozen north. *Milbank Q.* 1988;66(1):1–64.

25. Kirkman-Liff BL. Physician payment and cost-containment strategies in West Germany: suggestions for Medicare reform. *J Health Polit Policy Law.* 1990;15:69–99.

26. Rice T. Physician-induced demand for medical care: new evidence from the Medicare program. In: Scheffler RM, ed. *Advances in Health Economics and Health Services Research.* Greenwich, Conn: JAI Press Inc; 1984;5.

27. Fuchs V. The supply of surgeons and the demand for operations. *J Hum Resources.* 1978;13(suppl): 35–36.

28. Sloan FA, Schwartz WB. More doctors: what will they cost? *JAMA.* 1983;249:766–769.

29. Kletke PR, Marder WD, Silberger AB. The growing proportion of female physicians: implications for U.S. physician supply. *Am J Public Health.* 1990;80:300–304.

30. Rachlis M. Understanding the Ca-

nadian health care system. Presented at the Pew Health Policy Program National Meeting; May 20, 1990; Toronto, Ontario.

31. Himmelstein DU, Woolhandler S. Cost without benefit: administrative waste in U.S. health care. *N Engl J Med.* 1986;314:441–445.

32. Evans RG, Lomas J, Barer M, et al. Controlling health care expenditures: the Canadian reality. *N Engl J Med.* 1989;320:571–577.

The "family" of health workers resembles nothing so clearly as the family itself, with women playing subordinate and nurturant roles, men playing dominant and instructive roles— . . . a kind of institutional sexism.
— Barbara Ehrenreich

Physician Payment Review Commission

Medicare Physicians Payment

Six years ago, the Congress created the Physician Payment Review Commission to advise it on physician payment under the Medicare program. At that time, concern was growing over the escalation in program expenditures for physicians' services; beneficiaries' increasing financial liability; and the fact that Medicare's method of paying physicians on the basis of their historical charges had severely distorted the pattern of relative payment across different physician specialties, services, and geographic areas. Moreover, many also saw a need for the medical profession to address issues of apparent inappropriate and variable utilization of medical services.

The Commission recommended a set of proposals to respond to these problems, which served as the basis for the physician payment reform provisions enacted by the Congress in the Omnibus Budget Reconciliation Act of 1989 (OBRA89). The major elements of the comprehensive law include the Medicare Fee Schedule, limits on the amounts physicians may charge beneficiaries above the Medicare approved fee, and Volume Performance Standards (VPSs) to control expenditure growth. The legislation also expanded federal funding for effectiveness research and the development of practice guidelines.

The enactment of physician payment reform ushered in a new era for Medicare, but many expect the changes will have a more widespread impact. Already, a number of private payers and state Medicaid programs are giving serious consideration to adopting a similar method of paying physicians. In looking further into the future, many see the Medicare payment model as an essential part of comprehensive health care reform. With Medicare's physician payment system in its early stages of implementation, the national policy agenda has shifted to focus on concerns regarding both the absolute level and rate of growth of national health care expenditures as well as barriers to access faced by many of the nation's citizens. Consideration of broader system reform has been accompanied by a growing recogni-

---

The Physician Payment Review Commission (PPRC) was established by Congress in 1985 to advise and recommend methods to reform payment to physicians under Medicare and to conduct research and report on related expenditure and utilization issues. Abridged from Physician Payment Review Commission. (1992). *Medicare Physicians Payment: Report to Congress.* Washington, DC: The Commission. Used with permission.

tion of the limitations of exclusive reliance on financial incentives to control expenditures and ensure appropriate use of services. . . .

REFINING THE MEDICARE FEE SCHEDULE

After two years of preparation, the Medicare Fee Schedule was implemented on January 1, 1992. . . . Reports in the media suggest that many physicians have found the payment rates to be lower than expected. This may reflect a number of aspects of the policy, including the unexpectedly low dollar conversion factor that translates relative values into fees; the impact of not paying for interpretation of electrocardiograms (EKGs); discounted payments for new physicians; and some aspects of the payment reform that are less well understood, such as the absence of a transition for the elimination of specialty differentials. In addition, the implementation of new visit codes increases physicians' uncertainty about how their revenues will change.

While the broad effects of payment reform are progressing in line with congressional intent, issues related to coding, payment policies, and relative values remain. Some of these will have a substantial impact on certain physicians and threaten the system's ability to make equitable and acceptable payments to them. With [the Health Care Financing Administration] HCFA committed to continued refinement of the Medicare Fee Schedule, the Commission believes that problems anticipated by different specialties or groups of physicians are better solved by further refining the fee schedule than by creating exceptions or exemptions for narrow classes of providers. Furthermore, issues such as compensating physicians for the costs of medical education, research, or uncompensated care should be addressed separately from refinement of the fee schedule.

In defining global payment policies for major and minor surgery, HCFA has made substantial progress in distinguishing clearly which services belong in which category and allocating payment in ways that accurately reflect the appropriate bundle of services. The Commission does remain concerned that physicians may not understand how the policies apply and urges an increased effort to educate both physicians and carriers. It is also important for HCFA to refine and clarify its payment policies for special types of surgery, such as trauma surgery, that routinely involve multiple operations and more than one physician providing care.

Coding issues still present difficulties. The Commission remains especially concerned about coding for evaluation and management services. With content descriptions and typical times often not congruent, the new codes may send mixed messages to physicians and carriers concerning what is the appropriate code for a given service. The Commission plans to monitor use of the new visit codes to determine whether the goals of coding reform—using codes in a predictable and uniform manner—are being accomplished.

The assignment of accurate relative values remains a key issue as well. In assessing the refinements published in the Final Rule, the Commission has found that significant improvements have been made. It is pleased that HCFA has established an ongoing process for reviewing relative values that may remain out of line. A particular area that needs more attention is the pattern of relative work values for EM services, especially the differences in intensities (work per unit of time) for different visit classes. Currently, virtually the same intensity is assigned for all types of visits in the office and the hospital. The two exceptions are a substantially lower intensity for initial inpatient consultations and a substantially higher intensity for inpatient follow-up consultations. This pattern is inconsistent with both analysis of survey data and the opinions of clinicians obtained through a structured consensus process.

The absence of patient factors, such as severity of illness, may present an additional obstacle to equitable payment. The introduction of a Medicare adjuster and research on the feasibility of incorporating a severity modifier would help address this issue.

HCFA will reduce the practice expense relative values by 50 percent for selected services that are provided primarily in physician offices when those services are delivered in hospital outpatient departments. This site-of-service differential reflects the fact that hospitals furnish and are paid for some resources required in performing these services. The Commission applauds HCFA's effort to introduce site-of-service differentials into the fee schedule, but suggests that it should attempt to develop service-specific estimates of practice expense differences by site. In the longer term, the Commission supports basing the practice expense component of the fee schedule on estimates of the resources required to provide individual services instead of historical charge levels as specified in OBRA89.

OBRA89 called for the initial conversion factor for the fee schedule to be budget neutral. HCFA initially proposed an unexpectedly low amount of $26.87, which according to its interpretation of the law was required to maintain budget neutrality. Various factors affected HCFA's calculation of the conversion factor, including its interpretation of how to adjust payments to maintain budget neutrality and its assumptions about physician responses to changes in payment rates. The Commission previously recommended changes to restore the conversion factor to a level more consistent with congressional intent. The final conversion factor of $30.42 (updated to $31.00 for 1992) reflects numerous modifications in its calculation. But it still includes an adjustment for an estimated 6.5 percent net increase in the volume of services that HCFA assumes will occur in response to changes in payment rates. The Commission regards the magnitude of this adjustment as excessive.

The Commission also recommends changes that will require congressional action in several areas. Specifically, the Commission recommends separate payment for EKGs, elimination of differential payment for new physicians, and resource-based payment for assistants-at-surgery.

As increasing numbers of other payers incorporate elements of the Medicare Fee Schedule into their own policies, the importance of broadening the applicability of the fee schedule beyond Medicare is heightened. Already some state Medicaid programs and private payers are taking steps to adopt fee schedules based on Medicare relative values, a trend that seems certain to continue. Adjustments to relative values or new relative values are needed for services provided to certain distinct patient populations—such as obstetrical services and services to children—and for services not covered by Medicare—such as some preventive services.

The prospects for use of major elements of the fee schedule beyond Medicare highlight the urgency of refining the fee schedule. While HCFA is continuing to improve its refinement process, it should take further steps to make certain that the process is an open one, with disclosure of the basis for making changes. The process should include the wide spectrum of interested parties that will be affected by the refinement of the Medicare Fee Schedule and its broader use—physicians, other practitioners, consumers, private payers, and Medicaid programs.

Everyone who is born holds dual citizenship, in the kingdom of the well and in the kingdom of the sick.
— Susan Sontag

8

Nurse Labor Market

*Public health nursing
crisis intervention*

Linda H. Aiken

The Hospital Nursing Shortage: A Paradox of Increasing Supply and Increasing Vacancy Rates

Vacancy rates for nurses in the nation's hospitals have almost tripled since 1984. More than 75% of all hospitals report a shortage of nurses; almost one in five describes their shortage as severe. Nearly a third of hospitals in urban areas (30%) and 15% of rural hospitals reported closing hospital beds in 1987 as a result of the nursing shortage. The U.S. Department of Health and Human Services Secretary's Commission on Nursing concluded recently that the reported shortage of nurses is "real, widespread, and of significant magnitude."[1]

There have been cyclical shortages of nurses since World War II, but the current shortage is particularly perplexing. The supply of nurses in the United States has increased substantially in recent years to about 1 registered nurse for every 135 Americans (most of whom are healthy). Moreover, during the period in which the current shortage developed, the use of hospital inpatient facilities declined notably. There were 50 million fewer inpatient hospital days in 1987 than in 1981. This scenario would suggest a surplus of nurses rather than a shortage. As recently as the fall of 1988, the Department of Health and Human Services, in its report to the President and Congress, concluded that the supply of nurses was in balance with requirements until into the next century.[2]

THE PARADOX OF MORE NURSES AND MORE VACANCIES

There are several commonly held misconceptions about the causes of the nursing shortage. One is that dissatisfied nurses are leaving the profession

Linda H. Aiken, Ph.D., R.N., F.A.A.N., is Trustee Professor of Nursing, Professor of Sociology, Director of the Center for Health Services and Policy Research, and Associate Director of the Leonard Davis Institute of Health Economics at the University of Pennsylvania, Philadelphia.

From Aiken, L. (1989). The hospital nursing shortage: A paradox of increasing supply and increasing vacancy rates. *Western J Med* 151(1):87–92. Reprinted by permission from *The Western Journal of Medicine*.

in large numbers. While job dissatisfaction is common among nurses,[3] approximately 80% are employed, which is a high employment rate for a predominantly female occupation. Only about 5% of registered nurses work in non-health-related jobs, suggesting that the specialized nature of nursing education does not permit nurses to move easily into other occupations of comparable status.

It has also been suggested that the growing number of jobs for nurses in ambulatory care and new jobs in the health industry, including insurance claims review, hospital preadmission screening programs, risk management, quality assurance, and others, have siphoned nurses away from hospital practice. To the contrary, hospitals have increased the number of nurses employed in the aggregate and the ratio of nurses to patients by more than 25% since 1982.

Enrollments in nursing schools have fallen substantially—26% since 1983—causing great alarm as to the future supply of nurses. Despite declining numbers of graduates, however, there are still many more new graduates coming into the employment pool each year than nurses leaving. Even if the trend in lower enrollments continues, the actual supply of employed nurses is expected to continue to increase until after the turn of the century.[2]

The current nursing shortage, then, has not been caused by a decline in the number of nurses working in hospitals but by an increase in the number of additional nursing positions offered by hospitals.[1] In economic terms, the nursing shortage is demand driven. The increased employment of nurses by more competitively positioned hospitals has resulted in substantial shortages in less competitive hospitals and during unpopular night and weekend hours and leaves fewer nurses available for positions in nursing homes and other settings.

The increased demand for hospital nurses can be explained in part by changing patterns of hospital care. The average length of a hospital stay has fallen by 7% since 1982. Discretionary admissions have been reduced as a result of preadmission screening programs, improvements in noninvasive diagnostic technology, and other changes in medical practice, including the increased use of ambulatory surgical procedures. On the one hand, these changes reduce the demand for nurses because inpatient days are fewer. On the other hand, the nursing care needs of the average patient in hospital are reported to be greater. These two changes should be offsetting in terms of nursing hours required overall.

Another factor affecting the demand for nurses is the doubling of the number of intensive care unit (ICU) beds since 1973 from more than 40,000 to 90,000 today. Hospitals have added more than 17,000 new ICU beds just since 1980. The percentage of intensive care days and neonatal intensive care days relative to the total impatient days has increased. Some research suggests that ICU beds are often used for patients who do not benefit, either because they are not sick enough or because they are termi-nally ill.[4] Nevertheless, ICU beds commit hospitals to a higher ratio of nurses to patients because, on average, it takes four nurses to staff each ICU patient around the clock, compared with one nurse for each patient on a general hospital unit.

The above factors partially account for the increased employment of nurses by hospitals since 1982, but they fail to provide a convincing expla-nation for all of the substantial increase in nurse employment during a period of notable reduction in hospital capacities nationally. In essence, employers are hiring more nurses than can be accounted for solely on the basis of population need. This explains why federal staffing analysts con-clude that the supply of nurses is in balance with national requirements in the midst of a perceived nursing shortage.[2] The federal model is based on estimates of national requirements for nurses, not employer demand.

Widespread Substitution of Nurses

A major determinant of the demand for any kind of worker is the cost of hiring that worker compared with possible alternatives. Nurses are versa-tile in a hospital context. They perform a wide range of functions in addi-tion to nursing care and require little supervision. As a consequence, the number of nurses employed is determined, in part, by nurses' wages com-pared with those of alternative workers or compared with the cost of alternative systems such as computers. When there is a narrow difference between the market wage rates for nurses and those for other kinds of hospital employees, hospitals prefer to hire nurses.

Over the past two decades, nurses have replaced large numbers of licensed practical nurses (LPNs) and aides in hospitals. In 1968 approxi-mately a third of nursing service personnel were nurses; today more than 60% are nurses. Many hospitals have adopted all registered nurse (RN) staffs. One important explanation for this shift toward more nurses was a narrowing of the wage differences between nurses and LPNs and aides.[5] The wages of LPNs, for example, are now about 73% of those of RNs.[6] When costs of supervision and limitations of legal practice are factored in, at current wage rates nurses are a more economical choice for hospitals than LPNs or aides. Under the wage rates that have prevailed over the past two decades, it was cost-effective for hospitals to move toward all nurse staffs.[7,8]

The introduction of Medicare's prospective payment system in 1983–1984 appears to have escalated previous trends and resulted in substan-tial changes in the labor mix in hospitals. Between 1979 and 1982, hospi-tals employed 3.2 RNs per LPN. Beginning in 1983–1984, the ratio began to climb, reaching 5 RNs per LPN by 1986. Between 1982 and 1987, hospitals reduced LPN employment by more than 67,000 full-time-equivalent positions. Over the same period, the number of RN full-time-equivalent positions per 1,000 adjusted patient-days increased by 18%. Clearly, the introduction of the prospective payment system resulted in a substantial escalation of the trend to substitute RNs for LPNs.

In addition, in the early years of the prospective payment system, hospitals reduced the size of the overall work force, cutting more than 300,000 non-RN and non-LPN full-time-equivalent positions between 1982 and 1985. In contrast, the number of full-time-equivalent nurses increased by 40,000 during the same period and by 137,000 during the longer period of 1980 to 1987. Hence, a picture emerges of a restructuring of the work force in hospitals, with a greater reliance on nurses.

When wage patterns are examined, some of the reasons for the substitution are clear. Figure 1 traces the relationship between nurses' wages and those of other hospital employees since 1980 in a panel of 73 hospitals, medical centers, and medical schools.[6] In 1983, nurses' salaries on average were 12% higher than those of a group of non-nurse hospital workers, including administrative assistants, computer operators, medical technicians, personnel specialists, pharmacists, physical therapists, physician assistants, respiratory therapists, social workers, and unit managers. Following the introduction of Medicare's prospective payment system, nurses' annual wage increases fell behind those of other hospital workers. Despite a national shortage, nurses' salaries increased only 4.3% in 1986 and 3.1% in 1987. By 1987 nurses' salaries were less than 97% of those of other hospital employees. Preliminary data from 1988 indicate that nurses' salaries have begun to rise again. To prevent a widespread substitution of nurses for others, nurses' salaries would probably have to be substantially higher than those of alternative workers because nurses are so versatile in a hospital context and because they are viewed as contributing to good quality care, a matter of considerable value in an increasingly competitive hospital industry.[9]

Cost-containment programs such as Medicare's prospective payment system appear to have more of a dampening effect on nurses' salaries than on those of other hospital employees (figure 1).[10] Nursing service is often the largest single labor component in hospitals' budgets, which makes nursing an obvious target when budget reductions are required. Health economists have described nursing as a captive labor market.[11,12] Most nurses are tied to local labor markets because of family considerations. There is little demand for nurses outside traditional health care settings. Most of the jobs for nurses in the ambulatory sector remain filled because nurses prefer the more regular hours. Thus most nurses, if they want to work, are left with the options of hospitals or nursing homes. Nursing homes cannot compete with hospitals on a salary basis, and hospitals tend not to compete with one another for staff on this basis except in highly competitive local labor markets with many hospitals.

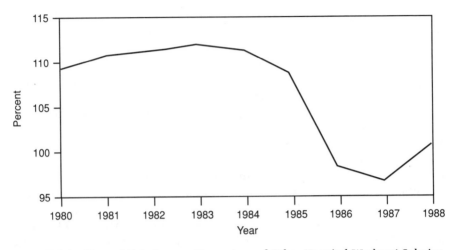

FIGURE 1   Nurses' Salaries as a Percentage of Other Hospital Workers' Salaries, by Year.

The artificial depression of nurses' salaries can be seen most clearly in the lifetime earnings potential of different occupational groups. The maximum salary hospital nurses can expect to earn is only 36% higher than starting salaries, about a $7,000 difference in current dollars. This compares to a salary progression of 72% for secretaries, 89% for personnel directors, 110% for purchasing clerks, 193% for accountants, and 226% for attorneys.[13] For nurses, 20 years' experience has been estimated to have a salary premium of about 5 cents an hour.[14] The low relative lifetime earnings potential of nurses is thought to be a factor in declining enrollments in nursing schools and in the erosion in the quality of the applicant pool. Nursing students have lower average Scholastic Aptitude Test scores than university students in other majors, and the gap between nursing students and others on college campuses is increasing. The possibility of an erosion in the nurse applicant pool is a source of concern, given the ever-increasing complexity of medical care.

Those in occupations with wage problems similar to those of nurses, such as teachers, have resorted to aggressive collective bargaining. A minority of nurses belong to unions, and many are reluctant to support strikes because of the possible adverse effects on patients. Recent rule changes proposed by the National Labor Relations Board that permit bargaining units to consist of all RNs may stimulate greater unionization of nurses in the future, however.[15]

We have documented elsewhere that over the past 25 years, there has been an inverse relationship between nurses' relative wages and hospital nurse vacancy rates.[16] The decline in nurses' relative wages over this period can be traced to various cost-containment efforts, from hospital wage and price controls in the Nixon administration to hospitals' voluntary cost-containment efforts of the 1970s, state rate setting, and finally by the prospective payment system in the 1980s. The evidence suggests that nurses' relative wage rates are inversely related to hospital vacancy rates, primarily because low relative nurses' wages lead to the substitution of nurses for others. We are not suggesting that some nurses have entirely different roles in hospitals as a result of substitution. Rather, we contend that every nurse is spending a substantial portion of his or her time in non-nursing activities that could be done by others. Time and motion studies of nurses show that nurses spend only about 25% to 35% of their time in the direct care of patients.[17,18] Most of the remainder is spent in indirect patient care activities, including charting and clerical work, administrative functions, patient transport, and communicating.

POSSIBLE SOLUTIONS

A recent Gallup poll indicates that only 20% of hospital chief executive officers believe substantial pay increases for nurses would solve the shortage (*Health Week,* August 8, 1988, p. 26). In general, hospital administrators do not think that pay increases attract additional nurses into local labor markets, and the evidence suggests that this is correct because 80% of nurses are already working. The point that is often overlooked, however, is that when nurses' wages rise substantially, there are increased incentives to use them more appropriately. For example, there seems to have been a notable increase in nurses' salaries in Boston in 1988, and it is there that the idea of nurse case managers as replacements for primary nursing has been most aggressively promoted. The assumption underlying the concept of case management is that fewer nurses will be needed than in a primary nurse model of staffing.

Increased salaries may also contribute to solving the shortage by encouraging the more than 500,000 nurses who work part-time to increase the number of hours they work. Many of the popular short-term solutions to shortages of nurses on nights and weekends offer full-time pay for part-time work, which encourages nurses to work part-time or to leave hospitals for work through agencies where they can command these same high hourly wages for full-time work. In addition, trends over the past 25 years suggest that higher wages have an effect on enrollments in nursing schools. Each major increase in nurses' relative wages has been accompanied by increased enrollments in nursing schools. Preliminary reports from nursing schools across the country indicate that enrollments increased in 1988 for the first time in five years, particularly in baccalaureate programs. It is too early to tell whether the increase will be a trend and whether it can be linked with recent increases in nurses' wages.

Increasing salaries in response to the current nursing shortage is likely to reduce or eliminate nursing vacancies because hospitals would have a strong economic incentive to provide care using fewer nurses. If this happens naturally, it is likely to happen first in local labor markets where many hospitals compete for a limited pool of nurses.[9] From a public policy perspective, it appears that an unintended consequence of hospital cost containment is the creation of nurse shortages due to a depression of nurses' wages relative to those of other occupations. Solving that problem, however, is a challenge. A hospital rate increase would be costly and would not necessarily be used to adjust nurses' wages. Also, earmarking funds for nurses runs counter to the underlying rationale of the prospective payment system. If the market fails to make a correction on its own over the next year or two, however, some form of intervention may be in the public interest.

Even in the absence of economic incentives, hospitals should be restructured to enhance their use of nursing resources. There are simply not enough people who want to be nurses to continue to use nurses so indiscriminately. The objective of restructuring is to reduce the number of nurses required without reducing direct nursing-care hours per patient day. This requires building a support system around nurses that enables them to increase the percentage of their time spent in direct patient care. The following changes would help accomplish this.

Administrative Support

It is hard to imagine another industry of the size and complexity of hospitals that has so few support personnel for its professional staff. Many head nurses run the equivalent of multimillion dollar businesses without even a secretary. The addition of a modest complement of secretaries or administrative assistants to nurses could go a long way in freeing nurses to spend their time with patients.

Unit Management

Nurses and physicians cannot take care of patients efficiently unless other departments meet reasonable performance standards. Yet nurses often have little recourse in cases of poor performance of support services but to take time away from nursing care to provide the services themselves. Providing fresh water, transporting patients to tests and therapy, preparing rooms for new admissions, handling food trays, obtaining drugs and supplies, and providing directions and assistance to visitors are all examples of things that need to be done but not by a nurse. At the least, nurses must have more influence over the performance of hospital support services. An improved management structure could be developed to remove these responsibilities from nurses.

The original concept of unit management, as pioneered at the University of Florida in the 1960s, seems applicable to solving this problem. Unit managers were to be professional hospital administrators with the designated authority from central hospital management to control support services at the unit level. Unit managers were to hold a position of authority in the organization comparable to that of the head nurse or clinical nursing director. Physicians would be represented at the unit by a clinical medical director. This team of three representing nursing, medicine, and administration would jointly make the decisions necessary to maintain an environment conducive to efficient, high-quality patient care.

The concept of unit management as originally envisioned was not widely implemented. There were not enough hospital administrators in the 1960s to recruit them to such positions as unit managers, and nurses were a less expensive substitute. Unit managers have become, for the most part, glorified ward clerks without the power and authority from central administration to get things done. There are now many more people beginning careers in hospital administration who could benefit from experiencing management closer to the basic product of hospitals—patient care. For this concept to work, however, unit managers must be responsible 24 hours a day every day and must function in an organizational context that balances the requirements and priorities of nurses and physicians with those of the support services.

Assistants to Nurses

New strategies are needed for the effective use of non-nurses in activities related to patient care. Aides and LPNs could be used more creatively to help nurses provide care—in essence, to serve as another pair of hands. Patients in hospitals today are too sick to have their care delegated to technical and informally trained staff, but assistants to nurses could enhance nurses' productivity and effectiveness and improve the overall quality of care.

Improved Systems

According to testimony by Ernst and Whinney, Inc, before the U.S. Department of Health and Human Services Secretary's Commission on Nursing in September 1988, hospitals invest only 2.4% of their operating budgets on information technologies compared with 8% for banks and 11% for insurance companies. Much of the existing computer capacity in hospitals is directed toward billing and third-party reimbursement, not clinical care.

Nurses spend an estimated 40% of their time on paperwork, and much of the overtime paid to nurses is for charting. A greater investment in clinically based computer systems could lead to a more cost-effective use of personnel in hospitals and also provide a more systematic data base on which to make clinical decisions and conduct research.

Shared Professional Values

The nursing turnover is estimated to range between 11% and 30% annually, at a cost to hospitals of as much as $3 billion.[1] While nursing is an occupation with a relatively high degree of inherent stress due to the psychological demands of caring for sick and dying people, much of the stress perceived by nurses is organizationally induced. Nurses report that they have little control over their work environment and the factors affecting the quality of care provided to patients, yet they hold themselves accountable for their patients' outcomes. They want less central decision making, self-contained clinical units where a cohesive professional staff can be developed without constant reassignments to cover shortages in other parts of the hospital, a greater flexibility in working hours, and greater autonomy in the practice of their profession. Indeed, hospitals that have been successful in recruiting and retaining nurses during times of national shortages have these organizational dimensions.[19]

Several blue-ribbon panels convened to study the nursing shortage over the past decade have directed recommendations concerning these organizational dimensions to hospital chief executive officers and boards.[20,21] With a few notable exceptions, these recommendations have been ignored and the shortage has persisted. Recent evidence suggests that nurses are still largely outside the decision-making structure of hospitals, which probably accounts for the lack of responsiveness of hospitals to proposals for organizational change. At the request of the Department of Health and Human Services Secretary's Commission on Nursing, the Office of the Inspector General recently did a study of nurse participation in hospital decision making.[22] The study consisted of a telephone survey to chief executive officers and chief nurse officers of a random sample of hospitals selected from the universe of Medicare-certified, acute care nonspecialty hospitals in the United States.

Chief executive officers were the only members of hospital management who consistently attended meetings of their governing bodies. Some 85% of them were members of the governing body, and about 65% voted. In contrast, less than 2% of all nurse executives were voting members of hospital boards, and only a third regularly attended board meetings. Chief executive officers appear to be the major conduit of information on nursing and patient care to their boards. The Inspector General's findings do not reassure us that the chief executive officers of hospitals routinely have access to the best information on nursing. For example, less than 5% of chief nurse officers were members of their hospital's executive committee, and none of those surveyed voted. Of chief nurse officers surveyed, 6% were members of the finance committee. Only half were voting members of joint conference committees, and only a third participated on planning committees. Excluding nurses from policy-making roles in hospitals limits the availability of information on nursing and related patient care issues and reduces the flow of information to nurses about institutional objectives and challenges.

One of the most frequent and persistent criticisms of hospitals is that services are fragmented, inefficient, and impersonal. Public opinion polls suggest that consumers feel increasingly that hospitals put too much emphasis on the financial aspects of their institutions and too little on the reason for their existence—the care of sick people. The more businesslike hospitals have become in the public's mind, the lower the level of trust and confidence the public has in hospital administrators and physicians. As a result, the quality of hospital care in the United States is ranked by the public somewhat better than that of automotive repair shops but worse than that of supermarkets and airlines.[23] The business model adopted by many hospitals needs to be balanced by the patient care perspectives that nurses and physicians bring.

Nurse-Physician Joint Practice

Unsatisfactory relationships with physicians are a major source of dissatisfaction among nurses and a common reason for resignations.[24] Moreover, it is increasingly clear that patient outcomes depend on the nature and quality of communication between nurses and physicians. A recent multi-hospital study of the effectiveness of intensive care concluded that the differences in mortality rates among hospitals could be attributed in large part to the nature of the communications and decision-making partnerships between nurses and physicians.[4] This finding is not at all surprising when we consider how rapidly the condition of critically ill patients changes and the importance of anticipating and preventing a catastrophic event rather than treating it under emergency conditions.

Nurses and physicians often do not fully appreciate the responsibilities and obligations that each holds for patients. This could be overcome by organizational arrangements for patient care in which specific nurses and physicians have longitudinal responsibility for the same groups of patients, as is the case in intensive care units where the relationships between nurses and physicians are consistently better than on the general medical and surgical units. Nurses often let their responsibilities for "managing" the unit divert them from maintaining the kinds of longitudinal responsibilities that physicians usually have for patients. It would be much more productive for physicians to support and participate in the restructuring of hospitals to reduce the administrative burden on nurses, enabling them to more fully participate in direct patient care than to propose an alternative bedside provider.

The Registered Care Technologist Proposal

Bringing an end to the persistent shortage of nurses requires the active involvement of physicians. The recent proposal developed unilaterally by the American Medical Association (AMA), however, to train a new category of health care worker as a solution to the nursing shortage diverts attention and resources from the pursuit of a permanent solution.

The proposal calls for the education of a new category of "bedside care givers" to execute medical protocols with special emphasis on technical skills.[25] A registered care technologist (RCT) would receive on-the-job training of from 2 to 18 months' duration. Basic RCT training for 9 months would qualify the graduate to provide bedside care to patients in hospitals and nursing homes. Advanced RCT training of 18 months would qualify high school graduates to care for patients in all types of critical care units, including administering intravenous drugs. Training RCTs is envisioned as hospital-based, following the model of diploma nurse education and with stipends for those in training. Registered nurses "who wish to remain at the bedside" would be eligible to be certified as advanced RCTs. The AMA anticipates that RCTs would be paid between $15,000 and $18,000 a year and that the new career would appeal to a pool of applicants not currently considering nursing, namely men and those persons requiring an income during their training period.

The major problem of the RCT proposal is that it does not address the root cause of the nursing shortage—the excess demand for nurses. Moreover, there are some 900,000 licensed practical nurses already trained and experienced in hospital care that hospitals have shunned in favor of registered nurses. The expected wage rates of RCTs are even closer to the wage rates of nurses than those of LPNs, a difference of only a few thousand dollars a year at current wage rates.

It is not clear why there would be a demand for RCTs since the demand for LPNs has declined dramatically. The better solution is moderating the demand for nurses by reducing nurses' responsibilities for unit administration. If the time nurses spend in direct patient care were doubled from the current between 25% and 35% to between 50% and 70%, the nursing shortage would be over. It makes much more sense to substitute clerical, administrative, and support personnel for nurses in nonclinical roles than to have less qualified personnel delivering bedside care to critically ill patients.

The AMA proposal is yet another example of the failure of nurses and physicians to develop mutually acceptable solutions to problems that affect the professional practice of both groups. Nurses primarily support and complement medical care. The expanded clinical responsibilities of nurses have freed physicians to perform medical functions that require their unique expertise and that tend to be more remunerative than most functions that nurses perform. Because nurses' remuneration derives from the hospital budget, whereas physicians' incomes are primarily fee-for-service, gains for nurses are unlikely to affect the economic status of physicians. A continuing shortage of nurses may adversely affect physicians' incomes, though, if the number of hospital admissions and surgical procedures is reduced because of the shortage. Thus, physicians and nurses both have a stake in solving the hospital nursing shortage and, working together, can promote their mutual interests and those of their patients.

REFERENCES

1. Secretary's Commission on Nursing: Final Report. Washington, DC, US Dept of Health and Human Services (DHHS), December 1988.

2. Sixth Report to the President and Congress on the Status of Health Personnel in the United States. Washington, DC, Bureau of Health Professions, Health Resources Administration, US DHHS, 1988.

3. Weisman CS, Alexander CS, Chase GA: Determinants of hospital staff nurse turnover. Med Care 1981; 19:431–443.

4. Knaus WA, Draper EA, Wagner DP, et al: An evaluation of outcome from intensive care in major medical centers. Ann Intern Med 1986; 104:410–418.

5. Aiken LH, Blendon RJ, Rogers DE: The shortage of hospital nurses: A new perspective. Ann Intern Med 1981; 95:365–373.

6. National Survey of Hospital and Medical School Salaries. Galveston, Texas, University of Texas Medical Branch at Galveston, 1987.

7. Burt ML: The cost of all RN staffing, In Alfano G (Ed): All-RN Nursing Staff. Wakefield, Mass, Nursing Resources, 1980.

8. Hinshaw AS, Scofield R, Atwood JR: Staff, patient, and cost outcomes of all-registered nurse staffing. J Nurs Adm 1981; 11:30–36.

9. Robinson JC: Hospital competition and hospital nursing. Nurs Econ 1988; 6:116–124.

10. Aiken LH: Breaking the shortage cycles. Am J Nurs 1987; 87:1616–1620.

11. Yett DE: An Economic Analysis of the Nurse Shortage. Lexington, Mass, Lexington Books, 1975.

12. Feldstein PJ: Health Care Economics. New York, John Wiley, 1979.

13. McKibbin RC: Analysis of Career Earnings in Nursing and Other Occupations. Presented at a meeting of the American Nurses' Association, March 11, 1988, Kansas City, MO.

14. Link C: Nurses for the future: What does a BS degree buy? Am J Nurs 1987; 87:1621–1627.

15. New upsurge in bargaining seen in wake of NLRB action. Am J Nurs 1988; 88:1409–1410.

16. Aiken LH, Mullinix CF: The nurse shortage: Myth or reality? N Engl J Med 1987; 317:641–646.

17. Misener TR, Frelin AJ, Twist PA: Sampling nursing time pinpoints staffing needs. Nurs Health Care, 1978 Apr. pp 233–237.

18. Rieder KA, Leasing SB: Nursing productivity: Evolution of a systems model. Nurs Management 1978; 18:13–44.

19. Kramer M, Schmalenberg C: Magnet hospitals: Institutions of excellence. J Nurs Adm 1988; 18(1):13–24; 18(2):11–19.

20. National Commission on Nursing: Summary Report and Recommendations. Chicago, Hospital Research and Educational Trust, 1983.

21. Institute of Medicine: Nursing and Nursing Education: Public Policies and Private Actions. Washington, DC, National Academy Press, 1983.

22. Management Advisory Report: Nurse Participation in Hospital Decision-making. Office of Inspector General, US DHHS publication No. OAI-03-88-01120, July 22, 1988.

23. Blendon RJ: The public's view of the future of health care. JAMA 1988; 259:3587–3593.

24. Mechanic D. Aiken LH: A cooperative agenda for medicine and nursing. N Engl J Med 1982; 307:747–750.

25. House of Delegates Report SS. Chicago, American Medical Association, June 1988.

I want to change the way we think about health—*by putting prevention first.*
— Joycelyn Elders,
U.S. Surgeon General

Claire M. Fagin

Cost-effectiveness of Nursing Care Revisited: 1981–1990

Despite increasingly aggressive efforts to contain health care costs over the decade of the 1980s, expenditures continue to increase at rates well over the growth in the general economy. Mounting concern on the part of government, employers, and insurers suggests that the 1990s may lead to more powerful efforts to examine alternatives for quality health care at reduced cost. Nursing is in a unique position among health care providers to respond to these efforts and is ready to provide evidence of its cost-effectiveness.

In earlier articles (Fagin, 1982a,b; Fagin & Jacobsen, 1985) I discussed the pro-competition environment of the early 1980s. The cumulative evidence showed that nurses provided cost-effective care that substituted for physician services in many situations and new and important services in long-term care and nursing homes. These findings led me to call for increased third-party reimbursement for nurses in areas where efficacy had been proved. There has been considerable progress in the reimbursement of nurses over this decade, but not nearly enough in view of the growing evidence from research that nurses achieve outcomes as good as or better than physicians in broad areas of primary care and midwifery, and at lower overall costs.

The purpose of this article is to update my previous synthesis of research on the cost-effectiveness of nursing care. It focuses on research published in the 1980s and reexamines the issues of costs and outcomes from professional and policy perspectives.

Claire M. Fagin, Ph.D., R.N., F.A.A.N., is Margaret Bond Simon Dean and Professor, School of Nursing and Director of a World Health Organization Global Collaborating Center at the University of Pennsylvania, Philadelphia.
From Fagin, C. M. (1992). Cost-effectiveness of nursing care revisited. In L. H. Aiken and C. M. Fagin, eds., *Charting Nursing's Future* (pp. 13–28). Philadelphia: J. B. Lippincott. Used with permission of the publisher.

NURSING IN HOSPITALS

Hospital care is the largest health care expenditure. Thus cost-containment pressures have and will continue to focus on inpatient care. Quality and cost trade-offs in hospitals dominate the literature, with concerns about diminished quality resulting from cost constraints, early discharge, the nursing shortage, and managed care expressed by professionals and consumers alike.

There is a growing body of research linking surgical volume (hence experience) with lower inpatient mortality (Bennett et al., 1989; Hannan et al., 1989). Similarly, a comparative study of 30 hospital emergency departments showed a positive correlation between hospital size and the quality of both medical and nursing care (Georgopoulos, 1985).

Several studies have pointed to the importance of nurses or nurse-physician relationships in patient outcome. One study found "significant associations between higher mortality rates among inpatients and the stringency of state programs to review hospital rates . . . the stringency of certificate-of-need legislation . . . and the intensity of competition in the marketplace, as measured by enrollment in health maintenance organizations" (Shortell & Hughes, 1988). The higher the percentage of registered nurses, the lower the mortality rates were. This finding is substantiated by other studies showing that hospitals with a high proportion of registered nurses provide a better quality of care, as measured by lower mortality rates (Hartz, Krakauer, & Kuhn, 1989).

These studies suggest that the greater the experience of the "medical" team, the better the patient outcomes. The specific contributions of nurses to these improved outcomes have not been well documented. Nor is it clear what specific impact nurses' experience or level of education has on improved outcomes. More targeted research is necessary to clarify the relationships.

In addition, more recent publications often document cost savings resulting from a higher productivity of registered nurses in institutions employing a large number of registered nurses. For example, in one hospital, researchers compared the changes in dependency needs of patients between 1969 and 1985 and the percentage of registered nurses during the same time periods. The study showed that although there was a 13 percent decrease in occupancy on medical units in the two time periods, acuity had indeed risen sharply. "In 1972, the nursing salary budget supported 1,169 full-time equivalents (FTEs), of whom 36 percent were registered nurses. In 1985, the nursing salary budget supported 1,618 FTEs, of whom 94 percent were registered nurses (approximately 15 percent with master's or doctoral degrees). In 1972 the nursing salary budget represented 17.8 percent of the corporate budget; in 1985, however, nursing accounted for only 14.7 percent of the corporate budget" (Donovan & Lewis, 1987). Nursing productivity increased sharply between the two time periods in that more than twice the amount of patient care was given in the same amount of time during the second period. Other studies support the same conclusion and indicate that lower turnover among nurses results from increased job satisfaction derived from the more professional work force with concomitant increases in autonomy and flexibility (Dahlen & Gregor, 1985; Wolf et al., 1986).

Concern regarding collaboration between physicians and nurses continues. Whether real progress has been made in further developing the relationships between nurses and physicians is not clear; however, there are indications that in certain areas the collaborative relationship is vital and thriving. Many authors show positive results when nurses and physicians collaborate in care of the elderly, in discovering ameliorative procedures for managing pressure sores, in the administration of analgesia, and in other inpatient and out-of-hospital health and medical care activities. Further exploration is needed of the dynamics of the nurse-physician relationship in the areas of the barriers to collaboration and the outcome of successful and unsuccessful interactions (DeFede et al., 1989; Kitz et al., 1989).

One of the most important recent studies on the impact of nurse-physician collaboration was an evaluation of mortality in intensive care units in 13 tertiary care hospitals. The researchers compared actual and predicted death rates for 5,030 patients in intensive care units and found significant differences in mortality among the hospitals. Taking into account the severity of illness of patients across these hospitals, the most important factor contributing to differences in mortality rates was physician-nurse communication. This factor was even more important than teaching status or the presence of an intensive care unit medical director (Knaus, Draper, Wagner, & Zimmerman, 1986).

Many articles were published during the 1980s that described specific and new nursing interventions. Some have evaluated the cost-effectiveness of these nursing interventions. Nurse investigators have discussed the use of restraints and ways to improve the individual's capacity for daily living (Evans, Stumpf, & Williams, 1991). Numerous papers have been published describing nursing programs to help patients with cancer and their families deal with the illness and treatment. Many of these studies show positive outcomes with regard to patient attitude, compliance, and tension reduction.

One interesting study reports the implementation of a surgical nurse coordinator program utilizing operating room nurses to improve communication for patients and their families during the perioperative period (Watson & Hickey, 1984). Since the program did not require additions of nursing staff, it was viewed as "cost-effective." The quality outcomes are clear: ". . . the families now gather in one area to await information instead of being scattered throughout the hospital. . . . The recovery room notes fewer calls from patient units, and anxious parents or spouses seldom wait outside the doors to catch a glimpse of the patient. . . . The time spent by floor nurses and evening supervisors in pacifying angry relatives is virtually eliminated" (Watson & Hickey, 1984).

Other innovative nursing interventions that have been evaluated include programs of shorter stays for patients, with heavy reliance on nursing care and observation (Balik et al., 1988; Boland, 1985); competitive programs with monetary incentives; and alternative nursing schedules or flextime, which contributed to increased productivity and cost-effective outcomes (Elliott, 1989).

Several studies examine nursing costs from the standpoint of diagnostic related groups (DRGs) or other patient classification systems. These studies indicate the extreme cost-effectiveness of nursing personnel and, in some instances, suggest that nursing care is far less costly than nurses themselves might think (Bailie, 1986; McKibben, 1982; Mitchell et al., 1984; Riley & Schaefers, 1983; Sovie et al., 1985; Walker, 1985; "What's the cost," 1986; Wilson et al., 1988).

Far fewer articles about the benefits of primary nursing and all registered nursing staffs were found in this current review than in the review 10 years ago. Some nursing administrators believe that a staff of all registered nurses has become almost a luxury in this time of nursing shortage.

A larger study using the database of the Medicus Nursing Productivity and Quality system found productivity and quality improvement, even in the face of staff cutting and cost reduction. They attribute this finding to the "widespread increase in the use of RNs. Every nursing manager . . . cited this as a significant factor in improved quality in their institution" (Helt & Jelinek, 1988). The hospitals in the study were mostly large, urban, teaching facilities using the Medicus Nursing Productivity and Quality system, whose "production-unit-based information systems" are reported to receive high marks from the users at all levels. Other studies support these findings and suggest that cost savings are demonstrated in staff turnover, low sick time, length of patient hospital stay, and overtime (LaForme, 1982; Hinshaw et al., 1981).

Over this decade considerable interest has been shown in the concept of primary nursing in many parts of the world. Research in this area has been reported in all English language nursing journals. Although results of studies of primary nursing are somewhat mixed as to cost-effectiveness, there appears to be a sizable body of literature supporting the view that primary nursing is worth trying, that its implementation is a worthwhile experience for both patients and nurses, and that the outcomes may be significantly better than for other forms of nursing organization (MacDonald, 1988; Sellick et al., 1983).

Overall, these studies of organization of nursing services have revealed important outcomes in quality and cost resulting from volume of care, experience of providers, collaboration between nurses and physicians, and the cost-effectiveness of nursing care in hospitals (as a portion of hospital charges); they have also expressed an overall positive view of an all registered nurse staff and of primary nursing and the positive effects of schedule flexibility, autonomy, and monetary incentives. Further research is necessary to quantify and evaluate the clinical efficacy of nursing interventions, the value of experience and education of nurses in improving patients outcomes, and the organizational designs that work best to facilitate nursing and patient satisfaction. These kinds of studies will greatly strengthen nursing's participation in technology assessment.

The lack of uniform standards for outcome evaluation is interesting to consider in light of the need to quantify nursing's contributions to health care. The Nursing Minimum Data Set (NMDS) was an initial effort to establish such standards and "draws on the documentation of the nursing process that occurs whenever nurses provide care to people in any setting" (Werley & Zorn, 1989). The NMDS includes specific items used on a regular basis by the majority of nurses involved in health care delivery. Its purposes are "(1) to establish comparability of nursing across clinical populations, settings, geographic areas, and time; (2) to describe the nursing care of patients or clients and their families in a variety of settings; . . . (3) to demonstrate or project trends regarding nursing care needs and allocation of nursing resources . . . ; and (4) to stimulate nursing research through links to the detailed data existing in nursing information systems . . ." (Werley & Zorn, 1989). Werley has been engaged in the process of developing and testing the concept of the NMDS for over 10 years and there is, currently, considerable interest in the method in the United States and internationally.

The NMDS includes nursing care, patient or client demographics, and service elements. There is not yet an acceptable scheme for categorizing nursing interventions, and research and development are urgently recommended by Werley and associates. Germane to this chapter is the view that an NMDS would provide improved data for quality assurance and costing of nursing services. Health policy debates frequently do not include nursing concerns and recommendations because data on nursing are incomplete.

The NMDS is said to be invaluable to nurse researchers interested in the "broad areas of the process, outcome or cost of nursing care." A review of the literature did not reveal studies that utilized the NMDS in the way proposed by Werley and others interested in this method. It may be that NMDS is what is needed to give similarity of form to outcome studies, but work is needed to determine the efficacy of this method for this purpose.

SUBSTITUTION OF NURSES FOR OTHER PROVIDERS

Two major reviews of the practice and cost-effectiveness of nurse practitioners were published during the decade. In 1983, the American Nurses

Association (ANA) published a review of the literature on the impact of nurse practitioners (NPs), and in 1986 the Office of Technology Assessment (OTA) published its review of the work of NPs and other non-physician providers. The OTA concluded that NPs, physician assistants, and certified nurse-midwives (CNMs) provide care of quality comparable to physician care, and that "NPs and CNMs are more adept than physicians at providing services that depend on communication with patients and preventive actions." The Office of Technology Assessment report recommends extending reimbursement to these nurses and believes that in some settings this "could benefit the health status of . . . segments of the population currently not receiving appropriate care [and that among the] long-term effects could be a decrease in total costs."

The results of the ANA (1983) review of the literature on NPs indicated consistent findings of cost-effectiveness, evidence of better control of obesity and hypertension among clients of NPs as compared with clients of physicians, relief of symptoms, compliance with appointments and treatment regimen, and continuity of care. Further, the review indicated that clients of NPs had fewer emergency room visits and documented an increase in clients returning to work and better results in a variety of other areas. Other studies carried out during the decade support these data. For example, one study showed that nurses provide more health education than physician providers and more follow-up care (Bibb, 1982), whereas others documented reductions in health-related costs, diagnostic tests, and medication use while maintaining quality of care. The latter studies also refuted a commonly held assumption that NPs take more time with patients, thus eliminating the cost differential between nurses and physicians. Indeed, in one study it was found that physicians' initial visit times were shorter than those of NPs but follow-up visit times were similar for both. Per episode, costs when NPs were the initial providers were 20 to 50 percent lower than when physicians were the initial providers (Salkever, Skinner, Steinwachs, & Katz, 1982).

In a review of evaluation research on nurse practitioners, Prescott and Driscoll concluded that the majority of studies reported no difference between nurse practitioners and physicians on many measures but that "the findings which indicated nurse practitioners score higher than physicians have been frequently overlooked." These included such areas as discussion about child care, preventive health, amount of advice offered, therapeutic listening and support, completeness of history taken, interviewing skills, and patients' knowledge about their management plan (Prescott & Driscoll, 1980). Wanting to understand whether and why such differences occur, the study compared outcomes in two groups of patients attending a hypertension clinic (Ramsay, McKenzie, & Fish, 1986). One group was seen by physicians and the other by nurses. Treatment outcome variables and patient compliance were compared, and the findings indicated superior outcomes in the nurse-staffed clinic for weight reduction, blood pressure reduction, and patient attrition. It is interesting to note that even though physicians referred nearly half of their patients to dietitians, weight control was poorer in this group.

During the 1980s, Ginsberg, Marks, and Waters continued their comparative studies of the use of nurse psychotherapists. Their most recent work was a randomized, controlled trial of behavioral psychotherapy provided by nurse therapists compared with routine management by the patient's general practitioner. Most of the patients had phobic disorders. At the end of one year, clinical outcomes "were significantly better in patients cared for by the nurse therapist" (Ginsberg et al., 1984). Economic outcomes were also better for the nursing group because the general practitioners prescribed more drugs and hospital treatment.

Studies that examined the use of NPs in occupational health settings also documented improved outcomes at lower costs. Annual cost savings were achieved by more effective handling of employee health problems and reductions in related health care utilization. One study reported a benefit/cost ratio of 2.1:1.0 for in-house primary care delivered by NPs as compared with physicians (Scharon & Bernacki, 1984).

There is no need to repeat the strong conclusions regarding the cost-effectiveness and quality of care of nurse-midwives reported in earlier articles. Suffice it to say that over 25 years of study of the practice of nurse-midwives has revealed excellent results for both cost and quality (Diers, 1982). The latest survey of maternity care costs makes the argument for midwife care of healthy maternal patients even more compelling. This report of findings of a 1989 survey of 173 community hospitals, 70 childbirth centers, and 153 licensed midwives reveals that the average cost of a nurse-midwife's services is $994 compared with physicians' fees for a normal pregnancy and delivery of $1,492. The cost of a cesarean section averages $7,186 (Minor, 1989).

Sufficient evidence is available to conclude that the NP is a provider who can maintain or increase quality of care at lower cost than physicians in a number of areas of vital importance. In this section I have discussed NPs as replacements for physicians in care traditionally provided in our health care system. I will discuss NPs further in terms of new and alternative modes of care in the section that follows.

ALTERNATIVE MODELS OF PRACTICE

The studies relating to alternative modes of practice deal with innovative practices of care of the elderly and with home or community care. Early patient discharge from the hospital with nurse follow-up, home nursing care with a variety of populations, and care of teen-aged mothers and their children are also included in this survey. Nurses are engaged in solving the most pressing health problems of our society, and their work is exemplary in cost and outcome. In addition to reviewing individual studies, I will discuss three large-scale, systematic studies and several review articles about the cost-effectiveness of home care. In addition, I have included here a study that describes a system of nursing care management that implements a nursing network of all care services.

Nursing Homes and Geriatric Nurse Practitioners

The evaluation of the Robert Wood Johnson National Teaching Nursing Home (TNH) Program offers important insights about the value of professional nursing. The evaluation of this experiment at 11 sites, which tested the outcomes of affiliation between nursing homes and university schools of nursing, found that the TNH approach reduced hospitalization rates for nursing home patients and fostered an environment conducive to maximizing patients' physical and cognitive functioning (Shaughnessy, Kramer, & Hittle, 1988). These accomplishments occurred at no additional cost, and reductions in hospitalization created substantial savings for Medicare. The evaluators recommended that the teaching nursing home approach be encouraged on a more widespread basis by Medicare and Medicaid. Specifically, they recommended reimbursement for the cost of nurse clinicians, education for aides, and selected educational programs, since these resulted in lower hospitalization rates for TNH patients in contrast with those in the comparison nursing homes (Shaughnessy et al., 1988).

Another comparative study examined quality of care and health services utilization in 30 nursing homes employing geriatric nurse practitioners versus those in 30 matched control homes (Kane et al., 1989). There were a number of quality improvements in the geriatric nurse practitioner group, including reduction in hospital admissions, reduction in use of restraints, and increase in the number of patients discharged to their homes. The potential to reduce total costs of care "is suggested by the data on hospital utilization, especially the reduction in hospital days. The savings occur through fewer hospitalizations and less emergency room use" (Kane et al., 1989).

An interesting analysis modeled outcomes of nursing home care by demonstrating that use of resources, as measured by minutes of nursing time, is associated with patient outcomes (Rohrer & Hogan, 1987). The results of this study indicated that care given by nurses, psychosocial care, and physician care were related to future functional status. The study does not differentiate among nurses offering "basic services" and does not investigate the cost/quality possibilities of upgrading nursing credentials versus adding other providers, such as physicians or others offering psychosocial care.

Community and Home Care

The effectiveness of a team approach to outpatient geriatric care was established through a randomized controlled clinical trial. The experimental group was cared for by a team that included physicians, nurses, social workers, and nutritionists. The control group was cared for by physicians alone. The team assessed the patients' physical, mental, and social functioning and provided counseling and family support to the experimental group as compared with the control intervention of only physician care. Hospital lengths of stay were 39 percent shorter for the experimental group over a 12-month period. The net result was a 25 percent reduction in cost for the treatment group. There was no reduction in satisfaction or functional level of the patient.

The literature has been greatly enriched during this decade by a number of studies of the cost-effectiveness of community and home care. The weakness in most of the series reviewed was that community care did not substitute for nursing home or hospital care but rather added to existing care. Thus, costs were increased overall (Berkeley Planning Associates, 1987). The Channeling Demonstration is an example of this phenomenon. It was ". . . a rigorous test of the effectiveness of comprehensive case management and expanded community services . . . as a way to contain the costs of long-term care of the elderly and to improve the quality of life of elderly clients . . ." and their caretakers (Carcagno & Kemper, 1988). Ten sites were included in the final evaluation. The evaluation found that average costs of caring for these patients increased because the cost of expanding case management and formal community services was not offset by reductions in nursing home or other types of care. The Channeling Demonstration did produce some increase in the measured well-being of clients and caretakers (Thornton, Dunston, & Kemper, 1988).

Weissert's review of a decade of research on home and community-based care concludes that "Community care rarely reduces nursing home or hospital use; it provides only limited outcome benefits; and to this point, it has usually raised overall use of health services as well as total expenditures" (Weissert, 1985).

The questions about cost in these studies appears conclusive. However, the assumption that community care would reduce cost was, in my opinion, erroneous in the first place because the demonstrations did not mandate specific populations where such care would more likely be substitutive. Further, at this time, there is considerable interest in community services for all functionally dependent people, including the elderly.

Recognition that services to this population should not be compared with costs for a nursing home alternative is proposed by Weissert and others. Other writers examining the same or additional information stress the "need for additional methodologically rigorous research to assess the effectiveness of home care" (Green, 1989; Hedrick & Inui, 1986).

Besides cost reduction, there are important reasons for providing home care and other forms of community care. The outcry on the part of some of the public in response to Medicare's Catastrophic Care Coverage was, in part, related to a correct perception that this coverage would not provide for long-term or chronic care in the home and community. There are programs that have demonstrated considerable savings when community care is *substituted* for institutional long-term care. The OnLok Senior Health Services Community Care Organization, which manages and delivers all long-term care services to its clients, finds community care 26 percent lower in costs than institutional care (Berkeley Planning Associates, 1987). The Nursing Home Without Walls Program in New York State has shown that it can provide care for patients in the community at 50 percent of the cost of institutional care. Thus, despite the negative conclusions reported by many of the studies cited above and in other reviews (General Accounting Office Report, 1983), many private and state payers draw different conclusions from their experiences.

The Health Insurance Association of America, Blue Cross and Blue Shield Association, Aetna Life and Casualty, and others appear convinced that home care is a cost-effective offering. Several states and counties and Visiting Nurse Associations have instituted and studied programs offering community care and have found them to be uniformly successful in reducing costs *if they have served as an alternative for other care.* Such services to the chronically ill and the functionally impaired appear to private and governmental payers to be cost-effective alternatives (Cabin, 1985). Kramer and coworkers provide data to support the views of the payers. After assessing the mix of patients currently treated in nursing homes and home health agencies, they drew inferences about the cost-effectiveness of the two modalities (Kramer, Shaughnessy, & Pettigrew, 1985). They concluded that home health care is a cost-effective alternative to acute care hospital use at the end of a hospital stay and may prevent exacerbations of medical problems resulting in rehospitalization (Kramer et al., 1985). Also, home health care might be a more viable option in the care of patients who are neither severely disabled nor have profound functional problems.

It is important to note here that these studies are not nursing studies per se; however, any study of home care or community care of a functionally impaired population at risk must be presumed to lean heavily on nursing because these are the services this population requires directly from nurses or services that are managed by nurses.

Nurses have done important research on home and community care during this decade. Most of these studies utilized clinical nurse specialists working with a variety of populations in innovative ways to shorten hospitalization, improve outcomes of care, or both.

McCorkle (McCorkle et al., 1989) studied home nursing care follow-up of a group of patients with progressive lung cancer by master's-prepared oncology nurses. The results of this study indicated that patients receiving home care had less symptom distress and social dependency than a group receiving only office care. The total length of hospital stays was lower among the specialized home care group as compared with the control groups. The quality outcomes are clear and obviously resulted in cost reductions because of decreased rates of complications and hospitalizations.

Another study of home follow-up services by clinical nurse specialists was done by Burgess (Burgess et al., 1987). When master's-prepared nurse specialists followed up postmyocardial infarction patients at home, the patients suffered less psychological distress and were less dependent on family supports than the control group.

The aforementioned populations are particularly amenable to innovative nursing interventions, and more recent studies can be expected to examine cost directly rather than by implication of outcome. For example, Naylor's (Naylor, 1990) randomized clinical trial compared the effects of a comprehensive discharge planning protocol implemented by a gerontologic nurse specialist with the hospital's standard discharge planning procedure. Rehospitalizations and total costs were reduced in the experimental group. Naylor's current research involves a large sample of elderly patients and addresses the cost issues in more detail and more extensively.

Teen-aged pregnancy and low birth weight infants are problems of great concern to American society and to health care providers. Nurses are making major contributions in these important areas through practice and research. O'Sullivan's (O'Sullivan & Jacobsen, unpublished) randomized trial of a health care program for infants of first-time adolescent mothers demonstrated that this comprehensive program reduced dropout rates from school, repeat pregnancies, and emergency room use. The number of fully immunized infants increased. The experimental group received routine and additional services, including counseling about returning to school, use of family planning methods, and extra health care teaching from pediatric nurse practitioners and trained volunteers. The public cost of teenage childbearing has been estimated at $15,620 per child (Burt, 1986). Thus the 18 prevented pregnancies in this group could be said to have resulted in savings of $281,160. The most interesting factor of the special program was that it not only reduced system costs by the outcome, but the program itself was less expensive by $16.00 per client per visit than routine care for the following reasons: volunteer teaching of self-care for certain procedures; the pediatric nurse practitioner and the physician gave the immunizations rather than an additional registered nurse; less space was needed per provider; and no teaching of residents was involved. Clearly, even with teaching costs added, the program would be less costly than routine care because of the change in style of health care delivery. The effectiveness of this program in cost and quality is impressive even without attempting to quantify the increase in accountability among volunteers and clients.

A recent study of women in a rural area near Elmira, New York, showed that home visits by nurses to low-income women during and after pregnancy to teach them the basics of childrearing resulted in less child abuse, healthier babies, and better employment and educational achievements by the mothers. The vast majority of the women were teenagers and unmarried (Olds, Henderson, Tatelbaum, & Chamberlin, 1988). As in the O'Sullivan study, the subsequent pregnancies were 43 percent lower than in the control group, and the young women in the experimental group returned to school more rapidly. Both of these studies reveal the weaknesses in our current reimbursement policies, in which these nurse practitioners must be "hidden" in the system rather than accessed directly by clients for their valuable services of health promotion, counseling, direct care, and education.

The definitive work in cost and quality during this decade is that of Brooten (Brooten et al., 1986) dealing with early discharge of very low birth weight infants, with home follow-up by nurse specialists. In this study, very low birth weight infants were discharged from the hospital early and received home follow-up services from a master's-prepared perinatal nurse specialist. The group of infants was discharged a mean of 11 days earlier, 200 g less in weight, and 2 weeks younger than the control group. There was a mean saving of $18,560 per infant over conventional care.

Brooten's work highlights the need for randomized clinical trials of nursing interventions and alternatives to traditional practices. She provides a useful model for study using master's-prepared clinical specialists with advanced practice skills. Although there is a growing body of literature on home care using similar models, there is a paucity of such work attesting to the cost-effective practice of in-hospital clinical specialists. Many writers believe that clinical specialists with advanced practice skills are cost-effective providers in hospitals. Others report positive results in influencing care delivery through nurse specialists' interaction with staff. Despite a consensus on the high value of clinical nurse specialists among nurses, additional research is crucial for understanding and providing a rationale for the support of clinical nurse specialists during an era of cost containment.

Case Management

Many articles during this decade discuss case management as an organizational strategy for improving the cost-effectiveness of nursing in hospitals. However, the authors do not present their work in a way that allows us to draw conclusions as to cost-effectiveness or quality outcomes. Some articles describe case management as an organizational structure for hospital patient care. Others define case management as "a set of logical steps and a process of interaction with service networks, which assures that a client receives needed services in a supportive, effective, efficient, and cost-effective manner" (Weil & Karls, 1985). Concerned about the increased number of patients with complicated care needs, one ambulatory care center established a case management system using registered nurses to make primary care more accessible. Preliminary findings show improved quality of care and cost reduction through reduced hospitalization. There was also an increase in patient counseling and health education and promotion activities (Winder, 1988).

One article offers an interesting model that has implications for the future world of health care delivery. It describes a nursing network that includes acute care inpatient services, extended care/long-term services, home care, hospice, and ambulatory care services. The last group includes both traditional physician services and nurse-managed community based clinics (Ethridge & Lamb, 1989). Preliminary analysis of data indicates that "nurse case managers appear to exert a financial impact through decreased length of stay . . . even though case-managed patients had a higher average acuity . . . than non-case-managed patients."

The alternative care models identified during this decade and summarized here have important benefits for patients and have been shown to be cost-effective additions or alternatives to traditional care.

CONCLUSION

During the decade of the 1980s, nurses and others have examined many aspects of nursing interventions from the perspective of cost and quality. This work has covered the gamut of clinical care integral to the broadest definition of nursing and dealt with patient populations from the neonate and the pregnant woman to the extreme elderly. Stimulated by the changes in hospital reimbursement, a great deal of attention has been paid to the organization and cost of nursing services within hospitals. This article has summarized the papers reviewed in three categories: (1) those dealing with nursing care in hospitals; (2) those dealing with nurse practitioners substituting for other providers; and (3) alternatives to traditional modes of care. There are some areas where more work is needed to flesh out strong impressions and beginning data. This is particularly the case in relation to the clinical nurse specialist, community care, and organization of nursing services in nursing homes. However, even in these areas, the data are accumulating to attest to the powerful contribution nurses are making to enhancing the quality of care, promoting health, and lowering total system costs. What is very clear is that nursing is a bargain, in and out of hospitals. We need to make the results of these studies available to policymakers and the public, since they strongly support nursing's political agenda and provide a solution to the cost problems plaguing our country.

Many believe the myth that increasing nursing compensation is not affordable given cost constraints. Yet, a cursory glance at the many articles examining cost of nursing care in this [article] and others . . . will debunk that myth and force exploration of where the money for health care is currently going. It is not going to nursing care. Nurse administrators in hospitals have shown both their accountability and loyalty as they have worked diligently to contain costs without sacrificing quality. However, hospital boards need to be familiar with the facts about nursing's small share of the hospital dollar as they plan and implement hospital policy for spending and saving.

Reviewing the data on nurse practitioners and nurse midwives gives rise to the reaction: Enough! There is no excuse for the perpetuation of policies that restrict the practices of NPs. Although there has been progress on a state-by-state basis in reimbursement for NPs, the limited public awareness of nursing's unique contribution has not been much improved in this decade.

As was said earlier, "Lack of public access to nursing outcome data . . . nursing's reluctance to make their contributions known, [and] . . . the way payment for institutional nursing services is handled in most settings" support nursing's low profile in all areas but the nursing shortage in hospitals. It is ironic that the extreme shortage of registered nurses in nursing homes is barely mentioned in the press.

The invisibility of nursing is causing problems more serious than those affecting the individual nurse's image. It is creating a dangerous situation with regard to the future pool of nurses, since fewer young people want a career in which practitioners appear unappreciated and unable to practice at their full potential. Nurses have the knowledge and skill to act independently, cost-effectively, and accountably in a vast array of services needed by the American people. The articles reviewed here attest to this fact.

In *Poor Richard's Almanac,* Benjamin Franklin wrote:

> Hide not your talents
> They for use were made
> What's a sundial in the shade?

REFERENCES

American Nurses' Association (1983). *Nurse practitioners: A review of the literature (1965–1982).* Kansas City, MO: American Nurses' Association.

Bailie, J.S. (1986). *Determining nursing costs: The nursing intensity index* (pp. 199–211). New York: National League for Nursing Publication, No. 20-2155.

Balik, B., Seitz, C.H., & Gilliam, T. (1988). When the patient requires observation not hospitalization. *Journal of Nursing Administration, 18*(10), 20–23.

Bennett, C.L., Garfinkle, J.B., Greenfield, S., Draper, D., Williams, R., Matthews, W.C., & Kanouse, D.E. (Eds.) (1989). The relation between hospital experience and in-hospital mortality for patients for AIDS-related PCP. *Journal of the American Medical Association, 261,* 2975–2979.

Berkeley Planning Associates (1987). *Evaluation of community-oriented long-term care demonstration projects.* Health Care Financing Extramural Report. Health Care Financing Administration Pub. No. 0342, Washington, DC: U.S. Government Printing Office.

Bibb, B. (1982). Comparing nurse practitioners and physicians on processes of care. *Evaluation and Health Professions, 6*(3), 28–42.

Boland, L.S. (1985). An interim stay unit reduces costs. *Journal of Nursing Administration, 18,* 42–45.

Brooten, D., Kumar, S., Brown, L., Butts, P., Finkler, S.A., Bakewell-Sachs, J., Gibbons, A., & Delivoria-Papadopoulos, M. (1986). A randomized clinical trial of early hospital discharge and home follow up of very low birthweight infants. *New England Journal of Medicine, 315* (15), 934–939.

Burgess, A.W., Lerner, D.J., D'Agostino, R.B., Vokonas, P.S., Hartman, C.R., & Gaccione, P. (1987). A randomized control trial of cardiac rehabilitation. *Social Science and Medicine, 24,* 359–370.

Burt, M.R. (1986). *Estimates of public costs of teenage childbearing: A review of recent studies and estimates of 1985 public cost.* Washington, DC: Center for Population Options.

Cabin, W. (1985, May). Some evidence of the cost-effectiveness of home care. *Caring, 4,* 62–67, 70.

Carcagno, G.J., & Kemper, P. (1988). The evaluation of the national long-term care demonstration 1: An overview of the channeling demonstration and its evaluation. *Health Services Research, 23*(1), 2.

Dahlen, A.L., & Gregor, J.R. (1985). Nursing costs by DRG with an all-RN staff. In F.A. Shaffer, (Ed.), *Costing out nursing: Pricing our Product* (pp. 113–122). New York: National League for Nursing Publication, No. 20-1982.

DeFede, J.P., Dhanens, B.E., & Keltner, N.L. (1989). Cost benefits of patient-controlled analgesia. *Nursing Management, 20,* 5.

Diers, D. (1982). Future of nurse-midwives in American health care. In L. Aiken, (Ed.), *Nursing in the 1980s: Crises, opportunities, challenges* (pp. 267–295). Philadelphia: J.B. Lippincott.

Donovan, M.I., & Lewis, G. (1987). Increasing productivity and decreasing costs: The value of RNs. *Journal of Nursing Administration, 17*(9), 17.

Elliott, T.L. (1989). Cost analysis of alternative scheduling. *Nursing Management, 20,* 4.

Ethridge, P., & Lamb, G.S. (1989). Professional nursing case management improves quality, access and costs. *Nursing Management, 20*(3), 33.

Evans, L., Strumpf, N., & Williams, C. (1991). Re-defining a standard of care for frail older people: Alternatives to reduce routine physical restraint. In P. Katz, R. Kane, & M. Mezey (Eds.), *Advances in long term care,* vol. 1 (pp. 81–108). New York: Springer.

Fagin, C.M. (1982a). Nursing's pivotal role in American health care. In L. Aiken (Ed.), *Nursing in the 1980s: Crisis, opportunities, challenges* (pp. 459–475). Philadelphia: J.B. Lippincott.

Fagin, C.M. (1982b). The economic value of nursing research. *American Journal of Nursing, 82*(12), 1844–1849.

Fagin, C.M., & Jacobsen, B.J. (1985). The economic value of nursing research: A critical review. In H. Werley (Ed.), *Annual review of nursing research,* 3 (pp. 215–238). New York: Springer.

General Accounting Office Report (May, 1983). GAO/IPE 83, 1: Washington, DC, December 7, 1982. *Health policy alternatives: Expansion of cost-effective home health care.* Washington, DC: Government Printing Office.

Georgopoulos, B.S. (1985). Organization structure and the performance of hospital emergency services. *Annals of Emergency Medicine 14*(7), 677–684.

Ginsberg, G., Marks, I., & Waters, H. (1984). Cost-benefit analysis of a controlled trial of nurse therapy for neuroses in primary care. *Psychiatric Medicine 14,* 683–690.

Green, J.H. (1989). Long-term care research. *Nursing and Health Care, 10*(3), 139–144.

Hannan, E.L., O'Donnell, J.F., Kilburn, H., Jr., Bernard, H.R., & Yazici, A. (1989). Investigation of the relationship between volume and mortality for surgical procedures performed in New York state hospitals. *Journal of the American Medical Association, 262*(4), 503–510.

Hartz, A.J., Krakauer, H., & Kuhn, E.M. (1989). Hospital characteristics and mortality rates. *New England Journal of Medicine, 321,* 1720–1725.

Hedrick, S.C., & Inui, T.S. (1986). The effectiveness and cost of home care:

An information synthesis. *Health Services Research, 20*(6), part II, 876.

Helt, E.H., & Jelinek, R.C. (1988). In the wake of cost cutting, nursing productivity and quality improve. *Nursing Management, 19*(6), 42.

Hinshaw, A.S., Scofield, R., & Atwood, J.R. (1981, November/December). Staff, patient, and cost outcomes of all-registered nurse staffing. *Journal of Nursing Administration, 11*(11,12), 30–36.

Kane, R.L., Garrard, J., Skay, C.L., Radosevich, D.M., Buchanon, J.L., McDermott, S.M., Arnold, S.B., & Kepferle, L. (1989). Effects of a geriatric nurse practitioner on process and outcome of nursing home care. *American Journal of Public Health, 79*(9), 1271–1277.

Kitz, D.S., McCartney, M., Kissick, J.E., & Townsend, R. (1989). Examining nursing personnel costs: Controlled versus noncontrolled oral analgesic agents. *Journal of Nursing Administration, 19*(1), 10–14.

Knaus, W.A., Draper, E.A., Wagner, D.P., & Zimmerman, J.E. (1986). An evaluation of outcome from intensive care in major medical centers. *Annals of Internal Medicine, 104*(3), 410–418.

Kramer, A.M., Shaughnessy, P.W., & Pettigrew, M.L. (1985). Cost-effectiveness implications based on a comparison of nursing home and home health care mix. *Health Services Research, 20*(4), 387–405.

LaForme, S. (1982, April). Primary nursing. Does good care cost more? *The Canadian Nurse, 74*(4), a46–47; b47–49.

MacDonald, M. (1988). Primary nursing: Is it worth it? *Journal of Advanced Nursing, 13,* 797–806.

McCorkle, R., Benoliel, J.Q., Donaldson, G., Georgiadou, F., Moinpour, C., & Goodell, B. (1989). A randomized clinical trial of home nursing care for lung cancer patients. *Cancer, 66,* 1375–1382.

McKibben, R. (1982). Registered nurses'

wages have minor effects on total hospital costs. *American Journal of Nursing, 12.*

Minor, A.F. (1989). The cost of maternity care and childbirth in the United States 1989. Washington, DC: *Health Insurance Administration of America.*

Mitchell, M., Miller, J., Welches, L., & Walker, D. (1984). Determining cost of direct nursing care by DRGs. *Nursing Management, 15*(4), 29–32.

Naylor, M. (1990, May/June). Comprehensive discharge planning for hospitalized elderly: A pilot study. *Nursing Research, 39*(3), 156–160.

O'Sullivan, A.L., & Jacobsen, B.S. *A randomized trial of a health care program of first-time adolescent mothers.* Philadelphia: University of Pennsylvania School of Nursing, unpublished.

Office of Technology Assessment (1986). *Physicians assistants and certified nurse-midwives: A policy analysis* (a, p6; b, p66). Washington, DC: U.S. Government Printing Office.

Olds, D.L., Henderson, C.R., Tatelbaum, R., & Chamberlin, R. (1988). Improving the life-course development of socially disadvantaged mothers: A randomized trial of nurse home visitation. *American Journal of Public Health, 78*(11), 1436–1445.

Prescott, P.A., & Driscoll, L. (1980, July–August). Evaluating nurse practitioner performance. *The Nurse Practitioner, 5*(4), 28–29, 31–32.

Ramsay, J.A., McKenzie, J.K., & Fish, D.G. (1986). Physicians and nurse practitioners: Do they provide equivalent health care? *American Journal of Public Health, 72*(1), 55–56.

Riley, W., & Schaefers, V. (1983, December). Costing nursing services. *Nursing Management, 14*(12), 40.

Rohrer, J.E., & Hogan, A.J. (1987). Modeling the outcomes of nursing home care. *Social Science and Medicine, 24*(3), 219–223.

Salkever, D.S., Skinner, E.A., Steinwachs, D.M., & Katz, H. (1982). Episode based efficiency comparisons for physicians and nurse practitioners. *Medical Care, 20*(2), 143–153.

Scharon, G.M., & Bernacki, E.J. (1984). A corporate role for nurse practitioners. *Business and Health, 1*(9), 26–27.

Sellick, K.J., Russell, S., & Beckmann, J.L. (1983). Primary nursing: An evaluation of its effects on patient perception of care and staff satisfaction. *International Journal of Nursing Studies, 20*(4), 265–273.

Shaughnessy, P.W., Kramer, A.M., & Hittle, D.F. (1988). *The teaching nursing home experiment: Its effects and implications.* Study Paper 6, December 1988. Denver: Center for Health Services Research, University of Colorado Health Sciences Center, unpublished paper.

Shortell, S.M., & Hughes, F.X. (1988). The effects of regulation, competition, and ownership on mortality rates among hospital inpatients. *New England Journal of Medicine, 318,* 1100–1107.

Sovie, M.D., Tarcinale, M.A., Vanputee, A.W., & Stunden, A.E. (1985, March). Amalgam of nursing acuity DRGs and costs. *Nursing Management, 16*(3), a, p22; b, p34; c, p38; d, p42.

Stevenson, B. (1948). *The home book of proverbs, maxims, and familiar phrases* (p. 2275). New York: Macmillan.

Thornton, C., Dunstan, S.M., & Kemper, P. (1988). The evaluation of the national long-term care demonstration 8: The effect of channeling on health and long-term care costs. *Health Services Research, 23,* 130.

Walker, D. (1985). The cost of nursing care in hospitals. *Journal of Nursing Administration, 13,* 13–18.

Watson, S., & Hickey, P. (1984). Help for the family in waiting. *American Journal of Nursing, 84*(5), 604–607.

Weil, M., & Karls, J. (1985). Historical origins and recent developments. In M. Weil, & J. Karls (Eds.), *Case management in human service practice* (p. 2). San Francisco: Jossey-Bass.

Weissert, W.G. (1985). Seven reasons why it is so difficult to make community-based long-term care cost-effective. *Health Services Research, 20*(4), 424.

Werley, H.H., & Zorn, C.R. (1989). The nursing minimum data set: Benefits and implications. *Perspectives in nursing*—1987–1989 (pp. 105–114). New York: National League for Nursing Publication, No. 19–229.

What's the cost of nursing care? (1986, November 5). *Hospitals,* p. 49.

Wilson, L., Prescott, P.A., & Aleksandrowicz, L. (1988). Nursing: A major hospital cost component. *Health Services Research, 22*(6), 773–796.

Winder, P.G. (1988, July). Case management by nurse at a county facility. *QRB, 14*(7), 215–219.

Wolf, G.A., Lesic, L.K., & Leak, A.G. (1986). Primary nursing. The impact on nursing costs within DRGs. [Financial Management Services]. *Journal of Nursing Administration, 16*(3), 9–11.

When you're doing your best to make a patient comfortable, that's all you can do. . . . I enjoy that kind of nursing. I've always worked in areas where people were very sick. Where people died. That's where I feel the most useful.
— Peggy Anderson

Zane Robinson Wolf

Uncovering the Hidden Work of Nursing

Nurses, the nation's largest group of health practitioners, are extremely important people in today's health care system. However, the occupation of nursing has low status in this hierarchical system (Dachelet, 1978). Our sheer numbers have failed to net us position, respect, or power. This may be due, in part, because much of the work of nursing is unnoticed.

The fine structures of nursing work are largely undisclosed to the public and shielded from professional outsiders. Many of our care activities are hidden, private, taken for granted, and noticed only when they are not delivered. The personal and private nature of some of nurses' work necessitates some seclusion. Because of this, the public does not know the complexity of nurses' work, including the direct and indirect actions performed as nurses care for their patients. We should make our hidden work noticeable, more explicit, so that the public's regard of the work is closer to our clinical reality.

When patient and nurse problems are described in the literature, they are often treated abstractly. Much of the lived experience is condensed, leaving clinical aspects of nurses' work missing. Nursing's importance, worth, and contributions often are obscured along with the hidden work. The hidden work of nursing includes those invisible activities that are either unseen, by virtue of their being-taken-for-grantedness or silence of expression, or dishonored and ignored, because of their association with working with the body and its products.

Now, as a result of the nursing shortage, "we have the public's attention. We're in the spotlight—the place we always said we wanted to be. For once, they're listening" (Barnum, 1989, p. 21). It is crucial that we examine the factors that contribute to our anonymity and invisibility in order to shine in the spotlight, to more clearly express what we do and who we are.

Zane Robinson Wolf, Ph.D., R.N., is Professor, School of Nursing at La Salle University, Philadelphia.

Abridged from Wolf, Z.R. (1989). Uncovering the hidden work of nursing. *Nursing & Health Care* 10(8):463–467. Copyright 1989. Reprinted with permission from the National League for Nursing.

UNSEEN WORK

The hidden work of nursing is directed toward improving the welfare of patients. Part of this work can be categorized as unseen; it includes the unapparent and undiscernible aspects of nursing activities. Examples of unseen work are caring, system maintenance, safety, comforting, privacy, and sacred work.

Common Sense, Caring Work

Many see nurses' work as common sense work. They do not appreciate that common sense is not really very common (McBride, 1988). Nursing is equated with everyday women's work. Our low wages may still be connected to the fact that in the economic sense, a housewife does not work (Saunders, 1981). Similar to unpaid housewives, nurses do caring work. Like others who do "women's work," the caring work performed is ". . . difficult to define and even harder to control" (Reverby, 1987, p. 5). Reverby, a historian, proposes that nurses have taken on caring more as the nursing identity rather than the nursing work. Over time, nurses' altruistic devotion to duty has not brought power. By using the rhetoric of feminism, earning university degrees, employing assertiveness techniques, and other strategies, and making certain that nurses' caring work does not suffer, nurses may ultimately snare the carrot of autonomy (Reverby, 1987). However, our devotion to a caring identity, our possession of caring attitudes, and our performance of caring actions goes unseen and unappreciated.

Consider for a moment what nurse caring work is composed of. Patients see nurse caring when they perceive that nurses recognize individual qualities and needs, provide a reassuring presence, give information, assist with pain control, spend time, promote individual autonomy, and demonstrate surveillance activities (Brown, 1986). These actions are frequently not associated with improved patient outcomes in our research literature. However, human caring research conducted by nurses has increased dramatically over the last decade. Furthermore, the caring components of nursing work are subtle and increase or decrease in response to the needs of our patients as we perceive, validate, and act on them. We fear losing our caring orientation. For example, high-technology nurses have reacted to the impact of technology and cost containment on their caring work. Caring for machines rather than for patients frustrates and evokes fear in us, since we do see our identity closely entwined with caring, even though this caring is not readily discernible.

System Maintenance and Safety Work

Nurses are still the right-hand women and men for physicians in the health care system (Hughes, 1971). They are the glue that keeps the hospital together (Thomas, 1983). "She does tasks of people below her or outside the role hierarchy of medicine. It hurts her, but she does it. Her place in the division of labor is essentially that of doing in a responsible way whatever necessary things are in danger of not being done at all" (Hughes, 1971, p. 308). Glue can be invisible, and taking care of things to maintain the flow of work goes unnoticed. Generally the public pays attention only when mistakes are made, not when silent actions maintain patient safety. Nursing's commitment to the value, to first do no harm, is enacted daily during direct and indirect care activities. It is incorporated under the umbrella of safety work.

Interpersonal Work

Psychiatric-mental health nurses who work independently of health care institutions are reimbursed for interpersonal nursing work in some states. Their work takes place in the interpersonal space between nurses and patients, and it is intangible. However, little of this work is heralded or monitored by quality assurance personnel when performed by hospital nurses (Volk, 1989, personal communication). Psychological, culturally specific, and social nursing care is elusive, and seldom documented (Dachelet, 1978). For example, how often is listening to patients included in the costing of nursing services? Listening may include paying attention to direct or indirect meanings in patient communications, waiting enough time for patient responses to an invitation to speak, accepting what patients say, and building on what the patient has said with the next nurse communication (Epstein, 1975). These and other actions should be made more explicit, and we should describe them as interventions as we document our care. At the present time, it is doubtful that these interpersonal actions are included very often, if at all, in patient acuity estimates.

Comforting Work

Nurses often make their patients more comfortable. The state of comfort is achieved by physical, physiological, psychological, culturally appropriate, and socially oriented nursing interventions. "Failure to do comfort work (that is to minimize the discomforts associated with pain, nausea, etc.) to the satisfaction of patients when they are hospitalized is a major source of their anger and frustration" (Strauss, Fagerhaugh, Suczek, & Weiner, 1985). But the comfort work of nurses has not been well explained in our literature. Few have studied nurses' comforting actions . . . (Wilby, 1988). This work may focus solely on the alleviation of patient symptoms and it serves as another example of unseen nursing work.

Privacy Work

Nurses believe that patients have the right to withhold themselves and their lives from public scrutiny (Kozier & Erb, 1979). However, gathering information about patients goes with the territory in health care agencies. Nurses keep patient records secure to protect patients against invasion of privacy.

Another side of nurses' privacy work with patients involves making sure that they have their hygienic needs met. Hygienic care is a personal matter, and nurses provide privacy by draping body parts, drawing curtains, and closing doors. Much nursing work is done under the screen of privacy, and is obscure to outsiders.

Sacred Work

Nurses' work is also concerned with sacred aspects of life. Daily they deal with moral and ethical problems. Early on, trained nurses in the United States were urged to think of their work with the sick as holy and sacred (Wolf, 1986). Today technology and chronic illness have complicated the health care environment for nurses. Values are often in conflict. For example, the values of life at any cost, quality of life, death with dignity, and conservation of limited resources may coexist and be opposed in the same patient. These problems are displayed in the common do-not-resuscitate/ resuscitate decisions with which nurses are involved.

Another example of sacred nursing work takes place as nurses offer patients hope when cancer makes comfort difficult to achieve. Sharing a hopeful attitude is common as nurses quietly encourage chronically ill patients to live.

COGNITIVE WORK

Some react to nursing work as technical, procedural, and ritualistic in a mindless, repetitive sense. It comes as no surprise to nurses, but it is amazing to others that nursing is a complex enterprise that requires an educated intellect, sharpened by experience. Part of this may be related to the public's lack of information about nursing. The cognitive activity that goes on as we work is seldom recognized. This may be connected to tenacious ideas that women's ways of solving problems are illogical, even mysterious.

DIRTY WORK

Also centered on improving patients' welfare, the dirty work of nursing shares much with the unseen work. This work is on the nonsocial side of things. For nurses, dirty work involves caring for people tacitly identified by society as unclean, either by infection or by lifestyle, or handling bodily products considered polluted. By association, nursing may have taken on the attributes of the unclean substances and the unclean people of society.

NURSING: A STIGMATIZED PROFESSION

On the positive side, many nurses feel valued by families, friends, patients, and communities. Since this is not a universal perception, it is necessary to reflect on the sources of our invisibility and anonymity.

The social role of nurse brings status problems to our work. Societal stigmas related to nursing services may cause the public to have a negative perception of nursing as an occupation. The salience or importance of our work as conceptualized by society is related to our low status. Low status and low salience yield low self-esteem (Jones et al., 1984; Plummer, 1975; Walsh, 1975, p. 28).

Nursing's corporate self-esteem is low. As a subculture and as a reflection of U.S. society, we share our fellow Americans' views that nursing is not so important as other occupations. Often nurses praise other health care workers above themselves and their nurse colleagues. The occupational designation of "nurse" may be an unsatisfactory one for some members of our society. People ask, often with voices tinged with repugnance, "How can you bear to be a nurse?" (Mallinson, 1987, p. 419).

Our work is evaluated by our society's cultural standards. Even though our language, customs, and values differ in some respects from the larger culture, and at times we shake off the ideas that we are unimportant, nevertheless we cannot escape the low self-esteem that pulls us down. We are self-deprecatory, having internalized the views of the larger society.

Similar to other cases of the oppressor and oppressed, dominant groups may have imposed their norms and values on us as the right ones. We have succumbed and behaved as the oppressed in response to the oppressor (Friere, 1970). We have joined our oppressors by internalizing their norms and by believing that becoming like them will lead to power and control (Hedin, 1986, p. 54; Roberts, 1983, p. 22).

Dirty Work and Dirty Workers

Nurses share a bad rap with other dirty workers. The socially deviant or "spoiled identities" of our society are not the only ones performing dirty work (Goffman, 1963). . . . Failing to acknowledge the dirty work makes it hidden.

Society has assigned dirty work to nurses. Doing "sometimes repulsive and socially stigmatized labor" (Bernstein, 1979) is part of what we call nursing, and it is incorporated into the whole of nurses' work. Performing this work helps us to delineate and define ourselves (Fraser, 1968). Not doing it eliminates us from the in-crowd of respected nurses (Wolf, 1988). Refusal to handle excretia, secretions, and blood and the products of infection in order to keep patients clean, and to accomplish other care agendas such as caring for alcoholics, drug addicts, infected patients, and individuals with otherwise unacceptable lifestyles, violates nursing's standards of conduct.

Women: Society's Unclean

It is clear in some "primitive" societies that unclean or polluted persons, menstruating women for example, take care of people and their secretions and excretions (Lev. 15:19). Acknowledging this archaic notion may assist in dealing more openly with discrimination against nurses as dirty workers. "Few outside of nursing or within nursing explicitly label nurses as dirty workers" (Wolf, 1986). However, making this deeply based association more explicit could help nurses sort their status problems and ultimately reveal the clinical realities of nurses' work. Some of nursing's contributions are obscured by the dirty work that we do; some people are unable to get past their first reaction to the profane parts of nurses' work.

BODY WORK

The body work that nurses do includes the therapeutic ritual of the bath. It also serves as the stage for the nurse to check skin and mental functioning, and to listen to the patient's lived experience and reasons for seeking health care. This and other types of body work are personal, so intimate and so embarrassing for the patient, and at times for the nurse, that little is shared publicly in the nursing arena of change of shift report or outside of the veiled events as nurses care for patients.

The body work of nurses is associated with their privacy work. It is manual work, with low symbolic prestige outside of nursing, which may be related to society's view of the materials or equipment used in body work tasks. Body work involves profane areas of human life. Accepted as commonplace, it lies hidden, and it is taken for granted. However, this body work requires knowledge and skill that is refined by experience. Seasoned nurses help neophyte nurses grow in the art of body work. Skillfully bathing an incontinent cancer patient with bone pain resulting from metastasis is an art that can only be appreciated by the patient who may never be able to acknowledge her or his satisfaction with the results.

DEATH WORK

Death work has also been associated with the hidden work of nursing. Few outside of the profession realize that nurses care for patients after death. Nurses treat their patients with respect, remove traces of suffering by cleansing, and hope that the family and friends see past the suffering of the loved one (Wolf, 1988). It is easy to see nurses' death work as dirty work. Nurses do not ignore this work; they assume responsibility for care after death.

STRATEGIES TO UNCOVER HIDDEN WORK
AND AT THE SAME TIME TO EMPOWER
NURSES PERSONALLY AND PROFESSIONALLY

We need to develop "dignifying rationalizations" and "collective pretensions" (Hughes, 1964), not only to elevate the status of our work, but to clarify the boundaries, shared domains, and areas of nursing expertise. We are our own constructivists, capable of creating the social environment that we share with our patients and others. We need enhancers and embellishers of our practice.

We need to tell our own stories, so that others appreciate the clinical reality of nursing. First, we rarely share our war stories with those not introduced into our world. However, we are capable of helping others understand. Our literature needs to be full of clinical case descriptions that are concerned with patients' lived experiences, their problems, and nursing solutions. We can start on a small scale with these cases. It is respectable to begin with a few at a time. We need to observe and describe the mundane of nursing. Others will be fascinated with it.

We must realize that we are fascinating people workers. As nurses, we witness and participate in some of the most dramatic situations of human existence. The actualities and the contexts of these experiences should be described and explained.

Nurses spend a lot of clinical time doing safety work. Checking three times is a tenaciously held behavior pattern associated with the administration of medications. We check and recheck physician orders, medication and treatment kardexes, and patients during our surveillance activities. Other routines and procedures are devoted to safe patient care. We must specify the many patterns and specific actions of our safety work.

It is time to stop undervaluing the "soft side" of nursing. We can reframe our views and note that caring makes a difference to the individuals and families whom we serve. While caring does not use technological equipment, it may improve client outcomes. Future nursing research may connect nurse caring to healthier patients. Cost savings could accompany improved patient outcomes.

We must start praising ourselves in our professional organizations and informal groups. Some of us have started this already. We can create our own *Center to Promote Nursing*. Instead of originating as a response to the nursing shortage, our center should promote nursing and nurses in general (*American Nurse*, March 1989, p. 5).

We must stop hiding our expert practitioners. How many health care agencies fail to encourage periodic meetings among expert nurses? Expert nurses could initiate these meetings with administrative support. How many expert nurses do not document their weekly activities by using checklists and audits? Our experts may be expendable because they do not keep records about what they do daily, weekly, and monthly. In addition, new nurses need experts' support as they gain skill and experience.

We must make our values more explicit. One of our predominant values, to first do no harm, is not thought of at times in the clinical setting. The do-not-resuscitate/resuscitate dilemma provides a frequently occurring situation to illustrate this value. Many nurses are frustrated with the repeated resuscitations of their chronically ill patients. They do not explore the options with some patients and their families. They respect the family's silent decision to resuscitate the loved one. Rather than clarifying the nursing position and negotiating with physicians and families in order to influence the DNR (do-not-resuscitate) or no-code decision, they persist, shift after shift, day after day, in a stalemate. Nurse resentment and impotence and patient suffering build, at least in the minds of nurses (Wolf, 1988). In this situation, the value of "quality of life" is also threatened. We should seek different strategies to solve this and other examples in which our values are violated. We must explain our position and frustration.

Nursing's body work is integrated along with other types of care. Despite the fact that our body work may be seen as menial and "low tech," we should capitalize on it. We should realize that the bath is more than a ritual and practice it and other body work skills, such as therapeutic massage techniques in order to get back to basics. Presently, time constraints limit our practice of body therapies in institutions (Dossey, Keegan, Guzzetta, & Kolkmeier, 1988, p. 339). In addition, we have to realize that some of our patients and the public are in awe of the body work we do. They are impressed by our skills.

Nurses owe it to themselves to destigmatize nurses' work. All professions and occupations share the fact that dirty work is part of the whole job. If dirty work is performed with grace and dignity by nurses, the people we serve feel graceful and dignified. Furthermore, another aspect of our dirty work lies in its coexistence with our sacred work. Who beside nurses perform both types of human caring?

How important is nursing care to patients? Rather than being taken for granted, much like the background music of a movie, our work helps people. Lynaugh and Fagin (1988) exhort us to celebrate the ". . . care-giving, safety, competence and continuity" that nurses have provided their patients (p. 184). These accomplishments persist in a society that consistently undervalues care. We must point out these successes to patients, family members, other health care workers, and to anyone who will listen. We must tell our clients and patients that they are being taken care of by registered nurses. Often, patients complain that they do not know who their nurses are. One simple solution is to use name tags with large, white print on a black background, with the designation "RN" clearly seen. When we introduce ourselves, we should tell our patients that we are registered nurses. And, nurses should shock our public and coworkers with our thoughts, judgments, and opinions by exposing them to interesting conversations about ourselves, other nurse colleagues, and the cognitive side of our clinical practice.

Even though today nurses are better educated, in greater demand, and self-governing, we have difficulty articulating our hidden, taken-for-granted work, both the unseen work and the dirty work. Nurses can no longer afford to do this. Visibility accompanies autonomy and responsibility. The hidden dimensions of nurses' work must be made more explicit. Subtle, obscure actions are part of the clinical realities of nursing, and they should be celebrated in research, nursing education programs, and in clinical agencies.

REFERENCES

American Nurse. (1989). Hospital association creates center to promote nursing. *American Nurse 21* (3), 5.

Barnum, B. (1989). Nursing's image and the future. *Nursing & Health Care, 10*(1), 18–21.

Bernstein, P. (1979). Alienation and self-management. *Contemporary Psychology, 24*(6), 501.

Brown, L. (1986). The experience of care: Patient perspectives. *Topics in Clinical Nursing, 8*(2), 56–62.

Dachelet, C.Z. (1978). Nursing's bid for increased status. *Nursing Forum, 17*(1), 18–45.

Davis, D.S. (1984). Good people doing dirty work: A study of social isolation. *Symbolic Interaction, 7,* 233–247.

Dossey, B.M., Keegan, L., Guzzetta, C.E., & Kolkmeier, L.G. (1988). *Holistic nursing: A handbook for practice.* Rockville, MD: Aspen.

Epstein, C. (1975). *Nursing the dying patient.* Reston, VA: Reston, p. 171.

Fraser, R. (Ed.). (1968). *Work.* Penguin Books.

Friere, P. (1970). *Pedagogy of the oppressed* (M.B. Ramos, Trans.). New York: Continuum Press. (Original work published 1968.)

Goffman, E. (1963). *Stigma: Notes on the management of spoiled identity.* Englewood Cliffs, NJ: Prentice-Hall.

Hedin, B.A. (1986). A case study of oppressed group behavior in nurses. *Image, 18*(2), 53–57.

Hughes, E.C. (1971). Social role and the division of labor. In E.C.

Hughes. *The Sociological eye: Selected papers* (pp. 304–347). Chicago: Aldine Atherton.

Jones, E.E., Farina, A., Hastorf, A.H., Markus, H., Miller, D.T., Scott, R.A., & French, R. deS. (1984). *Social stigma: The psychology of marked relationships.* New York: W. H. Freeman.

Kozier, B., & Erb, G.L. (1979). *Fundamentals of nursing: Concepts and procedures.* Menlo Park, CA: Addison-Wesley.

Lev. 15:19.

Lynaugh, J.M., & Fagin, C.M. (1988). Nursing comes of age. *Image, 20*(4), 184–190.

Mallinson, M.B. (1987). Editorial: How can you bear to be a nurse? *American Journal of Nursing, 87*(4), 419.

McBride, A.B. (1988). Mosby nursing calendar. St. Louis: C. V. Mosby.

Plummer, K. (1975). *Sexual stigma: An interactionist account.* Boston, MA: Routledge and Kegan Paul.

Reverby, S. (1987). A caring dilemma: Womanhood and nursing in historical perspective. *Nursing Research, 36*(1), 5–11.

Roberts, S.J. (1983). Oppressed group behavior: Implications for nursing.

Advances in Nursing Science, 5(4), 21–30.

Saunders, C. (1981). *Social stigma of occupations.* Westmead, England: Gower, pp. 1–53.

Strauss, S., Fagerhaugh, S., Suczek, B., & Wiener, C. (1985). *Social organization of medical work.* Chicago: University of Chicago Press.

Thomas, L. (1983). *The youngest science.* New York: Viking Press.

Volk, E. (1989). Personal communication. Quality Assurance Director, Moss Rehabilitation Hospital, Philadelphia, PA.

Walsh, E.J. (1975). *Dirty work, race, and self-esteem.* Ann Arbor, MI: Institute of Labor and Industrial Relations.

Wilby, M. (1988). Cancer patients' descriptions of comforting and discomforting nursing actions. Unpublished manuscript, La Salle University, Philadelphia, master's research proposal.

Wolf, Z.R. (1986). Nurses' work: The sacred and the profane. *Holistic Nursing Practice, 1*(1), 29–35.

Wolf, Z.R. (1988). *Nurses' work: The sacred and the profane.* Philadelphia: University of Pennsylvania Press.

The holistic assumption is that the body knows how to heal itself, is a natural "healing system" intent on good health.
— *The Nurse's Almanac, Second Edition*

Pamela C. Mittelstadt

Federal Reimbursement of Advanced Practice Nurses' Services Empowers the Profession

Significant changes in the 1980s and early 1990s in federal laws governing health programs have enabled advanced practice nurses to be directly reimbursed for their services. This reimbursement has assisted in breaking down the barriers to full utilization of advanced practice nurses (APNs) as primary care providers. Changes in reimbursement have also enabled advanced practice nurses to play a more direct role in the delivery of health care. Advanced practice nurses are defined as nurse practitioners, clinical nurse specialists, certified nurse midwives and certified registered nurse anesthetists. (A summary of federal reimbursement for APNs is given in table 1.)

IMPORTANCE OF DIRECT REIMBURSEMENT TO APNS

Paying APNs directly allows them to provide care and, therefore, allows them to improve needed access to care. Many of the recent changes in federal health programs enacted by Congress were made to improve health care access to underserved populations, such as nursing-home residents, low-income women and children, and people in rural areas. Direct reimbursement gives APNs primary care provider recognition and visibility. More than 35 million people in this country lack health insurance, and most of these people lack access to primary care.[1] To meet the needs of this uninsured population, additional primary care practitioners will be needed. Directly reimbursing APNs breaks down one of the most significant barriers to the greater utilization of these nurses.

Pamela C. Mittelstadt, M.P.H., R.N., is Director of Medical Affairs at the Group Health Association of America, Washington, D.C.

Abridged from Mittelstadt, P.C. (1993). Federal reimbursement of advanced practice nurses' services empowers the profession. *Nurse Practitioner* 18(1):43, 47–49. Copyright 1993 by Elsevier Science Publishing Co., Inc. Reprinted by permission of the publisher.

TABLE 1   Federal Reimbursement for Nurses in Advanced Practice: Current Status

	Advanced Practice Nurses			
Federal Programs	*Nurse Practitioner*	*Certified Nurse Midwife*	*Certified Registered Nurse Anesthetist*	*Clinical Nurse Specialist*
Medicare Part B	Yes[1]	Yes	Yes	Yes[2]
Medicaid	Yes[3]	Yes	State discretion	State discretion
CHAMPUS[5]	Yes	Yes	Yes	Yes[4]
FEHB[6]	Yes	Yes	Yes	Yes

[1] Limited to nursing facilities and rural areas
[2] Limited to rural areas
[3] Limited to pediatric NPs and family NPs
[4] Limited to certified psychiatric nurse specialists
[5] CHAMPUS is the Civilian Health and Medical Program of Uniformed Services
[6] FEHB is the Federal Employee Health Benefit Program
Source: American Nurses Association, Division of Governmental Affairs, 1992.

Direct payment to APNs recognizes them as independent health care practitioners. This puts APNs on an equal footing with other practitioners who are paid directly for their services. Direct payment also provides recognition for APNs as unique providers in the health care system.

Direct billing and payment puts a price and value on the service provided. The ability to bill directly allows nurses to be self-employed or to enhance the revenue of their employers. Direct billing also improves the data available on the services provided and improves the ability to conduct research on the costs and outcomes of APN care. In addition, direct payment increases APNs' autonomy and authority to act on behalf of their patients. The ability to bill for APN services allows these practitioners to provide the needed services and coordinate and manage care. Direct reimbursement empowers APNs within the health care system by giving them greater control over their practices. With increased recognition as primary care providers, APNs have greater decision-making power in the care of their patients.

BARRIERS TO RECEIVING DIRECT REIMBURSEMENT

Since 1948 the American Nurses Association has advocated direct reimbursement of nursing services; however, this was not realized in a significant way until the early 1990s.[2] There have been many barriers that have prevented nurses from receiving direct payment for their services over the last 40 years.

Organized medicine has been opposed to APNs receiving direct reimbursement because it would allow nurses to practice independently. Organized medicine's opposition has been expressed through questions about the quality of the services provided by APNs and the requirement that their practice be under the supervision of a physician. These views were expressed by several physician groups at a 1986 hearing of the Subcommittee on Compensation and Employee Benefits of the House Committee on Post Office and Civil Service. The hearing focused on direct reimbursement for nonphysician providers under the Federal Employee Health Benefit Plan. Physician groups historically have claimed that APNs do not provide the same quality of care as physicians. The physician groups say APNs need to be directly supervised by physicians. The myth about quality of care was publicly dispelled at a congressional hearing through a study conducted by a congressional advisory board.[3] In recent years, physician opposition on Capitol Hill has not been as great as was experienced in earlier years, because the physicians have been affected by a major change in Medicare's payment for their services. This change in the law, called Medicare Physician Payment Reform, has kept the physicians occupied with overseeing the implementation of a new system of payment that will redistribute (and in some cases decrease) the payment for their services. However, many states still experience opposition from organized medicine when state nurses' associations lobby to change state health insurance laws regarding APN reimbursement.

The extraordinary rise in health care costs and nursing's inability to show cost savings has been a barrier to obtaining direct payment. Health care's portion of the gross national product has grown from 5.3 percent in 1960 to 12.5 percent in 1990, increasing from $42 billion to almost $647 billion.[4] Congress has shown its concern about the rise in the health care budget by enacting new cost-containing Medicare payment systems for hospitals and physician services. In addition, Congress has exhibited restraint in the annual funding of other health programs, frequently only increasing funding to cover inflation. Reimbursement legislation for APN services is almost always seen as a cost item. The Congressional Budget Office believes that if the number of providers is increased, the costs for health care will increase because of the greater number of services provided. In an effort to contain costs, members of Congress have been reluctant, until recent years, to give APNs the authority to bill directly for their services.

Congress is concerned about the rise in health care costs and the looming federal deficit. With the large deficit being blamed for a sluggish economy, members of Congress are reluctant to increase spending on health care.

One of the significant barriers to APNs receiving direct reimbursement has been a lack of consumer demand for their services. For example, consumers have not written their representatives in Congress to ask for NP Medicare coverage. Senators and representatives are influenced by their constituents' requests. It is difficult for members of Congress to support APN reimbursement when the recipients of the Medicare program are not calling for this change. Improving the reimbursement of nurses would be more effective if nursing had more consumer advocates. Many consumers are unaware of the unique and valuable primary care services delivered by APNs. This lack of awareness contributes to the exclusion of APN services from many health insurance plans.

MEDICARE

Despite the barriers, successful lobbying by the American Nurses Association and other nurse specialty groups has brought about major changes in the Medicare program. Medicare now reimburses APNs in a variety of settings. However, the reimbursement varies considerably by the type of APN, the health care setting and the payment level. This is due to numerous amendments that have been enacted at different times over the last decade, written by different legislators and enacted for different reasons.

Medicare covers the services of nurse practitioners in nursing homes, rural areas, rural health clinics, health maintenance organizations, Federally Qualified Health Centers (FQHCs), and ambulatory care settings when the service is "incident to" a physician's service. The nursing-home and rural-area provisions are the only direct-reimbursement provisions under Medicare.

As part of the Omnibus Budget Reconciliation Act (OBRA) of 1989, Congress recognized NPs as direct providers of services to residents of nursing homes.[5] Congress enacted this law in order to improve access to care for nursing-home residents. A federal demonstration project had shown that if NPs were reimbursed for their services, nursing home residents would receive more comprehensive care, thus avoiding unnecessary hospitalizations and emergency department visits. This law was enacted at a time when Congress was focusing attention on nursing-home standards of care. To receive payment, the NP must be an employee of a physician, nursing home or hospital, and must be practicing in collaboration with a physician. The payment goes to the employer of the NP; the payment level is 85 percent of the Medicare fee schedule.

In 1990 Congress enacted another significant change through OBRA of 1990, allowing NP and clinical nurse specialist services to be reimbursed when provided in a rural area.[6] This law was enacted because Congress wanted to improve access to care for rural Medicare beneficiaries. Though the NP and CNS must work in collaboration with a physician, they do not have to submit claims through their employer; they may submit claims directly. The payment level is at 85 percent of the fee schedule for outpatient services and at 75 percent for inpatient services. Rural areas are defined as counties that are in nonmetropolitan statistical areas.

In 1990 Congress established a new Medicare benefit through the Federally Qualified Health Centers to encourage the delivery of more community-based care and to improve the financing of these centers.[6] The services of NPs and certified nurse midwives are reimbursed when provided in an FQHC. The ANA has urged the Health Care Financing Administration (the federal agency administrating these programs) to include CNSs in their final regulations for FQHCs.

The FQHCs are significant because they offer a broad range of Medicare- and Medicaid-covered preventive services, including physical examinations, screening and diagnostic testing, vision and hearing screening, health education, prenatal and post-partum care, well-child care, immunizations, and family planning services. Community health centers, migrant health centers and homeless centers qualify, and can receive cost-based reimbursement for Medicare and Medicaid services. Other centers meeting the same criteria can also qualify by being a look-alike center.

Certified nurse midwifery services are covered in rural health clinics and in FQHCs. Since 1987, CNMs have had their services covered under the Medicare program as direct providers. This authority was given through OBRA of 1986.[7] The covered services are only those related to the maternity cycle. However, the American College of Nurse Midwives is lobbying Congress to have them expanded to include reproductive health services. To be covered, the CNMs must work in collaboration with physicians; CNMs receive direct payment for their services at 65 percent of the fee schedule.

OBRA of 1986 also gave authority to certified registered nurse anesthetists to bill directly and be direct providers of Medicare services.[8] Although the law was passed in 1986, it was not effective until January 1989. Payment to CRNAs is at two levels. Nonmedically directed CRNAs' payment levels are in transition, and, in 1996, their payment will be the same as anesthesiologists for the same service. This reflects the new principles of payment for Medicare services. Under the Medicare Physician Payment Reform Law, the amount of payment for a service is based on the type of service and not on the type of provider. Under the new system, neurologists and family physicians are paid the same for delivering the same service. CRNAs are the first group of APNs to be paid under the new principles of payment and in 1996 will be paid the same as physicians for delivering the same service. Medically directed CRNA services receive 30 percent less than the nonmedically directed services.

Health maintenance organizations that have Medicare contracts may use NPs to deliver direct services to enrollees. To be eligible, the NP must work in collaboration with a physician. The payment is not direct, since Medicare HMOs receive a monthly capitated amount from the federal government regardless of the number of services delivered. NPs contract with the HMO to deliver the services; they are paid by the HMO according to the individual HMO payment policies.

The services of all APNs are covered under the Medicare provision of services furnished incident to a physician's service. This is an often misunderstood provision by Medicare carriers and APNs alike because the federal instructions for the rule are vague and do not reflect current practice. However, recent communication with the federal agency has clarified that the "incident to" provision covers the services of a physician's employee delivered in an ambulatory setting if the following three criteria are met:

1. The service is within the scope of practice of that employee.
2. The physician is on site at the time the service is being rendered.
3. The service is related to the physician's plan of care for the client and is related to the primary condition that the client was first treated for by the physician.

For example, an NP may deliver a follow-up service to a client being treated for hypertension who was originally seen by the physician for the same condition. This service would be considered an "incident to" service and the physician would receive payment as if s/he had delivered the service. However, if the same client came into the office with a new condition (e.g., a respiratory infection), the service delivered by the NP would not be covered because this service is not related to the original condition treated by the physician. This requirement leads to barriers to APN practice because it requires physician supervision and does not allow APNs to treat all conditions within their scope of practice.

MEDICAID

In 1989 Congress mandated the coverage of pediatric nurse practitioners and family nurse practitioners in an effort to improve access to care for the population of women and children served by Medicaid and decrease our nation's high infant mortality rate.[5] The PNP and FNP provision does not require supervision or collaboration by any other health professional. The payment rate is determined by the states. The "1992–93 Update: How Each State Stands on Legislative Issues Affecting Advanced Nursing Practice," includes information about those states that cover PNP and FNP services at the same rate as the physician's services.

States have always had the option of covering the services of any health professional.

In 1980 Congress gave authority for CNMs to be reimbursed under all state Medicaid programs.[9] The services are limited to those of the maternity cycle and do not require the supervision of any health care provider. The coverage of CRNA services has not been mandated by Congress. However, 31 states do cover their services under the Medicaid program.[10]

CHAMPUS

The Civilian Health and Medical Program of the Uniformed Services (CHAMPUS) provides services to members of the uniformed services and their families when these people cannot obtain care from a military hospital. Certified nurse practitioners, certified psychiatric nurse specialists, CNMs and CRNAs are authorized to provide CHAMPUS services, and are directly reimbursed. Certified psychiatric nurse specialists are similar to CNSs in that they must be licensed as registered nurses and have at least a master's degree in nursing. To meet the CHAMPUS criteria the nurse's master's degree must be in psychiatry or mental-health nursing. The payment level is at the same rate as the physician's, not at a discounted rate as it is in the Medicare program. A physician referral is required for a CRNA service to be reimbursed.

FEDERAL EMPLOYEE HEALTH BENEFIT PLAN

The Federal Employee Health Benefit Plan determines the policies and contracts for the health insurance companies that offer health plans to federal employees. The plan is operated by the federal Office of Personnel Management (OPM). The ANA worked with Congress beginning in 1986 to effect a change in these plans and mandate the coverage of advanced practice nurses' services. In 1990 Congress finally included a provision in a House appropriation bill.[11] This mandate called for the coverage of NPs, CNSs and CNMs; the OPM has included CRNAs in the classification of NPs. The provision includes direct payment of APN services with no supervision required. The payment level is determined by the individual health insurance plan, Blue Shield for example.

CONCLUSION

Direct reimbursement of APN services empowers APNs to be major players in the health care system. Direct reimbursement makes APN services more visible to consumers, policymakers and health database systems, and recognizes APNs as primary care providers. This recognition comes none too soon since the United States is considering national health care reform.

APNs should be recognized in the old system in order to have a role in the evolving new system. A new system of care should provide basic health care to people who have not previously received it. APNs can help serve as needed primary care providers.

To ensure their role in the new system, APNs must ask their senators and representatives to support legislation that will complete the APN reimbursement authority in the Medicare and Medicaid programs. APNs should continue to educate consumers about the basic, primary health care services APNs provide and work to create consumer demand for their services.

REFERENCES

1. Lewin/ICF: "To the Rescue: Toward Solving America's Health Care Crisis," Families USA Foundation, Washington, D.C., 1990, p. 13.

2. American Nurses Association: "Reimbursement for Nursing Services: Position Statement of the Commission on Economic and General Welfare," Kansas City, Mo., 1977.

3. U.S. Congress, Office of Technology Assessment: "Nurse Practitioners, Physicians' Assistants and Certified Nurse-Midwives: Policy Analysis," Washington, D.C., 1986.

4. Levit, K.R., et al.: "National Health Care Spending, 1989," Health Affairs, Spring 1991, 10:1, p. 117.

5. Omnibus Budget Reconciliation Act of 1989, Public Law No. 101–239.

6. Omnibus Budget Reconciliation Act of 1990, Public Law No. 101–508.

7. Omnibus Budget Reconciliation Act of 1987, Public Law No. 100–203.

8. Omnibus Budget Reconciliation Act of 1986, Public Law No. 99–509.

9. Omnibus Budget Reconciliation Act of 1980, Public Law No. 96–499.

10. American Association of Nurse Anesthetists, personal correspondence, 1992.

11. Public Law No. 101–509.

The kinds of society we invent and particularly the way we handle issues of life, health, suffering, and death arise from the way . . . we perceive this essential part of our humanness. And how we perceive it, how we behave in relation to the biological base, also affects our destiny as social beings, for there is no doubt about the social creation of illness and suffering as well as the social construction of the knowledge about it.
— Margaret Stacey

Part III

Outcomes of the U.S. Health Care Delivery System

The need for a national health care plan is clearly evident when we acknowledge the shocking increase in the number of uninsured people among both employed and unemployed persons living in poverty; it is becoming a national scandal. Inequities in access to health care also are well documented, especially for African Americans and other minority racial and ethnic groups. Lack of access reduces or prevents some people from receiving services and negatively affects health status.

Historically, it has been difficult for women to obtain health services and receive care for problems that primarily affect them such as osteoporosis and heart disease. The need is urgent for research on the many health care issues women face. In addition to their own health problems, women also bear the heaviest burden of informal caregiving to others. Older women are also at greater risk because of financial problems they often experience at the same time their health begins to fail.

Quality of care is a growing concern at all levels and at all health service sites. Quality of care in hospitals is problematic, particularly for Medicare patients who are being discharged "quicker and sicker" under the prospective payment system. Research documents measurable negative effects on mortality rates for Medicare patients who are discharged in unstable conditions. Even now, monitoring of hospital quality of care is minimal. Nursing home and home care quality, discussed in previous chapters, continues to be unacceptable in many areas. Unnecessary surgery and inappropriate medical care also are growing problems that need attention. Devising approaches to gain control of this critical area of concern will remain difficult as long as the medical profession continues to police its own behavior through professional review organizations and state medical boards. All levels of the health service system badly need consumer control and oversight to improve quality of care.

Part III illustrates how the outcomes of health care services become a key focus of health policy when costs increase and access to services is constrained. Chapter 9 examines the current literature on the number of uninsured persons in the United States and identifies the groups that lack access to health care services because they have no private or public health insurance. The chapter also describes the situation of minority and special population groups that not only lack health insurance but face other financial, social, cultural, and geographic barriers to obtaining health services and are most at risk for exposure to disease and other problems.

Chapter 10 examines the special health status and health service issues facing women in the United States. The role of women as consumers of health services as well as major providers of both informal and formal health care services is explored. Public policymakers' attention to the particular needs of women also is discussed. Chapter 11 examines quality of care as a major outcome issue. The role of nurses and other professionals as major change agents in improving the quality of health care services is discussed along with public policies addressing quality-of-care and quality-of-life issues. The chapter illustrates how an understanding of quality problem areas, such as unnecessary surgeries, can contribute to improvements in care outcomes not only for individual clients but for organizations and health professionals as well.

9

Health Status and Access to Care

Waiting for care

M. Eugene Moyer

A Revised Look at the Number of Uninsured Americans

The preliminary March 1988 Current Population Survey (CPS) shows that a total of 31.1 million Americans lacked health insurance during 1987. This is considerably fewer than the 37 million reported earlier. The number of uninsured is smaller for two major reasons: (1) the health insurance questions on the CPS were reordered and asked of more adults; and (2) additional questions were added to the survey about coverage of children by Medicaid or by private health insurance.

The CPS has been conducted each month by the Bureau of the Census continuously since 1942, although from 1942 to 1948 the survey was called the Monthly Report on the Labor Force. From 1940 to 1942, essentially the same survey was conducted by the Works Progress Administration.[1] The main purpose of the CPS is to collect monthly statistics on the number of employed and unemployed persons in the nation. The current sample consists of about 60,000 households containing just under 156,000 individuals, which represents the 241.2 million persons in the noninstitutionalized civilian population plus military personnel who live either off post or on post with their families.

During March of each year, the Bureau of the Census conducts a supplement to the CPS on family income and work experience during the previous year. Since March 1980, the supplement has included questions on the health insurance coverage of each adult family member. In March 1988, the census bureau made major changes in the CPS, including a reconstruction of the health insurance questions. The revisions coincided with a completely new processing system, which is likely to be completed by late summer 1989. By that time, results from the March 1989 CPS are also likely to be available. For these reasons, the census bureau provided a preliminary file to the Department of Health and Human Services (HHS) and others. The census bureau had edited the questions available on the March 1987 survey but had done nothing to the new questions. HHS

M. Eugene Moyer is an economist at the Office of the Assistant Secretary for Planning and Evaluation, U.S. Department of Health and Human Services.

Abridged from Moyer, M. E. (1989). A revised look at the number of uninsured Americans. *Health Affairs* 8(2):102–110. Used with permission from Project HOPE.

augmented already existing coverage codes using the new questions; the results are presented in this article.[2] The census bureau found our methodology and the resulting estimates of covered persons to be acceptable but is continuing to edit its file. Differences remain between the file the census bureau will have in the late summer and the file HHS has now.

We publish these results now because the CPS is the most consistently cited source of data on the number and characteristics of the uninsured and because these data are important to the current policy debate over the best method of providing medical care to uninsured Americans.

METHODS

For the CPS, addresses are chosen for interview and an attempt is made to conduct a face-to-face interview with all adults in selected households. Often, however, a reference adult will respond for all persons in the household. An adult, usually a parent, always responds for children under age 15 since children are not interviewed.

The March 1988 CPS represents a departure from previous surveys in its questions about the health insurance coverage of the U.S. population. Respondents to earlier surveys were asked about employer-sponsored insurance only if they reported having worked during the previous year. Nonworking adults were asked if they had other health insurance coverage in a final question. No provisions were made to ask about the coverage of children except to the extent that parents in the household had insurance covering their children. Anecdotal evidence indicated that some respondents were confused by the sequence of questions and that some felt they were not asked pertinent questions about their coverage.

In the March 1988 survey, all adult respondents were asked whether they were covered by Medicare, by Medicaid, and (a single question) by CHAMPUS, Veterans Administration (VA) medical programs, or Military Health Care. Having responded to these questions about government-provided health insurance, all adults were asked a series of questions about their private coverage: whether they were covered by a private health insurance plan; whether the plan was in their own name; whether the plan was offered through a current or former employer or union; whether an employer paid all, part, or none of the cost of the plan; and finally, whether the plan covered other persons inside or outside the household. This change of sequence alone apparently accounted for a reduction in the reported number of uninsured persons to 14.7 percent of the March 1988 population, from 15.8 percent in March 1985 and 15.7 percent in March 1986 and March 1987.[3]

In addition to the change in the sequence of questions, households containing children under age 15 were asked new questions about the coverage of children in the household by Medicaid and by private health insurance. A third question (conditioned on the second) asked whether the private health insurance was provided by someone outside the household, presumably in most cases by an absent parent. Finally, additional households were imputed coverage to parallel a census procedure attributing coverage to military personnel and their families and to households that failed to respond to the household coverage questions.

RESULTS

Number of Uninsured

The preliminary March 1988 CPS shows a total of 31.1 million uninsured persons (12.9 percent of the population) in the United States during 1987 (exhibit 1). This is considerably fewer than the 37 million shown on the March 1987 and earlier versions of the CPS.[4] These preliminary results are much more consistent with other recent estimates of the number of uninsured persons in the nation.[5] However, they differ from the preliminary findings from the new National Medical Expenditure Survey (NMES)— 36.8 million persons uninsured during the first four months of 1987. The difference between NMES and CPS estimates (besides time differences) appears to be related mainly to the treatment of persons eligible for VA medical benefits. The NMES counts as uninsured those persons eligible only for VA benefits.[6] The CPS, which cannot separate such persons from those with coverage by some sort of military health care, has always included them among the insured. The CPS shows about four million persons insured only by VA or military health care. Other differences remain unexplained.

As a subset of private health insurance, employer-sponsored health insurance covered 148 million Americans, but this number will be much larger on the final CPS because of census edits not done on the preliminary file. Other information suggests that many people are covered both by individually purchased health insurance and by employer-sponsored insurance. The survey did not ask about such dual private coverage.

Characteristics of the Uninsured

Exhibit 2 shows that 6.8 million of the uninsured were under age 15 and that 7.7 million were not employed or were employed part-time but usually worked under 18 hours per week. This leaves 16.6 million who were employed at least 18 hours per week for all or part of 1987. Fewer than one-third of the uninsured were poor; an additional 9 percent were near-poor (in families with incomes below 125 percent of the poverty threshold). The

EXHIBIT 1 Persons Covered by Medicaid and Health Insurance, by Age, Millions of Persons, 1987

Type of Coverage	Total	Under 15	15–17	18–24	25–34	35–64	65 and Older
Total population	241.2	52.7	10.8	26.1	43.0	80.1	28.5
Private health insurance							
Persons covered	181.4	38.3	8.0	17.5	32.3	65.2	20.1
Percent covered	100.0%	21.1%	4.4%	9.6%	17.8%	35.9%	11.1%
Percent of population	75.2	72.7	74.3	67.1	75.3	81.3	70.5
Employer-sponsored health insurance							
Persons covered	147.6	33.0	6.5	13.3	29.1	57.0	8.6
Percent covered	100.0%	22.4%	4.4%	9.0%	19.7%	38.6%	5.8%
Percent of population	61.2	62.7	60.3	51.1	67.7	71.1	30.2
Medicaid							
Persons covered	20.9	8.6	1.1	2.1	2.9	3.8	2.5
Percent covered	100.0%	40.9%	5.4%	10.0%	13.8%	18.1%	11.8%
Percent of population	8.7	16.3	10.5	8.0	6.7	4.7	8.6
Any private or public insurance							
Persons covered	210.0	45.9	9.2	20.0	35.8	70.9	28.3
Percent covered	100.0%	21.9%	4.4%	9.5%	17.0%	33.8%	13.5%
Percent of population	87.1	87.1	85.5	76.7	83.2	88.5	99.1
Uninsured							
Persons not covered	31.1	6.8	1.6	6.1	7.2	9.2	0.3
Percent not covered	100.0%	21.8%	5.0%	19.5%	23.1%	29.7%	0.9%
Percent of population	12.9	12.9	14.5	23.3	16.8	11.5	0.9

Note: Medicare and other coverages are not shown separately. Persons can be in more than one insurance category.

Source: Preliminary tabulations from the March 1988 Current Population Survey, 17 April 1989.

EXHIBIT 2   Characteristics of the Uninsured Population, Millions
of Persons, 1987

	Uninsured	Percent of Uninsured	Probability of Being Uninsured
Annual work experience			
Total	31.1	100.0%	12.9%
None	7.7	24.8	11.1
Full-time, all year	7.7	24.7	10.0
Part-time, all year[a]	1.4	4.4	16.5
Full-time, part year	5.4	17.4	23.3
Part-time, part year[a]	2.1	6.9	20.3
Under age 15	6.8	21.8	12.9
Employed subtotal	16.6	53.3	13.9
Poverty status of family			
In poverty	9.4	30.1%	28.7%
100–124 percent	2.9	9.3	26.3
125–149 percent	2.7	8.8	25.0
150–184 percent	3.3	10.7	20.9
185 percent or more	12.8	41.1	7.5
Family type			
Single with children	5.1	16.4%	19.2%
Husband and wife with children	11.2	36.1	11.0
Single, no children	8.9	28.6	18.9
Two or more adults, no children	5.9	18.9	9.0
Census region			
Northeast	4.4	14.1%	8.8%
Midwest	5.5	17.7	9.3
South	13.4	43.1	16.3
West	7.8	25.1	15.7

[a]Part-time workers must work eighteen or more hours per week.

Source: Preliminary tabulations from the March 1988 Current Population Survey, 17 April 1989.

largest group of the uninsured were in families with incomes above 185 percent of the poverty level. Over half of the uninsured were children or in families with children. Over half of the uninsured were concentrated in the South and the West census regions.[7]

... The 16.6 million employed uninsured includ[e] 1.8 million persons who were self-employed. We chose to include the self-employed, although for some purposes they could have been excluded. Almost half of the 16.6 million employed uninsured worked full time during all of 1987, but another one-third worked full time for only a part of 1987.

Over 43 percent of the employed uninsured worked for firms with fewer than 25 employees. This percentage is somewhat misleading, since 15 percent did not answer the question on employer size. The final census file will attribute an employer size to nonrespondents; . . . we included them in the group who worked for firms of 25 or more employees. . . . About 80 percent of the uninsured either were employed or were dependents of an employed person in 1987. This is approximately the group that might be affected by any of the proposed approaches to mandating that employers provide health insurance to employees and their dependents. This employment definition includes those who were self-employed and excludes part-time workers who usually worked fewer than 18 hours per week. About 25 percent of these uninsured persons were poor, while almost half were in families with incomes above 185 percent of the poverty standard.

Definition of Employment

The term "employment" may be defined in many ways to indicate a continuing attachment to work and the labor force. For example, in this article, we decided at the outset to exclude part-time workers who worked under 18 hours per week because their attachment to the labor force was thought to be too tenuous. We could have excluded other workers, such as those who work for very small employers or who earn very low hourly wages, for similar reasons. For policy purposes, proposals define employment in various ways in an attempt to include only workers with a relatively strong attachment to work and the labor force.

If the employment definition were to include only employees who worked for (or were the owners of) firms with 25 employees or more, the number of uninsured would fall to about 15 million. Of these, only about 3.3 million (21 percent) would be poor, but 7.5 million (49 percent) would be in families with incomes above 185 percent of poverty. If the employment definition excluded those who earned under five dollars an hour, the number of the employed uninsured and their dependents would fall to 12.5 million persons, of whom only 1.4 million (11.5 percent) would be poor, but 7.5 million (60 percent) would be in families with incomes above 185 percent of the poverty standard. If the definition were to exclude employees earning five dollars an hour or less who worked for employers with fewer than 25 employees, the number of uninsured workers would fall to 8.5 million. Of these, under a million (10 percent) would be poor and 5.3 million (63 percent) would be in families with incomes above 185 percent of the poverty level.

A POLICY BASELINE

The March 1988 CPS is a rich source of data on the economic status of American families, including their insurance coverage, during 1987. It is difficult to describe the complex information available on the file in these exhibits. We chose them for their relevance to policy options for helping the uninsured to gain access to medical care. Among the leading options in this regard are proposals to allow poor (or poor and near-poor) persons to participate in state Medicaid programs at little or no cost or to require that employers provide health insurance to all or some of their employees and their dependents.

While the data shown here do not allow an analysis of any specific proposal, they do provide a baseline reference on the number of uninsured persons who might have been eligible for such plans in 1987 and how well different proposals would have targeted insurance coverage on the poor uninsured.

NOTES

1. Bureau of Labor Statistics, *BLS Handbook of Methods,* vol. 1 (U.S. Department of Labor, BLS, December, 1982), 3.

2. Some households reported coverage of children in the household question on health insurance, but indicated neither that the coverage was provided outside the family nor that an adult in the family was covering children. We counted children in those households as insured.

3. Unpublished census memoranda.

4. Estimates of the uninsured from the March 1987 CPS from K. Swartz, *The Uninsured and Workers Without Employer-Group Health Insurance,* Urban Institute Project Report, August 1988; and D. Chollet, *Uninsured in the United States: The Nonelderly Population Without Health Insurance, 1986* (Washington, D.C.: Employee Benefit Research Institute, 5 October 1988), 26. Their estimates do not include a small number of uninsured age 65 or older.

5. See K.E. Ladenheim and G.R. Wilensky, "Trends in the Number and Characteristics of the Uninsured," presented at the American Public Health Association, New Orleans, Louisiana, 19 October 1987, for a comparison of the numbers of uninsured persons under age 65 shown on several data sets during the 1970s and 1980s.

6. According to papers given at the 13–18 November 1988 meetings of the American Public Health Association, the National Medical Expenditure Survey (NMES) showed 36.8 million uninsured during the first four months of 1987. See, for example, P.F. Short, A. Monheit, and K. Beauregard, "Uninsured Americans: A 1987 Profile."

7. Most studies of the uninsured have shown similar results. For example, see Swartz, *The Uninsured and Workers Without Employer-Group Health Insurance,* Table 1; and Chollet, *Uninsured in the United States.*

Karen Davis

Inequality and Access
to Health Care

Inequality in health outcomes and access to health care services has been a central issue in public health policy and health services research over the last 20 years. The recognition that health status and utilization of health services varied significantly depending upon one's income, race, and geographic location was an important factor in support for national health policies to expand health care programs for the poor and other vulnerable population groups in the 1960s and 1970s. Legislative proposals for national health insurance were introduced and debated in the 1970s, but failed to gather sufficient support for passage.

In the 1980s public policymakers became preoccupied with the rising cost of health care, and access to health care received relatively less attention. Cutbacks in funding for public programs and attempts to foster competition and cost consciousness in the health care system came to the forefront. Yet the continued attention in the research literature to the gaps that remained for especially vulnerable subpopulations helped lay the groundwork for some continued modest expansions in programs such as Medicaid and community health center funding.

As the nation enters the decade of the 1990s, national public policy debate has again focused on the need for a universal health plan to ensure access to health care for all Americans. The health services research literature promises to play an important contribution to this debate through its increasingly sophisticated analyses of the multiple determinants of health outcomes and access to health care. . . .

EQUITY AND NATIONAL HEALTH INSURANCE

The passage of Medicare and Medicaid in 1965 and the establishment of federal funding for community and migrant health centers in the 1960s

Karen Davis, Ph.D., is Executive Vice-President of the Commonwealth Fund, New York.

Abridged from Davis, K. (1991). Inequality and access to health care. *Milbank Q* 69(2):253–273. Used with permission of the Milbank Memorial Fund.

greatly expanded the role of the federal government in assuring access to health care services for the poor and elderly people. Despite the significance of these programs, it was widely recognized that more fundamental reforms would be necessary to ensure that all Americans received adequate health care.

Somers and Somers (1972) were among the earliest analysts of national health insurance legislative reform proposals. They set forth nine criteria for the evaluation of competing proposals:

1. Universal coverage
2. Comprehensive benefits
3. Equitable financing
4. Incentives for efficiency and effectiveness
5. Regulated competition in insurance underwriting and administration
6. Consumer choice of provider
7. Administrative simplicity
8. Flexibility
9. General acceptability to providers and consumers

Health insurance legislative proposals were characterized as falling into four types:

1. Incentives to purchase private health insurance voluntarily (supported by the American Hospital Association, American Medical Association, Health Insurance Association of America)
2. Employer-mandated private health insurance for workers and dependents, public programs for low-income families and children, and voluntary purchase of private health insurance for others outside the workplace (Nixon administration)
3. Extension of Medicare to the entire population with the option for employers and nonworking families to opt out of Medicare coverage by purchasing private health insurance (Javits bill)
4. A single public plan for all (Kennedy-Griffiths bill)

It is striking to see how closely these early proposals capture the range of options currently under consideration. Somers and Somers expressed concern that the debate would split supporters of a national health insurance plan into two camps: those favoring a purely public financing system and those willing to accommodate a major role for private insurers. Their analysis could just as easily have been written today.

Fein (1972) provided an important conceptual framework for the national health insurance debate by setting forth the importance of achieving equity in access to health care services. This goal could be defined as equal health outcomes for all (e.g., by income group), equal expenditures per capita (e.g., across income groups), or the elimination of income as a rationing device. Fein concluded that a national health insurance plan with comprehensive benefits and no deductibles or other cost sharing by patients was the most likely to achieve equitable access to health services. He also noted that national health insurance schemes with a progressive financing source were more equitable than those that placed a greater burden on lower-income families. He stressed the importance of linking a system of universal financing with a reformed health care delivery system in which financial incentives for physicians to treat patients would not depend upon income of patients or quantity of services tendered, but rather would compensate physicians on a salaried basis for providing quality health care services. White (1972) stressed the importance of assuring an adequate primary health care delivery system to reduce inequalities in access to care.

These pathbreaking articles . . . helped shape the debate over the need for national health insurance in the early 1970s and the merits of different legislative proposals. My own work (Davis 1975b) was greatly influenced by their conceptual framework. Using the criteria set forth by Somers and Somers and by Fein, I contrasted the major national health insurance legislative proposals and analyzed their benefits, costs, and consequences. In addition, I stressed the importance of designing a national health insurance plan that would eliminate disparities by income, race, and geographic location. This would be achieved by coupling universal financing with health system reform and a health resources development fund to develop additional health services in underserved areas.

Although the legislative debate over national health insurance died at the end of the legislative session in 1974, this analysis was instrumental in the design of the Carter National Health Plan in 1979 (U.S. Department of Health and Human Services, 1980). The Carter plan, like the Nixon and Javits plans, was for universal public-private national health insurance, creating a new public plan called HealthCare to replace Medicare and Medicaid and to cover other groups of uninsured. Employers were required to purchase either HealthCare or comparable private health insurance coverage for workers and dependents. However, this plan, too, died in the Senate Finance Committee in the spring of 1980—in large part because of concern with the federal budgetary cost of expanding coverage to all low-income uninsured.

IMPACT OF MEDICARE AND MEDICAID
ON ACCESS

While the debate over national health insurance continued to be a major policy issue through the 1970s, attention in the research literature shifted to analyzing the impact of the Medicare and Medicaid programs on improving access to health care services. This analysis was fostered by a growing concern over major inequities in access to health care and health outcomes.

The classic analysis of socioeconomic differentials in mortality by Kitagawa and Hauser (1973) was a major factor in underscoring concern about inequalities in health. They linked death certificates with 1960 census information on income, education, and race and provided an exhaustive examination of the link between socioeconomic status and mortality. Kosa and Zola (1975) had a similarly significant impact with their examination of the sociological relationships between poverty and health.

Socioeconomic differences in utilization of health care services received major attention with national surveys analyzed by researchers at the Center for Health Administration Studies at the University of Chicago (Aday 1976; Aday and Andersen 1975; Aday, Andersen, and Fleming 1980; Aday, Fleming, and Andersen 1984; Andersen and Aday 1978; Andersen et al. 1972, 1987). Andersen, Aday, and their colleagues developed a conceptual framework for analyzing access to health care services and stressed the importance of identifying predisposing and enabling factors as well as the need for health care as determinants of utilization of health care services. Operationally, this concept has led researchers to measure access to health care services as the relation of level of utilization to the need for health care as measured by health status (Berki and Aschraft 1979; Freeman et al. 1987; Hershey, Luft, and Gianaris 1975; Kronenfeld 1980; Vladeck 1981).

Aday (1976) . . . emphasized the need for developing accurate measures of access that include the need for care rather than just utilization rates. She proposed the ratio of health care utilization to disability days as an indicator of equitable access to care. Based on this indicator, she found that between 1963 and 1970, while Medicare and Medicaid improved utilization of medical services by low-income people, the improvement was not commensurate with level of illness. The use of physician services divided by disability days during the year continued to be lowest for low-income persons in 1970. The Aday analysis, however, did not break down the analysis of low-income persons into those who were covered by Medicare or Medicaid and those who were not. Aday stressed that those who had a usual source of care and a way of entry into the health system were most likely to benefit from health financing coverage.

The pathbreaking work by Andersen, Aday, and their colleagues had a similarly strong influence on my own work. With colleagues at the Brookings Institution (Davis 1975a, 1976a,b; Davis and Reynolds 1976; Davis and Schoen 1978) I pursued an econometric approach to the analysis of utilization of health care services, simultaneously holding constant for health financing coverage such as Medicare, Medicaid, and private health insurance, income, several measures of health status, and other determinants. We found that need for health care as measured by such health status variables as presence of chronic conditions, disability days, and self-assessment of health status was the most important determinant of utilization. However, after holding constant for the need for care, significant differences existed between lower-income persons who were not covered by either a public program of health insurance like Medicaid or Medicare or private health insurance and higher-income individuals in use of health care services. In the framework of Fein's definition of equity, low-income persons without Medicaid coverage did not have equitable access to health care services. Medicaid beneficiaries, by contrast, used health care services at a rate similar to higher-income persons after adjustment for health status differences.

The Medicare program was also a subject of great interest to researchers. Although Medicare was a uniform program with standard benefits for all beneficiaries, the presence of deductibles and coinsurance meant that financial barriers to care might be greater for low-income beneficiaries. Other barriers to care, such as racial discrimination or geographical availability of health care services, could also influence actual utilization of health care services. In one early study, . . . I analyzed differentials in the distribution of Medicare benefits by race, geographic location, and income and found that despite the uniform benefits afforded by Medicare, actual receipt of benefits was very uneven (Davis 1975a). Higher-income elderly (those with incomes over $15,000 in 1969) received 60 percent more physician services and 45 percent more days of hospital care than lower-income elderly (incomes under $5,000) not covered by Medicaid—holding constant for health status as measured by chronic conditions, limited activity, restricted activity days, age, race, geographic location, and supply of physicians and hospitals. Although it improved access for elderly blacks, in the early years of the program black beneficiaries of Medicare were still less likely to receive health care services than white beneficiaries.

Studies on the Medicaid program also investigated the impact of the program on beneficiaries. Early studies showed that Medicaid was successful in increasing utilization of beneficiaries up to a level comparable to that of higher-income persons, holding constant for health differences (Davis 1976a, b; Davis and Reynolds 1976; and Davis and Schoen 1978). Further research documented that care for Medicaid beneficiaries was not more costly than care for all Americans (Blendon and Moloney 1982; Davis and Schoen 1978; Rogers, Blendon, and Moloney 1982). This helped establish that Medicaid costs were high because health care was costly, not because of any flaws specific to the program.

Zwick (1972) . . . documented the importance of community health centers in improving access to health care services—despite the strong opposition of organized medicine. Another pathbreaking study by Reynolds

(1976) . . . found that community health centers improved access to health care for those most in need: the young, blacks, and seriously ill people. His analysis of data from 32 community health centers for the period from October 1972 to September 1973 found that they provided more preventive care and stressed continuity of care to a greater degree than care delivered to comparable persons outside of community health centers. The greatest problems community health centers faced was inadequate funding and the difficulty of attracting and retaining physicians.

These early studies helped establish the importance of programs like Medicare, Medicaid, and community health centers in improving access to health care services for the poor and the elderly. At the same time, they stressed the incomplete nature of the progress to date and the need to continue to expand access to health care.

New studies in the early 1980s updating some of the early work of the 1970s with more recent data found that substantial disparities among Medicare and Medicaid beneficiaries had been reduced. Long and Settle (1984) reported . . . results of an analysis of utilization of health care services by the elderly in 1977, using data from the Current Medicare Survey. They found that no significant differences continued to exist across income groups in use by the elderly of hospital and physician services. Elderly whites in the South continued to receive more hospital care than elderly blacks, but the differentials in use were sharply reduced from the 1969 levels I had found (Davis 1975a). A parallel study by the authors using 1977 Health Interview Survey data found similar results (Link, Long, and Settle 1982b).

In an important analysis of utilization of health services by the elderly . . . , Wan (1982) conducted a multivariate analysis of the factors affecting the use of ambulatory care and short-term hospitalization by the noninstitutionalized elderly based on interviews conducted in five neighborhood health center service areas. Indicators of the determinants of access used as independent variables in the analysis included regular source of care, health insurance coverage, and family income. To adjust for health status, Wan included a number of episodic illnesses within a year and limitations in major activities resulting from chronic conditions. He found that the elderly who were more likely to use private physicians included those over 80 years of age, white females with higher levels of education, minor chronic disability, and private supplemental insurance. Elderly users of neighborhood health centers were more likely to be black, female, less educated, annual family income less than $5,000, persons with moderate disability, and those with Medicaid to supplement Medicare. The elderly with severe chronic disability were more likely to be older, nonwhite, with lower incomes, and to have Medicaid coverage. Wan found that for ambulatory care utilization, chronic disability and acute illness were the most predictive of use. For hospitalization, he found that usual source of care, number of episodic illnesses, and chronic disability determined admission. Those with a regular source of care had more hospital days and more physician visits. Insurance coverage also correlated with more frequent physician visits. He found that, for a given level of health, elderly blacks with a regular source of care had more physician visits than elderly whites, but blacks had shorter lengths of stay in the hospital. This may be the result of racial disparities in insurance benefits, greater use of outpatient services, or discriminatory practices of hospitals.

Link, Long, and Settle (1982a) replicated my earlier study of the distribution of Medicaid benefits among beneficiaries using 1969 Health Interview Survey data and contrasted those results with data from the 1976 Health Interview Survey. They found that between 1969 and 1976 Medicaid beneficiaries increased their use of physician services to a greater extent than the nonelderly U.S. population, and that this was true for Medicaid beneficiaries regardless of race, region, or health status. By 1976 they found that nonelderly blacks on Medicaid used physician services at a rate comparable to nonelderly whites on Medicaid. Only in the South did blacks on Medicaid receive lower hospital services than whites. This effect, however, was not statistically significant for those with serious health problems.

Kasper (1986b) also investigated health status and utilization of Medicaid beneficiaries compared with others. Using 1980 data from the National Medical Care Utilization and Expenditure Survey, she found that Medicaid beneficiaries in poor health used health services at the same rate as those of similar health status who were not poor. Those poor not covered by Medicaid, however, were less likely to see a physician or to purchase a prescribed drug.

THE UNINSURED AND ACCESS TO HEALTH CARE

With the finding that disparities in benefits among beneficiaries of Medicare and Medicaid had been reduced, if not eliminated, in the first 10 years of the programs, attention shifted to examining barriers to access to health services for the uninsured. Some argued that Medicare and Medicaid had not only achieved equity in access for covered beneficiaries, but had also eliminated inequities in access to health care services generally (Aday, Andersen, and Fleming 1980).

This view was challenged by Kleinman, Gold, and Makuc (1981), who found that more sophisticated approaches to adjusting for age and health status using 1976–1978 Health Interview Survey data still revealed significant differences in use of services between the poor and nonpoor and between blacks and whites. They also found that even among the elderly in fair or poor health, blacks and the poor had lower utilization of services.

Given the conflicting views on whether public policy efforts to date had been adequate to achieve equitable access to care, my colleagues and I conducted a review of the literature in the early 1980s (Davis, Gold, and Makuc 1981). We concluded that, although gaps had been narrowed in access to care, significant differentials still existed.

Increasingly, the research focus shifted to the uninsured—those without coverage under either private health insurance or public programs like Medicare and Medicaid—as the group continuing to experience the most serious difficulties in obtaining health services.

The President's Commission on ethics highlighted the degree to which those without health insurance coverage continued to lag well behind others (President's Commission 1983). Analysis that I conducted for the President's Commission with Rowland . . . (Davis and Rowland 1983), using data from the 1977 National Medical Care Expenditure Survey, . . . found that the poor, minorities, and young adults continued to be the groups most likely to be uninsured. People with health insurance received 54 percent more ambulatory care and 90 percent more inpatient hospital care than those without health insurance coverage. Race and geographic location were also important independent determinants of differences in health care utilization, but were of less importance than insurance coverage.

The nature of health insurance coverage also became a focus of research concern. . . . Farley (1985) stressed the importance of examining the adequacy of health insurance coverage, not just the existence of any coverage. Using data from the 1977 National Medical Care Expenditure Survey, she found that approximately 13 percent of those with private insurance are underinsured. The underinsured are most likely to be poor, a member of a family that does not have a worker, a woman and her dependents, a person with nongroup health insurance coverage, between the ages of 55 and 65 in fair or poor health, and reside in the South or outside metropolitan areas.

Turnover in Medicaid enrollment is also a growing source of concern. Recent studies have shown that a high fraction of Medicaid beneficiaries are covered for relatively brief periods of time (Short, Cantor, and Monheit 1988). For example, only 43 percent of Medicaid beneficiaries at the beginning of a three-year period were still covered 32 months later. Over one-third were enrolled less than eight months. Changes in employment and earnings are major factors affecting Medicaid enrollment. The majority of newly covered Medicaid enrollees were uninsured before qualifying for Medicaid, and the majority of individuals leaving Medicaid were subsequently uninsured.

VULNERABLE SUBPOPULATION GROUPS

The importance of more disaggregated analysis spurred health services researchers to focus their attention on the particular problems of vulnerable subpopulation groups. Access to health care services for children became an especially important focus of research (Dutton 1985; Kasper 1987; Newacheck 1988; Orr and Miller 1981; Wolfe 1980). Using data from the 1980 National Medical Care Utilization and Expenditure Survey, for example, Kasper (1987) found that children who were poor or without insurance coverage were less likely to see a physician. Medicaid children, on the other hand, saw physicians slightly more often than other children (4 percent)—holding constant for multiple determinants of utilization. Rosenbach also found that low-income children without either private health insurance or Medicaid were the least likely to receive physician care (36 percent), which made them considerably worse off than Medicaid children (25 percent) (Rosenbach 1985).

Concern with barriers to health care for children was heightened by a growing body of literature documenting the importance of medical care for health outcomes of children (Starfield 1985a,b).

Research also began to focus on the importance of established relationships with a primary care physician. Having a usual source of care both increases the amount and kind of care used as well as satisfaction with care (Andersen, Mullner, and Cornelius 1987; Hulka and Wheat 1985; Kasper 1986a,b, 1987; Walden, Wilensky, and Kasper 1985). Kasper (1987) found that children who used a physician's office as their regular source of care had lower health expenditures than children who relied on hospital outpatient departments or emergency rooms and had no regular physician.

Rosenbaum and Johnson (1986) examined the contribution of Medicaid, especially its Early Periodic Screening Diagnosis and Treatment (EPSDT) program, in improving preventive care among low-income children. They found that Medicaid has played an important role in improving access to care for poor children, but that only one-third of poor children are covered. EPSDT preventive care has proven to be cost-effective, yet has fallen short of reaching all Medicaid children. A Children's Defense Fund survey of 50 states analyzed by Rosenbaum and Johnson found that no state had a supplemental funding program for children to guarantee coverage beyond Medicaid eligibility. The absence of national standards for EPSDT was also found to be a barrier to effective preventive care.

The problems of access to health care in rural areas also received greater attention in the research literature in the 1980s. Rowland, Lyons, and Edwards (1988) found that residents in rural areas were more likely to be poor and uninsured. Coupled with the reduced availability of health services in rural areas, rural residents receive fewer physician and hospital services than urban residents.

A further analysis by Patrick et al. (1988) of the interplay of poverty, health status, and health services in rural America was [based on] . . . a cross-sectional analysis from interviews at 36 rural sites of users and non-users of community health centers and found that symptoms of mobility impairment increased with poverty. The poor uninsured in poor health had fewer visits than the poor with insurance coverage (typically from Medicaid). Patrick et al. found that providing equal access through community health centers, however, was not sufficient to eradicate the differences in health status between poor and nonpoor, and called for additional steps to alter the disparity.

In a special supplement to the [*Milbank*] *Quarterly* devoted to the issue of the health of black Americans, several authors investigated health status differentials, health insurance coverage, and the contribution of private insurance and public programs to improving access to health care (Andersen, Mullner, and Cornelius 1987; Baquet and Ringen 1987; Davis et al. 1987; Ewbank 1987; Gibson and Jackson 1987; Long 1987; Manton, Patrick, and Johnson 1987; Miller 1987; Schlesinger 1987). The issue identified the gains in health status made by blacks since the early 1960s and the contributions of Medicaid, Medicare, community health centers, and federal minority health professional programs to those gains. However, the authors note the gaps in these programs and how recent cuts in funding threaten any further progress in improving the health status of blacks (Davis et al. 1987).

More recent work . . . has highlighted the barriers in access to health care of Hispanics (Wolinsky et al. 1989). Based on national Health Interview Surveys from 1976 and 1984, Wolinsky and coworkers found that utilization of hospital care is somewhat more equal between Hispanics and non-Hispanics than ambulatory care. Significant differences exist among Hispanics in number of disability days and frequency of hospital use, with Cuban Americans showing relatively better health status and lower hospital utilization.

COMPETITION AND COST CONTAINMENT

In the 1980s greater emphasis was placed on containing health care costs through competition among health care providers and increasing emphasis upon cost-containment measures. This squeeze, coupled with rising unemployment and poverty in the early 1980s, caused a deterioration in access to health care for many low-income persons.

. . . Feder, Hadley, and Mullner (1984) examined the role of hospital charity care for the uninsured at public and private hospitals using data from the American Hospital Association/Urban Institute surveys on hospital finances in 1980 and 1982. They found that, although the number of uninsured increased between 1980 and 1982, the amount of charity care essentially remained unchanged. Public hospitals made more of an effort to maintain care, but those facing financial difficulties only modestly expanded their charity care. They noted that hospitals may ration free care by directly discouraging use by those unable to pay, and by cutting the services used most by uninsured poor, such as outpatient clinics. They suggested two ways to improve access to hospital care: expand health insurance coverage or pay hospitals to provide free care. Although they found the first option preferable, they note that public policy is doing neither and it appears most politically feasible to patch the system of charity care by providing special aid to hospitals providing a disproportionate share of charity care.

Schlesinger et al. (1987) also examined . . . the impact of competition and cost-containment pressures on access to care. They analyzed a 1984 survey of physicians by the American Medical Association and found that physicians reported that they were discouraged from admitting unprofitable patients to hospitals. The findings for Medicaid and the uninsured were similar, but stronger for the uninsured. Access was particularly discouraged at for-profit hospitals and health systems where there is increased competition. The authors cautioned that the study is largely based on physician perceptions, but the results are consistent with other studies suggesting that the trends toward greater cost pressure will lead to decreased access for the uninsured.

Other studies found that hospitals reduced care for Medicaid patients in the early 1980s as Medicaid hospital payment rates failed to keep pace with that of other payers (Davis et al. 1990; Rowland 1987; Rowland, Lyons, and Edwards 1988). For-profit hospitals markedly reduced their share of Medicaid patients over the period. In general, the impact of cost-containment efforts was largely to make health care less accessible to the uninsured and, to some extent, those covered by Medicaid.

Freeman et al. (1987) found that access to health care deteriorated substantially between 1982 and 1986. Using national surveys of access to health care, they found that the gap in utilization of physician services between the insured and uninsured widened over the period, as did the differences between blacks and whites. A minority of uninsured with serious health symptoms sought health care from a physician in 1986.

Cutbacks in Medicaid funding at the federal and state level also markedly curtailed access to health care (Blendon and Moloney 1982; Rowland and Gaus 1982; Rowland, Lyons, and Edwards 1988). States not only failed to increase income eligibility levels with inflation, but they also cut benefits by limiting covered services. Swartz (1988) found that, between 1979 and 1983, poverty among children increased 35 percent whereas children on Medicaid increased by 4 percent. Similarly, although poverty among women aged 18 to 40 increased 60 percent, the number of young women on Medicaid increased by only 20 percent.

States instituted a number of measures to encourage Medicaid benefi-ciaries to enroll in health maintenance organizations or other managed care systems (Anderson and Fox 1987; Spitz 1982). Although early studies (see Berkanovic et al. 1975) found little to distinguish care received by Medicaid beneficiaries in prepaid health plans from that provided to the fee-for-service sector, later studies suggested that health outcomes were disturbingly worse for low-income persons enrolled in health mainte-nance organizations (Ware et al. 1986).

Rosenbaum et al. (1988) conducted a nationwide survey of states that provide managed care plans in their Medicaid programs. They reported that, of 41 managed care contracts reviewed, none guaranteed continued coverage for pregnant women if Medicaid eligibility stopped, few expe-dited enrollment, few provided high-risk specialists, and only five had specific quality-of-care controls.

HEALTH OUTCOMES AND ACCESS TO CARE

The most recent development in the health services research literature on access to health care is the trend toward more disaggregated studies that look at specific services and the link between access to health services and health outcomes.

Lurie et al. (1984) found that low-income persons who were dropped from Medi-Cal coverage experienced a marked deterioration in access to health care. As a result, the incidence of untreated diabetes and hyperten-sion increased, and the probability of death was significantly greater for those losing coverage than for a control group who retained coverage.

Hadley, Steinberg, and Feder (1991) found that the uninsured who are hospitalized are less likely to get specialized services and are more likely to die while hospitalized. Using hospital discharge abstract data on almost 600,000 patients from a national sample of hospitals in 1987, they found that the uninsured had a 44 to 124 percent higher risk of in-hospital mortality at the time of admission than did the privately insured. The actual in-hospital death rate was 1.2 to 3.2 times higher among uninsured patients than privately insured patients, after controlling for their poor health status upon admission. The uninsured were less likely to receive high-cost or high-discretion procedures.

. . . Baquet and Ringen (1987) analyzed data from the National Cancer Institute/SEER program. They found that the incidence and mortality of cervical cancer is two to three times higher in blacks than in whites, and that the distribution of cases mirrors other inequities in the health care system. Between 1975 and 1984 the incidence of invasive cervical cancer declined in both black and white women, but black women continued to have much higher rates. The age-specific rates for elderly black females was highest. Those least likely to have received a Pap smear are poor, black, and reside in rural areas. The major reason for differentials in rates are inequities in the distribution of health resources, not genetic or biological factors. The authors recommend better delivery of services, quality improvements, programs targeted to high-risk populations, and better data collection and monitoring.

CONTRIBUTION OF RESEARCH TO POLICY AND FUTURE ISSUES

Research on inequalities in health outcomes and access to health care services in the last two decades has made an important contribution to the public policy debate. Research documenting the success of Medicaid in improving access to health care for covered beneficiaries at a cost comparable to that of privately insured people helped lead to political acceptance of Medicaid as an essential and effective program that ensures access to needed health care services for millions of impoverished Americans.

Research on access to health care for children and the importance of prenatal care and well-baby care in improving health outcomes also contributed to legislative expansions of Medicaid to greater numbers of low-income pregnant women and children. Documentation of the disparities in use of health services of the elderly by income highlighted the need for legislation to expand Medicaid to supplement Medicare for all poor elderly—a legislative change that was enacted in the late 1980s.

Research on the adverse impact of cost-containment measures applied exclusively or excessively to health programs for the poor has also helped underscore the importance of comprehensive health system reform. Such reform needs to guarantee universal health coverage while removing or reducing differentials in the rates of compensation to physicians, hospitals, and other health care providers.

More detailed research on the consequences for health outcomes of barriers to care for the uninsured should help build the case for universal health insurance coverage. Increasingly, policymakers want to know not just that insurance makes a difference in utilization of health care services, but also what the implications are for the health of the uninsured.

... The coming decade should prove even more challenging as the nation turns once again to the policy goal of assuring universal health insurance coverage.

REFERENCES

Aday, L.A. 1976. The Impact of Health Policy on Access to Medical Care. *Milbank Memorial Fund Quarterly/ Health and Society* 54(2):215–33.

Aday, L.A., and R. Andersen. 1975. *Development of Indices of Access to Medical Care.* Ann Arbor, Mich.: University of Michigan Health Administration Press.

Aday, L.A., and R. Andersen. 1984. The National Profile of Access to Medical Care: Where Do We Stand? *American Journal of Public Health* 74(12):1331–8.

Aday, L.A., R. Andersen, and G.V. Fleming. 1980. *Health Care in the U.S.: Equitable for Whom?* Beverly Hills, Calif.: Sage Publications.

Aday, L.A., G. Fleming, and R. Andersen. 1984. *Access to Medical Care in the U.S.: Who Has It, Who Doesn't.* Chicago: Pluribus Press.

Andersen, R., and L.A. Aday. 1978. Access to Medical Care in the U.S.: Realized and Potential. *Medical Care* 16(7):533–46.

Andersen, R., L.A. Aday, C. Lyttle, et al. 1987. *Ambulatory Care and Insurance in an Era of Constraints.* Chicago: Pluribus Press.

Andersen, R., R. Greeley, J. Kravatts, and O.W. Anderson. 1972. *Health Service Use: National Trends and Variations, 1953–1971,* DHEW pub. no. 73-3004. Rockville, Md.: National Center for Health Services Research and Development.

Andersen, R.M., A. McCutcheon, L.A. Aday, G.Y. Chiu, and R. Bell. 1983. Exploring Dimensions of Access to Medical Care. *Health Services Research* 18(1):49–74.

Andersen, R.M., R.M. Mullner, and L.J. Cornelius. 1987. Black-White Differences in Health Status: Methods or Substance? *Milbank Quarterly* 65(suppl. 1):72–99.

Anderson, M.D., and P.D. Fox. 1987. Lessons Learned from Medicaid

Managed Care Approaches. *Health Affairs* 6(1):71–86.

Baquet, C., and K. Ringen. 1987. Health Policy: Gaps in Access, Delivery, and Utilization of the Pap Smear in the United States. *Milbank Quarterly* 65(suppl. 2):322–47.

Berkanovic, E., L.G. Reeder, A.C. Marcus, and S. Schwartz. 1975. The Effects of Prepayment on Access to Medical Care: The PACC Experience. *Milbank Memorial Fund Quarterly/Health and Society* 53(2):241–54.

Berki, M., and M. Aschraft. 1979. On the Analysis of Ambulatory Utilization: An Investigation of the Roles of Need, Access, and Price as Predictors of Illness and Preventive Visits. *Medical Care* 17:1163–81.

Blendon, Robert J., and Thomas W. Moloney. 1982. Perspectives on the Medicaid Crisis. In *New Approaches to the Medicaid Crisis,* eds. R.J. Blendon and T.W. Moloney. New York: Frost and Sullivan Press.

Davis, K. 1975a. Equal Treatment and Unequal Benefits: The Medicare Program. *Milbank Memorial Fund Quarterly/Health and Society* 53(4):449–88.

———. 1975b. *National Health Insurance: Benefits, Costs, and Consequences.* Washington: Brookings Institution.

———. 1976a. Achievements and Problems of Medicaid. *Public Health Reports* 912(4):309–16.

———. 1976b. Medicaid Payments and Utilization of Medical Services by the Poor. *Inquiry* 13(2):122–35.

Davis, K., G. Anderson, D. Rowland, and E. Steinberg. 1990. *Health Care Cost Containment.* Baltimore: The Johns Hopkins Press.

Davis, K., M. Gold, and D. Makuc. 1981. Access to Health Care for the Poor: Does the Gap Remain? *Annual Review of Public Health* 2:159–82.

Davis, K., and R. Reynolds. 1976. The Impact of Medicare and Medicaid on Access to Medical Care. In *The*

Role of Health Insurance in the Health Services Sector, ed. R.N. Rosett, 391–435. New York: National Bureau of Economic Research.

Davis, K., and D. Rowland. 1983. Uninsured and Underserved: Inequities in Health Care in the United States. *Milbank Memorial Fund Quarterly/Health and Society* 61(2):149–76.

Davis, K., and C. Schoen. 1978. *Health and the War on Poverty: A Ten Year Appraisal.* Washington: Brookings Institution.

Davis, K., M. Lillie-Blanton, B. Lyons, F. Mullan, N. Powe, and D. Rowland. 1987. Health Care for Black Americans: The Public Sector Role. *Milbank Quarterly* 65(suppl. 1):213–47.

Dutton, D.B. 1985. Socioeconomic Status and Children's Health. *Medical Care* 23(2):142–56.

Ewbank, D.C. 1987. History of Black Mortality and Health before 1940. *Milbank Quarterly* 65(suppl. 1):100–28.

Farley, P.J. 1985. Who are the Underinsured? *Milbank Memorial Fund Quarterly/Health and Society* 63(3):476–503.

Feder, J., J. Hadley, and R. Mullner. 1984. Falling Through the Cracks: Poverty, Insurance Coverage, and Hospital Care for the Poor, 1980 and 1982. *Milbank Memorial Fund Quarterly/Health and Society* 62(4):544–66.

Fein, R. 1972. On Achieving Access and Equity in Health Care. *Milbank Memorial Fund Quarterly/Health and Society* 50(4,pt.2):157–90.

Freeman, H.E., R. Blendon, L. Aiken, S. Sudman, C. Mullinix, and C. Corey. 1987. Americans Report on Their Access to Health Care. *Health Affairs* 6(1):6–18.

Gibson, R.C., and J.S. Jackson. 1987. The Health, Physical Functioning, and Informal Supports of the Black Elderly. *Milbank Memorial Fund Quarterly/Health and Society* 65(suppl. 2):421–54.

Hadley, J., E.P. Steinberg, and J. Feder.

1991. Comparison of Uninsured and Privately Insured Hospital Patients. *Journal of the American Medical Association* 265(3):374–9.

Hershey, J., H. Luft, and J. Gianaris. 1975. Making Sense Out of Utilization Data. *Medical Care* 13(10):838–54.

Hulka, B., and J. Wheat. 1985. Patterns of Utilization: The Patient Perspective. *Medical Care* 23(5):438–60.

Kasper, J.D. 1986a. Children at Risk: The Uninsured and the Inadequately Insured. Paper presented at the annual meeting of the American Public Health Association, Maternal and Child Health Section, Las Vegas, September.

———. 1986b. Health Status and Utilization: Differences by Medicaid Coverage and Income. *Health Care Financing Review* 7(4):1–17.

———. 1987. The Importance of Type of Usual Source of Care for Children's Physician Access and Expenditures. *Medical Care* 25(5):386–98.

Kitagawa, E.M., and P.M. Hauser. 1973. *Differential Mortality in the United States: A Study in Socioeconomic Epidemiology.* Cambridge, Mass.: Harvard University Press.

Kleinman, J.C., M. Gold, and D. Makuc. 1981. Use of Ambulatory Medical Care by the Poor: Another Look at Equity. *Medical Care* 19(10):1011–36.

Kosa, J., and I.K. Zola. Eds. 1975. *Poverty and Health: A Sociological Analysis.* Cambridge, Mass.: Harvard University Press.

Kronenfeld, J.J. 1980. Sources of Ambulatory Care and Utilization Models. *Health Services Research* 15(1):3–20.

Link, C.R., S.H. Long, and R.F. Settle. 1982a. Access to Medical Care under Medicaid: Differentials by Race. *Journal of Health Politics, Policy, and Law* 7(2):345–65.

———. 1982b. Equity and the Utilization of Health Care Services by the Medicare Elderly. *Journal of Human Resources* 17:195–212.

Long, S.H. 1987. Public versus Employment-related Health Insurance: Experience and Implications for Black and Nonblack Americans. *Milbank Quarterly* 65(suppl. 1):200–12.

Long, S.H., and R.F. Settle. 1984. Medicare and the Disadvantaged Elderly: Objectives and Outcomes. *Milbank Memorial Fund Quarterly/Health and Society* 62(4):609–56.

Lurie, M., N.B. Ward, M.F. Shapiro, and R.H. Brook. 1984. Termination from Medi-Cal: Does It Affect Health? *New England Journal of Medicine* 311(7):480–4.

Manton, K.G., C.H. Patrick, and K.W. Johnson. 1987. Health Differentials between Blacks and Whites: Recent Trends in Mortality and Morbidity. *Milbank Quarterly* 65(suppl. 1):129–99.

Miller, S.M. 1987. Race in the Health of America. *Milbank Quarterly* 65 (suppl. 2):500–31.

Newacheck, P.W. 1988. Access to Ambulatory Care for Poor Persons. *Health Services Research* 23(3):401–19.

Orr, S.T., and C.A. Miller. 1981. Utilization of Health Services by Poor Children Since Advent of Medicaid. *Medical Care* 19(6):583–90.

Patrick, D.L., J. Stein, M. Porta, C.Q. Porter, and T.C. Ricketts. 1988. Poverty, Health Services, and Health Status in Rural America. *Milbank Quarterly* 66(1):105–36.

President's Commission for the Study of Ethical Problems in Medicine and Biomedical and Behavioral Research. 1983. *Securing Access to Health Care.* Washington.

Reynolds, R.A. 1976. Improving Access to Health Care Among the Poor: The Neighborhood Health Center Experience. *Milbank Memorial Fund Quarterly/Health and Society* 54(1):47–82.

Rogers, D.E., R.J. Blendon, and T.W. Moloney. 1982. Who Needs Medicaid? *New England Journal of Medicine* 307:13–18.

Rosenbach, M.L. 1985. *Insurance Coverage and Ambulatory Medical Care of Low-Income Children in the United States, 1980.* National Medical Care Utilization and Expenditure Survey, series C, analytical report no. 1, DHHS pub. no. 85-20401. Washington: National Center for Health Statistics.

Rosenbaum, S., D. Hughes, E. Butler, and D. Howard. 1988. Incantations in the Dark: Medicaid, Managed Care, and Maternity Care. *Milbank Quarterly* 66(4):661–93.

Rosenbaum, S., and K. Johnson. 1986. Providing Health Care for Low-Income Children: Reconciling Child Health Goals with Child Health Financing Realities. *Milbank Quarterly* 64(3):442–78.

Rowland, D. 1987. *Hospital Care for the Poor and Uninsured.* Doctoral dissertation, Johns Hopkins School of Hygiene and Public Health, Baltimore.

Rowland, D., and C.R. Gaus. 1982. Reducing Eligibility and Benefits: Current Policies and Alternatives. In *New Approaches to the Medicaid Crisis,* ed. R.J. Blendon and T.W. Moloney. New York: Frost and Sullivan Press.

Rowland, D., B. Lyons, and J. Edwards. 1988. Medicaid: Health Care for the Poor in the Reagan Era. *Annual Review of Public Health* 9:427–50.

Schlesinger, M. 1987. Paying the Price: Medical Care, Minorities, and the Newly Competitive Health Care System. *Milbank Quarterly* 65(suppl. 2):270–96.

Schlesinger, M., J. Bentkover, D. Blumenthal, R. Musacchio, and J. Willer. 1987. The Privatization of Health Care and Physicians' Perceptions of Access to Hospital Services. *Milbank Quarterly* 65(1):25–58.

Short, P.F., J.C. Cantor, and A.C. Monheit. 1988. The Dynamics of Medicaid Enrollment. *Inquiry* 25:504–16.

Somers, H.M., and A.R. Somers. 1972. Major Issues in National Health Insurance. *Milbank Memorial Fund*

Quarterly/Health and Society 50(2,pt. 1):177–210.

Spitz, B. 1982. A National Survey of Medicaid Case-Management Programs. *Health Affairs* 6(1):61–70.

Starfield, B. 1985a. *The Effectiveness of Medical Care: Validating Clinical Wisdom.* Baltimore, Md.: Johns Hopkins University Press.

———. 1985b. Motherhood and Apple Pie: The Effectiveness of Medical Care for Children. *Milbank Memorial Fund Quarterly/Health and Society* 63 (3):523–46.

Swartz, K. 1988. How the Overlap Between the Poverty and Medicaid Populations Changed Between 1979 and 1983, or Lessons for the Next Recession. *Journal of Human Resources* 24(2):319–30.

Thomas, J., and R. Penchansky. 1984. Relating Satisfaction with Access to Utilization of Services. *Medical Care* 22:553–68.

U.S. Department of Health and Human Services. 1980. *National Health Insurance Working Papers. Vol. I: Background Papers; Vol. II: Decision Papers for the Secretary.* Washington.

Vladeck, B. 1981. Equity, Access, and the Costs of Health Services. *Medical Care* 19(suppl.):69–80.

Walden, D., G. Wilensky, and J.D. Kasper. 1985. *Changes in Health Insurance Status: Full-Year and Part-Year Coverage.* National Medical Care Expenditure Survey, data preview no. 21. Rockville, Md.: National Center for Health Services Research.

Wan, T.T. 1982. Use of Health Services by the Elderly in Low-Income Communities. *Milbank Memorial Fund Quarterly/Health and Society* 60(1): 82–107.

Ware, J.E., Jr., R.H. Brook, W.H. Rogers et al. 1986. Comparison of Health Outcomes at a Health Maintenance Organisation with Those of Fee-For-Service Care. *Lancet* 1:1017–22.

White, K.L. 1972. Health Care Arrangements in the United States: A.D. 1972. *Milbank Memorial Fund Quarterly/Health and Society* 50(4,pt.2): 17–39.

Wolfe, B.L. 1980. Children's Utilization of Medical Care. *Medical Care* 18(12): 1196–1207.

Wolinsky, F.D., B.E. Aguirre, L.J. Fanns et al. 1989. Ethnic Differences in the Demand for Physician and Hospital Utilization among Older Adults in Major American Cities: Conspicuous Evidence of Considerable Inequalities. *Milbank Quarterly* 67(3–4):412–49.

Zwick, D.I. 1972. Some Accomplishments and Findings of Neighborhood Health Centers. *Milbank Memorial Fund Quarterly/Health and Society* 50(40,pt.1):387–416.

Basic health *care assures a person the preventive and curative measures generally available to permit full functioning during a normal life expectancy.*
— Charles Fried

Robert J. Blendon / Linda H. Aiken / Howard E. Freeman /
Christopher R. Corey

Access to Medical Care
for Black and White
Americans: A Matter
of Continuing Concern

Since the 1960s, access to medical care for black Americans has improved significantly. In 1963, the proportion of blacks who saw a physician was 18% lower than for whites; by 1982 this gap had been almost eliminated.[1] In addition, black-white differences in the use of virtually all types of health services also had narrowed during this time. For example, the proportion of pregnant black women who received prenatal care during the first three months of pregnancy increased from 42% in 1969 to 62% in 1985.[2]

These improvements in access to medical care for blacks were accompanied by improved health outcomes.[3] Infant mortality in two decades declined by over 50%, and the difference between white and black life expectancy rates narrowed from 7.4 years in 1960 to 5.8 years in 1985.[2]

Other researchers have pointed out, however, that the gains during the past two decades should not lead to overstating the progress made in use of health care and the burdens of death and illness of blacks compared with whites. Blacks, on the average, are in poorer health than whites, which may be a consequence of a life-course deficit in access to medical care as well as a generally lower level of living, as reflected by differences

---

Robert J. Blendon, Sc.D., is Professor and Chair, Department of Health Policy and Management at the Harvard School of Public Health, Boston.

Linda H. Aiken, Ph.D., is Trustee Professor of Nursing, Professor of Sociology, Director of the Center for Health Services and Policy Research, and Associate Director of the Leonard Davis Institute of Health Economics at the University of Pennsylvania, Philadelphia.

Howard E. Freeman, Ph.D., was Professor of Sociology, University of California, Los Angeles.

Christopher R. Corey is a doctoral student at the University of California, Los Angeles.

Abridged from Blendon, R.J., Aiken, L.H., Freeman, H.E., and Corey, C.R. (1989). Access to medical care for black and white Americans. *JAMA* 261:278–281. Copyright 1989, American Medical Association. Used with permission.

in average incomes and other indicators of socioeconomic status. Consequently, if there were real parity in access to medical care between the two racial groups, there would be a substantially higher use of health services on the average among black Americans.[4] Similarly, as reported by the Department of Health and Human Services' Secretary's Task Force on Black and Minority Health, black Americans continue to have a 1½ times higher death rate than whites of the same age, and the infant mortality rate for blacks is twice that of whites.[2,5]

Given this persistent disparity between white and black health, it is of considerable concern that a 1986 national survey finds a significant deficit remains in access to health care among blacks, compared with white Americans. The survey documents the existence of substantial unmet medical needs among black Americans.

METHODS

The data reported in this article come from a national telephone survey conducted in 1986.[6] Each respondent was interviewed for approximately 25 minutes about various aspects of access to medical care, including the availability of a regular source of care, the frequency of ambulatory visits, the presence of serious medical conditions, problems in paying for health services, and reports about the care received during his or her last ambulatory visit.

The survey consisted of interviews with 10,130 persons living in the continental United States. Some 76% of the persons selected for interviews cooperated. This completion rate compares favorably with other rates obtained in the health care field. People with chronic and serious illness were oversampled; the study group was weighted, however, so that the findings represent the U.S. population. Proxy interviews with an adult, generally a parent, were conducted to obtain information about children under 17 years of age. Also, in cases where the respondent was too sick or otherwise unable to be interviewed, proxy interviews with another household member were obtained. (Some of the figures reported differ from those obtained by the National Health Survey. A number of methodological differences between the surveys explain the differences in findings. National Health Survey information is collected in face-to-face interviews compared with telephone interviews in this survey; another difference is that proxy information is collected about all household members in the National Health Survey, while the information in this survey is usually obtained from the individual household member.)

Blacks constituted 12.2% of the weighted sample, approximately the percentage that they represent in the U.S. noninstitutionalized population. About one fourth of the study group are children; some 12% are 65 years of age or older. Differences in the black–white age distributions were examined when required in the analysis.

In this analysis of the progress of black Americans in achieving equitable access to care, the rates at which blacks and whites actually use health services are compared with one another. The approach of comparing the use of medical care by different populations to assess access to health services goes back to the landmark study of barriers to health care undertaken by the Committee on the Costs of Medical Care in 1932.[7] As recently as 1983, this approach was recommended by the President's Commission for the Study of Ethical Problems in Medicine and Behavioral Science Research as a useful and valid way to evaluate the impact of U.S. health care policies.[8]

This frequently used approach to assessing access to care is based on the assumption that, in the absence of barriers to care, use of health services among population groups primarily is a function of the incidence and prevalence of illness in population groups. Of course, social and cultural differences among population groups also are related to health care behavior. However, the volume of care received by low-income populations is highly sensitive both to the presence of financial barriers to health care and to the availability of medical resources in the community.[9,10] Although one would not expect all populations with similar health problems to use health services at identical rates, wide disparities between populations should be a cause for public concern.

This study relies on interviewees' self-reported health status as the principal measure of the need for health services. Prior studies have shown that health status is a sensitive indicator of the actual need for medical care.[11–13] Individuals' reports of their health status have been shown to be good predictors of their physical health, including the presence of chronic conditions and disabilities, the number of specific health problems and symptoms, sensory impairment and immobility, and limitations on normal activities due to illness. Thus, earlier studies justify the use of interviewees' perceptions of their health as an indicator of the need for medical care of different aggregates in the population.

RESULTS

In general, the 1986 survey found blacks worse off than whites in terms of access to physician care. As reported in table 1, blacks have a significantly higher rate than whites of not seeing a physician within a one-year period. The average annual number of physician visits among blacks compared with whites also is considerably lower (3.4 per year compared with 4.4). The proportion of blacks hospitalized one or more times during the year also is lower, although this difference is not statistically significant.

TABLE 1   Ambulatory and Hospital Experience in 1986

Variable	White	Black	P <
% Without ambulatory visit in year	31.7	37.2	.01
Mean number of ambulatory visits in year	4.4	3.4	.01
% Hospitalized in year	6.9	6.3	NS

The lower rate of visits to physicians by blacks than whites clearly is of major concern, given the evidence that serious illness is much more common among blacks than whites.[5,6] Moreover, . . . the lower access to health care of blacks compared with whites [has been documented] even when health status is taken into account. Both among persons reporting they are in good or excellent health and among those in fair or poor health, there are significantly more blacks than whites who have not seen a physician in a year. Likewise, there are significant differences in average number of visits, and this is the case particularly among persons in fair or poor health (10.1 visits compared with 6.9). The gap in the use of ambulatory services between blacks and whites is of particular concern because of the evidence that blacks have considerably higher rates of mortality and morbidity than whites.[2]

A key issue, of course, is whether these differences are explainable by the well-documented income differential between blacks and whites in the United States or the fact that blacks on average are younger than the white population. To examine this issue, multiple regression analyses were undertaken to assess whether differences in mean number of visits and in having at least one provider visit in a year are related to ethnicity over and above income level and other sociodemographic characteristics. Even after taking into account persons' income, health status, age, sex, and whether they had one or more chronic or serious illnesses, blacks have a statistically significantly lower mean number of annual ambulatory visits and are less likely to have seen a physician in a year.

The 1986 survey clearly establishes that there is significant underuse of medical care by black Americans. . . . One in 11 blacks reported not receiving health care for economic reasons compared with 1 in 20 whites. Likewise, 1 in 4 blacks who reported they had 1 of 10 chronic or serious illnesses about which they were specifically questioned did not have an ambulatory visit in the year preceding the survey, compared with 1 in 6 white persons surveyed. Among persons reporting they had hypertension, 30% of blacks had not had an annual blood pressure check compared with 19% of whites.

Moreover, the differences between whites and blacks in use of health services also extend to dental care. Some 50% of blacks, compared with 36% of whites, received no dental care in the year prior to the survey.

To understand the black-white differences in access to care, over and above the direct effects of poverty, a number of measures that reflect differences in health care arrangements were examined. In part, the black-white differences on these measures reflect the indirect consequences of economic level of living. In part, however, our analysis suggests more general, ethnic-related differences in health care arrangements and lifestyle.

For example, . . . not only are blacks less likely to have *any* insurance coverage, but they are considerably less likely to be covered by a private insurance carrier (85.1% compared with 72.5%). Moreover, on a recently developed measure of the breadth and generosity of states' Medicaid programs, blacks are significantly more likely to reside in states with the least generous programs, which tend to be the Southern and Southwestern states, many of which have a preponderance of black residents.[14]

Similarly, almost half of the blacks surveyed used hospital clinics, emergency departments, community health centers, or other organized settings for their last visit (if they had a visit in the past year) compared with only slightly more than one fourth of whites. Of note is that blacks are significantly more likely than whites to prefer to go to a different provider for their health care than they saw at their last visit.

Blacks are more likely than whites to live in one-adult households, which may impede accessing medical care (22.9% compared with 13.5%). Finally, although the percentages are small for both whites and blacks, three times as many blacks as whites report problems getting to their providers.

The undersupply of black physicians and of physicians in general in minority communities also may result in reduced opportunities for medical care. Studies by the Public Health Service on the availability of physicians in minority communities showed that many counties with dense minority populations have substantially lower ratios of health professionals than similar communities with primarily white populations.[2]

The survey did not include measures that directly reflect black-white cultural differences that might explain the access findings reported. However, the differences in health care arrangements just discussed are persistent features of the sociocultural milieux of the two racial groups. Consequently, it is a reasonable conjecture that underlying some of our findings are unmeasured sociocultural differences between blacks and whites that are associated with the findings on access to care.

Of course, the number of visits people make to physicians does not tell us all that we wish to know about medical care received by a population. The survey sought to go beyond the narrow framework of counting physician visits by exploring patients' perceptions about the care received. . . . Blacks were more likely than whites to report that during their last visit their physician did not inquire sufficiently about pain, did not tell them how long it would take for prescribed medicine to work, did not explain the seriousness of the illness or injury, and did not discuss test or examination findings.

An interesting exception was that blacks were *less* likely to report that their doctor failed to discuss preventive care with them (80.6% compared with 67.7%). However, *among* persons hospitalized one or more times, over twice as many blacks as whites (18.9% compared with 7.2%) reported that they believed their last hospitalization was for too short a time. On two items . . . , whether physicians explained future health changes *or* explained the cause of the illness, there are no significant differences between blacks and whites.

As a generalization, it appears that not only are there differences in access, but the care provided differs for blacks and whites along a number of dimensions.

Moreover, blacks are less satisfied with the care received both while hospitalized and during ambulatory visits. . . . Fewer than three-fifths of blacks are completely satisfied with care provided during their last hospitalization, compared with over three-fourths of whites. The differential is less for ambulatory visits but in the same direction and statistically significant. In addition, blacks are more likely than whites to have had to wait for more than half an hour before seeing a physician at their last ambulatory visit.

CONCLUSIONS

In 1983, one of the authors of this article (R.J.B.) wrote in *JAMA* that although the country had just passed through a period in which the availability of medical care for much of the population had been dramatically improved, growing restrictions on public spending for health care seemed inevitable in the future. Thus, there was a need to independently monitor the impact of these restrictions on the care available to patients, and to advise those who make decisions if the health of the nation's citizens appeared to be adversely affected by changes in the organization and financing of medical care.[15]

This study reports disturbing trends. There continues to be a lack of parity in access to health care, and a consequent excess of unmet medical needs for blacks compared with whites. The difficult economic circumstances of many black families clearly contribute to the lack of access to health services. However, the findings suggest that even blacks above the poverty line have less access to medical care than their white counterparts. Despite progress during the past two decades, the nation still has a long way to go in achieving equitable access to health care for all its citizens.

382   *Access to Medical Care for Americans*

REFERENCES

1. *Special Report: Updated Report on Access to Health Care for the American People.* Princeton, NJ, Robert Wood Johnson Foundation, 1983.

2. National Center for Health Statistics: *Health, United States, 1987,* DHHS publication (PHS) 88-1232. Dept of Health and Human Services, 1987.

3. Hadley J: *More Medical Care, Better Health?* Washington, DC, Urban Institute Press, 1982.

4. Kleinman JC, Gold M, Makuc D: Use of ambulatory medical care by the poor. Another look at equity. *Med Care* 1981;19:1011–1028.

5. *Report of the Secretary's Task Force on Black and Minority Health.* Dept of Health and Human Services, August 1985.

6. Freeman HE, Blendon RJ, Aiken LH, et al: Americans report on their access to care. *Health Aff* 1987;6:6–18.

7. Committee on the Costs of Medical Care: *Medical Care for the American People.* New York, Arno Press, 1972.

8. *Securing Access to Health Care.* President's Commission for the Study of Ethical Problems in Medicine

and Biomedical and Behavioral Research, 1983.

9. Blendon RJ, Aiken LH, Freeman HE, et al: Uncompensated care by hospitals or public insurance for the poor. *N Engl J Med* 1986;314:1160–1163.

10. Rogers DE, Blendon RJ, Moloney TW: Who needs Medicaid? *N Engl J Med* 1982;307:13–18.

11. Davies AR, Ware JE: *Measuring Health Perceptions in the Health Insurance Experiment.* Santa Monica, Calif, RAND Corp, 1981.

12. Maddox G, Douglass E: Self-assessment of health: A longitudinal study of elderly subjects. *J Health Soc Behav* 1983;14:87–93.

13. Yergan J, LoGerfo J, Shortell S, et al: Health status as a measure of need for medical care: A critique. *Med Care* 1981;19(suppl 12):57–68.

14. Erdman K, Wolfe S: *Poor Health Care for Poor Americans: A Ranking of State Medicaid Programs.* Washington, DC, Public Citizen Health Research Group, 1987.

15. Blendon RJ, Rogers DE: Cutting medical care costs: *Primum non nocere. JAMA* 1983;250:1880–1885.

Health: *A state of complete physical, mental and social well-being and not merely the absence of disease or infirmity.*
— World Health Organization

10

Women's Health

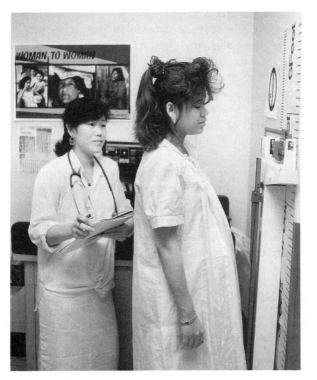

The Society for the Advancement of Women's
Health Research

Towards a Women's Health
Research Agenda

On April 23, 1991, the Society for the Advancement of Women's Health Research questioned the scientific and medical community regarding its priorities for the health needs of American women. Representatives of 25 medical specialities and professional organizations . . . identified the following topics of concern among all of the medical specialties:

- The alarming lack of information on a variety of diseases which primarily afflict women.
- The failure to include women in research study populations; and when women are included in research, the lack of analysis by gender, age, race, and socioeconomic factors.
- The failure to consider modulating factors such as endogenous or exogenous sex hormones, different life stages, lifestyles, or psychosocial issues when designing treatment regimens.
- The dearth of knowledge about the pharmacokinetics of drugs in women and the impact of age and hormonal status on drug metabolism.
- The underrepresentation of women professionals in both senior research and policy-making positions across the medical specialities.
- The importance of longitudinal studies to understand changes that occur with different life stages.
- The acknowledgment that the low self-esteem of many women, occurring as a result of the socialization process that begins during

The Society for the Advancement of Women's Health Research, established in 1990 in Washington, D.C., gathers, analyzes, and disseminates information about women's health research and conducts Scientific Advisory Meetings, Corporate Advisory Councils, and Roundtable Discussions with leaders of women's organizations, community-based women consumer groups, and health providers.

Abridged from The Society for the Advancement of Women's Health Research. (1991). *Towards a Women's Health Research Agenda: Findings of the Scientific Advisory Meeting*, edited by S. Blumenthal and E. Reavon. Washington, DC: The Society for the Advancement of Women's Health Research. Used with permission.

childhood and adolescence and continues into maturity, profoundly affects choices throughout a woman's life.

. . . This report reflects the issues discussed at the meeting and should not be viewed as a comprehensive or definitive women's health agenda. For the purposes of this report, topics are classified as either biomedical or psychosocial. It was understood by the participants, however, that when addressing women's health it is crucial to consider interactions between the biological, psychological, and social issues that impact on medical problems. When designing research protocols for any particular health issue, it is critical that behavioral factors, age, family, work roles, and gender attitudes, as well as race and class, be considered. The complexity of these interactions is enormous. However, since "health" is defined by all these variables in any given individual or population, we must continually strive toward this goal.

BIOMEDICAL HEALTH ISSUES

Cardiovascular Disease in Women

Heart disease is the leading cause of death for both men and women in the United States. In 1988, it was responsible for 765,000 deaths overall, 49% of which occurred in women. Its most common form, coronary heart disease (CHD), accounted for 245,000 deaths among women. CHD is predominantly a disease of older women, particularly after menopause. As the U.S. population ages, more women than men will live into old age (at 65, the ratio of women to men is 60:40; at 85, the ratio is 75:25). Thus, the burden of heart disease in terms of illness and health care costs is particularly significant for women.

Despite these facts, decisions regarding prevention, diagnosis, risk stratification, medical and surgical therapies, and prognosis of coronary heart disease are often derived from studies conducted predominantly or exclusively in middle-aged men. Presumably this is due to the mistaken belief that the 10–15 year lag in the development of CHD morbidity and mortality in women, as compared to men, means that women are not significantly affected by CHD. Women themselves are not aware of this risk for CHD because until recently the emphasis has been on the need for women to protect their husbands, brothers, and sons from CHD.

More information on women and heart disease is urgently needed and several critical areas for future research were identified.

- **Delayed onset of coronary artery disease in women.** Does the delayed onset of CHD in women relate to the early protective effects of the female sex hormones (estrogens and progestins)? Is this effect on the coronary arteries themselves, for example, or their vasoactivity or lipid disposal mechanisms?

Is the presumed hormonal protective effect related to different levels of circulating lipids (total cholesterol or triglycerides) or specific subpopulations of circulating lipoproteins (HDL and LDL) between men and women? Are the protective effects in young women due to heightened functions of other tissues of the body, for example, in the use of circulating lipids for production of high levels of hormones like estrogens and progestins?

- **Menopause and heart disease.** There is a large and growing body of literature which suggests that estrogen therapy is beneficial in preventing cardiovascular disease in women. A recent meta-analysis of studies on estrogen use and cardiovascular disease (CVD) reports that estrogen users have a 50% reduction in the occurrence of CVD as compared to nonusers. However, most of the studies were conducted in women using unopposed estrogen (estrogen without a progestin). This is an important issue since there is now strong evidence that estrogens protect against CVD by beneficially altering HDL-cholesterol levels. Progestin use, however, can negate the beneficial effects of estrogen on HDL cholesterol, and it is possible that the currently popular use of combined estrogen-progestin therapy may have a diminished protective effect, or no protective effect, on CVD occurrence. This issue requires further clarification.

- **Prognosis for women with CHD.** Studies have shown that women with myocardial infarctions have poorer outcomes than men. Does this relate to the older age of onset of CHD in women, or the fact that detection was delayed due to the misperception that women are not prone to CVD? Or are there other factors to consider, such as lack of information on proper drug therapy in women, especially older women?

- **Identification of CVD-risk factors unique to women.** More information is needed on the impact of age, pregnancy, supplemental hormone use, and stress (e.g., caregiver stress, economic burdens, and/or multiple life roles often experienced by women) on the prevalence of CVD. Since the age of onset of CVD in women is delayed as compared to men (and thus a major concern of the postmenopausal or older woman), what is the impact of diet, obesity, exercise, smoking, type II diabetes, and other age-related diseases, and how do these factors relate to age-associated or stress-associated CVD prevalence, treatment, and outcome?

- **The impact of hypertension.** Hypertension is more common in women than men, and carries a 2–3 fold increased risk of stroke, other cardiovascular disease, and death. Are there gender differences in the occurrence of isolated systolic hypertension? Are there gender differences in the efficacy and side effects of recommended treatments? What is the effect of pregnancy on recommended therapies? Are there significant hormonal-antihypertensive drug interactions?

- **Pregnancy and heart disease.** Methods need to be identified to prevent peripartum cardiomyopathy and to manage patients requiring anticoagulation during pregnancy. Strategies for pharmacologic testing must be found to remove the pregnant woman from the ranks of the medically disadvantaged.

Cancer in Women

Cancer is the second leading cause of death among women in the United States. This year alone, 250,000 women are expected to die from: lung cancer (51,000), breast cancer (45,000), colon cancer (30,500), ovarian cancer (12,500), uterine cancer (5,500), and others. The numbers are increasing each year for both breast cancer and lung cancer. Research is urgently needed to define the etiology, risk factors, detection, and effective treatment therapies for these diseases in an effort to reverse these frightening statistics.

Breast Cancer. Of the cancers afflicting women, breast cancer has the highest frequency and is responsible for 32% of all cancers with an estimated 175,000 new diagnoses [in 1991]. The incidence of breast cancer in the United States has risen 32% since 1982. Although the incidence of breast cancer is higher among Caucasian women, African-American women, once diagnosed, have less favorable outcomes. One in every 9 women will develop breast cancer at some point in her life. About 80% of women with breast cancer are over the age of 50; the median age for diagnosis is 63.

Risk factors, apart from increasing age, appear to include a family history of breast cancer in first-degree relatives, long-term supplemental sex hormone therapy (especially estrogen), preexisting benign fibrocystic disease, and may also include obesity, silicone implants, dietary fats, and caffeine. However, it is a striking fact that 70% of women newly diagnosed with breast cancer have none of these risk factors: therefore every woman is at risk for this disease.

There is growing evidence that long-term estrogen replacement therapy (ERT) after menopause increases risk. A recent meta-analysis of ERT shows breast cancer risk after menopause increased significantly with duration of estrogen use, estimated at approximately 30% after 15 years of estrogen use. When extrapolated to 3 million women in the United States, this translates to 4,700 new cases and 1,500 breast cancer deaths per year due to estrogen use. These numbers increase when specific risk factors (e.g., family history) are considered. Perhaps even more threatening is the fact that many women who have taken estrogen-containing contraceptives for years (since the introduction of oral contraceptives in the early sixties), are now likely to be exposed to postmenopausal hormones as well. The impact of 30 years of hormone-based contraception and 10–15 years of post-menopausal supplemental hormones on the incidence of breast cancer is simply unknown. Recommendations for future breast cancer research include:

- **Basic science research.** Research at the cellular and molecular level must continue to identify mechanisms of tumor development and the process by which tumor dissemination occurs. Current work that seeks to define the primary and interrelationships between specific DNA sites, oncogenes, tumor promoter and suppressor factors, growth and metastatic factors, hormones, antihormones, and various protein receptors must go forward. More information is needed on the mechanism(s) of tumor formation and metastases to permit the design of appropriate treatments to combat these processes.

- **Risk factors.** The impact of certain risk factors on the development of breast cancer must be studied. To what extent do innate (i.e., nonalterable) factors such as age, genetic propensities, and race modify the frequency or course of the disease, and to what extent do acquired (i.e., alterable) factors such as supplemental hormone use, obesity, alcohol, caffeine, and diet affect incidence? Well-planned, long-term clinical trials evaluating these and other risk factors need to be continued.

- **Imaging technology.** To aid in breast cancer detection, there is an urgent need for improved imaging technologies, especially as used in tumor detection in the dense breast (younger women), and in distinguishing between benign disease and malignancy. It is critical to develop national standards for mammography across the country and to develop appropriate guidelines for screening that take into consideration age and various risk factors. Despite current guidelines for mammography, only 30% of women follow these recommendations. Behavioral research is needed to better understand the fears and barriers to women obtaining mammography and to develop behavior-changing strategies targeted at high-risk groups.

- **Self Breast Examination (SBE).** Current figures show that 60% of all breast cancers are discovered by women themselves. Yet the value of SBE has been questioned in terms of its accuracy and its impact on the mental health of women who are constantly on the alert for disaster. Clearly, the benefits of SBE must be determined, the techniques of self-examination improved, and educational methods must be developed to deal with the associated emotional stress of SBE. There is an obvious need for more information on the natural history of breast tissue and its developmental relationship to benign fibrocystic disease and malignancy.

Breast cancers take many years to grow. It has been suggested that SBE techniques should be taught to adolescent girls who will become familiar with their cyclic changes and set baselines for their own life stages. We must learn how to inform young women and how to identify the high-risk groups among them.

Other Cancers.   Other major cancers that affect women are primarily age-related, and in some cases, incidence is also affected by specific risk factors. **Lung cancer,** for example, has now surpassed breast cancer as the major cancer killer of women. The death rate due to lung cancer has risen more than 100% since the early 1970s and virtually all the increase is correlated with increased rates of smoking by women. Though the prevalence of male smoking has dropped markedly in recent years, female smoking rates have not. An estimated 33% of women continue to smoke, and smoking among teenage girls is reportedly on the rise. Factors surrounding this gender-related resistance to stopping smoking must be identified and reversed.

Smoking prevention efforts have not focused on women because traditionally women have not been perceived as vulnerable to lung cancer, as with cardiovascular disease. Advertising directed at women, and relevant psychosocial factors (such as the link between cigarette smoking and weight loss) need to be examined.

The incidence of **uterine cancer** is four times higher in postmenopausal women on unopposed ERT than in women on combined estrogen and progestin therapies. Yet, the protective effect of estrogens on CVD may be negated if progestins are also used, and without ERT, the risk for osteoporosis increases. The risks involved increase with the number of years a woman is on ERT following menopause. Currently, a woman must weigh these grim factors in choosing a treatment regimen to follow. More research is clearly necessary to provide menopausal women with acute relief of perimenopausal symptoms, and at the same time provide her with a safe long-term regimen that will have beneficial effects on her bones, heart, uterus, and breasts. Well-designed, long-term trials evaluating nonhormonal-based drugs in combination with exercise programs (to minimize bone loss) and diet programs (to minimize CVD) should be considered.

The cure rate for **cervical cancer,** if detected early, nears 100%. The PAP test has led to a 50% drop in deaths from cervical cancer. Despite this, African-American women continue to die from cervical cancer at disproportionate rates and similar disparities are found in Hispanic, Asian, and Arab women. The inequities are linked to economic and cultural factors. The most significant gap in the research base is the lack of understanding of how to make Pap test technology accessible and acceptable to all women. Recommendations include: 1) identifying programs that target underserved populations and incorporating strategies in those programs to surmount cultural and economic barriers to routine screening, 2) exploring the impact of incentive programs in increasing equitable delivery of basic screening.

Over the previous 25 years there has been a growing incidence of **malignant melanoma.** There will be 32,000 new cases in 1991, 25% will be in people aged 39 or younger. Deaths this year are expected to be 6,500. By the year 2000, the lifetime risk of developing melanoma will be 1 in 90. On the whole, the prognosis for women is somewhat better than for men. Although it has been suspected that this advantage is due to women presenting earlier for medical treatment, this theory has not been borne out in studies. It is accepted that exposure to sunlight, particularly during childhood, is an important risk factor in the induction of this cancer. Prevention strategies are needed to teach and underscore the importance of proper protection against the sun's rays.

Other Diseases Affecting Women

Osteoporosis.   Osteoporosis affects one-third to one-half of all post-menopausal women. Each year there are over 1.5 million fractures of the hip, vertebrae, wrist, and other bones due to osteoporosis. The disease causes pain, deformity, and loss of independence, and leads to approximately 50,000 deaths a year. More research is needed to determine the impact of lifelong exercise and to find other nonhormonal methods to reduce bone loss. It is necessary to understand how estrogen works to maintain bone mass and to assess the benefits and problems associated with long-term ERT. Such studies must include the influence of age, race, body size, menopausal status, calcium intake, hormonal therapy, diet, smoking, and exercise.

AIDS.   The Centers for Disease Control has reported that the risk to women of contracting HIV is increasing so rapidly that it is expected to be the major cause of death among women by the next decade. AIDS is currently the primary killer of women during their reproductive years in New York City.

There appear to be a number of differences in the way AIDS affects men and women. For example, HIV-infected women are rarely afflicted with Kaposi's sarcoma. Studies also suggest that women with AIDS die sooner after diagnosis than men with AIDS. In addition, HIV-infected women die from cancers more rapidly and at a younger age than women without HIV infection. More research is critically needed on the natural history of HIV infection in women, as well as responses to therapies. Specific gynecologic considerations must be given to pregnancy, menstrual, and hormonal effects and sequelae, sexually transmitted diseases, fertility, cervical dysplasia, herpes simplex virus, and human papilloma virus infection. Moreover, psychological responses and neuropsychiatric sequelae to HIV infection in women must be explored. Behavioral strategies targeted to various high-risk groups of women to prevent the further spread of HIV infection are urgently needed.

In 1989, approximately 6,000 women infected with HIV gave birth in the United States. At the time of delivery, the risk of a child acquiring HIV infection from its mother is between 20–40%. Research is needed on mechanisms of maternal protection against infection of the fetus. Additionally, knowledge is needed to determine why 60–80% of mothers with HIV infections do not transmit the virus to their infants.

Gastrointestinal Diseases. Diseases of the gastrointestinal tract are the most common cause of days missed from work among the working population. Though many of these disorders are common in women, clinical investigations have been carried out mostly in men. Poorly understood diseases that occur more frequently in women include biliary tract diseases, gastrointestinal motility disorders, and alcoholic liver disease.

Gallstones occur earlier in women, and women continue to have a greater prevalence of stones throughout life. Biliary dyskinesia occurs more often in women. Two syndromes, irritable bowel syndrome and gastroparesis (delayed gastric emptying) are three times more common in women than men. Chronic constipation, which results in up to 2.5 million physician visits per year, is poorly studied, often multifactorial, and is commonly associated with previous obstetrical or gynecologic trauma. At one time many of these diseases were thought to be "functional"; more recent studies suggest that pathophysiologic factors are involved.

Women are more susceptible to the hepatotoxic effects of alcohol than are men. They develop liver disease after a shorter period of drinking and from drinking less than do their male counterparts. Cirrhosis occurs twice as frequently in women and African-American women are even more susceptible than Caucasian women. Safe levels of alcohol consumption for women should be recognized as approximately one-third that for men. The cause of this increased susceptibility is not known although some studies show that women possess lower levels of the enzyme alcohol dehydrogenase than men. More research is required on this subject.

Certain liver disorders are unique to pregnancy. Preeclampsia complicates up to 10% of pregnancies in Caucasian women and up to 20% in African-American women; in severe cases, the liver is affected.

Immunologic Disease.   Lupus erythematosus is a chronic autoimmune disease characterized by inflammation of the skin, joints, kidneys, central nervous system, heart, and lungs, affecting over 50,000 persons in the United States. The onset of the disease occurs earlier in women; 90% of lupus patients are women between the ages of 15 and 45. African Americans comprise 60% of lupus patients; those with systemic lupus erythematosus have a higher incidence of disfiguring scarring skin lesions, lung and kidney disease. Survival among African-American patients appears to be reduced compared to Caucasian patients. Children born to women with this disease are at risk for cardiac abnormalities.

Over the past three decades research has furthered understanding of the treatment of lupus. It is clear that early identification of individuals with lupus erythematosus permits treatment intervention against irreversible or life-threatening complications. Research efforts must continue in order to discover the cause of the disease, and research is also necessary to improve public awareness and access to therapy for all patients.

Urologic Disorders.   Urinary incontinence is a symptom of various conditions rather than a disease itself. It affects as many as three to four million older women. Twice as many women as men are at risk. Approximately 50% of nursing home residents are incontinent. Estimates for the total economic burden of urinary incontinence range from $1.8 to $8.0 billion a year.

The most common form of incontinence among young or middle-aged women is stress incontinence resulting in urine leakage due to a loss of normal pelvic support of the sphincter area. Stress incontinence occurs during sneezing, coughing, physical exertion, or any activity that increases intra-abdominal pressure. In the elderly, detrusor instability is even more common.

The research goals include better understanding of the mechanisms responsible for incontinence, and assessment of the predisposing factors such as disease, injury, and aging. It is hoped that research can lead to prevention strategies and training programs to lessen the incidence of this disorder.

In 1985, urinary tract infections were the number one urologic disorder requiring visits to physicians. Urinary tract infections are more common in females than in males. In children they are second in frequency only to infections of the respiratory tract. Strategies for research include the search for etiology, for more accurate, simpler and less expensive methods of detection, and for methods to prevent infection accompanying long-term indwelling bladder catheters.

Reproductive Health

Reproductive health issues cover the span of a woman's life beginning with awareness of sexuality, menstruation, conception (and contraception), pregnancies (including pregnancy loss or infertility), postpartum problems, menopause, and finally postmenopausal disorders. Each stage is associated with particular medical, ethical, psychological, social, economic, and often political issues that can shape the course of a woman's life. Yet, there has been a dearth of research on these issues. An in-depth examination of psychosocial-medical factors affecting reproductive health across the life span is urgently needed.

At the Scientific Advisory Meeting, reproductive issues relating to teenagers received special attention. Adolescents in the United States become sexually active at about the same age and at the same rate as those in Canada, Sweden, and other industrialized nations, but U.S. teens lead the industrialized world in pregnancies. For the most part these are unintended pregnancies resulting from a lack of contraception, lack of access to appropriate support and informational systems, denial of sexual activity, lack of skills in understanding and handling interpersonal relationships, lack of self-esteem, or hopelessness about other life options. These unintended pregnancies are disproportionately high among poor young women and reflect ambivalent societal attitudes toward sexuality in this country. Our society must concern itself with both the prevention and the outcome of these pregnancies. First, as a society we need to recognize the extent of the problem and its costs in terms of human suffering and welfare dollars. More contraceptive choices must become available for teens. Behavioral research is necessary in order to develop strategies to help teens modify high-risk sexual behavior, to assist them in accepting, preparing for, and taking responsibility for their sexuality, and to learn the best methods of information access.

Pharmacology

Relatively few studies have addressed the issue of gender differences in drug metabolism. Among the many questions that remain unanswered are the following: Do women, as a result of their unique physiology, absorb and or metabolize certain drugs (e.g., psychotropic drugs, cardiac medications) differently from men? How do the pharmacokinetics and pharmacodynamics of a drug change over time as a woman ages? What are the effects of a woman's cyclical hormonal phase and menstrual status and the use of exogenous hormones such as oral contraceptives or estrogen replacement therapy on drug metabolism and side effects? How can clinical trials be carried out during pregnancy? What other factors should be considered when medications are prescribed to women?

PSYCHOSOCIAL ISSUES

Violence Against Women

Of the many issues discussed at the Scientific Advisory Meeting, violence against women was underscored as a critical public health problem across all disciplines. Injury is the outcome of violence, and it is injury to women that places violence on the women's health research agenda.

The most frequent reason women present in emergency rooms today has to do with battering. Women are as likely to be injured by violence as by cancer. Every 15 seconds a woman in the United States is beaten in her home and every day at least four women are killed by their batterers. It is estimated that more than three million physical assaults on women occur each year. Health professionals often do not screen for violence in their practices so these figures may, in fact, be understated. As one participant stated "in this country, women's thought processes, freedom of movement, job choices, social-marital relationships, and general levels of anxiety are influenced by their efforts to avoid violence. We have come to view violence as normal in our lives, and we must change that."

Research must be an integral part of that change, and yet it has been said that more research is done on dog bites to the face than on psychiatric and medical problems resulting from battering. Clearly solutions to the problem require total community efforts. Scientific research is needed to determine effective processes that women can use to extricate themselves from abusive relationships or from potentially dangerous situations.

Research is also needed on women's responses to battering, and the impact that this may have on child abuse. Similarly, there is a need to determine whether low self-esteem of women impacts their willingness to accept abuse and whether early training experiences for girls will help develop their self-esteem, regard for their bodies, and recognition of potentially abusive situations. Would education on the consequences of abuse affect attitudes and behavior? Do existing social and legal policies in this country help shape attitudes toward women that lead to violence?

Depression

Depressive disorders are disabling illnesses affecting 10 million Americans. One in four women will experience a major form of depression at some time in her life. The interaction of negative life experiences (e.g., medical problems, social and cultural pressures, recent losses, low self-esteem, poverty) with underlying genetic vulnerability contributes to the onset of this disorder.

Women's risk for depression exceeds that of men by a ratio of 2:1. There are currently at least seven million women in the United States with diagnosable depression, and most go untreated. Some 15% commit suicide each year. The economic toll is staggering; all mental illnesses combined cost the United States $129 billion each year and depression represents a large portion of that cost.

Research is needed on depression at all stages of the life cycle in women. Studies are needed to understand why there is a rise in the incidence of depression in females compared to males during adolescence. Longitudinal research is needed to follow children into adolescence and sexual maturity, evaluating the impact of biological factors, changes in self-image, self-esteem, gender stereotypes, relationships with family members, stressful life events, including experiences of teenage pregnancy, violence, and other factors on the development of depression. Studies are needed to assess the impact of biological factors including hormonal changes and exogenous hormone use (at different stages of a woman's life) on the onset and course of depression.

Research is needed to evaluate whether women's higher vulnerability to depression can be explained by the large numbers of women who are physically or sexually abused (childhood sexual assault rates range from 22% to 37% among women). Research is needed to evaluate whether psychosocial and drug therapies for depression are equally effective for women and men, and whether there are gender differences in side effects. Finally, because poverty is one pathway to depression, studies should determine to what extent the associated poor nutrition, poor health care, feelings of powerlessness or victimization impact the development and course of depressive disorders.

Substance Abuse

Substance abuse and addiction (including alcohol, nicotine, prescription drug, and illegal drug dependency) is a growing problem in America affecting people of all ages and both sexes. To what extent women are particularly affected, or responsive to treatment, is often not clear because most of our knowledge about sources of addictions and treatments of addictions is based on male subjects. We do know that certain types of drugs in particular are consumed by women. For example, women use tranquilizers 2.5 times more often than men, and two-thirds of the prescriptions for psychotropic drugs are for women. Experts estimate that of the 10 million alcoholics in the United States, 30–50% are women. A significant number of women appear also to be cross-addicted to more than one drug. Anabolic steroid use in women is becoming more prevalent.

There is special concern for the pregnant substance abuser or addict. An estimated two infants of every 1,000 live births suffer from Fetal Alcohol Syndrome. Alcohol and other drugs cross the placenta and enter the fetal bloodstream, interfering with both the physical and mental development of the fetus resulting in reduced birth weight, birth defects, learning and behavioral disorders, and newborn distress. The developing fetus cannot detoxify these drugs because of its immature enzyme systems. A mother's physical dependence on alcohol or other drugs at the time of delivery may lead to withdrawal syndromes in the newborn as well as postpartum withdrawal in the mother.

Recommendations include an assessment of the unique physiological consequences of different levels of alcohol, nicotine, and specific drug use in women as compared to men as well as in various subpopulations of women. The latter would include women of different races, cultures, life stages, lifestyles, and women on hormone therapy or other medications. Research is needed to determine whether women respond differently than men to interventions and prevention techniques. For example, women have more difficulty quitting smoking than men do, and interventions designed specifically for women are crucial to any smoking cessation program. This may well be the case for other addictions involving women. Specific screening techniques are needed in various settings including clinics, doctor's offices, and hospitals to enhance early detection of substance abuse.

Behavioral Medicine

Chronic medical illnesses have replaced acute illnesses as the major causes of morbidity and mortality in the United States. Behavioral factors play an important role in the onset and course of medical and mental disorders. Additionally, psychosocial interventions may impact on the behavioral and lifestyle factors that are implicated in seven out of 10 of the leading causes of death in the United States including cancer, heart disease, diabetes, AIDS, and suicide. Conference participants underscored the importance of studying gender differences in behavioral and lifestyle factors such as diet, smoking, stress, and exercise as contributory variables in the onset and course of mental illnesses.

Additionally, behavioral research is needed on methods to change high-risk behavior in women. Treatment studies examining psychosocial and pharmacologic interventions, as well as combinations of these interventions are needed to alter the course of medical and mental illnesses in women.

OTHER ISSUES RELATED TO WOMEN'S HEALTH RESEARCH

In addition to the biomedical, psychosocial, and behavioral issues discussed above, meeting participants raised underlying issues of concern including the dearth of women in senior scientific research and health policy positions and women's different utilization of the health care system.

Leadership Issues

Between 1978 and 1989, the number of female faculty members in U.S. medical schools increased 76% while male faculty increased only 25%. However, female faculty members are concentrated in the lower ranks—only 3% of women compared to 12% of men attain professorship levels after 12 years. In professional and academic societies, women hold fewer leadership positions and top administrative positions. Women represent only 10.5% of the American Medical Associations's (AMA) members and only one woman currently sits on the AMA Board of Trustees. Various obstacles have been cited as barriers for women to reach the top rungs of their respective career ladders. These obstacles range from stereotypical attitudes of men and women, sex discrimination, lack of role models, different perceptions of family responsibilities, to lack of training in leadership and political skills.

To facilitate women's advancement in academia, the system must become more supportive. Child care centers and flexible hours are one step. In addition, mentorship relationships must be fostered to facilitate women's advancement in the institution. Women should be encouraged to enter elite programs (such as the combined M.D.-Ph.D. program) offered by many medical schools. Senior women must be appointed to search committees, which in turn should be held accountable for decisions when similarly qualified male and female candidates are considered for hiring and promotion. Women doctors should work closely with their medical societies to gain political experience and to assume policy-making positions.

One other side of this picture of women and leadership should also be considered. Women often assume that because the professional style of men is positively evaluated and rewarded they must attempt to embrace that style as their own. However, the "kinder, gentler" approach usually adopted by women may be just as effective (if not more effective) in leadership roles. Studies should be designed to specifically test this question.

Education of Health Care Professionals

To date, there is no medical specialty that provides primary health care for women. OB/GYN physicians are interested in the reproductive tract and are not necessarily informed about other medical or psychosocial health issues relevant to women. Likewise, physicians in other specialties may not be well informed about reproductive health. As a result, many women receive fragmentary care. Very often medical issues that have to do with the unique physiology of females (e.g., hormonal cycles) or gender roles are overlooked or neglected. Various medical professional groups are beginning to address these oversights. For example, the American Medical Women's Association (AMWA) has prepared a multidisciplinary, multispecialty postgraduate course specifically on the health care needs of women. The pressing issue is how to integrate this kind of core curriculum into the training experiences of physicians and other health care professionals.

The Health Care Delivery System

It has been reported that women tend to be more attentive to their own health and are more compliant with physicians' treatment regimens than men. They also report more illness, visit physicians more often, and take more prescription drugs. This behavior brings up interesting questions regarding women's health. Do women take better care of themselves, and is this (and perhaps other lifestyle issues) related to their greater longevity compared to men? Does a woman's greater personal involvement in her interaction with her physician influence the care she receives? Do women have relatively more chronic illnesses than men? Do women simply report more symptoms, or do they have more? Does a woman's willingness to visit physicians lead eventually to decreased mortality, or "do physicians stop listening and start prescribing"? In other words, what is the impact of the use of resources on health outcomes? Would the answer differ depending on whether the physician is male or female?

What factors affect use of health care resources? For example, good screening procedures for two common cancers in women exist, mammography and Pap smears. These techniques unequivocally save lives. The major obstacles are inadequate utilization and lack of access. Surveys indicate that many women would obtain a mammogram if their doctors told them to do so. Educating physicians is one approach; educating women directly is another. Access is often limited by financial status. Insurers in different states vary in terms of coverage for screening tests; and among the 40 million Americans who have no medical insurance at all, many are older, poor, and/or minority women.

Recommendations for improvement of the health care delivery system for women include:

- Efforts to support screening tests for early detection of diseases like breast cancer and cervical cancer;
- Educational campaigns against smoking to prevent growing numbers of women from contracting lung cancer and heart disease;
- Educational programs to ensure safe sexual practices to decrease the frequency of HIV infection in women;
- Educational campaigns for new approaches to contraception to prevent unintended pregnancies.

In terms of tax dollars spent, results from successful research in these four areas alone would far offset the costs of supporting the health care and/or welfare needs of hundreds of thousands of women.

CONCLUSION

It was not the role of the conference participants to assign priorities among women's health problems but some facts are clear. In sheer numbers, the morbidity and mortality from the diseases afflicting older women were of critical importance. Because many of the diseases of older women begin much earlier, it seems clear that better understanding of the etiology, risk factors, and mechanisms for the prevention of specific diseases in young women will lead to a healthier old age.

Equally compelling arguments could be made for making a priority of most of the health problems discussed. The conference participants underscored the need for a full spectrum of basic, clinical, and epidemiological research on diseases afflicting women. They highlighted the urgent need to increase prevention research, to improve the education of the public and health care professionals, and to increase access to health care services. For most of the health questions discussed, each of these areas of research is vital. For example, the success of preventing or treating a disease depends on how well it is understood. Understanding alone, however, is not sufficient if access to health care for millions of women is limited. More coordinated efforts . . . will be needed to establish priorities so that the gaps in knowledge about women's health problems can be filled. . . .

By health *I mean the power to live a full, adult, living, breathing life in close contact with the earth and the wonders thereof . . .*
— Katherine Mansfield

Nona Y. Glazer

The Home as Workshop: Women as Amateur Nurses and Medical Care Providers

There are really no data on what is best for the patient. I ask doctors why they discharge patients or keep them for different amounts of time and the physicians themselves admit that they do not know because there are no data. We make judgments that are convenient to administrative decisions. (Director, Home Health Agency)

Erving Goffman (1961, 321–86) called the hospital the physician's workshop. Today, the home is an expanding workshop for paid nursing personnel who care for patients just discharged from outpatient clinics, nursing homes, and acute care hospitals. It is also the workshop for amateurs, mostly women family members who are ancillary health care workers, doing unpaid labor essential to the U.S. health care system. Their unpaid labor has changed from housekeeping and minor nursing to encompass the administration and monitoring of complex nursing-medical regimens once done only in acute care hospitals by physicians or registered nurses (RNs) and specialists.

This organization of home health care delivery violates the sociological model of work as divided between the public and private spheres. Supposedly, the private sphere includes personal life and the family, where women do unpaid domestic labor, while the public sphere includes all else, including paid labor (Zaretsky 1976). While many sociologists recognize that the spheres are related, most focus on one or the other (Glazer 1984). They study health care delivery in the "public" sphere, from the perspective of paid providers such as physicians, hospitals, and insurers (Starr 1982), and less often, from that of patients (Corbin and Strauss 1988). As Olesen (1989) notes, informal caregivers in the private sphere in the United States have been neglected by sociologists, studied instead by gerontologists and nurse researchers (see, however, Abel 1989; Abel and

Nona Y. Glazer, Ph.D., is Professor, Department of Sociology at Portland State University, Portland, Oregon.

Abridged from Glazer, N.Y. (1990). The home as workshop: Women as amateur nurses and medical care providers. *Gender and Society* 4(4):479–499. Used with permission.

Nelson 1990). In this article, I abandon the concept of private and public spheres to reconceptualize health care delivery as a seamless web of social relations. . . .

THEORETICAL ISSUES

Three major interpretations of how unpaid domestic labor has fared under capitalism imply an indirect connection only to class relations, the political economy of capitalism, and the state. One view is that domestic labor was never brought into the process of capitalist *commodification*. Although women in the household use goods and services from the marketplace, their own labor power remains precapitalist (Bennholdt-Thomsen 1984; Mies 1986). The second view is that the energy spent by women in domestic labor has declined with the commodification of goods. However, given the loss of servants, ever-increasing consumption transforms wives and mothers into "cryptoservants" (Galbraith 1973) and makes "more work for mother" (Cowan 1983). My third view is that domestic labor is largely the *social reproduction* of the work force. On a daily basis, the labor of wives and mothers reproduces the present generation of workers and, by raising children, the next generation of workers (Laslett and Brenner 1989). These views of domestic labor as private, and "for" the family are exemplified in the now-superseded economists' definition of domestic labor as "leisure," in the classical Marxist view of housewives as outside capitalist relations of production (Glazer-Malbin 1976), and in the traditional sociological view of the family as a system of interacting personalities, integrated in society by the mediating role of the husband-father as breadwinner (Parsons and Bales 1955).

Critiques of theories of separate domains date back to the 1970s (Kelly 1979; Rapp, Ross, and Bridenthal 1979; Zaretsky 1976). The "domestic labor debates" were an attempt by Marxist feminists to reconceptualize the boundary between paid and unpaid labor and the relation of women's uncommodified labor to capitalist production (Glazer-Malbin 1976). Empirically, health care has been slighted in research on housewives (Lopata 1971; Oakley 1974) and the household gender division of labor (Berk and Berk 1979; Berk 1980; Vanck 1974); in estimates of the economic value of a housewife (W. Brody 1975); and in debates on domestic labor (Fox 1980). Hence, theoretical critiques have not led to empirical research on the connections between health care labor in the public and private spheres.

Historical Roots

What has been called the ideology of two spheres developed in Euro-American societies in the late eighteenth and early nineteenth centuries.

With variations by class, nationality, race, and ethnicity, men won status as citizens with individual political and civil rights and gained immunity from close government and church scrutiny (Habermas 1974, 89). In the nineteenth century, with the movement of free men and unmarried women into the factory system, household and commodity production became increasingly distinct. Yet the changes were uneven. For example, until the 1960s most married women worked in undercapitalized sectors, as "homeworkers," or in the informal economy as domestic workers, home launderers, and taking in boarders and lodgers (Lewis 1986). In the United States, married women entered the formal labor force in sizable numbers in the decades after World War II, with the growth of the service sector. Yet their domestic labor remains unwaged or in the paid informal underground economy. However, a "mutual infiltration" of private and public continues (Habermas 1989), and the use of women's unpaid work in the health care system is only a recent case.

Women's Work in Health Care Delivery

Conceptualizing women's unpaid labor in the home as one segment of health care work differs from most analyses, which treat technical health care as encounters between professionals and their clients, usually physicians and patients, sometimes RNs and patients. Because the dehospitalization of people with acute illnesses and the extended use of outpatient clinics is new, most research has been on home care of the chronically ill (cf. Archbold 1982; Jones and Vetter 1984; Matthews 1987). Only a few sociologists have examined the impact of unremitting care on families in the United States as welfare services declined (Corbin and Strauss 1988), conceptualized caregiving as "work" (Carpenter 1980; Glazer 1988), researched the use of high-tech medicine by caregivers (Fox and Swazey 1974), or connected changes in women's paid health service work to women's unpaid family work (Glazer 1988).

Within the family in capitalist societies, women are responsible for two major activities: (1) Women engage in the social reproduction of the labor force. Women's nontechnical and technical health care work for husbands, partners, children, and other kin is one among the many tasks of social reproduction. (2) Women develop and maintain social relations and ideologies that support family members in their relations with service institutions, such as the health care delivery system. Domestic labor, therefore, entails another contribution that few theorists of work recognize: women's care of family members who are socially and economically dependent, namely, the retired and the sick who need physical and emotional as well as financial help (Strong-Boag 1986).

A NEW LABOR PROCESS: THE WORK TRANSFER

Women's domestic labor is used for health care through the work transfer. Managers change the labor process, that is, how work is organized, and do so repeatedly in efforts to maximize worker productivity, accumulation, and profit. Their techniques include a detailed division of labor and automation, job consolidation (the tasks of two or more jobs are combined), upgrading skills (not pay), and speedups (increasing the pace of work, the length of the working day, dropping the piece-rate). In manufacturing, employers' attempts to increase worker productivity by these techniques depend on the objects of labor (the parts of goods) being standardized and made interchangeable and the work being done at a controlled pace. In service industries, the objects of labor are clients or patients who need services, but unlike manufacturing, their needs are not standardized or interchangeable and cannot easily be forced to a measured pace. People want food *when* they are hungry, to shop *when* they find it convenient, and medical and nursing care *when* they are ill. Service workers must be on call continually, even though users make demands intermittently.

The work transfer designates another labor process: waged workers are eliminated or given new tasks, and the work that they did before is transferred to women (and sometimes, men) as family members. Hence, the free labor of women in families substitutes for the once-waged labor of workers. In health services, the paid labor is that of nursing personnel. Family members are mothers, wives, adult daughters, and daughters-in-law of the sick, who provide the free domestic labor that completes a labor process begun outside the household. The completion is essential, not complementary.

Relying on the work of customers, clients, and their families has historical precedent in the United States. Starting in Chicago in the 1890s with "cafeterias," businesses adopted self-service to increase the productivity of their service workers (the cost of labor per unit cost of output). Retailers circumvented their inability to control shopper demands for services and overcame the "wasteful cost" of having sales clerks wait around for customers by replacing clerk-service with self-service shopping. They understood that the customer's labor could "contribut[e] to company and industry productivity" (Heskett 1986, 106) and that productivity could be increased by substituting the free work of customers for that of waged workers.

Managers in public agencies and nonprofit organizations, such as health care facilities, also have substituted "client" labor (and that of their families) for waged workers (Lovelock and Young 1979, 66). Historically, family members relied on each other, especially on women, for health care; but with the development of science-based medicine and the modern hospital, an elaborate hierarchy of workers developed to sell health care. Managers tried to increase the productivity of these workers: hospital administrators by reassigning work to patients and family caregivers, freeing waged professionals and ancillary health workers to do other work, but without reducing direct costs to patients (Blitzer 1981). In the United States, hospitals experimented with "hospitals without walls" (Koren 1986), "ambulant wings" (Tunstall 1960), "cooperative care" units ("New care unit" 1979; Gibson and Pulliam 1987), and "care-by-parent" units (Evans and Robinson 1983). Family members nursed, and patients and family caregivers did housekeeping, arranged treatments, and prepared meals (Tunstall 1960).

Queuing theory gives managers improved predictions of client demands for services but does not allow them to force patients, for example, to distribute their demands evenly over the working day to improve the productivity of hospital workers. Managers can, however, use the labor of clients (or their surrogates) and employ fewer service workers. Sending recovering (or dying) patients home to be serviced by family caregivers is just such a use of client labor.

Equally important, the sale of medical goods adds more to corporate profits and accumulation than the sale of service labor, given the difficulties of increasing productivity (Mandel 1975). Hence, in anticipation of an enormous market, corporations supplying home care goods tried to form partnerships with nonprofit visiting nurse associations, who would have provided all services. Most associations refused, well aware that federal reimbursements for supplies and equipment, not for their services, would support care for Medicare and Medicaid patients.

EFFECTS OF THE DRG REIMBURSEMENT SYSTEM

The new federal reimbursement system for Medicare and Medicaid patients applies business practices to human services and results in a work transfer. The DRG reimbursement system brings together assumptions from the manufacturing sector about standardization with those from the service sector about consumer labor. Hospital services are conceptualized as if treatments are identical and as if sick people are interchangeable, with identical needs and responses to treatments. Legislators know this homogenization is false, that some patients need longer hospital stays, more costly treatments, and so on, but concluded "that hospitals would make a few dollars on some patients and . . . lose a few dollars on others" (Committee on Aging 1984, 47).

Congress intended that the DRGs would force hospitals to be more efficient, but the flat fee simply gives them an incentive to discharge patients quickly and do as much as possible outside the hospital. The result, deliberately or inadvertently, is the work transfer with new work for women as family members.

The DRGs accelerated the long-term decline in average length of hospital stays and the greater use of nursing homes, home health service agencies, family caregivers, and self-care. Before the DRGs, the use of home health services rose from 8 per 1,000 Medicare enrollees in 1970 to 27 per 1,000 in 1980, but jumped sharply within two years of its start-up to 51 per 1,000 in 1985 (Health Care Financing Administration 1988a, 28; Health Care Financing Administration 1988b, 4; U.S. Bureau of the Census 1985, 371; U.S. Bureau of the Census 1987, 347). Furthermore, treatments such as knee surgery and cataract removal now must be done on an outpatient basis. Patients who once would have recovered in the hospital go home to self-care or family caregivers, with or without formal home health services. Health care will probably continue to be delivered in these ways as long as it is considered cost-effective to insurers, who ignore the hidden cost of the transfer of work to family members (see U.S. General Accounting Office [1982] and Hammond [1979] for assessments of home health services, from 1965 to 1981, as not cost-effective, though patients may prefer them).

Whether or not it costs insurers less, it costs families more. According to federal estimates, "for every $120 of taxpayer money spent by home care agencies, an estimated $287 worth of unpaid services is provided by the homebound person's family and friends" (U.S. Department of Commerce 1978, 490). The industry estimates a $10 billion savings in wages because of unpaid family work (Paringer 1985). Of course, the "family and friends" are mostly women.

WOMEN AS CAREGIVERS

Changing reimbursement policies make more work for women; and the family, the sex-gender system, and race-class subordination make the work transfer possible. In the United States (and other societies with weak welfare systems), citizens have access to social resources, such as health care, through their membership in families. The ideology of "individualism: self-help, self-support, self-sufficiency" appears to reject dependency on other people and social groups, but "in practice, the unit of self-support is not the individual but the family" (Barrett and McIntosh 1984, 45). Those whose families lack money and know-how rely on welfare institutions or go without, while those who lack families buy help if they can afford it (Barrett and McIntosh 1984). In capitalist societies with stronger welfare systems, such as Sweden and the Netherlands, ironically, citizens claim social resources as individuals (Bystydzienski 1989, 678; Folbre 1987). To curtail welfare spending, the United States has been reducing state services and enlarging dependency on families. Canada and the United Kingdom, with their dissimilar welfare systems, have also been "dehospitalizing," shifting financial and work responsibilities to the family and the women within them. Dehospitalization is currently being discussed in Sweden.

Health care can be shifted from the formal health care delivery system to the family and the women within it because of ideologies and practices of the "social relations of family tending," and because women continue to be responsible for unpaid domestic labor. Hospital administrators, middle-level managers, and discharge planners view "the family" as responsible for patients, for taking over when hospitals no longer give nursing care.

The Prevalence of Women as Caregivers

Women caregivers enable the family to be a "provider" unit (Jones and Vetter 1984; Littman 1974) and help prevent rehospitalization (Pesznecker et al. 1987). The price, however, may be the disruption of their personal lives (Finch and Groves 1980; Haber 1986). Because the extensive use of home health services for the acutely ill is new, available studies have examined only the chronically ill, but there is no reason to expect many differences. (In 1989, the U.S. federal government issued a request for proposals to study the household gender division of labor in home health care of the acutely ill.)

Women constitute from two-thirds to three-quarters of unpaid providers (Stone et al. 1987), as primary caregivers (Archbold 1983; E. Brody 1985) and even when family members share care (Matthews 1987). Women provide most of the care when men help ("Eldercare survey" 1988; Haber 1986), when a spouse (the wife or husband) is unable to care (E. Brody and Schoonover 1986), and when they are employed outside the home (Stoller and Stoller 1983). Men rather than women are likely to be the primary caregivers when patients have no daughters living close to them or when sons are their only children (Horowitz 1985). However, men caregivers are more likely than women to use support networks to relieve them of full-time responsibilities (Miller 1990).

Race and Class

Not all women experience the work transfer in the same way, because recent changes in hospital use differ by age, race, and family income. Between 1983 and 1985, the admission of children dropped more than for others, 19 percent compared to 11 percent (Moss and Moien 1987, 5), presumably with mothers doing more home care. The admission of

African-American patients decreased over twice as much as European-Americans, 27 percent compared to 11 percent. Admission rates of those with family incomes under $10,000 declined by 19 percent, compared with 11 percent for those with incomes over $35,000 (Moss and Moien 1987, 7). Patients with private insurance stayed in nursing homes longer than Medicare patients who went home sicker (as measured by a case-mix index), whether or not home health services were available (Morrissey, Sloan, and Valvona 1988, Exhibit 3, 59).

Women cope differently, depending on class. Women from upper strata are less likely than others to care continuously for their elderly parents (who also rely on friends) and are less likely than the poor to be in the same community as their parents. Women from households with high incomes may hire substitutes for themselves, such as private-duty RNs, nurse assistants, and attendants. In contrast, working-class women rely on home care nurses and home health aides. Finally, the government discriminates against the poor, giving less service to indigent Medicaid patients than to elderly Medicare patients.

GOING HOME SICKER: WHAT AMATEURS DO

> We joke. We say, "Patients will go from ICU [the intensive care unit] to the home" or "We will be operating on the patient's kitchen table." (Director, Home Health Services)

Home care has been conceptualized by sociologists in such a way that they ignore the medical and nursing content of the work and see it as a variation on the usual domestic chores of women—transportation, emotional and social support, homemaking, and personal care. But "care" now encompasses a range of nursing-medical tasks as well. Most important, family caregivers "practice" nursing and medicine, monitoring patients for everything from reactions to change in medication to medical crises requiring emergency readmission to hospital. Women use high-tech equipment to deliver treatments for acute and chronic conditions and to treat systemic infection and cancer. They supervise exercises and give mechanical relief to patients with breathing disorders, feed by tubes those unable to take food orally or digest normally, give intramuscular injections and more tricky intravenous injections, and monitor patients after antibiotic and chemotherapy treatments.

The work can be difficult for families to do, made more so because of hospital-staff cuts. Because patients are sent home sicker and because there are no aides to help them do so in the hospital, patients must also recover basic functions at home. Hence, there is more work for both family caregivers and home care RNs. . . .

HOME CARE AND THE WEB OF SOCIAL
RELATIONSHIPS

In the current practice of home health care, delivery work is a seamless web of social relations that spills over any purported boundary between public and private spheres. In this web, women's work as family members is critical but semivisible, partly because whatever women do is devalued, even if it may be romanticized too. But the cloudy perceptions of how women's work in the family shores up capitalist social relations has another source: It is the continuing theoretical commitment of the social sciences to a bifurcated view of the social world.

Tending to patients under the formal supervision of home health service agencies requires coordination, willingly or not, between professional health care workers and family caregivers, who do much more than glorified housekeeping. Health care workers, mostly women, and family members, also mostly women, are locked together in the performance of highly technical health care. Recognizing the real and lived links between the performances of unpaid and paid workers would give a more accurate picture of the contemporary U.S. health services industry and the continued dependence of capitalism on women's unpaid domestic labor.

Conceptualizing the social world as neatly divided into the private and the public spheres may have made sense of social change in the late eighteenth and nineteenth centuries. The factory system replaced the household economy as a basic form of subsistence, the marketplace became a major source of goods and services, and political and civil rights were extended to propertyless men. The dichotomy had an ideological meaning that was used to justify the development of civil society with its realm of intellectual and moral privacy (Habermas 1989) and to justify the household as free from state and religious authority.

Today this archaic view of the privacy of the home and its separation from the core of social life (the economy, politics, education, and so on) obfuscates our understanding of social relations. It hides the labor of women (Weinbaum and Bridges 1976). It masks the success of corporations in redefining human services according to business values and practices and in reconstructing the home as a new health care marketplace that depends on self-care and women's domestic labor.

The public and private spheres may make intuitive sense to medical sociologists who have observed the emergence of the modern hospital, the professionalization of medicine and nursing, and the transformation of hospitals from poorhouses and small businesses into corporate investments (Bergthold 1987). But the dichotomy hides the complexity of the health care labor force, the work of women as family members in home care, and how social policies depend for their implementation on the everyday activities and unpaid labor of women (Glazer forthcoming). It continues the outdated concept of the family as some remnant of the preindustrial world, rather than as a fundamental unit from whence women's domestic labor can be drawn for use by corporate capitalism, enabling consumption of goods with the least social costs to businesses.

The work transfer focuses on the changing relationship between paid and unpaid work, particularly between the paid service work and unwaged domestic service labor done by women. But the social processes by which changes are constituted in women's paid service labor and women's unwaged domestic labor reflect microcosms of class, racial and ethnic, and gender relations in advanced capitalism. The changing relations between paid and unpaid service labor reflect also the hegemony of capitalism, demonstrating the power of corporate capitalism to redefine family responsibilities and to extend women's responsibilities for tending without provoking organized resistance by the public.

Furthermore, the work transfer is not limited to health care: The redesign of work in which the customer or client must do tasks once done by waged workers has been used to change other female-typed service jobs. For example, automatic teller machines in banking displaced women clerical workers and substituted a new division of labor, between men who work as cash-replenishers of the machines and women and men bank customers. Nor is health care the only human service affected. After budget cuts in Portland, Oregon, the police adopted a new policy of do-it-yourself reporting of home burglaries, vandalism, and petty property crimes, requiring victims to go to their local precincts to file reports. Some are more problematic: relying on mothers and fathers to fill in for the teachers lost to the schools when budgets have been rejected by voters; expecting would-be welfare clients to complete do-it-yourself intake forms on the reception room computer, when the information so obtained is used to decide on their eligibility for services. Supposedly more efficient and evenhanded than welfare aides, the computer also eliminates the humane judgments of the aides and may force would-be aides into the ranks of those they could have serviced.

The paid and unpaid service work reorganized by the work transfer shows a seamless web of work done by women. Change in one, paid work, prompts a change in the other, unpaid work. Health care was always partly work done in the home, but modern medicine and a highly profitable health care industry kept the unpaid work of women as family members marginal. The new changes in reimbursement have brought the family and women back to the forefront of the invisible support for continuing profits in the health services industry and placed the low-waged service work of health workers at risk. Changes via the work transfer are cumulative and interconnected, forcing more self-service work from women in the alleged service society and expelling some women from low-paid service work. But the changes may continue to hide those services done for free under the rubric of the private work of consumption.

BIBLIOGRAPHY

Abel, Emily K. 1989. Family care of the frail elderly: Framing an agenda. *Women's Studies Quarterly* 1(2):75–86.

Abel, Emily K., and Margaret Nelson. 1990. *Circles of care.* Albany: SUNY Press.

Archbold, Patricia C. 1982. An analysis of parentcaring by women. *Home Health Care Services Quarterly* 3:5–26.

Barrett, Michelle, and Mary McIntosh. 1984. *The anti-social family.* London: Verso.

Bennholdt-Thomsen, Veronika. 1984. Subsistence production and extended production. In *Of marriage and the market,* edited by Kate Young, Carol Wolkowitz, and Roslyn McCullogh. London: Routledge & Kegan Paul.

Bergthold, Linda A. 1987. Business and the pushcart vendors in an age of supermarkets. *International Journal of Health Services* 17:7–27.

Berk, Richard, and Sarah Fenstermaker Berk. 1979. *Labor and leisure at home.* Beverly Hills, CA: Sage.

Berk, Sarah Fenstermaker, ed. 1980. *Women and household labor.* Beverly Hills, CA: Sage.

Blitzer, Carol. 1981. Cooperative care unit cuts costs 40% at NYU hospital. *Business Insurance* 15(28 December): 3, 27.

Brody, Elaine. 1985. Parent care as a normative family stress. *Gerontologist* 25:19–29.

Brody, Elaine, and Claire Schoonover. 1986. Patterns of parent-care when adult daughters work and when they do not. *Gerontologist* 26:372–81.

Brody, Wendyce H. 1975. Economic value of a housewife. *Research and statistics note.* DHEW Pub. No. (SSA) 75-11701. Washington, DC: GPO.

Bystydzienski, Jill M. 1989. Women

and socialism: A comparative study of women in Poland and the USSR. *Signs* 14:668–84.

Carpenter, Eugenia S. 1980. Children's health care and the changing role of women. *Medical Care* 18:1208–18.

Committee on Aging. Select Committee, United States House of Representatives. 1984. *Building a long-term care policy: Home care data and implications.* Comm. Pub. No. 98-484. Washington, DC, December.

Corbin, Julie, and Anselm Strauss. 1988. *Unending work and care.* San Francisco: Jossey-Bass.

Cowan, Ruth. 1983. *More work for mother.* New York: Basic Books.

Creative teaching. 1985. *Caring* 4:17.

Eldercare survey shows need for benefits. 1988. *Employee Benefit Plan Review* 43(September):13–14.

Evans, Robert, and Geoffrey Robinson. 1983. An economic study of cost savings on a care-by-parent ward. *Medical Care* 21:768–82.

Finch, Janet, and Dulcie Groves, eds. 1980. *Labor of love: Women, work, and caring.* Boston: Routledge & Kegan Paul.

Folbre, Nancy. 1987. The pauperization of motherhood: Patriarchy and public policy in the United States. In *Families and work,* edited by Naomi Gerstel and Harriet Gross. Philadelphia: Temple University Press.

Fox, Bonnie, ed. 1980. *Hidden in the household.* Toronto: Women's Press.

Fox, Renee, and Judith Swazey. 1974. *The courage to fail.* Chicago: University of Chicago Press.

Galbraith, John Kenneth, 1973. *Economics and the public purpose.* Boston: Houghton Mifflin.

Gibson, Kathy R., and C. Beth Pulliam. 1987. Cooperative care: The time has come. *Journal of Nursing Administration* 17(3):19–21.

Glaser, Barney, and Anselm Strauss. 1967. *The development of grounded theory.* New York: Aldine.

Glazer, Nona Y. 1984. Servants to capital: Unpaid domestic labor and paid work. *Review of Radical Political Economics* 16:61–87.

———. 1988. Overlooked and overworked: Women's paid and unpaid labor in the U.S. "cost crisis." *International Journal of Health Services* 18:119–37.

———. Forthcoming. *Servants to capital: Women's paid and unpaid work in retailing and health services.* Philadelphia: Temple University Press.

Glazer-Malbin, N. 1976. Housework. *Signs* 1:905–21.

Goffman, Erving. 1961. The medical model and mental hospitalization. In *Asylums.* Garden City, NY: Doubleday Anchor.

Haber, David. 1986. In-home and community-based long-term care services. *Journal of Applied Gerontology* 5:37–50.

Habermas, Jurgen. 1974. The public sphere (1964). *New German Critique* 3:46–55.

———. 1989. *The structural transformation of the public sphere.* Cambridge: MIT Press.

Hammond, John. 1979. Home health care cost effectiveness. *Public Health Reports* 9:305–11.

Health Care Financing Administration. 1988a. *Use and cost of home health agency services under Medicare: Selected calendar years 1974–86.* Research brief No. 88-4. Washington, DC.

———. 1988b. *1988 HCFA statistics.* HCFA Pub. No. 03271. Washington, DC, December.

Heskett, James. 1986. *Managing the service economy.* Boston: Harvard Business School Press.

Horowitz, A. 1985. Sons and daughters as caregivers to older parents. *Gerontologist* 25:612–17.

Jones, Dee A., and Norman J. Vetter. 1984. A survey of those who care for the elderly at home: Their problems and their needs. *Social Science in Medicine* 19:511–14.

Kelly, Joan. 1979. The doubled vision of feminist theory. *Feminist Studies* 5:221–27.

Kind, A. C., D. N. Williams, G. Persons, and J. Gibson. 1979. Intravenous antibiotic therapy at home. *Archives of Internal Medicine* 139:413–15.

Koren, Mary Jane. 1986. Home care—who cares? *New England Journal of Medicine* 314:917–20.

Laslett, Barbara, and Johanna Brenner. 1989. Gender and social reproduction: Historical perspectives. In *Annual review of sociology, Vol. 15,* edited by W. Richard Scott. Palo Alto, CA: Annual Reviews.

Lewis, Jane. 1986. The working-class wife and mother and state intervention, 1870–1918. In *Labour and love,* edited by Jane Lewis. Oxford: Basil Blackwell.

Littman, Theodor J. 1974. The family as a basic unit in health and medical care: A social behavioral overview. *Social Science Medicine* 8:495–519.

Lopata, Helena Z. 1971. *Occupation: Housewife.* New York: Oxford University Press.

Lovelock, Christopher, and Robert F. Young. 1979. Look to consumers to increase productivity. *Harvard Business Review* 57(3):66–76.

Mandel, Ernest. 1975. *Late capitalism.* London: New Left Books.

Matthews, Sarah H. 1987. Provision of care to old parents. *Research on Aging* 9:45–60.

Mies, Maria. 1986. *Patriarchy and accumulation on a world scale.* London: Zed.

Miller, Baila. 1990. Gender differences in the spouse management of the caregiver role. In *Circles of care,* edited by Emily K. Abel and Margaret K. Nelson. Albany: SUNY Press.

Morrissey-Ross, Mary. 1988. Documentation: If you haven't written it, you haven't done it. *Nursing Clinics of North America* 23:363–71.

412   *The Home as Workshop*

Morrissey, Michael, Frank A. Sloan, and Joseph Valvona. 1988. Shifting Medicare patients out of the hospital. *Health Affairs* (Winter):52–63.

Moss, Abigail J., and Mary A. Moien. 1987. *Recent declines in hospitalization: United States, 1982–86.* Advanced data no. 140, 1–15. Washington, DC: National Center for Health Statistics, U.S. Dept. Health and Human Services, 24 September.

New care unit to cut hospital costs by 40%. 1979. *American Nurse* 11(20 May):1–6.

Oakley, Ann. 1974. *Woman's work.* New York: Vintage.

Olesen, Virginia. 1989. Caregiving, ethical and informal: Emergent challenges in the sociology of health and illness. *Journal of Health and Social Behavior* 30:1–10.

Paringer, L. 1985. Forgotten costs of informal long-term care. *Generations* 9:55–58.

Parsons, Talcott, and Robert F. Bales. 1955. *Family, socialization and interaction process.* Glencoe, IL: Free Press.

Pesznecker, Betty, Barbara Horn, Joanne Werner, and Virginia Kenyon. 1987. Home health services in a climate of cost containment. *Home Health Care Services Quarterly* 8:5–21.

Rapp, Rayna, Ellen Ross, and Renate Bridenthal. 1979. Examining family history. *Feminist Studies* 5:174–200.

Starr, Paul. 1982. *The social transformation of American medicine.* New York: Basic Books.

Stoller, E., and E. L. Stoller. 1983. Help with activities of everyday life: Sources of support for the non-institutionalized elderly. *Gerontologist* 28:64–70.

Stone, Robyn, Gail Lee Cafferata, and Judith Sangl. 1987. *Caregivers of the frail elderly: A national profile.* Washington, DC: National Center for Health Services Research.

Strong-Boag, Veronica. 1986. Keeping house in God's country: Canadian women at work in the home. In *On the job,* edited by Craig Heron and Robert Storey. Montreal: McGill-Queen's University Press.

Tunstall, Patricia. 1960. Hospitals without nurses. *Practical Nursing* 10(5): 14–15.

U.S. Bureau of the Census. 1985. *Statistical abstract of the United States, 1986.* Washington, DC: GPO.

———. 1987. *Statistical abstract of the United States, 1988.* Washington, DC: GPO.

U.S. Department of Commerce. 1978. *U.S. industrial outlook, 1960–1987* (excludes 1981). Washington, DC: GPO.

U.S. General Accounting Office. 1982. *The elderly should benefit from expanded home health care but increasing those services will not insure cost reductions.* Washington, DC: GPO.

Vanck, Joanne. 1974. Time spent in housework. *Scientific American* 231: 116–20.

Weinbaum, Batya, and Amy Bridges. 1976. The other side of the paycheck: Monopoly capital and the structure of consumption. *Monthly Review* 28:88–103.

Zaretsky, Eli. 1976. *Capitalism, the family and personal life.* New York: Harper & Row.

Health *has its science as well as disease.*
— Elizabeth Blackwell

Terry Arendell / Carroll L. Estes

Older Women in the Post-Reagan Era

Gender and minority status are crucial in explaining differences in the economic and health issues confronted by the aged. Significantly, the situation of older women is a result not of old age, but of lifelong patterns of socioeconomic and gender stratification in the larger society. The social origins of the disadvantaged status of older women are not mysterious; they reside in the institutions and structures of the family (the informal sector), the labor market, and the state and its social policy (both parts of the formal sector). Each of these areas has received independent study; however, the consequences for older women flow from the complex and often subtle interrelationships among and across these social institutions.[1] Women's family roles, particularly their caregiving, directly impinge upon their economic status. Not only does economic status directly affect access to health care, but social class and socioeconomic status have repeatedly been shown to be strongly linked to health status as measured by mortality, disability, chronic illness, and institutionalization.[2-6]

Because of the structural embeddedness and complexity of these institutional arrangements and interrelationships that adversely affect women, the resolution of older women's economic and health issues cannot be achieved by providing services alone. While a more comprehensive and integrated health and social service delivery system is needed for older females, this need is shared by all individuals who are asked to provide caregiving up and down, within and between the generations in the growing number of three and four generational families. Although state support of access, availability, and financing of services remains vitally important, changes in service provision alone will do little to address the gendered division of labor and the capitalist mode of production that have played a pivotal role in socially creating the jeopardized situation in which older

Terry Arendell, Ph.D., is Assistant Professor of Child and Family Studies at the University of Wisconsin, Madison.
Carroll L. Estes, Ph.D., is Director of the Institute for Health & Aging, and Professor, Department of Social and Behavioral Sciences, School of Nursing at the University of California, San Francisco.

From Arendell, T., and Estes, C.L. (1991). Older women in the post-Reagan era. *International Journal of Health Services* 21(1):59–73. Reprinted by permission of Baywood Publishing Co., Inc.

women find themselves. The analytical framework proposed here acknowledges the link between income and health needs in a life course perspective, delicately balancing health and well-being. For women, this raises the need for broad-based solutions that address sex, race, and age discrimination in the labor market, unequal pay for comparable worth, and the invidious quality of income security programs for older women that are predicated on ideological and inaccurate assumptions, wage discrimination, and a lifetime of devalued caregiving work.

A key element of women's precarious economic status in old age is their family responsibility across the lifespan for which they bear a significant and continuous burden of work. Lodged primarily in what has been socially constructed as the private sphere of the family, women have been responsible for providing care and nurturing both the very young and the very old in a social and political context that romanticizes but provides no financial remunerations for their caring activities. Because caring takes place within millions of individual family units, it is neither recognized nor valorized because of the historic neglect and devaluation of women's unpaid labor, and the ideological dichotomy between the "public" and "private" in which the family is defined as private, autonomous, and self-sufficient. As a result, the place of women and children in the gendered division of labor and the costs of caring activities tend to be ignored and obscured. Although women have entered the wage labor force in unprecedented numbers over the last two decades, the wage differentials between men and women have not improved or changed significantly in the past 30 years; a significant number of women hold part-time jobs; and most wives remain economically dependent on husbands.[7]

In old age, many women discover that the structural conditions and the normative expectations that have promoted and maintained their economic dependence converge, resulting in poverty or near-poverty and economic uncertainty. Indeed, poverty is the central problem facing older women.[8]

The aged are not a homogeneous population, despite recent reports asserting the economic gains made by the elderly. While there has been a decline in the overall rate of poverty among the aged in the past 15 years, major pockets of poverty and conditions of economic hardship persist.[7,9,10] Indeed, because so many aged persons are near poverty (150 percent of the poverty level and below), the proportion of aged who are poor and near-poor is larger than the combined proportion of nonaged who are poor and near-poor.[7] Well over 50 percent of older women will find themselves facing economic hardships.

DEMOGRAPHIC CHARACTERISTICS

The older population is disproportionately female: nearly 60 percent of all Americans 66 years and older, and nearly 70 percent of those 80 and over, are female. Because women typically outlive their husbands, fewer than 40 percent of older women are married, whereas nearly 80 percent of older men are married and live with their wives. Marital status—especially being widowed but also being divorced or separated—is a primary explanation for the high percentage (41 percent) of older women who live alone.[7] These gender differences in marital status and living arrangements for older women are significant because women's economic status in later life (as well as throughout the lifespan) is directly related to marital status.

Life expectancy, both at birth and at age 65, is higher for women than men. In 1986, total remaining life expectancy for men at age 65 was estimated at 14.4 years, while that for women was estimated at 18.7 years. For those born in 1986, life expectancy was estimated at 71.3 years for males and 78.3 years for females. Although improvements in mortality rates have been shared by both males and females over the last three decades, women have experienced more rapid improvements for most leading causes of death. Yet, proportionately more elderly women are limited in their activities of daily living than men, and elderly women visit physicians more frequently and use more days of hospital and nursing home care than men.[11] Older women have more acute and chronic conditions than men and these diseases limit their activity, but they are seldom life-threatening.[12,13] Women also bear a greater burden of health care costs than men; older women's health care expenditures constitute 63 percent of the total of the elderly's health care costs, although women make up 59 percent of the population.[11]

The availability of adult children, particularly daughters, to give care is the significant factor in keeping the frail and disabled elderly out of residential care.[14,15] Indeed, researchers have found that "the critical variable in the elderly's living arrangement was not the degree of the elderly's functional impairment but rather the access to family care."[15] Some 1.3 million elderly persons reside in institutions, three-quarters of whom are women.[7] Several factors account for this phenomenon: women live longer than men, and older women have a higher prevalence of chronic disability and are less likely than men to have a spouse from whom to receive care. Because the majority of older men have living spouses, they typically receive informal care from their wives; "females [depend on] care from offspring and relatives."[16] The importance of such family support in preventing institutionalization is shown in the statistic that persons living alone who are single, divorced, or separated have a ten times greater probability of being institutionalized than those who are married.[17]

Based on demographic projections, the greatest growth in the potential population in need of long-term care is for unmarried females aged 75 and over, with the largest increase (both absolute and relative) projected for the population of women over age 85.[16] The oldest old—generally women—can, and will, be disadvantaged not only by increasing infirmity, but also by outliving their closest relatives.

ECONOMIC STATUS OF THE AGED:
A GENDER STORY

It is a myth that the old are financially well-off and that their economic status has been achieved at the expense of the young. The best illustration of this point is the case of older women. Older women were 59 percent of the elderly population and 71 percent of its poor in 1984.[18] Significantly, over half of all older women live marginally close to, if not actually below, the poverty level.[7,19] In 1987, the median annual income was $11,854 for older men and $6,734 for older women. Even using the low official poverty line of $5,447 a year ($105 a week for a single individual), older women have almost double the poverty rate of older men.[7] Additionally, significant racial differences exist in the economic status of older women. Being old, female, and a member of a minority group represents a "triple jeopardy."[18,20] More research, especially longitudinal studies, needs to be conducted to fully identify the nature and extent of jeopardy.

Women's poverty in old age is significantly related to their marital status, added to the cumulative effects of wage discrimination and their unpaid work. Unmarried women between the ages of 65 and 69 receive approximately 40 percent of the total income of their married counterparts.[7] The substantial differences in poverty rates between married and unmarried older women reflect the economic vulnerability of a large majority of older women. Most women outlive their husbands, and for most women widowhood is accompanied by a dramatic fall in overall income. Further, these economic problems are compounded with age. With increasing age, there is a real drop in income, such that the oldest elderly have the lowest money incomes. Medical expenditures increase with age. People aged 85 and older were found in 1984 to have an average income that was 36 percent less than that of people aged 65 to 69, while Medicare costs of elders aged 80 and older were 77 percent higher than those of elders 66 to 69 years of age.[21] The "oldest old" tend to be female and, with increasing age, women are more likely to be widowed and in a precarious economic circumstance.

The impoverishment of women, however, is not unique to old age. Indeed, women of all ages are at risk of being poor, as denoted by the concept of "the feminization of poverty." Factors in the impoverishment of women include: the effects of wage discrimination and occupational segregation; lack of comparable pay; the increase in numbers of female-headed households; child care costs; inequitable divorce statutes and the extensive noncompliance with the support orders; the "widow's gap" in Social Security; the rapid increase in numbers of displaced homemakers who are especially disadvantaged in reentering the employment sector as a result of both ageism and sexism; the inadequacy of social programs; cutbacks in domestic programs; increased health care costs; and biases in pension and retirement programs for the aged.[22-26] Due to a combination of these various social processes, women are actively being pushed into low-income and poverty conditions. It should be noted here that the feminization of poverty and the marginality of older women cannot be fully understood without taking race into account. As Dressel[27] has shown, a comprehensive explanation of economic inequality and impoverishment, as well as the situation of older women within it, requires attention to the complex interrelations between gender, race, and class. This is particularly important for policy and programmatic actions, since policies designed to address female poverty alone will be insufficient to address the economic issues of older black women and older women of other racial–ethnic groups.

FACTORS IN THE ECONOMIC GENDER GAP

Older women's low income status reflects the culmination of a lifetime of secondary economic status. Contemporary wage and social policies are still based on the underlying assumption that women are economically dependent on a wage-earning male head-of-household, who theoretically shares with his wife and other dependents his higher earnings, retirement pension, and other employment-related benefits. The eligibility rules for public entitlement programs reflect the male model of work[28] and male patterns of labor force participation. The non–means-tested entitlement programs such as Social Security give men greater access to benefits and reward continuous participation in the primary labor force, while the more penurious means-tested and state-variable social assistance programs, including Supplemental Security Income (SSI), primarily support women.[29]

Thus, public and private sector policies have contributed to the perpetuation of both the gender-structured wage and public pension systems. Most women are employed in secondary jobs, receiving substantially lower wages and fewer work-related benefits (for example, health insurance coverage and retirement pensions) than their male counterparts, and women's earnings continue to average approximately three-fifths of those of men. Older women's incomes average even less. Women who invested the majority of their efforts and time in homemaking and caring for children—traditional women's roles that are socially expected—discover in old age or when they divorce or are widowed in mid-life that they are economically penalized for having performed these traditional gender role activities. As displaced homemakers these women, who expected continued economic security in their marriages, find themselves living in conditions of genuine economic hardship, victims of sexism, ageism, wage discrimination, lack of recent employment experience, and inadequate (if any) spousal support after divorce or inadequate widow's benefits after a husband's death.

The increase in numbers of mid-life and older women who suddenly need to be self-supporting after having been economically dependent in marriage is due largely to the high rate of divorce. Over one-third of the more than one million divorces annually occur between couples married 10 or more years, and 20 percent of all divorces involve couples married 15 or more years. The divorce rate among couples of long-term marriages and among those middle-aged or older continues to rise.[23,30] Divorce has profound, often lasting, effects on women's standard of living. Studies show that men recover economically from divorce, and in fact, improve their financial status after divorce. Women, however, generally experience no such recovery—unless they remarry, which few women over age 40 do.[23,30,31] While the economic effects of divorce adversely affect women of all ages, mid-life and older women have even fewer options for reversing the downward mobility prompted by divorce than do younger women.[22,23] "The dramatic increase in divorce, especially in marriages of long duration, predicts an increase in the number of older women living alone and in poverty in the next generation."[8]

Widowhood also puts some women in the status of displaced homemakers. The average age at which a woman becomes widowed in the United States is about 56, yet no Social Security widow's benefits are available until age 60.[32,33] The time between becoming widowed and turning age 60, referred to as the "widow's gap," is a time of desperate economic uncertainty for many widowed women. Coupled with the unfavorable labor market for mid-life and older reentry women, the lack of economic protection pushes many widowed women—who were economically secure during marriage—into harsh and unremitting economic conditions.

There are essentially no public funds available for providing temporary support to women, without minor children, who suddenly lose their economic base. Displaced homemakers themselves qualify for no unemployment compensation, since their family and home work is unpaid labor. They do not qualify for Social Security disability benefits. Despite the increased numbers of displaced homemakers, now estimated at nearly 11.5 million American women (70 percent of whom are over age 55),[34, p. 37] no programs have been initiated to provide economic support for these women, no matter how desperate their economic situations. Federal cuts in employment and training programs have brought these programs to their lowest funding levels in 15 years.[35] Women attempting to reenter the employment sector during mid-life or later years are directly harmed by the lack of training programs.

Sources of Income

Women's disadvantaged economic status in old age is directly related to the sources of income available to them, primarily Social Security benefits, asset income, private pension benefits, and employment earnings. These income sources are themselves directly related to women's earlier family and work activities and women's secondary status in the employment and policy sectors.

Dependency on Social Security as the primary, or often only, source of income is a major factor in older women's precarious economic standing. One in three unmarried older women receiving Social Security depends on it for more than 90 percent of her income.[36] In 1987, the average old age Social Security benefit was $6,924 annually for men and $5,292 for women.[34, p. 28] Not only are women's Social Security payments less, but women rely to a much greater extent than do men on Social Security as their primary, and often only, source of old age income.

The gender inequities of the Social Security program and its disadvantages for women are well documented.[26,36] Income inequalities throughout the basic social structure of society, based on gender and class status, are both reproduced and reinforced through the Social Security program. Because Social Security is modeled on an insurance scheme, wage earners who remain attached to the labor force throughout their adult years until retirement age—usually men—secure relatively greater protection through this public pension system. Women's lower earning records and interrupted work histories—for parenting and caring of older dependents—and their consequent economic dependency on husbands result in their lower Social Security benefits. Further, over 70 percent of women take early retirement at age 62, either to care for elderly family members or because of ill health, and so receive reduced monthly benefits. Yet, even though most women who reach age 62 will live another two or more decades, their Social Security benefits remain at the lower amount. The average Social Security monthly benefit paid to retired men in 1987 was $577, compared with $441 paid to retired women, $265 paid to dependent wives, and $342 paid to widows.[37]

Several Social Security reforms of the 1980s will adversely affect women, including those who will enter old age in the coming years: (*a*) the 1983 and other intermittent periods during which Social Security cost-of-living adjustments (COLAs) have been frozen, even for limited periods of time (for example, it has been projected that a delay in the COLA for only one year would bring 500,000 more elderly, mostly women, below the poverty level; (*b*) the gradual increase of the retirement age to 67 and the stepped-up penalties for early retirement (which nearly three-quarters of older women take); (*c*) the termination of the widow's benefit when the youngest child reaches age 16 rather than 18; (*d*) the phase-out of student benefits for children of retired, disabled, or deceased workers, all of which affect older women; and (*e*) the elimination of the minimum Social Security benefit (which earlier had been only $122 per month) for persons retiring after January 1982, which further disadvantages the poorest women by removing them from the respectability of Social Security coverage and forcing many to seek public assistance in the form of SSI.[7] The major policy changes that are likely to positively affect older women were in the pension reforms, particularly those of 1984 and 1986 that reduced the time for pension vesting (from ten to five years) and required the signature of the pensioner spouse who wishes to receive higher pension benefits during his lifetime by resigning the rights to a pension for the surviving spouse. In addition, one of the few remaining provisions of the repealed Catastrophic Coverage Act was a provision on spousal impoverishment to protect a minimum income and assets for spouses of those who are institutionalized in nursing homes.

Income from private pensions does not compensate for women's low Social Security payments. Only about 13 percent of older women receive income from private pensions and, even then, the amounts received are less than half the amounts received by men. According to Moon's[38] estimate, women's pensions averaged 59 percent of men's in amount. Women's lower earnings and intermittent attachment to the wage labor force contribute to their lower pension coverage. As noted, many women who become widowed or divorced are inadequately protected with regard to legal claim to their husband's accrued pension funds, even though the "pension accrued by the working spouse is often the single largest asset of an older married couple."[39] Assets contribute relatively little to older women's overall income. Even though approximately one-half of the older population receives income from assets, most people receive very small amounts of asset income, and the proportion of total income that it represents is low.[26] Evidence indicates that individuals whose lifetime incomes are high will accumulate more assets than those whose incomes are relatively low. This means that women, whose lifetime incomes are significantly lower than men's and whose economic status depends primarily on their marital status, are not likely to benefit from asset income during old age. Only 7.2 percent of older women improved their economic status through employment in 1986, and the majority of these women had only part-time employment.[7] Thus, the total amounts of income derived by older women from pensions, assets, and employment generally do not significantly add to Social Security benefits. Most older men, however, rely on a combination of income sources and are relatively secure in their economic status.

Income Supports for the Very Poor

The SSI program is a federal–state cash assistance program for the poor aged, blind, and disabled. Eligibility for SSI benefits requires extreme poverty and almost no assets (a maximum of $2,000). Nationally there are four and a half million beneficiaries, about three-quarters of whom qualify on the basis of age. Three-quarters of the aged SSI recipients are women—not surprisingly, given the much higher poverty rate of older women compared with men.[7] The income assistance provided through the SSI program is so minimal that its recipients remain below the poverty level.[40] The monthly federal benefit level for SSI for aged persons living alone was $354 in 1988, and only 26 states supplemented this amount (but at a very limited level, averaging about $1.00 a day).[34, p. 28] In nominal dollars, this supplementation has been cut 16 percent since 1980, and it has been eroded by an estimated 40 percent due to inflation.[34] Further, SSI benefit levels discriminate against single individuals by setting the maximum federal benefit level at 76 percent of the poverty line for individuals (mostly women) and at 90 percent of the poverty line for couples. Eligibility requirements for SSI are so rigid that, once a woman becomes a beneficiary, few options exist for moving off this program,[14,41] and it is estimated that only half of those eligible for this assistance receive it. Further, state Medicaid programs have tightened eligibility requirements in the last decade, contributing to a decline in the proportion of poor who are eligible for Medicaid, from 63 percent in 1975 to 40 percent in 1987. Among the aged, an even lower percentage of those below the poverty level are covered, and the percentage of poor aged (again, largely women) in the Medicaid program has also declined.[39,42]

The deleterious economic status of older women of the future must remain a serious cause for concern, particularly in view of the projections of the Commonwealth Fund[43] that, by 2020, the percentage of older men living alone who are poor or near-poor will decline rapidly (from 38 to 6 percent), while the proportion of poor and near-poor older women will change little (declining from 45 to 38 percent).

HEALTH CARE

A large body of data has consistently shown that social class and health are correlated, with the poor and near-poor most compromised. Older women's lower incomes are coupled with ill health and the likelihood of increased need for medical care. Medical and health care costs have increased for older women owing to higher patient cost-sharing and the greater need for care with age. As aggregate medical care costs continue to rise, publicly financed health programs have been faced with growing constraints. Yet, older women's available income remains relatively fixed and will fall with the death of a spouse. It has been well documented that Medicare meets only 44 percent of the elderly's health care costs.[44,45] However, a recent study showed that, while Medicare meets about 44 percent of the health care expenditures of elderly married couples, it meets only about 33 percent of these costs for an elderly single woman.[45] This is easily understood in the context of Medicare's acute care policy that, on average, pays out more in both Part A (hospital) and Part B (physician) benefits to men than to women, and shortchanges women in terms of the chronic illness care they need.[46]

Few private insurance dollars (less than 16 percent) go to health services for the aged.[25] Because most private health insurance coverage is a benefit of employment, those who are unemployed, retired, or low-wage casual employees are not likely to have private health insurance coverage. "The lack of health insurance is most common among those least able to afford the consequences of poor health or lack of preventive health care."[25] Further, because women's marital status is a more significant predictor of their health insurance coverage than is their own employment status, older women lose access to health coverage when they lose their spouse through death or divorce.[47] Because older women make up the majority of the older poor and those who are not married, it is women who are least able to cover out-of-pocket expenses or to afford supplementary private insurance coverage.

Because of escalating health care costs, aged persons actually expend a greater share of their income on health care costs now than they did prior to the enactment of Medicare.[36,40] A Congressional report in March 1984 stated that the average out-of-pocket costs for doctors' bills was "virtually the same for older persons with incomes under $5,000 as for those few older persons with incomes of $36,000 and up."[24] Older women, who are at greater risk for chronic disability and disadvantaged economic status, bear a heavier out-of-pocket burden for health care costs, in terms of both absolute dollars and proportion of income expended. An elderly married couple paid about 9 percent of its income on direct out-of-pocket payments and health insurance premiums in 1986, compared with the almost double out-of-pocket expenses paid by single elderly women (over 16 percent of their incomes).[45] Most older men are in couples, whereas most older women are not. Further, single women's spending increases proportionately with age, with monthly out-of-pocket expenses being greater for the oldest old. Although the average income of people aged 85 and older is 36 percent less than the income of people aged 65 to 69, Medicare costs for those over 80 have been shown to be 77 percent greater than those between 65 and 69.[21]

Older women must purchase supplementary medical insurance (Part B premiums for physicians' services and Medigap coverage to cushion the cost of hospital and physician deductibles and copayments not covered by Medicare), or else they must pay out-of-pocket for the costs that are not covered by Medicare directly. Out-of-pocket and cost-sharing expenses for all elderly receiving hospital and physician services increased substantially in the 1980s. Obviously, low-income individuals are handicapped the most by these changes. Aged recipients of SSI cash assistance may qualify for publicly financed health coverage through the Medicaid program, but the eligibility requirements of many states are more restrictive than those for SSI.[48] Thus, many who are poor and near-poor are denied this health coverage.[35,49] Over $15 billion was cut from the Medicaid program between 1980 and 1987. Medicaid cuts were implemented through reductions in the federal share of the costs and incentives provided to states to constrain expenditures and access in this program for the poor. One result has been that the variability among the states in their eligibility and utilization has increased, as the percentage below poverty who are covered by Medicaid has declined.[50,51]

No publicly financed health coverage exists for nondisabled American adults prior to their eligibility age for Medicare (age 65), unless they are economically destitute or qualify as medically needy under Medicaid. Women below age 65 and past the years of raising minor children cannot qualify for Medicare coverage unless they are disabled. Given that displaced homemakers are more likely to have no private health insurance, because most of it is a benefit of husbands' employment, divorced women are twice as likely as any other group to be without any kind of health insurance coverage.[47] Recent legislation (COBRA) has been adopted to require employers to offer conversion plans to retain health insurance for women for a limited time period (18 months) following widowhood or divorce, but they must be able to afford to purchase it (paying both their own and their employer's share of the insurance). Following this, women attempting to obtain *new* coverage will be particularly disadvantaged if they have preexisting medical conditions because of the exclusions that insurers typically impose. Lack of money and the presence of certain medical conditions simply preclude access to private health insurance for many unmarried mid-life and older women. In future years, not only are more women likely to enter old age already poor, but—without major health reform—more women will enter old age without having had access to adequate preventive medical care during important periods earlier in their lifetimes.

Several limited advances have occurred in health care that are of import to older women. These include the ability to extend health insurance coverage under COBRA, the inclusion under Medicare of coverage for Pap smears, and the requirement that, for the elderly poor, Medicaid programs cover copayments, deductibles, and premiums. However, the continuing omission of long-term care coverage under Medicare is particularly damaging for women because they are asked to provide 80 percent of these services, and the individual costs of women's doing so have begun to be documented.

CAREGIVING, WOMEN, AND IDEOLOGY: THE CONSEQUENCES

The 1980s have been marked by an ideological revolution in which the New Right that was forged promoted a simultaneous revival of the free market (under neoliberalism) and a return of the (now-mythical) patriarchal autonomous family (under neoconservatism). The former ideological strain is distinctly oriented toward a "minimalist state" in being hostile to anything that may impede the (natural) order of the market (and its natural superiority). The latter appeals to authority, allegiance, tradition, and to "nature." "A corollary . . . is that the [traditional nuclear] family is central to maintaining the state."[52] Because this New Right model "squares the circle between an intellectual adherence to the free market and the emotional attachment to authority and imposed tradition,"[53] it melds the interests of capitalism and patriarchy. Further, the New Right has reminded us that the primary, if not the only, justification for government intervention is the national defense and law enforcement.

Natural rights individualism is the "ideological cement" binding together contemporary neoconservative and neoliberal ideas and U.S. politics,[54, p. 232] supporting principles of self-help based on economic initiative and productivity, individual autonomy, and voluntary association. The difficulty in restoring "both the giant corporation and the autonomous family . . . to their 'rightful place' in American life [requires] . . . faith and patriotism,"[54, p. 237] but it is a project whose stunning success is one of the most significant hallmarks of Ronald Reagan's presidency. Reagan's ideological project was operationalized through a policy agenda designed to promote both privatization of the welfare state and the isolation of the "family" from "society."[55] Privatization policies promote the belief that the "proper" and best form of health and social services to the elderly is nongovernmental. In U.S. health and social policy, privatization has operated hand-in-glove with the increased informalization of care bolstered by the rhetoric of family responsibility. The message once again was that women workers should return home to care for their elderly;[56] yet there was a contradictory message that those who do not achieve labor market participation on the male model will not be helped by the state. Phrases such as the "sandwich generation," the "daughter shortage," the "baby dearth" were bemoaned, yet policymakers remained firm in their refusal to move toward a long-term care policy and beyond reaffirmations of the need for continuing family support.[57]

As a consequence, every American woman can expect to spend 18 years of her life helping an aging parent and 17 years caring for children.[57] It has been estimated that over 27 million days of unpaid caregiving are provided for older Americans every week. Women's caregiving directly affects both their economic status and health in old age. These effects again point to the structural conditions that contribute to women's lower socio-economic status and to the direct and indirect economic costs of caregiving. The women who give care to their disabled spouses may have to drain their savings and assets acquired during the marriage, "spending them down" on their spouse's or parent's needs. Family labor—more precisely, women's unpaid labor—is viewed as free labor (if recognized as labor at all). Yet, it is in government's interest to secure as much of this free work as possible since it relieves the government of the costs of having to provide adequate long-term care. It is noteworthy that "over 40 percent of adult offspring participating in one survey reported that the time spent on caregiving tasks was equivalent to the time required by a full-time job."[15]

Additionally, there are "opportunity costs"—costs that may well be the greatest economic expense of caregiving. The women who take early retirement or otherwise modify their employment to provide care lose not only wages and wage-related benefits, but also additional Social Security credits. Studies suggest that changing work patterns and even quitting work are common coping strategies of caregivers.[58] Data from the Informal Caregivers Survey, a component of the larger National Long-Term Care Survey, indicate that a majority of caregiving women had either reduced their paid working hours, rearranged their work schedules, taken time off without pay, or quit their jobs to resolve conflicting demands of caregiving and employment.[59] Caregiver women jeopardize their own sources of income for their later years: Social Security and private pension benefits are directly tied to wages and employment patterns. In these ways, female caregivers' own economic dependency is reproduced. Because a total of only five years can be dropped out from the averaging of accrued Social Security credits, women who quit their employment to caretake (either their children or elders) directly affect their future Social Security benefits, and perhaps even their eligibility. These caregiving women find themselves in a no-win situation: they are expected to provide care to their husbands or elderly relatives, yet public policy economically penalizes them for doing so. Because the majority of older women's economic situations are precarious, at best, the added costs from caregiving are significant.

Caregiving carries high physical health risks.[58,60] Physical labor, sometimes excessive, is part of caregiving, and disabled persons need various kinds of assistance. Because many caregivers themselves are old, or approaching old age,[59] they too are vulnerable to, and may be experiencing, chronic ailments. Older women have more health problems than do older men,[11,12] yet it is women who do most caregiving work. Additionally, there are somatic outcomes of high levels of stress: high blood pressure, fatigue and exhaustion, and greater susceptibility to physical illness are some of the physical health risks.[12] Lack of respite and relief from responsiblities, lack of assistance in performing physical tasks, and emotional fatigue and overload thwart a caregiver's recovery from illness.[61] Their physical health is also endangered by a lack of preventive health care resulting from inadequate financial resources, time, and attention to the onset of disabilities.[58,60]

UNSETTLED FUTURE

Social policies are shaped largely by requirements of the economy and the politics surrounding it. Women's position as female workers, caregivers, and beneficiaries of public policies continues to be systematically unequal to that of men. By failing to address these structural inequities, social policies perpetuate, both directly and indirectly, the disadvantaged economic and health situation of older women thoughout old age.

Under the policies and fiscal retrenchment of the 1980s, the position of women has been undermined, and there has been a distinct shift of resources away from women to men and from minorities to whites. The most important elements of the Reagan legacy for older women[57] are: (*a*) intensified commodification and medicalization of care for the aging in ways that are consistent with capitalist expansion of the medical-industrial complex;[62] (*b*) the continuing refusal of the State to provide meaningful long-term care benefits to the elderly and disabled; (*c*) the accumulation of multiple pressures on a beleagured network of traditionally nonprofit home and community-based health and social service providers, thinly stretched by the demands of very sick and very old patients discharged from the hospital earlier than ever before[63] and a growing population of oldest old (85 and over); and (*d*) the use of policies to promote family responsibility and increase the informalization of care. These efforts to restore and regulate family life (primarily women) are congruent with the deep concerns of the state and capital to minimize state costs for the elderly, and concerns of the New Right to restore patriarchal family arrangements to assure a continuing supply of women's free labor essential to the reproduction and maintenance of the work force.[64] The Reagan Administration's resistance to a federal policy solution to the problem of long-term care and its unstated policy of informalization must be understood as part of a larger austerity strategy in the context of the state's need for women (regardless of their labor force participation) to continue to perform large (and increasing) amounts of unpaid servicing work.[28]

The economic and health situations of older women require deep structural and policy changes that redress inequities and provide access to basic resources, including Social Security, housing, health and long-term care, and broad-based social reforms aimed at ending the social and economic inequities experienced by women. The economic and health issues confronted by aging and aged women will challenge the very structure of our social institutions. In conclusion, some points warrant reemphasis. The relationship between the private and public spheres has a profound effect on the economic and health condition of women. This effect will vary across different critical periods of older women's lives as their overall health status declines and available financial and social resources become more limited. The opportunity for responding to these increasing needs varies, not only by gender, but by class and race.

The austerity imposed on publicly funded programs has redirected attention away from the prior decade's concern for increasing access to a comprehensive system of health and social services. Today, the greater emphasis upon individual self-reliance, private insurance, and the ability to save for and purchase health care makes the issue of an adequate income policy more important than ever. Health must be regarded in the broad sense to include well-being and not merely the absence of disease. Thus, women's income issues cannot be ignored in the health policy debate. Public commitment to a strong state role remains essential because of the deep structural origins and potential solutions to the problems identified here. Key issues for older women are not only state policies that provide adequate income, health, and long-term care, but also policies that abridge (and compensate for) the gendered division of labor and lifelong discrimination that women experience.

REFERENCES

1. Estes, C., Gerard, J., and Clark, A. Women and the economics of aging. *Int. J. Health Serv.* 14: 55–68, 1984.

2. Marmot, M. G., Kogevinas, M., and Elston, M. A. Social/economic status and disease. *Annu. Rev. Public Health* 8: 111–135, 1987.

3. Dutton, D. B. Social class, health and fitness. In *Applications of Social Science to Clinical Medicine and Health Policy,* edited by L. H. Aiken and D. Mechanic, pp. 31–62. Rutgers University Press, New Brunswick, N.J., 1986.

4. Butler, L. H., and Newacheck, P. W. Health and social factors relevant to long-term care policy. In *Policy Options in Long-term Care,* edited by J. Meltzer, F. Farrow, and H. Richman, pp. 38–77. University of Chicago Press, Chicago, 1981.

5. Kane, R. A., and Kane, R. L. *Long-term Care: Principle, Programs, and Policies.* Springer, New York, 1987.

6. Luft, H. S. *Poverty and Health: Economic Causes and Consequences of Health Problems.* Ballinger, Cambridge, Mass., 1978.

7. United States Bureau of the Census. *Statistical Abstract of the United States, 1988. National Data Book and Guide to Sources.* U.S. Government Printing Office, Washington, D.C., 1989.

8. King, N., and Marvel, M. *Issues, Policies, and Programs for Midlife and Older Women,* p. 44. Center for Women's Policy Studies, Washington, D.C., 1982.

9. Schultz, J. *The Economics of Aging.* Van Nostrand Reinhold, New York, 1985.

10. Stone, R. *Recent Developments in Respite Care Services for Caregivers of*

the Impaired Elderly. The Institute for Health and Aging, University of California, San Francisco, July 1985.

11. Rice, D., and Estes, C. Health of the elderly: Policy issue and challenges. *Health Aff.* 3: 25–49, 1984.

12. Verbrugge, L. Women and men: Mortality and health of older people. In *Aging in Society: Selected Reviews of Recent Research,* edited by M. Riley, B. Hess, and K. Bond. Lawrence Erlbauns Association, London, 1983.

13. Rice, D. Sex differences in mortality and morbidity: Some aspects of the economic burden. In *Sex Differentials in Mortality: Trends, Determinants, and Consequences,* edited by A. Lopez and L. Ruzicka. Department of Demography, Canberra, Australia, 1983.

14. Vladeck, B. *Unloving Care: The Nursing Home Tragedy.* Basic Books, New York, 1980.

15. Feldblum, C. Home health care for the elderly: Programs, problems, and potential. *Harvard J. Legislation* 22: 194–254, 1985.

16. Manton, K., and Soldo, B. Dynamics of health change in the oldest old. *Milbank Mem. Fund. Q. Health Soc.* 63: 252, 1985.

17. Butler, L., and Newacheck, P. W. Health and social factors relevant to long term care policy. In *Policy Options in Long-term Care,* edited by J. Meltzer, F. Farrow, and H. Richman, pp. 38–77. University of Chicago Press, Chicago, 1981.

18. Minkler, M., and Stone, R. The feminization of poverty and older women. *Gerontologist* 25: 351–357, 1985.

19. Grad, S. Incomes of the aged and nonaged, 1950–82. *Social Security Bull.* 47(6), 1984.

20. Markides, K. S., and Mindel, C. H. *Aging and ethnicity,* pp. 31–35. Sage, Beverly Hills, 1987.

21. Torrey, B. Sharing increasing costs on declining income: The visible dilemma of the invisible aged. *Milbank Mem. Fund Q. Health Soc.* 63: 385–387, 1985.

22. Arendell, T. *Mothers and Divorce: Legal, Economic, and Social Dilemmas.* University of California Press, Berkeley, 1986.

23. Arendell, T. A review: Women and the economics of divorce in the contemporary United States. *Signs: Journal of Women in Culture and Society,* Winter 1987.

24. Coalition on Women and the Budget. *Inequality of Sacrifice: The Impact of the Reagan Budget on Women.* National Women's Law Center, Washington, D.C., March 1984.

25. Kasper, A., and Soldinger, E. Falling between the cracks: How health insurance discriminates against women. *Women Health* 8: 77–93, 1983.

26. Rix, S. *Older Women: The Economics of Aging.* Women's Research and Education Institute of the Congressional Caucus for Women's Issues, Washington, D.C., 1984.

27. Dressel, P. L. Gender, race, and class: Beyond the feminization of poverty in later life. *Gerontologist* 28: 177–180, 1988.

28. Sassoon, A. S. Women's new social role: Contradictions of the welfare state. In *Women and the State,* edited by A. S. Sassoon, pp. 166–167. Hutchinson, London, 1987.

29. Quadagno, J. Race, class, and gender in the U.S. welfare state: Nixon's failed Family Assistance Plan. *Am. Sociol. Rev.* 55: 11–28, 1990.

30. National Center for Health Statistics. *Monthly Vital Statistics Report.* U.S. Department of Health and Human Services, Washington, D.C., 1985.

31. Weitzman, L. *The Divorce Revolu-*

tion. The Free Press, New York, 1985.

32. U.S. Senate Special Committee on Aging. *Aging America: Trends and Projections, 1985–86*. U.S. Department of Health and Human Services, Washington, D.C., 1986.

33. Markson, E. *Older Women: Issues and Prospects*. Lexington Books, Lexington, Mass., 1985.

34. Families U.S.A. Foundation. *Three Year Report (1986–1987–1988)*. Washington, D.C., 1989.

35. United States Congress. *Problems of Working Women*. Hearing before the Joint Economic Commissions, April 4. U.S. Government Printing Office, Washington, D.C., 1984.

36. Women's Equity Action League (WEAL). *WEAL Facts: Letter to the Editor, Equity for Women*. Washington, D.C., 1985.

37. Social Security Bulletin. *Annual Statistical Supplement, 1988*. U.S. Department of Health and Human Services, Social Security Administration, Washington, D.C., 1988.

38. Moon, M. Economic Issues Facing a Growing Population of Older Women. Paper presented at the American Sociological Association, New York, September 1986.

39. United States Senate, Special Committee on Aging. *The Future of Medicine*. U.S. Government Printing Office, Washington, D.C., 1983.

40. United States Congress. *An Analysis of the President's Budgetary Proposals for Fiscal Year 1986*. Congressional Budget Office, U.S. Government Printing Office, Washington, D.C., February 1986.

41. Crystal, S. *America's Old Age Crisis: Public Policy and the Two Worlds of Aging*. Basic Books, New York, 1982.

42. Estes, C. Long-term care and public policy in an era of austerity.
J. Public Health Policy 6: 464–475, 1985.

43. Commonwealth Fund Commission on the Elderly People Living Alone. Testimony of Karen Davis, Director, to House of Representatives, Select Committee on Aging. *Report on the Quality of Life for Older Women: Older Women Living Alone*. U.S. Government Printing Office, Washington, D.C., 1988.

44. National Health Law Program. *In Poor Health: The Administration's 1985 Health Budget*. Los Angeles, 1985.

45. ICF, Inc. *Medicare's Role in Financing the Health Care of Older Women*. Submitted to the American Association of Retired Persons, July 1985.

46. United States Department of Health and Human Services, Health Care Financing Administration, Division of Program Statistics. Unpublished data for 1984.

47. Berk, M., and Taylor, A. Women and Divorce: Health Insurance Coverage, Utilization, and Health Care Expenditures: National Health Care Expenditures Study. Paper presented at the Annual Meeting of the American Public Health Association, Dallas, November 1983.

48. Estes, C., et al. *Organizational and Community Responses to Medicare Policy: Consequences for Health and Social Services for the Elderly. Project Summary*. The Institute for Health and Aging, University of California, San Francisco, 1985.

49. Davis, K., and Rowland, D. Uninsured and underserved: Inequities in health care in the United States. In *Securing Access to Health Care 3*. Presidential Commission for the Study of Ethical Problems in Medicine and Biomedical and Behavior Research. U.S. Government Printing Office, Washington, D.C., March 1983.

50. Holahan, J. F., and Cohen, J. W. *Medicaid: The Trade-off Between Cost Containment and Access to Care.* Urban Institute, Washington, D.C., 1984.

51. Darling, H. The role of the federal government in assuring access to health care. *Inquiry* 23: 286–295, 1986.

52. Levitas, R. Competition and compliance: The utopias of the New Right. In *The Ideology of the New Right,* edited by R. Levitas, p. 93. Polity Press, Cambridge, Mass., 1986.

53. Edgar, D. The free or the good. In *The Ideology of the New Right,* edited by R. Levitas, pp. 74–75. Polity Press, Cambridge, Mass., 1986.

54. O'Connor, J. *Accumulation Crisis.* Basil Blackwell, New York, 1984.

55. Myles, J. Personal communication, March 1989.

56. Binney, E. A., Estes, C. L., and Humphers, S. Informalization and Community Services for the Elderly. Paper presented at the American Sociological Association, San Francisco, 1989.

57. Estes, C. L. The Reagan legacy: Privatization, the welfare state, and aging. In *States, Labor Markets, and the Future of Old Age,* edited by J. Myles and J. Quadagno. Temple University Press, Philadelphia, 1991.

58. Brody, E. Parent care as a normative family stress. *Gerontologist* 25: 19–29, 1985.

59. Stone, R., Cafferata, G., and Sangl, J. *Caregivers of the Frail Elderly: A National Profile.* National Center for Health Services Research, Rockville, Md., 1986.

60. Bader, J. Respite care: Temporary relief for caregivers. *Women Health* [*Special Issue*] 10(2/3): 39–52, 1985.

61. Corbin, J., and Strauss, A. Issues concerning regime management in the home. *Ageing and Society* 5: 249–265, 1985.

62. Estes, C. L., and Binney, E. A. The biomedicalization of aging: Dangers and dilemmas. *Gerontologist* 29: 587–596, 1990.

63. Wood, J. B., and Estes, C. L. The impact of DRGs on community-based service providers: Implications for the elderly. *Am. J. Public Health* 80: 840–843, 1990.

64. Abramovitz, M. *Regulating the Lives of Women,* pp. 349–379. South End Press, Boston, 1988.

Resolve to think of nothing but . . . health *in the first place and . . . honor and comfort in the second, because in this fickle world we can do nothing else.*
— Isabella D'Este, Sixteenth century

11

Quality of Care

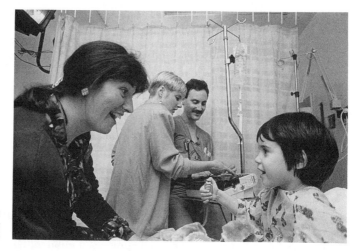

Care of high quality—a nursing priority

William L. Holzemer

Quality and Cost of Nursing Care: Is Anybody Out There Listening?

The well-being of our society is threatened by the health problems we are facing: the homeless, drug use, high infant mortality rate, and the HIV/AIDS epidemic. In addition, the health care needs of the estimated 37 million Americans without health insurance—mostly women and children—are not currently being met by our delivery and reimbursement systems. Yet the costs of health care to this nation continue to escalate—DRGs notwithstanding. A coordinated program of nursing research is required that will contribute to documenting the impact of nursing interventions on patient outcomes and the cost-effectiveness of those outcomes. Maraldo (1989) wrote that nursing must "assume responsibility for its own actions and that means assuming its rightful role in hospitals, in health care delivery, and in shaping the policies that determine the future of health care delivery" (p. 2).

QUALITY OF CARE

A prominent theme in health care in the 1980s has been quality of care. Beyers (1988) wrote:

> The common measure in health care delivery services today from a clinical perspective is the quality of care provided. Consequently, in the midst of variations in delivery systems, quality provides stability. Quality serves as the balance that demonstrates professional commitment to patient care. This balance is needed in the formidable process of unbundling and restructuring health care. Clinical providers now depend on quality measures to ensure that the financial and organizational changes do, in fact, serve patients

William L. Holzemer, Ph.D., R.N., F.A.A.N., is Professor, Department of Mental Health, Community Health, and Administrative Nursing, and Associate Dean for Research, School of Nursing at the University of California, San Francisco.

From Holzemer, W. L. (1990). Quality and cost of nursing care: Is anybody out there listening? *Nursing & Health Care* 10(8):412–415. Copyright 1989. Reprinted with permission from the National League for Nursing.

well. Quality outcomes are used to balance organizational prerogatives. Quality is the vehicle to ensure public trust in health care delivery (p. 618).

Although quality of care was an important theme in the 1980s, it is not yet adequately defined.

Donabedian (1968) reported that it was very difficult to define the quality of care but that it could be promoted by evaluating process and outcome variables. By 1980, he stated that an adequate definition of quality of care remained a mystery. Donabedian (1980) was clear to note that quality of care could not be defined without taking into account issues of cost. In a review of current issues in quality of care, Lohr, Yordy, and Thier (1988) wrote, "Implicit in the concept of quality of care is the idea that service should be provided in a cost-efficient and cost-effective manner . . ." (p. 17). Wilson (1986) related this discussion to nursing research when she wrote, "the amount and type of published research providing documentation of those outcomes related to nursing care have increased significantly, but the literature reports little about cost-effective nursing practice" (p. 57). More recently, we have the call from the Secretary's Commission on Nursing (Commission on Nursing, 1988) to conduct research on the relationship of health care financing and nursing practice" (Recommendation 15, p. 69).

Some suggest that quality can be quantified on some type of scale, and, hence, we see in the literature phrases like "promoting high-quality care." Most definitions of the quality of care, however, recognize both the art and technology of the health sciences. These definitions reflect concerns for caring behaviors and technical skills. Merry (1987) discussed several subjective aspects involved with the measurement of the quality of care. Subjective aspects were defined with examples such as the patients' perceptions of the degree of caring provided by the nursing staff. Merry also discussed objective aspects of quality of care including items like the numbers of deaths and infections. Health care providers agree that these objective indicators are important aspects of care. Only recently, however, has there been a growing consensus that the quality of care is also defined by the recipient of that care. The Joint Commission on Accreditation of Health Care Organizations (JCAHO) now recognizes the importance of measures of patient satisfaction as indicators of quality care.

A national panel of health care experts recently defined quality of care as the:

Evaluation of the performance of medical providers according to the degree to which the process of care increases the probability of outcomes desired by patients and reduces the probability of undesired outcomes, given the state of medical knowledge. Which elements of patient outcomes predominate depends on the patient condition (U.S. Congress, 1988, p. xi).

One might expect that the definition of such a prestigious group would reflect a concept of quality of care that includes the contributions of all types of providers. Unfortunately, the authors of many of the recent federal reports provide only a physician's definition of quality of care, not a definition that encompasses all the components of care from patients' and other providers' perspectives.

These congressional reports appear to ignore the interdisciplinary nature of health care delivery and the real nature of patients' health problems. A list of indicators of quality of care, categorized by the type of medical provider and by the assessment approach used, was presented. Many of the structure, process, and outcome indicators discussed are significantly affected by nursing and other care providers, yet there was no mention of nursing or other providers. Two examples illustrate this point. Adverse events that occur within a hospital setting, such as falls (a process indicator) and complete discharge patient assessments (an outcome indicator), are suggested as significant indicators of quality of care at an institutional level by this congressional report. The report, however, did not discuss or even mention that it is nurses who complete incident reports and nurses or social workers who often manage discharge planning.

THE SILENT VOICES

Recent governmental reports demonstrate the need to expand the research by nursing and other disciplines on the quality and cost of care. The report to the Ranking Minority Member, Special Committee on Aging, U.S. Senate (1988) titled, *MEDICARE: Improved Patient Outcome Analyses Could Enhance Quality Assessment,* discussed the need to enhance the available measures of patient outcomes. The actual or potential contribution by nursing or other providers to the measurement of patient care is *not* addressed. The report stated, "None [of the nine analytical approaches available to measure patient outcomes] have yet been adequately validated for effectiveness in targeting cases for quality review" (p. 4). It does not appear to occur to these authors that these measures may not be reliable measures of the quality of patient care because of their lack of input from health care providers besides physicians.

A synthesis of the measurement strategies to assess quality of care was recently released by the U.S. Congress (1988), titled *The Quality of Medical Care: Information for Consumers.* The report discussed the six generic quality screens developed by the Health Care Financing Administration. Four of these screens reflect patient outcome indicators that are dramatically affected by nursing and other providers. These four indicators include the adequacy of discharge planning, the status of patient at discharge, the presence of nosocomial infections, and the potential trauma suffered in the hospital (e.g. falls). The potential relationships among nursing assessments, interventions, and patient outcomes relative to these four screens were not addressed! The contributions of dieticians, social workers, or respiratory therapists were not addressed. It is unconscionable that such a document could be prepared with no recognition of the contributions to quality care by many health care providers.

The recent summary report on the *Physician Payment Review Commission* (1988) was charged to recommend reforms on the methods of payment for physician services provided by Medicare payments. Their report has become well known for promoting a relative value concept that may result in increasing payments to some groups of physicians, such as general practitioners and psychiatrists, and lowering payments to other groups, such as surgeons.

The authors developed their recommendations working under the assumption that the available Medicare dollars should be redistributed among physician specialities—and potentially among surgical assistants and those who provide nonphysician diagnostic services. The report fails to recognize that two of their goals, maximum access to care and quality of care, might have been compromised by their competing goal of promoting equity among physicians. There were no discussions of strategies to enhance the quality of care that might result in the redistribution of Medicare dollars to provide payments to other types of providers, such as nurse practitioners, midwives, or chiropractors. There was no discussion on how the consumer would like these limited Medicare dollars redistributed.

A final example of the silent voices in these reports on health and health care in the United States is illustrated by a recent American Medical Association report. Ring (1988) examined the use of severity of illness data by hospitals and concluded that although there were several well-developed severity systems, the concept of severity of illness should not be considered a quality indicator. The nurse scientist's role in the development, utilization, and analyses of these severity of illness scales in hospital settings was not discussed. The opportunity to evaluate the changes in the severity of illness indicators as a potential measure of quality of care was dismissed.

The theme that develops in these medically driven quality-of-care studies is the invisibility of nursing and other health care providers. Reports are written that covertly suggest the minimal or nonexistent contribution of nursing and others to quality of patient care.

CURRENT WORK IN NURSING

Nursing leaders such as Abdellah (1961) have long recognized the need to conduct research on the cost-effectiveness of nursing interventions.

However, recently Larson and Peters (1986) warned that there have been too many studies that have separated assessment of quality of care from costs. Lang and Clinton (1984) reviewed the literature on the quality of care from 1974 to 1982 within a framework of structure, process, and outcome and reported that there were only a few studies that related nursing interventions with cost. The factors in these quality-of-care studies that were related to cost analyses included health care agency expenditures of salaries, nurse absenteeism and turnover, unscheduled overtime and sick pay, temporary nursing personnel, supplies, patient care episode costs, patient day costs, administrative expenditures, audit costs, and patient education costs. Health services utilization costs included length of stay, hospitalization rate, emergency room use, and clinic visit costs. Lang and Clinton's conclusions agreed with Fagin's (1982) earlier work. There is only modest evidence to support the conclusion that nursing interventions have been documented to be effective and cost-effective.

Fagin and Jacobsen (1985) found only six studies that examined innovative nursing interventions within a cost-effectiveness framework. Each study was unique and, hence, not helpful in developing a model to examine the relationship between nursing interventions and cost-effectiveness. More recent work on costing has focused on the direct and indirect nursing costs per DRG (McLain & Selhat, 1984; Mowry & Korpman, 1985; Reschak et al., 1983).

Efforts to classify the nature and outcomes of nursing interventions have developed largely independent of studies of costing outcomes. For example, Smith (1988) presented a unique meta-analysis of nursing intervention research. Based upon her criteria for selecting intervention studies, 42 studies were located. Seventeen of the 42 studies (40%) used instruction, teaching, or information explanation as their type of nursing intervention. Smith aggregated these interventions to three levels, including: doing for/to/with, teaching, and both doing and teaching. Holzemer (1988) recently categorized 1,139 interventions noted by nurses in a primary health care project in Nigeria into seven categories with education accounting for 46% of the interventions. These works and others (Bulechek and McCloskey, 1985; Campbell, 1984) provide background for developing a conceptual model of nursing interventions, which must be linked to patient outcomes.

Work on classifying patient outcomes is preliminary and equally provocative. The development, approval mechanisms, and dissemination activities of the North American Nursing Diagnoses Association provides a classification system for the conceptualization of patient problems (Kim et al., 1987). It is possible to define outcomes as the change in status of patient problems.

Smith's (1988) analyses of patient outcomes paralleled her report on interventions and 17 of the 42 outcomes focused upon learning as an outcome. Holzemer (1988) made a judgment about the nature of the outcome of nursing interventions by examining the relationship between initial problem and reported results. Outcomes were classified for each identified problem as: problem resolved, problem less severe, problem unresolved, and problem worsened. Waltz and Strickland (1988) and Strickland and Waltz (1988) present several strategies used by investigators to measure outcomes, yet there does not appear to be a conceptual framework robust enough for the task of explaining patient outcomes resulting from nursing interventions.

The work of Werley and Devine (1987) on the development of the nursing minimum data set provides a framework for the structure necessary to develop a classification scheme that is supposed to relate interventions, outcomes, and costs. However, the nursing minimum data set is not helpful in understanding how to link conceptually interventions with outcomes, only that it is important to record them in a data system. The integration of costing outcome studies within these existing classification schemes of patient problems, nursing interventions, and outcomes is critical to our ability to evaluate the quality and cost of nursing care.

THE CHALLENGE

Ellwood's (1988) recent presentation on outcomes management in the *New England Journal of Medicine* is fascinating. He suggests that patients are uninformed today, the payers of health care—government, unions, and business—are very skeptical, physicians are frustrated with the pressures of DRGs and cost-containment, and health care executives are besieged. He calls for the development of a measure of functional status and well-being to enhance our ability to assess quality of care, yet is unaware of the work by nurses in acuity systems. He calls for a national database that would include new outcome measures, yet makes no mention of the nursing minimum data set. He refers to the health care system as an organism desperately in need of a central nervous system that can help it cope with the complexities of today's health care system.

Nursing research has begun to link quality patient outcome studies with cost-effectiveness in an interdisciplinary approach that is drawing the attention of the health care community (Brooten et. al, 1986). And, nurse researchers are active in speaking out at the federal level through the Tri-Council, the ANA-PAC, and other mechanisms. Yet we have not been effective in placing on the national agenda the contributions of nursing to the nation's health. The recent federal reports discussed above uniformly disregard nursing in their discussions of the quality of health care in the United States. As federal agencies begin to develop strategies to collect and distribute information on the quality of health care in the United States

(Roper et al., 1988), we have an obligation to contribute our knowledge of health care quality and cost-effectiveness for the benefit of the U.S. public.

REFERENCES

Abdellah, F. G. (1961). Criterion measures in nursing. *Nursing Research, 10*, 21–26.

Beyers, M. (1988). Quality: The banner of the 1980s. *Nursing Clinics of North America, 23*, 617–623.

Brooten, D., et al. (1986). A randomized clinical trial of early hospital discharge and home follow-up of very-low-birth-weight infants. *New England Journal of Medicine, 315*, 934–939.

Bulechek, G. M., & McCloskey, J. C. (1985). *Nursing interventions. Treatment for nursing diagnoses.* Philadelphia: W. B. Saunders.

Campbell, C. (1984). *Nursing diagnosis and intervention in nursing practice.* New York: John Wiley & Sons.

Donabedian, A. (1968). Promoting quality through evaluating the process of patient care. *Medical Care, VI*, 181–202.

Donabedian, A. (1980). *Explorations in quality assessment and monitoring: The definition of quality and approaches to its assessment.* Ann Arbor, MI: Health Administration Press.

Ellwood, P. M. (1988). Shattuck Lecture—outcomes management, a technology of patient experience. *New England Journal of Medicine, 318*, 1549–1556.

Fagin, C. M. (1982). The economic value of nursing research. *American Journal of Nursing, 82*, 1844–1849.

Fagin, C. M., & Jacobsen, B. S. (1985). Cost-effectiveness analysis in nursing research. In: H. H. Werley & J. J. Fitzpatrick (eds.), *Annual Review of Nursing Research,* Vol. 3 (pp. 215–238). New York: Springer.

Holzemer, W. L. (1988). *The Enugu village experience, National Association of Nigeria Nurses & Midwives, Nigeria.*

Geneva: International Council of Nurses.

Kim, M., McFarland, G., & McLane, A. (1987). *Pocket guide to nursing diagnosis* (2nd Ed.). St. Louis: C. V. Mosby Co.

Lang, N. M., & Clinton, J. F. (1984). Assessment of quality of nursing care. In H. H. Werley & J. J. Fitzpatrick (eds.), *Annual Review of Nursing Research,* Vol. 2 (pp. 135–163). New York: Springer.

Larson, E. L., & Peters, D. A. (1986). Integrating cost analysis in quality assurance. *Journal of Nursing Quality Assurance, 1*, 1–7.

Lohr, K. N., Yordy K. D., & Thier, S. O. (1988). Current issues in quality of care. *Health Affairs, 7*, 5–18.

Maraldo, P. J. (1989, Winter). *Executive Director Wire.* New York: National League of Nurses.

McLain, R. L., & Selhat, M. S. (1984). Twenty cases: What nursing costs per DRG. *Nursing Management, 15*, 27–34.

Merry, M. D. (1987). What is quality care? A model for measuring health care excellence. *Quality Review Bulletin, 13*, 298–301.

Mowry, M. N., & Korpman, R. A. (1985). Do DRG reimbursement rates reflect nursing costs? *The Journal of Nursing Administration, 15*, 29–35.

Physician Payment Review Commission, (1988). *Summary report.* Annual Report to Congress, Washington, DC.

Reschak, G. L. C., Biordi, D., Holm, K., & Santucci, N. (1983). Accounting for nursing costs by DRG. *The Journal of Nursing Administration, 15*, 15–20.

Ring, J. J. (1988). *Study of Uses of*

Severity of Illness Data by Hospitals. Report of the Board of Trustees, Report: O. Chicago: American Medical Association.

Roper, W. L., Winkenwerder, W., Hackborth, G.M., & Krakauer, H. (1988). Effectiveness in health care; An initiative to evaluate and improve medical practice. *The New England Journal of Medicine, 319,* 1197–1202.

Scitovsky, A., & Rice, D. (1987). Estimates of direct and indirect costs of Acquired Immunodeficiency Syndrome in the United States, 1985, 1986, & 1991. *Public Health Reports, 102,* 5–17.

Secretary's Commission on Nursing (1988). *Commission on Nursing.* Final Report, Vol. 1, Washington, DC.

Smith, M.C. (1988). *Meta-Analysis of Nursing Intervention Research.* Birmingham, Alabama.

Strickland, O. L., & Waltz, C. F. (1988). *Measurement of Nursing Outcomes— Measuring Nursing Performance: Practice Education & Research,* Vol. 2. New York: Springer Publishing Co.

The Report to the Ranking Minority Member, Special Committee on Aging. U.S. Senate, (1988). *MEDICARE: Improved Patient Outcome Analyses Could Enhance Quality Assessment.* GAO/PEMD-88-23 Medicare Patient Outcome Analyses, Washington, DC.

U.S. Congress, Office of Technology Assessment (1988). *The Quality of Medical Care: Information for Consumers.* Washington, DC.

Waltz, C. F., & Strickland, O. L. (1988). *Measurement of Nursing Outcomes— Measuring Client Outcomes,* Vol. 1. New York: Springer.

Werley, H. H., & Devine, E. C. (1987). The nursing minimum data set: Status and implications. In K. J. Hannah, M. Reimer, W. C. Mills, & S. Letourneau (eds.), *Clinical judgement and decision making: The future with nursing diagnosis* (pp. 540–551). New York: Wiley & Sons.

Wilson, C. K. (1986). Strategies for monitoring the cost and quality of care. *Journal of Nursing Quality Assurance, 1,* 55–65.

Health *is that pattern of disease which is accepted by a culture or society in a particular historical time.*
— Eugene Pumpian-Mindlin

William H. Rogers / David Draper / Katherine L. Kahn /
Emmett B. Keeler / Lisa V. Rubenstein /
Jacqueline Kosecoff / Robert H. Brook

Quality of Care Before and After Implementation of the DRG-based Prospective Payment System: A Summary of Effects

In 1984, the Health Care Financing Administration made a remarkable change in the Medicare system for financing hospital care for the elderly in the United States. Instead of paying for hospitalization on a cost basis, the Health Care Financing Administration developed a fixed-fee prospective payment system (PPS) based on diagnosis-related groups. Because the new payment system contains incentives to reduce length of stay and substitute lower-cost services for more expensive ones, concern has arisen that quality may have declined under the PPS.[1-4]

We have conducted a nationally representative study of the effects of the PPS on the quality of care given to hospitalized Medicare patients.[5-13] Our study had two purposes: (1) to evaluate the quality of care given to the nation's Medicare patients before and after the introduction of the PPS and (2) to compare observed quality after the introduction of the PPS with predictions of what quality might have been in the same period in the absence of the PPS intervention. In previous articles ... we have documented significant differences in sickness at admission,[9] processes of care,[10] unstable conditions at discharge,[12] and outcomes[13] for Medicare patients hospitalized before and after the implementation of the PPS. Spe-

William H. Rogers, Ph.D., David Draper, Ph.D., Katherine L. Kahn, M.D., Emmett B. Keeler, Ph.D., Lisa V. Rubenstein, M.D., and Robert H. Brook, M.D., Sc.D., are members of the Health Program of the RAND Corporation, Santa Monica, California; Jacqueline Kosecoff, Ph.D., is with Value Health Sciences, Inc., Santa Monica, California.

Drs. Kahn, Rubenstein, Kosecoff, and Brook are also in the Departments of Medicine and Health Services at the University of California, Los Angeles.

Abridged from Rogers, W. H., Draper, D., Kahn, K. L., Keeler, E. B., et al. (1990). Quality of care before and after implementation of the DRG-based prospective payment system. *JAMA* 264(15):1989–1994. Copyright 1990. American Medical Association. Used with permission.

cifically, we demonstrated that, during the 1985–1986 study period, after the introduction of the PPS, the incidence of sickness at admission was higher, in-hospital processes of care were better, the number of patients discharged in unstable condition was higher, and mortality rates both 30 and 180 days following admission were lower or unchanged compared with 1981–1982, before the introduction of the PPS. In this report we attempt to sort out which of these differences may have been caused by PPS and which by other changes that occurred during the same period.[14]

For instance, in the last 10 years the number of patients treated in outpatient settings has risen and the average burden of illness of such patients has also increased. The use of do-not-resuscitate (DNR) orders has grown.[15,16] Professional review organizations were established and have been extending their reach and insisting on better accountability. New technologies and medical knowledge have become available, and as time passes older physicians are continually being replaced by younger physicians who have more thorough training in the use of newly developed medical technology.

We report on three types of analyses that supplement our previous descriptive before-and-after comparisons and help us determine which of the observed changes were caused by the PPS. First, we estimate the impact on mortality of each of the previously described changes associated with the PPS. Second, for the important changes, we examine patterns of change among patient subsets to see whether the changes are consistent across all patient groups or are concentrated in particular types of patients and hospitals. Third, we extend our before-and-after comparisons to a time series analysis with multiple points before and after introduction of the PPS and examine trends within and across the 1981–1982 and 1985–1986 periods to determine whether values after the introduction of the PPS are consistent with trends before the PPS. . . .[17–19]

Impact on Mortality of Changes After the Introduction of the PPS

The major effects on 180-day mortality associated with changes after the introduction of the PPS are concentrated in four variables: sickness at admission, initial DNR status, in-hospital process of care, and discharge status. . . . The effects on 30-day mortality rates are very similar. . . . Increases in sickness at admission, adjusting for changes in demographics, had an especially pronounced predicted effect on mortality for patients with pneumonia (an expected rise of 3.0 percentage points in the 180-day mortality rate) and hip fracture. After adjusting for changes in demographics and sickness at admission, the rise in the initial use of DNR orders was associated with a modest increase (0.2 to 0.7 percentage points) in expected mortality for all five diseases.

Improvements in in-hospital process of care after the introduction of the PPS (after accounting for changes in demographics, sickness at admission, and initial DNR orders) were associated with noticeable decreases in expected mortality for all five diseases (0.5 to 1.3 percentage points). These changes were significant for all conditions but hip fracture. There was a statistically significant rise in expected mortality associated with adverse changes in one or more discharge variables in four of the five diseases. Changes in the number of patients in unstable condition at discharge and the number of patients with abnormal last laboratory values were significant for three of the five diseases. Taken together, problems at discharge after the introduction of the PPS have increased enough to raise expected death rates by an amount that varies from a total of 0.2 percentage points for patients with acute myocardial infarction to 0.9 percentage points for patients with pneumonia.

Generally, interactions between the effect of death on the variables . . . and the period before or after the introduction of the PPS were statistically insignificant. For unstable condition at discharge, however, the differential in mortality rates associated with discharge in unstable condition in 1985–1986 was about 60% as large as the differential in mortality rates in 1981–1982. This interaction effect was insignificant for individual diseases but significant ($p < .05$) when combined across all five diseases.

. . . Our analysis explains only a portion of the actual differences. The discrepancies could be due either to sampling variability (the SEs for the changes in death rates are about 2 percentage points for each disease) or to systematic effects unaccounted for in our analysis of the sources of change. For example, our analysis does not address the contribution of new technology to lower death rates because we specifically excluded new technologies from our process measures.

Patient and Hospital Subset Analyses

. . . Across all five diseases we observed a consistent and significant pattern of differences by hospital setting in improvements in the process of care after the introduction of the PPS. Rural nonteaching hospitals showed the biggest gains in in-hospital process of care, and urban teaching facilities showed the smallest gains. In contrast, the initial use of DNR orders and the number of patients in unstable condition at discharge showed consistent increases across the three hospital types after the introduction of the PPS.

We found some differences in the magnitude of the increase in use of DNR orders after the introduction of the PPS as a function of patient characteristics. The biggest increase was in patients with poor function and high levels of acute sickness at admission. Using the variables mentioned [previously] . . . to define patient and hospital subgroups, we were not able to find any types of patients for any of our five study diseases for whom the rise in the number of patients in unstable condition at discharge after the introduction of the PPS differed significantly from the average increase in the number of patients in unstable condition for all patients with that disease.

Trend Analyses

The quality of the in-hospital process of care was on the rise before the introduction of the PPS ($p < .01$) and continued to rise after the introduction of the PPS, although at a slightly slower rate (the difference between the rates is not significant). Use of initial DNR orders was increasing in 1981–1982 ($p < .05$) and this increase continued in 1985–1986. The percentage of patients discharged in unstable condition was reasonably flat both in 1981–1982 and in 1985–1986, with a jump between these two periods. Sickness at discharge and discharge to a nursing home also had jumps between these periods (data not shown). . . . The adjusted mortality values after the introduction of the PPS were consistent with values before the PPS.

COMMENT

After adjusting for sickness at admission, mortality was unchanged or lower in 1985–1986 after the introduction of the PPS than in 1981–1982. We believe this was the result of two counterbalancing forces: sharp improvements in in-hospital process of care from 1981 to 1986 that acted to lower mortality rates, offset by increases during the same period in sickness at admission,[9] the use of DNR orders,[15,16] and patients in unstable condition at discharge that acted to raise mortality.[12] However, most of the improvements in the process of care we have documented were probably not caused by the PPS. Two types of evidence presented herein support this conclusion: the presence of a significant upward trend in the process of care in 1981–1982, before the PPS was introduced, and the lack of uniformity of improvements in the care process across different types of patients and hospitals after the introduction of the PPS. It is difficult to understand why, if the PPS caused the gains in the process of care we have demonstrated, it did so with substantially more force in rural nonteaching facilities than in urban teaching hospitals. Rather, it seems more plausible that ongoing trends in medicine, such as diffusion of newer methods into outlying areas, were responsible for the observed improvement. On this score the PPS may be judged a success: the care process did not deteriorate in the effort to save money.

An increased rate of use of DNR orders at admission after the introduction of the PPS was associated with somewhat higher death rates. Do-not-resuscitate orders potentially save the hospital money and save the patients pain, but increased usage of DNR orders is associated with an increase in death rates. The patient subgroups in which the biggest changes in use of DNR orders were concentrated—those who were both acutely ill and functioning poorly—suggest that the potential benefits of medical care are being examined more closely for these patients. This makes sense and does not implicate the PPS.

The number of patients in unstable condition at discharge and related factors have risen in temporal association with the PPS. Furthermore, the number of patients in unstable condition at discharge is increasing across the board rather than in any specific patient or hospital subgroup and has increased in ways we believe are not due to changes in recording.[12] Both results implicate the PPS. On the face of it, this problem needs attention.

There is room, however, for substantial debate about how serious a problem this is. First, should *unstable condition* be defined broadly or narrowly? If unstable condition is defined narrowly to include only factors that are clearly remediable, the increase in the number of patients discharged in unstable condition after the introduction of the PPS may be responsible for a 0.5 percentage point increase in the mortality rate, depending on the disease. If unstable condition is defined broadly to include sickness at discharge and discharge to a nursing home, the associated rise in death rates may be as high as 0.9 percentage points. We do not know how fixable these problems are, but we do know that we measured only a fraction of the problems that should be fixed before discharge.

Second, there is no guarantee that the hospital would be able to reduce mortality by holding patients in unstable condition longer. Third, the effects of unstable condition might be reduced by more cost-effective mechanisms than increasing hospital length of stay. For example, patients in unstable condition could be given special consideration in nursing homes or could be part of well-designed posthospitalization home nursing programs. Indeed, the impact on mortality of discharge in unstable condition does not appear to be as great in 1985–1986 as it was in 1981–1982; this may be a result of improvements in care after hospitalization. Fourth, the length of stay has remained relatively constant since 1986, so any contribution of inappropriately short hospital stays to discharge problems has probably stabilized.[20]

On the other hand, entirely eliminating discharges of patients in unstable condition (not just the effect after the introduction of the PPS) might have a large impact on the effectiveness of hospital care. For the five diseases studied, patients in unstable condition at discharge after the introduction of the PPS have a mortality rate 30% higher than that of patients discharged in stable condition. This translates into additional mortality of 4.4 percentage points in the 90 days following admission for patients in unstable condition at discharge. An observational study such as ours cannot definitely estimate the effects of better discharge monitoring on patient outcomes; a controlled experiment with specific discharge protocols is required.

Between 1981–1982 and 1985–1986 there were also important changes in the demographics and sickness of patients. Patients with pneumonia are much sicker at admission now than before. For other diseases, the nature of the change in sickness at admission is less clear. As we mentioned above and have documented elsewhere,[9] some of the apparent increase in sickness appears to be a recording bias. When we move from recording-sensitive sickness indicators (such as functional status and acute and chronic sickness measures) to the recording-insensitive indicators used in the remainder of this study's analyses (such as our 30- and 180-day scales), the apparent rise in sickness at admission is smaller. Part of the rise in severity, however, may be due to efforts by the professional review organizations to restrict admissions of less-sick patients. For two diseases (acute myocardial infarction and pneumonia), admissions of the least-sick patients appear to be down about 30%.

In conclusion, because the PPS was not introduced as an experiment, our observational time series study can provide only limited answers about the changes in quality of care that the PPS, and the PPS alone, caused. As we have noted elsewhere . . . ,[13] three other caveats are also worth bearing in mind when considering our results: (1) We studied only five diseases, albeit five important diseases in the Medicare cohort. (2) Our study design allowed us only to assess differences in quality of care once patients are hospitalized, so that, for example, we cannot comment on any changes in *access* to hospital care the PPS may have caused. (3) Our study covers the era after the introduction of the PPS only through June 1986. Since that time hospital payments under the PPS have been tightened.[7]

Even so, two key policy conclusions appear clear: (1) At least through mid-1986, the PPS did not interrupt an important long-term trend toward better processes of in-hospital care, a trend that has led to somewhat lower death rates. (2) On the other hand, we believe that the PPS has had an adverse effect on the condition in which patients are discharged.

These conclusions lead to three major policy recommendations: (1) To eliminate any possible problems with patients in unstable condition at discharge, a more systematic assessment should be made of the readiness of a patient to leave the hospital and be cared for as an outpatient or in an institution other than an acute-care hospital. Perhaps our instability-at-discharge scale would be a good place to start. (2) If further investigation suggests that some discharges of patients in unstable condition may be acceptable with suitable follow-up or could be prevented by a longer hospital stay, we recommend that clinical trials be undertaken to evaluate the impact of such changes on mortality. (3) To provide current information about the effects of Medicare's payment methods on quality of care, we also recommend the continued collection of clinically detailed data that monitor sickness at admission, processes of care, discharge status, and outcomes on a regular basis as long as prospective payment is in place.

REFERENCES

1. Omenn GS, Conrad DA. Implications of DRGs for clinicians. *N Engl J Med.* 1984;311:1314–1317.

2. Smits HL, Watson RE. DRGs and the future of surgical practice. *N Engl J Med.* 1984;311:1612–1615.

3. Stern RS, Epstein AM. Institutional responses to prospective payment based on diagnosis-related groups: implications for cost, quality, and access. *N Engl J Med.* 1985;312:621–627.

4. Iglehart JK. Early experience with prospective payment of hospitals. *N Engl J Med.* 1986;314:1460–1464.

5. McCarthy CM. DRGs: five years later. *N Engl J Med.* 1988;318:1683–1686.

6. Schramm CJ. Prospective payment: some retrospective observations. *N Engl J Med.* 1988;318:1681–1683.

7. Kahn KL, Rubenstein LV, Draper D, et al. The effects of the DRG-based prospective payment system on quality of care for hospitalized Medicare patients: an introduction to the series. *JAMA.* 1990;264:1953–1955.

8. Draper D, Kahn KL, Reinisch EJ, et al. Studying the effects of the DRG-based prospective payment system on quality of care: Design, sampling, and fieldwork. *JAMA.* 1990;264:1956–1961.

9. Keeler EB, Kahn KL, Draper D, et al. Changes in sickness at admission following the introduction of the prospective payment system. *JAMA.* 1990;264:1962–1968.

10. Kahn KL, Rogers WH, Rubenstein LV, et al. Measuring quality of care with explicit process criteria before and after implementation of the DRG-based prospective payment system. *JAMA.* 1990;264:1969–1973.

11. Rubenstein LV, Kahn KL, Reinisch EJ, et al. Changes in quality of care for five diseases measured by implicit review, 1981 to 1986. *JAMA.* 1990;264:1974–1979.

12. Kosecoff J, Kahn KL, Rogers WH, et al. Prospective payment system and impairment at discharge: the 'quicker-and-sicker' story revisited. *JAMA.* 1990;264:1980–1983.

13. Kahn KL, Keeler EB, Sherwood MJ, et al. Comparing outcomes of care before and after implementation of the DRG-based prospective payment system. *JAMA.* 1990;264:1984–1988.

14. Vladeck BC. Hospital prospective payment and the quality of care. *N Engl J Med.* 1988;319:1411–1413.

15. Scheidermayer DL. The decision to forgo CPR in the elderly patient. *JAMA.* 1988;260:2096–2097.

16. Bedell SE, Delbanco TL. Choices about cardiopulmonary resuscitation in the hospital: when do physicians talk with patients? *N Engl J Med.* 1984;310:1089–1093.

17. Kahn KL, Draper D, Keeler EB, et al. *The Effects of the DRG-based Prospective Payment System on Quality of Care for Hospitalized Medicare*

Patients: Design, Methods, and Results. Santa Monica, Calif: RAND Corp; 1990-2. R-3931-HCFA.

18. Wonnacott TH, Wonnacott RJ. *Introductory Statistics for Business and Economics.* 3rd ed. New York, NY: John Wiley & Sons Inc; 1984:377–379, 686.

19. Scheffe H. *The Analysis of Variance.* New York, NY: John Wiley & Sons Inc; 1959.

20. Witaberger C, Kominski G. *Recent Trends in Length of Stay for Medicare Surgical Patients.* Santa Monica, Calif: RAND Corp; 1990. R-3940-HCFA.

Every culture evolves a set of remedies that are given for dis-ease . . . but no remedy, in and of itself, will restore good health.

— Mary Howell

Lucian L. Leape

Unnecessary Surgery

INTRODUCTION

In 1974, the Congressional Committee on Interstate and Foreign Commerce held hearings on unnecessary surgery. McCarthy et al.[35] presented the most important evidence. Their findings from the first surgical second opinion program (SSOP) indicated that 17.6% of recommendations for surgery were not confirmed. The Congressional Subcommittee on Oversight and Investigations extrapolated these figures to estimate that nationwide there were 2.4 million unnecessary operations performed annually, resulting in a cost of $3.9 billion and 11,900 deaths.[47]

This claim fell on the receptive ears of payers, including the Health Care Financing Administration (HCFA), who were beginning to feel the burden of accelerating increases in health care costs. Reducing costs by 15–20% was an appealing prospect, and several payers subsequently instituted mandatory SSOP. About the same time, HCFA and commercial insurance companies implemented preprocedural review programs for operations widely considered overutilized.

It is worth recalling that before 1970 public policy was concerned not with overuse, but with the problems of underuse of health services and perceived shortages of doctors and hospitals.[16] But, as the full costs of Medicare became evident, cost containment entered the public agenda. Increasing cost pressures in the private sector, which resulted from technologic advances, also led private payers to search for ways to reduce health care expenditures. Unnecessary surgery was an obvious target. Doctors have had less interest in unnecessary surgery, because they have tended to dissociate themselves from the debates concerning cost containment and because most do not recognize unnecessary surgery as a significant problem. No surgeon believes that what he or she does is unnecessary, and physicians are generally reluctant to pass judgment on their colleagues. The 1970s witnessed a remarkable profusion of mechanisms designed to change, or at least challenge, physicians' decisions. In addi-

Lucian L. Leape, is Lecturer in the Department of Health Policy and Management at the Harvard School of Public Health, Boston.

tion to SSOP and precertification programs, analysis of geographic variations of use of procedures was provided to physicians as "feedback" with the hope of influencing their patterns of use. "Managed care" was invented: an overt second-guessing of doctors' decisions aimed at reducing days of hospitalization and use of expensive services. The government provided subsidies for the development of health maintenance organizations (HMO) and began to encourage Medicare patients to enroll in them.

Although significant reductions have subsequently been reported in hospital stay or in the use of a particular procedure, it has been difficult to demonstrate that these programs have had the significant effects on utilization and costs that were anticipated. In fact, health care costs have continued to rise at two or more times the inflation rate. More importantly, there is no evidence that these attempts to reduce utilization have had any affect on the quality of care. Recent reports suggest high (10–20%) rates of inappropriate use of a variety of services.[3,9,20,29,37,58,59] Clearly, unnecessary surgery is still with us.

Surgery has been a primary focus of attention for those interested in overuse of health care services for several reasons. First, it is easy to study: Most operations are reasonably standardized, outcomes are obvious, and the delivery of the service can be reliably ascertained from discharge or payment claims data. Second, operations are costly, in terms of both surgical fees and hospitalizations. More can be saved by reducing rates of surgery than by curtailing the use of most other therapeutic or diagnostic services. Third, surgical care is generally riskier than other forms of therapy. There is a finite mortality risk associated with almost every major operation. The combination of risk and potential for dramatic cure gives surgery an aura of excitement lacking in other forms of therapy. Abuse is, therefore, more serious and more intriguing.

Finally, the current interest in unnecessary surgery also reflects recent increases in the number and types of operations performed in the United States. Many operations that are now performed frequently, such as coronary artery bypass, hip replacements, carotid endarterectomy, arthroscopy, laparoscopy, and heart and liver transplantation, were unknown just 25 years ago. Not surprisingly, some of the indications for these procedures are controversial. There has also been a substantial increase in the rates of performance of well-established operations, such as cataract extraction and cesarean section, which raises questions of overuse.[3] Overall, the surgery rate grew at twice the rate of the population from 1979 to 1986.[27] Unnecessary surgery is, in many ways, a "disease of medical progress," which reflects the hazards, as well as the benefits, of technological advances. A concern about its impact is timely, because the implications of unnecessary surgery are greater than ever, in terms of both the number of patients at risk and the aggregate cost.

Recently, there has been a deliberate shift in federal emphasis. Responding to imprecations from the research community, Congress established the Agency for Health Care Policy and Research (AHCPR) in 1989. This new agency within the Public Health Service supervises and funds research into clinical outcomes and the development of practice guidelines, and it has launched a major effort in both areas. In addition, HCFA has pursued the development and implementation of analysis of large clinical data bases to demonstrate patterns of use that can be fed back to physicians or used by the Peer Review Organizations (PRO) as quality measures.

Physicians have also become concerned about unnecessary surgery, as their colleagues have produced more convincing and sophisticated evidence of inappropriate use of some operations and procedures.[8,59] Professional specialty societies, individually and through the Council of Medical Specialty Societies and the American Medical Association, have started to develop practice guidelines to help physicians choose appropriate care. . . .[50]

WHAT IS UNNECESSARY SURGERY?

The term "unnecessary surgery" has many meanings. The person who has had an operation that failed to relieve his symptoms may understandably conclude that the operation was unnecessary, even if the operation is successful in most individuals and its use is unquestioned. Others confuse unnecessary with "elective," a term used by doctors in reference to timing, not as a synonym for "optional." In contrast to an "urgent" or "emergent" operation, an elective operation is one that can be scheduled at a time of convenience, because the underlying condition does not pose an immediate threat to life or health.

The most common association of the term unnecessary surgery is with high frequency of use. Some cesarean sections are considered unnecessary when the rate of performance in a region exceeds some threshold number. One learns that there are "too many" hysterectomies performed, or that Dr. X performs unnecessary surgery because he does a higher number of a certain operation than his colleagues. Some carry this type of thinking to the extreme: Lower rates of surgery of all types must be evidence of higher quality medical care! This stands in interesting contrast to the use of vaccines, for example, for which most people associate higher use with better quality care. The difference is that vaccines are considered an unequivocal low-risk good, whereas operations carry greater risk and have been suspected of overuse.

Although it might seem simplest to consider as unnecessary any operation that is not clearly necessary, this definition creates more problems than it solves. Webster defines necessary as something that "must be by reason of the nature of things," "cannot be otherwise," or "determined and fixed and inevitable."[53] No operation qualifies, for the simple reason that no operation "must be" or is "inevitable" for any patient. A host of variables enter into the decision for surgery, of which the patient's own values are among the most important. Individuals vary in their tolerance of risk, fear of surgery, desired activity level, tolerance of pain, and fear of death. They also vary in how they value different probabilities of good and bad outcomes. Clearly, it is not possible to define what is necessary for an individual—what is necessary for me may be totally unacceptable to you.

In contrast, *Webster*'s definition of unnecessary, "useless," is easy to use, as it can be based entirely on objective data. No operation is necessary if it is ineffective, i.e. if it does not accomplish its objective for a given clinical situation. For example, if the objectives of coronary artery bypass graft (CABG) surgery are to relieve pain and prolong life, CABG is ineffective—and, therefore, unnecessary—for an asymptomatic patient with coronary artery disease that causes blockage of only one of the three coronary arteries, because studies have shown that CABG does not increase longevity in patients with single vessel disease. An unnecessary operation, then, is one that is ineffective or useless. An operation is also unnecessary if it confers no clear advantage over a less risky alternative. In both instances, the operation does not represent a net benefit to the patient. The patient will not be better off. This is the definition we will use.

One other aspect of ineffectiveness must be considered: occult or unrecognizable unnecessary surgery. For many indications for operations, the evidence for effectiveness is clear-cut. But, there are other indications for some operations for which the evidence is absent or equivocal, and expert judgments are divided on its benefit. Some indications in this "gray zone" of effectiveness will one day be found to be inappropriate. Therefore, these operations represent occult unnecessary surgery, unrecognizable at the present state of knowledge. Operations performed for indications in this uncertain or equivocal category cannot now be fairly labeled as unnecessary, but some of them eventually will be. Other operations currently labeled as effective will be found to have only marginal benefit as more data are accumulated from outcome studies. These, too, represent occult unnecessary surgery.

Clearly, we cannot measure what is not recognizable, so it would be highly speculative to estimate the extent of occult unnecessary surgery. However, the implication is clear that the full extent of unnecessary surgery is greater than is measured by any of the current methods. For now, we must confine our analysis to what is known, i.e., to clinical situations in which the best available evidence or informed expert judgment indicates that an operation is ineffective or useless. What do we know?

THE EVIDENCE

Evidence for unnecessary surgery comes from three types of studies: circumstantial evidence from studies of variations of rates of use of various operations among different geographic regions and between different types of practices, denial rates of second opinion and precertification programs, and attempts to measure inappropriate use directly.

Geographic Variations

It is not unreasonable to assume that if an operation is being performed ten times as frequently in one area as in another, the high use must represent unnecessary surgery, although an equally logical conclusion is that the low rate represents underuse. There is probably some truth in both interpretations. . . . [1,4–6,8–9,13,22,25,29–31,33,36,42–46,51,54–57,59]

. . . Although geographic variations in the use of surgical procedures result from a multitude of factors, the most important seems to be variations in physician perceptions of the value of the operation in question. These differences result from lack of professional consensus about the value of many procedures for many potential indications. Thus, geographic variations are primarily a measure of professional uncertainty. In the few instances in which unnecessary surgery has been directly measured, the extent is greatest for procedures about which there is little professional consensus. Thus, large geographic variations in the use of an operation suggest that a significant fraction is unnecessary. The extent of variation is not a direct measure of the extent of unnecessary surgery, however, as inappropriate use represents only a minor share of the differences.

Variations by Method of Payment

Another type of variation in practice patterns that has been cited as evidence of inappropriate care is the difference in surgical rates between HMOs and private practice. Patients who receive care in HMOs are one-half to one-fourth as likely to be operated on as patients in the fee-for-service sector.[32,49] Overall, reductions in use of medical services in HMOs does not have a deleterious effect on outcomes,[10] so it can be inferred that the difference in surgical rates is at least partly due to unnecessary surgery.

Second Surgical Opinion Programs

. . . What does the experience with second opinion programs tell us about the extent of unnecessary surgery? Unfortunately, less than one might hope. Although many studies have been made of nonconfirmation rates and cost savings, none have directly addressed the question of whether nonconfirmation accurately identifies operations that should not be performed. In the absence of controls, it is not even possible to tell if the supposed benefits of forgone operations are, in fact, realized. The absence of outcome data even prevents evaluation of the supposed benefits to SSOP patients of nonconfirmation. More fundamentally, the characteristics of second opinion programs make it unlikely that they either identify or diminish the rate of unnecessary surgery. . . .[28,34,39,41,48]

Precertification Programs

. . . Recently, several large insurance companies have instituted computerized preprocedural review programs by using a commercial product that applies highly detailed criteria that have been developed with the RAND/UCLA appropriateness methodology. Blue Cross/Blue Shield reported the results of a pilot program that used these criteria for 21 procedures in six states over a one-year period ending in July 1990. The overall rate of inappropriate proposed use was 11.2%; individual rates of inappropriateness varied from 0% for CABG to 21.5% for hysterectomy and 27.1% for tonsillectomy.[27]

Direct Measurement

. . . The evidence for unnecessary surgery is largely circumstantial. Geographic variations reflect uncertainty and, thus, indicate the presence of unnecessary surgery, but do not measure its extent. Second opinion program results represent only differences of opinion between two individuals, a thin reed upon which to make a judgment of inappropriate use. Criteria studies, and the results from the related use of explicit criteria for precertification programs, do provide concrete evidence of unnecessary surgery. From these studies, it is reasonable to conclude that 10% or more of surgical procedures are unnecessary. For controversial operations, the fraction may be substantially higher.[2,11,17,38]

WHY DOES UNNECESSARY SURGERY OCCUR?

Why do surgeons perform unnecessary surgery? It is difficult to believe that many do so deliberately, out of greed or malice. A judgment that a physician is performing unnecessary surgery implies that the operation is known to be inappropriate for a given condition. But, no one knowingly performs a useless operation. Therefore, the surgeon either does not know that it is inappropriate or does not accept the evidence.

Unfortunately, it is often not clear what is "known" in medicine. Contrary to popular assumptions, most accepted medical therapy is not based on scientific evidence of effectiveness. Acceptable therapy, therefore, includes both those treatments for which there is good evidence of effectiveness and those for which the evidence is scant, but the weight of professional opinion is favorable. Further, science is what scientists say it is, so even the acceptability of scientific data relies on the belief that the conclusions are valid. In the absence of a consensus, whether based on evidence or expert opinion, a judgment regarding the necessity of a given treatment is impossible.

Several considerations determine whether a consensus will develop and whether an individual physician will know and accept the consensus judgment on the appropriate use of any treatment: the methods by which scientific knowledge is developed, the manner by which it is disseminated, and a host of social and psychological factors.

WHAT CAN BE DONE ABOUT UNNECESSARY SURGERY?

It is evident that utilization review, second surgical opinion programs and geographic variation analysis with feedback are blunt instruments for improving quality. Each takes advantage of the pervasive uncertainty in medical practice to intimidate or exert peer pressure on physicians to conform. Although these programs may decrease the volume of services that are provided, they do so unselectively. As we have seen, there is no evidence that any of these programs specifically reduces inappropriate care, and, in the case of SSOP, it possibly increases. Without a focus, these programs are unlikely to lead to identifiable improvements in quality.

To decrease unnecessary surgery, it is first necessary to define it. Physicians need better information on effectiveness and better dissemination and use of that information. Finally, attention must be given to developing more effective ways to get doctors to accept and use new information. Outcomes research attempts to improve the information base, whereas practice guidelines make it more accessible to physicians.

Outcomes Research

The randomized clinical trial is widely accepted as the gold standard for measuring effectiveness, but the costs and logistic problems of conducting these trials limit their applicability. In recent years, the effectiveness of a treatment has increasingly been evaluated by sophisticated analyses of patient outcomes. As noted, the AHCPR has launched a major effort—the Medical Treatment Effectiveness Program—to evaluate the outcomes of treatment of several important diseases, such as cataract, myocardial infarction, and back pain.

Although the importance of studying outcomes is unassailable, expectations regarding the usefulness of this information may be exaggerated. Meaningful information from outcomes studies requires evaluation of numerous health factors in addition to the presence of disease. Controlling for these variables can be difficult and expensive; thus, effectiveness studies of all variants of patient and disease are not possible. Consequently, it is unlikely that outcomes studies can ever provide information on more than a minor fraction of the thousands of diseases and treatments.

This is not to say that outcomes studies should not be carried out. On the contrary, they offer the most practical hope of obtaining valuable information that will both validate treatments that work and lead to elimination of those that do not. But for maximum efficiency, outcomes studies should be focused on specific treatments for which the information will be of greatest value, i.e., on those that are performed in large numbers, show wide geographic variations, and are controversial. Despite its limitations, outcomes research is the best current hope for improvement in knowledge generation.

Practice Guidelines

The other challenge, getting physicians to accept and use effectiveness information, may be more difficult. The current movement to develop practice guidelines is an attempt to accomplish this mission. The objective of practice guidelines is to make effectiveness information accessible and acceptable to doctors by providing authoritative statements regarding the appropriateness of a procedure for all of its possible indications. These statements are based on available evidence and expert opinion. As we have seen, even when there is good scientific data, guidelines are needed to translate that information into a useable form. If well done, guidelines provide practicing physicians with a better informed, more objective, and, therefore, wiser evaluation than they can readily obtain from the literature and personal experience. The development of comprehensive practice guidelines is an urgent first priority for anyone who wishes to decrease the rate of unnecessary surgery. Fortunately, the urgency of that need has risen to national attention within the past several years and has been accepted both within the medical profession and by the government.

Practice guideline development is the second major responsibility of the AHCPR. Recently, at the agency's behest, a committee of the Institute of Medicine issued a set of attributes and principles for the guideline development process.[23] The report stressed the importance of credibility and accountability and the need for the link between guidelines and scientific evidence to be explicit. It strongly recommended that the guideline development process "include participation by representatives of key affected groups and disciplines" to ensure that all relevant evidence is located, that practical problems are identified, and that affected groups will cooperate in implementation.[23]

Professional specialty societies have also begun to develop comprehensive and highly specific practice guidelines.[50] Early experience suggests that these guidelines will be used and will make a difference. For example, following the 1987 universal adoption by Massachusetts anesthetists of the American Society of Anesthesiologists' "Standards for Basic Intra-Operative Monitoring," the number of deaths from hypoxia decreased to zero in the following year, and for the first time no lawsuits were filed for hypoxic damage.[40]

Ultimately, the validity of practice guidelines will depend on the advances in scientific knowledge provided by randomized clinical trials and outcomes studies. The commitment of Congress to support outcomes studies is, therefore, encouraging. These efforts are complementary. Outcomes data provide evidence to be used in guideline development, while the guideline process helps focus outcomes research by identifying common clinical conditions for which effectiveness information is lacking.

POLICY IMPLICATIONS

As Eddy[12] has described, medical practice is in the middle of a profound transition. Once it was assumed that physician's decisions were, by definition, correct; however, evidence now indicates that many are not, and mechanisms have been established to second-guess physician judgments. Eddy points out, however, that much of medical care is effective, doctors are not practicing fraud, and the problems are no one's fault. Physicians make errors because they must make decisions every day on the basis of inadequate information. And, they must deal not only with vagaries of scientific knowledge, but also with variations in patient preferences and expectations, changing systems of reimbursement, threats of malpractice, and peer pressure.

The pace of technologic progress is now such that it has become impossible for researchers to provide the information on effectiveness of new treatments as rapidly as they are developed. Further, our methods of information dissemination are not adequate to make even that which is known accessible to the physician. As a result, it is not surprising that evidence from a variety of sources suggests a substantial amount of surgery is unnecessary. The solutions to these problems will not come quickly or easily, but the movement to practice guidelines should ultimately lead to more rational and more acceptable medical decision making.

Credibility of practice guidelines requires that the judgments be made by respected clinical experts, leaders in their fields. But, that may not be enough. Surgeons, in particular, are unlikely to accept these recommendations without professional endorsement. Surgical leaders must accept the process and support the results. The AHCPR has been slow to enlist the support or participation of organized medicine—either the American Medical Association or the relevant specialty societies. Also, the academic establishment's position is unclear. Some health services researchers are very interested in various aspects of guideline development, but they have had limited input into the federal process. Without either professional or academic support, it is hard to believe that federal guidelines will be accepted. A related question is whether the government will require physicians to follow the federally developed guidelines. Such a requirement would result in the de facto nullification of one of the highest functions of a profession: control of its standards. It seems improbable that either organized medicine or individual doctors will readily accept such an outcome. If the legitimacy of federal guidelines is challenged, as it almost certainly will be, it is not likely that either Congress or the courts will support the right of the federal government to practice medicine. To be viable, therefore, practice guidelines must be supported by either the academic establishment or organized medicine, preferably both.

The use of practice guidelines will result in significant changes in the way doctors practice medicine. For the first time, the identification and significant reduction of inappropriate care and unnecessary surgery will be possible. Whether this potential will be realized will be determined within the next few years by the interplay of government policies and professional reactions. If means to cooperate cannot be found, reductions in unnecessary surgery may be long in coming.

BIBLIOGRAPHY

1. Am. Coll. Surg. and Am. Surg. Assoc. 1975. *Surgery in the United States: A Summary Report of the Study on Surgical Services for the United States.* Chicago: Am. Coll. Surg./Am. Surg. Assoc.

2. Barrett, J.F.R., Jarvis, G.J., Macdonald, H.N., Buchan, P.C., Tyrrell, S.N., et al. 1990. Inconsistencies in clinical decisions in obstetrics. *Lancet* 336:549–51.

3. Barron, J. Apr. 16, 1989. Unnecessary surgery. *NY Times Mag.*

4. Bombardier, C., Fuchs, V.R., Lillard, L.A., Warner, K.E. 1977. Socioeconomic factors affecting the utilization of surgical operations. *N. Engl. J. Med.* 297:699–705.

5. Bunker, J.P. 1970. Surgical manpower. A comparison of operations and surgeons in the United States and in England and Wales. *N. Engl. J. Med.* 282:135–44.

6. Bunker, J.P., Brown, B.W. 1974. The physician-patient as an informed consumer of surgical services. *N. Engl. J. Med.* 290:1051–55.

7. Chalmers, T.C. 1987. Meta-analysis in clinical medicine. *Trans. Am. Clin. Climatol. Assoc.* 99:144–50.

8. Chassin, M.R., Brook, R.H., Park, R.E., Keesey, J., Fink, A., et al. 1986. Variations in the use of medical and surgical services by the Medicare population. *N. Engl. J. Med.* 314:285–90.

9. Chassin, M.R., Kosecoff, J., Park, R.E., Winslow, C.M., Kahn, K.L. 1987. Does inappropriate use explain geographic variations in the use of health care services? *J. Am. Med. Assoc.* 258:2533–37.

10. Dorsey, J.L. 1983. Use of diagnostic resources in health maintenance organizations and fee-for-service practice settings. *Arch. Int. Med.* 143:1863–65.

11. Doyle, J.C. 1953. Unnecessary hysterectomies. *J. Am. Med. Assoc.* 151:360–65.

12. Eddy, D.M. 1990. The challenge. *J. Am. Med. Assoc.* 263:287.

13. Eddy, D.M. 1984. Variations in physician practice: The role of uncertainty. *Health Aff.* 3:74–89.

14. Eisenberg, J.M. 1985. Physician utilization: The state of research about physicians' practice patterns. *Med. Care* 23:461–83.

15. Eisenberg, J.M., Nicklin, D. 1981. Use of diagnostic services by physicians in community practice. *Med. Care* 19:297.

16. Evans, R.G., Barer, M.L., Hertzman, C. 1991. The 20-year experiment: Accounting for, explaining, and evaluating health care cost containment in Canada and the United States. *Annu. Rev. Public Health* 12:481–518.

17. Fink, A., Kosecoff, J., Chassin, M., Brook, R.H. 1984. Consensus methods: characteristics and guidelines for use. *Am. J. Public Health* 74:979–83.

18. Gambone, J.C., Reiter, R.C., Lench, J.B. 1990. Quality assurance indicators and short-term outcome of hysterectomy. *Obstet. Gynecol.* 76:841–45.

19. Gray, D., Hampton, J.R., Bernstein, S.J., Kosecoff, J., Brook, R.H. 1990. Audit of coronary angiography and bypass surgery. *Lancet* 335:1317–20.

20. Greenspan, A.M., Kay, H.R., Berger, B.C., Greenberg, R.M., Greenspan, A.J., et al. 1988. Incidence of unwarranted implantation of permanent cardiac pacemakers in a large medical population. *N. Engl. J. Med.* 318:158–63.

21. Greer, A.L. 1988. The state of the art versus the state of the science. *Int. J. Tech. Assess. Health Care* 4:5–25.

22. Hulka, B.S., Wheat, J.R. 1985. Patterns of utilization: The patient persepctive. *Med. Care* 23:438–60.

23. Inst. Med. 1990. Clinical practice guidelines: directions for a new program. Washington, DC: Nat. Acad. Press.

24. Kanouse, D.E., Winkler, J.D., Berry, S.H., Brook, R.H. 1987. *Physician Awareness of the NIH Consensus Development Program.* R-2980 3060 Santa Monica: RAND.

25. Keller, R.B., Soule, D.N., Wennberg, J.E., Hanley, D.F. 1990. Dealing with geographic variations in the use of hospitals. *J. Bone Joint Surg.* 72-A:1286–93.

26. Kellie, S.E., Kellie, J.T. 1991. Medicare Peer Review Organization preprocedure review criteria. *J. Am. Med. Assoc.* 265:1265–70.

27. Kramon, G. Feb. 24, 1991. Medical second-guessing—in advance. *NY Times.*

28. Leape, L.L. 1989. Unnecessary surgery. A Pew Memorial trust policy synthesis: 7. HSR: Health Serv. Res. 24 (3):351–407.

29. Leape, L.L., Park, R.E., Solomon, D.H., Chassin, M.R., Kosecoff, J., Brook, R.H. 1990. Does inappropriate use explain small area variations in the use of health care

services? *J. Am. Med. Assoc.* 263:669–72.

30. Leape, L.L., Park, R.E., Solomon, D.H., Chassin, M.R., Kosecoff, J., Brook, R.H. 1989. Relation between surgeons' practice volumes and geographic variation in the rate of carotid endarterectomy. *N. Engl. J. Med.* 321:653–57.

31. Lewis, C.E. 1969. Variations in the incidence of surgery. *N. Eng. J. Med.* 281:880–84.

32. LoGerfo, J.P., Efird, R.A., Diehr, P.K., Richardson, W.C. 1979. Rates of surgical care in prepaid group practices and the independent setting. *Med. Care* 17:1–10.

33. Manning, W.G., Leibowitz, A., Goldberg, G.A., Rogers, W.H., Newhouse, J.P. 1984. A controlled trial of the effect of a prepaid group practice on use of services. *N. Engl. J. Med.* 310:1505–10.

34. McCarthy, E.G., Finkel, M.L. 1978. Second opinion elective surgery programs: Outcome status over time. *Med. Care* 16:984–94.

35. McCarthy, E.G., Widmer, G.W. 1974. Effects of screening by consultants on recommended elective surgical procedures. *N. Engl. J. Med.* 291:1331–35.

36. McPherson, K., Wennberg, J.E., Hovind, D.B., Clifford, P. 1982. Small-area variations in the use of common surgical procedures: An international comparison of New England, England, and Norway. *N. Engl. J. Med.* 307:1310–14.

37. Merrick, N.J., Brook, R.H., Fink, A., Solomon, D.H. 1986. Use of carotid endarterectomy in five California Veterans Administration medical centers. *J. Am. Med. Assoc.* 256:2531–35.

38. Park, R.E., Fink, A., Brook, R.H., Chassin, M.R., Kahn, K.L. et al. 1986. Physician ratings of appropriate indications for six medical and surgical procedures. *Am. J. Public Health* 76:766–72.

39. Peebles, R.J. 1991. Second opinions and cost-effectiveness: the questions continue. *Am. Coll. Surg. Bull.* 76:18–25.

40. Pierce, E.C. 1990. The development of anesthesia guidelines and standards. *QRB* 16:61–64.

41. Poggio, E., Goldberg, H.B., Kronick, R., Schmitz, R., Van Harrison, R., Ertel, P. 1985. *Second Surgical Opinion Programs: An Analysis of Public Policy Options.* Natl. Tech. Inf. Serv.

42. Roos, N.P. 1984. Hysterectomy: Variations in rates across small areas and across physicians' practices. *Am. J. Public Health* 74:327–34.

43. Roos, N.P., Roos, L.L. 1982. Surgical rate variations: Do they reflect the health or socioeconomic characteristics of the population? *Med. Care* 20:945–58.

44. Roos, N.P., Roos, L.L. 1981. High and low surgical rates: Risk factors for area residents *Am. J. Public Health* 71:591–600.

45. Roos, N.P., Roos, L.L., Henteleff, P.D. 1977. Elective surgical rates—do high rates mean lower standards? *N. Engl. J. Med.* 297:360–65.

46. Stockwell, H., Vayda, E. 1979. Variations in surgery in Ontario. *Med. Care* 17:390–96.

47. US Congr. House Subcomm. Oversight Invest. 1976. *Cost and Quality of Health Care: Unnecessary Surgery.* Washington, DC: GPO.

48. US Congr. Senate Comm. Aging. 1985. *Unnecessary Surgery: Double Jeopardy for Older Americans.* Washington, DC: GPO.

49. US Dep. Health Educ. Welf. 1971. *The Federal Employees Health Benefits Program—Enrollment and Utilization of Health Services, 1961–1968.* Washington, DC: GPO.

50. US Gen. Account. Off. 1991. *Practice Guidelines: The Experience of Medical Specialty Societies.* Publ. GAO/PEMD-91-11. Washington, DC: GAO.

51. Vayda, E., Barnsley, J.M., Mindell, W.R., Cardillo, B. 1984. Five-year study of surgical rates in Ontario's counties. *Can. Med. Assoc. J.* 131:111–15.

52. Deleted in proof.

53. *Webster's 3rd New International Dictionary.* 1976. Springfield: Merriam.

54. Wennberg, J.E. 1984. Dealing with medical practice variations: a proposal for action. *Health Aff.* 3:6–31.

55. Wennberg, J.E., Gittelsohn, A. 1982. Variations in medical care among small areas. *Sci. Am.* 246:120–34.

56. Wennberg, J.E., Gittelsohn, A. 1975. Health care delivery in Main I: Patterns of use of common surgical procedures. *J. Main. Med. Assoc.* 66:123–49.

57. Wennberg, J., Gittelsohn, A. 1973. Small area variations in health care delivery. *Science* 142:1102–8.

58. Winslow, C.M., Kosecoff, J.B., Chassin, M., Kanouse, D.E., Brook, R.H. 1988. The appropriateness of performing coronary artery bypass surgery. *J. Am. Med. Assoc.* 260:505–9.

59. Winslow, C.M., Solomon, D.H., Chassin, M.R., Kosecoff, J., Merrick, N.J. et al. 1988. The appropriateness of carotid endarterectomy. *N. Engl. J. Med.* 31:721–27.

Healthism, simply put, is an overemphasis on keeping healthy . . . many persons today are too focused on staying healthy, . . . preoccupied with controlling the more manageable health factors like smoking or diet because they feel powerless to change major factors like financial uncertainty or potential nuclear disaster. When we are overly focused on healthiness or a "healthy lifestyle" as goals to strive for (or as the measure of a "healthy" society), we deflect attention from the more important goals of social justice and peace.
— The Boston Women's Health Book Collective

Part IV

Reforming the U.S. Health Care Delivery System

Although strengthening the economy is the nation's first priority, health care reform is certainly second on the list. The many legislative, executive, professional, and consumer group proposals are confusing and complex. The American Nurses' Association, the National League for Nursing, and many other nursing organizations propose a mandated employer-based insurance system that would continue the current public and private financing system. This plan is similar to that proposed by the American Medical Association and a number of legislators.

A more comprehensive approach is a single-payer government system proposed by the Physicians for a National Health Program and by a number of federal legislators. This plan would ensure coverage for everyone under a government-financed system like the Medicare program. Such an approach would save enough in administrative cost to assist in financing coverage for the uninsured. Although the public favors major reform and a public program, politics dictate that some type of compromise plan be developed. Health reform is not only about who is going to pay for coverage (businesses, individuals, and families—tax payers), but also about who is going to manage the plan (private companies or government agencies).

461

A managed competition approach would be financed by employers and employees. This "play-or-pay" system, would mandate that all businesses purchase minimal health plans for workers through private companies or pay into a public health plan. Unemployed persons would be covered by the public plan. If this approach is implemented, it would allow the continuation of the private health insurance industry and still extend health coverage to the entire U.S. population.

Although there are many options available for reforming the U.S. health care system, the question is whether changes will be substantive or cosmetic, incremental or transformative in nature and in scope. The key questions are who is to be covered, what the benefits are to be, and how much they will cost. Political and economic considerations no doubt will determine the outcomes of legislative debates.

Part IV presents three approaches to national health care reform. The first approach, prepared by the major nursing organizations, is an employer-mandated health system similar to plans presented by other health care provider organizations. The second approach is a single-payer model described in one article on basic health services and one on long-term care services. Finally, President Clinton's proposal for health reform, developed when he was a candidate, is presented even though it was later modified and expanded. A comparison of the various approaches illustrates that the long and difficult process of developing a plan to bring about national health care reform inevitably represents political compromise. This chapter does not seek to predict how reform is to be designed and implemented, but rather attempts to clarify the kinds of options that form the foundation for political decision making.

12

National Health Care

*American Nurses'
Association president
Batts endorsing 1992
U.S. presidential
candidate Clinton*

American Nurses' Association

Nursing's Agenda for Health Care Reform

Nurses provide a unique perspective on the health care system. Our constant presence in a variety of settings places us in contact with individuals who reap the benefits of the system's most sophisticated services as well as those individuals seriously compromised by the system's inefficiencies.

More and more, nurses' observe the effects of inadequate services and the declining quality of care on the nation's health. Firsthand experience tells us that the time has come for change. Patchwork approaches to health care reform have not worked. While preserving the best elements of the existing system, we must build a new foundation for health care in America. . . .

Nursing's plan for reform converts a system that focuses on the costly treatment of illness to a system that emphasizes primary health care services and the promotion, restoration, and maintenance of health. It increases the consumer's responsibility and role in health care decision making and focuses on partnerships between consumers and providers. It sets forth new delivery arrangements that make health care a more vital part of individual and community life. And it ensures that health services are appropriate, effective, cost efficient, and focused on consumer needs. . . .

THE FRAMEWORK FOR CHANGE

Nurses strongly believe that the health care system must be restructured, reoriented, and decentralized in order to guarantee access to services, contain costs, and ensure quality care. Our plan—the product of consensus building within organized nursing—is designed to achieve this goal. It

---

The American Nurses' Association (ANA), representing 200,000 individuals and registered nurse associations, sponsors the American Academy of Nursing and other research, education, credentialing, and rights centers and publishes journals, reports, proceedings, and statistics on nursing and health care.

Abridged from American Nurses' Association. (1991). *Nursing's Agenda for Health Care Reform: Executive Summary*. Washington, DC: American Nurses' Association. Used with permission.

provides central control in the form of federal minimum standards for essential services and federally defined eligibility requirements. At the same time, it makes allowances for decentralized decision making that will permit local areas to develop specific programs and arrangements best suited to consumer needs.

Nursing's plan is built around several basic premises, including the following:

- All citizens and residents of the United States must have equitable access to essential health care services (a core of care).
- Primary health care services must play a very basic and prominent role in service delivery.
- Consumers must be the central focus of the health care system. Assessment of health care needs must be the determining factor in the ultimate structuring and delivery of programs and services.
- Consumers must be guaranteed direct access to a full range of qualified health care providers who offer their services in a variety of delivery arrangements at sites that are accessible, convenient, and familiar to the consumer.
- Consumers must assume more responsibility for their own care and become better informed about the range of providers and the potential options for services. Working in partnership with providers, consumers must actively participate in choices that best meet their needs.
- Health care services must be restructured to create a better balance between the prevailing orientation toward illness and cure and a new commitment to wellness and care.
- The health care system must assure that appropriate, effective care is delivered through the efficient use of resources.
- A standardized package of essential health care services must be provided and financed through an integration of public and private plans and sources.
- Mechanisms must be implemented to protect against catastrophic costs and impoverishment.

The cornerstone of nursing's plan for reform is the delivery of primary health care services to households and individuals in convenient, familiar places. If health is to be a true national priority, it is logical to provide services in the places where people work and live. Maximizing the use of these sites can help eliminate the fragmentation and lack of coordination that have come to characterize the existing health care system. It can also promote a more "consumer friendly" system where services, such as health education, screening, immunizations, well-child care, and prenatal care, would be readily accessible.

At the same time, consumers must be the focus of the health care system. Individuals must be given incentives to assume more responsibility for their health. They must develop both the motivation and capability to be more prudent buyers of health services. Promotion of healthy lifestyles and better informed consumer decisions can contribute to effective and economical health care delivery.

Finally, in implementing reforms, attention must be directed to the unique needs of special population groups whose health care needs have been neglected. These individuals include children, pregnant women, and vulnerable groups, such as the poor, minorities, AIDS victims, and those who have difficulty securing insurance because of preexisting conditions. Lack of preventive and primary care for this sector has cost the nation enormously—both in terms of lives lost or impaired and dollars spent to treat problems that could have been avoided or treated less expensively through appropriate intervention.

Access to care alone may not be sufficient to resolve the problems of these vulnerable groups. For those individuals whose health has been seriously compromised, a "catch-up" program characterized by enriched services is justified. Coverage of pregnant women and children is critical. This first step represents a cost-effective investment in the future health and prosperity of the nation.

It is this set of values that distinguishes nursing's plan from other proposals and offers a realistic approach to health care reform.

A PLAN FOR REFORM

Nursing's plan for health care reform builds a new foundation for health care in America. It shifts the emphasis of the health care system from illness and cure to wellness and care. While preserving key components of the existing system, it sets forth new strategies for guaranteeing universal coverage; making health care a more vital part of community life; and ensuring that the health care services provided are appropriate, effective, and cost efficient. . . .

Universal Access to a Standard Package of Essential Services

Nursing's plan envisions a new and bold approach to universal access to a standard package of essential health care services and the manner in which these services are delivered.

The federal government will delineate the essential services (core of care) that must be provided to all U.S. citizens and residents. This standard package will include defined levels of:

- Primary health care services, hospital care, emergency treatment, inpatient and outpatient professional services, and home care services
- Prevention services, including prenatal and perinatal care; infant and well-child care; school-based disease prevention programs; speech therapy, hearing, dental, and eye care for children up to age 18; screening procedures; and other preventive services with proven effectiveness
- Prescription drugs, medical supplies and equipment, and laboratory and radiology services
- Mental health services and substance abuse treatment and rehabilitation
- Hospice care
- Long-term care services of relatively short duration
- Restorative services determined to be essential to the prevention of long-term institutionalization

By taking this approach, traditional illness services are balanced with provisions for health maintenance services that prevent illness, reduce cost, and avoid institutionalization. Thus, hospital coverage and emergency care are covered, as are such services as immunizations, physical examinations, and prenatal and perinatal care.

The creation of federal minimum standards for essential services will necessitate modifications in existing public programs. The ultimate goal will be, over time, to merge all government-sponsored health programs into a single public program.

Coverage Options.   Universal coverage for the federally defined package of essential services will be accessed through an integration of public and private plans and resources.

- A public plan, administered by the states, will provide coverage for the poor (those below 200% of the federal poverty level), high-risk populations, and the potentially medically indigent. Any employer or individual will also have the option of buying into this plan as their source of coverage.
- Private plans (employment-based health benefit programs and commercial health insurance) will be required to offer, at a minimum, the nationally standardized package of essential services. This package could be enriched as a benefit of employment or individuals could purchase additional services from commercial insurers if they so choose.

All citizens and residents will be required to be covered by one of these options. Under both the public plan and private plans, no one will be denied insurance because of preexisting conditions. If employers do not offer private coverage, they will be required to pay into the public plan for their employees. Employer payments will be actuarially equivalent to the costs of employee and dependent coverage. Financial relief will be made available to small businesses (25 employees or less) for whom this provision would not be feasible. Individuals with no source of private coverage could also buy into the public plan. To assure universal access to essential services, systems will be developed to identify the insurance option through which each individual's needs are met.

Premiums and Payment Rates.   Access to health care services will be enhanced by offering insurance premiums that the public can afford and payment rates to providers that are equitable and inclusive.

Both the public and private plans will utilize deductibles and copayments to ensure that beneficiaries continue to pay for a portion of their own care and, therefore, have financial incentives to be economical in their use of services. Deductible amounts and copayment rates, however, will never serve as barriers to care. Provisions will be made to waive or subsidize deductions and copayments for households with incomes below 200% of the federal poverty level. Deductibles for certain types of programs and services (e.g., health promotion, such as well-child care, immunizations, and mammograms; managed care plans) will be held to a minimum to encourage wider use of cost-efficient wellness-oriented options.

Public and private payers will be required to offer fair and consistent rates of payment to providers. To protect access to care, providers will not seek payment at the point of service; nor will they be permitted to engage in balance billing. Because providers will be reimbursed fairly through insurance and the problems of uncompensated care will be largely eliminated, there will be no need for providers to charge consumers amounts above the established rate. Consequently, consumers' financial responsibility for health care services will be more predictable.

To make insurance more affordable to individuals and to reduce costs to insurers and employers, nursing's plan calls for reforms in the private insurance market. These reforms may encompass a variety of strategies, including:

- Community rating for all insurers.
- A cap on the out-of-pocket expenses individuals must pay for catastrophic care, including nursing home and other long-term care.
- State reinsurance pools to protect insurers and consumers against the high costs of insuring a broader range of patients.

Special Programs for Vulnerable Groups.　Countless individuals suffer from long-term health problems associated with inadequate access to basic health services over time. Often the poor and many members of minority groups are in this category. Special programs will provide services and outreach to vulnerable populations in order to compensate for formerly inadequate care and its consequences.

For infants and children (e.g., low birthweight babies, battered and neglected children, pregnant teenagers, children who abuse drugs, and young victims of violence and homelessness) such programing could be viewed as a health service (Healthstart) equivalent to the Head Start Program for those who are educationally disadvantaged. An expanded version of the Women's, Infants and Children (WIC) Program may be needed to produce quality outcomes in maternal–child health for poor and minority populations. Other special population groups may also warrant compensatory health programs beyond the scope of essential health benefits and services.

It is important to note that the ultimate goal of improved health is not achievable exclusively within the confines of the health sector. Social failures have serious health consequences. Improvements in the broader environment have a major impact on health status and health care costs. While the focus of this plan is on the health care system, nursing's long-term policy agenda for the nation is much broader. National health reform must also consider the interrelationships between health and such factors as education, behavior, income, housing and sanitation, social support networks, and attitudes about health. Better health cannot be the nation's only goal when hunger, crime, drugs, and other social problems remain. Consequently, nursing is committed to pursuing reform in other areas affecting health. Discussion of such reform, however, is beyond the scope of this paper.

Long-term Care.　High costs of long-term care often threaten to impoverish patients and their families. Nursing's plan seeks to prevent impoverishment and the potential loss of dignity by recognizing both public responsibility for long-term care and continued personal commitment to planning for such care. Financing arrangements will provide "front-end" coverage for chronic care and long-term care services of short duration through a variety of public and private options.

Beyond addressing short-term needs, individuals will be expected to assume personal responsibility for long-term care through strengthened private insurance programs and a variety of innovative financing arrangements. Such strategies will include privately purchased long-term care insurance, new savings and tax incentives, and home equity conversion opportunities. Such steps are essential to prevent individuals and their families from becoming impoverished by necessary care that can be anticipated and planned for. Emphasis on personal responsibility, however, does not ignore the fact that there always will be some individuals who will be left without resources who must reach out for public assistance.

Catastrophic Expenses.   Length and/or intensity of illness may generate catastrophic costs. Given this fact, limits will be placed on individuals' out-of-pocket payments for catastrophic health care expenses. Costs to insurers or individuals that exceed preset limits will be covered through a state reinsurance pool, to which all insurers must contribute. Under nursing's plan, insurers will tap into the pool when their total costs or costs per patient exceed preset limits. When costs decline, they will resume normal financing.

Decentralized Delivery System.   Although standards for essential health services and eligibility requirements are to be mandated at the federal level, delivery mechanisms for health services will be decentralized in terms of planning and administration to foster greater consumer orientation. Because local needs differ, states will have the authority to modify implementation to reflect geographical diversity.

To promote greater use of disease prevention and primary health care, services will be delivered, whenever possible, in convenient, familiar sites readily accessible to households and individuals. Maximizing the use of local settings, including schools, homes, places of work, and other community facilities, will help reduce the fragmentation of primary health care delivery and promote a more consumer-friendly system.

Cost-effective, Quality Care

By properly balancing individual health needs and self-care responsibilities with provider capabilities, care can be provided in a more efficient and coordinated manner. It can be more effectively directed at health promotion activities that will ultimately improve outcomes and reduce costs. Nursing's plan for reform is designed to achieve such balance.

Provider Availability.   Financial and regulatory obstacles, as well as institutional barriers, that deny consumer access to all qualified health professionals will be removed. The wider use of a range of qualified health professionals will increase access to care, particularly in understaffed specialties, such as primary health care, and in underserved urban and rural geographical areas. It will also facilitate selection of the most cost-effective option for care.

Under this arrangement, health providers must be reasonably and fairly compensated for their services. Where fee-for-service payment arrangements continue, payments for patient services must be made directly to providers.

Consumer Involvement. Consumers will be encouraged to assume more responsibility for their own health. Health professionals will work in partnership with consumers to evaluate the full range of their needs and the available services. Together the consumer and the health professional will determine a course of action that is based on an understanding of the effectiveness of treatment.

Outcome and Effectiveness Measures. Development of multidisciplinary clinical practice guidelines is essential to the proper functioning of the health care system. These guidelines will be used to sensitize providers and others to the proven effectiveness of practices and technologies. With clear-cut information on the value of various procedures, payers, providers, and consumers can work together to eliminate wasteful and unnecessary services. Moreover, increased dissemination of research findings regarding health care outcomes will enhance provider and consumer involvement in making the most effective choices about care and treatment. By taking this approach, the likelihood of serious disputes or litigation over appropriateness of care will be minimized. Likewise, the need for defensive practices designed to protect providers against malpractice suits will be greatly reduced.

Practice guidelines and directives derived from research, while providing an element of control, will be supportive of innovation. Coverage will be extended to procedures shown to be significantly more effective, less costly than existing approaches, and/or useful in improving patient outcomes and quality of life. At the same time, an effort will be made to carefully weigh new therapeutic approaches with high start-up costs that may ultimately be less expensive than present methods.

Use of advancements in clinical practice and technology will be conditioned on satisfying criteria related to cost efficiency and therapeutic effectiveness. Such an approach will not deny people essential services. It will, however, assess carefully the appropriateness of providing high-tech curative medical care to those who simply require comfort, relief from pain, supportive care, or a peaceful death.

Review Mechanisms. State and local review bodies, representative of the public and private sectors and composed of payers, providers, and consumers, will be established. These groups, operating under federal guidelines, will determine resource allocation, cost-reduction approaches, allowable insurance premiums, and fair and consistent reimbursement levels for providers. Such review will be sensitive to ethical issues.

Managed Care. Managed care will be instituted both to reduce costs and assure consumer access to the most effective treatments. Nursing's plan envisions managed care as organized delivery systems that link the financing of health care to the delivery of services, serving to maximize the quality of care while minimizing costs. To promote the use of managed care, enrollment in approved provider networks will be a requirement for those covered by the public plan. Managed care will also be encouraged for recipients of private coverage through reductions in deductibles and co-payments.

In the past, managed care has been used, in many instances, to protect the pocketbooks of insurers rather than the rights of consumers. Managed care must be restructured to retain the maximum possible consumer choice and to place a premium on services that address the health of consumers.

Case Management.   In contrast to managed care systems, case management is rooted in the client-provider relationship. Case management services will be used to integrate, coordinate, and advocate for people requiring extensive services. The aim of case management is to make health care less fragmented and more holistic for those individuals with complex health care needs. A variety of health care professionals are qualified to provide this service. The first allegiance of these providers will be to their clients. Acting as advocates, they will provide both direct care and negotiate with systems on behalf of their clients. They will be authorized to access services for a given client.

Both case management (provider) and managed care (delivery systems) models are important to the smooth functioning of the health care system.

A Realistic Plan of Action

Under nursing's plan, universal coverage will be achieved through implementation of both the public plan and private plan options. Employers will be motivated to collaborate with employees in shaping private plans that best satisfy their needs. At the same time, as larger numbers of more diverse groups participate in the public plan, the attractiveness of this option in terms of cost, quality, and image will be enhanced.

While the public and private sector plans can move forward simultaneously, it may be necessary to expand coverage to segments of the population in sequential steps. These steps would be introduced at an acceptable and financially reasonable rate until the ultimate goal of universal coverage is achieved. This approach would avoid excessive shocks to the health care system and allow the public to adjust to changing patterns of service.

Given this perspective, the first targeted population would include all pregnant women, children under age 6, and those individuals who demonstrate health status seriously compromised by a history of inadequate care. Improvements in coverage and benefits for these groups will have the greatest impact on the nation's future health and productivity.

As expeditiously as possible, other segments of the population would be covered. These groups might be approached as outlined below. This sequence, however, is not necessarily intended as a rigid order.

- All children and young people, ages 6–18
- All those above age 18 with incomes below 100% of the federal poverty level
- All employees and dependents
- All those with incomes below 200% of the federal poverty level

The process will culminate with the merger of all entitlement plans into a single public program to provide coverage to all citizens and residents who do not have or cannot obtain coverage through a private plan.

The Fiscal Implications of Reform

It is impossible to predict the dollar amount that will be associated with the expansion of services or the efficiencies in nursing's plan. It is predictable that additional funding will be necessary to support start-up costs and transition. It is also possible that such expenditures will be recaptured over time.

A number of proposals for reform have been introduced. Among those proposals with cost estimates, additional health care costs range from $60–90 billion.[3,4] Although nursing's plan for expanded coverage is similar in a number of ways to some of these proposals, offsetting proposed efficiencies integral to the plan will create significant dollars for real location. These resources will be directed to areas currently underfunded or excluded, including long-term care and primary-care services.

Although precise financial estimates are impossible at this time, several general observations can be made.

Cost Impact.   Extension of coverage for essential services to the uninsured and underinsured will result in the dedication of more dollars. One source estimated that such coverage, if provided in 1990, would have added approximately $12 billion to health spending.[5]

It will also be necessary to dedicate more dollars to the expansion of long-term care services. Cost estimates for improved long-term care coverage vary. One 1990 study suggests that provision of comprehensive long-term care services, if implemented in 1990, would have cost $45 billion, $34 billion of which would have been new costs.[6] Nursing's plan, however, calls for more limited coverage supported through a combination of public dollars and enhanced personal responsibility.

In the initial phases of nursing's health care reform, the emphasis on preventive services will require dollars. Over time, however, improved health resulting from the availability of comprehensive primary care services will produce a cost-reducing "health dividend." By placing greater emphasis on health promotion and disease prevention in community-based settings, the system will reach out aggressively to individuals and households to foster an increased commitment to healthy lifestyles, prevention of disease, periodic screening for early detection of illness, and earlier treatment and promote informed decision making by the consumer. All of this will contribute to cost-effective, early interventions that, over time, will reduce the need for more costly care.

Cost Savings.   New costs associated with nursing's plan will be offset to a considerable degree by the following cost-saving initiatives:

- Required usage of managed care in the public plan and encouraged use in private plans.
- Incentives for consumers and providers to utilize managed-care arrangements.
- Controlled growth of the health care system through planning and prudent resource allocation.
- Assurance of direct access to a full range of qualified providers.
- Development of health care policies based on effectiveness and outcome research.
- Incentives for consumers and providers to be more cost efficient in selecting health care options.
- Elimination of unnecessary bureaucratic controls and administrative procedures through such measures as standardized billing, simplified utilization review, streamlined administrative procedures, regulatory reforms, and consolidation of plans.

Sources of Revenue.   To the extent that any additional dollars are needed, sources can be found. Responsibility for financing health care reform must be distributed equitably among individuals, employers, and government.

Individuals will continue to pay a portion of health costs through co-payments by households and individuals with incomes above 200% of the poverty level, and through reduced co-payments for those whose incomes are 100–200% of the poverty level.

Employers will provide private health insurance that meets or exceeds minimum federal standards for their employees and dependents or provide coverage through the public plan. Accommodations will be made to provide small businesses with the necessary financial relief to meet this obligation.

State governments currently pay a portion of health care expenses for the poor and fund certain other health programs. Nursing's health reform plan calls for consolidation of existing government health plans into a single public program. When this occurs, all states will contribute revenues to the program through maintenance-of-effort arrangements.

Revenues to pay for any increased costs could be derived from some combination of higher tobacco and alcohol taxes, additional payroll taxes, higher marginal income tax rates, and the increase or elimination of the income ceiling for FICA tax collection. A value-added tax (similar to a national sales tax) could also be considered.

A LOOK TOWARD THE FUTURE

The existing health care system stands as evidence of the futility of patchwork approaches to health care reform. America's nurses' say it is time to frame a new vision for reform—time for a bold departure from the present. Reform of any single component of the system will not do the job. Insurance reform alone will not guarantee access to care if the health care delivery system is not restructured. Conversely, many people will remain unserved or underserved if health care services are so costly that millions of Americans cannot afford to purchase care. To be most effective, a health care system must do more than provide equipment, supplies, facilities, and manpower. It must guarantee universal access to an assured standard of care. It must use health resources effectively and efficiently—balancing efforts to promote health with the capacity to cure disease. It must provide care in convenient, familiar locations. And it must make full use of the range of qualified health professionals and diverse settings for care. It is this insight that underlies nursing's plan for reform, making it the most viable solution to the health care crisis.

BIBLIOGRAPHY

1. U.S. Department of Commerce, *U.S. Industrial Outlook 1991,* Chapter 44, Health and Medical Services, 1–6.
2. National Leadership Coalition for Health Care Reform, A Comprehensive Reform Plan for the Health Care System, 2.
3. *The Pepper Commission, A Call for Action: Final Report,* September 1990, 137.
4. Mark G. Battle, National Association of Social Workers, Remarks During NASW's National Health Care Press Conference, January 8, 1991.
5. Lewin/ICF estimates in *To the Rescue: Toward Solving America's Health Care Crisis,* Families USA Foundation, November 1990, 13.
6. Pepper Commission, 151.

*David U. Himmelstein / Steffie Woolhandler / Writing
Committee of the Working Group on Program Design,
Physicians for a National Health Program*

A National Health Program
for the United States:
A Physicians' Proposal

Our health care system is failing. It denies access to many in need and is expensive, inefficient, and increasingly bureaucratic. The pressures of cost control, competition, and profit threaten the traditional tenets of medical practice. For patients, the misfortune of illness is often amplified by the fear of financial ruin. For physicians, the gratifications of healing often give way to anger and alienation. Patchwork reforms succeed only in exchanging old problems for new ones. It is time to change fundamentally the trajectory of American medicine—to develop a comprehensive national health program for the United States.

We are physicians active in the full range of medical endeavors. We are primary care doctors and surgeons, psychiatrists and public health specialists, pathologists and administrators. We work in hospitals, clinics, private practices, health maintenance organizations (HMOs), universities, corporations, and public agencies. Some of us are young, still in training; others are greatly experienced, and some have held senior positions in American medicine.

As physicians, we constantly confront the irrationality of the present health care system. In private practice, we waste countless hours on billing and bureaucracy. For uninsured patients, we avoid procedures, consultations, and costly medications. Diagnosis-related groups (DRGs) have placed us between administrators demanding early discharge and elderly patients with no one to help at home—all the while glancing over our shoulders at the peer-review organization. In HMOs we walk a tightrope between thrift and penuriousness, too often under the pressure of surveillance by bureaucrats more concerned with the bottom line than with other

David U. Himmelstein, M.D., and Steffie Woolhandler, M.D., M.P.H., serve on the Writing Committee of the Working Group on Program Design, Physicians for a National Health Program, Chicago, Illinois.

From Himmelstein, D.U., and Woolhandler, S. (1989). A national health program for the United States. *N Eng J Med* 320(2):102–108. Used with permission from *The New England Journal of Medicine.*

measures of achievement. In public health work we are frustrated in the face of plenty; the world's richest health care system is unable to ensure such basic services as prenatal care and immunizations.

Despite our disparate perspectives, we are united by dismay at the current state of medicine and by the conviction that an alternative must be developed. We hope to spark debate, to transform disaffection with what exists into a vision of what might be. To this end, we submit for public review, comment, and revision a working plan for a rational and humane health care system—a national health program.

We envisage a program that would be federally mandated and ultimately funded by the federal government but administered largely at the state and local level. The proposed system would eliminate financial barriers to care; minimize economic incentives for both excessive and insufficient care, discourage administrative interference and expense, improve the distribution of health facilities, and control costs by curtailing bureaucracy and fostering health planning. Our plan borrows many features from the Canadian national health program and adapts them to the unique circumstances of the United States. We suggest that, as in Canada's provinces, the national health program be tested initially in statewide demonstration projects. Thus, our proposal addresses both the structure of the national health program and the transition process necessary to implement the program in a single state. In each section below, we present a key feature of the proposal, followed by the rationale for our approach. Areas such as long-term care; public, occupational, environmental, and mental health; and medical education need much more development and will be addressed in detail in future proposals.

COVERAGE

Everyone would be included in a single public plan covering all medically necessary services, including acute, rehabilitative, long-term, and home care; mental health services; dental services; occupational health care; prescription drugs and medical supplies; and preventive and public health measures. Boards of experts and community representatives would determine which services were unnecessary or ineffective, and these would be excluded from coverage. As in Canada, alternative insurance coverage for services included under the national health program would be eliminated, as would patient copayments and deductibles.

Universal coverage would solve the gravest problem in health care by eliminating financial barriers to care. A single comprehensive program is necessary both to ensure equal access to care and to minimize the complexity and expense of billing and administration. The public administration of insurance funds would save tens of billions of dollars each year. The more than 1500 private health insurers in the United States now consume about 8 percent of revenues for overhead, whereas both the Medicare program and the Canadian national health program have overhead costs of only 2 to 3 percent. The complexity of our current insurance system, with its multiplicity of payers, forces U.S. hospitals to spend more than twice as much as Canadian hospitals on billing and administration and requires U.S. physicians to spend about 10 percent of their gross incomes on excess billing costs.[1] Eliminating insurance programs that duplicated the national health program coverage, though politically thorny, would clearly be within the prerogative of the Congress.[2] Failure to do so would require the continuation of the costly bureaucracy necessary to administer and deal with such programs.

Copayments and deductibles endanger the health of poor people who are sick,[3] decrease the use of vital inpatient medical services as much as they discourage the use of unnecessary ones,[4] discourage preventive care,[5] and are unwieldy and expensive to administer. Canada has few such charges, yet health costs are lower than in the United States and have risen slowly.[6,7] In the United States, in contrast, increasing copayments and deductibles have failed to slow the escalation of costs.

Instead of the confused and often unjust dictates of insurance companies, a greatly expanded program of technology assessment and cost-effectiveness evaluation would guide decisions about covered services, as well as about the allocation of funds for capital spending, drug formularies, and other issues.

PAYMENT FOR HOSPITAL SERVICES

Each hospital would receive an annual lump-sum payment to cover all operating expenses—a "global" budget. The amount of this payment would be negotiated with the state national health program payment board and would be based on past expenditures, previous financial and clinical performance, projected changes in levels of services, wages and other costs, and proposed new and innovative programs. Hospitals would not bill for services covered by the national health program. No part of the operating budget could be used for hospital expansion, profit, marketing, or major capital purchases or leases. These expenditures would also come from the national health program fund, but monies for them would be appropriated separately.

Global prospective budgeting would simplify hospital administration and virtually eliminate billing, thus freeing up substantial resources for increased clinical care. Before the nationwide implementation of the national health program, hospitals in the states with demonstration programs could bill out-of-state patients on a simple per diem basis. Prohibiting the use of operating funds for capital purchases or profit would eliminate the main financial incentive for both excessive intervention (under fee-for-service payment) and skimping on care (under DRG-type prospective-payment systems), since neither inflating revenues nor limiting care could result in gain for the institution. The separate appropriation of funds explicitly designated for capital expenditures would facilitate rational health planning. In Canada, this method of hospital payment has been successful in containing costs, minimizing bureaucracy, improving the distribution of health resources, and maintaining the quality of care.[6-9] It shifts the focus of hospital administration away from the bottom line and toward the provision of optimal clinical services.

PAYMENT FOR PHYSICIANS' SERVICES, AMBULATORY CARE, AND MEDICAL HOME CARE

To minimize the disruption of existing patterns of care, the national health program would include three payment options for physicians and other practitioners: fee-for-service payment, salaried positions in institutions receiving global budgets, and salared positions within group practices or HMOs receiving per capita (capitation) payments.

Fee-for-Service Payment

The state national health program payment board and a representative of the fee-for-service practitioners (perhaps the state medical society) would negotiate a simplified, binding fee schedule. Physicians would submit bills to the national health program on a simple form or by computer and would receive extra payment for any bill not paid within 30 days. Payments to physicians would cover only the services provided by physicians and their support staff and would exclude reimbursement for costly capital purchases of equipment for the office, such as CT scanners. Physicians who accepted payment from the national health program could bill patients directly only for uncovered services (as is done for cosmetic surgery in Canada).

Global Budgets

Institutions such as hospitals, health centers, group practices, clinics serving migrant workers, and medical home care agencies could elect to receive a global budget for the delivery of outpatient, home care, and physicians' services, as well as for preventive health care and patient-education programs. The negotiation process and the regulations covering capital expenditures and profits would be similar to those for inpatient hospital services. Physicians employed in such institutions would be salaried.

Capitation

HMOs, group practices, and other institutions could elect to be paid fees on a per capita basis to cover all outpatient care, physicians' services, and medical home care. The regulations covering the use of such payments for capital expenditures and for profits would be similar to those that would apply to hospitals. The capitation fee would not cover inpatient services (except care provided by a physician), which would be included in hospitals' global budgets. Selective enrollment policies would be prohibited, and patients would be permitted to leave an HMO or other health plan with appropriate notice. Physicians working in HMOs would be salaried, and financial incentives to physicians based on the HMO's financial performance would be prohibited.

The diversity of existing practice arrangements, each with strong proponents, necessitates a pluralistic approach. Under all three proposed options, capital purchases and profits would be uncoupled from payments to physicians and other operating costs—a feature that is essential for minimizing entrepreneurial incentives, containing costs, and facilitating health planning.

Under the fee-for-service option, physicians' office overhead would be reduced by the simplification of billing.[1] The improved coverage would encourage preventive care.[10] In Canada, fee-for-service practice with negotiated fee schedules and mandatory assignment (acceptance of the assigned fee as total payment) has proved to be compatible with cost containment, adequate incomes for physicians, and a high level of access to and satisfaction with care on the part of patients.[6,7] The Canadian provinces have responded to the inflationary potential of fee-for-service payment in various ways: by limiting the number of physicians, by monitoring physicians for outlandish practice patterns, by setting overall limits on a province's spending for physicians' services (thus relying on the profession to police itself), and even by capping the total reimbursement of individual physicians. These regulatory options have been made possible (and have not required an extensive bureaucracy) because all payment comes from a single source. Similar measures might be needed in the United States, although our penchant for bureaucratic hypertrophy might require a concomitant cap on spending for the regulatory apparatus. For example, spending for program administration and reimbursement bureaucracy might be restricted to 3 percent of total costs.

Global budgets for institutional providers would eliminate billing, while providing a predictable and stable source of income. Such funding could also encourage the development of preventive health programs in the community, such as education programs on the acquired immunodeficiency syndrome (AIDS), whose costs are difficult to attribute and bill to individual patients.

Continuity of care would no longer be disrupted when patients' insurance coverage changed as a result of retirement or a job change. Incentives for providers receiving capitation payments to skimp on care would be minimized, since unused operating funds could not be devoted to expansion or profit.

PAYMENT FOR LONG-TERM CARE

A separate proposal for long-term care is under development, guided by three principles. First, access to care should be based on need rather than on age or ability to pay. Second, social and community-based services should be expanded and integrated with institutional care. Third, bureaucracy and entrepreneurial incentives should be minimized through global budgeting with separate funding for capital expenses.

ALLOCATION OF CAPITAL FUNDS, HEALTH PLANNING, AND RETURN ON EQUITY

Funds for the construction or renovation of health facilities and for purchases of major equipment would be appropriated from the national health program budget. The funds would be distributed by state and regional health-planning boards composed of both experts and community representatives. Capital projects funded by private donations would require approval by the health-planning board if they entailed an increase in future operating expenses.

The national health program would pay owners of for-profit hospitals, nursing homes, and clinics a reasonable fixed rate of return on existing equity. Since virtually all new capital investment would be funded by the national health program, it would not be included in calculating the return on equity.

Current capital spending greatly affects future operating costs, as well as the distribution of resources. Effective health planning requires that funds go to high-quality, efficient programs in the areas of greatest need. Under the existing reimbursement system, which combines operating and capital payments, prosperous hospitals can expand and modernize, whereas impoverished ones cannot, regardless of the health needs of the population they serve or the quality of services they provide. The national health program would replace this implicit mechanism for distributing capital with an explicit one, which would facilitate (though not guarantee) allocation on the basis of need and quality. Insulating these crucial decisions from distortion by narrow interests would require the rigorous evaluation of the technology and assessment of needs, as well as the active involvement of providers and patients.

For-profit providers would be compensated for existing investments. Since new for-profit investment would be barred, the proprietary sector would gradually shrink.

PUBLIC, ENVIRONMENTAL, AND OCCUPATIONAL HEALTH SERVICES

Existing arrangements for public, occupational, and environmental health services would be retained in the short term. Funding for preventive health care would be expanded. Additional proposals dealing with these issues are planned.

PRESCRIPTION DRUGS AND SUPPLIES

An expert panel would establish and regularly update a list of all necessary and useful drugs and out-patient equipment. Suppliers would bill the national health program directly for the wholesale cost, plus a reasonable dispensing fee, of any item in the list that was prescribed by a licensed practitioner. The substitution of generic for proprietary drugs would be encouraged.

FUNDING

The national health program would disburse virtually all payments for health services. The total expenditure would be set at the same proportion of the gross national product as health costs represented in the year preceding the establishment of the national health program. Funds for the national health program could be raised through a variety of mechanisms. In the long run, funding based on an income tax or other progressive tax might be the fairest and most efficient solution, because tax-based funding is the least cumbersome and least expensive mechanism for collecting money. During the transition period in states with demonstration programs, the following structure would mimic existing funding patterns and minimize economic disruption.

Medicare and Medicaid

All current federal funds allocated to Medicare and Medicaid would be paid to the national health program. The contribution of each program would be based on the previous year's expenditures, adjusted for inflation. Using Medicare and Medicaid funds in this manner would require a federal waiver.

State and Local Funds

All current state and local funds for health care expenditures, adjusted for inflation, would be paid to the national health program.

Employer Contributions

A tax earmarked for the national health program would be levied on all employers. The tax rate would be set so that total collections equaled the previous year's statewide total of employers' expenditures for health benefits, adjusted for inflation. Employers obligated by preexisting contracts to provide health benefits could credit the cost of those benefits toward their national health program tax liability.

Private Insurance Revenues

Private health insurance plans duplicating the coverage of the national health program would be phased out over three years. During this transition period, all revenues from such plans would be turned over to the national health program, after the deduction of a reasonable fee to cover the costs of collecting premiums.

General Tax Revenues

Additional taxes, equivalent to the amount now spent by individual citizens for insurance premiums and out-of-pocket health costs, would be levied.

It would be critical for all funds for health care to flow through the national health program. Such single-source payment (monopsony) has been the cornerstone of cost containment and health planning in Canada. The mechanism of raising funds for the national health program would be a matter of tax policy, largely separate from the organization of the health care system itself. As in Canada, federal funding could attenuate inequalities among the states in financial and medical resources.

The transitional proposal for demonstration programs in selected states illustrates how monopsony payment could be established with limited disruption of existing patterns of health care funding. The employers' contribution would represent a decrease in costs for most firms that now provide health insurance and an increase for those that do not currently pay for benefits. Some provision might be needed to cushion the impact of the change on financially strapped small businesses. Decreased individual spending for health care would offset the additional tax burden on individual citizens. Private health insurance, with its attendant inefficiency and waste, would be largely eliminated. A program of job placement and retraining for insurance and hospital-billing employees would be an important component of the program during the transition period.

DISCUSSION

The Patient's View

The national health program would establish a right to comprehensive health care. As in Canada, each person would receive a national health program card entitling him or her to all necessary medical care without copayments or deductibles. The card could be used with any fee-for-service practitioner and at any institution receiving a global budget. HMO members could receive nonemergency care only through their HMO, although they could readily transfer to the non-HMO option.

Thus, patients would have a free choice of providers, and the financial threat of illness would be eliminated. Taxes would increase by an amount equivalent to the current total of medical expenditures by individuals. Conversely, individuals' aggregate payments for medical care would decrease by the same amount.

The Practitioner's View

Physicians would have a free choice of practice settings. Treatment would no longer be constrained by the patient's insurance status or by bureaucratic dicta. On the basis of the Canadian experience, we anticipate that the average physician's income would change little, although differences among specialties might be attenuated.

Fee-for-service practitioners would be paid for the care of anyone not enrolled in an HMO. The entrepreneurial aspects of medicine—with the attendant problems as well as the possibilities—would be limited. Physicians could concentrate on medicine; every patient would be fully insured, but physicians could increase their incomes only by providing more care.

Billing would involve imprinting the patient's national health program card on a charge slip, checking a box to indicate the complexity of the procedure or service, and sending the slip (or a computer record) to the physician-payment board. This simplification of billing would save thousands of dollars per practitioner in annual office expenses.[1]

Bureaucratic interference in clinical decision making would sharply diminish. Costs would be contained by controlling overall spending and by limiting entrepreneurial incentives, thus obviating the need for the kind of detailed administrative oversight that is characteristic of the DRG program and similar schemes. Indeed, there is much less administrative intrusion in day-to-day clinical practice in Canada (and most other countries with national health programs) than in the United States.[11,12]

Salaried practitioners would be insulated from the financial consequences of clinical decisions. Because savings on patient care could no longer be used for institutional expansion or profits, the pressure to skimp on care would be minimized.

The Effect on Other Health Workers

Nurses and other health care personnel would enjoy a more humane and efficient clinical milieu. The burdens of paperwork associated with billing would be lightened. The jobs of many administrative and insurance employees would be eliminated, necessitating a major effort at job placement and retraining. We advocate that many of these displaced workers be deployed in expanded programs of public health, health promotion and education, and home care and as support personnel to free nurses for clinical tasks.

The Effect on Hospitals

Hospitals' revenues would become stable and predictable. More than half the current hospital bureaucracy would be eliminated,[1] and the remaining administrators could focus on facilitating clinical care and planning for future health needs.

The capital budget requests of hospitals would be weighed against other priorities for health care investment. Hospitals would neither grow because they were profitable nor fail because of unpaid bills—although regional health planning would undoubtedly mandate that some expand and others close or be put to other uses. Responsiveness to community needs, the quality of care, efficiency, and innovation would replace financial performance as the bottom line. The elimination of new for-profit investment would lead to a gradual conversion of proprietary hospitals to not-for-profit status.

The Effect on the Insurance Industry

The insurance industry would feel the greatest impact of this proposal. Private insurance firms would have no role in health care financing, since the public administration of insurance is more efficient,[1,13] and single-source payment is the key to both equal access and cost control. Indeed, most of the extra funds needed to finance the expansion of care would come from eliminating the overhead and profits of insurance companies and abolishing the billing apparatus necessary to apportion costs among the various plans.

The Effect on Corporate America

Firms that now provide generous employee health benefits would realize savings, because their contribution to the national health program would be less than their current health insurance costs. For example, health care expenditures by Chrysler, currently $5,300 annually per employee,[14] would fall to about $1,600, a figure calculated by dividing the total current U.S. spending on health by private employers by the total number of full-time-equivalent, nongovernment employees. Since most firms that compete in international markets would save money, the competitiveness of U.S. products would be enhanced. However, costs would increase for companies that do not now provide health benefits. The average health care costs for employers would be unchanged in the short run. In the long run, overall health costs would rise less steeply because of improved health planning and greater efficiency. The funding mechanism ultimately adopted would determine the corporate share of those costs.

Health Benefits and Financial Costs

There is ample evidence that removing financial barriers to health care encourages timely care and improves health. After Canada instituted a national health program, visits to physicians increased among patients with serious symptoms.[15] Mortality rates, which were higher than U.S. rates through the 1950s and early 1960s, fell below those in the United States.[16] In the Rand Health Insurance Experiment, free care reduced the annual risk of dying by 10 percent among the 25 percent of U.S. adults at highest risk.[3] Conversely, cuts in California's Medicaid program led to worsening health.[17] Strong circumstantial evidence links the poor U.S. record on infant mortality with inadequate access to prenatal care.[18]

We expect that the national health program would cause little change in the total costs of ambulatory and hospital care; savings on administration and billing (about 10 percent of current health spending[1]) would approximately offset the costs of expanded services.[19,20] Indeed, current low hospital-occupancy rates suggest that the additional care could be provided at low cost. Similarly, many physicians with empty appointment slots could take on more patients without added office, secretarial, or other overhead costs. However, the expansion of long-term care (under any system) would increase costs. The experience in Canada suggests that the increased demand for acute care would be modest after an initial surge[21,22] and that improvements in health planning[8] and cost containment made possible by single-source payment[9] would slow the escalation of health care costs. Vigilance would be needed to stem the regrowth of costly and intrusive bureaucracy.

Unsolved Problems

Our brief proposal leaves many vexing problems unsolved. Much detailed planning would be needed to ease dislocations during the implementation of the program. Neither the encouragement of preventive health care and healthful lifestyles nor improvements in occupational and environmental health would automatically follow from the institution of a national health program. Similarly, racial, linguistic, geographic, and other nonfinancial barriers to access would persist. The need for quality assurance and continuing medical education would be no less pressing. High medical school tuitions that skew specialty choices and discourage low-income applicants, the underrepresentation of minorities, the role of foreign medical graduates, and other issues in medical education would remain. Some patients would still seek inappropriate emergency care, and some physicians might still succumb to the temptation to increase their incomes by encouraging unneeded services. The malpractice crisis would be only partially ameliorated. The 25 percent of judgments now awarded for future medical costs would be eliminated, but our society would remain litigious, and legal and insurance fees would still consume about two thirds of all malpractice premiums.[23] Establishing research priorities and directing funds to high-quality investigations would be no easier. Much further work in the area of long-term care would be required. Regional health planning and capital allocation would make possible, but not ensure, the fair and efficient allocation of resources. Finally, although insurance coverage for patients with AIDS would be ensured, the need for expanded prevention and research and for new models of care would continue. Although all these problems would not be solved, a national health program would establish a framework for addressing them.

Political Prospects

Our proposal will undoubtedly encounter powerful opponents in the health insurance industry, firms that do not now provide health benefits to employees, and medical entrepreneurs. However, we also have allies. Most physicians (56 percent) support some form of national health program, although 74 percent are convinced that most other doctors oppose it.[24] Many of the largest corporations would enjoy substantial savings if our proposal were adopted. Most significant, the great majority of Americans support a universal, comprehensive, publicly administered national health program, as shown by virtually every opinion poll in the past 30 years.[25,26] Indeed, a 1986 referendum question in Massachusetts calling for a national health program was approved two to one, carrying all 39 cities and 307 of the 312 towns in the Commonwealth.[27] If mobilized, such public conviction would override even the most strenuous private opposition.

REFERENCES

1. Himmelstein DU, Woolhandler S. Cost without benefit: administrative waste in U.S. health care. N Engl J Med 1986: 314:441–5.

2. Advisory opinion regarding House of Representatives Bill 85-H-7748 (No. 86-269-MP, R.I. Sup. Ct. Jan 5, 1987).

3. Brook RH, Ware JE Jr, Rogers WH, et al. Does free care improve adults' health? Results from a randomized controlled trial. N Engl J Med 1983; 309:1426–34.

4. Siu AL, Sonnenberg FA, Manning WG, et al. Inappropriate use of hospitals in a randomized trial of health insurance plans. N Engl J Med 1986 315:1259–66.

5. Brian EW, Gibbens SF. California's Medi-Cal copayment experiment. Med Care 1974; 12:Suppl 12:1–303.

6. Iglehart JK. Canada's health care system. N Engl J Med 1986; 315:202-8, 778–84.

7. *Idem.* Canada's health care system: addressing the problem of physician supply. N Engl J Med 1986: 315:1623–8.

8. Detsky AS, Stacey SR, Bombardier C. The effectiveness of a regulatory strategy in containing hospital costs: the Ontario experi-

ence, 1967–1981. N Engl J Med 1983: 309:151–9.

9. Evans RG. Health care in Canada: patterns of funding and regulation. In: McLachlan G, Maynard A, eds. The public/private mix for health: the relevance and effects of change. London: Nuffield Provincial Hospitals Trust, 1982: 369–424.

10. Woolhandler S, Himmelstein DU. Reverse targeting of preventive care due to lack of health insurance. JAMA 1988; 259:2872–4.

11. Reinhardt UE. Resource allocation in health care: the allocation of lifestyles to providers. Milbank Q 1987; 65:153–76.

12. Hoffenberg R. Clinical freedom. London: Nuffield Provincial Hospitals Trust, 1987.

13. Horne JM, Beck RG. Further evidence on public versus private administration of health insurance. J Public Health Policy 1981; 2:274–90.

14. Cronin C. Next Congress to grapple with U.S. health policy, competitiveness abroad. Bus Health 1986; 4(2):55

15. Enterline PE, Salter V, McDonald AD, McDonald JC. The distribution of medical services before

and after "free" medical care—the Quebec experience. N Engl J Med 1973; 289:1174–8.

16. Roemer R, Roemer MI. Health manpower policy under national health insurance: the Canadian experience. Hyattsville, Md.: Health Resources Administration, 1977. (DHEW publication no. (HRA) 77-37.)

17. Lurie N, Ward NB, Shapiro MF, et al. Termination of Medi-Cal benefits: a follow-up study one year later. N Engl J Med 1986; 314:1266–8.

18. Institute of Medicine. Preventing low birthweight. Washington, D.C.: National Academy Press, 1985.

19. Newhouse JP, Manning WG, Morris CN, et al. Some interim results from a controlled trial of cost sharing in health insurance. N Engl J Med 1981; 305:1501–7.

20. Himmelstein DU, Woolhandler S. Free care: a quantitative analysis of the health and cost effects of a national health program. Int J Health Serv 1988; 18:393–9.

21. LeClair M. The Canadian health care system. In: Andreopoulos S, ed. National health insurance: can we learn from Canada? New York: John Wiley, 1975:11–92.

22. Evans RG. Beyond the medical marketplace: expenditure, utilization and pricing of insured health care in Canada. In: Andreopoulos S, ed. National health insurance: can we learn from Canada? New York: John Wiley, 1975:129–78.

23. Danzon PM. Medical malpractice: theory, evidence, and public policy. Cambridge, Mass.: Harvard University Press, 1985.

24. Colombotas J, Kirchner C. Physicians and social change. New York: Oxford University Press, 1986.

25. Navarro V. Where is the popular mandate? N Engl J Med 1982; 307:1516–8.

26. Pokorny G. Report card on health care. Health Manage Q 1988; 10(1):3–7.

27. Danielson DA, Mazer A. Results of the Massachusetts Referendum on a national health program. J Public Health Policy 1987; 8:28–35.

The last thing we should do is try to curb technology in our attempt to deal with costs or to slow down our investment in research. . . . Rather, . . . we need to get scientists and administrators to think about the more appropriate use of it.
— Donna Shalala, U.S. Secretary of Health

*Charlene Harrington / Christine Cassel / Carroll L. Estes /
Steffie Woolhandler / David U. Himmelstein / Working
Group on Long-term Care Program Design, Physicians
for a National Health Program*

A National Long-term Care
Program for the United States:
A Caring Vision

American medicine often cures but too rarely cares. Technical sophistica-
tion in therapy for acute illnesses coexists with neglet for many of the
disabled. New hospitals that lie one-third empty house thousands of
chronic-care patients because even the shabbiest nursing homes remain
constantly full.[1] If the fabric of our acute care is marred by the stain of the
uninsured and underinsured, the cloth of our long-term care (LTC) is a
threadbare and tattered remnant.

For millions with disabilities, the assistance that would enable independent living is unobtainable. Nursing homes offered as alternatives to the
fortunate few with Medicaid or savings are often little more than ware-
houses. In the home, relatives and friends labor unaided, uncompensated
and without respite. Geriatric training is woefully underfunded and carries
little prestige.[2] Hence, too few physicians are well equipped to address
remediable medical problems that contribute to disability,[3,4] while many are
called on to assume responsibility for care that has more to do with personal
maintenance and hygiene than with more familiar medical terrain; even
when they know what should be done, the needed resources are often
unavailable. The experts in providing care—nurses, homemakers, social
workers, and the like—are locked in a hierarchy inappropriate for caring.

With the aging of the population and improved survival of disabled
people of all ages, the need for a cogent LTC policy will become even more

Charlene Harrington, Ph.D., R.N., F.A.A.N., Christine Cassel, M.D., Carroll L. Estes,
Ph.D., Steffie Woolhandler, M.D., M.P.H., and David U. Himmelstein, M.D., serve in the
Working Group on Long-term Care Program Design, Physicians for a National Health
Program, Chicago, Illinois.

pressing. Yet policymakers have neglected LTC, for a number of reasons. (1) They have been unwilling to accept LTC as a federal responsibility in an era of cost containment. (2) Meeting routine living needs is a central feature of LTC, with biomedical issues often secondary. Hence, logic dictates that the system emphasize social services, not just medical ones, with social service and nursing personnel rather than physicians often coordinating care—a model that some physicians and policymakers may find threatening.[5] And, (3) LTC needs are largely invisible to policymakers because the majority of services for disabled people—of any age—are provided by "informal" (unpaid) caregivers, mainly female family members, neighbors, or friends.

Long-term care services are those health, social, housing, transportation, and other supportive services needed by persons with physical, mental, or cognitive limitations sufficient to compromise independent living. The United States has a complicated and overlapping array of financing and service programs for LTC. Financing for LTC is largely independent of financing for acute care and varies depending on whether the need is intermittent or continuous, short or long term, posthospital or unrelated to hospitalization.[6-8] Private insurance companies have made only tentative efforts to market LTC insurance and currently insure less than 1% of Americans.[9] Insurance for LTC is unaffordable to most who need it and rarely covers all necessary services.[10-12] Thus, about half of LTC expenses are paid out-of-pocket, with most of the remainder paid by Medicaid.

Presently the elderly spend 18% of their income for medical care, with out-of-pocket costs rising twice as fast as Social Security payments. Medical expenses cost the average elder 4.5 months of his or her Social Security checks.[13] The financial burden for LTC falls most heavily on disabled people without Medicaid coverage.[14] To qualify for Medicaid, families must either be destitute or "spend down" their personal funds until they are impoverished. Furthermore, Medicaid is institutionally biased, funding nursing home care far more extensively than home and community-based services.

Age restrictions on many LTC programs arbitrarily limit access, because about a third of the LTC population is not elderly.[9,15,16] Seventy-eight percent of the disabled who receive Social Security disability benefits, 14% of nursing home residents, and 34% of the noninstitutionalized population reporting limitations in activity due to chronic conditions are under 65 years.[17,18] Children constitute 5% of the severely disabled, yet generally are not eligible for LTC under public programs unless they are poor.

Informal services are vital to millions but are neither supported nor encouraged by current programs. More than 70% of those receiving LTC (3.2 million people) rely exclusively on unpaid caregivers.[19] Almost 22% use both formal and informal care, while 5% use only formal care.[19-22] Of the more than 7 million informal caregivers, three fourths are women, 35% are themselves over 65 years old, a third are in poor health, 10% have given up paid employment to assume the care of their loved one, and 8 of 10 spend at least 4 hours every day providing care.[9] Such personal devotion can never be replaced by the assistance of even the kindest of strangers. It must be valued and supported, not supplanted by formal care.

We believe that a government-financed program will be required in order to ensure adequate LTC for most Americans. At most 40%, and perhaps as few as 6%, of older Americans could afford private LTC insurance.[9,10,23–25] The average nursing home costs of $20,000 to $40,000 per year would bankrupt the majority of Americans within 3 years.[26]

There is growing recognition that the crisis in LTC, as in acute care, calls for bold and fundamental change. We propose the incorporation of LTC into a publicly funded national health program (NHP). We borrow from the experience in the Canadian provinces of Manitoba and British Columbia,[27] where LTC is part of the basic health care entitlement regardless of age or income.[27] Case managers and specialists in needs assessment (largely nonphysicians) evaluate the need for LTC and authorize payment for services. This mechanism for directing appropriate services to those in need has allowed broad access to nursing home and community-based services without runaway inflation.

We also incorporate elements from several recent LTC proposals for the United States.[9,10,14,24,28–30] Most of these, however, have three important flaws: (1) they focus primarily on the aged and would exclude the 40% to 51% of those who need LTC but are under the age of 65 years[15,16]; (2) while most would expand Medicare, they would provide a major role for private insurers, perpetuating fragmented and inefficient financing mechanisms; and (3) they exclude nurses and social workers from certifying and prescribing nonmedical LTC services, inappropriately burdening physicians with responsibilities that are often outside their areas of interest and expertise.

Our proposal is designed as a major component of the NHP proposed by Physicians for a National Health Program.[31] The NHP would provide universal coverage for preventive, acute, and LTC services for all age groups through a public insurance program, pooling funds in existing public programs with new federal revenues raised through progressive taxation. This approach would improve access to the acute care that could ameliorate much disability, eliminate the costly substitution of acute care for LTC, prevent unnecessary nursing home placements, and provide a genuine safety net, both medical and financial, for people of all ages.

GOALS FOR LTC

Nine principles are central to our proposal:

- Long-term care should be a *right* of all Americans, not a commodity available only to the wealthy and the destitute.

- Coverage should be universal, with access to services based on need rather than age, cause of disability, or income.
- Long-term care should provide a continuum of social and medical services aimed at maximizing functional independence.
- Medically and socially oriented LTC should be coordinated with acute inpatient and ambulatory care.
- The program should encourage the development of accessible, efficient, and innovative systems of health care delivery.
- The program should promote high-quality services and appropriate utilization, in the least restrictive environment possible.
- The financial risk should be spread across the entire population using a progressive financing system rather than compounding the misfortune of disability with the specter of financial ruin.
- The importance of "informal" care should be acknowledged, and support, financial and other, should be offered to assist rather than supplant home and community caregivers.
- Consumers should have a range of choices and options for LTC that are culturally appropriate.

COVERAGE

Everyone would be covered for all medically and socially necessary services under a single public plan. Home- and community-based benefits would include nursing, therapy services, case management, meals, information and referral, in-home support (homemaker and attendant) services, respite, transportation services, adult day health, social day care, psychiatric day care, hospice, community mental health, and other related services. Residential services would include foster care, board and care, assisted living, and residential care facilities. Institutional care would include nursing homes, chronic care hospitals, and rehabilitation facilities. Drug and alcohol treatment, outpatient rehabilitation, and independent living programs would also be covered. In special circumstances, other services might be covered such as supported employment and training, financial management, legal services, protective services, senior companions, and payment for informal caregivers.

Preventive services would be covered in an effort to minimize avoidable deterioration in physical and mental functioning. The reluctance of some individuals to seek such preventive services requires sensitive outreach programs. Supportive housing environments, although essential for many who are frail and disabled, should be financed separately as part of housing rather than medical programs. Long-term care services would supplement and be integrated with the acute care services provided by the NHP, such as medical, dental, and nursing care; drugs and medical devices; and preventive services.[31]

The public program, with a single, uniform benefit package, would consolidate all current federal and state programs for LTC. At present, 80 federal programs finance LTC services, including Medicare, Medicaid, the Department of Veterans Affairs, the Older Americans Act, and Title XX Social Services.[21] Other public programs finance LTC for the developmentally disabled, the mentally disabled, substance abusers, and crippled children. State disability insurance programs also finance some LTC. This multiplicity of programs leaves enormous gaps in both access and coverage, confuses consumers attempting to gain access to the system, and drives up administrative costs. Furthermore, the system is grossly out of balance, biased toward acute and institutional care and away from community-based health and social services. In contrast, the proposed LTC program would be comprehensive, administratively spare, and "user friendly."

Comprehensive coverage permits use of the most appropriate services and may prevent unnecessary hospitalization or institutional placement. Because most individuals needing LTC prefer to remain at home,[24,26] services should promote independent living and support informal caregivers, using nursing homes as the last resort rather than as the primary approach to LTC. Services must be culturally appropriate for special population groups including ethnic, cultural, and religious minorities; the oldest old; individuals who are mentally impaired or developmentally disabled; children; and young adults.

ADMINISTRATIVE STRUCTURE AND ELIGIBILITY FOR CARE

With a federal mandate, each state would set up an LTC system with a state LTC Planning and Payment Board and a network of local public LTC agencies. These local agencies would employ specialized panels of social workers, nurses, therapists, and physicians responsible for assessing individuals' LTC needs, service planning, care coordination, provider certification, and, in some cases, provision of services. These agencies would serve as the entry points to LTC within local communities, certify eligibility for specific services, and assign a case manager when appropriate.

The LTC Planning and Payment Board and the local LTC agencies in each state would pay for the full continuum of covered LTC services. Each state's LTC operating budget would be allocated to the local LTC agencies based on population, the number of elderly and disabled, the economic status of the population, case-mix, and cost of living. Each local LTC agency would apportion the available budget to cover the operating costs of approved providers in its community—although the actual payment apparatus would be centralized in the state's LTC Planning and Payment Board to avoid duplication of administrative functions.

Each institutional provider, e.g., community agency, nursing home, home care agency, or social service organization, would negotiate a global operating budget with the local LTC agency. The budget would be based on past expenditures, financial and clinical performance, utilization, and projected changes in services, wages, and other related factors. Alternatively, institutional providers could contract to provide comprehensive LTC services (or integrated LTC and acute care services) on a capitated basis. No part of the operating budget or capitation fee could be used for expansion, profit, marketing, or major capital purchases or leases. Capital expenditures for new, expanded, or updated LTC facilities and programs would be allocated based on explicit health planning goals separately from operating budgets by the state LTC agency. For-profit providers would be paid a fixed return on existing equity, and new for-profit investment would be proscribed. As Physicians for a National Health Program has previously proposed,[31] physicians could be paid on a fee-for-service basis, or receive salaries from institutional providers. Physicians and other providers would be prohibited from referring patients to facilities or services in which they held a proprietary interest. Providers participating in the public program would be required to accept the public payments as payment in full and would not be allowed to charge patients directly for any covered service. Federal and state budget allocations for LTC services would be separate from those for acute care, as in Canada.

Coverage would extend to anyone, regardless of age or income, needing assistance with one or more activity of daily living (ADL) or instrumental activity of daily living (IADL), (ADLs are basic self-maintenance activities [i.e., bathing, dressing, going to the toilet, getting outside, walking, transferring from bed to chair, or eating]; IADLs relate to a person's ability to be independent [cooking, cleaning, shopping, taking medications, doing laundry, making telephone calls, or managing money].) High-risk patients not strictly meeting this definition would be eligible for services needed to prevent worsening disability and subsequent costly institutional care. Local panels would have the flexibility, within their defined budgets, to authorize a wide range of services, taking into account such social factors as the availability of informal care.

When case management or care coordination is needed, the local agencies would assume these tasks or delegate them to appropriate providers, e.g., capitated providers offering comprehensive services. Not all those needing LTC require case management.[32] Case managers and care coordinators would work with the client, family, and other caregivers to assess adequacy and appropriateness of services, promote efficiency, and respond to changing needs. Progressive decline in function characterizes many chronic illnesses, while full recovery is possible in others. Thus, change in need is a nearly universal aspect of LTC and mandates frequent reevaluation and flexibility. In all cases, programs should encourage independence and minimize professional intrusion into daily life.

A universal need-based entitlement to LTC would replace the current irrational patchwork of public and private programs, each with its own eligibility criteria, by age, cause of disability, and income. All income groups would be covered without means testing, which is cumbersome and costly to administer, may increase costs in the long run by causing people to postpone needed care, creates a stigma against recipients, and narrows the base of political support for the program.[28] There are scant data on how to set simple eligibility standards that ensure coverage for all in need, while excluding those for whom LTC services are a luxury rather than a necessity. We have chosen an inclusive general criterion (one ADL or IADL) and have left fine tuning to local agencies able to individualize decisions.

In all, approximately 3.9% of the population (9.3 million people in 1985) would be eligible for covered LTC services. An estimated 3.6% (7.6 million persons) of the total noninstitutionalized population need assistance with ADLs or IADLs,[15] including only 8% of those aged 65 to 69 years but 46% of those aged 85 years and over.[15] Another 1.5 million people are in nursing homes and residential care facilities,[17] and 200,000 people are in psychiatric and long-stay hospitals.[33]

UTILIZATION AND COST CONTROLS

Removing financial barriers to LTC will increase demand for formal services. Long-term care insurance could legitimately result in a 20% increase in nursing home utilization and a 50% to 100% increase in use of community and home health care by the elderly.[9,24] Increases in utilization might be expected to level off after about 3 years, as occurred in Saskatchewan's LTC program.[27]

Our program would be financed entirely by tax revenues, without premiums, deductibles, copayments, or coinsurance. However, people permanently residing in residential care would use part of their basic Social Security or Supplemental Security Income to contribute to "hotel" costs. Although other cost-sharing methods raise revenues and discourage utilization, these regressive financing mechanisms disproportionately burden the poor and the sick and reduce the use of preventive and other essential services.[28,34,35]

Although we eschew financial barriers to care, utilization controls are essential since many LTC services (e.g., "meals on wheels," homemakers) are desirable to people without disabilities. Several states' Medicaid programs have demonstrated that screening and utilization controls can both control costs and improve care by preventing unnecessary institutionalization, coordinating services, and ensuring the use of the most appropriate care.[35,36]

The local LTC agencies, each with a defined catchment area and budget, would apportion the finite resources for LTC among those in need. These local agencies, serving as the single point of entry for LTC service authorization, would work with clients and caregivers to select and coordinate appropriate services from a comprehensive listing of providers. This approach relies on enforceable overall budgetary ceilings to contain costs. The local agencies would have strong incentives to support more cost-effective informal providers and community-based services that might forestall institutionalization.

INNOVATION IN THE PROVISION OF LTC

Broad changes in the provision of LTC are essential.[37] The current system is fragmented among many acute care in-patient, ambulatory, and LTC providers. This fragmentation creates higher costs through the duplication of bureaucracy and the failure to achieve administrative economies of scale. More important, the lack of coordination compromises the quality of care. A unified financing system would foster the integration, or at least coordination, of acute care and LTC—an essential step, because virtually everyone needing LTC also needs acute care. Financing the full continuum of care from a common source might also enable a more rational targeting of resources, with emphasis on preventive services, early intervention, vigorous rehabilitation, and restorative care. Expanded community-based services would allow earlier discharge for many hospitalized patients and might forestall hospitalization for many others.

The goal of the national LTC program would be to support and assist informal caregivers, not to replace them. However, informal caregivers should not be expected to undertake an overwhelming burden of care and would be offered predictable respite care and other supportive services, such as counseling, training, and support groups.

The program would encourage the provision of LTC by multidisciplinary teams of social workers, nurses, therapists, physicians, attendants, transportation workers, and other providers. Collegial relationships and teamwork should be the rule, with leadership from nurses and social workers as well as from an expanded cadre of well-trained geriatricians, rather than the traditional hierarchical relationships between physicians and nonphysicians.[38]

The availability of capitated funding would foster organizations providing consolidated and comprehensive LTC and acute care services. Two LTC demonstrations that have employed such a model are the social health maintenance organizations and the On Lok Senior Health Service in San

Francisco, California. Both provide a full range of acute, ambulatory, and LTC services with a capitated financing system.[39,40]

Although such coordinated care may be optimal,[41] individual providers could continue to operate on a contractual or fee-for-service basis. In some cases, family members or other informal caregivers could be approved as providers. However, in these situations responsibility for case management and care coordination would ordinarily rest with the local LTC agency.

Innovation would be supported by earmarked extra funding that the state LTC boards would award to local agencies offering the most promising proposals. Although each local agency would be required to provide a standard set of services with uniform eligibility criteria and reimbursement rates, this supplemental funding would encourage state and local agencies to develop services beyond the basic level and to seek and reward innovation. This is particularly important for improving services to different age groups, disability categories, and cultural and racial minorities.

Finally, missteps are inevitable in the course of the major reform we envision. Funding for ongoing evaluation is essential to rapidly disclose problems and allow their timely correction. Particular attention should be focused on key policy questions where current expert opinion has not been fully tested by rigorous research. In what situations does case management improve outcomes or efficiency? What organizational framework best ensures appropriate attention to both medical and social needs? What, if any, preventive measures minimize deterioration in mental or physical function? Are categories such as ADLs and IADLs optimal for targeting care?

QUALITY OF CARE

No other segment of the health care system has as many documented quality-of-care problems as the nursing home industry, and concern is growing about the quality of home care.[42–44] As many as one third of all nursing homes are operating below the minimum federal standards.[45] Monitoring the quality of LTC has been hindered by variability in state regulatory programs and the lack of well-validated regulatory standards and procedures.[46]

Each LTC provider (including home care agencies) would be required to meet uniform national quality standards in order to be paid by the NHP. These standards would include structural measures (e.g., staffing levels, educational requirements), process measures (e.g., individualized planning and provision of care), and outcome measures (e.g., changes in functional or mental status, incontinence, mortality, and hospital admission rates). Earmarked funds from the federal LTC budget would support urgently needed research to validate and improve these standards and to develop new approaches to quality assurance.

Each LTC organization and agency would be required to establish a quality assurance program meeting national standards and a quality assurance committee with representatives of each category of service provider (e.g., social workers, homemakers, nurses, physicians, and so forth), clients and their family members or other caregivers, and community representatives. The committee would meet regularly to review quality of care and to resolve problems and disputes, with unresolved issues reported to the public regulatory system discussed below.

All regulatory activities of the current licensing and certification agencies, peer review organizations, Medicare inspection of care, and other agencies that monitor LTC would be combined into a single program. This unified monitoring system would enforce regulations and have the power to sanction and decertify providers. This program would be administered at the federal and state levels, with input from the local LTC agencies and provider quality assurance committees. Consumer complaint systems and telephone hotlines for quality concerns would be mandated. The regulatory agency would be required to employ sufficient staff to conduct periodic surveys of each provider and to investigate complaints in a timely fashion. Providers would be required to disclose financial data and other management information such as staff turnover rates, incident rates, and patient outcome data.

Improving the training, wages, and morale of LTC workers is also crucial to improving the quality of care. Long-term care workers currently earn 15% to 45% less than comparable hospital employees (US Department of Health and Human Services, Division of Nursing, unpublished data, 1988), and 20% of nursing home workers have no health insurance.[47] Nursing homes are not currently required to provide around-the-clock registered nursing care, few have specialized staff such as geriatric nurse practitioners, and aides are often inadequately trained. Many home care agencies have no professional staff or consultants. Wages in LTC organizations receiving payment from the NHP would be regulated to achieve parity with the acute care sector, with funding for this increase phased in over 5 years.

Funding would also be allocated for training and inservice education of LTC professionals, paraprofessionals, and informal caregivers. Formal providers would be required to meet minimum training and competency standards. Augmented training is particularly important for nurses and physicians, who often lack experience in working with the frail elderly, the disabled, and the mentally impaired and in working with multidisciplinary teams to develop community services. The development of a cadre of physicians and nurses with special training in gerontology and geriatrics is essential. These professionals would play key clinical and managerial roles in integrating LTC for the elderly with acute care, as in Great Britain and other countries.[48]

CONSUMER CHOICE

Consumer choice would be explicitly fostered by the national LTC program. Each individual eligible for LTC services would choose among the certified providers in her or his area. Individuals would select a primary provider organization and/or individual care provider, including a primary care physician, and could switch providers if they desired. An independent ombudsman would resolve consumer grievances over provider choice. Consumers and/or their delegated representatives would be encouraged to assume control over decisions regarding their care and would be given assurance that durable power of attorney and living will provisions would be honored.

COSTS AND FINANCING

Estimates of current expenditures for LTC are imprecise because of the diversity of payment sources. In 1990 an estimated $54.5 billion was spent for nursing homes, $14.1 billion for equipment and appliances, and $10.6 billion for home health services.[49] In addition, about 10% ($25 billion) of total hospital costs were spent on psychiatric, rehabilitative, and chronic care services.[49] Thus, the total LTC expenditures were at least $104 billion in 1990 (16% of total health spending), excluding informal LTC services. Public programs, primarily Medicaid, currently finance about half of formal LTC. Medicaid pays for 48% of nursing home care, Medicare for 2%, and other public payers for 3%.[50] Private insurance covers less than 2% of nursing home costs, while consumers pay 45% directly out-of-pocket.[50-53] Consumers pay out-of-pocket for 40% of home services in the United States.[54]

Our program would replace almost all of the $52 billion (all figures in 1990 dollars) currently spent each year on private LTC insurance and out-of-pocket costs with public expenditures. Additional funding would be needed, particularly in the first few years, to pay for the increased utilization of LTC for previously unmet needs. The expected utilization increases of 20% for nursing homes and 50% to 100% for home health care[9,24] would cost between $16 billion and $21.5 billion annually.

Further funding would be needed to improve quality through increased training, wages, and staffing levels. However, some of these costs would be offset by reduced administrative costs and improved program efficiency. Additional savings may result from reductions in disability and inappropriate hospitalizations. Precise estimates of these costs and savings are impossible. For our estimates, we assume that the net increase needed for the quality improvement measures (after subtracting potential administrative and other savings) amounts to $2 billion per year.

Overall, a total of $70 to $75.5 billion in new tax revenues ($380 to $410 per adult) would be needed to finance our program. Of this total, $52 billion represents money that is currently spent privately that would be shifted onto the public ledger. In effect, a broad-based tax would replace payments by the chronically ill. Because LTC has been seriously underfunded, $18 to $23.5 billion in truly new spending ($100 to $130 per adult) would be needed to expand care and improve its quality. Because almost every family will use such services at some point, this seems a reasonable price for financial protection and improved services for the disabled and aged.

These revenues could be raised from several sources, including the Social Security system, general taxes, and estate taxes. Expanding Social Security payroll taxes that currently fund Medicare would build upon the existing tax system and ensure a broad tax base. For example, a 1% increase in payroll taxes for both employers and employees would raise about $50 billion.[10] Increasing the earned income tax credit for lower-income workers to lower their payroll tax and removing the current ceiling on Social Security taxes would generate about $49 billion in additional revenue, while making such taxes less regressive.[10,28] Federal estate taxes are another logical source of funds for LTC and would have little negative impact on low-income groups. A 10% surcharge on gifts and estates above $200,000 would raise $2 to $4 billion,[9,10] and taxing capital gains at death would raise about $5.5 billion.[10]

COMMENT

Our proposed LTC program would be integrated with the NHP, creating a single comprehensive and universal public program for acute care and LTC. The program would be federally mandated and funded but administered at the state and local levels. A single state board would contract directly with providers through a network of local public agencies responsible for LTC eligibility determination and for case management and/or care coordination. All payments would be channeled through the single payment agency in each state.

Single-source payment is key to controlling costs, streamlining administration, and minimizing inequalities in care.[31,55] Private insurance duplicating the public program would be eliminated in order to decrease administrative costs, prevent insurers from electing to cover only the healthiest (hence leaving only the most difficult and expensive tasks for the public sector), and guard against the emergence of two-class care.[30,56]

502 A National Long-term Care Program

Prospective global budgeting for nursing homes and community-based services would simplify administration and virtually eliminate billing and eligibility determination. Prohibiting the use of operating funds for capital purchases or profit would minimize financial incentives both for skimping on care (as under the current per-diem nursing home payment system) and for excessive intervention (as under the fee-for-service payments received by many home care providers). The separate appropriation of capital funds would facilitate rational health planning.

Current capital spending largely determines future operating costs, as well as the distribution of facilities and programs. Combining operating and capital payments, as under the existing reimbursement system, allows prosperous providers to expand and modernize, whereas impoverished ones cannot, regardless of their quality or the needs of the population they serve. The NHP would replace this implicit mechanism for distributing capital with an explicit one. Capital funds would be allocated on the basis of a comprehensive planning process, with the involvement of health planners, community members, and providers. Priority would be given to underserved regions and populations and to the development of home- and community-based services, to correct the current bias toward institutional care. While funds for sheltered and supportive housing are more appropriately part of a housing rather than a medical care program, coordination in planning of housing and LTC is essential.

Issues of profit-making are particularly problematic in LTC, where 75% of the nursing homes and a growing proportion of home care agencies are proprietary.[17] There is ample documentation of LTC providers' skimping on basic services and staffing in order to maximize profits.[46,57] As previously proposed,[31] the NHP would pay owners of for-profit providers a reasonable fixed rate of return on existing equity. Since virtually all new capital investment would be funded by the NHP, it would not be included in calculating return on equity. The proprietary sector would gradually shrink because new for-profit investment would be proscribed.

We advocate fully public financing of LTC for four reasons: (1) single-source public funding facilitates cost containment through administrative streamlining and the ability to set and enforce an overall budget; (2) financial risk is spread across the entire population (who are all ultimately at risk for needing services) rather than falling only on the disabled and elderly; (3) few people today are covered by private LTC insurance, and there is little reason to believe that widespread private coverage is practicable; and (4) there is a need for clear public accountability.

Public insurance programs are far more efficient than private plans. Administration consumes 5% of total Medicaid spending[24] and only 2% of the Medicare budget. In contrast, in 1986 Blue Cross/Blue Shield and self-insured plans had overhead of 8%, prepaid plans averaged 11.7%, and commercial insurers averaged 18.9%.[52] Many Medicare supplemental policies (medigap insurance) have notoriously low payout ratios, 60% or less.[58] Payout rates for private LTC insurance are low[10] and virtually unregulated. According to the General Accounting Office, of the 33 states with minimum payout ratios for general health insurance, most do not report benefit and premium data separately for LTC insurance, only 20 states even monitor payout ratios, and 12 states have established minimum LTC insurance payout ratios.[13]

The multiplicity of public and private insurers in the United States results in exorbitant administrative costs. Health insurance overhead alone costs $106 per capita in the United States (0.66% of gross national product) compared with $15 per capita (0.11% of gross national product) in Canada.[59] Additional unnecessary administrative costs accrue to providers who must determine eligibility, attribute costs and charges to individual patients and insurers, and send and collect bills for myriad insurers and individual patients.[60] Overall, administration accounts for almost one fourth of U.S. health spending, but only 11% in Canada.[60]

Finally, public opinion strongly supports public financing of LTC. Eighty-seven percent of Americans consider the absence of LTC financing a crisis, the majority prefer public over private funding, federal administration is favored over private insurance programs by a 3 to 2 margin, and two thirds believe that private insurance companies would undermine quality of care because of their emphasis on profits.[26] While respondents want a federally financed program, they support the administration of such a program at the state level.[26]

The oft-stated view that the public wants LTC coverage but is unwilling to pay for it is inaccurate.[61] The 1987 poll conducted by the American Association of Retired Persons and the Villers Foundation found that 86% of the sample supported government action for a universal LTC program that would finance care for all income groups, and not just the poor. Overall, 75% would agree to increased taxes for LTC.[26] A 1988 Harris poll reached virtually identical conclusions.[62]

CONCLUSIONS

In summary, we recommend that LTC be incorporated into a publicly financed NHP. We urge that a comprehensive public model be adopted as a single mandatory plan for the entire population and that new public revenues be combined with existing public program dollars. This approach would ensure universal access, comprehensive benefits, improved quality, and greater cost control. Most important, the financial costs would be spread across the entire population rather than borne by the disabled themselves. Our nation has the resources to provide better care for the disabled and elderly, and it has a responsibility to develop a reasonable system of LTC. The public supports this type of approach. Health and human services professionals and the makers of public policy need the vision and courage to implement such a system.

REFERENCES

1. Holahan J, Dubay LC, Kenney G, Welch WP, Bishop C, Dor A. Should Medicare compensate hospitals for administratively necessary days? *Milbank Q.* 1989;67: 137–167.

2. Hazzard WR. A report card on academic geriatrics in 1991: a struggle for academic respectability. *Ann Intern Med.* 1991;115: 229–230.

3. Rowe JW, Drossman, E. Bond E. Academic geriatrics for the year 2000: an Institute of Medicine report. *N Engl J Med.* 1987;316: 1425–1428.

4. Kane R. Solomon D, Beck J, Keeler E, Kane R. The future need for geriatric manpower in the United States. *N Engl J Med.* 1980;302:1327–1332.

5. Estes CL, Binney EA. The biomedicalization of aging: dangers and dilemmas. *Gerontologist.* 1989; 29:587–596.

6. Kane RA, Kane RL. *Long-term Care: Principles, Programs, and Policies.* New York, NY: Springer Publishing Co Inc; 1987.

7. Estes CL, Newcomer RJ, Benjamin AE, et al. *Fiscal Austerity and Aging.* Beverly Hills, Calif: Sage Publications; 1983.

8. Harrington C, Newcomer RJ, Estes CL, et al. *Long-term Care of the Elderly: Public Policy Issues.* Beverly Hills, Calif: Sage Publications; 1985.

9. *A Call for Action: Final Report.* Washington, DC: US Bipartisan Commission on Comprehensive Health Care; 1990.

10. Ball RM, Bethell TN. *Because We're All in This Together: The Case for a National Long-term Care Insurance Policy.* Washington, DC: Families U.S.A. Foundation; 1989.

11. Firman J, Weissert W, Wilson CE. *Private Long-term Care Insurance: How Well Is It Meeting Consumer Needs and Public Policy Concerns?* Washington, DC: United Seniors Health Cooperative; 1988.

12. Estes CL. *Long-term Care: Requiem for Commercial Private Insurance.* San Francisco, Calif: Institute for Health and Aging; 1990. Study prepared for the Annual Meeting of the Gray Panthers.

13. *Private Long-term Care Insurance: Unfit for Sale? A Report of the Chairman to the Subcommittee on Health and Long-term Care.* Washington, DC: US House Select Committee on Aging; 1989.

14. *InterStudy's Long-term Care Expansion Program: A Proposal for Reform.* Excelsior, Minn: InterStudy; 1988;1

15. LaPlante MP. *Data on Disability from the National Health Interview Survey, 1983–85.* Washington, DC: US Dept of Education; 1988. Prepared for the National Institute on Disability and Rehabilitation Research.

16. *Issues Concerning the Financing and Delivery of Long-term Care 1989.* Washington, DC: Employee Benefit Research Institute; 1989. No. 86

17. National Center for Health Statistics, Hing E, Sekscenski E, Strahan G. The National Nursing Home Survey: 1985 summary for

the United States. *Vital Health Stat* [13]. 1987;No. 97. DHHS publication (PHS) 89-1758.

18. National Center for Health Statistics, Schoenborn CA, Marano M. Current estimates from the National Health Interview Survey: United States, 1987. *Vital Health Stat [10]*. 1988;No. 166. DHHS publication (PHS) 88-1594.

19. Liu K, Manton KG, Liu BM. Home care expenses for the disabled elderly. *HCF Rev.* 1985;7:51–57.

20. Stone R, Cafferata GL, Sangl J. Caregivers of the frail elderly: a national profile. *Gerontologist.* 1987;27:616–626.

21. *Developments in Aging: 1988: A Report of the Special Committee on Aging, United States Senate.* Washington, DC: US Senate; 1989;1–3.

22. Stone R. Aging in the eighties, age 65 years and over—use of community services: preliminary data from the supplement on aging to the National Health Interview Survey: United States January–June 1985. *NCHS Adv Data.* 1986;124.

23. Families USA Foundation calls for a FTC investigation of insurance industry abuse of frail elderly nursing home insurance buyers. Press release. Washington DC: Families USA Foundation; February 26, 1990.

24. Rivlin AM, Weiner JM. *Caring for the Disabled Elderly: Who Will Pay?* Washington, DC: Brookings Institution; 1988.

25. *Source Book of Health Insurance Data: Update.* Washington, DC: Health Insurance Association of America; 1988.

26. *The American Public Views Long-term Care: A Survey Conducted for the American Association of Retired Persons and the Villers Foundation.* Princeton, NJ: R.L. Associates; October 1987.

27. Kane RL, Kane RA. *A Will and a Way: What the United States Can Learn from Canada About Care of the Elderly.* New York, NY: Columbia University Press; 1985.

28. Blumenthal D, Schlesinger M, Drumbeller PB. *Renewing the Promise: Medicare and Its Reform.* New York, NY: Oxford University Press Inc; 1988.

29. *Long-term Care Conference.* Washington, DC: Villers Foundation; 1987.

30. *Draft Proposal Long-term Care Social Insurance Program Initiative.* Washington, DC: Lewin & Associates; 1987. Prepared for Advisory Committee on Long-term Care, sponsored by the American Association of Retired Persons, Older Women's League, and the Villers Foundation.

31. Himmelstein DU, Woolhandler S, and the Writing Committee of the Working Group of Program Design of Physicians for a National Health Program. A national health program for the United States: a physicians' proposal. *N Engl J Med.* 1989; 320:102–108.

32. Callahan JJ. Case management for the elderly: a panacea? *J Aging Social Pol.* 1989;1:181–195.

33. *Hospital Statistics: 1986 Edition.* Chicago, Ill: American Hospital Association; 1986.

34. Estes CL. The United States: long-term care and federal policy. In: Reif L, Trager B, eds. *International Perspectives on Long-term Care.* New York, NY: The Haworth Press; 1985;315–328.

35. *InterStudy's Long-term Care Expansion Program: Issue Papers.* Excelsior, Minn: InterStudy; 1988;2.

36. Justice D. *State Long-term Care Reform: Development of Community Care Systems in Six States.* Washington, DC: National Governor's Association; 1988.

37. Kane RL, Kane RA. A nursing home in your future? *N Engl J Med.* 1991;324:627–629.

38. Freidson E. *Professional Dominance.* Chicago, Ill: Aldine Publishing Co; 1970.

39. Newcomer RJ, Harrington C, Friedlob A, et al. *Evaluation of the Social Health Maintenance Organization Demonstration.* Washington, DC: US Dept of Health and Human Services, Health Care Financing Administration; 1989. Publication 03283.

40. Zawadski RT. The long-term care demonstration projects: what they are and why they came into being. *Home Health Care Services Q.* Fall/Winter 1983;4:3–19.

41. Campbell LJ, Cole KD. Geriatric assessment teams. *Clin Geriatr Med.* 1987;3(1):99–117.

42. *Hearings Before the Special Committee on Aging of the US Senate,* 99th Cong. 2nd Sess (1986).

43. *Hearings Before the US House Committee on Ways and Means,* 99th Cong, 2nd Sess (1986).

44. Kusserow RP. *Home Health Aide Services for Medicare Patients.* Washington, DC: US Dept of Health and Human Services; 1987. Unpublished report OA101-86-00010.

45. *Report to the Chairman, Subcommittee on Health and Long-term Care, Select Committee on Aging, US House of Representatives: Medicare and Medicaid: Stronger Enforcement of Nursing Home Requirements Needed.* Washington, DC: US General Accounting Office; 1987.

46. Institute of Medicine. *Improving the Quality of Care in Nursing Homes.* Washington, DC: National Academy Press; 1986.

47. Himmelstein DU, Woolhandler S. Who cares for the care givers? Lack of health insurance among health and insurance personnel. *JAMA.* 1991;266:399–401.

48. Barker WH. *Adding Life to Years: Organized Geriatric Services in Great Britain and Implications for the United States.* Baltimore, Md: The Johns Hopkins University Press; 1987.

49. US Dept of Commerce, International Trade Administration. *Health and Medical Services: U.S. Industrial Outlook 1990.* Washington, DC: US Dept of Commerce; 1990.

50. *Hearings Before the Health Task Force Committee on the Budget, US House of Representatives,* 100th Cong, 2nd Sess (1987) (testimony of Nancy Gordon, assistant director for Human Resources and Community Dept).

51. Task Force on Long-term Care Policies. *Report to Congress and the Secretary: Long-term Health Care Policies.* Washington, DC: US Dept of Health and Human Services; 1987.

52. Division of National Cost Estimates, Office of the Actuary, Health Care Financing Administration. *National Health Expenditures, 1986–2000.* Washington, DC: Health Care Financing Administration; 1987;8:1–36.

53. Levit KR, Freedland MS. National medical care spending. *Health Aff.* 1988;7:124–136.

54. Price RJ, O'Shaughnessy C. *Long-term Care for the Elderly.* Washington, DC: The Library of Congress; 1990. Congressional Research Service Issue Brief.

55. Harrington C, Newcomer RJ, Friedlob A. Medicare beneficiary enrollment in S/HMO. In: *Social/Health Maintenance Organization Demonstration Evaluation: Report on the First Thirty Months.* Washington, DC: Health Care Financing Administration; 1987;chap 4. Contract HCFA 85-034/CP.

56. Bodenheimer T. Should we abolish the private health insurance

industry? *Int J Health Serv.* 1990; 20:199–220.

57.	Hawes C, Phillips CD. The changing structure of the nursing home industry and the impact of ownership on quality, cost, and access. In: Gray BH, McNerney WJ, eds. *For-Profit Enterprise in Health Care.* Washington, DC: Academy Press; 1986:492–538.

58.	*Report to the Subcommittee on Health, Committee on Ways and Means, House of Representatives: Medigap Insurance Law Has Increased Protection Against Substandard and Overpriced Policies.* Washington, DC: US General Accounting Office; 1986.

59.	Evans RG, Lomas J, Barer ML, et al. Controlling health expenditures—the Canadian reality. *N Engl J Med.* 1989;320:571–577.

60.	Woolhandler S, Himmelstein DU. The deteriorating administrative efficiency of the U.S. health care system. *N Engl J Med.* 1991;324:1253–1258.

61.	Blendon RJ. The public's view of the future of health care. *JAMA.* 1988;259:3587–3593.

62.	Harris L. *Majorities Favor Passage of Long-term Health Care Legislation.* New York, NY: Louis Harris & Associates; 1988.

The establishment of a national health *plan . . . was a good idea when it was proposed . . . in 1934. . . . It's been a good idea for a long while. Let's get it on the books!*
— Arthur Flemming

Governor Bill Clinton

The Clinton Health Care Plan

The American health care system has the potential to provide every citizen with the best care in the world. Yet the system as currently financed and organized is plagued by two problems: health care costs are increasing at unsustainable rates, and Americans cannot be sure that they will have health care coverage when they need it.

We cannot afford four more years of political gridlock on health care. We must reform the health care system so that all American families have access to affordable high-quality health care. My plan offers a framework for this reform, and, as president, I will bring together health care providers, consumers, employers, and the government to work toward our common goal.

PROBLEMS: HIGH COSTS AND LIMITED ACCESS

Costs

Spending for health care continues to increase at a rate that exceeds growth in the rest of the economy. The statistics on the rise in costs have been cited so often that many have become inured to them, but the numbers are staggering. Every measure that I have seen illustrates the same thing—unsustainable increases in spending.

Spending for health care in the United States has reached more than $800 billion per year. Spending per person has tripled in the past 12 years, increasing from $1,059 in 1980 to $3,057 this year. There is no end in sight to this inflation: at the current rate, spending will reach $1.6 *trillion* by the year 2000—$5,712 for every person in this country. Health care, which consumed 9.1 percent of our gross national product in 1980, today consumes more than 13 percent, and will account for more than 16 percent of the gross national product by the year 2000 unless action is taken.[1]

These costs are overwhelming our society. Families face increased insurance premiums and reduced benefits, and they fear they may not be able to afford care when they need it. The caring relationships between

From Clinton, B. (1992). The Clinton health care plan. *N Engl J. Med* 327(11):804–806. Used with permission from *The New England Journal of Medicine.*

health professionals and their patients are also placed at risk by concern over cost.

The international competitiveness of our businesses is threatened by health care costs in the United States that far exceed those in other nations. Health care costs are now the number-one cause of bankruptcy and of labor disputes. In 1990 they added $1,086 to the cost of every car made in America. Experts warn that over the coming decades, every dollar workers might earn in higher wages could go instead to pay for rising health care costs.[2]

Federal and state governments devote an ever-increasing share of their resources to health care. The amount consumed by Medicare and Medicaid alone has grown from 8 percent of the federal budget in fiscal year 1980 to 13.5 percent today. In the next five years, they may consume 20 percent of the entire federal budget, absorbing more than half of its growth.[3] This rate of increase in the costs of health care is unacceptable, and we cannot allow it to continue.

Access

What is especially troubling about the unending escalation in spending is that we have not even provided basic health benefits to all our citizens. A large number of Americans lack such protection; more than 35 million people were uninsured in 1990. An even more troubling indicator of the uncertainty facing the American people is that more than 60 million people—about 1 in every 4 of our citizens—were without health benefits at some time during a 28-month period.[4] As employers reduce or drop health benefits and insurers limit or eliminate coverage for those who are the sickest, families cannot be assured of health coverage when they need it.

PUTTING PEOPLE FIRST: AFFORDABLE, HIGH-QUALITY HEALTH CARE

The cost and coverage problems are only the visible symptoms of a system that requires fundamental change. As I argued in a previous article on my health care plan,[5] the worst choice for addressing our trouble is sticking with the status quo or simply trying to fine-tune the system. Under our current system, private and public coverage is stretched to the limit in providing benefits to our citizens, and the structure and incentives of the financing and delivery system yield total spending increases that cannot be sustained.

We must carefully design health care reforms under which every American family has a right to affordable, high-quality health care. In doing so, we must set and keep our sights on three goals: controlling rising health care costs, covering every American with at least a basic health benefits package, and maintaing consumer choice in coverage and care.

"Putting People First," my national economic strategy, lays out a five-part approach to revitalizing the national economy: create jobs, reward work and restructure welfare, support lifelong learning, revolutionize government, and provide affordable, high-quality health care.[6] The health plan is a central component of that national economic strategy. Any economic plan that fails to control inflation in health care costs will not succeed.

Many suggest that we must choose between two extremes in reforming the health care system: we can have either a government-run regulatory system or a private, market-based, competitive system. Although that may be traditional and politically convenient rhetoric, it is the type of thinking that has resulted in gridlock in the national debate on health care and across the nation's entire domestic-policy agenda. I reject such polarizing rhetoric in domestic economic policy, and I reject it in health care.

Putting people first in health care calls for a fundamental reform of the system. It requires that we combine an appropriate and revised governmental role with a reliance on the private sector to provide care and to compete to serve every person in this country. But that competition must take place under a restructured set of ground rules that foster competition to provide the best care at the best price, not to avoid covering the less healthy and to raise prices fastest for the sickest.

The following are the key elements of my health care plan.[7]

Overall Structure to Contain Costs and Ensure Access

We will establish a National Health Board composed of consumers, providers, and representatives of business, labor, and government. That board will establish annual budget targets and define a core benefit package that must be available to every American. Benefits will be provided by employers and public programs through a reformed insurance system and the use of collaborative health care networks that serve those in both private and public plans. The networks and other insurers will offer health care within the global budgets. States may establish consistent rates applying to all payers for services provided outside managed-care networks as a backup mechanism to meet the global budget targets. An intensified program of health education will strive to persuade Americans to change unhealthful, and costly, personal behavior.

Core Benefit Package

The board will establish national and state budget targets for health care to guide expenditures in the public and private sectors. It will also establish a core benefit package for private and public plans that will include ambulatory care, inpatient hospital care, prescription drugs, basic mental health care, and important preventive benefits, such as prenatal care and screening mammography.

Universal Health Benefits Coverage

Universal coverage will be phased in by building on the public–private partnership that is uniquely American. Employers and employees will either purchase private health benefits directly or participate in the publicly sponsored alternatives that offer the core benefits package established by the National Health Board. Those not covered through their employers will participate in the publicly sponsored alternatives. Medicare will remain an independent program but will benefit from the cost-containment provisions of the plan. With universal coverage, no family will fear bankruptcy as a result of needed care for their loved ones, and providers can be assured that every patient they see will be able to pay for high-quality care.

Health Networks

Insurers, physicians, and health care institutions will be given strong incentives to collaborate in developing local health networks. Such networks will negotiate fees with participating providers and institutions, which will be responsible for the total care of the patients served. They will compete for patients enrolled in private or public health plans on the basis of both cost and quality. This structured form of competition will yield results far more productive than today's competition to avoid covering the sickest. Moreover, collaborative networks of health care providers operating within global budgetary constraints could shelter the provider–patient relationship from some of the intrusive methods of many of today's efforts to control costs.

Insurance Reform

Today's needlessly complicated and wasteful insurance system will be reformed. Competition based on risk selection will be eliminated, and the medical-underwriting practices that divide Americans into smaller and smaller risk groups will be banned. Insurers will be required to guarantee access to health care to all groups and to all persons within those groups, regardless of their medical condition, and insurers will be required to employ "community rating" (in which premiums are based on the expected costs for all policyholders, not on a particular group's historical costs ["experience rating"]). A single standardized claim form for all private and public plans will lessen administrative complexities for physicians.

Special Provisions for Small Employers

As all businesses begin to participate in making health care available to all workers, that care must be made more affordable. The cost-containment features of the plan will lower the rate of increase in future health care costs, and universal coverage will eliminate the shifting of costs for uninsured patients to the insurance bills paid by employers and others. Nevertheless, for businesses that do not now provide health benefits, especially small businesses, the new requirements impose new costs. My plan provides for such small businesses the option of purchasing benefits from the publicly sponsored plan if doing so will save money.

Medical-Malpractice Reform

Physicians are forced to spend hundreds of millions of dollars to insure themselves against malpractice litigation. Even more troubling, our current system results in the practice of "defensive medicine," whereby unnecessary procedures are ordered to protect against a malpractice suit. Alternative mechanisms for resolving disputes will be made available in every state—mechanisms that take disputes out of the court system and effectively and fairly address the concerns of patients and physicians. We will also encourage the development of medical-practice guidelines to help eliminate improper care and to help physicians defend against charges of negligence.

Other Cost-Containment Features

To control costs and trim the "paper hospital," my plan will replace expensive billing, coding, and utilization-review functions with a simplified billing system. Everyone will carry "smart cards" coded with his or her personal medical information.

We will slow price increases for prescription drugs that force Americans to pay more than Europeans or Canadians pay for the same drugs. We need a robust American pharmaceutical industry that will continue to lead the world in research and development but not in marketing expenses. Therefore, we will maintain the research-and-development tax credit, but we will seek to limit the deductibility of marketing and lobbying costs. Finally, we will work to accelerate the approval process for new drugs, especially those for AIDS.

In addition, the proliferation of duplicative technology will be controlled. The National Health Board will develop recommendations and incentives for the shared use of new forms of technology where appropriate.

Enhanced Preventive and Primary Care

Preventive and primary care saves lives and dollars. For this reason, preventive care will be part of the core benefits package, and access to preventive and primary care will be expanded. This requires more primary care clinics and providers—including school-based clinics where needed, community health centers in underserved areas, training support for nurse practitioners and nurse-midwives, and an expanded National Health Service Corps sending professionals to serve these areas.

Long-term Care

No American should have to become impoverished to qualify for long-term health care. No family should ever have to choose between long-term care for the grandparents and education for the children.

We can provide more services to the elderly and disabled by expanding Medicare. Long-term care benefits will be phased in, starting with the most neglected area—care in the home and community. In Arkansas, we've launched a popular pilot program called ElderChoices, which gives the elderly the right to take money previously available only for nursing home care and spend it instead on home health care, personal care, transportation to senior centers, a nurse's services, or attendance at an adult day care center.

Health Education and Personal Responsibility

An intensified health-education system must be designed to educate and encourage the American people to change behavior that results in ill health and high costs. The right to affordable health care—a right that is the cornerstone of my plan—must be accompanied by the responsibility to maintain our own health and to use the system wisely.

A PLAN FOR CHANGE

I fully recognize that the path to health care reform is difficult. Some have described it as the "black hole" of American politics. But I am committed to implementing a plan that will constrain increases in spending for health care while providing coverage for all Americans. In addition, I believe we need a health care system that stresses preventive and primary care, including drug and health education; meets the challenges of the HIV epidemic, women's health concerns, and long-term care; and invests in medical research. My plan presents a framework for meeting those objectives.

As president, I will work with everyone involved to shape this plan and submit it to Congress in the first 100 days of my administration. We must all be willing to rethink our views and compromise where necessary. But we must conclude with a plan under which every American finally has the right to affordable, high-quality health care.

I look forward to the day when I sign that plan into law, and I invite you to join with me in this effort.

REFERENCES

1. Sonnefeld ST, Waldo DR, Lemieux JA, McKusick DR. Projections of national health expenditures through the year 2000. Health Care Financ Rev 1991; 13(1):1–27.

2. Advisory Council on Social Security. Income security and health care: economic implications, 1991–2020: an Expert Panel Report to the Advisory Council Report on Social Security. Washington, D.C.: Department of Health and Human Services, 1991.

3. Congressional Budget Office. An analysis of the President's budgetary proposals for fiscal year 1993. Washington, D.C.: Government Printing Office, 1992.

4. Bureau of the Census. Health insurance coverage, 1986–1988. Household economic studies. Current population reports. Series P-70. No. 17. Washington, D.C.: Government Printing Office, 1990.

5. Clinton B. Health care reform: the worst choice is the status quo. Cincinnati Journal of Medicine. July 31, 1992:9.

6. *Idem.* Putting people first: a national economic strategy for America. Little Rock, Ark.: Bill Clinton for President Committee, 1992.

7. Bill Clinton's American Health Care Plan. Little Rock, Ark.: Bill Clinton for President Committee, 1992.

Now is our chance to beat the historical odds and give the American people the health *security they need and deserve.*
— Hillary Rodham Clinton

Conclusion

NATIONAL HEALTH POLICY

Health policy is the art and science of making public policy decisions about financing organizations and delivery systems for health care services. As the nation embarks on major reform, policymakers have many options for the future. Options for change are limitless. Dramatic change is bound to occur and needs to be addressed with creativity and courage.

If national health care reform adopts a play-or-pay approach (the use of private health plans to insure and manage the health care system rather than a public national health plan), this scenario for the future can be envisioned: Health care would be financed through private health plans, and businesses would be mandated to pay for basic coverage for employees through either private or government insurance plans. The federal government would pay for individuals not otherwise covered. Under this approach, the private insurance industry would be forced to increase its efficiency, resulting in the elimination of small or disreputable companies and streamlining of billing procedures and other administrative practices. The private health insurance industry would be a major player in a play-or-pay approach, but overall, the industry is unlikely to accept a reduction in its profits and administrative costs, which currently absorb 14 percent of total premiums.

In contrast, a government-run health plan, such as Medicare or Canada's single-payer system, would be significantly and dramatically less expensive than private health plans. Moreover, a government plan would be more open and equitable in its policies, delivery, and management of services than private plans. The current health insurance industry violently opposes any public plan that would prevent maintaining and expanding its profits. Opposition to a government health plan is joined by the medical profession, which fears the power of a single-payer approach to reduce not only physician incomes, but physician management and control over the health care system. The health insurance and provider

515

lobbies continue to assert great political influence in Congress through campaign contributions and political action committees.

The advantage of a play-or-pay approach is that less direct tax money is necessary to finance the system. Politicians do not believe the public will understand or accept a shift of private health dollars into the tax system. Moreover, U.S. taxpayers, who want health insurance but are unwilling to have taxes increased, are convinced that private-sector management is better than public-sector management. Thus, a public–private partnership approach is born of the political expediency of policymakers.

A national plan based on employer mandates is unlikely to satisfy anyone except those currently uninsured, who often do not participate in the political process. If major corporations are required to give up their tax breaks on health insurance, their costs will increase and this is likely to result in reduced health care coverage. In a *back-to-basics* plan, employees may have to pay for all health care costs beyond the minimum required plan. Thus, middle-class employees who enjoy good health benefits at the present time would no doubt have to pay for larger and larger proportions of their health care costs through supplemental insurance policies. If small businesses are required to pay for basic plans they would incur new costs and might either reduce the number of employees or be forced out of business. Businesses and government agencies of all types might increase the proportion of part-time and temporary employees hired in order to stay below the level at which health benefits would be required. In the long run, the population would have greater access to health care coverage but would be paying for most of it directly out of pocket.

With the strengthening of cost controls, the lobbying efforts by physicians, hospitals, pharmaceutical companies, and health insurers will intensify. All elements of the health industry will continue to fight for maximum funding with minimal government control over administration and service patterns. Groups with the greatest power within the health industry—physicians and health insurers—will force cost reductions on other health professionals and workers in order to protect their own incomes and profits.

Incremental health policy changes can modify existing premiums, benefits, and other components of public or private insurance. Innovative alterations in eligibility, means testing, and rationing could be introduced. Finally, a revolution or fundamental change could revise the entire health financing and delivery system. The United States is facing an economic and a health crisis in the 1990s. The response will shape the system of health care delivery and the entire health of the nation for the twenty-first century.

Perhaps, in complex societies, there is no alternative to incremental change. Thus, health reform efforts inevitably may need to move slowly through a transition from the current chaos to a public–private approach before a more rational government-financed national health plan can be developed. In any case, the process and the speed of health care reform will be determined by the legislative and policy efforts of the day. Such reform will build a transformed system and a healthier nation in the future.

NURSING AND HEALTH POLICY

Nurses have had an important impact on health policies at the national, state, and local levels. The priority focus of nursing organizations naturally has been on national health insurance reform because the problems of access, quality, and costs can best be addressed through a major reform of health care financing. The American Nurses' Association and other national nursing organizations have become major players at the federal level in health policy reform. They have developed a sophisticated and informed membership and an effective lobbying operation in Washington so that they have been able to make changes in legislative proposals and final legislation. The Association has been active in presenting testimony at hearings, lobbying key congressional representatives, presenting legislative proposals, and monitoring the implementation of legislation.

Nurses have been actively involved in many state efforts to provide health care coverage through legislative reform of state laws. Some states have passed such legislation and others continue to work for legislative reform. National legislative reforms for health care plans no doubt will allow state discretion in formulating approaches that meet the particular needs of individual states. Thus, even with national health reform, state legislation will continue to be important in specifying health policies and professional practice patterns. Under the Clinton administration of the mid-nineties, nurses are encouraged by the emphasis placed on health reform and believe that new leadership by women—in the Congress, at the head of the Department of Health and Human Services, and in the White House—will address women's health issues with vigor and strengthen the role of women in the health professions.

Nevertheless, nurses must be vigilant at all levels to ensure that they are active participants in new programs and that they and their clients are treated fairly under health reform. The most effective approach both to learning how to be a part of the legislative process and to influence health policy is for nurses to work through organizations. The American Nurses' Association and state nurses' associations are far more effective and able to influence decisions in the large and complex political arena than individual nurses. On the other hand, a few informed and committed nurses can influence the policies and approaches of nursing organizations. Having an impact depends not only on being informed and active participants in the process but also on making campaign contributions. Participating in the political process requires both knowledge and commitment and is a responsibility of nursing leaders.

Index

Aaron, H. J., 11
Abdellah, F. G., 435
Abel, Emily K., 400–401
Access to health care, 359
  for black and white Americans, 376–381
  and competition and cost containment, 368–370
  contributions of research to policy and future issues in, 371
  and equity and national health insurance, 359–361
  health outcomes and, 370–371
  impact of Medicare and Medicaid on, 361–365, 371
  uninsured and, 365–366
  and vulnerable subpopulation groups, 367–368
Aday, L. A., 362, 365
Administrative costs, health care, study on, 80–82, 85–88
Advanced practice nurses (APNs), reimbursement of, 341, 347–348
  barriers to receiving direct, 342–344
  by CHAMPUS, 347
  by Federal Employee Health Benefit Plan, 347
  importance of direct, 341–342
  by Medicaid and Medicare, 344–347
Advertising, by physicians, 74, 76
Aetna Life and Casualty, 322
Agency for Health Care Policy and Research (AHCPR), 450, 454, 455, 457

Aging and Social Services, 238, 240
Aid to Families with Dependent Children (AFDC), 25, 26, 119
Aides, *see* Nurse aides
AIDS (acquired immune deficiency syndrome), 95, 163–164, 432
  in women, 390–391
Aiken, Linda H., 300, 376
Altman, D., 95, 276
Altman, Stuart H., 37, 92, 97
Ambulatory care centers, 60–61
American Association of Homes for the Aging, 200
American Association of Retired Persons, 262, 503
American Bar Association, 238, 240
American College of Nurse Midwives, 345
American Health Care Association, 200
American Hospital Association (AHA), 56, 59, 61, 150, 166, 214, 360
  Annual Survey of Hospitals of the, 164, 165
  and uncompensated care, 183, 184–185
  and Urban Institute surveys, 369
American Medical Association (AMA), 74, 75, 76, 200, 269, 285–286, 360
  and health care reform, 461
  Principles of Medical Ethics of, 70
  and quality of care, 435
  and RCT proposal, 310–311
  survey of physicians by, 369